# THE
# TELEVISION YEARBOOK

## COMPLETE, DETAILED LISTINGS
## FOR THE 1990–1991 SEASON

# FRANK LOVECE

A PERIGEE BOOK

*To Barbara, who believes*

Perigee Books
are published by
The Putnam Publishing Group
200 Madison Avenue
New York, NY 10016

Library of Congress Cataloging-in-Publication Data

Lovece, Frank.
The television yearbook / Frank Lovece.
p.     cm.
ISBN 0-399-51702-2
1. Television programs—United States.    I. Title.
PN1992.3.U5L68    1992
791.45′75′0973—dc20          91-27977 CIP

Printed in the United States of America
1   2   3   4   5   6   7   8   9   10

# INTRODUCTION

**T**elevision, next to the nuclear bomb, is the most powerful thing on earth. It influences how we dress, how we speak, what we buy, what we know, and what we think we know.

Consider: A TV movie about missing children galvanized a nation and a movement. The bounty of *Dynasty* and *Dallas* helped make Eastern Europeans covet capitalism. A generation who grew up on *The Mary Tyler Moore Show* was reminded and reinforced it's OK for women to have careers. *Miami Vice* had us wearing T-shirts with jackets. Bart Simpson's phrases? New American colloquialisms.

And TV doesn't just influence us -- it mirrors us. Watch a show in 1992, and get a slice of what the world is like here and now -- even in such slight entertainments as *Matlock*: "A couple is accused of killing a surrogate mom who's changed her mind about giving up her child." This is not *Mannix*, or *The Mod Squad*.

Television does tend to reinforce attitudes more than change them -- half the audience thought Archie Bunker an ignorant bigot, the other half, a sensible plain-talker. Even so, TV still influences us tremendously: When 30 million people watch *The Cosby Show* week after week after week, and see a middle-class black family unlike the inner-city stereotype, with the same hopes and fears as any other family, that image begins to sink in. How could it not?

And yet...for all that influence, there's been no place to look up the plots of the stories we're fed, the images we're subjected to, day in, day out. There's been no ready way to see who creates these programs that influence our language, our fashions, our social mores. Aside from a handful of famous names, TV's creators work with an anonymity that would do the CIA proud. Their credits fly by so fast onscreen, only VCR junkies and Evelyn Wood could have any idea who they are.

And there are the actors -- not just the stars, but the army of familiar faces who entertain us but whose names we never know. Those who appear in movies, we can look up in any of three popular, regularly published film yearbooks. Yet television, powerful and omnipresent as it is, rolls along in strange secrecy.

Now that's changing. Thanks to VCRs, museum retrospectives and the blurring of lines between "movie people" and "TV people," television has acquired a critical cachet. (Reacquired, actually, but that's another story.) Oscar-winners like Whoopi Goldberg and Glenn Close regularly do TV; so do such prominent movie directors as David Lynch, Robert Zemeckis, Walter Hill, and Allan Arkush. Pulitzer Prize-winner David Mamet wrote a *Hill Street Blues*; a book of *thirtysomething* scripts was a critically lauded best-seller. How

can we disregard the boob tube, the idiot box, the vast wasteland, when some of our best and most talented minds are working in it?

One reason: There's never been a reference book to let us know who's who and what's what.

**The Television Yearbook** is a record of the most recent full year in television: The title, airdate, plot, cast, guest cast, characters, writer and director of every episode of every primetime network-TV comedy, drama and variety series, plus selected cable and syndicated shows.

Now TV buffs and media students, journalists and publicists, even producers and casting directors can finally sort out the credits of actors, writers and directors who say they've worked here or there, knowing it was almost impossible to check. Fans of *Cheers* or *L.A. Law* can at last organize and title their video collections. John Goodman fans can see what TV work he did this year besides *Roseanne*. There's finally a place we can look up Tasha Yar's home planet on *Star Trek: The Next Generation*, or the correct spelling of Steven Bochco ("v," not "ph").

Regrettably, for reasons of space, we couldn't include TV-movies or miniseries, news, documentary, or "reality-based" programs, nor the treasures on PBS; future editions will. The enormous area we do attack is covered in microscopic detail. Even the briefest of bit players are here, as are many performers and creators who by choice or oversight were uncredited onscreen.

All this proved a Herculean task. Unlike with movies or theater, where a press kit or a *Playbill* gives all the information in a single place, television credits are a complete and utter looney bin.

Network press materials are incomplete and often incorrect, usually since they're written so far in advance. (Though not always: One ABC release had an episode of *thirtysomething* written by "Lewis Hamilton." Onscreen it was revealed as *Ann* Lewis Hamilton -- one of the producers, not a transient freelancer.) Production-company records are better, but even these can be incomplete. And even onscreen credits are incomplete: Unlike movies, few TV shows give titles onscreen -- and most TV dramas list major guest stars without giving their characters' names.

Yet dig hard enough, and the data does surface. And in coming years, as the TV community continues to realize the historical importance of its work, that pride will translate to credits as readily available as it is for the cinema and the legitimate theater.

TV is important. TV matters. And *The Television Yearbook* will continue to bring it all home.

# SOME NOTES ON USING THIS BOOK

*The Television Yearbook* covers primetime comedy, drama and variety shows from Sept. 17, 1990 (the official start of last year's season) to Sept. 1, 1991 (the official end), with extensions where appropriate.

Included are ABC, CBS, NBC and Fox series; selected primetime series on the cable services HBO (*Dream On, 1st & Ten, Tales from the Crypt*), USA Network (*The Ray Bradbury Theater, The Hitchhiker, Swamp Thing, Counterstrike*) and Lifetime (*The Days and Nights of Molly Dodd*), plus selected primetime, first-run syndicated series (*Star Trek: The Next Generation, Shades of LA, They Came from Outer Space, She-Wolf of London*).

The parameters of a show's run -- its start and end dates, and the night of the week it ran -- are listed at the head of each entry. Within these parameters are:
1) The new, first-run episodes you see listed.
2) Preemption dates, noted in boldface.
3) Reruns (the gaps between the dates).

Sometimes a show is preempted at the last moment because of a news bulletin or somesuch. These are noted in boldface as "unscheduled preemptions."

**Cast-members** are those performers listed in a series' standard opening credits. On one or two series, for arcane contractual and ego reasons, some cast-members are listed in the end-credits, and are so noted here.

**Recurring guests** we generally define as those who appear three or more times in a season. Some, such as Bebe Neuwirth (Lilith on *Cheers*) are as popular and recognizable as cast-members. Others, such as recurring judges on *L.A. Law*, have smaller roles. Major or minor, recurring guests are listed in a separate section just below the regular cast-members, along with a list of the specific episodes in which they appear.

We also list all **guest performers** for every episode of every show. For space reasons, the final performers on each credit list may be given paragraph style, rather than on separate lines. No lesser status is implied.

Information was gathered from onscreen credits -- our final arbiter -- plus network press materials, production-company data, and print and interview sources. **The front and end credits of virtually every episode of every show was videotaped, freeze-framed, scrutinized, and cross-checked.** (About 1% of the more than 2,000 telecast episodes here were unable to be completely taped; these are noted by cast listings headed "Announced cast includes.")

Gathering the names of the actors and creators is one step; gathering the names of the characters, quite another. Incredibly, network press materials regularly leave out the names of writers, directors and even major guest-stars listed in the onscreen credits! This necessitates going back to the production company for characters' names in particular. Yet when a show is cancelled, casting directors' files go into boxes and warehouses, rarely if ever to be seen again -- a big problem when a show is cancelled in November, and unused episodes pop up the following June, long after the files are stored away.

Even when production-company records *are* available, they, too, don't always list all the characters -- sometimes, amazingly, not even all the principal actors! When this happens, and a character name isn't otherwise available, the *Yearbook* lists the performer on a line beginning "With:" This is placed to correspond with the actor's place in the onscreen credits -- a more accurate reflection of a performer's role than shunting him or her to the end with the bit players.

For all these reasons, *TV Guide* sometimes publishes erroneous information. Since TV researchers traditionally use *TV Guide* as a primary source, we've taken pains to note inaccuracies. Likewise, *TV Guide* and network press materials both often list performers dropped from a show, or who choose to go uncredited, or whose credit, for inadvertent or nefarious reasons, was left off. Thus, we've indicated where a performer was "also originally announced." On occasions where we've recognized an actor who went uncredited onscreen (usually after having been announced), we've noted that, too.

Particular attention has been given to confirming proper names -- a formidable task. Leonard Maltin, in his annual movie reference book, noted he'd spoken to actor Daniel Day-Lewis' agent, who'd confirmed his client's name had no hyphen. But upon meeting the actor and asking him, Maltin found there *is* a hyphen, and that Mr. Day-Lewis was happy he could stop people from calling him "Mr. Lewis." (I imagine Mark Linn-Baker of *Perfect Strangers* feels the same way.) *The Television Yearbook* has likewise made all efforts at confirming spellings short of speaking to the stars themselves (except for Patti LuPone, for which we're grateful). In virtually all cases, onscreen spellings (which are occasionally wrong) have been confirmed with at least one and preferably two print sources.

Even this can be exasperating: Melanie Mayron's actress sister spells her name Gale Mayron for her recurring role on *Shades of LA*, but Gail Mayron when she guested on *thirtysomething*. Actress Kim Ulrich is also known as Kim Johnston Ulrich a.k.a. Kim Johnston-Ulrich. In such cases, the first full name we give is the one onscreen this particular episode, followed by other names by which the person has been credited. It's critical to be accurate when you consider that Michael J. Fox and Michael Fox are two very different actors, as are white teen actress Jenny Lewis, and black adult actress Jenifer (one "n") Lewis.

A final spelling note: For exactly six of the more than 20,000 names in this book, the upper and lower case arrangement could not be verified. In these rare instances, a person who might be either deMarco or DeMarco is given all in caps: DEMARCO. In such cases, we *have* confirmed onscreen whether the name is two words (DE NIRO) or one (DEVITO).

Odds and ends: When available, we've include episodes production numbers, which give some insight into the order in which episodes were made, as opposed to aired.

Finally, writing and "created by" credits are determined by a formula of the Writers Guild of America. When partners craft a script together, their names are separated by an ampersand (&). When another writer works on a script -- a rewrite, an initial draft, whatever -- that name is separated by the word "and." Writing credits are also sometimes divided into "story" (the plot) and "teleplay" (the script adapted from it).

Enjoy the book, and send us your suggestions and (shudder) corrections. See you next edition.

Frank Lovece

# ACKNOWLEDGMENTS

This book cannot possibly exist -- the information to put it together is too scattered, too hidden. That it does exist is thanks to a convocation of professionals who gave generously of their time, resources and fax numbers. In no particular order, I gratefully thank:

At ABC: Richard J. Connelly, David Horowitz, Jeff De Rome, Anne Marie Riccitelli, Janice Gretemeyer, Leslie Clark, Dan Doran, Eileen Kurtz, Jasper Vance, Bill Wilkins, Gayle Vrooman and Patty McTeague; at CBS: Ed Devlin, Lori Huhn, Bernice Green, Sarah Holt, Leslie Jones, Emily Rubin, Hali Simon, Michael DiPasquale, and Kathy Juan; at NBC: Curt Block, Elizabeth McDermott, Dorothy Austin, Barry Cherin, Merry Aronson, Carol Janson, Rosemary Keenan, Rob Maynor, Bob Meyer, Rosemary O'Brien, Brian Robinette, Margo Zinberg, Dalina DeSoto, Kim Donlon, and Kathy Fern-Banks; at Fox Broadcasting: Cindy Ronzoni, Antonia Coffman, Dom Giofre, Joan-Ellen Delaney, Janine Jones, Phil Gonzales, Monica Bouldin, Andrew Shipps, and Sharan Magnuson.

The extraordinarily helpful production-company and publicity sources: David Stapf, Jeannie Heldoorn, Diane DeStefano, Nan Sumski, and Paul Gendreau at Lorimar Television; Arigon Starr and Bill Barron at Viacom; Leah Krantzler, her assistant Michelle, Chris Dektar, Tracy Harper and Mitch Zamarin at the Lippin Group; James A. Gordon and Lauren Tobin at Steven Bochco Productions; James Anderson, Diann Shaw and Richie Solomon at the Carsey-Werner Co.; Claire Lee, Bette Ashley, Ellen Gonzalez and Carla Princi at Warner Bros.; Nancy Burnette at Gil Grant Productions; Kim Reed and Cindy Marvin at MGM/UA Television; Harriet Margulies and Robin Torodor at Belisarius Productions; Sara La Lowe at the Family Channel; Karen Blythe, Joshua Stern and Jody Milano at Wolf Films; Cynthia Lieberman, Andy St. James, Chuck Panama, and Kelly Klein at Twentieth Century Fox; Anthony Williams, Howard Borim, and Linda Morton at Paramount; Robert Pini, Debbie Gangwer, Dana Friedman, Sue Roth and Steve Belgard at Bender Goldman & Helper; Alex Wagner, Tracy Colletti, Abby Gans, and Carmina Marcial at Lifetime; Tobe Becker at HBO; Faye Katz and Larry Landsman at Showtime; Anna Maria Nuccilli and Kathy Devlin at Alliance Entertainment; Frank Anni-no, Debbie Darr, Georgia Scott and Rhonda Reyes at MCA/Universal; Ellen Morganstern at WWOR; Diane Passarelli, Ennette Nusbaum and Mike Testa at Stephen J. Cannell Productions; Jeff Mackler, Bill Bence, and Connie Stout at Jeff Mackler Communications; Laurie Talbot, Maggie Bagley and Trisha Cardoso at Mahoney Communications; Patrick McFarland at Arts & Entertainment; Pam Giddon and Dina Ligorski at Pamela Giddon & Co.; Rosemary Amendola and Lynn White at Rachel McCallister & Associates; Stuart Fink and Julie Roberts at Touchstone/Walt Disney; CiCi Harris at TNT/WTBS; LeslieAnne Wade, Bonnie Hammer, Cee Cee Fallon, Paul Reader and Lou Fazio at USA Network; Bill Wright at Nickelodeon; Jim Sirmans; David Sherry; and Bob Blake at the National Academy of Television Arts and Sciences. Sincere apologies to anyone I may have inadvertently overlooked.

For information available nowhere else: performers Peter Falk, Gil Gerard, Patti LuPone, Gerald McRaney and Joe Penny; producers Norman Lear, Stan Rogow, Boris Malden, Wendy Grean, Clyde Phillips, and Walter F. Parkes, and Michael Leeson and his assistant, Tina.

My editors and colleagues at NEA Syndicate gave moral and logistical support, and valued friendship: Diana Loevy, Lynn Hoogenboom, Chris Hull, Wendy Wallace, Kirk Nicewonger, and the late Robert DiMatteo. Other friends who gave of themselves, both in favors and in patience: Andy Edelstein, Mark Fleischmann, Jules Franco, Lisa Vartuli, Tony Perrotti, and in particular Tom Gillian and Michael Isbell, whose patient modification of my computer wordware saved more worker-hours than it took to build the Sphinx.

Finally, special thanks to my wife, Toni, and my son, Vincent; Gene Brissie, my editor, who shepherded this massive project with grace and humor; copy editor Claire Winecoff, she of the laser eyes; Liz Stein; Diane Lomonaco; Lori Perkins, who championed the *Yearbook* early on; and my agent, Barbara Lowenstein, who for a commission could probably negotiate peace in the Middle East.

## Against the Law

Fox  Sept. 23-Nov. 11  Sundays, 10-11 p.m.
Nov. 16-April 12  Fridays, 9-10 p.m.

Series premiere: Sept. 23, 1990
Final telecast: April 12, 1991

Law drama of a maverick Boston attorney who has broken from his father's blue-blood firm to challenge a judicial system he sees as inequitable and class-conscious. Filmed in Boston.

Simon MacHeath.............................................Michael O'Keefe
Yvette (ep. 2-on).........................................Suzzanne Douglas
Meigs..........................................................M.C. Gainey
Elizabeth Verhagen........................................Elizabeth Ruscio
Also orig. announced:
Toy Feng......................................................Rosalind Chao

*Recurring:*
Phoebe Haverhill MacHeath, Mac's
ex-wife (ep. 1,3,4,6)...............................Barbara Williams
Wexford (ep. 1,4,8).................................Richard Jenkins
Prosecutor Beth Connor (ep. 10,13,17)..........Tovah Feldshuh
Samantha (ep. 12,14,16-17)..............................Annie Corley

Sarabande Productions and MGM/UA Television (early in season); Daniel H. Blatt Productions and MGM/UA Television (later in season)
Executive producers: David Manson, Michael Butler (both ep. 1-on), Daniel H. Blatt (added later)
Producers: Marcus Viscidi (ep. 1-on), John Landgraf (early in season), Elia J. Katz, Wayne Powers, Donna Dottley Powers (latter three added later)
Supervising producers: Jan Egleson, Frederick Rappaport (both early in season); Steve Feke, Sam Pillsbury (both later in season)
Executive story editors (variously, occasionally in combination): Howard Chesley; Arla Mae Nudelman; Fern Hill
Associate producers: Vanessa Hayes (ep. 2-on), William A. Anderson (early in season)
Director of photography (variously): Paul Goldsmith (ep. 1); Misha Suslov; Tom Priestly, Jr.
Technical advisor (legal): Robert Jonathan Kurtz
Music: Thomas Newman (ep. 1); Jay Gruska
Theme (instrumental): Thomas Newman
Creators: Michael Butler & David Manson

---

1. "Against the Law"  Sept. 23, 1990  9:30-11 p.m.

MacHeath represents a woman (Rush) divorcing a Mafia don, and faces his former father-in-law (Weaver) when he defends a former mental patient.

Haverhill....................................................Fritz Weaver
Walter Littlefield.............................................Tom Atkins
Richey Littlefield.........................................Rodney Eastman
Shraker......................................................Paul Guilfoyle
Louise Ciardi...............................................Deborah Rush
Wisher.............................................William Martin Brennan
Al Caridi.......................................................Joe Hindy
Judge Wall................................................Stuart Burney
Mrs. Littlefield.......................................Marcia Jean Kurtz

Director: Jan Egleson  Writer: Michael Butler

2. "Where Truth Lies"  Sept. 30, 1990

A pathological liar is accused of murdering a wealthy Bostoni-

an; an older couple is busted for selling erotic pastries.

Timmy Lowell...............................................Steve Buscemi
Grainger.....................................................Anthony Heald
Jill.............................................................Melissa Leo
Sonia Kolowicz..........................................Laura Harrington
Delaney.......................................................Gus Johnson
Forbes.........................................................Mark Ziesler
Stewart...................................................Jeremiah Kissel
Kendall.......................................................Wiley Moore
Ida Timmons..................................................Alice Duffy
Also originally announced: Leonard Zola (Ben Buckman), June Lion (Shirley Buckman)

Director: Eugene Corr  Writer: Frederick Rappaport

3. "The Price of Life"  Oct. 7, 1990

Mac represents a mother (Gregorio) whose son died during an appendectomy. Weaver reprises his role from ep. 1.

Haverhill......................................................Fritz Weaver
Risa Ferrante..............................................Rose Gregorio
Fenstrom....................................................Greg Germann
Dr. Schulman..................................................Joe Urla
Sean...........................................................Ben Affleck
And: Joe Costa (Dr. Sciovone), Dee Nelson (Marcie Shulman), Chris Nylan (Peterbilt), Deb Parmet (Felicia Kelly)

Director: Francis Delia  Writer: Howard Chesley

4. "The Women"  Oct. 14, 1990

Mac becomes the fifth lawyer to try to defend a powerful Boston business mogul (Walker) with a heartless reputation.

Paulette....................................................Kathryn Walker
Mariella...................................................Marita Geraghty
Fenstrom....................................................Greg Germann
Horne........................................................Ken Cheeseman
And: Joan Quinn Eastman (Diane Regis), Gustave Johnson (Delaney), Richard Snee (Judge Stonlitz), David Wheeler (Judge Lyman), William Young (Fulton)

Director: Jan Egleson
Writer: Fern Hill (Arla Mae Nudleman orig. announced)

**preempted Oct. 21**

5. "The Second Man"  Oct. 28, 1990

Mac's mentor, now his co-counsel (Converse) in a two-defendant murder case, tries have Mac's client take the fall.

Gordon Leary.............................................Frank Converse
Piccaccio....................................................Roxanne Hart
Joey O'Brien..................................................Brian Burke
Barnett...................................................Bill Chamberlain
Armored car driver.......................................Richard Ferrone
Cavanaugh....................................................Bill McCann
Turlock..............................................Christopher McCann
Frank O'Brien...............................................Fred Sullivan

Director: Fred Gerber  Teleplay: Michael Butler
Story: Cynthia Saunders

6. "Requiem in B Flat"  Nov. 4, 1990

In a story told in reverse chronology, Mac fights to win a reprieve from execution for a jazz-musician friend (David). Guest Foote is the actress daughter of writer Horton Foote.

Otis..............................................................Keith David
Sister Byrne................................................Deborah Hedwall
Mrs. Jackson...................................................Hallie Foote
Sgt. Chase.....................................................Earl Hindman
Priest...........................................................Norm Buerkin
Prosecutor Pickens.......................................William Miller
Governor.............................................Charles Werner Moore
Amy Jackson..............................................Shannon Tyree
Chairperson...................................Bronia Stefan Wheeler
    Also originally announced:
    Ricardo Pitts-Wiley (Jimmy Knowles)

Director: Jan Egleson        Writer: Sandy Kroopf

7. "Contempt" Nov. 16, 1990

Mac defends a shock comic (Sizemore). Orig. scheduled for
Oct. 7 and Nov. 11. Hart reprises her role from ep. 5.

Jill................................................................Melissa Leo
Rainey Fults.................................................Tom Sizemore
Judge Webb................................................Philip Bosco
And: Guy Mirano (Sascha), Roxanne Hart (Piccaccio)

Director: Jan Egleson        Writer: Michael Butler

8. "A Safe, New World" Nov. 23, 1990

Mac represents a teen (Klein) to emancipate him from his Ma-
fia-connected dad (Lisi). Burney reprises his role from ep. 1.

Peter Cantrell.....................................................Joe Lisi
Sam Lime....................................................Michael Mantell
Judge Wall....................................................Stuart Burney
Johnny Rainbow..........................................Michael Balcanoff
And: Daniel Von Bargen (Terry Meade), Jack Ferren (FBI agent
    Sellers), Dean Harrison (FBI agent Johnson), Paul Kaup
    (Jack Gold), Steven Klein (Andrew Cantrell)
    Also orig. announced: John Fiore (Wakefield)

Director: Sam Pillsbury
Writers: Sam Denver & Elia J. Katz (Barry Pullman orig. an-
    nounced)

9. "Nature Now" Dec. 7, 1990

In New Hampshire, MacHeath defends a former flame and
classmate accused of attempted murder for tree-spiking.

Announced cast includes:
Jessica...........................................................Jo Anderson
Jeff Travis.......................................................Eric Lutes
Maddie Skoggins.....................................Stephanie Clayman
Sherman Dewitt...........Robert Clohesse a.k.a. Robert Clohessy
And: Neal Brown (Sam Welch), Leon B. Stevens (Judge Fickett)

Director: Don Scardino
Writers: Donna Dottley Powers & Wayne Powers

10. "We, the Jury" Dec. 21, 1990

A desperate, homeless family man (Coates), barricaded with
hostages, consents to use them as jury in an impromptu trial.

Eddie Grover...................................................Kim Coates
Police Captain.................................................Brad Sullivan
Martha Dean...............................................Ann McDonough
Mayor............................................................James Rebhorn
Emily Martindale...............................................Peg Flaherty
And: Ray Ashley Ford (RJ242), Dorothy Gallagher (Betty By-
    num), Sakina Jaffrey (Ava), Peter Kovner (Bob Bynum)

Also orig. announced: Richard Jenkins (Wexford), Sheila
Stasack (Jill), Gary Hoffman (Eddie, Jr.), Brenda Chro-
naik (Melinda)

Director: Sam Pillsbury
Writers: William Bentley & Steven Whitney

11. "The Indictment" Jan. 11, 1991

Mac's fellow lawyers in a civil suit against a major corporation,
frustrated by Mac, have him framed for rape to discredit him.

Gloria........................................................Jenny Robertson
Kenneth Richardson..........................................Bruce Altman
Malcolm Bramwell.............................................Robert Fields
Warden...........................................................W.T. Martin
Tony...........................................................Michael Galardi
Detectives....................................Ron Ryan, Michael Fennimore
And: Dossy Peabody (Katherine Dunwoody) Linda Peterson
    (Judge Smathers), Guy Strauss (Winstead)

Director: Peter Ellis        Writer: Elia J. Katz

12. "Hoops" Feb. 1, 1991 (AL-117)

A carried-along, barely literate college athlete (Martin), whose
scholarship is revoked upon an injury, sues his famous coach.

Ben Gale........................................................Delroy Lindo
Michael Gale....................................................Duane Martin
Coach Leary...................................................Robert Lansing
Clarissa Moore......................................................Liz Leisek
And: R. Sebastian Russ (Hunt), William Ball (Commissioner)
    Also orig. announced:
    Frank Biacamano (Slim Rite defense), Warren Peace (Dr.
    Rushman), Robert Jacobs (Charles)

Director: Rob Bowman
Writers: Barry Beckerman & Michell Gallagher

13. "The Union Label" Feb. 8, 1991

Mac helps the daughter (Emmenlin) of a missing union official
(North). Mantell and Balcanoff reprisee their roles from ep. 8.

Announced cast includes:
Megan........................................................Georgia Emmenlin
Sean O'Hara........................................................Alan North
Donovan.......................................................Pat McNamary
And: Michael Mantell (Sam Lime), Robert Hogan (Paddy Bren-
    nen), Michael Balcanoff (Johnny Rainbow)

Director: Peter Ellis
Writers: Steven Whitney & William Bentley

14. "Damages" Feb. 15, 1991

The widow (Corrillo) of a boxer killed in a fight alleges a corruption scandal extending to the boxing commissioner.

Linda Martin...............................................Elpidia Corrillo
Spider Martin, her husband.....................Leon Isaac Kennedy
Tom Rosario...................................................Tom Signorelli
Sonny...........................................................Michael Milan
"Buster" Duke....................................................Geoff Pierson
And: Chuck Cooper (A.J. Calhoun), Steve Marcus (Eddie Side-
    pockets), Walter Covell (Dr. Spangler), Glenn Ordway
    (Sports announcer), Scott Richards (Joshua Meek)

Director: Armand Mastroianni
Writers: Steven Whitney & William Bentley

**preempted Feb. 22**

15. "Past, Present" March 1, 1991

Mac and his girlfriend (Moore) are stalked by an ex-con (Keats) he put away years before. Orig. scheduled for Jan. 11 and 18.

Dartman Charles Hampton...................................Steven Keats
Vanessa.......................................................Christine Moore
Cleon.................................................................Jason Boyd
Detective Shaner..............................John Grant-Phillips
    Also orig. announced:
      Darliesha Lyons (Luisa), Patrick Shea (Hingham)

Director: Jan Egleson
Writer: Maurice Jules (Yale Udoff orig. announced)

16. "Miss Mass" March 8, 1991

Old, revealing photos of a beauty-queen client (Krakowski) may cost her her crown. Working title: "Miss New England."

Colleen Hanrahan..........................................Jane Krakowski
Maureen Hanrahan................................................Fran Brill
Doris Campbell.....................................................Ann Dowd
Harvey Jameson............................................Graeme Malcolm
Kathy Dinova....................................................Susan Crook
Frank Hilden (orig. Hiller)..................................Munson Hicks
Dr. Sandra Kingsley.....................................Geraldine Librandi
Judge Medfield.............................................Linda Peterson
Jeffrey Smathers (orig. Smith)..............................Chris Wilder
    Also orig. announced: Cope Murray (Murry Stein), Paula
    Plum (PR director), Kelsey Nichols (Chelsea)

Director: Victor Lobl       Teleplay: Michael A. Graham
Story: Michael A. Graham & E. Gail Willhardt

17. "Evil Conduct" April 5, 1991

The father (Joyce) of a date-raped woman (Coppola) kills the perpetrator. Burney reprises his role from ep. 1 and 8.

Terence Finnegan...............................................Stephen Joyce
Patrick Randolph...Reed Edward Diamond a.k.a. Reed Edward
Kathleen Finnegan.............................................Alicia Coppola
Judge Wall.....................................................Stuart Burney
    Also orig. announced:
      John Picardi (Garrison), Bud Williams (Priest)

Director: Armand Mastroianni       Writer: Yale Udoff

# Amen

NBC       Saturdays, 8-8:30 p.m.

Series premiere: Sept. 27, 1986
Final telecast: July 27, 1991

Comedy of the deacon and the minister of the First Community Church of Philadelphia.

Deacon Ernest J. Frye................................Sherman Hemsley
Rev. Reuben Gregory..................................Clifton Davis
Thelma Frye Gregory, his wife................Anna Maria Horsford
Church trustee Amelia Hetebrink............................Roz Ryan
Church elder Rolly Forbes, Thelma's uncle.......Jester Hairston

*Recurring:*
Clarence (ep. 4-5,8,11-12,16,18,20-21)........Bumper Robinson
Darla (10, 19-20).............................................La Wanda Page

Tommy McAllister (ep. 3,5,17,21)..............Nicholas Rutherford

Stein & Illes Productions and Carson Productions
Executive producers: Robert Illes, James R. Stein
Supervising producer: Jim Geoghan
Producers: Ken Johnston, Bob Peete, Marilynn Loncar
Co-producer (later in season): Beverly Cashen a.k.a. Beverly
    Spalding Cashen
Consulting producer: Ken Hecht
Associate producers: Beverly Cashen a.k.a. Beverly Spalding
    Cashen (early in season), Joni Rhodes (later in season)
Co-associate producer: Tracy L. Foster
Story editors: David Pitlik, Barry Gurstein
Executive consultant: Sherman Hemsley
Consultants: Darice Rollins, Rev. Madison Shockley, Dr.
    Thomas Kilgore, Jr.
Director of photography: Donald A. Morgan
Music: uncredited; only a music "director" listed
Theme: "Shine on Me" by Andrae Crouch; performed by
    Vanessa Bell Armstrong
Creator: Ed. Weinberger

---

1. "Love, Deacon Style" Nov. 17, 1990   8:30-9 p.m.

Thelma, on her sixth-month anniversary, feels neglected now that Reuben has the additional task of teaching night school. The role of Leola had formerly been played on a recurring basis by Rosetta LeNoire, now a cast-member of *Family Matters.*

Leola Forbes, Thelma's aunt/Rolly's wife........Montrose Hagins
Dean Barnsworthy................................................Ben Hartigan

Director: Jules Lichtman
Writers: Barry Gurstein & David Pitlik

**preempted Nov. 24**

2. "Two Men, One Woman and a Baby" Dec. 1, 1990

Thelma wants to keep abandoned baby; Frye is tax-audited.

Stephanie Harris....................................................Anne Gagen
McAllister............................................................Wesley Mann
Tonya...............................................................Yvonne Farrow
Jeffrey (infant)...............................................Devin/Deon Bush

Director: John Sgueglia       Writer: Robin J. Stein

3. "Child's Play" Dec. 8, 1990

Frye begins running a day-care center, Deaconland.

Max................................................................Michael Oliver
Max's mother....................................................Patti Cohoon
And: Marissa Rosen (Jennifer), Nichole Francois (Paula)

Director: Jules Lichtman       Writer: Bob Peete

4. "Yo, Deak" Dec. 15, 1990

Frye takes in a trouble-prone teen (new recurring guest Robinson), a would-be rapper dubbed "Clarence So Fine."

Judge Stoneham.....................................................John Ingle
And: Richard Camphuis (Police officer), Joe Banks (Bailiff),
    Lyvingston Holmes (Glenda Simpson), Lou Cutell (Sid)

Director: John Sgueglia
Writers: Robert Illes & James R. Stein

5. "Miracle on 134th Street" Dec. 22, 1990 8-9 p.m.

In an homage to the film *Miracle on 34th Street* (1947), Frye backs a man (Windom) claiming to be Santa Claus. Hagins reprises her role from ep. 1, Holmes from last episode.

Nick St. Nicholas..............................................William Windom
Jason Lockwood.........................................................Ron Glass
Josephine Gregory, Reuben's mother.....................Jane White
Judge Kalenski....................................................William Lanteau
Martin......................................................................Ron Orbach
Bruno..............................................................Richard Karron
Leola Forbes.................................................Montrose Hagins
Glenda Simpson.........................................Lyvingston Holmes
And: David Correia (Bailiff), Joseph Darrell (Guard), Rick Marotta (Prisoner), Robin Goodrin Nordli (Reporter), Mary Fanaro (Elf helper), Lora Temple (Stenographer)

Director: Gary Shimokawa
Writers: Barry Gurstein & David Pitlik (part 1); Robert Illes & James R. Stein (part 2)

6. "Judge Deacon Frye" Dec. 29, 1990

Newly appointed to the bench and power-drunk, Judge Frye aims to throw the book at all who come before him.

Heather Fetlock..................................................Lu Leonard
Prosecutor...........................................................Barbara Pariot
McAllister........................................................Patrick O. Brien
And: James R. Sweeney (Attorney), Christopher Michael (Bailiff), Renata Scott (Mrs. Thatcher), Nicholas Worth (Joey Fetlock)

Director: Robert Lally          Writer: Ken Hecht

7. "The Gospel Truth" Jan. 5, 1991

Reuben's visiting niece reveals she's leaving seminary school to become a singer, and Frye enters her in a gospelfest.

Charise..............................................................Siedah Garrett
Barney..................................................................Mark Lonow
Rick..............................................................................Rick Illes
Deacon Willis...................................................D'Mitch Davis

Director: John Sgueglia          Writer: Jim Geoghan

8. "Lights, Camera, Deacon" Jan. 12, 1991

Frye sees publicity in a televised trial involving writer-comedian Steve Allen in a suit against a fried-chicken mogul (Marino).

Himself......................................................................Steve Allen
Talk-show hostess............................................Melody Rogers
Attorneys....................................John McCann, Gary Grossman
Police official.....................................................James Mathers
Bailiff.......................................................Christopher Michael
Waiter.............................................................Wayne Federman
Capt. Chicken/Commander Cluck.....................Frank Marino

Director: John Sgueglia
Writer: David Pitlik & Barry Gurstein

9. "Unforgettable" Jan. 19, 1991

Frye dates a beautiful, much younger environmentalist (Berry).

Claire....................................................................Halle Berry
Vernon............................................................Dwayne Kennedy
And: Suzanne Stone (Gladys), Claudia Bloom (Waitress)

Director: Gary Shimokawa          Writer: Ken Hecht

10. "Ernie and the Sublimes" Feb. 2, 1991

Frye reunites with his old doo-wop group (Mayo, Foree, Dortch, Taylor), torn apart by a former femme fatale (new recurring guest Page). Radio personality Kasem and pop-rock singer Checker play themselves.

Swifty................................................................Whitman Mayo
Ax...........................................................................Ken Foree
Einstein...............................................................Ron Dortch
String Bean..........................................................Ron Taylor
Bob........................................................................Larry Harpel
Themselves...............................Chubby Checker, Casey Kasem

Director: John Sgueglia
Writers: David Pitlik & Barry Gurstein

11. "The Deacon's Slam Dunk" Feb. 9, 1991

A retired basketball star (former pro Abdul-Jabbar) begins dating Amelia. According to NBC, the series' 100th episode.

James "The Wizard" Anderson................Kareem Abdul-Jabbar
Benito Laguttula.................................................John Costanza
Lorenzo Laguttula..............................................Tony Pandolfo

Director: John Sgueglia          Writer: Bill Streib

**preempted Feb. 16**

12. "Three Men and a Hammer" Feb. 23, 1991

Rap singer M.C. Hammer, shows potential dropout Clarence what life might be like without a high school diploma.

Himself [and] Rev. Pressure, Reuben's
    former seminary roommate............M.C. Hammer (Stanley Kirk Burrell)
Guard.....................................................Jacques Apollo Bolton

Director: John Sgueglia
Writers: Robert Illes & James R. Stein

13. "Nothing Says Lovin'..." March 2, 1991

On her and Reuben's first anniversary, Thelma reveals she's expecting a child. Orig. scheduled for Feb. 23, 8:30-9 p.m.

Father at restaurant................................Andrew Hill Newman
Mother at restaurant......................................Jeanine Jackson
Janet Johnson..................................................Susan Beaubian
Brittany...........................................................................Thora
Jonathan............................................................Michael Ciotti
Waitress...............................................................Nancy Rubin

Director: John Sgueglia          Writer: Robin J. Stein

14. "My Fair Homeboy" March 9, 1991

Frye's panicky when Clarence dates the daughter (Johnson) of his rich college clum (Hancock). Orig. scheduled for March 2.

Announced cast includes: John Hancock (Marshall Whittaker), A.J. Johnson

Director: John Sgueglia
Writers: Robert Illes & James R. Stein

**preempted March 16**

15. "A Star is Burned"  March 23, 1991

Thelma gets her own local TV cooking show.  Hancock reprises his role from last episode.

Marshall Whittaker............................................John Hancock
Eileen..........................................................Katharine Van Loan
Ralph................................................................Hank Berring
Stage manager............................................John Timothy Botka

Director: John Sgueglia
Writers: Darice Rollins and Allison Abner

16. "Deak-Scam"  March 30, 1991

An old nemesis (Glass) invites Frye to join a country club, where the Deacon wanders into a sting operation.  Guest Fabian is a singer.  Orig. scheduled for March 9 and March 16.

Prosecutor Jason Lockwood....................................Ron Glass
Himself...............................................................Fabian [Forte]
Al............................................................Peter Van Norden
And: Barry Dennen (Headwaiter), Jack Ryland (Collins), Oscar Dillon (Zeus), Senait (Tami)

Director: Michael Dimich            Writer: Darice Rollins

17. "The Wild Deak"  April 6, 1991

Itching for adventure, Frye dons leathers and joins a geriatric motorcycle gang.  Dortch reprises his role from ep. 10.

Earl........................................................................Earl Boen
Einstein..............................................................Ron Dortch
Cashmere................................................................Don Gibb
And: Fred Stoller (Bull), Pat Crawford Brown (Winnie)

Director: John Sgueglia              Writer: Bob Peete

18. "Three's a Crowd"  April 13, 1991

Frye begins dating a teacher (Moody) with whom Clarence is smitten; Reuben straps on a pregnancy simulator.

Amy Cassidy......................................................Lynne Moody
Waitress............................................................Nancy Rubin
Ice Pick..................................................................Joe Torry

Director: John Sgueglia              Writer: Jim Geoghan

19. "Date with an Angel"  April 27, 1991

At a charity bachelor auction, Frye is snagged by the insufferable Darla, newly separated from her jealous husband (Mayo, reprising his role from ep. 10).

Swifty............................................................Whitman Mayo
Floozy..............................................................Robbi Chong
Francine...................................................Bambola Allen-Blaine
Yolanda........................................................Sylvia Bronson
Waitress............................................................Nancy Rubin

Director: John Sgueglia
Writers: Barry Gurstein & David Pitlik

20. "Deliverance" Part 1  May 4, 1991

Frye and Clarence try raising church funds by dating wealthy Darla and her equally unattractive granddaughter.

Pamela.................................................................Connie Ray

Peter....................................................................Ron Fassler
Watkins..............................................................Wesley Mann
Darletta, Darla's granddaughter..........................Renee Cross
And: Nancy Rubin (Waitress), Reggie Douglas (Reggie)

Director: John Sgueglia            Writer: Jim Geoghan

21. "Deliverance" Part 2  May 11, 1991

On a telethon, soul singer James Brown (as himself, singing "I Feel Good") helps save the financially troubled church; Thelma delivers a baby boy.  Guests Lewis and Price are singers.

Himself............................................................James Brown
Herself....................Mrs. James Brown [sic] (Adrienne Brown)
Himself..............................................................Butch Lewis
Himself.............................................................Lloyd Price
Woman..........................................................Barbara Pariot
Thelma and Rueben's baby.........Crystal/Cherish/Byron Davis

Director: John Sgueglia
Writers: Robert Illes & James R. Stein

**preempted May 18**

## American Dreamer

NBC          Sept. 22-Dec. 22    Saturdays, 10:30-11 p.m.
             May 25-June 22      Saturdays, 8:30-9 p.m.

Series Premiere: Sept. 20, 1990
Final telecast: June 22, 1991

Seriocomedy of a TV reporter turned Chicago newspaper columnist, living in a small Wisconsin town with his two children and taking frequent impressionistic forays into memory.

Tom Nash................................................................Robert Urich
Lillian Abernathy, his secretary..............................Carol Kane
Rachel Nash (15)...................................................Chay Lentin
Danny Nash......................................................Johnny Galecki
Holly..................................................................Margaret Welsh
Joe Baines, Tom's editor....................................Jeffrey Tambor

*Recurring:*
Bill Abernathy, Lillian's ex-husband
     (ep. 5,13-14,17)............................................John Glover
Nelson Abernathy, Bill and Lillian's son
     (ep. 13-14,17).............................................Brice Beckham

UBU Productions in assoc. with Paramount Television
Executive producers: Gary David Goldberg, Susan Seeger
Supervising producer: Seth Freeman
Producers: Linda Nieber, Sam Weisman
Associate producer: Diane Edwards Thorington
Story editors: Brad Hall, Theresa Rebeck
Creative consultant: Bruce Helford
Director of photography (variously): Robert F. Liu, A.S.C.;
     Mikel Neirs
Music arranged and performed by: Tom Scott
Theme: Peter Leinheiser (words & music); performer
     uncredited
Director: Sam Weisman
Creator: Susan Seeger

1. (pilot)  Thursday, Sept. 20, 1990  9:30-10 p.m.

Tom interviews his old high-school sweetheart (Banes).

Jessica.................................................................Lisa Banes

Margaret Thatcher................................................Erica Rogers
Young Jessica....................................................Carla Gugino

Writer: Susan Seeger

2. "Guys Just Wanna Have Fun" Sept. 22, 1990

Tom organizes an encounter group after Lillian remarks about men not sharing their true feelings with each other.

Terry................................................James Cromwell
Rick................................................Sal Viscuso
Davey................................................Michael G. Hagerty
Warren................................................Brian Nestor

Writer: Gary David Goldberg

3. "Flight of the Dodo" Sept. 29, 1990

A disillusioned cartoonist quits his newspaper job and seeks a hideaway from reality with Tom.

Teddy................................................Austin Pendleton
Bud................................................Terry Wills

Writer: Brad Hall

4. "All God's Children Go to Wisconsin" Oct. 6, 1990

The arrival of a new Episcopal minister causes former Catholic Tom to rethink his plans for his children's religious training.

Reverend Janet................................................Stephanie Dunnam
Father Mahoney................................................Richard Venture
Boys....................Dustin Berkovitz, Micah Rowe, Adam Ryen
Girl................................................Remy Ryan

Writer: Bruce Helford

5. "Corvette Man" Oct. 13, 1990

Lillian's visited by her ne'er-do-well car salesperson ex-husband (recurring guest Glover).

Writer: Theresa Rebeck

6. "Over the Hill?" Oct. 20, 1990

Tom ponders his mortality after a worrisome medical checkup.

Dr. Timmy Greer................................................Geoffrey Nauffts
Pop................................................Michael Alldredge
Susie................................................Jenny Drugan
Eddie................................................Christopher Castile

Writer: Brad Hall

7. "Mr. Wizard" Oct. 27, 1990

Tom fills in as a substitute high school English teacher.

Larry/"Mr. W"................................................Scott Paulin
Mrs. Palmieri................................................Shirley Prestia
John................................................Jason Horst
Kate................................................Nicki Vannice
And: Heather Green (Stephanie), Yunoka Doyle (Christine), Christopher Blank (Mark)

Writer: David Owen

8. "Divorce American Dreamer Style" Nov. 3, 1990

On the first anniversary of her divorce, Lillian winds up in a motel room with Joe.

Mom................................................Pamela Winslow
Rita................................................Jennifer Nash

Writer: Susan Seeger & Brad Hall

9. "In from the Cold" Part 1   Nov. 10, 1990

A suspected spy offers to turn himself in to the FBI if Tom will tell his side of the story.  Orig. scheduled for Oct. 13.

Kathleen Ryan................................................Christine Ebersole
FBI agent Ralph Short................................................Leslie Jordan
Reporters....................Richard McGonagle, Charles Stransky
Pres. Richard M. Nixon................................................John Roarke

Writer: Seth Freeman

**preempted Nov. 17**

10. "In from the Cold" Part 2   Nov. 24, 1990

Faber shows up, and Kathleen is revealed as a rival reporter.

Kathleen Ryan................................................Christine Ebersole
FBI agent Ralph Short................................................Leslie Jordan
Carl S. Faber................................................Joe Spano
Reporters....................Richard McGonagle, Charles Stransky

Writer: Seth Freeman

11. "The Fabulous Baker Girls"  Dec. 1, 1990

Holly's charismatic, free-spirited sister (Matthews) visits.

Drew................................................DeLane Matthews
Customer................................................Max Delgado
Jesse................................................Justin Shenkarow

Writer: Theresa Rebeck

12. "A Face in the Cloud"  Dec. 8, 1990

Still-grieving Rachel and Danny are upset at Tom's plan to write a column about their late mom (Menzies, Urich's real-life wife).  Orig. scheduled for Nov. 10.

Elizabeth................................................Heather Menzies
Kurt................................................Eric Champnella

Writer: Gordon Farr

**preempted Dec. 15
on hiatus after Dec. 22 rerun**

13. "Don't Drink the Water"  May 25, 1991

Tom's kids take a part-time job with Lillian's hustling ex-husband, now a local bottled-water entrepreneur.

Water Dept. person................................................Sam Lloyd
Principal Lucchesi................................................Brian Smiar

Writer: Theresa Rebeck

14. "Mother Knows Best"  June 1, 1991

A panicky Lillian begs Tom to pretend they're married when she learns her mother (Brennan) is coming to visit.

Beatrice............................................................Eileen Brennan
Natalie................................................................Susan Hess

Writers: Brad Hall & Theresa Rebeck

15. "Papa Joe" June 8, 1991

Joe's rare weekend with his 15-year-old daughter (Warren) is spoiled when he finds his ex plans to move to Paris with her.

Lisa Baines....................................................Kiersten Warren
Little Lisa.......................................................Noley Thornton

Writer: Seth Freeman

16. "Heartbreak Diner" June 15, 1991

Tom's well-meant intervention in Rachel's crush on a college student (Barnes) just winds up embarrassing her.

Jamie.............................................Christopher Daniel Barnes
Davey...............................................Michael G. Hagerty

Writer: Susan Seeger

17. "They Shoot Ducks, Don't They?" June 22, 1991

Danny disobeys his father and sneaks off to go duck hunting.

Pop.................................................................Michael Alldredge
Rev. Bates.....................................................Andrew McCullough

Writer: Brad Hall

## The Antagonists

CBS                    Thursdays, 9-10 p.m.

Series premiere: March 26, 1991
Final telecast: May 30, 1991

Law drama of the volatile personal relationship between a straightlaced prosecutor (Holly) and a flamboyant, unpredictable attorney (Andrews) often opposing her in court.

Jonathan (Jack) Scarlett....................................David Andrews
Kate Ward.............................................................Lauren Holly
Clark Munsinger.....................................................Matt Roth
Joanie Rutledge (ep. 2-on).............................Lisa Jane Persky
Asst. D.A. Marvin Thompson..........................Brent Jennings

*Recurring*
Mona Feldman (ep.1-2,4)...................................Dey Young
Philip Van Petton (ep. 1-2,7,9)..........................Erich Anderson
Larry Eccles (ep. 1,7,9).......................................Tony Simotes

Universal Television, an MCA Co.
Executive producers: William Sackheim, Daniel Pyne
Supervising producers (ep. 2-on): Les Carter, Susan Sisko
Producer (ep. 2-on): Aaron Lipstadt
Co-producer (ep. 2-on): Jack Terry
Associate producer: Todd Pinsky (ep. 1); Janice Cooke-Leonard (ep. 2-on)
Director of photography: Roy H. Wagner, A.S.C. (ep. 1); Stevan Larner, A.S.C.
Technical advisors: Harold Rosenthal, Elizabeth A. Lippet
Music [and] Theme (instrumental): Michael Convertino
Creator: Daniel Pyne

1. "The Antagonists" Tuesday, March 26, 1991 9:30-11 p.m.

A woman (Bauer) arrested for drunk driving has a necklace belonging to a recent murder victim. Wahl, the 1983 *Penthouse* Pet of the Year, is the estranged wife of actor Ken Wahl.

Gretchen..........................................................Belinda Bauer
Dieter Thurman...............................................Stephen Davies
D.A. Klein.........................................................Harris Laskawy
Detective Hodges.................................................Will Leskin
Mario Escobar................................................Geoffrey Rivas
Simon................................................................Al Pugliese
Gardner...............................................Christopher McDonald
Gary.......................................................................Sean Faro
Dry cleaner.......................................................Shelly DeSai
Florence Howard..........................................Patience Cleveland
Judge Leipzig...............................................Nicholas Kepros
Press guy............................................................Lance Davis
Bruce...................................................................Micah Grant
Secretary............................................................Eileen Conn
Older woman...................................................Bunny Summers
Kelly....................................Corinne Wahl a.k.a. Corinne Alphen
Judge Burt.........................................................Rich Crater
Police officers...................Cheryl Wheeler-Dixon, Shane Dixon
Night watch.....................................................Don Brunner
Japanese businesspeople.............Kit Wong, Hayward Soo Hoo
    Also orig. announced:
    Diane Fisk (Party hostess), Jake Jacobs (Banker), Timothy Charles (Accountant), DeeDee Michaels (Deliveryperson), Scott LaRose (Cab Driver), Maria Diaz (Susie)

Director: Rob Cohen                    Writer: Daniel Pyne

2. "Silent Beef" March 28, 1991

Jack defends a college pal (Salem) on an apparently self-defense murder charge, though Kate is determined to convict.

Rafe Sassa..........................................................Kario Salem
Nick Ramos.......................................................David Proval
Red Wilson...........................................................Jack Carter
Marty Lorber......................................................Paul Willson
Arturo Medina..............................................Mario Roccuzzo
Joe Collela....................................................Scott Burkholder
Bartender.......................................................Thomas Wagner
Detective Roy Shroyer.....................................Peder Melhuse
Judge Terrence Bannon...................................Tom Dahlgren
Rene Gilette...................................................Jonathan Fuller
Vanetta Gray...................................................Kathryn Kimler
Police officer....................................................Ron Troncatty
Nigel Dee...................................................Sean Francis Howse
Clarence (orig. Walter) Bishop, Jr......................Robert Munns

Director: Aaron Lipstadt      Writers: Les Carter & Susan Sisko

3. "Full Disclosure" April 4, 1991

Jack is court-appointed advisor to an ex-con (Maruzzo) defending himself for his sister's murder. Orig. scheduled for April 11.

Frank Scarpo.......................................................Joe Maruzzo
Judge Theresa Foxworth..................................Caroline Kava
Mrs. Lewinger..................................................Helen Stenborg
Detective Haley.................................................Mitch Pileggi
Janet Scarpo...................................................Kristina Loggia
And: David M. Parker (Detective Dandrich), Daniel O'Shea (Deputy Terry Arthur), Russell Lunday (Bailiff Luchinski), Kevin McDermott (D.A. Roper), Francois Chau (Deekin), Mark Daneri (Detective), Ken Medlock (Cop)

Director: James Quinn          Writer: Robert Cochran

**4. "Con Safos"** April 11, 1991

A teen gang-member (Coca) is accused of a drive-by shooting.

Big Mike Petoskey..............................................Michael Alldredge
Reuben Ramos/El Dreamer...............................Richard Coca
Armando Ramos, Sr., his father.......................Eloy Casados
Judge Wallace Gaines.......................................J.A. Preston
Insane Duane.....................................................Bruce Beatty
Sam Garmo.........................................................Alan Fudge
Judge Josh Kahn ..............................................Pierre Epstein
Sister Delourdes................................................Anne Betancourt
Woody Hitchcock...............................................Michael Ayr
And: Thomas Virtue (Artie Reznik) Edward Jackman (Juggling
     cowboy), Elizabeth Storm (Andrea Kasdan), Ann Gee
     Byrd (Judge Candace Feury), Karon Wright (Internal Af-
     fairs officer), Dave A.R. White (Off. Kootch), Mark Adair
     (Gang member), Dorothy Constantine, Adrian de la Garza

Director: Brad Silberling
Teleplay: Les Carter & Susan Sisko
Story: Steve Wasserman & Jessica Klein and Les Carter &
     Susan Sisko

**5. "Variations on a Theme"** April 18, 1991

A con artist (Auberjonois) who specializes in ripping off elderly
ladies is accused of murder when a mark is found dead. Director Haid is a former cast-member of *Hill Street Blues*.

Alistar Lombard...............................................Rene Auberjonois
Emil Kutcher.....................................................Mark Margolis
Mrs. Reinfield...................................................Claudette Nevins
Detective Reese................................................John Putch
Judges..........................Abraham Alvarez, Silvana Gallardo
Esther...............................................................Patricia Huston
And: Hanna Hertelendy (Ilka Shad), Marjorie Lovett (Astrid
     Kronauer), Elisabeth Harmon (Woman), Paul Ganus
     (Man), Frank Giarardeau (Detective), Homeselle Smith,
     Buster Jones (Clerks), Larry Barrett (Guard)

Director: Charles Haid
Writers: Carolyn Shelby & Christopher Ames

**6. "Lawyers, Guns and Money"** April 25, 1991

Despite videotaped evidence otherwise, Jack tries to prove his
mentor and old boss (Rich) is innocent of drug charges.

Moses Metzler...................................................Allan Rich
Gary Zandonella................................................Richard Cox
Annie Drew........................................................Laurie O'Brien
Judge F.V. Pierotti............................................Raymond Serra
Warren Selby.....................................................Randy Polk
Owen Smith Gallagher.....................................Erick Avari
Randy.................................................................Jahary Bennett
Judge W. Garcia.................................................Norma Donaldson
Fenstry...............................................................Hank Stone
And: Sonya Hunt (Young mom), Marilyn Fox (Knitting juror),
     Orlando Bonner (Bailiff Bob), Charles Douglass (Clerk),
     James Dalesandro (Paco), Gloria Hendry (Court clerk),
     Loren Farmer (Dentist), James Parkes (Barry), Warren
     Rice, Joey Hamilton, Mary Maldonado (Jurors)

Director: Deborah Reinisch
Writer: Harold Rosenthal (also orig. announced: Daniel Pyne)

**7. "Unnatural Acts"** May 2, 1991

A Latino political refugee (DeSoto) is tried for the murder of
her American lover. Melhuse reprises his role from ep. 2.

Zulena Godoy.....................................................Rosanna DeSoto
Gil Arenque........................................................Tony Plana
Gary Eccles........................................................Sean Faro
Sgt. Zaruq..........................................................Eli Danker
Detective Roy Shroyer........................................Peder Melhuse
Matthew Binyon..................................................Joe Kell
Shirley Benning...................................................Lisa Marie Russell
And: Abraham Alvarez (Judge), Stephen Tobolowsky (Raymond
     Dumas), Robert Wightman (Translator), Maryanne McGar-
     ry (Judge), Endre Hules (Chairperson), Dana Williams
     (Feminist), Tom Challis (Long hair), Joe Viviani (Reporter)

Director: Aaron Lipstadt          Teleplay: Jeff Cazanov
Story: Melinda Snodgrass

**preempted May 15**

**8. "State of Mind"** May 23, 1991

As Kate argues murder for a woman (Plunkett) on trial for killing her husband and his mistress, Jack seeks manslaughter.
Kava reprises her role from ep. 3. Orig. scheduled for May 2.

Lisa Ames...........................................................Maryann Plunkett
Judge Theresa Foxworth....................................Caroline Kava
Marsha Manning.................................................Nancy Harewood
Sally Gilchrest....................................................Jane Alden
Millsteen............................................................Jeffrey Allan Chandler
Dr. Robert West..................................................Paul Collins
Dr. Eugene Walsh...............................................Ping Wu
Charles Ames.....................................................Stephen Mendel
Nancy Ames.......................................................Juliet Sorcey
Sarah McKenna..................................................Elaine Kagan
Lewis Kleist........................................................Robert David Hall
Thelma (orig. Ella) White...................................Lynn Wanlass
And: Andrew Castillo (Duran), Shelly Desai (Danny Stiles),
     Nick Jameson (Arza Schwartz), Doreene Hamilton (Court
     clerk), Tom Wideline (John McKenna), Maryann Powell
     (Stenographer), Chris Cole, Lawrence McNeal III (Cops),
     Johnny Crear (Ballistics expert), Rebecca Friedman (Bev-
     erly Ames), Maria Pecci (Denise Ranken)

Director: Charles Haid
Writer: Melinda Snodgrass (Les Carter, Susan Sisko also orig.
     announced)

**9. "Brother to Brother"** May 30, 1991

Jack appeals when a convicted murderer's (Steinmetz) brother
(Baltz) confesses to the crime. O'Brien reprises her role from
ep. 6, Faro from ep. 7. Orig. scheduled for April 25.

Leon Riker.........................................................Kirk Baltz
Benjamin Riker..................................................Richard Steinmetz
Annie Drew........................................................Laurie O'Brien
Gary Eccles........................................................Sean Faro
Judge Brock........................................................Phil Rubenstein
Doreen Messner..................................................Kitty Swink
Sam Riker...........................................................Philip Baker Hall
Caryn (orig. Cathy) Clifton.................................Greta Blackburn
Allan Binaud (orig. Alan Binder)........................Bob Delegall
Bruno Grimaldi...................................................Peter Esfakis
Kenji Masuoka....................................................Darrell Kunitomi
Operator.............................................................Tim McCormack
     Also orig. announced:
     Desiree Russell.....................................Mychelle Charters

Director: Chip Chalmers          Story: Tracy Friedman
Teleplay: Tracy Friedman and Les Carter & Susan Sisko
(Orig. announced: Writers: Tracy Friedman, Les Carter & Su-
san Sisko and Daniel Pyne)

## Anything But Love

ABC
Feb. 6-April 17, May 8-June 5          Wednesdays, 9:30-10 p.m.
Aug. 7-on                              Wednesdays, 10-10:30 p.m.

Series premiere: March 7, 1989

Comedy of two writers for *Chicago Weekly* magazine, on their
journey from friends to lovers. Robin's ex-husband: Kenny.
Hannah and Robin's nickname for each other: Mrs. Schmenk-
man. Curtis is the daughter of performers Tony Curtis and
Janet Leigh, and the wife of producer Christopher Guest.

Hannah Miller...............................................Jamie Lee Curtis
Martin E. (Marty) Gold..............................Richard Lewis
Editor Catherine Hughes.................................Ann Magnuson
Columnist Mike Urbanek.......................................Bruce Weitz
Jules Bennett, Catherine's assistant.................Richard Frank
Robin Dulitski, Hannah's best friend.....................Holly Fulger

*Recurring:*
Patrick Serreau (ep. 1-3)...........................................John Ritter

Adam Productions in assoc. with 20th Century Fox Television
Executive producers: Peter Noah, Robert M. Myman
Co-executive producer: Janis Hirsch
Producer: Peter Schindler
Co-producers: Bill Bryan, Clare Witt
Story editor: Bill Barol
Executive consultant: Eric Cohen
Creative consultant: Richard Lewis
Director of photography: Richard Hissong
Music: Jeremy Lubbock
Theme (instrumental): John David Souther
Director unless otherwise noted: Robert Berlinger
Creator: Wendy Kout
Developed by: Dennis Koenig and Peter Noah

1. "Say It Again, Han"  Feb. 6, 1991

Hannah and Marty's initial tryst is complicated by the arrival
of a dashing, world-famous photographer (recurring guest Ritter, a principal of the series' production company).

Writer: Peter Noah

2. "Martus Interruptus"  Feb. 13, 1991

Marty panics when Serreau asks Hannah to accompany him
on a photo shoot in West Africa.

Writer: Janis Hirsch

**preempted Feb. 20**

3. "Hello...Mali?"  Feb. 27, 1991

Before she leaves for West Africa with Patrick, Hannah anticipates a night of lovemaking with Marty.

Jake...........................................................Andre Rosey Brown
Beepo.....................................................................Tony Longo

Writers: Billy Van Zandt & Jane Milmore

**unscheduled preemption March 6**

4. "Long Day's Journey Into...What?"  March 13, 1991

After their first night together, Hannah and Marty fantasize

about how they'll behave in the office -- *a la* Ben Hecht (*The
Front Page*), Tennessee Williams (*A Streetcar Named Desire*),
Noel Coward (*Design for Living*) and David Lynch (*Twin Peaks*).
Orig. scheduled for March 6.

Writer: Peter Noah

5. "The Day After"  March 20, 1991

At work, Hannah and Marty try to separate their personal and
professional lives.  Orig. scheduled for March 13.

Writer: Janis Hirsch

6. "The Torrid Zone"  March 27, 1991

Catherine sends Marty and a beautiful model (Waterman) on a
tropical swimsuit shoot.  Orig. scheduled for March 20.

Nicole Dupre.............................................Felicity Waterman
Steve.......................................................Patrick Warburton
Co-worker Louis....................................................David Allyn

Writer: Bill Bryan

7. "My New Best Friend"  Monday, April 1, 1991
   10:30-11 p.m.

Hannah tests her integrity when she befriends an aerobics
classmate to learn about her famous billionaire boyfriend.

Tara Wetherly.......................................................Brenda Strong
Louis...................................................................David Allyn

Writer: Bill Barol

**preempted April 3**

8. "Adventures in Babysitting"  April 10, 1991

Marty falls ill while babysitting Hannah's young cousin (Haun).

Nikki........................................................................Lindsey Haun
And: Ellen Ratner, Joel Cason

Writer: Janis Hirsch

9. "Isn't It Romantic?"  April 17, 1991

Hannah wants to break up with Marty. Lubbock, in a cameo,
is the series' music composer.

Louis [no lines]......................................................David Allyn
Orchestra conductor [no lines].......................Jeremy Lubbock

Director: Richard Marion    Writer: Bill Barol

**on hiatus**

10. "Scream a Little Scream"  May 8, 1991

Robin begins to feel unwanted; Catherine begins scream therapy.  Unscheduled preemption of *My Life and Times*.

Office cleaner (no lines)............................................Linda Lutz

Writer: Bill Bryan

11. "Pot of Gold"  May 15, 1991

Marty's jealous when Catherine promises Hannah a big raise.

Louis..................................................David Allyn
Bootmaker...................................Marius Mazmanian

Writer: Bill Bryan

**on hiatus after June 5 rerun; reruns begin again Aug. 7**

**renewed for 1991-92; new episodes begin Sept. 25, 1991**

## Babes

Fox          Sept. 13-June 13  Thursdays, 8:30-9 p.m.
             July 13-Aug. 10   Saturdays, 9:30-10 p.m.

Series premiere: Sept. 13, 1990
Final telecast: Aug. 10, 1991

Comedy of three very overweight sisters sharing a cramped
New York City apartment.  Initial cast-member Overton was
listed as a guest performer ep. 10.

Charlene Gilbert...........................Wendy Jo Sperber
Marlene Gilbert.....................................Lesley Boone
Darlene Gilbert.....................................Susan Peretz
Ronnie Underwood (ep. 1-9)...............Rick Overton

*Recurring:*
Neighbor Mrs. Newman (ep. 10-11,15,17,19,22).......Nedra Volz
Neighbor child Billy (ep. 11-13,15)....................Miko Hughes
Lisa (ep. 20-22).........................................Shea Fowler
Denise (ep. 20-22).......................................Molly Orr

Sandollar in assoc. with 20th Century Fox Television
Executive producers: Sandy Gallin, Candace Farrell, Brian
    Levant (early in season), Jordan Moffet (ep. 2-on)
Producers: Tracy Jackson, Marsha Posner Williams (ep. 1);
    Patricia Rickey, Cindy Begel, Lesa Kita, Michael Lessac
    (latter four most of season); Geralyn Maddern (later in
    season)
Associate producer (variously): Alan Padula; Geralyn Maddern
Story editors: David A. Goodman, Rick Copp (Tracey Jackson
    orig. announced as Executive story editor)
Executive script consultants: David Silverman, Stephen
    Sustarsic
Executive story consultant: Dava Savel (early in season)
Creative consultants: Stephen Neigher, Robert DeLaurentis,
    Eric Cohen (latter two early in season), Buddy Sheffield
    (later in season)
Director of photography: Richard Brown
Theme: Jay Gruska (words and music)
Music (variously): Jay Gruska; Steve Orich
Director unless otherwise noted: Michael Lessac
Creators: Gail Parent and Tracey Jackson

--------

1. "Babes" Sept. 13, 1990

Newly separated Darlene and newly unemployed Marlene
move in with sis Charlene.  Orig. scheduled for Aug. 23.

Tyrone.................................................Richard Poe
Maxmillion..........................................S.A. Griffin
Ivan Ivanstein.....................................Murray Rubin
Shula...............................................Donna Ponterotto
Jimmi............................................William De Acutis
Juju.....................................................Kevin West
And: Michelle Haupert (Gloria), Melissa Young (Blonde)

Writer: Tracey Jackson

2. "Bend Me, Shape Me" Sept. 20, 1990

The sisters face weight prejudice when they join a health club.

Suzanne.............................................Riley Bowman
Vince......................................................Ben Reed
Naomi..........................................Jennifer Convy
Ann...............................................Lynn Danielson
And: Erica Yohn (Joan), Debbie Barker (Holly)

Writers: Rick Copp & David A. Goodman

3. "Everything But Love" Sept. 27, 1990

Darlene's tempted to return to her seemingly repentant ex.

Wilbur, Darlene's ex-husband......................Brandon Maggert
Greg..........................................J.C. MacKenzie
Tony.........................................Marc DeCarlo

Writers: Stephen Sustarsic and David Silverman

**preempted Oct. 4**

4. "The One Where Charlene Meets Ronnie's Mother"
   Oct. 11, 1990

The one where Charlene meets Ronnie's mother.

Doris Underwood..............................Dena Dietrich
Bartender.......................................Randall Carver
SWAT officer.....................................Ken Wright

Writer: Dennis Snee

5. "Temper, Temper" Oct. 18, 1990

Darlene, trying to control her temper, explodes when her ex-
husband (Maggert, reprising his role from ep. 3) uses under-
handed divorce tactics.  Orig. scheduled for Oct. 11.

Wilbur............................................Brandon Maggert
Dr. Ramirez.....................................Candace Azzara
Mr. Anderson..................................Armin Shimerman
And: Tom Fridley (Joey), Valente Rodriguez (Underground
    Avenger), Derek Loughran (Mime)

Writers: Lesa Kite & Cindy Begel

6. "No Regrets" Oct. 25, 1990

Following the death of a friend, the ladies each set out to do
the things they most regret never having done.  TV kid's-show
pioneer Buffalo Bob Smith was orig. announced to guest-star.

Wranglin' Rick Roundup...........................Jeff Corey
Mrs. Werber.......................................Peggy Pope
Detective O'Grady.............................John Del Regno
Richard Werber..................................Jim Doughan
And: Gretchen Wyler (Mrs. McNair), Jennifer Banko (Audrey)

Writer: Greg Phillips

7. "Dream Vacation" Nov. 1, 1990

The sisters find romance on a low-rent island vacation.

Resort-director Sandoval........................Cesar Romero
Dave..............................................Walter Olkewicz
Jack...................................................Jack Riley
Joey...............................................Doug Ballard

And: Earl Boen (Sheldon), Joe Gieb (Spittoon), Angelo Tiffe (Rick), Jennifer Ashleigh (Knockout)

Writer: Al Aidekman

8. "Marlene's Problem"  Nov. 8, 1990

Marlene gets hired and fired as the Hefty Hose model, Darlene's dog-grooming assistant, and a bit-part actress.

| | |
|---|---|
| Marsha | Rhonda Aldrich |
| Crellin | Jack Blessing |
| Patient | Tom Hallick |
| Mrs. Pomerantz | Randee Heller |
| Merit | Matt McCoy |
| Doctor | Lyman Ward |
| Voice of English announcer | Peter Brooks |
| Voice of clapboard person | Eric Head |
| Voice of TV announcer | Jeffrey Myers |
| Big Mike | Tom Williams |

Writers: Lesa Kite & Cindy Begel

9. "The Thanksgiving Show"  Nov. 22, 1990

The sisters share the holiday with a homeless orphan (Baby D).

| | |
|---|---|
| Nicky | Baby D |
| Ralph | Basil Hoffman |
| Aunt Marion | Rhoda Gemignani |
| Marla | Cheri Caspari |
| Bobby | Ken Wright |

Teleplay: Jordan Moffet
Story: Jordan Moffet & Jeff Stein

10. "Ronnie's Rib Joint" a.k.a. "Ribs"
    Dec. 6, 1990  8:33-9 p.m.

When Ronnie goes out of town for the weekend (returning married), Charlene runs his restaurant.  Orig. scheduled for Nov. 15.  Late start due to previous show (*The Simpsons*) running overtime.

| | |
|---|---|
| Joyce Healy | Margaret Reed |
| Jake | Tom Silardi |
| Sheila | Alicia Brandt |
| Bea | Dona Hardy |
| Dr. Roberts | Tom Henschel |
| Gil | John Hostetter |
| Businessperson | Wayne Armstrong |

And: Holly Butler (Mary), Kimberly Grey (Gina), Richmond Harrison (Brian), John Hawkes (Lloyd), Lawrence Parks (Roy), Diane Robin (Irma), Greg Thriloway (John)

Director: Don Corvan
Writer: Jeff Stein (Dava Savill orig. announced)

11. "Rent Strike"  Dec. 20, 1990

Charlene organizes a rent strike against the building owner. Azaria is a recurring voiceover guest on *The Simpsons*.

| | |
|---|---|
| Bud | Tracey Walter |
| Tony | Hank Azaria |
| Howard | Oliver Clark |
| Maria | Cheri Casprari |
| Massey | Dan Gilvezan |
| Wally | Peter Iacangelo |

And: Barry Kivel (Fred), Michael Durrette (Bailiff), Katherine Henryk (Leona), Ed Morgan (Judge Howell)

Director: Howard Murray
Writers: Stephen Sustarsic and David Silverman

12. "Most Likely to Succeed"  Jan. 10, 1991

Charlene tries to convince her reunion classmates she's lived up to her old "Succeed" label.  Nahan is a sportscaster.

| | |
|---|---|
| Sheila Marie | Denny Dillon |
| Roberta | Mary Lou Childs |
| Preston | Donn Simione |
| Ellen | Caroline Williams |
| Himself | Stu Nahan |
| Billy Bob | Stuart Charno |

And: Karen Haber (Jane), Steve Lundquist (John), Michael McKenzie (Barry), Heather Wilson (Knockout)

Director: Don Corvan          Writers: Lesa Kite & Cindy Begel

**unscheduled preemption Jan. 17**

13. "All Bummed Out"  Jan. 24, 1991

The sisters turn a bum (Windom) into a ruthless executive.

| | |
|---|---|
| Darryl | William Windom |
| Langstrom | Barry Michlin |
| Sister Katherine | Elmarie Wendel |
| Bums | Carmen Filpi, Frank Noon |
| Voice of receptionist | Barbara Gannen |

Director: Howard Murray
Writers: David Silverman & Stephen Sustarsic

14. "babes, lies and videotape"  Jan. 31, 1991

The sisters compete for the same man (Carreiro). Guest Puck is a Los Angeles chef-restaurateur. Orig. scheduled for Feb. 7.

| | |
|---|---|
| Chris | Tony Carreiro |
| Himself | Wolfgang Puck |
| Alexis | Julie Payne |
| Francis | Brian Backer |
| Woman | Marsha Clark |

And: Frank Collison (Jeremiah), Doug Hale (Voice of Herb), Joe Lala (Waiter), Dane Ince, Joel Leder, Larry Parks

Director: Howard Murray                    Writer: Dava Savel

15. "Hello Dolly"  Feb. 7, 1991

Charlene becomes makeup artist to country-music singer Dolly Parton, and gets blamed for tabloid rumors. Parton (a principal of the show's production company), sings "Why'd You Come in Here Lookin' Like That?" in a music-video segment also featuring the three co-stars. Orig. scheduled for Jan. 31.

| | |
|---|---|
| Herself | Dolly Parton |
| Becky Higgins | Lucy Lee Flipin |
| Maury | Carmine Caridi |

Director: Howard Murray
Writers: Rick Copp & David A. Goodman

16. "Babes in Boyland"  Feb. 14, 1991

Fed up with New York City guys, the sisters try the men in Alaska.  Orig. scheduled for Jan. 24.

| | |
|---|---|
| Jacques | Nicholas Guest |
| Ed | Peter Marc |

Pierre................................................................Phil Proctor
And: Daniel Greene (Fantasy Rusty), Patrick T. O'Brien
(Rusty), Natalie Strauss (Vicky), Ivy Austin (Loretta)

Director: Howard Murray          Writer: Dava Savel

17. "Mom"  Feb. 21, 1991

The sisters' domineering -- and thin -- mother visits, and does
better with men than they do.

Mrs. Gilbert................................................Barbara Barrie
Fred...............................................................Peter Haskell

Director: Howard Murray          Writer: Chuck Upton

**preempted Feb. 28 and March 7**

18. "The Last Temptation of Marlene"  March 14, 1991

When their car breaks down out of town, Marlene and a nice,
wholesome guy (Witting) face temptation at an "adult" motel.

Leon...............................................................Steve Witting
Mo....................................................................Ernie Sabella
Chill..............................................................Lee Arenberg
Nun...............................................................Barbara Gannen

Director: Art Dielhenn
Writers: Rick Copp & David A. Goodman

19. "The House of Gilbert"  March 28, 1991

Charlene puts her money where her mouth is, and vice versa,
in helping Marlene set up a large-lady fashion business.

Mr. Clem.......................................................Leslie Jordan
Sloan............................................................Susan Kellerman
Salesperson...............................................Karla Tamburrelli
And: Gary Bolen (Dawson), Helen Siff (Olga)

Director: Art Dielhenn          Writer: Chuck Distler

**preempted April 18**

20. "Not Married...With Children"  April 25, 1991

When Darlene is arrested for fighting at a hockey game, she's
sentenced to perform community service at a children's center.
Riley reprises his role from ep. 7. Guest Berger is the series'
audience warm-up person. Orig. scheduled for April 18.

Jack.................................................................Jack Riley
Mrs. Lipnik...................................................Lois deBanzie
Allison........................................................Donna Ponterotto
Bobby..............................................................Jesse Stock
And: Abraham Verduzco, Michael Berger

Director: Rob Schiller          Writer: Suzanne Kay

21. "Eleven Angry Men...And Charlene"  May 2, 1991

Charlene tries to land a date with a handsome fellow juror
(Rich). Orig. scheduled for April 25.

Lowry...........................................................Christopher Rich
Milligan...........................................................Sal Viscuso
Mr. Neal.........................................................Lenny Wolpe
Judge Holser..................................................Patrick Cronin
And: Len Lesser (Eberhardt), Lee Brooks (Mark), Randall
Caldwell (Meyer), Denis Mandel (Mr. Logan)

Director: Howard Murray
Writers: David Silverman & Stephen Sustarsic

22. "Three's a Crowd"  May 9, 1991

When the apartment is deemed overcrowded, Marlene and
Darlene decide to move out and be on their own.

Caryn..............................................................Siobhan Fallon
Mike.....................................................Michael Gilbert Lewis
Brunhilda........................................................Moria Turner

Director: Howard Murray
Writers: Rick Copp & David A. Goodman

**preempted June 20, June 27 and July 3**

## Baby Talk

ABC          March 8-April 5     Fridays, 9:30-10 p.m.
             April 16-May 7      Tuesdays, 8:30-9 p.m.
             May 17              Friday, 9:30-10 p.m.
             Aug. 16             Friday, 8:30-9 p.m.

Series premiere: March 8, 1991

Comedy of a single mother in New York City's TriBeCa neighborhood, raising her infant son (whose adult-like thoughts we
hear) while she searches for a "perfect father." Based on the
movie *Look Who's Talking* (1989). Exteriors shot in New York
City. Connie Selleca, orig. announced to star, left due to contract differences, according to Columbia Pictures Television.
Clooney (nephew of singer Rosemary Clooney) left some weeks
later but returned for a few episodes after Duffy was cast.
Orig. scheduled to premiere fall 1990, on Tuesdays, 8:30 p.m.

Maggie Campbell.................................................Julia Duffy
Joe (ep. 1-4, 12)............................................George Clooney
Fogarty...........................................................William Hickey
Howard..............................................................Lenny Wolpe
Dr. Eliot Fleisher.......................................Tom Alan Robbins
Voice of Mickey Campbell...................................Tony Danza
*Cast-members listed in end-credits:*
Mickey Campbell (infant)...........................Paul/Ryan Jessup

*Recurring:*
Nurse Andrea (ep. 1,3,8-10,12).................Michelle Ashlee
Paul (ep. 5-6,10).................................................Paul Sand
Claire (ep. 5-6,10).............................................Paula Kelly
Stella (ep. 5-6,10).......................................Jackie Swanson
Regina (ep. 5-6,10)............................................Sue Giosa
Elizabeth (ep. 5-6,10)....................................Ann Wilkinson
Voice of Stan (ep. 5-6,10)...........................Perry Anzilotti
Voice of Zach (ep. 5-6,10)..............................John Bowman
Voice of Lisa (ep. 5-6,10)................................Dinah Lenney
Baby Stan (ep. 5-6,10)..................Daniel/Nicholas Yon
Baby Zach (ep. 5-6,10)................Michael/Richard Imsen
Baby Lisa (ep. 5-6,10).................Hannah/Elanna Giram
Baby Luther (ep. 5-6,10)...........Chay/Christian Kirkland

Columbia Pictures Television / The Weinberger Co.
Executive producer: Ed. Weinberger
Co-executive producer: Alan Kirschenbaum (Marshall Karp
    also orig. announced)
Producers: Maxine Lupiduss, Mark J. Greenberg, Dennis
    Gallegos; Arlene Grayson (ep. 1)
Co-producer (ep. 3-on): Portia Iverson
Associate producer: Eric Rhoden (ep. 2-on)
Executive story editors: Oliver Goldstick, Phil Rosenthal
Story editors: Chris Westphal, Deborah Markoe-Klein

Creative consultants: Mark Reisman, Jeremy Stevens
Director of photography: Daniel Flannery
Music: uncredited; only a music "supervisor" given
Theme: "Bread and Butter" by Jay Turnbow, Larry Parks
  (words and music); performed by Gene Miller
Director unless otherwise noted: John Bowab
Based on characters created by: Amy Heckerling •
Developed for television by: Ed. Weinberger

• On May 13, 1991, Federal District Court Judge William
Matthew Byrne Jr. approved an out-of-court settlement between Tri-Star Pictures and writer-producers Jeanne Meyers
and Rita Stern, re: their lawsuit alleging Heckerling plagiarized portions of their student film, *Special Delivery*.

---

1. "Baby Love" March 8, 1991  8:30-9 p.m.

Mickey likes a baby (Wrate) whose father (McGinley) Maggie is
dating. Watkins is the wife of executive producer Weinberger.

Craig Palmer........................................................Ted McGinley
Voice of Danielle................Carlene Watkins (Marti Muller orig.
  announced)
Voice of yuppie baby..............................................Dan Gerrity
Voice of hip baby girl..................................Laurnea Wilkerson
Danielle Palmer..............................Rebecca/Stephanie Wrate
Yuppie baby........................................Kevin/Taylor Hartstein
Hip baby girl........................................Lauren/Megan McElroy

Writer: Alan Kirschenbaum

2. "A Star is Newborn"  March 15, 1991

An ad executive (Bierko) suggests Mickey has a future as a TV
spokesbaby. Guest Gallegos is one of the series' producers.

Bill Noonan...............................................................Craig Bierko
Voice of Roscoe Miller................................Roscoe Lee Browne
Mrs. Miller..........................................................Deborah Offner
Gentleman.......................................Dennis Michael Gallegos
Sheryl.........................................................................Susan Varon
Mrs. Vitale......................................................................Amy Hill
Roscoe Miller (infant)..............................Trevor/Travis Gruhot
Baby Vitale.........................................................Gian Carlo Canale

Writers: Oliver Goldstick & Phil Rosenthal

3. "Womb With a View"  March 22, 1991

Mickey helps talk the unborn child of Maggie's time-conscious
friend (Horsford, a co-star of *Amen*) into arriving early.

Judge Cynthia Willoughby......................Anna Maria Horsford
Voice of newborn baby..Tommy Ford a.k.a. Thomas Mikal Ford
Newborn baby.............................................Koquanna Hatfield

Writers: Chris Westphal & Deborah Markoe-Klein

4. "Trading Places"  March 29, 1991

Maggie thinks Mickey may have been switched with that of
another family's at birth.

Clarice Valentine...........................................Kathleen Mitchell
Katia Sorrento...................................................Lisa Michelson
Voice of Baby Andre.............................................Michael Bell
Baby Andre Sorrento.............................Chadd/Cameron Cole
"The Soaring Sorrentos"..............Michael J. Hay, Leslie L. Hay,
  Miles A. Hay

Writers: Ron Lux & Eugene B. Stein

5. "Give a Sucker an Even Break"  Monday, April 1, 1991
  9:30-10 p.m.

At a "Mommy and Me" class, Mickey complains he's had to go
cold turkey since his mom has stopped breast-feeding him.
Orig. scheduled for March 29.

Voice of Luther..............................................Richard McGregor

Writer: Maxine Lapiduss

6. "The Whiz Kid"  April 5, 1991

Mickey tries out for a "gifted baby" academy. A different actor
than in ep. 5 and 10 provides the voice of baby Luther.

Announced cast:
Dr. Ezra Farr...........................................Stephen Tobolowsky
Voice of Luther............................................Billy "Sly" Williams
Voice of Sophie..............................................Jeanine Jackson
Voice of Robert.............................................Rodney Kageyama
Voice of Ernest......................................................Jim Pirri
Dr. Farr's assistant.................................................Terry Bolo
And: Seth Kinast (Himself), Jacquelyn Umoff (Violinist)

Director: John Sgueglia              Writer: Victor Levin

7. "One Night With Eliot"  April 12, 1991

Dr. Fleisher poses as Maggie's husband to help Maggie get
Mickey into a prep school. Grammer is a co-star of *Cheers*.

Voice of Russell..............................................Kelsey Grammer
Miss Newton......................................................Lois deBanzie
Tammy Morrison...............................................Valerie Mahaffey
Charles Morrison................................................Richmond Hoxie
Secretary..................................................................Flo Di Re
Baby Russell........................................Adam/Brian Harman

Director: John Rich
Writers: Oliver Goldstick & Phil Rosenthal

8. "The Fever"  April 16, 1991

Dr. Fleisher has to seek out Maggie, who's on a date with a
sleaze, when Mickey gets sick at the thought of her having sex.

Gary.........................................................................Erich Anderson

Director: John Sgueglia              Writer: Alan Kirschenbaum

9. "The Big 'One'"  April 23, 1991

Maggie reluctantly asks Mickey's father (Danza), who's never
met his son, to attend Mickey's first birthday party. Danza,
who provides Mickey's voice, is a star of *Who's the Boss?*.

Nick.......................................................................Tony Danza
Clucko the Clown.................................................Rod McCary
Voice of Duane....................................................George Kirby
Baby Duane........................................Trayvion/Davion Daniel

Director: John Sgueglia                Story: Maxine Lapiduss
Teleplay: Deborah Markoe-Klein & Chris Westphal

10. "Tooth and Nail"  April 30, 1991

Maggie worries when Mickey shows aggressive behavior at his
Mommy and Me group; Fogarty preps Howard for a hot date.

Lloyd..............................................Carl Ballantine
Voice of Luther.............................Richard McGregor

Director: John Sgueglia          Story: Alan Kirschenbaum
Teleplay: Victor Levin & Mike Rowe

11. "Once in Love With Cecil"  May 7, 1991

To Maggie's chagrin, her visiting, sad-sack aunt (Rae) has a
mad night on the town with Fogarty.

Aunt Beverly....................................Charlotte Rae
And: Maria Strova (Belly dancer), Victor H. Touzie (Busperson)

Director: John Sgueglia
Writers: Beverly Goldstick & Phil Rosenthal

12. "Out of Africa"  May 17, 1991

Joe falls for Maggie's friend (Visitor), making Mickey afraid
they'll get married and Joe won't come around anymore. Kirby and Daniel reprises their parts from ep. 9. Orig. scheduled
for May 14.

Robin Taylor......................................Nana Visitor
Voice of Duane..................................George Kirby
Minister...........................................Nicholas Kepros
Voice of baby girl...................Siobhan Fallan a.k.a. Siobhan
Baby girl......................Stephanie/Marguerite Campbell
Baby Duane.......................Trayvion/Davion Daniel

Writer: Dinah Kirgo

**on hiatus; reruns orig. scheduled from Aug. 16 into the
fall season, but *Growing Pains* reruns replaced it beginning Aug. 23; renewed for 1991-92, with Mary Page Keller
succeeding Julia Duffy, who joins the cast of *Designing
Women*; new episodes begin Sept. 20, 1991.**

## Bagdad Cafe

CBS          Sept. 28-Nov. 23   Fridays, 8:30-9 p.m.
             July 27            Saturday, 10-11 p.m.

Series premiere: March 30, 1989
Final telecast: July 27, 1991

Comedy of a Mohave Desert diner-motel owner (Goldberg) and
a perpetual guest (Stapleton) who arrives after being abandoned by her husband. Based on the 1988 movie. Guest
Cleavon Little is listed in the main credits when he appears.

Brenda............................................Whoopi Goldberg
Jasmine Zweibel................................Jean Stapleton
Rudy...............................................James Gammon
Debbie, Brenda's daughter (16)....................Monica Calhoun
Dewey Kunkle (ep. 2-on)........................Sam Whipple

*Recurring:*
Sheriff Wayne Highsmith (ep. 5-9)...............William Shockley
Bobby (ep. 3-5)................................Walter Olkewicz

CBS Entertainment Productions in assoc. with Zev Braun
    Pictures, New World Television and Patchett Kaufman
    Entertainment
Executive producers: Tom Patchett, Kenneth Kaufman
Co-executive producers: Thad Mumford, Paul Bogart
Supervising producer: James M. Jaffee
Coordinating producers: Stephanie Hagan, Steve Lamar

Producer: Vicki S. Horwits (Martin Pasko also orig. announced)
Co-producer: Rebecca Parr
Executive story consultant: Victor Fresco
Associate producers: Randy Sutter, Susan Polmanski
Creative consultant: Don Rhymer
Theme: "Calling You" by Bob Telson (words and music);
       performed by Jevetta Steele
Music: Mark Snow
Director: Paul Bogart
Based on characters created by Percy Adlon
Developed by: Mort Lachman & Sy Rosen

—————————————

1. "This Bird Has Flown"  Sept. 28, 1990

Brenda wants to sell the cafe; Jasmine's husband arrives from
Wisconsin.

Sal, Brenda's estranged husband.....................Cleavon Little
Herb, Jasmine's estranged husband...............Philip Baker Hall
Bob................................................Ebbe Roe Smith
Chuck.............................................Randy Oglesby
Rueben.............................................Rudy Ramos
Amarah (infant)..................................Serene/Shanai Hawkins

Writers: Tom Patchett and Vicki S. Horwits

2. "Not Enough Cooks"  Oct. 5, 1990

Brenda fires her cook, and Rudy's nephew (Whipple) signs on.

Amarah (infant)..................................Serene/Shanai Hawkins
Johnny.............................................Glenn Quinn
Bus driver.................................Paul Michael Brennan
Customer..........................................Walter Sylvest
Passengers.....................Montrose Hagins, Dona Hardy,
    Molly McClure, Amzie Strickland, Ben Kronen, Earl
    Theroux, Nick LaTour

Writer: Rebecca Parr

**preempted Oct. 12 and Oct. 19**

3. "City on a Hill"  Oct. 26. 1991

When the water supply is cut off, the locals declare cityhood,
with Brenda as mayor. Orig. scheduled for Oct. 12 and Nov. 9.

Earl...............................................Tim Choate
Clerk..............................................Julie Payne

Writer: Victor Fresco

4. "16 Candles"  Nov. 2, 1990

Debbie, turning 16, asserts her independence.

Calvin the Clown...................................Jeff Corey
Nancy..............................................Beth Hogan
And: Dan Eisenstein (Bobby Jr.), Kimiko Gelman (Stephanie)

Writer: Don Rhymer

5. "I've Got a Crush on You"  Nov. 9, 1990

The sheriff (Shockley, beginning his recurring role) woos Brenda, while Rudy tries to heat up his friendship with Jasmine.

Riley..............................................Lou Myers
Jesse.............................................Michael Dempsey

Writer: Thad Mumford

6. "Rainy Days and Mondays"  Nov. 16, 1990

The day Brenda finally decides to file divorce papers, a downpour floods the roads and the cafe.

Coxen...................................................................Ron Frazier
Gilbert............................................................Dan Castellaneta

Writer: Vicki S. Horwits

7. "Hell Hath No Fury"  Nov. 23, 1990

A waif (Joyner), en route to meet her estranged husband, arrives with a broken car, and a gun. Orig. scheduled for Oct. 26.

Beth.................................................................Michelle Joyner
Clyde...............................................................Geoffrey Blake
Monica.......................................................................Senait

Writer: Rebecca Parr

**cancelled**

8. "Over My Dead Body"  July 27, 1991  10-10:30 p.m.

When strange things occur after an Indian burial site is uncovered in the kitchen, Dewey believes the room is haunted. Orig. scheduled for Nov. 30 (preempted by an unscheduled *Evening Shade* rerun), and July 20, 8-8:30 p.m.

Fred...............................................................Jimmie F. Skaggs
Zach.......................................................................Ed Hooks
Kathy................................................................Ami Rothschild
Alex..............................................................Michael Dempsey
Lou....................................................................Stuart Grant
Ted.............................................................Bryan Brightcloud
Rich...........Sonny Skyhawk a.k.a. Sonny Skyhawk Robideaux

Writer: Don Rhymer

9. "Prisoner of Love"  July 27, 1991  10:30-11 p.m.

Jealous Sal (Little, reprising his role from ep. 1) threatens the sheriff.  Orig. scheduled for Dec. 21, and July 20, 8:30-9 p.m.

Sal..................................................................Cleavon Little

Writer: Victor Fresco

## Beverly Hills, 90210

Fox          Thursdays, 9-10 p.m.

Series premiere: Oct. 4, 1990

Drama of a Minneapolis family with 16-year-old twins, trying to adjust to life in a highly materialistic city and school (West Beverly Hills High). Cast-member Tori Spelling is the daughter of series' production-company head Aaron Spelling. Walsh address: 933 Hillcrest Ave. High school radio station: KWBH. Team: Wildcats. Working titles: *90210*; *The Class of Beverly Hills*. Beginning July 11, the series title dropped the comma.

Brandon Walsh................................................Jason Priestley
Brenda Walsh................................................Shannen Doherty
Cindy Walsh, their mother.......................................Carol Potter
Financial manager Jim Walsh, their father....James Eckhouse
Kelly Taylor.......................................................Jennie Garth

Steve Sanders........................................................Ian Ziering
Andrea Zuckerman.......................................Gabrielle Carteris
Dylan McKay (ep. 2-on)............................................Luke Perry
David Silver.................................................Brian Austin Green
Scott Scott..................................................Douglas Emerson
Donna Martin..........................................................Tori Spelling

*Recurring:*
Diner-owner Nat (ep. 3,5-6,9,12,14,16,
    20-22, summer season ep. 1,6)....................Joe E. Tata
Housekeeper Anna (ep. 3,8,14,22)....................Luisa Leschin
Laura Rye (ep. 2-3,7-8)...........................................Nancy Paul

Propaganda Films in assoc. with Torand Productions, a unit of
    Spelling Entertainment
Executive producer: Charles Rosin
Producers: Sigurjon Sighvatsson, Darren Star, Jay Roewe
    (latter ep. 1 only), Jeffrey White (latter ep. 2-on)
Supervising producer: David Stenn
Consulting producer: Paul Waigner (later in season)
Associate producer: Stuart Besser (ep. 1); Livia Hanich (ep.
    2-on)
Story editors: Jordan Budde, Amy Spies
Director of photography (variously): David Bridges (ep. 1);
    David Geddes; Robert New
Music (variously): John E. Davis; David Schwartz; Stacy
    Widelitz
Theme (instrumental): "Beverly Hills, 90210" by Jeffrey
    "Skunk" Baxter & Stacy Widelitz (as credited on original
    airing of pilot); by John E. Davis (as credited subsequently,
    including on rerun of pilot, March 31, 1991)
Creator: Darren Star

---

1. "Beverly Hills, 90210 -- Pilot"  Oct. 4, 1990  8:30-10 p.m.

The Walsh family faces culture shock when they set up house in Beverly Hills; Brenda dates a lawyer (Caulfield).

Jason...........................................................Maxwell Caulfield
Maryanne...............................................................Leslie Bega
Vice Principal Jack Clayton.................Richard Cummings, Jr.
Mr. Ridley..............................................................Josh Mostel
Ms. Montes De La Rosa.............................................Bel Sandre
Flasin.....................................................................Deon Sams
Overweight girl..............................................Jo Ann Henrich
Jock.............................................................Louie Sabatasso
Cathy.....................................................................Dulcie Hunt
Michelle..........................................................Jocelyn Peden
And: Glenn Quinn, Randy Matick (Party jocks), Jason Luckett
    (Kid), Djimon (Doorperson), Kim Lentz (Waitress), Ernesto
    Hernandez (Flower deliveryperson), Brian Evans, Darrin
    Dotson (Track kids), Brian Straub (Waiter)

Director: Tim Hunter              Writer: Darren Star

2. "The Green Room"  Oct. 11, 1990    (BH-101)

Brandon helps a girl in trouble; Brenda realizes she can't compete financially with her peers.

Betty............................................................Heather McAdam
Eric...............................................................Jonathan Pekar
Duane..............................................................Steve Messina
And: Troy Shire, Milt Tarver, Raoul N. Rizik, Nicholas Read,
    Helena Apothaker, Kelli Brook

Director: Michael Uno              Writer: David Stenn

3. "Every Dream Has Its Price (Tag)"  Oct. 18, 1990  (BH-102)

Brenda is caught shoplifting; Brandon, beleaguered as a bus-boy in a too-chic restaurant, becomes a waiter at Nat's diner.

Tiffany...............................................................Noelle Parker
Cathy Genson...............................................Valerie Landsburg
Janet.................................................................Jennifer Blanc
And: Michael Wolff, Noel Alumit, Taunie Vrenon

Director: Catlin Adams                Writer: Amy Spies

4. "The First Time"  Oct. 25, 1990  (BH-104)

Brandon loses his virginity with his visiting girlfriend (Irvine); Brenda has a crush on a married teacher (Dunigan).

Cheryl.................................................................Paula Irvine
Matt Brody...........................................................Tim Dunigan
And: Beth Taylor, Ross Malinger, Sara Rose Johnson, Sally Champlin, Duncan C. MacFarlane, Cathy Hwang

Director: Bethany Rooney Hillschafer        Writer: Darren Star

5. "One on One"  Nov. 1, 1990   (BH-103)

Brandon competes for a spot on the basketball team; Brenda takes a disastrous third stab at driver's training.

James.....................................................................Tico Wells
Coach Reilly..................................................Scott Williamson
Walker.................................................................Don Barnes
And: Joshua Karton, Roger Hampton, Greg Rusin, Patty Toy

Director: Artie Mandelburg            Writer: Charles Rosin

6. "Higher Education"  Nov. 15, 1990   (BH-105)

Brandon, close to failing history, joins Steve in cheating.

Danzel.....................................................................Bill Morey

Director: Artie Mandelburg            Writer: Jordan Budde

7. "Perfect Mom" Nov. 22, 1990  (BH-106)

Brenda is impressed by Kelly's outwardly hip mom (Gillespie), who unbeknownst to Brenda is a troubled alcoholic.

Jackie Taylor.....................................................Ann Gillespie
Nina...............................................................Linda Thompson
And: Jordana Capra

Director: Bethany Rooney Hillshafer        Writer: Darren Star

8. "The 17 Year Itch"  Nov. 29, 1990 (BH-107)

Cindy is attracted to an old college friend (Gray); Brandon and Brenda become subjects of a twins psychology study at UCLA.

Glenn Evans.........................................................Stan Ivar
Guidance counselor........Denise Dowse a.k.a. Denise Y. Dowse
And: Bruce Gray, Philip Arthur Ross, Steven Robert Ross

Director: Jefferson Kibbee            Writer: Amy Spies

9. "The Gentle Art of Listening"  Dec. 6, 1990  (BH-108)

Brenda, working a teen hotline, encounters a date-raped student (Ryan, a cast-member of Doogie Howser, M.D.); Brandon falls for a 23-year-old (Gillingham).

Bonnie..........................................................Lisa Dean Ryan

Nina..........................................................Kim Gillingham
Carol Banning.....................................................Dale Weston
And: Pat O'Neal, Michael Woolson, William Forward, Heather Hopper, Dina Dayrit, Curt Corelius, Heather Elias, Charles Emmett, Hope Levy

Director: Daniel Attias                Writer: Charles Rosin

**preempted Dec. 13**

10. "Isn't It Romantic"  Jan. 3, 1991

Brenda becomes infatuated with Dylan, straining his and Brandon's friendship.

Stacy Sloan........................................................Kathy Molter
Kravitz.........................................................Raymond Singer
Blonde.........................................................Jaclyn Gradinger
And: Terence Ford

Director: Nancy Malone                Writer: Karen Rosin

11. "B.Y.O.B."  Jan. 10, 1991  (BH-110)

After a wild party he and Brenda throw while their folks are away, Brandon wrecks his car is arrested for drunk driving.

Trudy.........................................................Bobbi Jo Lathan
Bob................................................................Richard Paul
Officer..............................................................Larry Marks
Drew.................................................................Gregg Rogen
Teenagers........................................Nathan Higgins, Dani Lee
Feena............................................................Susannah Todd

Director: Miles Watkins                Writer: Jordan Budde

**unscheduled preemption Jan. 17**

12. "One Man and a Baby"  Jan. 24, 1991  (BH-111)

Brandon falls for a senior (Dattilo) with a six-month-old infant; Brenda considers taking the sky-diving lessons she's won.

Melissa Coolidge..................................................Kristin Dattilo
Don.............................................................Paul Satterfield
And: Melinda Fee, Dianne Buck, Jaclyn Gradinger, Briana/ Kelsea Clark (infant), Daniel/William Van Duzer (infant)

Director: Burt Brinckerhoff
Writers: Amy Spies and Darren Star

13. "Slumber Party"  Jan. 31, 1991  (BH-112)

The girls tell each other their secrets at a slumber party; Brandon and Steve get ripped off by two beautiful con-artists.

Amanda Peyser...................................................Michele Abrams
Trina.............................................................Julie McCullough
Shelly..............................................................Judie Aronson
And: Michael Chieffo, Oscar Dillon

Director: Charles Braverman            Writer: Darren Star

14. "East Side Story"  Feb. 14, 1991  (BH-108)

Brandon falls for a student (Montana) from inner-city East Los Angeles.  Guest Gibson is a singer-songwriter-producer.

Carla Montez.....................................................Karla Montana
Becky Wilerson..................................................Joanne Astrow
Chick Schneider.....................................................Mark Lonow

Richard Rodriques................................................John Vargas
Herself................................................................Debbie Gibson

Director: Daniel Attias                 Teleplay: Charles Rosin
Story: Carmen Sternwood and Charles Rosin

15. "A Fling in Palm Springs" Feb. 21, 1991 (BH-116)

On a teen-filled Palm Springs weekend, Brenda plans to bed
Dylan, and David brings visitors to his grandparents' house;
back home, Brandon befriends a homeless boy (Graas).

Henry Silver, David's grandfather..............................Al Ruscio
David's grandmother.............................................Erica Yohn
Curtis..............................................John Christian Graas
Tuesday..............................................................Shana Furlow
Tom.....................................................................David Gail
Janie.................................................................Laurie Plaxen
Desk clerk..............................................................Bud Leslie

Director: Jefferson Kibbee           Writer: Jordan Budde

16. "Fame is Where You Find It" Feb. 28, 1991 (BH-113)

Brandon is wooed and dumped by the star (Kaplan) of a hit TV
show. Rivers is the daughter of talk-show host Joan Rivers.

Lydia...................................................................Marcy Kaplan
Director/Jake.....................................................Alan Blumenfeld
With: Amy Hill
Sean..............................................................Graham Galloway
Dude.............................................................Rowdy Metzger
Mackenzie........................................................Melissa Rivers
Tourist.....................................................................Julie Gill
Customers.............................Sean Moran, Maureen Macke

Director: Paul Schneider
Writers: Karen Rosin & Charles Rosin

17. "Stand (Up) & Deliver" March 7, 1991 9:03-10 p.m.
    (BH-116)

Brandon glad-hands in his campaign for junior class VP;
Brenda wants to get her equivalency degree and move out.
Guest Hamilton is the daughter of actress Carol Burnett. Late
start due to an episode of The Simpsons running overtime.

Sky.....................................................................Carrie Hamilton
Jack.....................................................................Tom McTigue
Repossessor.............................................................Mik Scriba
With: Scott Fults, Marion Ramsey
And: Carmen Mejia (Passerby), Beverly Nero (Teacher)

Director: Burt Brinckerhoff          Writer: Amy Spies

18. "It's Only a Test" March 28, 1991

Brenda fears the lump on her breast may be cancerous; the
SAT college-entry exams draw near at school.

Dr. Natalie Donner...........................................Melinda Culea
Mr. Parker.........................................................Bart Braverman
Proctor...................................................................Jay Levey

Director: Charles Braverman          Writer: Darren Star

19. "April Is the Cruelest Month" April 11, 1991 (BH-118)

Brandon's new friend (Perry), driven ruthlessly by his demand-
ing father (Coster), may be planning to murder the man.
Dowse reprises her role from ep. 8, Nero from ep. 17.

Roger Azarian....................................................Matthew Perry
Darla Diller..........................................................Sharon Case
Guidance counselor........Denise Y. Dowse a.k.a. Denise Dowse
George Azarian....................................................Nicolas Coster
Coach Markham..................................................Gregory Burns
Psychiatrist...........................................................David Charles
History teacher......................................................Beverly Nero

Director: Daniel Attias
Writers: Steve Wasserman & Jessica Klein

20. "Spring Training" April 25, 1991 (BH-119)

Brandon and Steve co-manage a Little League team of spoiled
Beverly Hills children; Brenda tries adopting a lost dog.

Dave Franklin (orig. Fletcher)............................Norman Parker
Davey, his son....................................................Damion Stevens
Noah..................................................................Davey Roberts
Corey....................................................................Paige Cosney
Nan Guersy.....................................................Georgina Lindsey
Crawford.................................................................Bo Sharon
Mannie...............................................................Jerrod Stevens
Umpire...............................................................Hank Robinson
Wally (dog)................................................................Magic

Director: Burt Brinckerhoff          Writer: Charles Rosin

21. "Spring Dance" May 2, 1991

As the spring dance approaches, Brenda and Dylan get closer,
and Kelly and Andrea both want Brandon as their date. Case
reprises her role from ep. 19.

Darla Diller..........................................................Sharon Case
"The Rave-Ups": Jimmer Podrasky, Terry Wilson, Tim Jimenez,
    Tommy Blatnik
    Also orig. announced: Mary Kay Bergman (Betty)

Writer-director: Darren Star

22. "Home Again" May 9, 1991

Jim accepts a job promotion requiring a move back to Minneapolis, though the rest of the family wants to stay put.

Henry Powell, head of Jim's company.................Linden Chiles
Ruth..........................................................Kendall Carly Brown
Dan Simons.......................................................Michael Stuno
Matt Fries................................................................Jack West
And: Steve Gagnon

Director: Charles Braverman          Writer: Amy Spies

**renewed for 1991-92, beginning July 11, 1991. Title punc-
tuation slightly changed to Beverly Hills 90210. Douglas
Emerson departed the cast, appearing as a guest in ep. 1
below. New recurring-guest and production-staff data below; other information the same as at beginning of entry.**

Recurring:
Henry Thomas, Brandon's boss
    (ep. 1-2,4-6)..........James Pickens, Jr. (uncredited, ep. 6)
Acting teaching Chris Suiter (ep. 1-3,6)......Michael St. Gerrard

90210 Productions and Propaganda Films in assoc. with
    Torand Productions, a unit of Spelling Entertainment
Executive produer: Charles Rosin
Producer: Paul Waigner
Supervising producer: Darren Star
Co-producer: Jonathan Roberts

Story editors: Steve Wasserman, Jessica Klein
Associate producer: Livia Hanich
Director of photography: Daniel McKinny
Music [and] Theme (instrumental): John E. Davis (SEE ALSO
    Theme information at beginning of entry)
Creator: Darren Star

---

1. "Beach Blanket Brandon" July 11, 1991

Brenda, in summer school, reassesses her relationship with
Dylan; Brandon gets work at the Beverly Hills Beach Club;
Scott reluctantly leaves to spend the summer in Oklahoma.

Scott Scott....................................................Douglas Emerson
With: Stephen Mendel
And: Debra Sullivan (Nurse), Karen Lew (Receptionist), David
    Tiefen (Potential lifeguard)

Director: Chuck (a.k.a. Charles) Braverman
Writer: Darren Star

2. "The Party Fish" July 18, 1991

Brandon strikes up a protege-mentor relationship with a
beach-club member (Sloyan), straining his ties with his dad.

Sandy......................................Deborah Goodrich
Jerry Rattinger....................................James Sloyan
And: Paul Linke, Timothy Blake, Tom Fuccello

Director: Dan Attias a.k.a. Daniel Attias  Writer: Charles Rosin

3. "Summer Storm" July 25, 1991

Dylan, seriously injured in a surfing accident, moves into the
Walsh home to recover; Kelly is rebuffed by a hunk (Lascher).
Gillespie reprises her role from ep. 7 of the previous cycle.

Jackie Taylor....................................Ann Gillespie
Kyle Conner....................................David Lascher
Jack McKay, Dylan's dad (fantasy sequence)......Arthur Brooks
And: Mary Ingersoll (News anchor), Nathan Lorch (Young Dy-
    lan), David Gibbs (Security guard), Rick Danielson (Bob)

Director: Charles Braverman
Writers: Steve Wasserman & Jessica Klein

4. "Anaconda" Aug. 1, 1991

Dylan, abandoned penniless by his mother, is suspected of
stealing from the beach club.

Danny......................................Jason Adams
Detective Pena....................................Arva Holt
With: Kathleen Freeman
And: Kim Delgado (Detective)

Director: Daniel Attias          Writer: Jonathan Roberts

5. "Play It Again, David" Aug. 8, 1991

Kelly's mom and David's dad become romantically involved;
Brandon becomes self-appointed big brother to an abused kid.
Gillespie reprises her role ep. 3 and from last season.

Jackie Taylor....................................Ann Gillespie
Dr. Silver....................................Matthew Laurance
Suzanne....................................Lenore Kasdorf
Felix....................................Coleby Lombardo

And: Claudia Bloom (Woman at pool), Neal Kaz (Bartender),
    Ian Petrella (Kid)

Director: Charles Braverman          Writer: Sherri Ziff

6. "Pass/Not Pass" Aug. 15, 1991

Brenda and Andrea compete for Suiter's affections; Brandon's
dream car is a nightmare, and Nat may have no job for him.

Simon....................................Royce E. (a.k.a. Royce) Applegate
And: Lucy Liu (Courtney), Lindsey Brianne (Lindsey)

Director: Jefferson Kibbee          Writer: Allison Adler

7. "Camping Trip" Aug. 29, 1991

A storm confines the camping friends to a rundown cabin.

Neil....................................Peter Marc
Alison....................................Gina Lamond
Customer....................................Earl Theroux

Director: Jeff Melman    Writer: Karen Rosin

**continues into fall season after Sept. 1 rerun**

## Blossom

NBC          Jan. 3-April 27; May 29-        Mondays, 8:30-9 p.m.
             June 17; Aug. 26-on             Various
             Aug. 12, 15, 17

Series premiere: Jan. 3, 1991

Comedy of a plain-looking but witty young teenage girl living
with her two older brothers and their divorced musician dad.

Blossom Russo....................................Mayim Bialik
Joey Russo....................................Joey Lawrence
Anthony Russo....................................Michael Stoyunov
Nick Russo, their father....................................Ted Wass

*Recurring:*
Six, Blossom's friend (ep. 1-8, 10-13)..................Jenna Von Oy
Neighbor Agnes (ep. 1-3)....................................Eileen Brennan

Impact Zone Productions, Witt/Thomas Productions and
    Touchstone Television
Executive producers: Gene Reynolds, Paul Junger Witt, Tony
    Thomas, Don Reo
Supervising producer: Paul Perlove (ep. 1); Judith D. Allison,
    Bill Richmond (both ep. 2-on)
Producer: John Ziffren (ep. 1-on), Racelle Rossett Schaefer
    (ep. 2-on)
Co-producers (ep. 2-on): David Landsberg, Josh Goldstein,
    Jonathan Prince
Associate producer: Susan Nessanbaum-Goldberg
Executive script consultant: Brenda Hampton-Cain (ep. 2-on)
Music: Mike Post (ep. 1); Frank Denson (ep. 2-on)
Theme: Mike Post and Stephen Geyer (music and lyrics); per-
    formed by Dr. John (Malcolm "Mac" Rebennack)
Director: Zane Buzby
Creator: Don Reo

---

1. "Blossom Blossoms" Thursday, Jan. 3, 1991

Blossom reaches puberty, and substitutes an older friend

(Brennan) for her absentee mother to talk about it.  Rashad is a cast-member of *The Cosby Show*.

Imaginary mother...........................................Phylicia Rashad
Mitchell...............................................................Vonii Ribisi

Writer: Racelle Rossett Schaefer

2. "My Sister's Keeper"  Jan. 7, 1991

Bloosom looks forward to her first prom date, with Joey's friend (Dorff), but Nick forbids her to date an older boy.  Dorff is a cast-member of the syndicated *What a Dummy*.

Bobby.......................................................Stephen Dorff

Writer: Bill Richmond

3. "Dad's Girlfriend"  Jan. 14, 1991

Blossom can't stand dad's new girlfriend (Engle).  Guest Perlman is a cast-member of *Cheers*.

Godmother in fantasy sequence..........................Rhea Perlman
Elaine...................................................................Debra Engle
15-year-old boy...................................................Jay Lambert

Writer: Judith D. Allison

4. "Who's in Charge Here?"  Jan. 21, 1991

Nick leaves Blossom in charge of home one night while he performs on a cruise ship.  Guest Little Richard is a rock singer.

Himself.............................................................Little Richard
Stephanie.........................................................Nile Lanning

Writer: Paul Perlove

**preempted Jan. 28**

5. "Sex, Lies and Teenagers"  Feb. 4, 1991

Guilty Blossom dreams discussion-show host Phil Donahue has her in a segment on "Women Who Lie to Their Parents."

Himself..............................................................Phil Donahue
Diane (erroneously given
  as Joanne in *TV Guide*)............................Brenda Strong
Jason..................................................................Shawn Phelan
Ricky....................................................................Ryan Francis
And: Tobey Maguire (Boy), Alitzah Weiner (Sheila)

Writer: Paul Perlove

6. "I Ain't Got No Buddy"  Feb. 11, 1991

Blossom feels left out when Six befriends a chic new student.  Getty's character crosses over from *The Golden Girls*.

Sophia Petrillo.................................................Estelle Getty
Doris................................................................Penina Segall
Adrian...............................................................Aimee Brooks
Bobby...............................................................Michael Landes
Boys......................................Jason Strickland, Xavier Garcia

Writer: David Landsberg

7. "Thanks for the Memorex"  Feb. 18, 1991

Prompted by old home videos, the family retreats to the cabin by the lake where they'd shared happier times in the past.

Maddy, Nick's ex-wife, and the kids' mother.........Paige Pengra
Young Anthony...............................................Aaron Freeman
Joey at 11...................................................Matthew Lawrence
Joey at 2.......................................................Andrew Lawrence

Writer: Racelle Rossett Schaefer

8. "The Geek"  Feb. 25, 1991

Blossom blames herself for getting tricked into a date with a school "geek" (Demetral).  ALF, created by Paul Fusco, is the puppet star of the series *ALF* (NBC, 1986-1990).

Himself (puppet character)..............................................ALF
Fred Fogerty..................................................Chris Demetral
Jordan Taylor....................................................Justin Whalin

Writers: Brenda Hampton-Cain and William C. Kenny

9. "Tough Love"  March 4, 1991

Nick gives Anthony an ultimatum: get a job or get out of the house; singer-mayor Sonny Bono helps Blossom write a song.

Himself.................................................................Sonny Bono
Mozart.................................................................David Knell
Bambi...................................................................Joely Fisher
Fisher................................................................John Apicella
And: Rex Ryon (Cop), Aaron Lohr (Student)

Writers: Josh Goldstein and Jonathan Prince

10. "Such a Night"  March 11, 1991

Blossom leans on Six for support while calling a boy for a date; Anthony tries to help a friend (Morrissette) stay sober.

Jeff................................................................Billy Morrissette

Writers: Don Reo & Judith D. Allison

**preempted March 18**

11. "School Daze"  March 25, 1991

Against her father's wishes, Blossom plans to drop out of her snooty private school and enroll in public school.

Dominique.................................................Judith-Marie Bergan
Mrs. Whiting...............................................Priscilla Morrill
Wendy..........................................................Nicole Huntington
And: Frank Como (Mike Henderson), Kris Newquist (Boy)

Writer: Don Reo

**preempted April 1**

12. "Papa's Little Dividend"  April 8, 1991

Blossom and Six spy on a woman (Gallagher) who claims Nick's the father of her child; Anthony preps for a blind date.

Arlene...............................................................Megan Gallagher
Maitre d'.................................................................Nick Ullett
Francois.............................................................Eric Poppick

Writer: Nancy Beverly

13. "Love Stinks!"  April 29, 1991

Blossom's brokenhearted over a breakup with a boy (Hoffman).

Sheila...............................................................Jane Leeves
Ricky (orig. Bobby)......................................Joshua Hoffman
Boy......................................................................Josh Goddard

Writer: Racelle Rossett Schaefer

**on hiatus until reruns begin, May 27; again until Aug. 12**

**preempted Sept. 9**

**renewed for 1991-92; new episodes begin Sept. 16, 1991**

## Broken Badges

CBS            Nov. 24-Dec. 22      Saturdays, 9-10 p.m.
               June 6-20            Thursdays, 9-10 p.m.

Series premiere: Nov. 24, 1990
Final telecast: June 20, 1991

Lighthearted action-drama of an eccentric New Orleans cop in fictional Bay City, Calif., in charge of a unit of officers removed from active duty for psychological/emotional problems. Star Ferrer is the son of actor Jose Ferrer and singer Rosemary Clooney. Filmed in Vancouver.

Beau Jack Bowman..........................................Miguel Ferrer
J.J. "Bullet" Tingreedes....................................Eileen Davidson
Stanley Jones (with puppet Officer Danny)..........Jay Johnson
Toby Baker...........................................................Ernie Hudson
Psychiatrist Dr. Priscilla Mathers (ep. 2-on)......Charlotte Lewis
Lt. Eleanor Hardwick (ep. 1)............................Teresa Donahoe

*Recurring:*
Chief Sterling (ep. 1,2,4,7).................Don S. (a.k.a Don) Davis
Officer Charlie Von Bork (ep. 1,5,6).....Forry Smith
Sgt. Ty Carter (ep. 1,4,5,6)..........Garry Chalk (misspelled Gary
      Chalk in *TV Guide*)

Stephen J. Cannell Productions
Executive producers: Stephen J. Cannel, Randall Wallace
Supervising producer: Jo Swerling, Jr.
Co-supervising producer (later in season): Jack Bernstein
Producers: John Peter Kousakis (ep. 1); Jack Bernstein (early in season), Joan Carson
Associate producers: Bruce Golin (ep. 2-on), Gary Skeen Hall (ep. 5-on)
Director of photography: Cyrus Block (early in season); John S. Bartley (later in season)
Music: Mike Post (early in season); Velton Ray Bunch (later in season)
Theme: Mike Post (music and lyrics); performer uncredited
Creators: Stephen J. Cannell & Randall Wallace

---

1. "Broken Badges" Nov. 24, 1990 8-10 p.m.

Bowman, arriving to deliver a murder suspect he believes innocent, encounters opposition from local authorities, and with Hardwick's help forms his own local unit, the Broken Badges.

Tina Cardenas....................................................Ada Maris
Frank Cardenas..................................................Carlos Gomez
Martin Valentine..................................................Tobin Bell
Dr. Morrison......................................................Richard Riehle
Capt. Adam LeFave...........................................Michael MacRae
Enrique Cardenas...............................................Ismael (East) Carlos

Augie Desau, Jack's New Orleans partner...................Tim Neil
Dr. Vietro.............................................................Leslie Carlson
Gordon Bacus.......................................................Gerry Bean
And: Rosanne Iverson (Stewardess), Jessica Marlowe, Rob Roy, R. Nelson Brown, Jon Cuthbert, Adrien Dorval, Terry Barclay, Dwight Koss, Michael Rogers, Howard Kruschke, Richard Sargent, Rob Johnson, Barbara Constantine, Phil Hayes, Michael Tiernan, Peter Bibby, Maureen Wilson, Pat Bermel, Kehli O'Byrne, Michael A. Jackson, Mitch Kosterman, Allan Lysell, Rosanne Hopkins

Director: Kim Manners
Writers: Stephen J. Cannell & Randall Wallace

2. "Westside Stories" Dec. 1, 1990

To catch a thief burglarizing high-society homes, the team goes undercover ammong the country-club set.

Graham Fitzgerald...........................................David Naughton
Melissa...............................................................Heidi Ziegler
Penelope Dupont...............................................Mary Jo Keenen
Andrew Witherspoon.........................................Peter Blackwood
Susan Clay.........................................................Merrilyn Gann
And: Rebecca Toolan (Katherine Finch), Sandra Carpenter (Buffy), Georgie Major (Alice), Paul Haddad (Squeaky)

Director: James Whitmore, Jr.          Writer: Jack Bernstein

3. "Strawberry" Dec. 8, 1990

Jack learns his old lover (Rose), whom he sent to prison, is out and looking for him. Neil reprises his role from ep. 1.

Sarah Bakum........................................................Jamie Rose
Augie Desau.........................................................Tim Neil
Prosecutor............................................................Jay Brazeau
Baloney................................................................Andrew Johnston
Fast Eddie Faldo..................................................Brent Stait
V.B. Ledbetter.....................................................Howard Jerome
Shelly.................................................................Sharlene Martin
And: Claudio De Victor (Desk Sergeant), Ken Budd (Attorney), Alex Taylor (Desk clerk), Celia Louise Martin (Reporter)
      Also orig. announced:
      Don S. [a.k.a. Don] Davis (Chief Sterling), Garry Chalk (Sgt. Ty Carter), Roman Padhura (Passerby), Ron Cartier (Doctor), Joyce Erikson (Elderly person)

Director: Jonathan Sanger          Writer: Randall Wallace

**preempted Dec. 15**

4. "Chucky" Dec. 22, 1990

When Toby is accused of murder, his colleagues and the dead man's son (Bader) go undercover to find the real killer. Guest Alzado is a former pro football player.

Tommy "Wide Load" Moran....................................Lyle Alzado
Chucky Moran, his son........................................Dietrich Bader
Joe Clerici..........................................................Clint Carmichael
Bud Covey...........................................................Alec Burden
Susan.................................................................Robin Smith
Paul Donnally.....................................................Steve Oatway
Hooper...............................................................Roger Crossley
Tracy.................................................................Veronica Lorenz
Judge Ritter.......................................................John Tierney
Susan Myers.......................................................Marcy Mellish
And: Lana Higgins (Little Eva), William MacDonald (Wade Parker), Steve Adams (Adam), Sharlene Martin (Denise), Graeme Kingston (Bailiff), Bruce Corkum (Deckhand)

Director: Kim Manners          Writer: Stephen J. Cannell

**cancelled**

5. "Meet Your Matchmaker"  June 6, 1991

Stanley joins an elite video dating service to try to catch a serial killer of businesspeople.  Orig. scheduled for Dec. 22.

Henry Little/Terri.................................................Brian L. Green
Brian Slade............................................................Paul Boretski
Melissa.................................................................Tamsin Kelsey
Kramer...............................................................French Tickner
Haverhilll.................................................................Larry Hill
Christine................................................................Ellie Harvie
And:  Glynis Davies (Alice), Norman Armour, Deryl Hayes  (Reporters), Terry Arrowsmith (Cop)

Director: Tucker Gates (Kim Manners orig. announced)
Writer: Jack Bernstein

6. "Argo the Venusian"  June 13, 1991

A cop (recurring guest Smith, who becomes one of the Badges) pretends to be an extraterrestrial when he's a suspect after having an affair with the wife of a mobster subsequently killed.

Chauffeur...........................................................Jano Frandsen
Francesca Bronzell.............................................Elena Stiteler
John "Buns" Bronzell.........................................James Kidnie
Prof. Higgs............................................................Sam Malkin
Brewster..............................................................Andre Daniels
Guards.........................................Terry King, Douglas Stewart

Director: Alan Cooke    Writer: Randall Wallace

7. "Can I Get a Witness?"  June 20, 1991

The group must protect a big-time money launderer (Newman) who's turning state's-evidence against a mobster (Betancourt).

Max Sloan.................................................Andrew Hill Newman
Gloria Castillo................................................Anne Betancourt
U.S. Attorney...................................................Jerry Wasserman
Felix.........................................................................Jason Scott
Enrique.............................................................Frank Ferrucci
Candy.....................................................................Suki Kaiser
And: Jack Ammon (Grandpa), Dwight McFee (Prison officer),
    Lon Katzmann (Smoker), Brent Chapman (Cop), Donna
    Carroll White (Judge), Pedro Salvin (Driver), Ahnee Boyce
    (Waitress), Lenno Britos (Pal)

Director: David Nutter          Writer: Jack Bernstein

## Carol & Company

NBC          March 31-May 4    Saturdays, 10-10:30 p.m.
             July 6-20         Saturday, 10:30-11 p.m.

Series premiere: March 31, 1990
Final telecast: July 20, 1991

Original repertory comedy.  Each playlet preceded by a question-and-answer session with Burnett and the studio audience.

Ensemble: Carol Burnett, Anita Barone, Meagen Fay,  Richard
    Kind, Terry Kiser, Peter Krause

Kalola and Wind Dancer Productions in assoc. Touchstone
    Television

Executive producers: Matt Williams, David McFadzean
Co-executive producer: Ian Praiser
Supervising producer: Bob Tischler
Producer: Robert Wright
Co-producer: Marcia Brandwynne
Associate producers: Gary S. Drews, Steve Schott
Director of photography: Richard Hissong
Creative consultant: Carmen Finestra
Executive story consultant: Lauren Eve Anderson
Executive story editors: Darrel Campbell, Billy Riback
Story editors: Terrie Collins, Peter Tolan
Music: Howard Pearl
Theme (instrumental): Dan Foliart & Howard Pearl
Director unless otherwise noted: Andrew D. Weyman
Developed by: Matt Williams & David McFadzean

1. "Grandma Gets It On"  Sept. 22, 1990

A woman tries to remove her sexually frisky mother (Burnett) from a nursing home.

Old man..................................................................Owen Bush

Writer: Peter Tolan

2. "Diary of a Really, Really Mad Housewife"  Sept. 29, 1990

After a series of mishaps, housewife Dorothy Tibbet (Burnett) is pushed to the brink of madness.

Writer: Bill Riback

3. "Goin' to the Chapel"  Oct. 6, 1990

Two weird events in one night in the life of Las Vegas Justice of the Peace Evelyn Sweets (Burnett).

Alfred Sternbacker.....................................................Lew Horn
Brandi Sternbacker.........................................Jennifer Richards
Pregnant woman................................................Ellen Gerstein
Marvin (dummy)................Chuck Wood (dummy); operated by
    David Strassman; voiced by Richard Kind

Writers:  Joyce  Costanza & Larry Moskowitz ("Dummy Dearest"); Terrie Collins ("Being Out There")

4. "Guns and Rosie"  Oct. 13, 1990

In a spoof of violent action films, three gun collectors debate who should kill a burglar.

Writer: David N. Weiss

5. "Stiff Competition"  Oct. 20, 1990

A woman's plan to leave her husband and marry her lover backfires after she confesses to her spouse.

Taxi drivers..................Michael Eugene Fairman, Eddie Hailey
And: Elaine Giftos

Writer: Darrel Campbell

6. "Here's to You, Mrs. Baldwin"  Oct. 27, 1990

A widow tries to resist romantic involvement with a much younger man (McKeon).

Bartender....................................................................Joe Lala
Ed.................................................................Robert Trumbull
And: Doug McKeon

Writers: Larry Moskowitz & Joyce Costanza

7. "Trisha Springs Eternal"  Nov. 3, 1990

Rosalind Burke (Burnett) employs desperate measures to escape a relentless old pal (White).

Trisha Durant......................................................Betty White
Frank...................................................................John Di Santi
Mr. Yamato...........................................................Jim Ishida

Writer: Lauren Eve Anderson

8. "Mom and Dad Day Afternoon"  Nov. 10, 1990

While applying for a loan, a couple is shocked to find the bank being robbed by their son.

Doogan........................................................John Cothran, Jr.
Evan...................................................................Marc Grapey
Teller..................................................................Valerie Spencer

Writer: Peter Tolan

9. "Driving Miss Crazy"  Nov. 17, 1990  10-11 p.m.

A woman recently released from an asylum tries to keep her sanity through the red tape of renewing a driver's license.  Followed by a rerun in the second half hour.

Writer: Billy Riback

10. "The Jingle Belles"  Nov. 24, 1990

A long-time jingle-writing duo breaks up when one partner (Peters) becomes a recording star.

Song: "The Next Dream" by Mark Mueller (lyrics) and Craig Safan (music)

Kay......................................................................Bernadette Peters

Writers: Joyce Costanza & Larry Moskowitz

11. "Teacher, Teacher"  Dec. 1, 1990

Two tales: A teacher is stopped for speeding by a former student; recollections of a beloved fifth-grade teacher (Brown).

Miss Underwood........................................Pat Crawford Brown
Mr. Carmen......................................Robert Urich (uncredited)

Writers: Darrel Campbell & Peter Tolan

12. "Spudnik"  Dec. 8, 1990

A flighty woman, preparing to rendezvous with a spaceship at a dock, confronts an angry woman (Carter) fishing there.

Dakota...................................................................Nell Carter

Writer: Darrel Campbell

**preempted Dec. 15**

13. "No News Is Bad News"  Jan. 5, 1991

A newscaster (Burnett) resists the flashy changes wrought by her new news director, a former game-show producer.

Harry Logan..........................................................Paul Napier

J.T.........................................................................Richard Karn
Wendy...................................................................Kelley Wright

Writer: David N. Weiss

**preempted Jan. 12**

14. "Turning Tables"  Jan. 19, 1991

A couple try to celebrate their one-year anniversary at a tony restaurant

Waiter.....................................................................I.M. Hobson
And: Terry Davis (Woman), Josef Powell (Pianist)

Writer: Diana Coen

15. "That Little Extra Something"  Jan. 26, 1991

Spoof of audience-interactive murder-mystery plays, with Burnett in three roles (including as an audience member).

Audience member..............................Tim Conway (uncredited)
Paul.........................................................................Paul Brett

Writer: Lauren Eve Anderson

16. "A Fall from Grace"  Feb. 2, 1991

A woman confronts the demons of her past when she's transported to another dimension by her clothes dryer.

Little Grace...........................................................Danielle Clegg

Writer: Ian Praiser & Peter Tolan

17. "Suture Self"  Feb. 9, 1991

Dorothy Tibbet, needing surgery, calls for Dr. Doogie Howser (Harris, in a spoof of his *Doogie Howser, M.D.* character).

Doogie Howser (as in end-credits; misidenti-
     fied as "Hoogie Dowser" in *TV Guide*)...Neil Patrick Harris

Writer: Darrel Campbell

18. "High on Life"  Feb. 16, 1991

A woman about to marry a dull, steady fellow is tempted by a free-spirited window-washer.

Writers: Larry Moskowitz & Joyce Costanza

**unscheduled preemption Feb. 23**

19. "Momma Needs a New Pair of Shoes"  March 2, 1991

Three sisters gather to bury their deceased mother, and to dig up old resentments while planning her burial attire.

Gladys Klein.........................................................Mimi Cozzens

Director: Marian Deaton       Writers: Ian Praiser & Peter Tolan

20. "Jewel of Denial"  March 9, 1991  10-11 p.m.

In a parody of detective movies, a woman has until midnight to solve an old crime and clear her deceased father's name. Followed by a rerun in the second half hour.

Announced cast includes: Jeremy Piven

Director: Asaad Kelada
Writers: Marilyn Anderson & Billy Riback

21. "Intimate Behavior" March 16, 1991

Vignettes and musical sketches satirizing contemporary life.

With: Hal Linden

Special musical material: Ken Welch, Mitzie Welch, Peter Tolan; music arranged and conducted by Peter Matz

Writers: Mitzie Welch & Ken Welch, Ian Praiser, Peter Tolan

**preempted March 23**

**preempted April 6**

22. "Noah's Place" April 13, 1991  10-11 p.m.

A waitress has an unexpected reunion with her convict husband, who stops at her coffee shop en route to a new prison. Followed by a rerun in the second half hour.

Rodney/Glen......................................................Jeremy Piven

Writer: Lynn Montgomery

23. "Overnight Male" April 27, 1991  10:30-11 p.m.

A postal worker is delighted with her fantasy dream lover (Reeve). Orig. scheduled for Feb. 23.

Dream lover/supervisor Bob Johnson..........Christopher Reeve
Maitre d'.................................................................Tom Urich
Postal worker...................................................Mark W. Scott

Choreographer: Don Chrichton

Writer: Billy Riback

24. "For Love or Money" May 4, 1991  10-11 p.m.

In a parody of 1940s gangster films, a woman reminisces about her romance with a gigolo aboard a luxury cruise ship.

Slappy...............................................................John Pinette
Steward...........................................................John Hoffman
Ward.....................................................................Gary Lahti

Director: NA   Writer: NA

**cancelled; reruns begin July 6**

## Cheers

NBC          Thursdays, 9-9:30 p.m.

Series premiere: Sept. 29, 1982

Comedy of a Boston sports bar, presided over by its womanizing bartender-owner (Danson), a former Red Sox pitcher, and his sexy but neurotic bar manager (Alley). The seafood restaurant upstairs is Melville's. Perlman is the wife of actor Danny DeVito; Alley, of actor Parker Stevenson. Occasional director Ackerman is also the series' film editor.

Sam Malone.........................................................Ted Danson
Rebecca Howe.....................................................Kirstie Alley
* Waitress Carla Tortelli LeBec............................Rhea Perlman

Norm Peterson.....................................................George Wendt
Cliff Clavin.......................................................John Ratzenberger
Bartender Woody Boyd.................................Woody Harrelson
Dr. Frasier Crane.............................................Kelsey Grammer

*Recurring:*
Dr. Lilith Sternin Crane (ep. 2,7-10,12,
     14-20,23-25)............................................Bebe Neuwirth
Robin Colcord (ep. 1,2,4,7,15).............................Roger Rees
John Allen Hill (ep. 8,12-13,18-19)......................Keene Curtis
Paul (ep. 4-5,7,10-11,13,15-17,21,23-25).............Paul Willson
Henri (ep. 11,19,24).........................................Anthony Cistaro

* Full name: Carla Maria Victoria Angelina Teresa Apollonia Lozupone Tortelli LeBec.

Charles Burrows Charles Productions in assoc. with
     Paramount Television
Executive producers: James Burrows, Glen Charles, Les
     Charles, Cheri Eichen, Bill Steinkellner, Phoef Sutton
Producers: Tim Berry
Co-producers: Andy Ackerman, Brian Pollack, Mert Rich, Dan
     O'Shannon, Tom Anderson, Larry Balmagia
Associate producer: Mary Fukuto
Creative consultant: David Lloyd
Executive script consultant: Bob Ellison
Creative consultants: Ken Levine, David Isaacs
Story editors: Dan Staley, Rob Long
Director of photography: John Finger
Music: Craig Safan
Theme: "Where Everybody Knows Your Name" by Judy Hart
     Angelo and Gary Portnoy (words and music); performed
     by Gary Portnoy
Director unless otherwise noted: James Burrows
Creators: Glen Charles & Les Charles and James Burrows

————————————

1. "Love is a Really, Really Perfectly Okay Thing"
    Sept. 20, 1990

Rebecca pledges her loyalty to a prison-bound Robin, after lying to him that she and Sam hadn't gone to bed together, and leaves Cheers to find a new job.

Father Barry..................................................Eric Christmas
Gary's Olde Towne Tavern bartender.............Edmund Gaynes
Customer.............................................Christopher Abraham

Writer: Phoef Sutton

2. "Cheers Fouls Out" Sept. 27, 1990  (195)

Woody accidentally injures Boston Celtics basketball player Kevin McHale, who's playing with the Cheers team against annual rival Gary's Olde Towne Tavern. Dedication: "To the memory of Stephen Kolzak, 1953-1990."

Himself..............................................................Kevin McHale
Gary.......................................................................Joel Polis
"Dr. Walter Froenmeyer"...............................James Hornbeck
And: James Nardini (James), Lee Vines (Father Conrad)

Writer: Larry Balmagia

3. "Rebecca Redux" Oct. 4, 1990  (197)

When Sam sees Rebecca working a menial job, he wants to rehire her as manager, but everyone loves new manager Earl.

Earl.......................................................................Bryan Clark

Promoter..............................................Perry Anzilotti
• Customer/Carla's brother................................Randy Pelish
Car show patron.......................................Timothy Fall
Tony.....................................................Tony Di Benedetto
Pete.....................................................Peter Schreiner
Deliverypersons......................Stanley Bennett Clay, Paul Cira
     Also orig. announced:
     Patrons...........................Lisa Robinson, Brandon Hooper

• Called Sal in a later episode.

Teleplay: Phoef Sutton and Bill Steinkellner & Cheri Eichen
Story: Bill Steinkellner

4. "Where Nobody Knows Your Name"  Oct. 11, 1990  (198)

Rebecca is incensed when Robin's former girlfriend poses as
the mystery woman for whom he gave up his money and freedom.  Talk-show host Hall appears as himself on the bar TV.

Himself..................................................Arsenio Hall
Sherman.................................................Ron Ulstad
     In end-credits but no speaking role in episode:
     Joanne................................................Catherine MacNeal

Director: Andy Ackerman
Writers: Dan O'Shannon & Tom Anderson

5. "Ma Always Liked You Best"  Oct. 18, 1990

Cliff's prodigal mother (Sternhagen, reprising her role from
previous seasons) rooms with Woody after a tiff with Cliff.

Esther Clavin.............................Frances Sternhagen
Construction worker Jeff.................................Rocky LAPORTE
Construction worker Lars.................................John Posey
Pete.....................................................Peter Schreiner
Police officers.................................Ken Foree, James F. Dean

Director: Andy Ackerman
Writers: Dan O'Shannon & Tom Anderson

6. "Grease"  Oct. 25, 1990

A devastated Norm learns the Hungry Heifer restaurant is
closing down; Robin's prison work-crew is just outside Cheers.

Hungry Heifer owner Sid Nelson.....................Sheldon Leonard
Vince...............................John Reger a.k.a John Patrick Reger

Writers: Brian Pollack & Mert Rich

7. "Breaking In is Hard to Do"  Nov. 1, 1990

Frasier and Lilith argue over who should give up their career
to be a full-time parent; Rebecca pays a conjugal visit to Robin. Guest Philip Perlman is the father of co-star Rhea Perlman;
he also appears as a background extra in many episodes.

Doug Aducci....................................Clive Rosengren
Prison guard.........................................John Boyle
Prisoner.............................................Edward Penn
Phil.................................................Philip Perlman
Frederick Crane, Frasier and Lilith's infant............(uncredited)

Director: Andy Ackerman  Writers: Ken Levine & David Isaacs

-- Nov. 8, 1990  9-10 p.m.

Special entitled *Cheers 200th* (title utilizing the series logo,
which has no apostrophe):  Retrospective commemorating the

series' 200th episode ("Bad Neighbor Sam," running Nov. 15),
with a panel of current cast-members, original co-star Shelley
Long, and recurring guests Bebe Neuwirth and Roger Rees on
a panel before a live audience, responding to questions by
syndicated public-affairs-show host John McLaughlin.

Directors: James Burrows, Andy Ackerman
Writers: Cheri Eichen & Bill Steinkellner and Phoef Sutton

8. "Bad Neighbor Sam"  Nov. 15, 1990

Sam gets in a property dispute with Melville's new owner (new
recurring guest Curtis); Woody gets a photo from his girlfriend
Kelly, studying in France.  The series' 200th episode, per NBC.

Jeffrey..................................................Carl Mueller
Hilary...................................................Sandy Edgerton
Martha...................................................Tamara Mark
Phil.....................................................Philip Perlman
     In end-credits but no speaking role in episode:
     Bradley..............................................E.E. Bell
     Mrs. Armstrong.......................................Aileen Fitzpatrick
     Patron...............................................Fred Slyter

Writers: Cheri Eichen & Bill Steinkellner

9. "Veggie-Boyd"  Nov. 22, 1990

Woody feels guilty about acting in a TV commercial for a
product he hates.

Director.................................................Tom Everett
Jill.....................................................Debbie Gregory
Technician...............................................John Cervenka
Phil.....................................................Philip Perlman
And: Michael Holden (Joe), Tony Di Benedetto (Tony)

Writers: Dan Staley & Rob Long

10. "Norm and Cliff's Excellent Adventure"  Dec. 6, 1990

Norm and Cliff's prank threatens to end Sam and Frasier's
friendship; Woody gets hooked on a home-shopping channel.
Dedication: "To the memory of Al Rosen, 1910-1990."

Heinrich.................................................Tom Klunis

Writers: Ken Levine & David Isaacs

11. "Woody Interruptus"  Dec. 13, 1990

Woody's girlfriend (Swanson, reprising her recurring role from
last season) returns from college abroad with an overly friendly French photographer friend (new recurring guest Cistaro).

Kelly....................................................Jackie Swanson
Dr. Eckworth (orig. Dr. Eugene Mendoza).........Michael Keenan
Motel night manager......................................Douglas MacHugh
Tony.....................................................Tony Di Benedetto

Writers: Dan Staley & Rob Long

12. "Honor Thy Mother"  Jan. 3, 1991

Carla's mother demands Carla rename one of her kids child
Benito Mussolini; Woody puts Cheers in an entertainment-
coupon book.  Pelish reprises his role from ep. 3.

Mama Mussolini Lozupone...........................Sada Thompson
Zia......................................................Oceana Marr
Gino, Carla's son........................................Josh Lozoff

Angeline, Carla's sister......................................Carol Ann Susi
Sal, Carla's brother.............................................Randy Pelish

Writers: Brian Pollack & Mert Rich

13. "Achilles Hill" Jan. 10, 1991

Sam vindictively dates the daughter (Mahaffey) of his nemesis Hill; Carla thinks the foosball table is possessed. Christmas reprises his role from ep. 1.

Valerie Hill........................................................Valerie Mahaffey
Father Barry.........................................................Eric Christmas

Director: Andy Ackerman
Writers: Ken Levine & David Isaacs

**unscheduled preemption Jan. 17**

14. "The Days of Wine and Neuroses" Jan. 24, 1991

Rebecca hits the bottle after getting cold feet when soon-to-be-free Robin proposes; Frasier gets hooked on the bar's new karaoke singalong machine. Orig. scheduled for Jan. 17.

Jukebox repairperson/Walter...............................Calvin Jung
Deliveryperson................................................Shad Willingham
Woman.........................................................Kristine Knudson

Writers: Brian Pollack & Mert Rich

15. "Wedding Bell Blues" Jan. 31, 1991

At her City Hall wedding, an anguished Rebecca declares she only loved Robin for his money, and calls off the marriage. Hatfield, of the singing duo The Righteous Brothers, sings part of their "Unchained Melody." Orig. scheduled for Jan. 24.

Himself..............................................................Bobby Hatfield
Justice of the Peace Ed.........................................Ray Stricklyn
Jonathan....................................................................Ron Abel
Security guard.......................................................George Case

Writers: Dan O'Shannon & Tom Anderson

16. "I'm Getting My Act Together and Sticking It in Your Face" Feb. 7, 1991

A broken Rebecca flies home to San Diego, along with Woody's credit cards; Frasier gives "updated" readings of Dickens. Orig. scheduled for Jan. 31.z

Leon.................................................................Jeff McCarthy
Flight attendant...................................................Jan Gan Boyd

Director: Andy Ackerman    Writers: Dan Staley & Rob Long

17. "Sam Time Next Year" Feb. 14, 1991

Sam mangles his back before embarking on his annual Valentine's Day tryst with his 20-year compatriot (Feldon). Massachusetts governor Dukakis has a silent cameo in the teaser.

Himself.....................................................Gov. Michael Dukakis
Lauren Hudson...............................................Barbara Feldon
Jules.........................................................Roger Eschbacher
And: Gibby Brand (Adam), Don Took (Edward)

Writer: Larry Balmagia

18. "Crash of the Titans" Feb. 21, 1991

Rebecca's plan to buy Cheers from Sam has Hill playing divide and conquer over the pool room and bathrooms (which he finally sells to new partners Rebecca and Sam for $30,000). Orig. scheduled for Feb. 7.

Harry................................................................Jeremiah Morris
Phil......................................................................Philip Perlman
Tony...........................................................Tony Di Benedetto
Pete..................................................................Peter Schreiner
Hope..................................................................Adele Baughn
Joy....................................................................Anadel Baughn

Writers: Dan Staley & Rob Long

19. "It's a Wonderful Wife" Feb. 28, 1991

Rebecca helps Norm's wife Vera get a job as hat-check person at Melville's; Lilith plans to give Frasier a birthday gift of sexy photos. Guest Birkett (Wendt's real-life wife) did an uncredited cameo as Vera (with her face covered) in a previous season's Thanksgiving episode.

Miss Kenderson...................................................Heather Lee
Pete..................................................................Peter Schreiner
Tony...........................................................Tony Di Benedetto
Voice of Vera Peterson.............Bernadette Birkett (uncredited)

Writer: Sue Herring

20. "Cheers Has Chili" March 14, 1991

Rebecca's latest business venture -- a tea room in the pool room -- is a hit when she serves up Woody's terrific chili.

Fire Marshal (erroneously given as
   "Bud" in *TV Guide*)..................................Robert Machray
Pete..................................................................Peter Schreiner
Albert.....................................................Stanley Bennett Clay
   Also orig. announced:
      Voice of Dorothy............................................Phyllis Katz

Director: Andy Ackerman
Writers: Cheri Eichen & Bill Steinkellner & Phoef Sutton

21. "Carla Loves Clavin" March 21, 1991

Carla, struggling to be nice so she can win the "Miss Boston Barmaid" contest, believes Cliff is one of the judges.

Emcee..............................................................Dante Di Loreto
Mr. Quincy.........................................................Nathan Davis
Shawnee Wilson......................................................Jessie Scott

Writer: Dan Staley & Rob Long

22. "Pitch It Again, Sam" March 28, 1991

Sam's old home run-hitting nemesis (Fairman) wants Sam to pitch to him at a baseball pre-game exhibition.

Former New York Yankee Dutch Kinkaid........Michael Fairman
Cap Richards, his manager...........................Henry Woronicz
Billy.............................................................Zachary Benjamin
Firefighter Jim........................................James Ellis Reynolds
Firefighter Peter.................................................Peter Kevoian
Firefighter Mike...............................................Michael Cannizzo
Ballplayer................................................................Joel Anderson
Victoria...........................................................Victoria Barrett
Leanne.............................................................Leanne Griffin

Writers: Dan O'Shannon & Tom Anderson

23. "Rat Girl"  April 4, 1991

Lilith takes the death of one of her lab rats distressingly hard;
Sam tries to figure why a shapely woman (Toussaint) spurns
him for portly barfly Paul.

Paula.................................................Beth Toussaint
School administrators.....Cheryl Lynn Bruce, Andre Miripolsky
Pete.................................................Peter Schreiner

Writers: Ken Levine & Dan Isaacs

24. "Home Malone"  April 25, 1991

Sam locks himself out while babysitting Frederick; Kelly (Swanson, reprising her role from ep. 11) works a shift at Cheers.

Kelly...............................................Jackie Swanson
Frederick Crane, Frasier and
      Lilith's toddler.........................Christopher/Kevin Graves
Pete.................................................Peter Schreiner
Phil (no lines)......................................Philip Perlman
Construction workers.............Gary Dee Davis, Norm Compton,
      Steve Hulin

Director: Andy Ackerman
Writers: Dan O'Shannon & Tom Anderson

25. "Uncle Sam Wants You"  May 2, 1991

Sam, enjoying all his free time with Frederick so much, tries to
find a mom for a child of his own, and asks Rebecca.

Elvis Presley (dream sequence)...............................Pete Wilcox
Frederick Crane...............................Christopher/Kevin Graves
Daria...............................................Tress MacNeille

Writers: Dan Staley & Rob Long

**renewed for 1991-92; new episodes begin Sept. 19, 1991**

## China Beach

ABC          Sept. 29-Dec. 8    Saturdays, 9-10 p.m.
             June 4-July 16     Tuesdays, 10-11 p.m.
             July 22            Monday, 9-11 p.m.

Series premiere: April 26, 1988
Final telecast: July 22, 1991

Vietnam War drama of Army nurse McMurphy, and the soldiers, medical staff, USO entertainers and others at the 510th
EVAC unit, China Beach, an R&R and medical center adjacent
to the U.S. base at Da Nang. Star Delany and series co-creator
Young are a couple in real life; co-creator Broyles is former
editor-in-chief of *Newsweek*.

Capt. Colleen McMurphy.....................................Dana Delany
Pvt. Sam Beckett.........................................Michael Boatman
Sarge Bub Pepper.........................................Troy Evans
Frankie Bunsen...........................................Nancy Giles
Ed "Dodger" Winslow......................................Jeff Kober
Dr. Dick Richard.........................................Robert Picardo
Lila Garreau.............................................Concetta Tomei
Boonie Lanier............................................Brian Wimmer
Camp prostitute K.C......................................Marg Helgenberger

*Recurring:*
Karen Lanier, K.C.'s/Boonie's daughter (1985)
      (ep. 1-2,14,16)........................................Christine Elise

Karen Lanier (1975) (ep. 11,13-14).........................Shay Astar
Joe (orig. Tom) Arneberg, Colleen's husband
      (ep. 10,15-16)...........................................Adam Arkin
Linda Matlock Lanier, Boonie's wife
      (ep. 1-2,8,16)...........................................Finn Carter
Dr. Colleen Flaherty Richard, Dr. Richard's wife
      (ep. 1,6,16).............................................Colleen Flynn
Trieu Au (ep. 3,11-12,14)....................................Kieu Chinh
Nurse Gloria Dawn (ep. 7,10,16)..............................Kathy Molter

Sacret, Inc. in assoc. with Warner Bros. Television
Executive producer: John Sacret Young
Co-executive producer: John Wells
Executive consultant: William Broyles, Jr.
Supervising producer: Mimi Leder
Producers: Carol Flint, Lydia Woodward, Geno Escarrega
Co-producer (later in season): Barbara Marshall
Associate producer: Barbara Marshall (early in season),
      Christopher Nelson, Darryl Levine (both later in season)
Executive story editor: Josef Anderson (early in season)
Director of photography: Richard Thorpe
Technical advisors: Betsy Jackson, Jan Wyatt
Music: Paul Chihara
Theme: "Reflections," performed by Diana Ross & The
      Supremes (the 1967 recording, a #2 hit on the *Billboard*
      pop chart)
End-theme: John Rubinstein
Stories (ep. 1-7) by: John Sacret Young & John Wells & Lydia
      Woodward & Carol Flint
Creators: William Broyles, Jr. and John Sacret Young

1. "The Big Bang"  Sept. 29, 1990

In flash-forward to 1985, Boonie and Dr. Richard have a reunion that stirs memories of their first days in Vietnam in 1966.
Part 1 of 2.  Working title: "History, Part I -- The Big Bang."

Lt. Col. Mac Miller...............................Wings Hauser
Dr. Singer.........................................Scott Jacek
Jan...............................................Debra Stricklin
Doctor.............................................Richard Green
Jake..............................................David Hollander
Grunt.............................................Oscar Jordan
Kid...............................................Sean Doherty
Gilliam...........................................Shannon Farrara
Boy...............................................Coleby Lombardo
And: Patrick Y. Malone (Nick Cheeks), Rick Marzan (Sergeant),
      Phi Nguyen (VC woman), Sean B. Ryan (Adam)

Director: John Sacret Young          Teleplay: John Wells

2. "History, Part II -- She Sells More Than Sea Shells"
      Oct. 6, 1990

In 1967, K.C. is pregnant, and when the baby's father is se-
verely wounded, turns to Boonie for help; in a flash-forward to
1985, Karen learns the truth about her natural mother.

Lt. Col. Mac Miller...............................Wings Hauser
Dr. Singer.........................................Scott Jacek
Angie.............................................Conni Marie Brazelton
      Also orig. announced: Martin Grey (Ciamacco)

Director: Mimi Leder          Teleplay: Carol Flint

3. "You, Babe"  Oct. 13, 1990

In Saigon with McMurphy, K.C. gives birth and hands the
child over to a foster mother (new recurring guest Kieu Chinh).

Nellie.............................................Kerry Noonan

General Duchesne..................................................Vic Polizos
Julie..................................................Ellen Crawford
Burly MP..................................................Patrick Lee James
Jim..................................................Richard Lineback
Scrawny MP..................................................Salvator Xuereb
Bellhop..................................................Chi-Muoi Lo
Ladies..................................Catherine Ai, Lee Mary Weilnau
Priest..................................Father James Phan Van Dai
Porter..................................................Quy Hoang
Bleary soldier..................................................Jeff Hudson
And: Christina Le, Viet Truong (Street kids), Louis Mandylor (Aussie), Tran Pham (Hooker), D. Thompson (Medic)

Director: Mimi Leder
Teleplay: Susan Rhinehart and Cathryn Michon

**preempted Oct. 20**

4. "Escape" Oct. 27, 1990

At his father's funeral in 1985, Beckett recalls his childhood, and his Vietnam assignment with the graves unit. Jacek reprises his role from ep. 1-2. Orig. scheduled for Oct. 13.

Dr. Singer..................................................Scott Jacek
Rev. Beckett..................................................Gilbert Lewis
Lynwood "Deadman" Crawford..........................Kenny Ransom
Dookie..................................................Everette Lamar
Cromwell..................................................Raynor Scheine
Soldier..................................................Peter Lewis
Young Beckett..................................................Tony T. Johnson
Pastor..................................................Orlando Bonner
Col. Broyles..............Ralph Meyering, Jr. (given as "Meyerling" in *TV Guide*)
And: Geoff Meed (Sergeant), Jimmy Lee Newman, Jr. (Young Dookie), Juan Padilla (MP)

Director: Christopher Leitch          Teleplay: Paris Qualles

5. "Fever" Nov. 3, 1990

In 1970, McMurphy returns to Lawrence, Kan. to take a nursing job and make peace with her mother (Fuller). Noonan reprises her role from ep. 3. Director Keaton, better known as an actress, previously directed the documentary *Heaven* and the *CBS Schoolbreak Special: The Girl with the Crazy Brother*.

Margaret Mary McMurphy, Colleen's mother........Penny Fuller
Nurse Webb..................................................Joanna Lipari
Nellie..................................................Kerry Noonan
Ralphie..................................................Drew Pillsbury
Mindy..................................................Christine Carman
Kieu..................................................Sany Chay
Folmsbee..................................................Nick De Mauro
And: Shawn Modrell (Young mother), Mary Ellen (E.R. nurse), Joe Lazenby (Man in E.R.), Michelle Mann (Charlotte), Pascal Marcotte (Driver), Tommy Morgan (Corpsman)

Director: Diane Keaton          Teleplay: Lydia Woodward

6. "Juice" Nov. 10, 1990

In 1972, Dr. Richard, a suburban physician on a weekend Florida fling with Colleen Flaherty, encounters a troubled, motorcycle-riding McMurphy working in a juice factory.

Noon Gantry..................................................Gavan O'Herlihy
Chaplain..................................................Andrew Buckley
Vietnam vet..................................................Joseph M. Hamilton

Director: John Sacret Young          Teleplay: John Sacret Young

7. "One Giant Leap" Nov. 17, 1990

In 1969, the joy of the first moon landing is overshadowed by Colleen's jealousy over Dick's infatuation with another nurse (Molter) and by the accident that will cost Boonie his leg.

USO singer Sweet Hula..........................Vanessa Bell Calloway
Everett, Jr...................................................Morgan Weisser
Soldier..................................................Charles Holman
The Palm Fronds (USO group)........April Grace, Gloria Reuben, Wynonna Smith

Director: Michael Katleman          Teleplay: Josef Anderson

**preempted Nov. 24**

8. "One Small Step" Dec. 1, 1990

Following the amputation of his leg, Boonie, with the help of Nurse Linda Matlock's affection, begins a long rehabilitation.

Stepakoff..................................................Michael Bowen
Kinnelt..................................................Alan Boyce
Dottie..................................................Sarah G. Buxton
Ricco..................................................William Gallo
Goldman..................................................Bernard White
Greene..................................................Rosalind Cash
Dr. Harbert..................................................Alan Haufrect
Navy nurse..................................................Andi Chapman
And: Raymond Cruz (Lopez), Christopher Murray (Navy surgeon), Michael Rapaport (Kravits), Phyllis Applegate (Nurse), Dalit Berkowitz (Red Cross worker), Wendy Bowers (Flight nurse), Owen Bush (Gen. Lee)

Director: Steven Dubin          Writer: John Wells

9. "The Call" Dec. 8, 1990

In 1969, aspiring standup comic Frankie returns to Chicago in time for the trial of the Chicago Seven; in Vietnam, McMurphy and Dodger try to help some Montagnard tribespeople. Lindfors is the mother of actor Kristoffer Tabori.

Ilsa..................................................Viveca Lindfors
Eddie..................................................Scott Lawrence
Rashid..................................................Basil Wallace
Darrin..................................................M.K. Harris
Gunner..................................................Michael Aron
Del..................................................Brian Markinson
Bobby Seale (real-life Chicago Seven defendant)........Tico Wells
Meg..................................................Kristine Blackburn
Judge Hoffman (real-life judge)..........................Steve Franken
William Kunstler (real-life defense attorney)........John Apicella
And: Darren Epton (G.I), David Simpson (Corpsman), Will Jeffries (Schultz), Christina Le (Child), Chantara Nop (Villager), Lee Mary Weilnau (Woman)

Director: Robert Ginty
Writers: Paris Qualles & Cathryn Michon

**on hiatus, then cancelled**

10. "I Could Have Danced All Night...But Didn't" June 4, 1991

In 1983, as a maid of honor, McMurphy meets future husband Joe (new recurring guest Arkin) and recalls the 1969 wedding plans of Lila and Sarge Pepper, and the end of her own relationship with Dr. Richard. Orig. scheduled for Dec. 15.

Director: Michael Fresco          Teleplay: Cathryn Michon
Story: Carol Flint

**11. "100 Klicks Out"  June 11, 1991**

As Saigon falls, Bangkok bordello-owner K.C. reunites with her daughter (Astar); in 1980s New Mexico, McMurphy tries to prevent child abuse.  Per Warner Bros., teleplay writer Rhineheart also wrote the story, though is uncredited onscreen.

Hector.................................................................Jesse Borrego
Joaquin.......................................................Randolph Mantooth
Cam Noi.................................................................Page Leong
Marines...........................................Ed Beechner, Peter Lewis
O'Bannion.................................................Patrick John Hurley
Innocencia..........................................................Petra Porras
Vietnamese clerk.....................................................Thau Chu
Neighbor.....................................................................Loc Do
And: Michael Ennis (Embassy clerk), Randy Kirby  (American),
     Donna Lew (Thai woman), Jean-Pierre C. Nguyen (Citi-
     zen), Kris Stevens (Joey), Huy T. Vu (NVA soldier)

Director: Mimi Leder            Teleplay: Susan Rhinehart

**12. "The Always Goodbye"  June 18, 1991**

In 1969 Bangkok, restaurant/bar-owner K.C.'s life is disrupted by the arrival of McMurphy and a young private (Newsom).

Turner....................................................................Pat Skipper
Loretta..............................................................Cynthia Gouw
Arnie Beachem.............................................Richmond Hoxie
PFC Leslie Maltbie...........................................David Newsom
Karen (2)...............................................Kelsey/Kirsten Dohring

Director: Gary Sinise            Writer: Lydia Woodward

**13. "Quest"  June 25, 1991**

In 1976, McMurphy helps K.C. re-enter the U.S., and visits Montana to see Dodger, who's converting a bus into a mobile church.  Astar reprises her role from ep. 11.

Squeaky Carver................................................Robert Knepper
Dad Winslow..................................................Richard Jaeckel
Archie...................................................Joseph Gordon-Levitt

Director: John Sacret Young      Story: John Sacret Young
Teleplay: John Sacret Young & Angela Ventresca

**preempted July 2**

**14. "Rewind"  July 9, 1991**

In 1985, Karen videotapes veterans who knew her mom, K.C. Hauser reprises his role from the two-part ep. 1-2; Lombardo played a different role, ep. 1.  Orig. scheduled for June 25.

Lt. Col. Mac Miller...............................................Wings Hauser
Marla.......................................................................Amy Steel
Gillian Lanier, Karen's little sister (1985).......Shannon Farrara
Lanier, Jr....................................................Coleby Lombardo

Director: Mimi Leder            Writers: Carol Flint & John Wells

**15. "Through and Through"  July 16, 1991**

In therapy in 1985, Colleen discovers she's suffering from post-traumatic stress syndrome.

Hyers.................................................................Ned Vaughn
Bill..........................................................Vondie Curtis-Hall
Owen......................................................................Ford Rainey
Norma..............................................................Lorinne Vozoff

Ray.............................................................Charles Noland
Franklin.......................................................Sy Richardson
And: James Staskel (Wags), Tom Wright (Robert), Don Hanmer
     (Kenneth),   Jack Ragotzy (Phil Sr.), Marcia Magus (Nurse
     Kass), Richard Zobel (Tony) Frederick Hall (P.F.C.), Nor-
     mal Nerrill (Dave), Mirron E. Willis (G.I.), Sean Gavigan
     (Tommy), Nurse (Laurie Souza)

Director: Mimi Leder            Writer: Carol Flint

**16. "Hello Goodbye"  July 22, 1991   9-11 p.m.**

At a 1988 reunion, Colleen, now married to Joe, recalls her final day at China Beach, and with others goes to the Vietnam Memorial. Gallagher is a former cast-member.  Final production filmed at Los Angeles' Indian Dunes facility, since closed.

Wayloo Marie Holmes.......................................Megan Gallagher
Dr. Bob..............................................................John Slattery
Lurch............................................................Neal McDonough
Top....................................................................Joseph Whipp
Malcolm Becket....................................................Troy Searcy
Archie Winslow.......................................................Tyrone Tan
And: Susan Byun (Receptionist), Jensen Daggett (Jennifer,
     Colleen and Joe's toddler), Michael D. Hall (Lifeguard)

Director: John Sacret Young      Teleplay: John Wells
Story:  John Sacret Young & John Wells & Lydia Woodward  &
     Carol Flint

## Coach

ABC              Tuesdays, 9:30-10 p.m.

Series premiere: Feb. 28, 1989

Comedy of a divorced college football coach (the Minnesota State University Screaming Eagles) and his staff, girlfriend, and married college-student daughter.  Luther's dog: Quincy.  Co-star Fabares is the wife of actor Mike Farrell, and the niece of singer Nanette Fabray.

Coach Hayden Fox...........................................Craig T. Nelson
Asst. Coach Luther Van Dam.........................Jerry Van Dyke
Newscaster Christine Armstrong.....................Shelley Fabares
Asst. Coach Michael "Dauber" Dybinski...........Bill Fagerbakke
Kelly Fox Rosebrock................................................Clare Carey
Stuart Rosebrock......................................................Kris Kamm

*Recurring:*
Athletic director Howard Burleigh
     (ep. 3-4, 19-20)................................................Ken Kimmins
Coach Judy Watkins (ep. 4,12-13,22).....................Pam Stone

Bungalow 78 Productions in assoc. with Unviersal Television
Executive producers: Barry Kemp, Sheldon Bull
Supervising producers: John Peaslee, Judd Pillot
Producer: Jay Kleckner
Associate producer: Craig Wyrick
Creative consultant: Mark Ganzel
Director of photography: Ronald W. Browne
Music: J.A.C. Redford
Theme: John Morris
Director unless otherwise noted: Alan Rafkin
Creator: Barry Kemp

**1. "That Shouldn't Happen"  Sept. 25, 1990**

Hayden, ecstatic about his team being ranked top-20 for the first time, meets Christine's mother (Fabray).

Mildred Armstrong.............................................Nanette Fabray
Bo Whitley......................................................Christopher Duncan
Bob Clifton.....................................................Joe Fowler
Skip.............................................................John R. Lacy
Jim..............................................................Jason Smith
      Also orig. announced: Bob Sorenson (Photographer)

Writers: Judd Pillot & John Peaslee

2. "Magnificent Abscession" Oct. 2, 1990 9:46-10:14 p.m.

When Hayden has to miss a game because of a bad tooth, Luther must coach via phone instructions from him. Late start due to a Presidential address.

Dr. Hibke......................................................Tom Poston
Announcer......................................................Joe Fowler

Writers: Barry Kemp & Mark Ganzel

3. "The Day That Moses Came to Town" Oct. 9, 1990

Hayden gets jealous when the university president woos a basketball coach with promises of grandiose perks. Guest Rick Barry is a sportcaster and former pro basketball player.

University president Dr. Elaine Tewksbury........Robin Strasser
Terrence Moses.................................................Bobby Hosea
Himself.........................................................Rick Barry
And: Penny Johnson (Susan), Mark Arnott (Carl)

Writer: Lyla Oliver

4. "Is This Your First Time on the Riverboat, Miss Watkins?" Oct. 16, 1990

Hayden reluctantly allows archrival Watkins (recurring guest Stone) to sit in on his poker night. Guest Kemp is the son of series creator Barry Kemp.

Billy...........................................................Justin Kemp

Writer: Sheldon Bull

5. "Hayden's in the Kitchen with Dinah" Oct. 23, 1990

Hayden promises to stay with a bedridden Christine, rather than attend a long-awaited team victory celebration.

Dinah...........................................................Marietta DePrima
Marion..........................................................K Callan
Tom.............................................................Gregory Itzin
Bo Whitley......................................................Christopher Duncan
Vince...........................................................Joshua Cadman

Writers: Judd Pillot & John Peaslee

6. "Hayden and Luther's Excellent Adventure" Oct. 30, 1990

Hayden and Luther get stranded out of town the night Hayden is to escort Christine to an awards banquet in her honor.

Leon............................................................Rocky Giordani
Floyd...........................................................Jeff Doucette
And: Beth Grant (Martha), F. Thom Spadaro (Man at the bar)

Writer: Sheldon Bull

7. "The Break Up" Nov. 6, 1990

Hayden and Christine decide to stop seeing each other.

Warren Graustark................................................Richard Sanders
Beverly Graustark...............................................Sandy Faison
Chaplain........................................................Joe Farago

Writers: Barry Kemp & Sheldon Bull

8. "The Iceman Goeth" Nov. 13, 1990

Even at a victory party, and with Elaine trying to seduce him, Hayden remains depressed over his breakup with Christine. Strasser reprises her role from ep. 3.

Dr. Elaine Tewksbury...........................................Robin Strasser
Bartender......................................................Mik Scriba

Writers: Mark Ganzel & Judd Pillot & John Peaslee

**preempted Nov. 20**

9. "Cabin Fever" Nov. 27, 1990

Christine wants all her belongings out of Hayden's house, and Luther might move in next-door.

Newbower........................................................Henry Jones
Fred Webb.......................................................Travis McKenna

Writer: Sheldon Bull

10. "Men Don't Heal" Dec. 4, 1990

Irritable over the breakup, Hayden attends a self-help group.

David...........................................................Stan Ivar
Hoyt............................................................Michael L. McManus
Ernie...........................................................Ernie Sabella

Writer: Mark Ganzel

11. "When Hayden Met Christine" Dec. 11, 1990

Dateless for a charity ball, Hayden flashes back four years to when he first met Christine, at the same affair.

Fred Webb.......................................................Travis McKenna
Stephen.........................................................Tom Hallick
Waiter in 1986..................................................Nicholas Shaffer

Writer: Sheldon Bull

12. "Christmas Brains" Dec. 18, 1990

Hayden's ex-wife (Kasdorf) unexpectedly shows up at his holiday party, and helps him decide to reunite with Christine.

Wilson Rosebrock, Stuart's father...............................James Staley
Beth Fox........................................................Lenore Kasdorf
Peg Rosebrock, Stuart's mother..................................Charlotte Stewart
Director........................................................Nick Toth

Writers: John Peaslee & Judd Pillot

**preempted Jan. 1**

13. "Dauber Graduates" Jan. 8, 1991

When Dauber finally graduates after eight years, Hayden promotes him to full-time coach, and their relationship changes.

Mr. Dybinski....................................................Jim Boeke
Elizabeth.......................................................Karen Bankhead

Writers: Judd Pillot & John Peaslee

14. "Puppy Love"  Jan. 22, 1991

Hayden concocts a wild tale to keep a promised $10 million donation from going to the basketball department instead.

Mrs. Rizendough...............................................Priscilla Morrill
Kennel attendant.................................................James Piddock
And: Dennis Patrick (Benjamin), Stu Levin (Charles)

Writer: Mark Ganzel

**preempted Jan. 29**

15. "The Marion Kind" Part 1  Feb. 5, 1991

Christine persuades Luther to have lunch with the reconciling best friend (Martin) who stole his girl 37 years ago. Callan played an apparently different character named Marion, ep. 5.

Peter Plunkett.......................................................Dick Martin
Marion Williamson......................................................K Callan

Writer: Sheldon Bull

16. "The Marion Kind" Part 2  Feb. 12, 1991

When Luther's old friend steals his girlfriend again, Hayden and Peter try to spare Luther's feelings by hiding the fact.

Peter Plunkett.......................................................Dick Martin
Marion Williamson......................................................K Callan
Airline clerk........................................................Kevyn Morrow

Writers: John Peaslee & Judd Pillot

17. "Leonard Kraleman: All-American"  Feb. 19, 1991

Hayden tries to discourage a scrawny, unpopular student (Schneider) who wants to try out for the football team. Director Dow co-starred in *Leave It to Beaver* (CBS, 1957-58; ABC, 1958-63), the TV-movie *Still the Beaver* (1983), and the cable series *Still the Beaver* and *The New Leave It to Beaver*.

Leonard Kraleman............................................Rob Schneider
And: D.C. Douglas (David), Christopher Abraham (Student)

Director: Tony Dow              Writer: Sheldon Bull

18. "2 BRs, MTN. VW."  Feb. 26, 1991

Whiny, well-meaning Stuart nearly drives Hayden to murder on a ski trip with Christine and Kelly.

Director: Tony Dow              Writer: Seth Weisbord

**preempted March 5**

19. "Hurley-Burleigh"  March 12, 1991

On his first trip to Las Vegas, athletic director Howard wants to sow some wild oats.

Shirley Burleigh, Howard's wife............................Georgia Engel
Club manager....................................................Ron Karabatsos
Cocktail waitress..................................................Helaine Hunter

Writers: John Peaslee & Judd Pillot

20. "Hayden Fox for Universal Jocks"  March 26, 1991

When Hayden discovers Christine's salary dwarfs his own, he decides to make extra cash as spokesperson for an athletic supporter company. Orig. scheduled for March 19.

Wally Krastack...................................................Ron Fassler

Writer: Sheldon Bull

21. "The Father and Son Reunion"  April 2, 1991

Hayden reunites Luther and his long-lost father.

Horace Van Dam.......................................................Paul Dooley

Writers: Judd Pillot & John Peaslee

22. "Diamonds Are a Dentist's Best Friend"  April 9, 1991

Cash-poor Hayden buys Christine's engagement ring from a cut-rate jeweler/dentist (Poston, reprising his role from ep. 2).

Dr. Hibke..................................................................Tom Poston

Writer: Sheldon Bull

**on hiatus until May 28**
**preempted July 2**

**renewed for 1991-92; new episodes begin Oct. 1, 1991**

## Columbo

ABC            Various

Series premiere:
    As the TV-movie *Prescription: Murder*: Feb. 20, 1968
    As a segment of *The NBC Mystery Movie*: Sept. 15, 1971
    As a series of TV-movies (first time): Nov. 21, 1977
    As a series of TV-movies (second time): Feb. 6, 1989

Lighthearted mystery-drama of a rumpled, pesky, seemingly slow-witted but brilliant Los Angeles Police detective with no revealed first name, who unravels complex murder cases involving the wealthy and powerful, with the audience privy to the killer's identity at the start. Executive producer Epstein died Nov. 24, 1990; his credit was retained on all episodes.

Lt. Columbo.............................................................Peter Falk

Universal Television, an MCA Co.
Executive producer: Jon Epstein
Co-executive producer: Peter Falk
Supervising producer: Alan J. Levi
Co-producer: Todd London
Executive story consultant: William Read Woodfield
Director of photography: George Koblasa
Music: James Di Pasquale (ep. 1); John Cavacas (ep. 2); Steve Dorff (ep. 3)
Creators: Richard Levinson & William Link

———————————

1. "Columbo Goes to College"  Sunday, Dec. 9, 1990  9-11 p.m.

Two privileged, calculating Freemont College seniors (Caffrey, Hershberger) murder a criminology professor (Sutorius) in a scheme that includes using Columbo for their alibi. Dedication: "In Memory of Executive Producer Jon Epstein."

Justin Rowe......................................................Stephen Caffrey

Cooper Redman............................................Gary Hershberger
Jordan Rowe, Justin's father...............................Robert Culp
Prof. D.E. Rusk.............................................James Sutorius
John (orig. Dominic) Doyle.............................William Lucking
Gretchen Clark.........................................Katherine Cannon
Mr. Redman.....................................................Alan Fudge
Justin's mother...........................................Maree Cheatham
Mrs. Raynes................................................Bridget Hanley
Joe Doyle.......................................................Jim Antonio
Medical examiner...........................................Steve Gilborn
Bartender....................................................Guy Stockwell
Malloy..........................................................Les Lannom
Sara.....................................................Elizabeth Swackhamer
Ollie Sachs.................................................Karl Wiedergott
And: James Ingersoll (John), Dick Balduzzi (Janitor), Robin Bach (Maitre d'), Gregg Rogen (Todd), Morgan Jones (Crime lab person), Jane Alden (Producer), Noel Conlon (Detective), Frank Farmer, Alfred Powers (Professor), Laurence Haddon (Dean Howard Gillespie), Larry McCormick (News anchor), George C. Simms, Aaron Seville (Police officers), Shauna Steiner (Newsperson), Jeremy McCollum (Toby), Troy Shire (Cary), David Cowgill (Crewperson), Robert R. Ross, Jr. (Norm), Tony Beninati (Charles), Mary Angela Shea, Casey Van Patten (Reporters), Darren Scott (Valet), Mary Maldonado (Maid)

Director: E.W. Swackhamer          Teleplay: Jeffrey Bloom
Story: Jeffrey Bloom & Frederick King Keller

2. "Caution: Murder Can be Hazardous to Your Health"
   Wednesday, Feb. 20, 1991  9-11 p.m.

The host (Hamilton) of the *CrimeAlert* "most-wanted" crime-re-enactment show murders his rival (Haskell) to avert blackmail. Locations include the Pasadena (Calif.) Civic Auditorium, where Falk had accepted an Emmy Award two days prior to shooting there. Working title: "Smokescreen."

Wade Anders.................................................George Hamilton
Budd Clarke.....................................................Peter Haskell
Maxine Jarrett...............................................Penny Johnson
Arnie............................................................Robert Donner
Medical examiner............................................Steven Gilborn
Henry Santos.....................................................Rick Najera
Lisa...........................................................Marie Chambers
Sgt. Lewis....................................................Dennis Bailey
Melanie.....................................................Patricia Allison
John...............................................................Jack Tate
Jack..............................................................Paul Ganus
"Barbara Baylor"..............................................Linda Dona
"Duke Dimarco"............................................Michael Russo
And: Louis Herthum (Technician), Emily Kuroda (Linda), Guerin Barry (Hairdresser), Barry O'Neill (Randy), Seth Foster (Al Morrow), Jim Jarrett (Production assistant), Mary Ingersoll (Sgt. Fitzwater), Lisa Marie Russell (Judy), Mimi Monaco (Wanda), Marabina Jaimes (Tisha), Mark Daneri (Customer), Brenda Isaacs (Redhead), Lawrence Scott Maki (Officer), Gary Kernick (SWAT officer), Aristides Priakos (Young Wade), Nicole Grey (Porno actress), Leesa Bryte (Phone woman), Joanne DiVito (Choreographer), Jan Hoag (Woman), Raymond Lynch (Detective Frank), Timothy Moran (Duke Dimarco), Tricia Long (Barbara Baylor), John Paul Ahearn (Male voice), Jennifer Asch, Barbara D'Altair (Female voices)

Director: Daryl Duke
Writer: Sonia Wolf & Patricia Ford & April Raynell •

• Latter writer orig. announced as Shelby Rose, the pen name for Raynell, Falk's personal assistant, who'd submitted the script to him psuedononymously.

3. "Columbo and the Murder of a Rock Star"
   Monday, April 29, 1991  9-11 p.m.

A famous criminal attorney (Coleman) murders his cheating live-in lover (Paris), a rock singer whose waning career led her to blackmail. Guest Danese is star Falk's actress wife; Little Richard is a rock/pop singer.

Hugh Creighton...........................................Dabney Coleman
Trish Fairbanks..............................................Shera Danese
Marcy Edwards..................................................Cheryl Paris
Neddy Malcomb.................................................Julian Stone
Sgt. Hubach..................................................Sondra Currie
Himself (orig. Trainwreck)...............................Little Richard
Sam Marlowe......................................................John Martin
With: Steven Gilborn, John Finnegan, Grant Heslov
And: Deborah Rose (Housekeeper), Tad Horino (Gardener Ando Miaki), Joseph Chapman (Prosecutor), Ann Weldon (Judge), B.J. Turner (Decorator Vito), Steve Tschudy (Defendant), Susie Singer (Darlene), Terrence Beasor (Contractor), Terry G. Warren (Police officer), Chad A. Bell (Kid), Mark Voland (Sergeant), Carolyn Carradine (Receptionist), Dorothy Constantine (Chief's secretary), Robert Terry Lee (Photographer), Robert Trumbull (D.A.), Bruce Marchiano (Tech), Michael Leopard (Bartender), Loren Blackwell (Waiter), Joe Faust (Stetson hat), Regina Leeds, Curt Booker (Reporters), William Chalmers (Client)

Director: Alan J. Levi          Writer: William Read Woodfield

**renewed as further TV movies for 1991-92**

# Comic Strip Live: Primetime

Fox          Sundays, 10-11 p.m.

Series premiere: Nov. 25, 1990
Final first-run telecast in this format: April 21, 1991
Final rerun edition: Aug. 23, 1991

Stand-up comedians, taped before audiences at various locations, with weekly guest hosts. First three installments titled *Comic Strip Live*, same as that of the latenight Fox syndicated series from which it spun off. Retitled **The Sunday Comics** April 28-on, with a change in format (see that entry). Reruns (from both primetime and latenight) ran Fridays, 9-10 p.m., Aug. 2-23.

Host (edition 1-3): Gary Kroeger
Comic Strip Live Band: Mike Chanslor, Denny Fongheiser, Mitch Reilly, Bob Wackerman

Fox Television Stations (edition 1-3); Manor House Productions (edition 3-on)
Executive producer: Ken Ceizler (edition 1-3); Kimber Rickabaugh (edition 3-on)
Producers (variously): Joe Revello, Jimmy Miller, Marilyn Seabury, Mark Adkins, Ben Hill, Nina Lederman
Coordinating producer: Marilyn Seabury (midseason); Kim Moses (later in season)
Associate producer (variously, sometimes in tandem): Linda Zwick, Bob Livengood, Glenn Stickley
Segment producers (early in season): Mike Colasuonno, Bruce Baum
Creative consultants (later in season): Rick Crom, Merle Kessler
Consultant (later in season): Jimmy Miller
Writers: Keith Kaczorek, Vince Calandra, Jr.
Director (variously): Ken Ceizler; Liz Plonka; Gene Crowe; Steve Binder

1. "Comic Strip Live on Campus" Nov. 25, 1990

Barry Sobel, Carol Leifer, Charles Fleischer, Bill Maher and Gilbert Gottfried at UCLA's Royce Hall.

2. "Comic Strip Live -- San Francisco" Dec. 2, 1990

Bobby Slayton, Ritch Shydner and Ellen DeGeneres at the Great American Music Hall.

3. "Comic Strip Live Celebrates the 10th Anniversary of the Laugh Factory" Dec. 9, 1990

Louie Anderson, Kevin Meany, Jeff Cesario, Darryl Sivad and Pam Matteson at the Los Angeles club; cameos by Sam Kinison, Roseanne Barr, Tom Arnold, George Carlin, Lenny Clarke, Gallagher, Rita Rudner, and the cast of *In Living Color*.

4. "Comic Strip Live: Christmas in New York" Dec. 16, 1990

Kim Coles, Mario Joyner, Cathy Ladman and Dom Irrera at Laura Belle, New York City. Musical guests: Buster Poindexter & His Banshees of Blue; The Boys Choir of Harlem (Dr. Walter Turnbull, director). Host: Robert Townsend.

5. "Frost Free in Key West" Jan. 6, 1991

Stephanie Hodge, Tom Kenny, Bob Nickman, Rick Overton and George Wallace at the Key West, Fla. Pier House. Musical guests: Kid Creole and the Coconuts. Host: Dave Thomas.

6. "Aspen Getaway" Jan. 13, 1991

Mark Curry, Evan Davis, John Mendoza and Diane Nichols at the Wheeler Opera House, Aspen, Colo. Musical guest: Three Blind Rats. Host: Martin Mull.

7. "Palm Springs" Jan. 27, 1991

Bill Hicks, Jeff Marder, Norm MacDonald, Michael Floorwax and Diane Ford. Musical guest: "Weird Al" Yankovic." Orig. scheduled for Jan. 20. Host: Victoria Jackson

8. "Celtic Celebration" Feb. 3, 1991

Jimmy Aleck, Rich Ceisler, Blake Clark, Mike Dugan and Jimmy Tingle at Hellenic College, Boston. Musical guest: Queen Latifah. Host: Joe Piscopo.

9. "Phi Beta Komics at Yale" Feb. 10, 1991

Paul Provenza, Kevin Rooney, Drake Sather, David Spade and John Riggi at the Repertory Theatre, Yale University, New Haven, Conn. Musical guest: Chubb Rock. Host: Dennis Miller.

10. "Mardi Gras Madness" Feb. 17, 1991

Lewis Dix, A.J. Jamal, Jedda Jones and John Witherspoon at the Orpheum Theater, New Orleans, during Mardi Gras. Musical guest: En Vogue. Host: Sinbad [David Atkins].

11. "Cruisin'" Feb. 24, 1991

Happy Cole, Lou DiMaggio, Danny Gans, Carol Leifer and Monica Piper on the cruise ship *M/S Southward*. (Mike Binder also orig. announced.) Cameos: Bernie Kopell, Ted Lange. Musical guest: The Shirelles. Host: Paul Rodriguez.

12. March 3, 1991

The Higgins Boys and Gruber, Joel Hodgson, Sue Kolinsky,

Cary Odes and Fred Stoller and at the World Theater, St. Paul, Minn. Musical guest: The Spinners. Host: Kevin Nealon.

13. "Spring Training" March 24, 1991

John Caponera, Tom Dreesen, Will Durst, John Mendoza, and Dom Irrera at the Compadre Stadium, Arizona. Musical guest: Betty D. and Sweet Sensation. Host: Bob Uecker. Cameos by several professional baseball players.

**preempted March 31**

14. "Spring Break" April 7, 1991

Charles Fleischer, Rich Jeni, Tom Parks, the Raspyni Brothers, and George Wallace at South Padre Island, Texas. Musical guest: Tommy Conwell and the Young Rumblers (The Road Kings orig. announced). Host: Julie Brown.

15. "Bobcat Goldthwait...and His Pals in Frisco" April 14, 1991

Blake Clark, Barry Crimmins, Jack Gallagher, Dan Spencer and Tony V in San Francisco. Musical guest: Too Much Joy. Host: Bob "Bobcat" Goldthwait.

16. "Houston Rodeo" April 21, 1991

Bill Engvall, Susan Norfleet, Ron Shock and Ritch Shydner at the Houston Livestock Show and Rodeo. Musical guest: T. Graham Brown. Host: Elayne Boosler Orig. scheduled for March 31.

**Changed format and title; SEE *The Sunday Comics***

# Cop Rock

ABC            Wednesdays, 10-11 p.m.

Series premiere: Sept. 26, 1990
Final episode: Dec. 26, 1990

Musical drama of Los Angeles police, featuring generally five original songs per episode. Co-producer Haid was a cast-member of co-creator Bochco's *Hill Street Blues* (NBC, 1981-87). Theme composer Newman appears performing the theme in the opening credits. Recurring guest Wilhoite is also one of the series' composers.

Chief Roger Kendrick................................Ronny Cox
Capt. John Hollander.............................Larry Joshua
Mayor Louise Plank..........................Barbara Bosson
Officer Vicki Quinn................................Anne Bobby *
Detective Ralph Ruskin, her husband...................Ron McLarty
Officer Andy Campo.....................David Gianopoulos
Officer Franklin Rose.......................James McDaniel
Detective Joseph Gaines.........................Mick Murray
Detective Vincent LaRusso....................Peter Onorati
Asst. Chief Warren Osborn (ep. 1).......................Ernie Hudson
Asst. Chief Warren Osborn (ep. 2-on)..........Vondie Curtis-Hall

*Recurring:*
Ray Rodbart (ep. 1-7,9,11)....................Jeffrey Allan Chandler
Detective Donald Potts (ep. 1-3,7-8,9,11)...William Thomas, Jr.
Patricia (Patti) Spence (ep.1,4-5)....................Kathleen Wilhoite
Trish Vaughn (ep. 2-11)...............................Teri Austin
Sidney Weitz (ep. 2,4,6-11)..........................Dennis Lipscomb
D.A. Willa Phelan (ep. 6,8-10)............................CCH Pounder

* Given as Anne Marie Bobby in initial press materials.

Steven Bochco Productions and 20th Century Fox Television
Executive producers: Steven Bochco (ep. 1-on), Gregory Hoblit (ep. 2-on)
Supervising producer: William M. Finkelstein
Senior producer: John Romano
Producers: Gregory Hoblit (ep. 1 only), Michael M. Robin, Charles Haid
Supervising associate producer: Craig Zisk (ep. 2-on)
Associate producer: Craig Zisk (ep. 1); Gigi Coello-Bannon
Director of photography: Tom Sigel (ep. 1); Roy H. Wagner, A.S.C.
Choreographer: Russell Clark
Technical consultant: Eddie Shore
Music producers: Mike Post, Greg Edmonson
Composers (variously, sometimes in partnership; several per episode): Ron Boustead, Greg Edmonson, Harvey Estrada, Stephen Geyer, Donald Markowitz, Amanda McBroom, Mike Post, Brock Walsh, Jim Wilhoite, Kathleen Wilhoite (Gerald Parrish also orig. announced)
Theme: "Under the Gun" by Randy Newman (words and music); performed by Randy Newman
Creators: Steven Bochco & William M. Finkelstein

1. "Cop Rock"
Sept. 26, 1990; Saturday, Sept. 29, 1990 10-11 p.m.

Loose cannon LaRusso kills in cold blood a drug pusher (Kimbro), released because of jail overcrowding, who'd murdered Rose's partner. All five songs composed by Randy Newman.

Tyrone Weeks......................................................Art Kimbro
Judge Walter Flynn.............................................Carl Anderson
Nelson Pine........................................................David Harris
Byron B..............................................................Glenn Plummer
Robert Appell......................................................Randal Patrick
Judge C.S. Adams................................................Dion Anderson
Asst. D.A. Keresy................................................Sharon Brown
Foreperson.........................................................Louis Price
Mersky..............................................................Armin Shimerman
Bivens...............................................................Gary Stockdale
Noonan..............................................................Lee Wilkof
Frank Newbold....................................................Luther Kent
Dave Handel.......................................................Rick Logan
Lou Sonnenscheim...............................................Scott Wojohn
Gilbert Braeden...................................................Kevin Skousen
Tommy Ryan.......................................................Dean Scofield
Angelo Poppi......................................................David Haid
Detective Rolfe...................................................Randy Harrington
And: David Byrd (Judge Weber), Dennis Cockrum (Glen), Josie Kim (Social worker), Shaun Baker (Street kid), Ellen Barber (Matron), Peter Slutsker (Reporter)

Director: Gregory Hoblit
Writers: Steven Bochco & William M. Finkelstein

2. "Ill-Gotten Gaines" Oct. 3, 1990

Gaines, demoted to Officer, is partnered with Rose; Hollander tries to unravel the cover-up of LaRusso's killing of Weeks.

Miriam Hernandez...............................................Lydia Nicole
Alan Lucas.........................................................Jeff Allin
Devon Lucas.......................................................Ann Gillespie
Jerome Brewster.................................................Jessie Lawrence Ferguson
Janey Hollander..................................................Gail Youngs
David (Davey) Hollander.......................................Josiah Berryhill
And: Rene Levant (Jamaal), Howard Mungo (Mustapha)

Director: Gregory Hoblit
Writers: Steven Bochco & William M. Finkelstein & John Romano

3. "Happy Mudder's Day" Oct. 10, 1990

Capt. Hollander increases pressure on Potts to testify against his partner LaRusso; LaRusso's mud-wrestling girlfriend (Tamburrelli) is endangered; Mayor Plank has cosmetic surgery; Gaines and Rose try to break up a violent marital dispute. David Haid had played a different role in ep. 1.

Gretchen............................................................Karla Tamburrelli
Dr. Watoon.........................................................Don Amendolia
Michael Weinstein...............................................Matthew Laurance
Eliot Weinstein...................................................Mitchell Laurance
Jimmy Smolan.....................................................Robert O'Reilly
Barney Rhoades...................................................James O'Sullivan
Florence.............................................................Kathy Hazzard
Walter................................................................Darryl Phinnessee
Armand Damiano..................................................Joseph Nasser
Phil....................................................................Frank Collison
Detective...........................................................David Haid
Ronnie...............................................................Jordan Lund
Big Johnnie Stain.................................................Johnny Cocktails
Yvonne...............................................................Pamela Runo
Perps.......................................Holly Sherwood, David Allen Morgan
Do Wop Cops.....................Carmen Carter, Charmaine Sylvers, Carmen Twillie
Nurses...............Tamela Gibbs, Kathy Singleton, Susie Hardy, Linda Esposito, Lori Hart, Stephanie Pope
Also orig. announced:
Anne Curry (Bobby), George Gerdes (Ray)

Director: Charles Haid
Writers: Steven Bochco & William M. Finkelstein & John Romano

4. "A Three-Corpse Meal" Oct. 17, 1990

LaRusso is charged with murder; Quinn and Campo pose as a married couple to nab the baby-sellers who bought Patti's daughter; Chief Kendrick takes the Mayor on a dinner date. Cockrum and Harrington reprise their roles from ep. 1.

Philip Beamer.....................................................Gordon Clapp
Glen...................................................................Dennis Cockrum
Tito....................................................................Gregory Norman Cruz
Asst. D.A. Karen Sharaga.....................................Katherine Cortez
Jody Lancaster....................................................Sherry Rooney
Bill Lancaster.....................................................William Forward
Judge.................................................................Kin Vassy
Tommy Ryan.......................................................Dean Scofield
Detective Rolfe...................................................Randy Harrington
Also orig. announced:
Paul McCrane (Detective Robert McIntyre), Robert F. Lyons (Detective)

Director: Fred Gerber
Teleplay: William M. Finkelstein & John Romano & Toni Graphia
Story: Steven Bochco & William M. Finkelstein & John Romano

5. "The Cocaine Mutiny" Oct. 24, 1990

LaRusso, free on bail and seeing a hard-hearted lawyer (Austin), uncovers cocaine users at a fundraiser; Gaines and Rose find yuppie coke snorters; Hollander uses the cokehead mistress (Harrington) of a lascivious city councilman (Cooper) to bring down her boss; Patti petitions the court for her baby.

Cassy Margolis....................................................Laura Harrington
Stacy Kane.........................................................Gina Gershon
Gary..................................................................John Putch
Councilman Culhane..............................................Charles Cooper

| | |
|---|---|
| Judge Neibaum | Ben Slack |
| John Wagnore | Bill Hayes |
| Assistant D.A. Danny Scott | Steven Anderson |
| E. Wilcox Tabscott | Joe Retta |
| Gordon Pollack | Jay Gerber |
| Carmen Ianello | Deborah Taylor |
| Larry Lyle | Thomas Knickerbocker |
| Maid | Donna-Jean Louden |

Also orig. announced:
Paul McCrane (Detective Robert McIntyre), Wortham Krimmer (Mitchell Sackheim)

Director: Arlene Sanford
Teleplay: Steven Bochco & William M. Finkelstein & John Romano
Story: Steven Bochco & William M. Finkelstein

6. "Oil of Ol' Lay" Oct. 31, 1990

Ruskin accuses Quinn of amorous feelings for her partner, Campo; Gaines tries to help a homeless man (Paymer); LaRusso's lawyers hire a PR firm to enhance his image; the Chief romances the Mayor. Co-creator Finkelstein has a bit part.

| | |
|---|---|
| Louie | David Paymer |
| Oscar Semjonovich | Graham Jarvis |
| Kevin Sturges | Duke Moosekian |
| Doris | Jan Hoag |
| Doctor | Mindy Seeger |
| Paul | Leigh C. Kim |
| Gil Garrity | William M. Finkelstein |
| Waitress | Lorna Scott |
| Hippie | T. Rodgers |
| Worker | Gray Daniels |
| Old wino | Jack Kutcher |
| Homeless persons | Theresa James, Suzanne Wallach, Dee Dee Bellson, Tommy Funderburk, Ricky Nelson |

Director: Michael Fresco
Teleplay: Steven Bochco & William M. Finkelstein & John Romano & Toni Graphia
Story: Steven Bochco & William M. Finkelstein & John Romano

7. "Cop-a-Feeliac" Nov. 7, 1990

LaRusso's PR firm gets to work; Potts receives violent threats; Ruskin follows his wife and Campo to a hotel room; a gay reporter (Bruneau) tries to "out" the Mayor's assistant (Chandler). Moosekian reprises his role from last episode; the character played by Sikking (a cast-member of co-creator Bochco's Doogie Howser, M.D.) crosses over from Hill Street Blues.

| | |
|---|---|
| Kevin Sturges | Duke Moosekian |
| Norm Chauncey | Pat McCormick |
| Alice Potts | Patricia Hodges |
| Lyle Barry | Ralph Bruneau |
| Lt. Kellogg | Mike Finnegan |
| Officer Cerruto | Rex Linn |
| Officer Sutton | Marlon Archey |
| Officer Brad Phelps | James McIntire |
| Officer Nissen | Mark Morales |
| Manny | Tony Genaro |
| Cops | Christopher Kriesa, Lou Palumbo |
| Valerie Gotbaum | Paula Venise |
| Allen Potts | Eric Drew Johnson |
| Rachel Potts | Christin Parker |
| Singing cops | Armando Compean, Michael Lanning, Marc Copage, Roger Freeland, Jim Gilstrap, Rick Riso |
| Band | Robbyn Kirmsse, Andrea Carol, Elizabeth Hooker, Liza Carbe, Karen Childs |
| Lt. Howard Hunter (no lines) | James B. Sikking (uncredited) |

Director: Arlene Sanford
Writers: Steven Bochco & William M. Finkelstein & John Romano & Michael Graham

**preempted Nov. 14**

8. "Potts Don't Fail Me Now" Nov. 21, 1990 (2108)

An intimidated Potts won't testify; Campo's attempt to placate Ruskin only provokes him; a racist cop (Connelly) enrages Gaines; Plank scolds Kendrick after he makes comments offensive to minorities. The characters played by Smits, Greene and Hancock cross over from L.A. Law; Hodges reprises her role from ep. 7, Berryhill from ep. 2; the unnamed cops played by Kriesa and Palumbo in ep. 7 appear here named.

| | |
|---|---|
| Judge Richard Armand | John Hancock |
| Detective Miller | John P. Connelly |
| Janey Hollander | Gail Youngs |
| Alice Potts | Patricia Hodges |
| Jerome | Tony Todd |
| Frank Downey | Bruce A. Young |
| Mustapha | Richard Allen |
| Dorothy Dugan | Gloria Cromwell |
| Harold Poe | Gilbert Lewis |
| David (Davey) Hollander | Josiah Berryhill |
| Marty | Duncan Gamble |
| Doug | Christopher Kriesa |
| Ted | Lou Palumbo |
| Cops | Clifton Powell, David Labiosa |
| Wife | Adrian Ricard |
| Reporters | Dawn Arnemann, Granville Ames, Tony Selznick, Kim Murdock |
| Singers: | Yvette Freeman, Yvonne Williams, Jackie Gouche, Maxi Anderson, Portia Griffin, Linda Tavani, Billie Barnum, Carmen Carter, Terry Wood, Mona Lisa Young, Gerald Parrish |
| Victor Sifuentes | Jimmy Smits (uncredited) |
| Abby Perkins | Michele Greene (uncredited) |

Director: Bradley Silberling
Writers: Steven Bochco & William M. Finkelstein & John Romano & Michael Graham

**preempted Nov. 28**

9. "Marital Blitz" Dec. 5, 1990 (2109)

In an attempt to save her marriage, Quinn gets a new partner; Ruskin and Potts take the stand in LaRusso's trial; Chief Kendrick alienates the media. Hancock reprises his role from ep. 8 and from L.A. Law; Linn appeared in a different role in ep. 7.

| | |
|---|---|
| Off. Dorothy Petrovich | Diane Delano |
| Judge Richard Armand | John Hancock |
| Off. Stillman | Zachary Throne |
| Jerome Hall | Willian Allen Young |
| Foreperson | Michael Pniewski |
| Jurors | Loretta Devine, Tim Russ, Dianne Rodgriguez, Carolyn Rainey Lewis |
| Sergeant | Rex Linn |
| Customers | Jordan Lund, David Powledge |
| Reporters | Paul Eiding, Elizabeth Harmon, Carlos Lacamara, Tony Selznick |
| Driver | Geldie Burns |
| And singers | Bobbi Page, Linda Harmon, Joe Esposito, Joseph Pizzulo, Reginald Burrell, Debbie McClendon Smith, Chris Farren, Jim Gilstrap, Randy Crenshaw, Robert David Hall |

Director: Gilbert Shilton

Teleplay: Steven Bochco & William M. Finkelstein & John
     Romano & Toni Graphia
Story: Steven Bochco & William M. Finkelstein & John Romano

10. "No Noose is Good Noose"  Dec. 12, 1990    (2110)

LaRusso takes the stand in his own defense, and eventually is found not guilty; Campo's new partner (Amerson) is a gorgeous blonde on undercover hooker detail; Quinn and Ruskin see a marriage counselor (Windust). Hancock reprises his role from ep. 8-9 and from *L.A. Law*; several jurors reprise their roles from last episode.

Jessica Wolfe..........................................Tammy Amerson
Judge Richard Armand.............................John Hancock
Jurors...................Loretta Devine, Tim Russ, Diane Rodriguez,
    Angela Paton, Carolyn Rainey Lewis
Host detective.......................................Robert F. Lyons
Foreperson...........................................Michael Pniewski
Therapist.............................................Penelope Windust
Lyle Pelt.....................................................Dell Yount
Angry people...................Charles Douglass, Marilyn Coleman
O'Rouke.................................................Peter Esfakis
Reporters.......................Paul Eiding, Dawn Arnemann
Stripper..................................................Dee Hengstler
Singers:  Arnold McCuller, Phil Perry, Lothair Eaton, Clydene
    Jackson, Sondra Baskin, Denise Stewart
    Also orig. announced: Carl Anderson (Nightmare judge)

Director: Michael M. Robin
Teleplay: Steven Bochco & William M. Finkelstein & John
     Romano & Toni Graphia
Story: Steven Bochco & William M. Finkelstein & John Romano

**preempted Dec. 19**

11. "Bang the Potts Slowly"  Dec. 26, 1989

LaRusso wants an enraged Potts as his partner again; Plank is media-groomed for a Senate run; Quinn prepares to leave her house and marriage; a rapist (Kehler) terrorizes a campus. O'Sullivan and the Laurance brothers reprise their roles from ep. 3, Throne from ep. 9, and Amerson from last episode; Harrington appeared in a different role in ep. 4, Anderson in ep. 5.

Jessica Wolfe..........................................Tammy Amerson
Off. Stillman..........................................Zachary Throne
Michael Weinstein..................................Matthew Laurance
Eliot Weinstein......................................Mitchell Laurance
Detective Lee........................................Randy Harrington
Donald Bruckner.........................................Jack Kehler
Barney Rhoades.....................................James O'Sullivan
Detective Ann Burroughs................................April Grace
Karen Markel..............................................Lenora May
Hilda................................................Viola Kates Stimpson
District Attorney...................................Steven Anderson
Elderly men.........................Alvin Hammer, Hank Worden
Camera assistant.................................Rosie Malek-Yonan
Fat lady who sings....................................Queen Yahna

Director: Fred Gerber
Teleplay: William M. Finkelstein & John Romano & Toni Graphia
Story: Steven Bochco & William M. Finkelstein & John Romano

## The Cosby Show

NBC          Thursdays, 8-8:30 p.m.

Series premiere: Sept. 20, 1984

Comedy of a Brooklyn obstetrician, his corporate-attorney wife, and their extended family. The original opening credits this season (ep. 1-4) used a mural based on one painted in Harlem by the Creative Arts Workshop for Homeless Children; the credits sequence was replaced after disagreements between the Carsey/Werner Co. and the Workshop over screen credit and compensation for use of the children's design. Cast-member Rashad is the wife of NBC sportscaster Ahmad Rashad (a guest in ep. 12 and 22). Cast-member Phillips had appeared as a different guest character in an episode several seasons ago. Recurring guests Hyman and Taylor reprise their roles from past seasons. Ep. 23 had significantly different production credits from all other episodes.

Dr. Cliff Huxtable......................................Bill Cosby
Clair Huxtable.......................................Phylicia Rashad
Theo Huxtable.............................Malcolm-Jamal Warner
Vanessa Huxtable...............................Tempestt Bledsoe
Rudy Huxtuble..........................Keshia Knight Pulliam
Sondra Huxtable Tibideaux........................Sabrina LeBeauf
Elvin Tibideaux.....................................Geoffrey Owens
Denise Huxtable Kendall...................................Lisa Bonet
Navy Lt. Martin Kendall.........................Joseph C. Phillips
Olivia Kendall (5), Martin's daughter
    from his first marriage...............................Raven-Symone
Pam Turner, Clair's distant cousin
    (ep. 1-22)............................................Erika Alexander

*Recurring:*
Russell Huxtable, Cliff's father (ep. 3,19-20,22)....Earle Hyman
Anna Huxtable, Cliff's mother (ep. 3,19-20).........Clarice Taylor
Charmaine (ep. 4,7,10-11,14,20-21)..........Karen Malina White
Lance (ep. 4,7,11,14,20)...................................Allen Payne
Slide (ep. 4,7,14).......Steven Mushond Lee a.k.a. Mushond Lee
Aaron (ep. 10-11, 20)..................................Seth Gilliam

The Carsey-Werner Co. in assoc. with Bill Cosby
Executive producers: Marcy Carsey, Tom Werner, Bernie
    Kukoff (ep. 1-22), John Markus (ep. 23)
Producers: Steve Kline (ep. 1-22, 24-25), Terri Guarnieri (all
    episodes), Elaine Arata (later in season), Matt Robinson
    (ep. 23)
Co-producer: Ehrich Van Lowe (ep. 1-22, 24-25)
Supervising producers (ep. 23): Gary Kott, Carmen Finestra
Associate producer: Mark Clark; Cissy Bedeian (ep. 23)
Creative consultant: Janet Leahy
Story editors: Lore Kimbrough, Bryan Winter (ep. 1-22);
    Ehrich Van Lowe (ep. 23)
Creative consultant: Mark St. German (ep. 23)
Script consultant: Matt Robinson
Production consultant: Alvin F. Poussaint, M.D.
Executive consultant: William H. Cosby, Jr.
Music: uncredited; only "musical directors" listed
Theme: Stu Gardner & Bill Cosby; trumpet performed by
    Lester Bowie; saxophone performance by Craig Handy
Creators: Ed. Weinberger & Michael Leeson and William H.
    Cosby Jr.

1. "Same Time Next Year"  Sept. 20, 1990

The kids start the new school year, with Rudy worried her bust's not ready for sixth grade. Orig. scheduled for Sept. 27.

Margie....................................................Bryce Barard
Amy......................................................Avanti Taylor

Director: Jay Sandrich          Writer: Ehrich Van Lowe

2. "Bird in the Hand"  Sept. 27, 1990

Jazz buff Cliff has to fill in as a "help-mom" at a day-care center, though he wants to concentrate on a record auction.

Mrs. Lebow...............................................Marge Redmond
James Harmon...........................................Sullivan Walker
Assistant.....................................................Ray DeMattis
Auctioneer...................................................L.B. Williams
Bidder....................................................Terry V. Williams
Day-care children............Kharisma Gooden, Keri Anne Gorley,
    Keivyn Graves, Jonathan Halyalkar, Tony Zeko

Director: Jay Sandrich
Writers: Steve Kline & Bryan Winter

3. "The Last Barbecue"  Oct. 4, 1990

Theo plans a belated bachelor party for Martin; Cliff hosts a
barbecue.  Originally scheduled for Sept. 20.

Kenny.....................................................Deon Richmond

Director: Ellen Falcon
Writers: Bernie Kukoff & Janet Leahy

4. "Period of Adjustment"  Oct. 11, 1990

The Huxtables take in Clair's teenage distant cousin Pam (new
cast-member Erika Alexander).

Director: Ellen Falcon
Writers: Lore Kimbrough & Gordon Gartrelle

5. "It's All in the Game"  Oct. 18, 1990

Cliff and Clair return from a Vermont vacation to once again
face the kids.

Director: Neema Barnette
Writer: Janet Leahy & Bryan Winter

6. "Getting the Story"  Oct. 25, 1990

Rudy and Kenny tape a day in the life of Cliff and Clair for a
school assignment.  Richmond reprises his role from ep. 3.

Steven Parnell ...................................Richard Woods
Kenny.....................................................Deon Richmond
Joanne Pruitt............................................Jodi Long
George Parker.........................................Ernest Abuba
And:  Beata Bal (Mathilde), Yamil Borges (Julia Arroyo), Fran-
    cisco Rivela (Mr. Arroyo), Paul Ukena (Security guard)

Director: Ellen Falcon                    Story: Mark St. Germain
Teleplay: Janet Leahy & Lore Kimbrough

7. "Just Thinking About It"  Nov. 1, 1990  8-9 p.m.

Pam, pressured by her boyfriend (recurring guest Lee) to have
sex, seeks Clair for advice and Cliff for a prescription for birth-
control pills. Guest Morales is a series production assistant.

Big fella....................................................Maurice Lauchner
Julio............................................................David Ilku
Skeeter....................................................Eagle-Eye Cherry
Shaniqua...............................................Cynthia Bailey
Jimmy.....................................................Gorlando Morales

Director: Jay Sandrich
Writer: Bernie Kukoff & Ehrich Van Lowe

8. "The Infantry Has Landed (And They've Fallen Off the Roof)"
Nov. 8, 1990

Rudy has her first period.

Danny McGee, Theo's friend..............................Keith Diamond
Susan, Rudy's friend....................................Rachel Hillman
Danielle, Rudy's friend..................................Nicole Leach

Director: John Bowab
Writers: Janet Leahy & Lore Kimbrough & Gordon Gartrelle

9. "You Can Go Home Again"  Nov. 15, 1990

Cliff and Clair recall their first apartment.

Director: Oz Scott
Writers: Bernie Kukoff & Steve Kline & Lore Kimbrough

10. "It's a Boy"  Nov. 29, 1990

When a neighbor (DeMattis) discovers he and his wife (Cox)
are having a boy, he seeks Cliff's advice in father-son bonding.
DeMattis appeared in a different role in ep. 2.

Alfred......................................................Ray DeMattis
Bernice....................................................Catherine Cox

Director: Chuck Vinson
Writers: Bernie Kukoff & Ehrich Van Lowe

11. "Clair's Liberation"  Dec. 6, 1990

When Clair announces she's beginning menopause, her concerned children begin treating her like an old woman.

Big fella....................................................Maurice Lauchner
Winnie Tibideaux (child)...........Monique/Dominique Reynolds
Nelson Tibideaux (child)................Christopher/Clayton Griggs
    Also orig. announced: Angela Hall (Diane)

Director: John Bowab
Writers: Bernie Kukoff & Ehrich Van Lowe

12. "It's Your Move"  Dec. 13, 1990

Sondra commits Elvin to helping friends move, on a day the
guys plan to watch a major football game.

Nancy......................................................Jackie Mari Roberts
Walter, her husband........................................Nathaniel Ritch
Announcer....................................................Ahmad Rashad

Director: Jay Sandrich
Writers: Steve Kline & Bryan Winter

13. "Theo's Final Final"  Jan. 3, 1991

With one exam to go, Theo's assured of making the Dean's list,
until he meets his distracting dream-woman (Williams). Diamond reprises his role from ep. 8; guest Vanessa Williams is
not the dethroned Miss America 1984.

Danny McGee.................................................Keith Diamond
Cheryl......................................................Vanessa Williams
Waitress......................................................Georgia Strauss
Cynthia.........................................................Rachel True
Lucy.............................................................Desirre Jones
    Also orig. announced:
    Deon Richmond (Kenny), Nicole Leach (Danielle)

Director: Neema Barnette                    Writer: Elaine Arata

14. "Attack of the Killer B's"  Jan. 10, 1991

Pam, wanting a college scholarship, works hard to earn good grades on her report card, making her friends jealous.

Mrs. Hobbs...............................................Shellye Broughton
And: Maurice Lauchner

Director: Art Dielhenn
Writers: Elaine Arata & Lore Kimbrough

**unscheduled preempted Jan. 17**

15. "Total Control" Jan. 31, 1991

A high school basketball coach (Ritter) tries to help his wife (Yasbeck) through labor.

Ray Evans................................................John Ritter
Alicia Evans.............................................Amy Yasbeck
Nurse Wrencher......................................Maureen Sadusk
        Also orig. announced: Ed Lover (Cabbie)

Director: Jay Sandrich
Writers: Bernie Kukoff & Ehrich Van Lowe

16. "Adventures in Babysitting" Feb. 7, 1991

With Cliff and Clair at a pinochle tournament, Rudy babysits Olivia. DeMattis reprises his role from ep. 10.

Dr. James Harmon.........................................Sullivan Walker
Nicole Harmon................................................Michele Shay
Jennings.....................................................Hortensia Colorado
Alfred..............................................................Ray DeMattis
Mrs. Thompson........................................Bern Nadette Stanis
And: Alvin Lum (Todd), Dale Shields (Photographer)

Director: Oz Scott                              Writer: Steve Kline

17. "Twenty-Seven and Still Cookin' " Feb. 14, 1991

Cliff's elaborate plans to recreate their Caribbean-honeymoon restaurant for his and Clair's 27th anniversary go awry.

Atkins.........................................................Clebert Ford
Musicians...........................Denroy Morgan, Roland Lawrence,
        Wayne Kirton, Alston Jack
Ricardo.................................................Richardo Alexander
Walter....................................................Walter Blanding

Director: Neema Barnette
Writers: Janet Leahy & Gordon Gartrelle

18. "The Return of the Clairettes" Feb. 21, 1991

Clair and her old school singing-group pal (real-life singer Uggams) reminisce; Rudy gets permission to go on a group date.

Kris...............................................................Leslie Uggams
And: Ron Foster (Husband Herb), Bemi Faison (Scott Williams)

Director: Neema Barnette                    Writer: Lisa Albert

19. "No More Mister Nice Guy" Feb. 28, 1991

Theo's plans to cook dinner for his girlfriend (Williams, reprising her role from ep. 13) go awry when family and friends keep popping up. Orig. scheduled for Nov. 8 and Jan. 17.

Denny.......................................................Troy Winbush
Cheryl.....Vanessa Williams (Julie Satterfield orig. announced)
Ellen..............................................................Troy Beyer

Director: Jay Sandrich
Writers: Steve Kline & Bryan Winter

20. "Home Remedies" March 7, 1991

When a cold threatens to ruin Olivia's anniversary song, the family tries to override doctor Cliff with home remedies.

Ralph............................................................Lee Weaver
Dave.........................................................Jerome Dempsey
And: Olivia Ward (Sybil), Ginny Yang (Mrs. Kim)

Director: Jay Sandrich                 Writer: Mark St. Germain

21. "Nightmare on Stigwood Avenue" March 21, 1991

Rudy dreams that Olivia bewitches the household and gets away with all kinds of kiddie mischief.

Marlon...........................................................Aaron Beener

Directors: Malcolm-Jamal Warner and Carl Lauten
Writers: Steve Kline & Lore Kimbrough

22. "There's Still No Joy in Mudville" April 4, 1991

Two retired Negro League baseball players (Hall of Famer Robinson and former Brooklyn Dodgers pitcher Black) reminisce with Cliff and pals. Walker reprises his role from ep. 16.

Carleton.......................................................Norman Beaton
Dr. James Harmon.........................................Sullivan Walker
Joe "Rubberarm" Simms.........................................Joe Black
Frank "Payday" Potter.................................Frank Robinson
Voiceover: Ahmad Rashad

Director: Carl Lauten
Writers: Matt Robinson & Gordon Gartrelle

23. "Cliff and Jake" April 11, 1991

A bride-to-be (Landers) recruits Cliff as peacemaker between feuding friends (Buttons, Marshall) about to become in-laws.

Jake................................................................Red Buttons
Angela (orig. Cookie), his daughter..................Audrey Landers
Seymour (orig. Stanley) Rappaport....................E.G. Marshall
Jonathan Rappaport......................................Kenneth Meseroll
Mrs. Henning.....................................................Angela Scott

Director: Jay Sandrich                 Writer: Mark St. Germain

24. "Theo and the Kids" Part 1 April 25, 1991

Theo's NYU course work requires him to spend a semester as counselor at a community center, where he discovers a rebellious 12-year-old (Santana) with dyslexia.

Mrs. Hudson.................................................Lynne Thigpen
Stanley........................................................Merlin Santana
Eugene..........................................................Eugene Byrd
Celeste..........................................................Lisa Arrindell
Leticia............................................................Yunoka Doyle
Carlos....................................................Edwin Maldonado Jr.
Loo..................................................................Lisa Tai
And: Kennan Scott

Director: John Bowab
Writers: Janet Leahy & Lore Kimbrough & Gordon Gartrelle

25. "Theo and the Kids" Part 2  May 2, 1991

Theo tries to help Stanley master his dyslexia. Beener reprises his role from ep. 21.

Mrs. Hudson....................................................Lynne Thigpen
Stanley.............................................................Merlin Santana
Eugene...............................................................Eugene Byrd
Leticia...............................................................Yunoka Doyle
Carlos.......................................................Edwin Maldonado Jr.
Loo...........................................................................Lisa Tai
Marlon...........................................................Aaron Beener
And: Kennan Scott
    Also orig. announced: Lisa Arrindell (Celeste)

Director: John Bowab
Writers: Bernie Kukoff & Ehrich Van Lowe

**renewed for 1991-92; new episodes begin Sept. 19, 1991**

## Counterstrike

USA July 1-Sept. 16, 1990    Sundays, 10-11 p.m. (rerun
                Saturdays, 7-8 p.m.)
    Sept. 23-Nov. 4, 1990    Sundays, 9-10 p.m. (rerun
                Saturdays, 7-8 p.m.)
    Nov. 10, 1990-on         Saturdays, 7-8 p.m. (rerun
                Sundays, 9-10 p.m.)

Series premiere: July 1, 1990

Adventure drama of a high-tech, international crime-fighting team organized by a billionaire (Plummer) whose wife and child had been victimized by terrorists. Filmed in Toronto and France. The series' initial cycle of first-run episodes was in progress when the fall season began Sept. 17, 1990; the first episode within the new season aired Oct. 7 (following reruns on Sept. 23 and 30). NOTE: The chronological premiere episode ("The Beginning") did not air first-run until Nov. 10.

Peter Sinclair.........................................Simon MacCorkindale
Nikki Beaumont.............................................Cyrielle Claire
Luke Brenner.............................................Stephen Shellen
Alexander Addington............................Christopher Plummer
*Cast-members listed in end-credits:*
Suzanne Addington, Alexander's daughter......Laurence Ashley
Bennett, Alexander's butler.............................Tom Kneebone
J.J...........................................................................Andre Mayers

USA Network, Alliance Communications, Compagnie
    Francaise Cinematographique, Grosso • Jacobson
    Productions
Executive producers: Robert Lantos, Denis Heroux, Sonny
    Grosso, Larry Jacobson
Supervising producer (later in season): Lionel E. Siegel
Producer: Julian Marks
Producer, France (later in season): Josette Perrotta
Line producer (later in season): Adam Haight
Associate producers (variously): Adam Haight (early in
    season); Lena Cordina; Lisa Parasyn
Consultants: Fern Field (ep. 1 only); Alan Wagner
Executive production consultant (later in season): Simon
    MacCorkindale
Series consultants: Christina-Avis Kraus, Keith Johnson
Executive story editor (later in season): Peter Mohan
Story editors: Shelly Altman, Michael Zettler (both ep. 1-on),
    Richard Oleksiak, Tony Di Franco, Debra Nathan (all
    added later)
Director of photography (variously): Miklos Lente, Ludek
    Bogner, Tony Thatcher, Claude Becognee, Ron Spannett
Music [and] Theme (instrumental): Domenic Troiano
Creator: uncredited; first episode written by Landen Parker

11. "Thanos"  Oct. 7, 1990

The wife (Pauly) and two daughers of an Islamic arms dealer (de Brugada) turns to old friend Nikki for help escaping him.

Philippe............................................................Michel Voletti
Jeanne.............................................................Rebacca Pauly
Duvall.....................................................................Yan Brian
Bouchareb.............................................Philippe de Brugada
Amman...............................................................Mandis Renos
And: Julie-Anne Rauth, Ludy Airs, Robin Lent, Anne Tihomir-
off

Director: Doug Jackson        Writer: Christian Watton

12. "Siege"  Oct. 14, 1990

Industrial leaders, meeting to discuss aid to Third World countries, are held hostage at the conference site by terrorists.

Gina.................................................................Beatrice Camurat
Akmed..................................................................Edwin Gerard
Ms. Haddad..........................................................Nabil Massad
And: Therese Cremieux, Carmela Valent, Betty Berr, Irene
    Fabry, Mimi Setin, Karim Salah, Yves Collignon, Vincent
    Lo Monaco, Guy-Pierre Mineur, Noel Hamann

Director: Bernard Dumont        Writer: Peter Mohan

13. "Escape Route"  Oct. 28, 1991

Two brothers (Witta, Wolkowitch) invent a phony terrorist organization as a cover to help facilitate a jail breakout.

Philippe Evran.....................................................Michael Voletti
Veronique.............................................................Corinne Touzet
Georges Verlaine....................................................Frederic Witta
Rene Verlaine...................................................Bruno Wolkowitch
And: Sebastian Roche, Karen Strassman

Director: Paolo Barzman        Writer: Chantal Renaud

14. "The Beginning"  Nov. 10, 1990

After a terrorist attack and the kidnapping of his wife (Law), Addington forms a private anti-terrorist team around a frustrated Scotland Yard investigator (MacCorkindale).

Lt. Samuelson.......................................................Vlasta Vrana
Chantal Addington..................................................Barbara Law
Kroger...............................................................Stephen Russel
And: Jim Morris, Doug Lennox, Arturo Fresolone

Director: Allan Eastman        Writer: Landen Parker

15. "Cry of the Children"  Nov. 17, 1990

Luke's old girlfriend (Taylor) appears with a baby she claims is his, but which turns out to be from an adoption black market.

Andrea...............................................................Laura Robinson
Mr. Laurence............................................................Kurt Reis
Zoe MacFarlane................................................Courtney Taylor
And: John Taylor (Manny), Ron White (Detective), Elizabeth
    Leslie, Amanda Lynn/Elizabeth Ann Smith (infant)

Director: Mario Azzopardi        Writer: Tony Di Franco

16. "Masks"  Nov. 24, 1990

A lookalike takes Alexander's place at a conference; the team hunts for a young witness (Moreau) to a politician's murder.

Gregor.................................................Nathaniel Moreau
Amanda Di Santo..................................Patricia Gage
And: Elizabeth Szathmary, Edward Juanz, Bill McDermott, John Lefebvre, Ellen Durbin

Director: Don Shebib          Writer: Christian Watton

17. "Mindbender"  Dec. 1, 1990

Luke, kidnapped and brainwashed by a Soviet Major and her associates, is programmed to assassinate the Soviet President.

Major Zukova.............................Heidi Von Palleske
Dr. Bruegel......................................Ned Vukovic
Boris..............................................Milan Cheyov
And: Bernard Behrens, Velkjo Pajkovic, Justine Campbell, David Lloyd Austin

Director: Allan Eastman          Writer: Richard Oleksiak

18. "Regal Connection"  Dec. 15, 1990

Suzanne's computer-science professor, the heir to an African throne, is kidnapped by an opposing faction.

Van Gelder.................................Maxwell Caulfield
Robert.........................................Anthony Sherwood
Yvonne...........................................Shawne Jackson
And: George Seremba, Adriane Willmer, Trevor Bain

Director: William Fruet          Writer: Tony Di Franco

19. "Cinema Verite"  Dec. 22, 1990

A famed mystery novelist (Smith) dies in a suspicious accident.

Scott.................................................Gene Glazer
Marlowe.............................................Cedric Smith
Samantha..........................................Eve Crawford
Sandy................................................Real Andrews
And: Michael Rhoades, Tracey Cook, Geordie Johnson, Kim Huffman, Mario Di Toro, Sandy Crawford, Mario Romano

Director: Rene Bonniere          Writer: Eric Watton

20. "Verathion"  Jan. 12, 1991

Suzanne obtains evidence of a drug company's plans to distribute to the Third World a drug with horrific side-effects.

Wylie.............................................Shawn Lawrence
Craver.............................................Victor Ertmanis
Clara..............................................Micki Maunsell
Detective Larwin.......................................Ron White
And: Declan Hill, Craig Gardner, Alexe Duncan, Sharon Dyer, Steve W. Smith

Director: Don Shebib          Writer: Chantal Renaud

21. "The Millerton Papers"  Jan. 19, 1991

Former cat-burglar Nikki runs into an old flame/accomplice (Fletcher, star of *The Hitchhiker*), who has swiped classified military blueprints from a toy mogul hoping to get a jump on the model toy market. Working title: "The Mendrake Papers."

Jason Denvers......................................Page Fletcher
Bernard Millerton.....................................J.P. Linton

Porzan.................................................Elias Zarou
Jemal..............................................Hrant Alianak
And: T.W. Schroeder, Carole Galloway

Director: George Mendeluk          Writer: Eric Watton

22. "The Dilemma"  Feb. 2, 1991

Recurring nightmares and a run-in with the British Secret Service over the team's methods prompt Peter to quit.

Col. Nathan........................................Scott Hylands
Robert.........................................Graeme Campbell
And: Janet-Laine Greene (Claire), Wayne Best, Matt Cooke, Martin Gorman, Bob Bainborough

Director: Jean-Pierre Prevost          Writer: Richard Oleksiak

23. "Extreme Measures"  Feb. 9, 1991

Former members of a '60s revolutionary group are being killed by order of a thieving compatriot turned Austrian politician.

Jean-Paul Grenier..............................Serge Feuillard
Nigel.............................................Nicolas Hawtrey
Jutar..............................................Trevor Stephens
Yamani.................................................................
And: Albert Pariente (Yamani), Vincent Grass, Patrick Tessari, Katie Vail, Melanie McCarty

Director: Michael Shock
Writers: Michael Zettler & Shelly Altman

**renewed for 1991-92; new episodes begin Sept. 21, 1991**

## Dallas

CBS          Nov. 2-Dec. 21     Fridays, 10-11 p.m.
             Jan. 4-May 3       Fridays, 9-10 p.m.

Series premiere: April 2, 1978
Final telecast: May 3, 1991

Prime-time soap opera of the Ewings, a wealthy oil and ranching family based at the Southfork Ranch near Dallas, Tex., centering on the gleefully Machiavellian manipulations of the power-hungry, treacherous, adulterous J.R. Ewing. Recurring guest Sherril Lynn Rettino is the daughter of executive producer Leonard Katzman, and former wife of associate producer John Ernest Rettino; producers Mitchell Wayne Katzman and Frank W. Katzman are the sons of executive producer Katzman. This season's opening episodes filmed partly in Paris.

John Ross (J.R.) Ewing.......................................Larry Hagman
Bobby Ewing, his brother....................................Patrick Duffy
Michelle Stevens...............................................Kimberly Foster
Clayton Farlow,
   J.R. and Bobby's stepfather........................Howard Keel
Carter McKay..................................................George Kennedy
Cliff Barnes.....................................................Ken Kercheval
James Richard Beaumont, J.R.'s son.................Sasha Mitchell
Cally Harper Ewing, J.R.'s new wife..................Cathy Podewell
Liz Adams........................................................Barbara Stock
April Stevens, Michelle's sister
   and Bobby's new wife............................Sheree J. Wilson

*Major recurring characters:*
"Sheila Foley"/Hillary Taylor (ep. 1-4,19-20).........Susan Lucci
Marjorie (Jory) Taylor,
   her daughter (ep. 13-15,17-21)..............Deirdre Imershein

LeeAnn Nelson De La Vega (ep. 8-12)..................Barbara Eden
Vanessa Beaumont,
    James' mother (ep. 6,8-12)....................Gayle Hunnicutt
Rose McKay, Carter's wife (ep. 5-9,11-12,21)............Jeri Gaile
Duke Carlisle (ep. 1-2,4-5)................................Clifton James
Johnny Dancer
    a.k.a. Johnny Danzig (ep. 4-7,11)..................Ramy Zada
Christopher Ewing,
    Bobby's adopted son (ep. 6-7,9,12-21)........Joshua Harris
John Ross Ewing, III,
    J.R.'s son (eps. 4,6-7,9,16-21)..........................Omri Katz
Sly Lovegren, J.R.'s secretary
    (ep. 1,3-8,10-11,13-15,17,19,21)..........Deborah Rennard
Secretary Phyllis (ep. 3,5,7-8,10,13,21).........Deborah Tranelli
Secretary Jackie (ep. 1,3-7,11-21)............Sherril Lynn Rettino
Secretary Kendall (ep. 5,7,10-18,20-21)........Danone Simpson
Detective Bussey (ep. 7,9-11,16,21)......................Buck Taylor
Debra Lynn Beaumont (ep. 16-20)..................Deborah Tucker

Lorimar Television
Executive producers: Leonard Katzman, Larry Hagman
Co-executive producer: Ken Horton
Supervising producer: Howard Lakin
Producer: Cliff Fenneman
Co-producer: Mitchell Wayne Katzman
Associate producers: Frank W. Katzman, John Rettino a.k.a.
    John Ernest Rettino
Executive story consultant: Lisa Seidman
Director of photography: Rick F. Gunter
Music (variously): John Parker; Lance Rubin; Richard Lewis
    Warren
Theme (instrumental): "Dallas" by Jerrold Immel
Creator: David Jacobs

---

1. "April in Paris"  Nov. 2, 1990

Bobby and April's Paris honeymoon is destroyed by a mysterious kidnapper (Lucci); Cally rethinks her conspiracy with James against J.R., who tries to escape the mental institution.

Dr. Wykoff........................................................Chelcie Ross
Morrisey.............................................................Mitch Pileggi
Jordan Lee.............................................................Don Starr
Keller.........................................................Michael P. Keenan
Goldman..........................................................Hugh Maguire
Ryan...................................................................Arthur Malet
Donia...................................................................Zane Lasky
Del Greco..............................................................Marty Schiff
And: Ken Foree (Howard), Shannon Wilcox (Anita), Rita Vassallo (Mary), Michael Hofland (Chauffeur), J.T. O'Connor

Writer-director: Leonard Katzman

2. "Charade"  Nov. 9, 1990

Sheila manipulates Bobby as he tries to rescue April, and he meets an enigmatic cyclist (Padraic Duffy, son of series co-star Patrick); James plays high-stakes poker with Duke; Cliff pushes Liz for a commitment; J.R. faces Morrisey in the asylum.

Control...............................................................John Harkins
Dr. Wykoff........................................................Chelcie Ross
Jordan Lee.............................................................Don Starr
Morrisey.............................................................Mitch Pileggi
Keller.........................................................Michael P. Keenan
Ryan...................................................................Arthur Malet
Donia...................................................................Zane Lasky
Goldman..........................................................Hugh Maguire
Del Greco..............................................................Marty Schiff

Anita...............................................................Shannon Wilcox
Mudcat...........................................................Clive Rosengren
Big H....................................................................Michael Clark
Mark Harris.......................................................Padraic Duffy
And: Rockwood (Tatoo artist), Bodine Balasco (Dealer), Jean Claudio (Inspector), Jacques Brunet (Phony De Rougement), Guy Chapellier (Artist), Jean Rougerie (Capt. De Rougement), J.T. O'Connor

Director: Irving J. Moore          Writer: Howard Lakin

3. "One Last Kiss"  Nov. 16, 1990

About to be given drug therapy, J.R. enlists his fellow patients in an escape scheme; Bobby turns to his cyclist friends to try to rescue April, and is forced to let Sheila pose as his bride.

Dr. Wykoff........................................................Chelcie Ross
Jordan Lee.............................................................Don Starr
Anita...............................................................Shannon Wilcox
Ryan...................................................................Arthur Malet
Keller.........................................................Michael P. Keenan
Donia...................................................................Zane Lasky
Goldman..........................................................Hugh Maguire
Del Greco..............................................................Marty Schiff
Tim.....................................................................Duane Davis
    Also orig. announced: Padraic Duffy (Mark Harris)

Director: Leonard Katzman          Writer: Lisa Seidman

4. "Terminus"  Nov. 23, 1990

Bobby attends an oil reception with Sheila, playing her charade; J.R., home from the asylum, makes a deal with Duke; James conspires with Sly against J.R.; April is shot dead.

Control...............................................................John Harkins
Jordan Lee.............................................................Don Starr
Pete Johnson...................................................David Crowley
Smith...................................................................Dierk Torsek
Jones....................................................................David Carlile
And: John Hoge (Ratagan), Frank Swann (Bartender/Mike)

Director: Irving J. Moore          Writer: Mitchell Wayne Katzman

5. "Tunnel of Love"  Nov. 30, 1990

April is buried in Paris, and Bobby returns home; Cliff proposes to Liz, who lies about her feelings to protect him from her ties to Dancer and the government; James seeks allies in his scheme to destroy J.R, who moves to blackmail Carter.

Control...............................................................John Harkins
Breslin....................................................................Peter White
Dora Mae..............................................................Pat Colbert
Mark Harris.......................................................Padraic Duffy
Garage owner/Alex...........................................Fred Stromsoe
Bartender/Mike..................................................Frank Swann
Inspector...............................................................Jean Claudio

Director: Michael Preece          Writer: Howard Lakin

6. "Heart and Soul"  Dec. 7, 1990

Bobby turns his back on Ewing Oil, and clashes with Michelle; Dancer is murdered after threatening Westar owner McKay, J.R.'s rival; J.R. sees his old love (Hunnicutt), and blackmails the McKay's wife; James offers McKay damaging information about J.R.; Clayton returns, to do business with McKay.

Breslin....................................................................Peter White

Gerhardt..................................................................David Gale
Dora Mae..............................................................Pat Colbert
O.R.C. members...................Robert Balderson, Peter Gonneau
Room service attendant........................................Jean Sincere

Director: Nick Havinga          Writer: Lisa Seidman

7. "The Fabulous Ewing Boys"  Dec. 14, 1990

Bobby accepts Michelle's apology, and both her and Liz's offer of help to find Sheila; J.R. hires back Sly; Vanessa confronts her son James, and meets with a pregnant Cally, who's left J.R.; a detective (Taylor) suspects a missing Cliff killed Dancer, and suspects Liz and McKay; Bobby vows to sell Ewing Oil.

Control..................................................................John Harkins
Ratagan...................................................................John Hoge
Tom...................................................................Doug Franklin
Brad...................................................................William Tucker
Bartender/Mike........................................................Frank Swann
Jeweler/John...........................................................Robert Chase

Director: Michael Preece          Writer: Leonard Katzman

8. "The Odessa File"  Dec. 21, 1990

Bobby sells the company to a Venezuelan oil magnate (Eden), and he and Michelle discover the woman they thought was Sheila isn't; Cliff returns; J.R. blackmails McKay and proposes to Vanessa.

Harv Smithfield.......................................................George O. Petrie
Breslin.....................................................................Peter White
Inagaki...............................................................Richard Narita
Toni Chastaine........................................................Susan Krebs
Casul.......................................................................Abel Franco
Nancy.................................................................Evelyn Guerrero
Dr. Banoff.............................................................Nick Eldredge
Sheila.............................................................Miranda Garrison
Sweeper.............................................................Michael Monks
Bellpersons.............................David Benbow, Nick Metropolis
Marquez.............................................................Enrique Sandino

Director: Nick Havinga          Writer: Howard Lakin

**preempted Dec. 28**

9. "Sail On"  Jan. 4, 1991

LeeAnn taunts J.R. with plans to sell Ewing Oil to Westar; Cliff tries to maintain his career despite being charged with Dancer's murder; J.R. and Vanessa announce their engagement; Cally leaves, telling J.R. she's pregnant with James' child.

Harv Smithfield.......................................................George O. Petrie
Dave Culver...........................................................Tom Fuccello
Dora Mae................................................................Pat Colbert
Stacy Byrnes........................................................Susan Edwards
Ratagan...................................................................John Hoge
Judge.................................................................William Porter

Director: Michael Preece          Writer: Lisa Seidman

10. "Lock, Stock and Jock"  Jan. 11, 1991

J.R.'s long-forgotten relationship with LeeAnn returns to haunt him; Michelle plots against J.R.; a jailed McKay is grilled by the police; Liz accepts Cliff's marriage proposal.

Ray King...........................................................Michael Alldredge
J.J. Carter............................................................Joseph Malone

Breslin.....................................................................Peter White
Janine..................................................................Patricia Barry
Teresa.......................................................Roseanna Christiansen
Garage owner/Alex................................................Fred Stromsoe
Waitress/Sue.............................................................Nikki Sands

Director: Nick Havinga          Writer: Mitchell Wayne Katzman

11. " 'S' is for Seduction"  Jan. 18, 1991

LeeAnn begins her plan to seduce J.R.; Bobby dreams of April, and he and Liz find a banker partner (Frank) of "Sheila" (real name: Hilary Taylor); after McKay is found guilty, Cliff privately confesses to the prosecutor of having killed Dancer.

Ray King...........................................................Michael Alldredge
J.J. Carter............................................................Joseph Malone
Jill.......................................................................Dorothy Parke
And:  Charles Frank (Paul Keats), Alan Weeks (Judge G. Thomas, Pat Colbert (Dora Mae), Frank Novak (Oil person)

Director: Michael Preece          Writer: Howard Lakin

**preempted Jan. 25**

12. "Designing Women"  Feb. 1, 1991

In Caracas, LeeAnn hands control of Ewing Oil to Michelle, who orders James to marry her as part of her battle with J.R.; Vanessa leaves J.R. after LeeAnn tells her of his infidelity; the D.A.'s office decides to keep Cliff's confession secret.

J.J. Carter............................................................Joseph Malone
Breslin.....................................................................Peter White
Frank Hillson.......................................................Richard Eastham
Judge G. Thomas.......................................................Alan Weeks

Director: Irving J. Moore          Writer: Lisa Seidman

13. "90265"  Feb. 8, 1991

J.R. finally realizes the company -- now De La Vega Oil -- is owned by Michelle, who fires him, Sly and Phyllis, and has married James; in Malibu, Bobby finds and pretends to woo the daughter (Imershein) of "Sheila Foley."

Dana.......................................................................Kelly Rowan
Kit Marlowe........................................................Shari Shattuck
Derrick...................................................................Paul Gannis
Garage owner/Alex................................................Fred Stromsoe
Justice of the Peace.................................................Gordon Wells

Writer-director: Leonard Katzman

14. "Smooth Operator"  Feb. 15, 1991

Bobby becomes unsure of his growing feelings for Jory, who is being stalked; J.R. learns of Michelle and James' psuedo-marriage and starts plotting to retake Ewing Oil, blackmailing a senator to postpone Cliff's government appointment.

Senator Garrity...................................................Charles Bateman
Kit Marlowe........................................................Shari Shattuck
John...............................................................Anthony Addabbu
Dana.......................................................................Kelly Rowan
Kinsey Richard......................................................Nancy Warren
Carmen Esperanza...................................................Barbara Luna
Derrick...................................................................Paul Gannis
Men......................Michael David Simms, Michael Ted Rooney
Gas station attendant............................................Michael Chieffo
And: Lloyd Battista (Ricardo), Kathleen Kinmont (Cookie)

Director: Larry Hagman          Writer: Lisa Seidman

**preempted Feb. 22**

15. "Win Some, Lose Some"  March 1, 1991

Bobby gives up his chance to get Hillary in order to save Jory, with whom he parts; James and Michelle play jealousy games with each other; Liz offers to sell her company to J.R. in exchange for Cliff's government appointment.

Dana.................................................................Kelly Rowan
Mark Harris....................................................Padraic Duffy
Kit Marlowe....................................................Shari Shattuck
DeeDee...............................................................Eva La Rue
Derrick............................................................Paul Gannis
Men...................Michael David Simms, Michael Ted Rooney
And: Graham Galloway (Surfer), Floyd Foster, Jr. (Harrigan)

Director: Patrick Duffy       Writer: Mitchell Wayne Katzman

16. "Fathers and Sons and Fathers and Sons"  March 8, 1991

Bobby and J.R. take their young sons on a cattle drive; Liz walks in on Cliff and a paramour; Cliff and Michelle plot against J.R.; a woman (Tucker) claims to be James' legal wife, in tow with a son, Jimmy. Per CBS, the series' 350th episode.

J.J. Carter....................................................Joseph Malone
Meg Callahan............................................Chris Weatherhead
Stephanie......................................................Mary Watson
Derrick............................................................Paul Gannis
Dora Mae........................................................Pat Colbert
Raoul........................................................William Marquez
Audrey Chase.................................................Julie Araskog
Reporter......................................................Catherine Dent
Man.............................................................Dusty Rhoads
Debbie....................................Deborah Marie Taylor
Lyle...............................................................William Jones
Woman............................................................Linda Dawson
Kitten.............................................................Kristy Talin
James Richard (Jimmy) Beaumont II (child)...........(uncredited)

Director: Larry Hagman        Writer: Arthur Bernard Lewis

**preempted March 15 and March 22**

17. "When the Wind Blows"  March 29, 1991

J.R. keeps Debra Lynn, James' legal wife, at bay while manipulating James into staying with Michelle, to keep a Ewing stake in the company; Cliff accuses Liz of fingering him as Dancer's murderer; Jory sets up a meeting with her mother.

David Stanley.................................................Bruce Gray
Derrick............................................................Paul Gannis
Raoul........................................................William Marquez
Frank..............................................................Don Maxwell
Debbie....................................Deborah Marie Taylor
Guard...........................................................Frank Kerman
Carla....................................................Carla Beachcomber
James Richard (Jimmy) Beaumont II (child)...........(uncredited)

Director: Patrick Duffy        Writer: Louella Lee Caraway

18. "Those Darned Ewings"  April 5, 1991

J.R., getting attached to James' and Debra Lynn's toddler, is torn between encouraging James to remain married to Debra Lynn, or to divorce and remarry Michelle; Bobby offers Jory a life in Dallas; J.R. learns he's the father of Cally's baby.

Dr. Kessler.......................................................Tony Miller
David Slade.......................................................Bill Smillie
Raoul........................................................William Marquez
Lawyer.........................................................Sheldon Kurtz
John Kane.........................................................Edson Stroll
James Richard (Jimmy)
          Beaumont II (child)...................Chuckie/Kenny Gravino
And: Norma Michaels (Sitter), Frank Swann (Bartender/Mike)

Director: Dwight Adair          Writer: Kenneth Horton

19. "Farewell, My Lovely"  April 12, 1991

J.R. searches for and finds Cally, but decides to stay out of her life; Clayton returns to reveal Miss Ellie has deeded Southfork soley to Bobby; James gets attached to Jimmy and Debra Lynn, while Michelle finds solace in Cliff, and Jory in Bobby.

Pat Connors....................................................Michael Bell
Kit Marlowe....................................................Shari Shattuck
Debbie....................................Deborah Marie Taylor
James Richard (Jimmy)
          Beaumont II (child)...................Chuckie/Kenny Gravino

Director: Patrick Duffy           Writer: Lisa Seidman

20. "Some Leave, Some Get Carried Out"  April 19, 1991

Hillary Taylor meets with Bobby at Southfork; James asks Debra Lynn to stay married and leave Dallas with him; John Ross announces he's moving to London to live with his mother; Michelle finds herself married to Cliff, and kills Hillary.

David Stanley.................................................Bruce Gray
Kit Marlowe....................................................Shari Shattuck
James Richard (Jimmy)
          Beaumont II (child)...................Chuckie/Kenny Gravino

Writer-director: Leonard Katzman

21. "The Decline and Fall of the Ewing Empire"  April 26, 1991

J.R. faces an old enemy (former cast-member Martin), and approaches a breakdown from his family's dispersing, losing Southfork to Bobby and Ewing Oil to Cliff, and the departure of Sly and Phyllis; Bobby bids Jory goodbye; Michelle is arrested for murder.

Dusty Farlow......................................................Jared Martin
Frank Hillson.................................................Richard Eastham
Robert MacCubbin.........................................Rob Youngblood
And: Doug Franklin (Cobb), Tom Fleetwood (Thompson)

Director: Ken Kercheval  Writer: Lisa Seidman

22. "Conundrum"  May 3, 1991  9-11 p.m.

An angelic emissary from Hell (Grey) shows the suicidal J.R. what the world would have been like had he never been born, culminating back in reality with Bobby hearing a shot from J.R.'s room and seeing J.R. (off-camera) having apparently shot himself in the head.  Shackelford and Van Ark are stars of the spinoff series *Knots Landing*; Mary Crosby a.k.a. Mary Francis Crosby is the daughter of singer Bing Crosby and his second wife, Katherine Grant.  Per CBS, the 356th episode.

Adam.................................................................Joel Grey
* Kristen Shepard.............................................Mary Crosby **
Sue Ellen Ewing..............................................Linda Gray **
Ray Krebbs.....................................................Steve Kanaly **
Nick................................................................Jack Scalia **

Gary Ewing.................................Ted Shackelford **
Valene (Val) Gibson.........................Joan Van Ark **
Bootsie Ewing.....................Kim Johnston Ulrich (a.k.a. Kim Johnston-Ulrich, Kim Ulrich)
Jeanne Lawrence..................................Leslie Bevis
Jason Ewing....................................Patrick Pankhurst
Judy..........................................Barbara Rhoades
Eb............................................Richard Lineback
Smith.........................................James Callahan
Jeff Peters...................................Anthony Addabbo
Alice Kingdom.................................Katherine Justice
Barbara Barnes..................................Tricia O'Neil
Annie Ewing...................................Rosalind Allen
Courtney.....................................Denise Gentile
Beth Krebbs...................................Katherine Cannon
Kimberly Kavanaugh............................Teri Ann Linn
Wally Ford....................................Herman Poppe
And: Jerry Potter (Bartender), Tony Auer (Ted), Edson Stroll (Charlie Haas), James Newell (Walter Kingdom), Robert Neches (Bob), Brioni Farrell (Alice Anne), Virginia Watson (Secretary), Dan Livingston (Edgar), Sylvia Brooks (Carol), Deborah Marie Taylor (Debbie), Christine Joan Taylor (Margaret), Gregory White (Kleever), Stephen Held (Young man), John Mueller (Harry), Kim Delgado (Stage manager), Wayne Chou (Servant), Conor Duffy (Little J.R.), Kate Horton (Little Ellie), David Katzman (Bobby, Jr.), Kenyon Moad (Cally's 3-year-old), Mike Simmrin (Andy), Nicolas Read (Cliff, Jr.), Michael Gonda, Jonathan Gonda (Cally's kids), Tim Eyster (Jock)

* J.R.'s former mistress, who shot him on the 1979-80 finale.
** Former cast-member.

Writer-director: Leonard Katzman

## Dark Shadows

NBC        Jan. 13-March 1   Fridays, 9-10 p.m.
           March 8-March 22  Fridays, 10-11 p.m.

Series premiere: Jan. 13, 1991
Final telecast: March 22, 1991

Serialized gothic-horror drama of vampire Barnabas Collins, and the denizens of the isolated Collinwood manor in fictional Collinsport, Maine. Cast-members Anthony and Pouget were listed as guest stars initially. Beginning a few episodes into the run, cast-members played both contemporary and 18th-century characters. Based on the 1966-71 ABC afternoon serial also created by Dan Curtis, also the basis for the films *House of Dark Shadows* (1970) and *Night of Dark Shadows* (1971). Partly filmed at the Greystone Mansion, Beverly Hills. The episode "titles" treat the two-hour ep. 2 as two episodes.

Barnabas Collins...................................Ben Cross
Elizabeth Collins Stoddard/
   Naomi Collins (1790)..........................Jean Simmons
Carolyn Stoddard, her daughter/
   Millicent Collins (1790)..................Barbara Blackburn
Willie Loomis/Ben Loomis (1790)....................Jim Fyfe
Victoria Winters, the governess/Josette
   Dupre (1790)...................................Joanna Going
David Collins, Roger's son/on/on/
   Daniel Collins (1790).....................Joseph Gordon-Levitt
Sarah Collins, the ghost of Barnabas' sister....Veronica Lauren
Maggie Evans (ep 2-on)............................Ely Pouget
Dr. Julia Hoffman/Countess Natalie
   Dupre (1790)..................................Barbara Steele
Roger Collins/Reverend Trask (1790)................Roy Thinnes
Joe Haskell/Peter Bradford (1790)..............Michael T. Weiss
Angelique (ep. 6-on)...........................Lysette Anthony

*Recurring:*
Housekeeper Mrs. Johnson/Abigail
   Collins (1790)...........................Julianna McCarthy *
Sheriff Patterson/Andre Dupre (1790)
   (ep. 1-3,5-11)..........................Michael Cavanaugh
Prof. Woodard/Joshua Collins,
   Barnabas' father (1790) (ep. 1-3,6-11)......Stefan Gierasch
Sam Evans, Maggie's father/Bailiff (1790)
   (ep. 1-2,4,8,10-11).........................Eddie Jones
Phyllis Wicke (ep. 5-8,11)......................Ellen Wheeler

* In every episode, though not technically a cast-member.

Dan Curtis Television Productions and MGM/UA Television
Executive producer: Dan Curtis
Supervising producer: Steve Feke
Producers: Jon Boorstin (ep. 1-on), Armand Mastroianni (added later; William Gray also orig. announced)
(Also orig. announced: Line producer: Norman Henry)
Associate producer: Bill Blunden
Executive story editors (ep. 3-on): Linda Campanelli, M.M. Shelly Moore, William Gray
Director of photography: Dietrich Lohmann (ep. 1); Chuy Elizando
Creative consultant (ep. 1): Sam Hall
Music [and] Theme (instrumental): Bob Cobert
Certain characters developed by: Art Wallace
Creator: Dan Curtis

---

1. "Dark Shadows" Part 1  Sunday, Jan. 13, 1991  9-11 p.m.

Upon separately arriving at Collinwood, the mysterious long-lost Barnabas and governess Victoria Winters discover a mutual attraction; Barnabas preys on distant relative Daphne.

Maggie Evans...........................................Ely Pouget
Daphne Stoddard....................................Rebecca Staab
Dr. Fisher.............................................Wayne Tippit
Gloria................................................Hope North
Local tough.........................................Michael Buice
Paramedics...................Rif Hutton, Steve Fletcher
Gardener/boy.......................................George Olden
Roadhouse band....................................J.B. and the Niteshift

Director: Dan Curtis
Story: Hall Powell & Bill Taub
Teleplay: Hall Powell & Bill Taub and Steve Feke & Dan Curtis

2. "Dark Shadows" Part 2   Monday, Jan. 14, 1991  9-11 p.m.

After a spate of murders, Woodard and the local police suspect a vampire lurks about; Sarah's ghost gives David a cryptic warning; Hoffman works on an experimental vampirism cure. Fletcher appeared in a different role last episode.

Daphne Stoddard....................................Rebecca Staab
Deputy Harker.......................................Steve Fletcher
Reverend.............................................Basil Langton

Director: Dan Curtis
Teleplay (first half): Hall Powell & Bill Taub and Steve Feke & Dan Curtis
Story (first half): Hall Powell & Bill Taub
Writer (second half): Jon Boorstin

3. "Episode 4"  Jan. 18, 1991  10-11 p.m.

Hoffman and Barnabas -- who can now see his reflection and walk in daylight -- try to stop Woodard from giving the police Julia's diary; Victoria learns of the Collins family history; David toys with voodoo. Orig. scheduled for 9-10 p.m.

Angelique......................................................Lysette Anthony
Dr. Fisher..............................................................Wayne Tippit
Deputy Harker.................................................Steve Fletcher

Director: Dan Curtis
Writers: Sam Hall and Steve Feke & Dan Curtis

4. "Episode 5" Jan. 25, 1991

Barnabas presents his long-lost love Josette's music box to Victoria; a jealous Hoffman alters her anti-vampirism serum.

Director: Armand Mastroianni
Writers: Matthew Hall and Steve Feke & Dan Curtis

5. "Episode 6" Feb. 1, 1991

Maggie asks a Ouija board to name the murderer terrorizing the town; Barnabas and Carolyn threaten Hoffman; Elizabeth, seeking information from Sarah, allows a seance. Anthony reprises her role from ep. 3, and joins the cast next episode.

Angelique......................................................Lysette Anthony
And: Charles Lane

Director: Armand Mastroianni
Writers: Jon Boorstin and Steve Feke & Dan Curtis

6. "Episode 7" Feb. 8, 1991

Victoria, transported to 1790, meets her 18th-century self, Josette Dupre; Angelique magically enlists Willie in her play for Barnabas.

Jeremiah Collins, Barnabas' brother......................Adrian Paul
And: Courtenay McWhinney (Crone), Laurel Wiley (Girl)

Director: Paul Lynch                    Writer: Jon Boorstin

7. "Episode 8" Feb. 15, 1991

In a duel over Josette, Barnabas and Jeremiah secretly plan to use no bullets, but Angelique magically loads Barnabas' pistol, leading to Jeremiah's death and accusations that Josette is a witch. Fletcher reprises his role from ep. 2, Paul from ep. 6.

Deputy Harker.................................................Steve Fletcher
Jeremiah Collins...................................................Adrian Paul

Director: Paul Lynch
Writers: M.M. Shelly Moore & Linda Campanelli and William Gray

**preempted Feb. 22**

8. "Episode 9" March 1, 1991

In 1790, Victoria is jailed for sorcery; Angelique turns Jeremiah into a zombie, and sends a vampire bat after Barnabas. Paul reprises his role from ep. 6-7.

Jeremiah Collins...................................................Adrian Paul
And: Apollo Dukakis

Director: Rob Bowman  Writer: Matthew Hall

9. "Episode 10" March 8, 1991

Joe tries convincing Sheriff Patterson a vampire controls Caro-

lyn; Angelique visits the present by possessing Julia; in 1790, Victoria may have found her link to new vampire Barnabas.

Director: Rob Bowman
Writers: M.M. Shelly Moore & Linda Campanelli

10. "Episode 11" March 15, 1991

Maggie is unaware of the results of her attempt to exorcise Angelique from Julia, who kills Joe; Victoria in 1790 receives a guilty verdict, as Barnabas prepares to wed and vampirize her.

Judge Isiah Braithwaite................................Brendan T. Dillon
Jury foreperson.................................................Dick Valentine

Director: Mark Sobel                    Writer: William Gray

11. "Episode 12" March 22, 1991

In 1790, Barnabas attacks Abigail; Naomi loses her mind; Sarah and Daniel suffer a potentially fatal fever; Joshua asks Barnabas to force Trask to withdraw the witchcraft charge against Victoria. Dillon reprises his role from last episode.

Judge Isiah Braithwaite................................Brendan T. Dillon
Nurse.................................................................Joanne Dorian
Dr. Roberts.......................................................Ralph Drischell
Minister.............................................................Donald Wayne

Director: Mark Sobel
Writers: M.M. Shelly Moore & Linda Campanelli & Matthew Hall

## Davis Rules

ABC Jan. 27-April 9, July 9-30          Tuesdays, 8:30-9 p.m.
    Aug. 7-Sept. 11                    Wednesdays, 9:30-10 p.m.

Series premiere: Jan. 27, 1991

Comedy of a committed, unconventional principal and single parent raising three sons with the help of his live-in father. School: Pomahac Elementary. Working titles: *The Principal*; *It's the Principal*; *Spiral Bound*; *The Dwight House*.

Dwight Davis......................................................Randy Quaid
Gunny Davis, his father.................................Jonathan Winters
Cosmo Yeargin.................................................Patricia Clarkson
Elaine Yamagami.................................................Tamayo Otsuki
Robbie Davis.......................................................Trevor Bullock
Charlie Davis.........................................................Luke Edwards
Ben Davis................................................................Nathan Watt

*Recurring, all or virtually all episodes:*
Rigo..................................................................Rigoberto Jimenez
Ms. Higgins.....................................................Debra Jo Rupp
Mrs. Rush.........................................................Debra Mooney
*Other recurring guests:*
Etta May Archimbault (ep. 1,3,9)............................Etta May *
Earl King (ep. 1,9,13)...........................................Kelly Connell
Debbie Kessler (ep. 4,5,10).........................Robin Lynn Heath
Alice Hansen (ep. 5-6,10,12)............................Angela Watson
Leo (ep. 2,12-13).................................................Bryan O'Byrne
Jerry (ep. 2,12-13)...........................................Arnold Johnson

* May be a psuedonym for Brenda Ferrari.

The Carsey-Werner Co.
Executive producers: Danny Jacobson, Marcy Carsey, Caryn Mandabach, Tom Werner, Norma Safford Vela

Supervising producer: Dale McRaven
Producers: Jon Spector, Fredi Towbin
Associate producers: Jean Hester-Lunt
Story editors: Kim C. Friese, Stephen Paymer
Theme (instrumental) and music: Mark Mothersbaugh
Director: Ellen Falcon
Creators: Norma Safford Vela & Danny Jacobson

————————————

1. "A Man for All Reasons"  Jan. 27, 1991  10:14-10:44 p.m.

The teachers and staff of his school vote a reluctant Dwight
into the principal's chair. Orig. scheduled for Jan. 8; odd time-
slot the result of scheduling to follow the Super Bowl, a tactic
used for the Jan. 31, 1988 premiere of *The Wonder Years*.

Mr. Clifford............................................................Ron Dortch
Mrs. Barrett..............................................Francesca P. Roberts
And: Tasha Scott, Dax Biagas, Jacob Kenner, Kristi Murakami

Writers: Danny Jacobson & Norma Safford Vela

2. "Rules of the Game"  Jan. 29, 1991

Romance may stir between Dwight and the algebra teacher
(Clarkson) he hires to tutor Robbie. Clarkson, listed as a cast-
member on ep. 1, though not appearing in it, debuts.

Writers: Fredi Towbin & Kim C. Friese

3. "The Trouble with Women"  Feb. 5, 1991

Dwight and Cosmo surrender to their mutual attraction; Robbie primes himself to protect Ben at school.

With: Ivory Ocean, Nick DeMauro, Hank Rolike, Jennette Feli-
ciano

Writers: Norma Safford Vela & Danny Jacobson

4. "Guys and Dolls"  Feb. 12, 1991

Dwight's jealous when Gunny says he saw Cosmo with another man; Rigo serenades his dream girl (recurring guest Heath).

Writers: Norma Safford Vela & Danny Jacobson

5. "Pomahac Day Massacre"  Feb. 19, 1991

Dwight wants to ask Cosmo to the Pomahac Day dance; Robbie gives Rigo dating tips. Dortch reprises his role from ep. 1.

Rae Nitschke....................................................Micole Mercurio
Mr. Clifford............................................................Ron Dortch
Mike Doovik.......................................................Jay Bradford

Writers: Danny Jacobson & Norma Safford Vela

6. "Yes, I'm the Great Pretender"  Feb. 26, 1991

Charlie pretends Cosmo is his new mother; Robbie's girlfriend
wants him to pierce his ear.

Belinda.................................................................Kristal Bivona
Jamie..................................................................Floyd B. Jones
Lucy..................................................................Bethany Allyn

Writers: Norma Safford Vela & Danny Jacobson

7. "Gimme the Ball"  March 5, 1991

As spring arrives, Robbie tries out for the baseball team, and
Charlie acquires a wooden dummy named Van Gogh.

Mr. Montecito.....................................................Reni Santoni
Beautiful neighbor Miss Kelly (no lines)..................(uncredited)
And: Tommy Tarantino

Writer: Kim C. Friese

8. "Twisted Sister"  March 5, 1991  9:30-10 p.m.

Davis' free-spirited sister (Hunt) visits from Florida.

Gwen...................................................................Bonnie Hunt
Waitress.........................................................Mary Pat Gleason
Cabbie/Julio.........................................................Israel Juarbe
Mike.....................................................................Bruce McGill

Writer: Kim C. Friese

9. "Take This Job and Love It"  March 12, 1991

Robbie rebels under the weight of being the principal's son;
Ms. Higgins fights teacher stress. Orig. scheduled for March 5.

Mr. Higgins, Sr.........................................................Mina Kolb
Mrs. Hilliard...........................................................Elsa Raven
Mr. Hilliard...............................................................John Ingle
    Also orig. announced:
    James Montague (Clyde), Dax Biagas (Student)

Writers: Danny Jacobson & Norma Safford Vela

10. "Sign of the Times"  March 19, 1991

Robbie and Rigo daringly scale the towering sign at the local
drive-in theater; Dwight includes women in his poker game.
McGill reprises his role from ep. 8.

Mike.....................................................................Bruce McGill

Writer: Fredi Towbin

11. "Habla Espanol"  March 26, 1991

Robbie and Spanish-student Dwight both end up in detention
hall after school.

Spanish teacher Ms. Chavez..................................Amy Aquino
Mrs. Moreno...................................................Irene Olga Lopez
Billy Bonafield..............................................Chris Demetral
Tom....................................................................Bruce Locke
Merle.....................................................................Tasha Scott
And: Diane Racine

Writers: Norma Safford Vela & Danny Jacobson

12. "Mission: Improbable"  April 2, 1991

Dwight tries to give his dad a birthday surprise party. Hunt
and Gleason reprise their roles from ep. 8, Mercurio from ep. 5.

Gwen...................................................................Bonnie Hunt
Rae Nitschke....................................................Micole Mercurio
Mrs. Catworthy.......................................................Fran Ryan
Waitress.........................................................Mary Pat Gleason
Stranger................................................................Jack McGee

Writer: Stephen Paymer

13. "Soap"  April 9, 1991

Charlie bets on how long he can avoid taking a shower; Dwight wants to confront a journalist; Gunny seeks romance.

With: Stephen Root

Writers: Norma Safford Vela & Danny Jacobson

**on hiatus until reruns begin July 9; scheduled as a 1991-92 midseason replacement series**

## The Days and Nights of Molly Dodd

Lifetime        Saturdays, 10:30-11 p.m.

Series premiere: May 21, 1987
Final telecast: July 13, 1991

Occasionally surreal seriocomedy of an attractive, intellectual, somewhat dilettantish divorced woman in her late 30s, working as an editor at a publishing house and coping with life on Manhattan's Upper West Side. Telecast on NBC from 1987-88 (26 episodes); picked up by Lifetime in January, 1989, first with NBC reruns, then with original episodes beginning April 6, 1989. Co-star McLerie and recurring guest Gaynes are married in real life. Filmed at Kaufman Astoria Studios, Queens, New York City. For episodes listed without guests, information (incomplete) is per Lifetime, and unconfirmed.

Molly Bickford Dodd..............................................Blair Brown

*Cast-members in end-credits:*
Florence Bickford, Molly's mother.................Allyn Ann McLerie
Doorperson Davey McQuinn.............................James Greene

*Recurring:*
Fred Dodd, Molly's ex-husband........William Converse-Roberts
Arthur Feldman, Florence's beau......................George Gaynes
Detective Nathaniel (Nate) Hawthorne..............Richard Lawson
Bookstore owner Moss Goodman...................David Strathairn
Ron Luchesse, Molly's neighbor..........................John Pankow
Ramona Luchesse, his wife.........................J. Smith-Cameron
Jimmy McQuinn, Davey's son............................James Gleason
Ghost of Edgar Dodd, Molly's father................Richard Venture

You & Me, Kid Productions
Executive producers: Jay Tarses, Bernie Brillstein
Supervising producer: Don Scardino
Co-producers: Elaine Arata, Richard Dresser
Coordinating producer: Leslie Dennis
Associate producer: Vivian Guardino
Executive consultant: Sandy Wernick
Director of photography: Michael Barrow
Music [and] Theme (instrumental): Patrick Williams
Creator: Jay Tarses

---

1. "Here's a Neat Way to Tie Up the Loose Ends" Jan. 19, 1991

When Molly tells Nate he's the father of her child, he proposes, prompting a dinner so that Florence can meet him.

With one or more recurring guests and: Arthur French, Harold Perrineau, Bill Damaschke, Angel Jemmon, Jeffrey Steefel

Director: Don Scardino        Writer: Richard Dresser

2. "Here's a New Way of Looking at Cappuccino" Jan. 26, 1991

At work, Molly discovers she hasn't been credited as the author of her book; at a cafe, Molly discusses childbearing.

Director: Steve Dubin        Writer: Elaine Arata

3. "Here's When the Fat Lady Sings" Feb. 2, 1991

In the afternoon, Nate gives Molly an engagement ring, but that evening, news arrives he's died from a medical condition.

With  one or more recurring guests and: Shawn Elliott (Nate's partner), David Lipman (Cabbie), Jodie Markell (Lillian)

Director: Steve Dubin
Writers: Richard Dresser & Elaine Arata

4. "Here Are Some Overnight Lows" Feb. 9, 1991

Molly tries to cope with Nate's death, and with jitters over impending motherhood.

Director: Steve Dubin
Writers: Elaine Arata & Richard Dresser

5. "Here's a Pregnant Pause" Feb. 16, 1991

Breaking through the fourth wall to speak directly to the audience, Molly fantasizes she's finally in control of her life.

With  one or more recurring guests and: Drew McVety (Brice, Molly's boss), Lewis Black, Anthony Farentino, Mary Joy (Sylvia), Rusty Magee, Sonia Ryzy-Ryski
Director: Don Scardino
Writers: Richard Dresser & Elaine Arata

6. "Here's a Good Excuse for Missing the Party" Feb. 23, 1991

Molly goes into labor on the street on the way to the hospital, while all her family and friends wait for her at a baby shower.

With  one or more recurring guests and: Maureen Anderman (Nina), John Glover (Cousin Mike), Jodie Markell (Lillian)

Director: Blair Brown
Writers: Richard Dresser & Elaine Arata

7. "Here's One Way to Fill Every Waking Moment" March 2, 1991

Molly spends her first few days of motherhood with her baby girl; Davey and Jimmy disagree about work styles.

With  one or more recurring guests and: Jean LeClerc, Daniel Dassin, Lynne Thigpen

Director: Don Scardino        Writer: James Ryan

8. "Here's a High Dive into a Shallow Pool" March 9, 1991

Molly, returning to work and finding herself now placed in human resources, is instructed to fire her friend Bernie.

Director: Ken Frankel        Writer: Richard Dresser

9. "Here's How to Break the Other Leg" March 16, 1991

Molly and Fred join Arthur and Florence for the opening of producer Arthur's play, *Breathless Angel*; Fred volunteers to help raise the baby.

Director: Don Scardino        Writer: Richard Dresser

10. "Here's How to Put an Egg in Your Shoe and Beat It"
   March 23, 1991

Ron and Ramona, now separated, are forced by economics to share their apartment; Fred ponders a music career in L.A.

Director: Blair Brown              Writer: Carl Capotorto

11. "Here's Why You Shouldn't Talk to Strangers in the Park"
   March 30, 1991

Florence and Arthur have big news; a mysterious woman makes disconcerting predictions about Molly's baby.

Director: Don Scardino           Writer: Cindy Lou Johnson

12. "Here's When Life Begins At" April 6, 1991

Molly celebrates her 40th birthday with old friend Nina, and unexpectedly meets garbage collector Nick (series creator Tarses, in his occasional role); Fred comes to say goodbye.

Director: Don Scardino           Writer: Cindy Lou Johnson

13. "Here's a Little Touch of Harry in the Night" April 13, 1991

Molly recalls her days in The Fred Dodd Quintet, and at a grocery recognizes her old guitarist (Friedman), of whom she was fond; Florence and Arthur leave on a cross-country trip.

Harry......................................................Peter Friedman
Voice of basset hound Dave..................Jay Tarses (uncredited)
Voice of horse......................................................(uncredited)

Writer-director: Jay Tarses

## DEA

Fox                Fridays, 9-10 p.m.

Series premiere: Sept. 7, 1990
Final telecast: June 14, 1991

Drama of U.S. Dept. of Justice Drug Enforcement Administration operatives, Group Nine, in their battles against narcotraffickers. From April 19 on, retitled *DEA: Special Task Force.*

Teresa Robles.........................................................Jenny Gago
Bill Stadler..............................................................Tom Mason
Jimmy Sanders...........................................Byron Keith Minns
Nick Biaggi..........................................................Chris Stanley
Group Nine Supervisor Phil Jacobs........................David Wohl

*Major recurring characters:*
Rafael Cordera (ep. 1)..............................................Joe Lala
Rafael Cordera (ep. 2-8)...............................Miguel Sandoval
The Confidential Informant (C.I.)
   (ep. 1-2,4,6,8,10-13).....................................Jorge L. Gil
Mrs. Clemente (ep. 1,3,4-5)...............................Ivonne Coll
Pascual Cordera (ep. 2-6)...........................Nate Esformes
Carl Schliemann (ep. 2-8,10)..............................Alan Scarfe
Ricky Prado (ep. 2-5)...........................................John Vargas
Greg Dyson (ep. 2-5)..............................Christopher Curry
Isabella Solana (ep. 4-8,10-11)..........................Roya Megnot
Michael Cambio (ep. 10-13)...................................Rene Assa
Dominic De Lasera (ep. 10-13)..........................Joseph Gian
Ginny Taylor (ep. 7,11-13)...............................Alyson Reed

Dark Ink and Gordon Freedman Productions in assoc. with
   Lorimar Television

Executive producer: Richard DiLello
Supervising producer: David Peckinpah
Producers: Banko Lusting (ep. 1); Gordon Freedman (ep.
   1-on); Christopher Chulack, Michael Ahnemann, Cyrus
   Nowrasteh (latter three, ep. 2-on)
Co-producer (ep. 2-on): Peter McCabe
Coordinating producer (later in season): Dean Barnes
Associate producer (early in season): Dean Barnes
Director of photography: Bryan Franklyn Greenberg
Consultant: Peter Werner
Theme (instrumental) and music: David Kurtz
Creator: Richard DiLello

---

1. "DEA"
   Sept. 7, 1990; Sunday, Sept. 9, 1990  10-11 p.m.  (DE-100)

In New York City, a rookie agent (Dobson) is killed by a Colombian drug lord.

Danny La Croix.....................................................Peter Dobson
Detective Tom Neally.................................................Ron Dean
Felix Loquera.................................................Ronald G. Joseph
Thomas Walthour..................................................Steve Kahan

Director: Peter Werner  Writer: Richard DiLello

2. "Aftermath" Sept. 14, 1990  (DE-101)

The agents hunt La Croix's killer, the Cordera crime family, while his widow seeks her own revenge.

Carlos Robles..................................................Abraham Alvarez
Producer.............................................................Sharon Brown
Danny La Croix...................................................Peter Dobson
Louis Calvatier.........................................................Bruce Gray
Felix Loquera.................................................Ronald G. Joseph
Clemente.......................................................William Marquez
Anne Kenner............................................Anne Elizabeth Ramsay
Darla Stadler..........................................................Rita Taggart
Julie La Croix..........................................................Kelly Wolf
Special Agent Clemmons....................................William Anton
DEA agents....................Michael Francis Clarke, Clifton Powell
And: Rosalia Hayakawa (Girl), Armando Molina (Angel), Michael Anthony Rawlins (punk), Michael Rider (Jools), Anthony Russell (Super), Marc Tubert (Gen. Guiterrez)

Director: Colin Bucksey            Writer: Richard DiLello

3. "Under Presidential Seal" Sept. 21, 1990  (DE-102)

Sanders takes down a Jamaican posse leader; a criminal's best friend (Curry) is arrested, and turns informer.

Gen. Vincente De Aza.......................................Castulo Guerra
Charlie Too-Bad....................................................David Harris
Clemente.......................................................William Marquez
Anne Kenner............................................Anne Elizabeth Ramsay
Samuel..............................................................Mark Robinson
Ellie.................................................................Gina Spellman
Oscar....................................................................Shaun Baker
Tina....................................................................Brigett Butler
Kim...................................................................Daphne Cheung
DEA agents....................Michael Francis Clarke, Clifton Powell
Ron Phelps................................Charles James Kahlenberg
Detective Alvarisio.................................................Robert Silver
NYPD detective........................................................Jake Turner
And: Carmen Mehia (Mariela), Mirron Edward Willis (Calvin)

Director: David Jackson           Writer: Michael Ahnemann

4. "Jumping the Trampoline" Sept. 28, 1990 (DE-103)

Theresa goes undercover in Mexico in an attempt to trap Ricky Prado in an extraditable country, but is kidnapped to Colombia. Part 1 of 2.

| | |
|---|---|
| Miguel Lorca | Carlos Gomez |
| Jack Martinez | Carlos Lacamara |
| Clemente | William Marquez |
| Rios | Garret Pearson |
| Cardena Solana | Phillip Pine |
| Fabio | Julian Reyes |
| Jorge Matta | Geno Silva |
| The Marshall | Robert Balderson |

And: Josh Cruz (Gen. Siqueros), Louis Rivera (Teco), Julia Calderon (Neighbor), Yvette Cruise (Griselda), Denis Marco (Girl), Elena Martinez (Maid), Noah Verduzco (Boy)

Director: Colin Bucksey
Writers: Ann Powell & Rose Schacht

5. "Prime Mover" Oct. 5, 1990 (DE-104)

Theresa gains the trust of the Colombian Cali cartel, and lures Ricky Prado to Costa Rica, an extraditable country. Part 2 of 2.

| | |
|---|---|
| Jack Martinez | Carlos Lacamara |
| Walter Hagen | Matt Landers |
| Rios | Garret Pearson |
| Cardena Solana | Phillip Pine |
| Capt. Morales | Carlos Carrasco |

And: Tom Klunis (Businessperson), Robert Madrid (El Loco), Denise Marco (Girl), Louis Rivera (Teco)

Director: Mark Sobel          Writer: David Peckinpah

6. "Bloodsport" Oct. 12, 1990 (DE-105)

Nick sees a dark side of himself personified in a bad cop when the two are paired to take down a Cali cartel hit man (Madrid).

| | |
|---|---|
| El Loco | Robert Madrid |
| Louis Calvatier | Bruce Gray |
| Rios | Garret Pearson |
| Ruben Monteban | Pepe Serna |
| Chuck Benninger | Robert Viharo |
| Diana | Mary Watson |
| Curro | Maurice Benard |

And: Dayton Callie (Cord), Ryan Cutrona (Lt. Fadiman), Robert Pucci (Cop), Dierk Torsek (Waltner)

Director: NA   Writer: Cyrus Nowrasteh

7. "MethLab" Oct. 26, 1990 (DE-106)

Nick and Theresa, undercover to bring down a drug manufacturer, become drawn to each other; Solana allies herself with Rafael Cordera to initiate a money-laundering scheme.

| | |
|---|---|
| Diana | Mary Watson |
| Oscar Lomax | Richard Marcus |
| Barry Stillman | Dennis Bailey |
| Errol | Scott Kraft |
| Ruben Monteban | Pepe Serna |
| Waitress | Stephanie Cushna |
| Joey Ruffin | Craig Gini |

And: Liza Whitcraft (Girl), Donald Willis (Desk clerk), Joel Gretsch (Stephen), Vic Trevino (Enrique), J. Andrew Bilgore (Walter Patchevsky), Gibby Brand (Paul Roscoe)

Director: Peter Ellis          Writer: Peter McCabe

8. "Moving Mary Jane" Nov. 2, 1990 (DE-107)

A huge Colombia marijuana shipment sparks an inter-agency squabble; Solana and Schliemann ally with a heroin trafficker.

| | |
|---|---|
| Sallie Ann | Jensen Daggett |
| Gen. De Aza's officer | Efrain Figueroa |
| Jack Randa | Steven Flynn |
| Jed (orig. Stanley) Kemp | Kenneth David Gilman |
| Baretto | Ricardo Gutierrez |
| Jackie Lansing | Franc Luz |
| Jonny Quan | Ping Wu |
| Edmons | Greg Almquist |

And: Teresa Dispina (Reya), Rudy Prieto (Guard), Jack Ryland (Augie Flynn), Walter Borchert (Alex), Cleo Blumberg (Alex's girlfriend), Cameron Hall (Prostitute), Marty Levy, Brian Mahoney (Agents), Patty Toy (Secretary)

Director: David Jackson   Writer: Michael Ahnemann

**on hiatus**

9. "The Fat Lady Sings Alone" April 19, 1991

Tom is thwarted by politics when he tries to apprehend the the Honduran druglord (Perez) who killed his friend (Brown).

| | |
|---|---|
| Paula Werner | Patricia Heaton |
| Sam Blankenship | Gregory Itzin |
| Valerie Rawlins | Felicity La Fortune |
| Stella McKay | Kathleen Kinmont |
| Severo Barillo | Tony Perez |
| Bob Ellis | Joel Anderson |
| CIA agents | James Asher-Salt, Dan Gerrity |
| Jack Rinaldi | Jack Stauffer |
| Tom Rawlins | Randy Brown |
| Agents | Darren Foreman, Robert Martin Steinberg, Greg Collins |
| Commanding officer | Joe Farago |

And: Gigi Groves, Debbie Foley (Girls), James Newell (Jameson), Melissa Young (Porn actress), Paul Collins (Man)

Director: Reynaldo Villalobos   Writer: Michael Ahnemann

10. "Dance with the Devil" April 26, 1991 (DE-108)

A Mafia boss (Boccelli), gunned down by rivals, gives information that could break open a heroin network; Nick begins dating high school teacher (Treas). Orig. scheduled for Nov. 16.

| | |
|---|---|
| Ruben Monteban | Pepe Serna |
| Jonny Quon | Ping Wu |
| Jed (orig. Stanley) Kemp | Kenneth David Gilman |
| Ellen Brunner | Terri Treas |
| Tony Maracotta | Dick Boccelli |
| Leonard | Michael Ralph |
| TV reporters | Jonathan Palmer, Rosanna Iversen, Francesca Rollins |
| Informant | Edward Carnevale |
| Kids | Marcus Brown, Garland Spencer |

Also orig. announced: Steven Flynn (Jack Randa)

Director: Peter Ellis          Writer: Peter McCabe

11. "The Connection" May 3, 1991 (DE-109)

European heroin link Isabella Solana is taken down, but not mob boss De Lasera, and the C.I. goes undercover after him.

| | |
|---|---|
| Anthony Maracotta Jr. | Joe Marinelli |
| Ruben Monteban | Pepe Serna |

And: Rachelle Carson (Girl), John David Conti (Clerk), Juan Garcia (Mando), Rosanne Iversen (Genele Jensen)

Director: James Quinn      Writer: Cyrus Nowrasteh

12. "White Lies"  May 10, 1991

Robles and Sanders arrest an attorney (Ziskie) possessing heroin; an informant (Gil) gets closer to druglord De Lasera.

Michael Stadler........................................................Chad Allen
Vicki Simon................................................Kim Morgan Greene
Visiglia...............................................................Joseph Sirola
Ellen Brunner.........................................................Terri Treas
Callahan...............................Daniel (a.k.a. Jeff Daniel) Ziskie
Chaya.............................................................Courtney Gibbs
Connie De Lasera................................................Eleni Kelakos
Joey/Gina.............................................David Shawn Michaels
Models.........................Sigal, Monika Schnarre, Roni Margolis
And: Jim Pirri (Bodyguard), Susanne Sullivan (Receptionist)

Director: Rob Bowman      Writer: David Peckinpah

**preempted May 17**

13. "Zero Sum Game"  May 24, 1991

De Lasera's drug empire topples, and the C.I. learns he has a debt to pay De Lasera after a recent heroin bust.

Michael Stadler........................................................Chad Allen
Mrs. Williams.......................................................Andi Chapman
David Rittenauer...............................................Matthew Laurance
Diana....................................................................Mary Watson
Johnny Fazio............................................................Jamie Alba
And: Francesca Rollins (Annie), Michael Raysses (Florist), Marissa Ribisi (Wendy), Dan Woren (Driver), Anthony De Fonte (Joseph Bebo), Alex Harris (Lamont Carson)

Director: Colin Bucksey      Writer: Garner Simmons

## Dear John...

NBC      Sept. 19-Dec. 26    Wednesdays, 9:30-10 p.m.
           Dec. 29-March 2    Saturdays, 10:30-11 p.m.
           March 13-June 19   Wednesdays, 9:30-10 p.m.
           July 6-27           Saturdays, 10-10:30
           Aug. 3-Sept. 7     Saturdays, 9:30-10 p.m.

Series premiere: Oct. 6, 1988

Ensemble comedy of the One-Two-One a.k.a. 1-2-1 singles support group at the Rego Park Community Center in the New York City borough of Queens, focusing on the recently divorced John Lacey. Series title is as appears onscreen.

John Lacey..............................................................Judd Hirsch
Kirk Morris................................................................Jere Burns
Louise Mercer..............................................................Jane Carr
Ralph Drang........................................................Harry Groener
Kate McCarren...............................................Isabella Hofmann
Mrs. Philbert................................................................Billie Bird
Mary Beth Sutton.................................................Susan Walters

*Recurring:*
Tom (ep. 1,3-21)....................................................Tom Willett
Denise (ep. 9-on).................................................Olivia Brown

Ed. Weinberger Productions in assoc. with Paramount Television

Executive producers: Hal Cooper, Rod Parker, Ed. Weinberger
Supervising producers: Mike Milligan, Jay Moriarty
Producers: Howard Meyers, Bob Ellison, George Sunga
Co-producer: Thomas Lofaro (a.k.a. Thomas Gold Lofaro, his additional credit as unit production manager)
Coordinating producer: Greg Giangregorio
Executive story editor: Rod Burton
Story editors: Marco Pennette, Efrem Seeger
Executive consultant: Judd Hirsch
Director of photography: George La Fountaine
Music: uncredited; only a "music supervisor" listed
Theme: "Dear John" by John Sullivan (music and lyrics); performed by Wendy Talbot
Director: Hal Cooper
Developed by: Bob Ellison & Peter Noah
Based on characters from the BBC television series *Dear John*, created by John Sullivan

--------------------

1. "Pretty Man"  Sept. 19, 1990

John goes on a blind double-date with Kirk, and finds himself mistaken for a professional escort.

Alexis...............................................................Christine Cattell
Blair...............................................................Valorie Armstrong

Writers: Diana Ayers & Susan Sebastian

2. "And Baby Makes Four, Part I"  Sept. 26, 1990

John hopes for a reconciliation when his ex-wife (Harmon) says she wants another child, but she only wants his sperm.
Wendy................................................................Deborah Harmon

Writer: Mike Milligan & Jay Moriarty

3. "And Baby Makes Four, Part II"  Oct. 3, 1990
    9:35-10:05 p.m.

Feeling pressured and rushed, John breaks into the insemination clinic to retrieve his sperm. The unusual time-slot derived from an apparent NBC experiment in beginning shows at five minutes after the hour *a la* Superstation TBS; see also *Unsolved Mysteries*, *The Fanelli Boys* and *Hunter* for this date.

Wendy................................................................Deborah Harmon
Young mother.............................................................Patty Toy
Husband................................................................Nathan Jung
Police officers..............................Pat Puccinelli, Anita Whitaker
And: Grace Albertson (Prim woman), Cliff Norton (Pilot)

Writer: Mike Milligan & Jay Moriarty

4. "A Priest's Story"  Oct. 10, 1990

John tries to mediate a fight over a woman between Kirk and his amazingly similar brother -- a priest.

Father Bob Morris..........................................................Kevin Dunn
Terry....................................................................Brynn Thayer
Boy...........................................................................Bo Sharon

Writer: Howard Meyers

**preempted Oct. 17**

5. "That's Big of Me"  Oct. 24, 1990

A new member (Sheehan) proposes to both Kate and Louise.

Jason Fowler..................................................Doug Sheehan
Chow Ling.....................................................Cu Ba Nguyen
Mindy..........................................................Karen Ironside
Minister..........................................................John O'Leary
And: Kyle-Scott Jackson (Desk Sergeant), Pat Puccinelli (Cop)

Writer: Rod Burton

6. "Hot Lips Lacey"  Oct. 31, 1990   9-9:30 p.m.

John sort of fulfills his dream of playing clarinet at Carnegie Hall.

Charlie Moura.....................................................Sab Shimono
Cab driver..........................................................Milton James
Billy...........................................Mitchell Gordon Bell
Girl..........................................................Megan McGinnis
Woman.........................................................Carrie Gordon
Heidi...........................................................Melissa Young
Marie (misidentified in end-credits as Lorraine).....Sandra Wild

Writer: Marco Pennette

7. "Hole in One"  Nov. 7, 1990

At her aunt's funeral, Kate confronts her ex-husand (Bernsen, of *L.A. Law*), a cad nonetheless loved by the rest of her family.

Blake McCarren..............................................Corbin Bernsen
Aunt Trudy..................................................Helen Page Camp
Minister..........................................................Jack Manning

Writers: Mark Reisman & Jeremy Stevens

8. "The Blunder Years"  Nov. 14, 1990

John seeks a reunion with a famous adventure author (Bevis) whom he recalls, via flashbacks, as the great love of his youth.

Matthew Lacey.....................................................Billy Cohen
Jessica Stone....................................................Leslie Bevis
Jessica (17 and 22)..............................................Paige Pengra
John (17 and 22)...............................................Peter A. Smith
Jessica (12)........................................................Erika Flores
John (12)........................................................Joshua Smith
Beasley.................................................................Ed Evanko
And:  Jason Strickland (Jimmy), Lori Fox (Nurse), Keith Allen
    Burns (Clerk), Jodie Mann, Laurel Ollstein (Patrons)

Writers: Diana M. Ayers & Susan Sebastian

**preempted Nov. 21**

9. "Down and Out in Rego Park"  Nov. 28, 1990

Despite interruptions by a newly svelte woman (new recurring guest Brown) from Overeaters Anonymous across the hall, the group tries to cheer up Mary Beth, who's lost her job.

Stacy.................................................Kathryn Danielle

Writer: Howard Meyers

**preempted Dec. 5**

10. "Homeward Bound"  Dec. 12, 1990

John wants his aging mother to move in with him.

Charlotte Lacey......................................................Nina Foch
Henry....................................................Miguel A. Nunez, Jr.

Millie Hanson.........................................................Meg Wyllie

Writers: Mike Milligan & Jay Moriarty

11. "A Matter of Trust"  Dec. 19, 1990  9-10 p.m.

John's job is jeopardized and the group disbands after a tabloid links him to a promiscuous movie star (Strasser).  Orig. scheduled as a two-part episode, Dec. 12 and 19.

Brooke Collins.....................................................Robin Strasser
Brad.................................................................Peter Jurasik
Dr. Hendricks..........................................................Raye Birk
Waiter.............................................................Timothy Jones
Amorous female student.............................................Ele Keats
Amorous male student.............................................Nicholas Katt
Students..............Laurie Plaxen, Larry Spinak, Patrick W. Day

Writer: Efrem Seeger

12. "Molly and Me"  Jan. 5, 1991

Ralph falls for a married fellow toll-taker (Mullally).

Molly............................................................Megan Mullally
Linda.............................................................Deasa Turner
Marcie..........................................................Victoria Howden

Writers: Diana M. Ayers & Susan Sebastian

**preempted Jan. 12**

13. "Love Stories" Part 1   Jan. 19, 1991

John meets a pretty periodontist (Matthews), Kate a suave South American (Lamas), and Kirk his fiesty match (Seeger).

Alejandro Braceros.............................................Lorenzo Lamas
Dr. Janet Benjamin......................................DeLane Matthews
Jackie.........................................................Mindy Seeger
Receptionist......................................................Laura Julian
Sexy woman (no lines)..........................Jennifer Van Buskirk
Patients...........................Robin Michael Cahal, Henry Holden

Writers: Rod Parker, Bob Ellison, Rod Burton

14. "Love Stories" Part 2   Jan. 26, 1991

Jackie agrees to live with Kirk, under exacting conditions; Louise gets a date with her IRS auditor (Davies).

Dr. Janet Benjamin......................................DeLane Matthews
Walter Harrison.......................................................Lane Davies
Jackie.........................................................Mindy Seeger
Danny...............................................................Glen Mauro
Donny...............................................................Gary Mauro

Writers: Rod Parker, Bob Ellison, Rod Burton

15. "Love Stories" Part 3   Feb. 2, 1991

Everyone gets dumped except Ralph; John's ex-wife brings news of a new baby.  Harmon reprises her role from the two part ep. 2-3, Mullally from ep. 2.

Dr. Janet Benjamin......................................DeLane Matthews
Molly............................................................Megan Mullally
Jackie.........................................................Mindy Seeger
Wendy.........................................................Deborah Harmon

Writers: Rod Parker, Bob Ellison, Rod Burton

16. "John and Kirk's Excellent Adventure"  Feb. 9, 1991

Kirk loses John's antique watch to a pretty thief (Ivy).

Betsy.............................................................Lela Ivy
Police officers.................................Bill Boyett, Clyde Kusatsu
Mrs. Spencer...................................................Eda Reiss Merin

Writer: Marco Pennette

17. "The Poet" Part 1   Feb. 16, 1991

John's college poetry teacher (Hearn) visits, and steals some of John's poems for a book; the group preps for a talent show.

Frank Hollander..................................................George Hearn
Voice of Sarah Donnelly at Patterson Publishing......uncredited

Choreography: Harry Groener

Writer: Howard Meyers

**unscheduled preemption Feb. 23**

18. "The Poet" Part 2  March 2, 1991

John huddles with the group-members over whether to expose the former professor (Hearn) who plagiarized his poems.  Orig. scheduled for Feb. 23.

Frank Hollander..................................................George Hearn
Orlando..............................................Ruben Santiago-Hudson
Emcee.....................................................Paul Eiding
The Newtones...............Howard McCrary, Perry Morgan, Alfred
    McCrary
Sarah Donnelly...................................................Lynne Thigpen

Choreography: Harry Groener

Writer: Howard Meyers

19. "Louise, the Hero"  March 13, 1991

After they learn she'd been institutionalized, the group scoffs at Louise's claim she can save the financially strapped center.

Natasha...........................................................Irina Davidoff
Mishka.........................................Mihaly Michu Meszaros
Florence Kellem.............................................Marlene Mancini
Fraternity member.......................................Chambers Stevens

Writers: Mike Milligan & Jay Moriarty

20. "Matthew and the Baby" March 20, 1991

John tries getting his son (Cohen, reprising his role from ep. 8) to discuss his hurt feelings about the baby his mom and John are having.  Orig. scheduled for March 6, 9:30-10 p.m.

Matthew Lacey......................................................Billy Cohen

Writer: Meredith Siler

**preempted April 10**

**preempted April 24**

21. "John's Week Off"  May 1, 1991

John is stranded in remote Hawaiian airports after buying a discount ticket from Kirk; Alejandro (Lamas, reprising his role

from ep. 13) proposes to Kate.

Alejandro Braceros..............................................Lorenzo Lamas
Woman......................................................Lisa Long
Harry the waiter................................................Richard Blum

Writer: Rod Burton

**preempted May 15 and May 22**

**preempted June 5 and June 12**

**renewed for 1991-92; new episodes begin Sept. 19, 1991**

## Designing Women

CBS          Mondays, 9:30-10 p.m.

Series premiere: Sept. 29, 1986

Comedy of four Atlanta women and the decorating firm, Sugarbaker's, they operate with their black, framed-ex-con employee (and, later, business partner). Burke, the wife of *Major Dad* costar Gerald McRaney, represented Florida in the 1974 Miss America pageant.  Carter is married to former recurring guest Hal Holbrook, now a cast-member of *Evening Shade*; Smart, to actor Richard Gilliland; and Potts, to *Northern Exposure* cinematographer James Hayman.  Recurring guest Ghostley reprises her occasional role from past seasons. Charlene's baby: Olivia.  Charlene's hometown: Poplar Bluff, Missouri.

Julia Sugarbaker....................................................Delta Burke
Suzanne Sugarbaker............................................Dixie Carter
Mary Jo Shively.......................................................Annie Potts
Charlene Frazier Stillfield......................................Jean Smart
Anthony Bouvier...............................................Meshach Taylor

*Recurring:*
Bernice (ep. 2,12,16,20,22-23)............................Alice Ghostley
Randa Oliver (ep. 3, 21-24)...................................Lexi Randall

Bloodworth/Thomason Mozark Productions in assoc. with
    Columbia Pictures Television / CPT Holdings
Executive producers: Harry Thomason, Linda Bloodworth-
    Thomason
Co-executive producer: Pam Norris
Producer: David Trainer
Supervising producers: Douglas Jackson, Tommy Thompson
Associate producer: Judith A. Burke
Story editors: Dee LaDuke, Mark Alton Brown
Director of photography: Edward Rio Rotunno
Music: Bruce Miller
Theme (instrumental): "Georgia on My Mind," a pop standard
    by Stuart Gorrell, Hoagy Carmichael; performed by Doc
    Severinsen
Director unless otherwise noted: David Trainer
Creator: Linda Bloodworth-Thomason

––––––––––––––––––

1. "A Blast from the Past"  Sept. 17, 1990

Sugarbaker's is beset by tourists when the building's Civil War foundation puts it on the Tour of Historical Homes; Mary Jo considers a marriage proposal from an old friend (Tabori, the son of actress Viveca Lindfors and director Don Siegel).

Karen Delaporte...........................................Mary Ann Mobley
Daryl..............................................................Kristoffer Tabori
Loud tourist.........................................................James Keane

Whining tourist..............................................Michele Buffone
Tourist with soda............................................Armand Asselin
Smoking tourist..............................................Frank DiElsi

Writer: Pam Norris

2. "Papa Was a Rolling Stone"  Sept. 24, 1990

The ladies hire a private investigator to find Anthony's long-lost father (Cobbs) as a 30th-birthday surprise.

Henry........................................................Bill Cobbs
Beefma.......................................................Tom Magee

Writers: Debbie Pearl & Cassandra Clark

3. "Working Mother"  Oct. 1, 1990

Resentment builds between Charlene and Mary Jo when Charlene wants to take a year off to look after her baby.

Adam.........................................................Adam Carl

Writer: Pam Norris

**preempted Oct. 8**

4. "Miss Trial"  Oct. 15, 1990

Julia's dinner plans with former President Jimmy Carter and his wife are put on hold when her jury gets sequestered.

Marshal......................................................Jessie Jones
DJ...........................................................John O'Connell
Tight Lips...................................................Ellen Albertini Dow
Janice.......................................................Kathryn Spitz

Writers: Dee LaDuke & Mark Alton Brown

5. "The Bachelor Auction"  Oct. 22, 1990

Suzanne reluctantly dates Anthony after winning him in a bachelor charity auction.

Emcee........................................................Rena Craig
Lenore.......................................................Donna Lynn Leavy
Cowboy.......................................................Tom Marvich
Woman with clipboard.........................................Kathy Connell
Women........................................................Joan Pirkle, Gyl Roland

Writer: Pam Norris

6. "Charlene Buys a House"  Oct. 29, 1990

And asks the Sugarbaker's crew to decorate it.

Marvin Sheinberg.............................................Charles Levin
Rusty........................................................Michael Goldfinger

Writer: Pam Norris

7. "Old Rebels and Young Models"  Nov. 5, 1990

Charlene's baby, Olivia, auditions for a modeling job; Mary Jo finds one of her former teachers (Wyllie) in a nursing home.

Miss Crown...................................................Meg Wyllie
And: Dona Hardy (Mrs. Chesley), Lorna Scott (Nurse)

Director: Iris Dugow
Writers: Dee LaDuke and Mark Alton Brown

8. "Nowhere to Run To"  Nov. 12, 1990

Mary Jo takes up jogging, and inadvertently helps turn Julia into a fitness zealot.   Per CBS, the series' 100th episode.

Davida Daniels...............................................Sandahl Bergman

Writers: Cassandra Clark & Debbie Pearl

9. "A Class Act"  Nov. 19, 1990

Anthony buys in to become a full partner; new student Charlene fends off an amorous psychology professsor (Sanders). Buffone played a different role, ep. 1.

Dr. Elliot Newhouse..........................................Richard Sanders
Ms. Gardner..................................................Michele Buffone
Gordon.......................................................Daniel Henning
And:  Susan Byun (Kathy), Kenneth Armstrong (Student),
      Adam Goldberg (Oreo person)

Director: Dwayne Hickman
Writers: Debbie Pearl & Cassandra Clark

10. "Keep the Home Fires Burning"  Nov. 26, 1990

With her husband away on a mission, Charlene guility draws close to a man (Crook) in her support group for military spouses.  Barr reprises his recurring role from past seasons.

Bill.........................................................Peter Crook
Soldiers.....................................................Robert Moran, Jerry Giles
Col. Bill Stillfield, Charlene's husband.....................Douglas Barr

"Don't Sit Under the Apple Tree" performed by: Angie Jaree,
      Patti Linsky, Mary Hylan

Writers: Dee LaDuke & Mark Alton Brown

11. "My Daughter, Myself"  Dec. 10, 1990

Mary Jo forbids her nearly 18-year-old daughter (Weems, reprising her recurring role from past seasons) to date a 34-year-old (Isbell), then dates him herself; Julia is forced to crash the men's room at a football stadium.

Jack.........................................................Tom Isbell
Claudia......................................................Priscilla Weems
Men..........................................................David James Alexander, Carl Beard
Mark.........................................................Michael B. Silver

Writer: Pam Norris

12. "And Now, Here's Bernice"  Dec. 17, 1990

Bernice gets a local cable show; Mary Jo has her heart broken by a client (Bernsen, brother of L.A. Law's Corbin Bernsen).

Donald Banks.................................................Collin Bernsen
Melinda......................................................Rebecca Balding
Susan........................................................Lois Hamilton
Ross.........................................................Tara Karsian
Phil.........................................................Jerry M. Hawkins
Nancy........................................................Lisa Long

Writers: Mark Alton Brown & Dee LaDuke

13. "Pearls of Wisdom"  Jan. 7, 1991

Mary Jo borrows and loses a string of pearls flaunted by Suzanne, subbing as a lifestyles reporter for local TV news.

Harley.........................................................Eliott Harold

Writer: Pam Norris

14. "High Noon in a Laundry Room"  Jan. 14, 1991

Anthony, concerned with his masculinity after working with the women so long, tries standing up to his bullying neighbor.

Billy Boy Swine.............................................Dennis Burkley
Party girl......................................................Christina Rich

Writers: Mark Alton Brown & Dee LaDuke

**preempted Jan. 21**

15. "How Long Has This Been Going On"  Jan. 28, 1991

Julia has covertly been signing at a nightclub.  Cast-member Carter is a longtime cabaret singer in real life.

May..............................................Patricia Ayame Thomson
Gary...........................................................................Bill Shick
And: David Heisey (Max), Hartley Silver (Sam)

Writers: Cassandra Clark & Debbie Pearl

16. "The Emperor's New Nose"  Feb. 4, 1991

Bernice gets an extraordinarily bad eye tuck and rhinoplasty.

Salesperson.............................................Kerry Leigh Michaels
Mother.........................................................Julie Ann Nesitt
Boy..................................................................Brady Bluhm

Writers: Michael Ross & Thom Bray

17. "Maybe Baby"  Feb. 11, 1991

Mary Jo, wanting a baby, turns to her friend and former beau (Gilliland, reprising his role from previous seasons); Suzanne takes up smoking as a way to diet.

J.D. Shackleford...........................................Richard Gilliland

Writer: Pam Norris

**preempted Feb. 18**

18. "This is Art?"  Feb. 25, 1991  10-10:30 p.m.

Julia inadvertently becomes the darling of Atlanta's art scene; Suzanne inadvertently glues her lips shut.

Roseland Price.............................................Claudette Nevins
Mrs. Fredhold...................................................Janice Kent
Mr. Fredhold.....................................................Terry Burns
Gentlemen...........................Sprague Theobald, Mike Regan
Delighted patron..........................................Joann B. Martin
Fruit bowl looker....................................Katherine Blackmon
Guard...............................................................Jon Huffman

Director: Roberta Sherry-Scelza
Writers: Steven Roth & Deanne Roth

19. "Blame It on New Orleans"  March 4, 1991

When the gang attends a convention in intoxicating New Orleans, Mary Jo unwittingly sleeps with a married man.

Garret Rossler.............................................Darrell Larson

Podiatrists........................................Kerry Stein, Frank DiElsi
Lolita LuPage.........................................David Shawn Michaels
And: Paula Trickey (Bikini model), Wade Patridge (Waiter)

Writers: Mark Alton Brown & Dee LaDuke

**preempted March 11**

20. "I'll See You in Court"  March 18, 1991

Mary Jo runs across the man who mugged her the year before, but faces horrendous judicial red tape to bring him to trial.

Sgt. Ramsey.................................................Donna Lynn Leavy
Judge.........................................................Laurence Haddon
Mary Jo's attorney...............................................Justin Dana
Norman's attorney..........................................George R. Parker
Norman Bates..........................................................P.R. Paul
Margaret.......................................................Dona Hardy
Attractive man..................................................Dan Dillon

Director: David Trainer (Iris Dugow orig. announced)
Writers: Debbie Pearl & Cassandra Clark

**preempted April 1**

21. "The Big Circle"  April 8, 1991

Julia tries coping with her boyfriend Reese's death by looking after the supremely spoiled child (recurring guest Randall) of a client couple on an extended vacation.

Ms. Tauber.......................................................Jennifer Rhodes
Miss Travis.......................................................Lyndsey Fields
And: Peter Jolly (Man), Joe Verroca (Taxi driver)

Writer: Pam Norris

22. "Friends and Husbands"  April 29, 1991

Charlene, readjusting to married life, quits her and Mary Jo's children's-book project when Bill returns from the war.  Barr reprises his role from ep. 10 and past seasons.

Col. Bill Stillfield..................................................Douglas Barr

Writers: Cassandra Clark & Debbie Pearl

23. "Fore!"  May 6, 1991

Suzanne is jealous when Anthony is invited to be the first black in the previously all-white Beaumont Country Club. Buffone played different roles, ep. 1 and 9.

Cissy Farenholt...............................................Gracie Harrison
Bitty Cantrell.......................................................Rena Craig
Bruz Duncan.........................................................Mark Neely
Stewart Crimmons.....................................................Jay Bell
And: Michele Buffone (Photographer), Monika Schnarre (Lady)

Writer: Pam Norris

24. "The Pride of Sugarbaker's"  May 13, 1991

Mary Jo and Julia demonstrate different coaching styles when their firm sponsors a Little League team.  Guest Burkley had played a different character in ep. 14.

Buford.............................................................Dennis Burkley
Quint.................................................................Brian Lando
Announcer.......................................Stuart Nelson (uncredited)

Director: Iris Dugow       Writers: Thom Bray & Michael Ross

**preempted June 17 and June 24**

**preempted Aug. 19**

**renewed for 1991-92; new episodes begin Sept. 16, 1991; Burke and Smart depart cast**

## A Different World

NBC          Thursdays, 8:30-9 p.m.

Comedy set at the predominantly black Hillman College.

Whitley Gilbert..........................................................Jasmine Guy
Jaleesa Vinson........................................................Dawnn Lewis
Dwayne Wayne.......................................................Kadeem Hardison
Mr. Gaines..............................................................Lou Myers
Ron Johnson...........................................................Darryl M. Bell
Walter Oakes..........................................................Sinbad (David Atkins)
Kim Reese..............................................................Charnele Brown
Winnifred "Freddie" Brooks...............................Cree Summer
Col. Clayton ("Dr. War") Taylor.........................Glynn Turman

*Recurring:*
Terrance Johann Taylor, the Colonel's
       son (ep. 1-2,6,9-10,14-15,17-21,23-24)............Cory Tyler
Kinu (ep. 1-2,5-7,20)....................................Alisa Gyse Dickens
Matthew (ep. 2,5-7,15-17,19-20,23-24)............Andrew Lowery
Professor Randolph (ep. 2-3,6,8-9)........Roger Guenveur Smith
Bianca Mack (ep. 1-3)....................................Toy Newkirk
Gina (ep. 17-18,21-23)........................................Ajai Sanders

The Carsey-Werner Co. in assoc. with Bill Cosby
Executive producers: Marcy Carsey, Tom Werner, Caryn
       Mandabach, Deborah Aal
Co-executive producer: Susan Fales
Producers: Debbie Allen, Joanne Curley Kerner
Co-producer (later in season): Yvette Denise Lee
Supervising producer: Gary H. Miller
Associate producer: Brenda Hanes-Berg
Executive story editor: Judi Ann Mason
Story editors: Yvette Denise Lee (early in season), Glenn
       Berenbeim, Jeannette Collins, Mimi Friedman
Executive consultant: William H. Cosby, Jr.
Production consultant: Alvin F. Poussaint, M.D.
Music: uncredited; only "musical direction" listed
Theme: "A Different World" by Stu Garnder, Bill Cosby
       (music); Dawnn Lewis (lyrics); performed by Aretha
       Franklin
Director unless otherwise noted: Debbie Allen
Creator: William H. Cosby, Jr. •

• As onscreen. Per NBC press release: "Created/developed by:
  Bill Cosby, John Markus, Carmen Finestra, Matt Williams."

———————————

1. "Everything Must Change" Sept. 20, 1990

Whitley finally decides she wants to date Dwayne, who mean-while has found a girlfriend (Dickens). The single-name per-former Pillow played a character of the same name.

"Herself"......................................................................Pillow

Writer: Susan Fales

2. "How Bittersweet It Is"  Sept. 27, 1990

Whitley dates Ron to try to make Dwayne jealous.

Kobie...................................Andrew Mariri a.k.a. Abner Mariri
D.J.........................................................................Anthony Kemp

Writer: Yvette Denise Lee

3. "Blues for Nobody's Child"  Oct. 4, 1990

Freddie befriends an orphaned foster child (Evans), whom she helps convince Prof. Randolph to adopt. Mariri reprises his role from last episode.

Alex..........................................................................T.J. Evans
Dion...................................................................Brandon Adams
Mr. Gordon......................................................George C. Simms
Kobie...................................Andrew Mariri a.k.a. Abner Mariri
Mr. Miles.......................................................Lanyard Williams

Writer: Judi Ann Mason

4. "Whitley's Last Supper"  Oct. 11, 1990

Whitley is put on a budget by her visiting dad (O'Neal, repris-ing his role from a previous season).

Mercer Gilbert..........................................................Ron O'Neal

Writers: Jeanette Collins & Mimi Friedman

5. "The Goodwill Games"  Oct. 18, 1990

Dwayne tutors Whitley for the college's All-Star Challenge quiz event, while giving emotional support to rival Kinu. Working title: "College Bowl."

Antonio.................................................Slaim "Slam" Tauwloos

Writer: Yvette Denise Lee

6. "Tales from the Exam Zone"  Oct. 25, 1990

Walter takes viewers on a *Twilight Zone*ish tour of the college before midterm exams.

Prof. Clayton............................................................Jenifer Lewis
Tony.................................................................Leroy Edwards III

Writer: Alonzo B. Lamont

**preempted Nov. 1**

7. "Good Help is Hard to Fire"  Nov. 8, 1990

Dwayne's mom visits; broke Whitley works as Dwayne's maid. Singer La Belle reprises her role from last season's last episode.

Adele Wayne, Dwayne's mother...........................Patti La Belle

Writer: Glenn Berenbeim

8. "Love Thy Neighbor"  Nov. 15, 1990

With Kinu out of the picture, Dwayne and Whitley awkwardly try to begin a relationship.

Ray Nay.....................................................................Lee Weaver

Director: Rob Schiller          Writer: Yvette Denise Lee

9. "Time Keeps on Slippin' "  Nov. 29, 1990

Dwayne, concentrating solely on Whitley, sees his grades decline and imagines how the relationship will affect his future.

Hope..................................................Eartha Robinson
Ron Mokwena...................................................Ron Mokwena

Director: Michael Peters          Writer: Glenn Berenbeim

10. "The Apple Doesn't Fall"  Dec. 13, 1990

Dwayne and Whitley take different sides when Ron is split between music or joining the family auto business; Terrance thinks his father shouldn't join a restricted country club.

Mr. Johnson..................................................Art Evans
Jim Howell.............................................Scott Williamson
Bill...........................................................Randy Kaplan

Director: Art Dielhenn          Writer: Gary H. Miller

11. "I'm Dreaming of a Wayne Christmas"  Dec. 20, 1990

Whitley tries to make a good impression on Dwayne's parents (La Belle, reprising her role from ep. 7, and Sylvester).

Adele Wayne..................................................Patti La Belle
Woodson Wayne............................................Harold Sylvester
Santa/mugger..................................................Stanley Brock
Singers: Oren Waters, Julia Waters, Maxine Waters, Josef Powell

"Nothing Could Be Better" performed by Patti La Belle

Writer: Judi Ann Mason

**preempted Jan. 3**

12. "War and Peace"  Jan. 10, 1991

Dwayne's old pal (L.A. Law cast-member Underwood), a reservist, is called to active duty in Saudi Arabia.  Co-writer Hoffman appeared last season as Whitley's boyfriend, Julian.

Zelmer Collier.................................................Blair Underwood

Director: Peter Werner
Writers: Dominic Hoffman & Jasmine Guy

**unscheduled preemption Jan. 17; preempted Jan. 24**

13. "Ex-communication or Fiance What?"  Jan. 31, 1991

Whitley visits a counselor (series producer Allen) with regrets about her ex-fiance (Hoffman, reprising his role from last season), who's about to be married.

Dr. Langhorn.......................................................Debbie Allen
Julian.............................................................Dominic Hoffman
Shelby..............................................................Yvette Holland
And: Michael Ralph (Waiter), Jan Crawford

Writers: Jeanette Collins & Mimi Friedman

14. "Risk Around the Dollar"  Feb. 7, 1991

Whitley and Ron plan to throw a rent party; Terrance wants to become a Muslim.  Orig. scheduled for Jan. 17.

Mr. Ludlow.......................................................Paul Benedict
Waiter..............................................................Michael Ralph
Tyrone.............................................................Haven Mitchell

Director: Art Dielhenn
Writers: Jeanette Collins & Mimi Friedman

15. "Love Hillman Style"  Feb. 14, 1991

With Valentine's Day in the air, Whitley wants to create and market a "Men of Hillman" beefcake calendar.

Brenda.............................................................Ja'net DuBois
Prof. Anderson................................................Frantz Turner
Jacklyn...............................................................Halle Berry
Waiter............................................................Michael Ralph
Lorna...........................................................Wynonna Smith
Patti..................................................................Keli Carter
Phil...................................................................Howard Dell

Director: Neema Barnette          Writer: Gary H. Miller

16. "A Word in Edgewise"  Feb. 21, 1991

Members of the National Theatre of the Deaf (as themselves) perform at Walter's outreach center; Dwayne bets Whitley she can't keep silent for one day.

Himself................................................................C.J. Jones
Kids........................................Brandon Adams, Raynelle Gipson
Prof. Burton...............................................Candy Ann Brown

Technical advisors: John Arce, Lisa Schway

"The Camel Dances" from Fables by Arnold Lobel

Writer: Glenn Berenbeim

17. "Ms. Understanding"  Feb. 28, 1991

A male student's treatise on sex roles on campus prompts most of the women to boycott the men.

Dean Hughes....................................................Rosalind Cash
Zulu...............................................................Gary Dourdan
Hamilton..........................................................Aaron Seville

Writers: Yvette Denise Lee & Judi Ann Mason

18. "The Cash Isn't Always Greener"  March 7, 1991

Dwayne ponders a high-paying corporate job after graduation, or grad school and teaching; Jaleesa's sister (Calloway) visits.

Danielle Vinson......................................Vanessa Bell Calloway
Mr. Kenemitsu.................................................Clyde Kusatsu

Director: Neema Barnette          Writer: Yvette Denise Lee

19. "How Great Thou Art"  March 14, 1991

Corporate-art intern Whitley buys a painting against the wishes of her boss (Premice); Freddie hosts a radio talk show.

Erdeen Abernathy......................................Josephine Premice
Auctioneer.....................................................Michael Ensign
Josie..............................................................Tisha Campbell

Director: Neema Barnette
Writers: Jeanette Collins and Mimi Friedman

20. "Showtime at Hillman"  March 21, 1991

Walter hosts a local-TV telethon to raise funds for a community center, but the phones are remarkably silent.

Larry......................................................Cleavant Derricks
Dion..........................................................Brandon Adams
Jameela.....................................................Raynelle Gipson
Beau Braxton..............................................Jonathan Webb
Brad Braxton........................................Edgar Godineaux, Jr.
Miguel.......................................................Raymond Maese
Outreach demons.........Ben Yusef Abdullah, Terrence Williams
Max...............................................................Max Miller
Vanna Black..................................................Kiki Shepard
Band: Whose Image?

Writer: Joe Fisch

21. "Sister to Sister, Sister"  March 28, 1991

Kim, pledging a sorority, discovers the pledge mistress over-
seeing her is Whitley. Smith reprises her role from ep. 15,
Seville from ep. 17.

Hamilton......................................................Aaron Seville
Pilar.....................................................Chantal Rivera Batisse
Lorna/pledge.................................................Wynonna Smith
Pledges...........Aydiee Vaughn, Michael Ball, Jimmy Hamilton,
    Derek Knight
Waiter........................................................Michael Ralph

Directors: Glynn R. Turman and John Rago
Writer: Judi Ann Mason

22. "Monet is the Root of All Evil"  April 4, 1991

Whitley is put in a censorship controversy when she sponsors
a classmate's work that a reactionary group labels obscene.
Working title: "Artistic Integrity."

Novian..........................................................K. Todd Freeman
Miller.........................................................Von Washington
Priscilla.....................................................Laverne Anderson

Director: John Rago            Writer: Ilunga Adell

23. "If I Should Die Before I Wake"  April 11, 1991

An oratory professor (Goldberg) has her students write their
own eulogies when one of their classmates contracts AIDS.
Episode introduced by Bill Cosby. Campbell reprises her role
from ep. 19. Dedication: "In Memory of Darryl Tribble."

Prof. Jordan.................................................Whoopi Goldberg
Josie..........................................................Tisha Campbell

Writer: Susan Fales

24. "Never Can Say Goodbye"  April 25, 1991

Ron begs the dean to let him make up a course he missed,
jeopardizing graduation; Walter is given a farewell "roast."
Miller and Gipson reprise their roles from ep. 20. Director
Chan is the series' videotape editor.

Dean Winston.................................................Robert Guillaume
Max...............................................................Max Miller
And: Raynelle Gipson (Jameela), Terrence Williams

Director: Henry Chan           Writer: Orlando Jones

25. "To Be Continued"  May 2, 1991

At graduation, Whitley must decide whether to leave valedictorian Dwayne for a New York City job; Ron and his dad (Evans,
reprising his role from ep. 10) negotiate with the dean (Guil-

laume, reprising his role from last ep.) for Ron's diploma.

Dean Winston.................................................Robert Guillaume
And: Art Evans (Mr. Johnson), Matthew Dickens (Steward)

Director: Michael Peters        Writer: Glenn Berenbeim

**preempted Aug. 15**

**preempted Sept. 12**

**renewed for 1991-92; new episodes begin Sept. 19, 1991;
Sinbad departs cast.**

## Dinosaurs

ABC          April 26-May 24    Fridays, 8:30-9 p.m.
             Aug. 21-on         Wednesdays, 8-8:30 p.m.

Series premiere: April 26, 1991

Live-action (animatronic) fantasy-comedy of a blue-collar dinosaur family in the year 60,000,003 B.C., headed by megalosaurus Earl Sinclair, a 43-year-old tree-pusher for the Wesay-
so Development Corp. Brian Henson is the son of the late Jim
Henson, the Muppets' creator; Hemsley is a co-star of Amen.

Voice of Earl Snead Sinclair (Megalosaurus).......Stuart Pankin
Voice of Fran Sinclair, his wife (Allosaurus)........Jessica Walter
Voice of Robbie Sinclair (14)..............................Jason Willinger
Voice of Charlene Sinclair (12)...........................Sally Struthers
Voice of Baby Sinclair..........................................Kevin Clash
Voice of Roy Hess, Earl's friend (Tyrannosaurus)..............Sam
    McMurray
Voice of Grandma Ethyl, Fran's mother (ep. 3-on).......Florence
    Stanly
Performers/operators, Earl Snead Sinclair.............Dave Goelz,
    Bill Baretta
Performers/operators, Fran Sinclair................Allan Trautman,
    Mitchell Young Evans
Performers/operators, Robbie Sinclair.......Steve Whitmire, Leif
    Tilden
Performers/operators, Charlene Sinclair..............Bruce Lanoil,
    Arlene Lorre (latter ep. 1), Michelan Sisti (latter ep. 2-on)
Performers/operators, Baby Sinclair............Kevin Clash, John
    Kennedy
Performers/operators, Roy Hess....David Greenway, Pons Maar
Performer/operator, Grandma Ethyl (ep. 3-on)................Kevin
    Clash, Brian Henson (latter added ep. 4)

*Recurring:*
Voice of B.P. Richfield, Earl's
    boss (Triceratops) (ep. 1,3)....................Sherman Hemsley
Performer/operator, B.P. Richfield....................Steve Whitmire
*Also:*
Additional dinosaur performers (variously, at least three per
    episode): Tom Fisher, Terri Hardin, Brian Henson, Arlene
    Lorre, Michelan Sisti, Jack Tate

Michael Jacobs Productions and Jim Henson Productions in
    assoc. with Touchstone Television (ep.1), with Walt
    Disney Television/Touchstone Television (ep. 2-on)
Executive producer: Michael Jacobs
Co-executive producer: Brian Henson
Supervising producer: Bob Young
Producer: Mark Brull
Co-producer and dinosaur designer: Kirk Thatcher
Co-producer (ep. 3-on): Jeff McCracken
Associate producer: Kim Rozenfeld
Executive story consultants: Rob Ulin, Victor Fresco, Dava Savel

Director of photography: Robert E. Collins
Music: Bruce Broughton (ep. 1); Ray Colcord (ep. 2-on)
Theme (instrumental): Bruce Broughton
Dinosaurs by: Jim Henson's Creature Shop (Creative
    supervisor: John Stephenson; production supervisor:
    William Plant; both uncredited onscreen)
Based on an idea by: Jim Henson
Creators: Michael Jacobs, Bob Young

---

1. "The Mighty Megalosaurus" April 26, 1991

When Earl is fired after 24 years, with Fran's new egg about to
hatch, the overwhelmed 'saur leaves to live in the wilderness
like his late granddad. Dedication: "In loving memory of Jim
Henson, whose creative genius made this series possible."

Arthur Rizzic (voice and operator).........................Brian Henson
Cavepeople.....................................Teri La Porte, Michelan Sisti

Director: William Dear    Writers: Michael Jacobs & Bob Young

2. "The Mating Dance" May 3, 1991

When Fran feels like a dowdy housewife, Earl has to relearn
the mating dance to woo her and make her feel attractive.

Voice of Mel Luster.........................................Richard Portnow
Performers/operators, Mel Luster........Bruce Lanoil, Jack Tate
Cavepeople.......Perry Anzilotti, Jeff Chayette, Julie Maddalena,
    Michelan Sisti

Director: Reza Badiyi    Writers: Michael Jacobs & Bob Young

3. "Hurling Day" May 10, 1991

Earl's anxious to toss his mother-in-law into the tar pit on her
imminent 72nd birthday, as is dinosaurs' euthanizing custom.

Voice of ancient dinosaur chief Bob LaBrea.........Harold Gould
Performers/operators, Bob LaBrea.........Kevin Clash, Michelan
    Sisti
Caveperson.......................................................Michelan Sisti

Director: Tom Trbovich                    Writer: Rob Ulin

4. "High Noon" May 17, 1991

When Gary, a gigantic dinosaur nine times Earl's size, covets
Fran, Earl must fight or flee. Orig. scheduled for May 24.

Voice of Gary................................................Steve Landesberg

Director: Tom Trbovich                    Writer: Victor Fresco

5. "The Howling" May 24, 1991

On his 15th birthday, Robbie rebels against the dinosaur tradition of howling as the adulthood rite-of-passage.

Director: Jay Dubin                       Writer: Rob Ulin

Unaired

"Employee of the Month"

The Sinclairs prepare for a visit from Earl's fearsome boss.
Orig. scheduled for May 17 and May 24.

**renewed for 1991-92; new episodes begin Sept. 18, 1991**

## Disney Presents The 100 Lives of Black Jack Savage

NBC     April 5-19     Fridays, 8-9 p.m.
            May 12-26    Sundays, 7-8 p.m.

Series premiere: March 31, 1991
Final telecast: May 26, 1991

Action-adventure fantasy of a billionaire white-collar fugitive
(Kelly) who flees to the fictional Caribbean island of San Pietro,
and sublets a castle haunted by a 17th-century pirate, who
informs his modern counterpart both face damnation unless
they can right the wrongs of their lives. Episodes introduced
by Disney chairman/CEO Michael Eisner. Filmed in Florida.

Barry Tarberry.............................................Daniel Hugh Kelly
Black Jack Savage.................................Stoney Jackson (ep. 1)
Black Jack Savage...........................Steven Williams (ep. 2-on)
Danielle St. Clair..............................................Roma Downey
Gov. Gen. Vasquez, the island dictator.................Bert Rosario
Logan "F.X." Murphy............................................Steve Hytner

Stephen J. Cannell Productions in assoc. with Walt Disney
    Television
Executive producer: Stephen J. Cannell
Co-executive producers: James Wong, Glen Morgan
Supervising producers: Jo Swerling Jr., Jack Bernstein (latter
    ep. 2-on)
Producer: John Peter Kousakis
Co-producers: Alan Cassidy, Daniel Hugh Kelly (latter
    ep. 4-on)
Story editor: Gary Rosen
Director of photography: Frank Johnson, A.S.C.
Theme (instrumental with uncredited voiceover) and music:
    Mike Post
Creators: James Wong & Glen Morgan and Stephen J. Cannell

1. "Disney Presents The 100 Lives of Black Jack Savage"
    Sunday, March 31, 1991 9-11 p.m.

Abetted by a genius tinkerer's (Hytner) high-tech boat, the duo
try to solve the disappearances of fishermen on a remote reef
amid sea caves containing Black Jack's buried treasure.

Tony Gianini................................................................Tobin Bell
Reya Montenegro.....................................................Roya Megnot
Jean Paul.................................................................SaMi Chester
Brigette...............................................................Veronica Lauren
Diggs Munroe...........................................................Ed Amatrudo
Napoleon Bird.........................................................W. Paul Bodie
Bobby Neusch................................................................Joe Hess
Quick Cunningham.............................................Marc Macaulay

Director: Kim Manners
Writer: Stephen J. Cannell (James Wong and Glen Morgan
    also orig. announced)

2. "A Pirate Story" April 5, 1991

The duo join forces to rescue an infant stranded on a scuttled
fishing boat after modern-day pirates kill the vessel's owners.

Christy............................................................Caroline Williams
Dave.......................................................................Scott Bryce
Harmon Willow....................................................William Horne
Zack Philips..........................................................Tom Schuster
Baby Jennifer............................................................Carly Rothlein
And: Kevin Quigley, Monica Zaffarano, Glenn Masra, Emiliano
    Diez, Craig Parrish, Kristy Feil, Omar Cabral, Julie Upton

Director: Kim Manners        Writer: Stephen J. Cannell

3. "A Day in the Life of Logan Murphy"  April 12, 1991

Special-effects expert Logan is the target of an escaped, convicted drug smuggler who once owned Barry's castle.

Hancock............................................................David Marciano
FBI agent Gwynn..........................................Julius J. Carry III
Menoc.................................................................Tom Nowiski
Officer Hograth...........................................Will Knickerbocker
McCrae........................................................................Ivan Cejas
Convicts....................................Matt Mearian, Ben Ferguson

Director: Tucker Gates
Writers: Glen Morgan & James Wong

4. "Deals Are Made to Be Broken"  April 19, 1991

When a fake Black Jack drives away terrified villagers, Tarberry suspects a real-estate scheme by his ex-wife (Adams). Megnot reprises her role from ep. 1. Orig. scheduled for April 12.

Marla.........................................................Mary Kay Adams
Otis Boot...................................................Michael Chiklis
Reya Montenegro...................................................Roya Megnot
Gustave...............................................Ismael (East) Carlos
Exorcist.................................................Alexander Panas
Ramon.................................................Robert Escobar
Sila.......................................................Yolanda Arenas
And:  John Archie (Villager), Elmer Bailey (Jail guard), Parris
     Buckner (FBI agent), Omar Cabral (Guard), Scott Gallin
     (Larry), Francisco Padura (Room service person)

Director: David Nutter
Writers: Glen Morgan & James Wong

**preempted April 26 and May 3**

5. "Look for the Union Label"  May 12, 1991

A Miami lawyer (Calloway) tries to organize natives in the island's untamed interior against encroaching ranchers.

Renee Horton.......................................Vanessa Bell Calloway
Julio..................................................................Carlos Gomez
Man.....................................................................Carlos Cestero
Sebastian.....................................................Guillermo Gentile
Father.....................................................................Julian Bevans
And: Dorette Young (Mother), W. Lawrence Flakes (Cop),  Bob-
     by Rodriguez (Masseur/Raoul), Tara Anderson (Blonde)

Director: James Whitmore, Jr.        Writer: Jack Bernstein

6. "The Not-So-Great Dictator"  May 19, 1991

The duo must try to save an exiled dictator (Djola) from rebel
forces, his mistress (Gorg), and his alleged friend Vasquez.

Premier Francois Benoit........................................Badja Djola
Luce..........................................................................Galyn Gorg
Commandos................................Tony Bolano, Steve Chambers
Otto...............................................................George Bustamante
Hugo.........................................................................Steve Carter
Corp. DuBois........................................................George Lauzardo
Priest.......................................................................Rex Benson
Vasquez's aide........................................................Omar Cabral
Military officer.......................................................Xavier Coronel
Soldier.................................................................Raul Santidrian

Director: Jorge Montesi        Writer: Gary Rosen

7. "For Whom the Wedding Bell Tolls"  May 26, 1991

While he tries to help a rejected groom (Ben-Victor), the bride-
to-be (Beck) falls for Tarberry.

Charlie.............................................................Paul Ben-Victor
Connie..............................................................Kimberly Beck
Charlie's father.......................................................Lou Bedford
Muggers..........................................Rene Rokk, Joe Camerieri
And: Mark McCracken (Freddie), Dave Corey (Bronco),  Antho-
     ny Giaimo (Bartender), David Morand (Waiter)

Director: Bruce Kessler        Writer: Gary Rosen

## Doctor Doctor

| CBS | Sept 19-Oct. 3 | Wednesdays, 8:30-9 p.m. |
| | Oct. 18-Jan. 3 | Thursdays, 9:30-10 p.m. |
| | June 8-July 6 | Saturdays, 10-10:30 p.m. |

Series premiere:  June 12, 1989
Final telecast: July 6, 1991

Comedy of an offbeat Rhode Island doctor and local-TV medical authority (on *Wake Up Providence...*, WNTW-TV).

Dr. Mike Stratford........................................................Matt Frewer
Dr. Abraham Butterfield...............................Julius J. Carry III
Dr. Grant Linowitz.......................................................Beau Gravitte
Dr. Dierdre Bennett........................................Maureen Mueller
Richard Stratford, Mike's brother......................Tony Carreiro
Nurse Faye Barylski..................................Audrie J. Neenan •
Dr. Leona Linowitz, Grant's sister
     (ep. 3-14, 16)...............................Anne Elizabeth Ramsay

• Neenan, upgraded within a few episodes from recurring
  guest to cast-member, is credited alternately as either, evidently because the airdate order differs from the order in
  which the episodes were produced.

Nikndaph productions and Reeves Entertainment, a Thames
     Television Co.
Executive producers: Norman Steinberg, David Frankel
Supervising producers: Martin Rips, Joseph Staretski
Producers: Bruce Chevillat
Co-producer: John Amodeo
Executive story editors: Terri Minsky, David Blum, Roberto
     Benabib, Karl Fink
Story editors: Joseph E. Toplyn, Jim Herzfeld, Jonathan
     Feldman (later in season)
Medical consultant: Leonard Schwartzman, M.D.
Director of photography: Tony Yarlett
Music: Artie Butler
Theme: "Good Lovin'" by Rudy Clark and Arthur Resnick;
     arranged by Artie Butler; performed by John Batdorf;
     formerly a 1966 #1 single by The Young Rascals, and
     originally recorded by the Olympics
Creator: Norman Steinberg

---

1. "Ch-Ch-Ch-Changes"  Sept. 19, 1990;
   Friday, Sept. 28, 1990  midnight-12:30 a.m.

Mike rebels when his partners revamp the practice to become
more cost-effective, heedless of patients' needs.

Ella Wilkes........................................................Ja'net DUBOIS
Carl Wilkes.........................................................Earl Billings
Laura..................................................................Darlene Vogel

Happy Hobart.................................................David Strassman
Harold.........Chuck Wood (Strassman's ventriloquist's dummy)

Director: Norman Steinberg
Writer: Norman Steinberg & David Frankel

2. "Murder, He Wrote"  Sept. 26, 1990

A mystery novelist's husband dies mysteriously after Mike helps the writer by prescribing an undetectable poison.

Olivia Judd.....................................................Maxine Stuart
Ramon..........................................................Andrew Roa
Bill Jansen....................................................Gary Riley
Officer Dickerson...........................................Duke Moosekian

Director: Robert Berlinger          Writer: Joseph E. Toplyn

3. "Who's Afraid of Leona Linowitz?"  Oct. 3, 1990

Mike meets Grant's neurotic divorced sister (Ramsay), who sets up a psychiatric practice in their medical building.

Emily Linowitz, Leona's daughter (8).....................Anna Slotky
Axel..............................................................Christopher Maleki
And: Jana Marie Hupp (Lita), David Arnott (Usher/Ken)

Director: David Frankel
Writers: Karl Fink & Roberto Benabib

**preempted Oct. 10**

4. "Making Mr. Right"  Oct. 18, 1990

Diedre's new boyfriend (Daughton), the playboy pilot of a private jet, dies after making love with her at the controls.

Pia Bismarck, Mike's TV co-host...........................Sarah Abrell
Kevin............................................................James Daughton
Bald driver....................................................Richard Dubin
          Also orig. announced: Charles W. Knapp (Bald man)

Director: Zane Buzby
Writers: Martin Rips & Joseph Staretski

5. "The Terminator"  Oct. 25, 1990

Mike is compelled to fire Leona's obnoxious new assistant (Rocket), complicated by his dating Mike's gay brother.

Charles.........................................................Charles Rocket
Vlad Alucard (erroneously given as
          "Alacarte" onscreen)...................................Time Winters

Director: James Widdoes          Writer: Ron Burla

6. "Providence"  Nov. 1, 1990

Mike attempts a reconciliation between his gay brother and his homophobic father, who gets into an accident on the way.

Connie Stratford, Mike and Richard's mother......Inga Swenson
Dr. Martin Tomkins.........................................Dan Martin
Hugh Persons..................................................Brian George

Director: Norman Steinberg
Writers: Norman Steinberg & David Frankel

7. "The Last Temptation of Mike"  Nov. 8, 1990

Mike and Leona, alone in his apartment, are drawn to each

other.   Guest Sagansky is president of CBS Entertainment.

Himself...........................................................Jeff Sagansky
Emily.............................................................Anna Slotsky

Director: James Widdoes
Writers: David Blum & Terri Minsky

8. "Ice Follies"  Nov. 15, 1990

At hockey practice, Mike accidentally hurts Abe's son (Taylor), apparently disabling him on the eve of a championship game. Abrell reprises her role from ep. 4.

Pia Bismarck...................................................Sarah Abrell
Justin Butterfield............................................Marlon A. Taylor
Coach.............................................................Mitch Pileggi

Director: Art Dielhenn          Teleplay: Joseph E. Toplyn
Story: Tom Spezialy & Alan Cross and Joseph E. Toplyn

9. "The Young and the Hopeless"  Nov. 22, 1990

Mike must fire the beautiful but unprofessional receptionist (Theiss) whom Grant is dating.  Orig. scheduled for Nov. 1.

Katie Benson...................................................Brookie Theiss
Candice..........................................................Samantha Kaye
Victor Caruso..................................................Rick Hall
Gina..............................................................Kimberly Neville
Dusty.............................................................Alejandro Quezada

Director: David Frankel          Writer: Jonathan Feldman

10. "Good Doc, Bad Doc"  Nov. 29, 1990

When a patient, who neglected to inform Mike she was already on medication, falls gravely ill, her niece sues for malpractice. Part 1 of 3.

Sheldon Boehm.................................................Don Lake
Sadie Mitchell.................................................Amzie Strickland
Attorney Suzanne Moore....................................Ann Marie Lee
Mr. Fujiyama...................................................Peter Kwong
Loman............................................................Michael Burger
Lance Link.......................................................Roger Nolan
          Also orig. announced: Jonathan Schmock (Karl)

Director: Art Dielhenn          Writer: Jim Herzfeld

11. "Malpractice Makes Imperfect"  Dec. 6, 1990

When Mike feuds publicly with the attorney (Lee) suing him for malpractice, his patients start canceling appointments. Part 2 of 3.

Sheldon Boehm.................................................Don Lake
Attorney Suzanne Moore....................................Ann Marie Lee
Hugh Persons...................................................Brian George
Mr. Ed...........................................................John Menick
Sarah Ballantyne..............................................Pearl Shear
Tiny boy.........................................................Thomas Hobson
Mrs. Cratchit..................................................Yvette Freeman

Director: John Neal          Writer: Jim Herzfeld

12. "Somewhere in the Berkshires"  Dec. 13, 1990

After being forced to settle out of court, Mike decides to give up medicine and go live in the mountains, where he finds himself compelled to treat the locals.  Part 3 of 3.

Hugh Persons.....................................................Brian George
Sam...............................................................Don Gibb
Casey..........................................................Beans Morocco
Dr. Julia Lawson...............................................Dana Stevens

Director: Norman Steinberg
Writers: Roberto Benabib & Karl Fink

13. "When Bad Books Happen to Good People"  Dec. 20, 1990

Mike's novel about a group of doctors hits too close to home.
George reprises his role from ep. 11-12, Burger from ep. 10.

Paisley Brookstone...................................Judith-Marie Bergan
Hugh Persons...................................................Brian George
Loman........................................................Michael Burger
Process server..................................................Gary Pagett

Director: Robert Berlinger
Writers: Terri Minsky & David Blum

**preempted Dec. 27**

14. "Sleeping Sickness"  Jan. 3, 1991

Richard, overwrought from a play he's directing, develops a
sleeping-pill addiction unknowingly fed by the doctors.

Miss Woonsocket (orig. Miss Westerly
       Pawtucket)...............................................Rhonda Shear
Mercutio..................................................Morgan Strickland

Director: James Widdoes          Writer: Eugene B. Stein

**on hiatus**

15. "Anatomy of Love"  June 8, 1991

Mike is again smitten by the photographer (Hillwood, wife of
star Frewer, reprising her role from last season) who'd dumped
him, and who now has a revealing photo of him in a show.

Jenna Lathrop...............................................Amanda Hillwood
Art gallery owner.................................................Jeff Austin

Director: Peter Bonerz          Writer: Joseph E. Toplyn

16. "Butterfields Are Free"  June 15, 1991

Mike's suggestion that Abe and his wife (Calloway) go off on a
romantic weekend backfires, and they wind up separated.
Orig. scheduled for Jan. 3 and June 22.

Gail Butterfield.....................................Vanessa Bell Calloway
       Also orig. announced:
       David Arnott (Warren Kaufman)

Director: Robert Berlinger          Writer: Neena Beber

17. "Butterfield's Complaint"  June 22, 1991

Mike sets up the separated Abe on his first date in more than
12 years.  Guest Strawberry is a pro baseball player with the
Los Angeles Dodgers, formerly with the New York Mets.

Himself...........................................................Darryl Strawberry
Rachel Patton....................................................Tracey Ross

Director: Robert Berlinger          Writer: Jonathan Feldman

**preempted June 29**

18. "Two Angry Men"  July 6, 1991

Mike and Richard discover their father is having an affair.
Orig. scheduled for June 15.  Matthews, a cast-member of
*Down Home*, reprises his role from the series' first six episodes
and the 1989-90 season premiere.

Dr. Harold Stratford.........................................Dakin Matthews
Roxanne Abrams...............................................Beth Broderick
       Also orig. announced
       Dana Steele, Faye's boyfriend..................Daniel McVicar

Director: Robert Berlinger          Writer: Terri Minsky

**on hiatus, then cancelled**

Unaired

"Long Day's Journey Into Deirdre"

Mike offers to marry Deirdre, who after a patient dies is left
shaken, depressed, and fearful of growing old alone.  Orig.
scheduled for July 13.  Abrell reprises her role from ep. 4.

Pia Bismarck.......................................................Sarah Abrell
Justice of the Peace............................................Basil Langton

Director: Robert Berlinger
Writers: Karl Fink & Roberto Benabib

## Doogie Howser, M.D.

ABC                    Wednesdays, 9-9:30 p.m.

Series premiere: Sept. 19, 1989

Seriocomedy of a teen-prodigy doctor, a third-year resident at
the large Eastman Medical Center in Los Angeles.

Douglas "Doogie" Howser (17)......................Neil Patrick Harris
Dr. David Howser, his father.......................James B. Sikking
Katherine O'Brien Howser, his mother......Belinda Montgomery
Vinnie Delpino.....................................................Max Casella
Dr. Canfield...............................................Lawrence Pressman
Dr. Jack McGuire.........................................Mitchell Anderson
Nurse Curly Spaulding.....................................Kathryn Layng
Janine Stewart......................................................Lucy Boryer
Wanda Plenn (ep. 2-on)...................................Lisa Dean Ryan
Raymond Alexander (ep. 2-on)......................Markus Redmond

*Recurring:*
Dr. Welch (ep. 2-3,11-12,16,21-22,25).....................Rif Hutton

Steven Bochco Productions in assoc. with Twentieth Century
       Fox
Executive producer: Steven Bochco
Supervising producers: Linda Morris, Vic Rauseo, Stephen
       Cragg
Senior producers: Scott Goldstein, Phil Kellard, Tom Moore
Producer: Joe Ann Fogle
Co-producers: Mark Horowitz (later in season), Mitchel Lee
       Katlin, Nat Bernstein
Supervising associate producer (early in season): Mark Horo-
       witz
Associate producer: Jeffrey A. Henry
Executive story editors: Nick Harding (later in season), Hollis
       Rich
Story editor (early in season): Nick Harding
Creative consultant: David E. Kelley
Director of photography: Michael D. O'Shea

Medical consultants: Gareth Wootton, M.D., Barbara M. Kadell, M.D.
Theme (instrumental) and music: Mike Post
Creators: Steven Bochco & David E. Kelley

---

1. "Doogenstein" Sept. 12, 1990 (1202)

Doogie's heavy third-year residency duties make him fear he's missing out on his youth.

Voice of Dr. Greenberg.............................Jay Gerber
Philip Leonetti...................................Paul Kent
Michael Leonetti..............................Michael Bendetti

Director: Eric Laneuville
Writers: Vic Rauseo & Linda Morris

2. "Guess Who's Coming to Doogie's" Sept. 19, 1990

A former gang-member (new cast-member Redmond, reprising his role from last season) gets a job at the hospital.

Archie Sullivan...................................Stan Kamber
Alvin...........................................SaMi Chester
Paramedic.........................................Al Septien

Director: Stephen Cragg
Writers: Mitchel Lee Katlin & Nat Bernstein

3. "Ask Dr. Doogie" Sept. 26, 1990 (1204)

Doogie becomes a media star when he appears in a series of teen-oriented TV public service announcements.

Director.........................................James Paradise
Janet.............................................Kendra Booth
Girl in shower............................Kathy Christopherson
Blondes......................................Tiffany Muxlow, Sharon Case

Director: Ed Sherin
Writers: Phil Kellard & Tom Moore

4. "C'est La Vinnie" Oct. 3, 1990

A panicky Vinnie gets stuck in an elevator with his pregnant French teacher (Kuzyk) as she goes into labor.

Claire Feldblum...................................Mimi Kuzyk
Father............................................Jeff Harlan
William Guillaume...............................Eugene Pack
Mechanic.........................................Harry Herman

Director: Joan Darling          Writer: Michael Swerdlick

5. "Car Wars" Oct. 10, 1990

Doogie brings home a classic '50s convertible, but his dad doesn't want to let him keep it.

Frank Murison.....................Kenneth David Gilman
Dr. Butterworth................................Jennifer Rhodes
Trish.............................................Kerry Remsen

Director: Brad Silberling          Writer: Nick Harding

6. "Doogie Sings the Blues" Oct. 17, 1990

The homeless old man Doogie treats for a hearing loss claims to be a legendary blues musician.

Blind Otis Lemon..................................Joe Seneca
Joe............................................Teddy Wilson
Jimmy...........................................Art Evans
Dr. Phil Stoessl................................Scanlon Gail
Nurse.........................................Louisa Abernathy

Director: Eric Laneuville          Teleplay: Michael B. Kaplan
Story: Vic Rauseo & Linda Morris and Nat Bernstein & Mitchel Lee Katlin

7. "Academia Nuts" Oct. 24, 1990 (1203)

Vinnie passes off one of Doogie's old biology papers as his own; Doogie balks at Canfield's suggestion he "find something wrong" with a wealthy hypochondriac (Bruce).

Mrs. Beatrice Portmeyer..........................Carol Bruce
Cathcart......................................Roy Brocksmith
Norman........................................Charles Levin
Animal trainer..................................John Miranda
Voice of Mr. Delpino............................Don Calfa (uncredited)

Director: Ed Sherin          Writer: Nick Harding

8. "Revenge of the Teenage Dead" Oct. 31, 1990

Vinnie recruits a young medical prodigy (Pettiet), placed in Doogie's care, to star in his amateur horror video.

Gregory Pelzman...........................Christopher Pettiet
Stuart Pelzman................................Edward Edwards
Prof. Laura Forrest............................Elyse Donalson

Director: Win Phelps
Writers: Mitchel Lee Katlin & Nat Bernstein

9. "Nautilus for Naught" Nov. 7, 1990

When Wanda becomes infatuated with a narcissistic art student/model (Cedar), Doogie tries to bulk up at the gym; Doogie treats a fashion model (Byrne) for bulimia.

Sasha.........................................Martha Byrne
Greg..........................................Jason Brooks
Dr. Rickett..................................Barry Livingston
Roger...........................................Larry Cedar
Waitress.......................................Holly Ryan
Muscle man..................................Troy L. Zuccolotto
Nurse Kidd...................................Sandy Rosenberg

Director: Matia Karrell
Writers: Neil Landau & Tara Ison and Nick Harding

10. "Don't Let the Turkeys Get You Down" Nov. 14, 1990

Mom's folks come for Thanksgiving, with grandpa irking Doogie's dad; Janine's folks want her to stop dating Vinnie.

Don O'Brien..................................Tim O'Connor
Irene O'Brien.................................Gloria Henry
Mr. Stewart....................................Noel Conlon
Patient.........................................Ben Kronen

Director: David Carson          Writer: Nick Harding

**preempted Nov. 21**

11. "Oh Very Young" Nov. 28, 1990

Age is at issue when young Doogie applies to a surgical training program, and "old" Canfield starts dating Nurse Spaulding.

Dr. Jonathan Reardon..............................Granville Van Dusen
Heather...............................................................Adrian Pearson
Girl in crowd..................................................Mauri Bernstein
Resident.................................................................Beverly Nero
  Also orig. announced:
  Max Grodenchik (Scalper)

Director: Joan Darling  Writers: Vic Rauseo & Linda Morris

12. "TV or Not TV"  Dec. 5, 1990

A hospitalized network-TV head (McCarthy) is besieged by med-center members with ideas for series based on their lives.

Bradford Eisner..................................................Jeff McCarthy
Karl....................................................................Paul Benvictor
Bob..............................................................................Ken Daly
Al...............................................................................Ron Perkins
Paramedic...............................................................Al Septien

Director: Joan Tewkesbury
Writers: Phil Kellard & Tom Moore

13. "A Woman Too Far"  Dec. 12, 1990

Doogie considers going behind Wanda's back to date a nursing student (McAdam), and helps a bigamist (McManus) keep his wives from meeting each other.  Preceded at 8:30 by a rerun.

Roy Lester......................................................Michael McManus
Lisa Fredericks..............................................Heather McAdam
Joanne Lester......................................................Candice Azzara
Marge Lester......................................................Patty McCormack
Heather...............................................................Shari Shattuck
Dennis.....................................................John Robert LaFleur
  Also orig. announced: Garth Wilton (Waiter)

Director: Victoria Hochberg
Writers: Phil Kellard & Tom Moore

14. "Presumed Guilty"  Jan. 2, 1991

Vinnie accidentally wrecks the Howsers' classic '57 convertible.

Clayton Wilburn.......................................Billy "Sly" Williams
Mechanic.............................................................Dave Conrades
Paramedic...........................................................Timothy Hughes

Director: Stephen Cragg
Writers: Phil Kellard & Tom Moore

15. "To Live and Die in Brentwood"  Jan. 9, 1990

When Wanda's mother is struck critically ill, a chastened Doogie learns of the emotions felt by his patients' loved ones.

Mr. Plenn, Wanda's father........................................Bill Hudson
Mrs. Plenn, Wanda's mother.............................Sherry Rooney
Funeral director............................................................Bill Shick
Mrs. Green..........................................................Linda LoPorto
Mr. Green..................................................................David Muir
Men......................................................Paul Ivy, Paul Navarra
Woman.........................................................Gwen Van Dam

Director: Scott Goldstein
Writers: Nat Bernstein & Mitchel Lee Katlin

16. "Air Doogie"  Jan. 23, 1991

The athletically unskilled Doogie joins a basketball game between his hospital and a rival.  Erving, in a dream sequence,

is a pro basketball player.  Orig. scheduled for Jan. 16.

Himself.................................................Julius "Dr. J." Erving
Trish Andrews...........................................................Jada Pinkett
Dr. Ramsey..............................................................Larry Gelman
Dr. Goodland......................................................Greg Callahan
Referee...........................................................Richard James Baker

Director: Rob Thompson
Writer: Mitchel Lee Katlin & Nat Bernstein

17. "A Life in Progress"  Jan. 30, 1991

A hospital mural project by children is blocked when the hospital learns the adult artist (Clohessy) supervising it has AIDS.

Jeff Moore....................Robert Clohessy a.k.a. Robert Clohesse
Phillip Lawrence..............................................James Callahan
Jerry Pierpont..............................................James McMullan
Samantha.............................................Danielle Zuckerman
Joy Curson.............................................................Mimi Bensinger
And: Thomas V. Mikkelsen (Reporter), Russ Bolinger (Big guy)

Director: Sandy Smolan  Writer: Hollis Rich

18. "My Two Dads"  Feb. 6, 1991

With Vinnie not getting along with his own dad (Calfa), Doogie and his father invite him on their annual father-son outing. Calfa had done a voiceover in ep. 7.

Carmine Delpino.........................................................Don Calfa
Pete..............................................................James Oden Hatch

Director: Bill D'Elia  Writer: Nick Harding

19. "Nobody Expects the Spanish Inquisition"  Feb. 13, 1991

When Doogie's caustic grandfather drives off workers remodeling the kitchen, he and Doogie take over the job.  O'Connor and Henry reprise their roles from ep. 10.

Don O'Brien...........................................................Tim O'Connor
Irene O'Brien...........................................................Gloria Henry
Bill Stapleton.............................................Christopher Collins
Nora McDonald.............................................Courtney Gebhart
Dennis McDonald.......Douglas McKay (Douglas Steindorff orig.
  announced)
Luis.................................................................Daniel Faraldo
Miguel...................................................................Rudy Prieto

Director: Stephen Cragg  Writer: Nick Harding

20. "Fatal Distraction"  Feb. 20, 1991  8-8:30 p.m.

With Wanda busy with new responsibilities following her mother's death, and Doogie attracted to a student nurse (Lively), Wanda and Doogie break up.  Orig. scheduled for Feb. 13.

Michele Faber.........................................................Robyn Lively
Maggie Plenn, Wanda's little sister....................Netahly Leddel
Janet...............................................................Deenie Dakota
Nurses.....Kimberly Neville, Kristine Blackburn, Amy Tenowich

Director: Gabrielle Beaumont
Writers: Phil Kellard & Tom Moore

**unscheduled preemption Feb. 27**

21. "The Doctor, The Wife, Her Son and Her Job"
  March 13, 1991

Katherine's decision to work at Eastman as a patient advocate disrupts her household and embarrasses Doogie. Kamber reprises his role from ep. 2. Orig. scheduled for Feb. 27.

Archie Sullivan......................................Stan Kamber
Mr. Quian...............................................James Hong
Mrs. Diaz..............................................Victoria Racimo
Patient..................................................Glen Vernon
Paramedic.............................................Carlease Burke

Director: Brad Silberling          Writer: Hollis Rich

22. "Planet of the Dateless"  March 20, 1991

Doogie lets mom arrange a blind date after Michele breaks up with him; McGuire's jealous of Doogie. Lively reprises her role from ep. 20; director Tabori, the son of actress Viveca Lindfors and director Don Siegel, is known primarily as an actor.

Michele Faber.......................................Robyn Lively
Dr. Michaels........................................David Selburg
Sarah...................................................Carla Gugino
Julie Kellogg.........................................Robin Gordon
April.....................................................Kimberly Sissons
Woman at airport...................................Nora Masterson
Patient at airport....................................Joel Lawrence

Director: Kris Tabori
Writers: Nat Bernstein & Mitchel Lee Katlin

23. "Doogie's Wager"  April 3, 1991  8:30-9 p.m.

Doogie delivers a premature baby struggling for its life; Vinnie gets rejection letters from film schools. Director Haid is a former cast-member of Hill Street Blues.

Albert Einstein......................................Rene Auberjonois
Mrs. Hollister.......................................Anne Lockhart
Mr. Hollister.........................................Alan McRae
Priest....................................................Tony Steedman
Madame Dorina....................................Carol Ann Susi
Dr. Biddison.........................................Pamela Roberts
Premature infant....................................Jacob Ulnick

Director: Charles Haid          Writer: Hollis Rich

24. "A Kiss Ain't Just a Kiss"  April 24, 1991

Vinnie "cheats" on Janine, who then turns to Doogie; Raymond's dad, who'd long abandoned him, appears in the E.R. Burke reprises her role from ep. 21.

John Alexander, Raymond's father.............Michael D. Roberts
Phyllis Maldarelli...................................Jennifer Gatti
Paramedic.............................................Carlease Burke

Director: Scott Goldstein     Story: Vic Rauseo & Linda Morris
Teleplay: Mitchel Lee Katlin & Nat Bernstein and Nick Harding

25. "Dances With Wanda"  May 1, 1991

Doogie has difficulty persuading a mourning Wanda to go to her senior prom with him.

Kelly....................................................Linda Larkin
Dr. Isaacs.............................................Ron Recasner
Nerds..................................Angelika Sequeira, Michael Bower
And: The USC Trojan Marching Band

Director: Steve Robman
Writers: Phil Kellard & Tom Moore

renewed for 1991-92; new episodes begin Sept. 25, 1991

## Down Home

NBC          Saturdays, 8:30-9 p.m.

Series premiere: April 12, 1990
Final telecast: Aug. 3, 1991

Comedy of a successful New York career woman who returns to her hometown fishing village of Hadley Cove, Texas to help save the family cafe-and-bait shop (McCrorey's Landing) from real-estate interests led by the boyfriend (Baker) she'd left 15 years ago. Co-executive producer Danson is a star of Cheers; story editor Sorkin is co-host of America's Funniest People; producer Christopher Lloyd is not the actor of the same name.

Kate McCrorey......................................Judith Ivey
Wade Prescott.......................................Ray Baker
Drew McCrorey, Kate's brother.................Eric Allan Kramer
Walt McCrorey, Kate's father...................Dakin Matthews
Grover, the Mayor..................................Timothy Scott
Tran Van Dinh, the cook..........................Gedde Watanabe

Savage Cake Productions and Jabberwocky Productions in
    assoc. with Paramount Television
Executive producers: Barton Dean, Dan Fauci, Ted Danson,
Producers: Christopher Lloyd, Jace Richdale
Co-producer: Ken Kuta
Coordinating producer: Bruce Kerner
Associate producer: Stephen K. Rose
Executive script consultant: Richard Day
Story editor (later in season): Arleen Sorkin
Director of photography: Thom Marshall
Theme (instrumental) and music: Stewart Levin
Creator: Barton Dean

———————————————

1. "Mail Order Tran"  Thursday, Feb. 28, 1991  9:30-10 p.m.

Tran faces jail or deportation for fooling a man (Tobolowsky) into bringing him to America as a mail-order bride.

Honis....................................................Stephen Tobolowsky
Priest....................................................Hal Landon, Jr.
Fisherman.............................................James Whitson
Deliveryperson.......................................J. Marvin Campbell

Director: Lee Shallat          Writer: Barton Dean

2. "This Has Been a Wade Political Announcement"
    March 2, 1991

Kate runs for mayor against Wade when it's revealed that Grover apparently is no longer eligible for reelection.

Lenny...................................................Harrison Young

Director: Lee Shallat          Writer: Ken Kuta

3. "Strange Bedfellows"  March 9, 1991

Country music star Randy Travis visits Hadley Cove for privacy; Kate and Wade fight against proposed off-shore oil drilling.

Himself.................................................Randy Travis
Swifcy..................................................Robert Machray
Bellperson............................................Patrick Shipstad
Nanci...................................................Nanci Kusley

Director: Lee Shallat       Writer: Richard Day

4. "Whatsamatta Drew" March 16, 1991  10:30-11 p.m.

A psychologist (Hearn) convinces Drew that his over-achieving, perfectionist sister is responsible for his personality problems. Orig. scheduled for March 2.

Dr. Gary Jacobs.................................................George Hearn

Writer-director: Douglas Wyman

5. "I'm Cooking as Fast as I Can" March 23, 1991

Kate oozes "helpless female" charm to prove she's not intimidating, then must reveal her true self to a catch (Kilner).

L.B. Taylor........................................................Kevin Kilner
Oil workers...............................Randall Oliver, Patrick Maguire
Sondra..............................................................Sondra Lieu

Director: Lee Shallat
Writers: Arleen Sorkin & Beth Milstein

6. "Don't Rock the Boat" March 30, 1991

The locals blame Kate for a disastrous Shrimp Day harvest since she defied local superstition by having sex on a shrimp boat. Director Ratzenberger is a cast-member of *Cheers*.

Officer.............................................................Larry Gilman
Floyd............................................................Hank Underwood

Director: John Ratzenberger       Writer: Richard Day

7. "The Good Fight" April 6, 1991

Kate loses her drive when Wade quits fighting with her over his condo scheme; Drew's new roommate is a wrestling bear. Underwood reprises his role from last episode.

Floyd............................................................Hank Underwood
Morris..............................................................Bennett Liss
Bear.......................................................Trishka (uncredited)

Director: Greg Antonacci       Writer: Jace Richdale

8. "You're Not Getting Older, You're Getting Deader"
    April 13, 1991

Kate hosts a party for the 100th birthday of the meanest man in town (Dotrice), who fakes dying to enjoy his funeral.

Jeremiah Hadley...................................................Roy Dotrice
Jeffrey..............................................................Fred Slyter
Father Fletcher...................................................Edward Penn
Baseball player.....................................................Jerry Giles

Director: Barton Dean       Writer: Christopher Lloyd

9. "Yipes, It's Snipes" April 20, 1991

To keep a 16-year-old wizard diesel mechanic (Bartok) from quitting his job, Kate reluctantly agrees to be his prom date.

Gunther Snipes..................................................Jayce Bartok
Augy...............................................................Ernie Lively
Fisherman.............................................George "Buck" Flower
Albert..............................................................Sean Whalen

Director: John Ratzenberger       Writer: Barton Dean

10. "Evian Spelled Backwards is Naive" April 27, 1991

Kate smells a scam when Drew quits his cafe job, goes to work for Wade's company, and quickly becomes Wade's boss.

Mr. Morton.......................................................Richard Doyle
Sandy..............................................................Deasa Turner
Customer......................................................Brad Blaisdell

Director: John Ratzenberger       Writer: Bruce Helford

11. "Dream Boat" May 4, 1991

Kate goes after her dad, upset he didn't say bye after finishing his 30-year boat project and sailing for the South Pacific. Joined in progress following an NBC News live telecast of a White House press conference.

Phoebe...........................................................Belle Calaway
Vendor...........................................................Tony Simotes

Director: Douglas Wyman       Writer: Ken Kuta

12. "Get Thee Back to a Nunnery" May 11, 1991

Tran objects to a budding romance between his visiting, convent-school sister (Gelman) and Drew; the guys participate in a Civil War reenactment. Orig. scheduled for April 27.

Trini Tran.......................................................Kimko Gelman

Director: Lee Shallat       Writer: Jace Richdale

13. "Black Widow" May 18, 1991

Walt becomes the romantic target of a widow (May) whose previous husbands reportedly suffered mysterious deaths.

Audrey...........................................................Deborah May
Emma.......................................................Patience Cleveland
Bagley...........................................................William Fuller
Paramedic........................................................David Homb

Director: Greg Antonacci       Writer: Christopher Lloyd

**cancelled; reruns begin June 29**

**preempted July 27**

## Dream On

HBO            Sundays  10-10:30 p.m.

Series premiere: July 1990

Comedy of a divorced New York City book editor, a TV child of the '50s whose thoughts we see expressed by clips of black-and-white TV shows (owned by MCA Television and including *General Electric Theater* and *Studio 57*). Each cycle of episodes runs July to October; only those within the yearbook's cut-off dates are listed. Information (incomplete) primarily per HBO.

Martin Tupper....................................................Brian Benben
Judith, his best-friend ex-wife.............................Wendie Malick
Toby, his secretary...............................................Denny Dillon
Jeremy Tupper, his son.......................................Chris Demetral
Talk-show host Eddie..........................................Dorien Wilson

Kevin Bright Productions in assoc. with MCA Televsion
Executive producer: John Landis, Kevin S. Bright

Co-executive producers (1991 season): David Crane, Marta
  Kauffman
Supervising producer: Bill Sanders
Producers (1991 season): Robb Idels, Ron Wolotzky
Producers (1990 season): Robb Idels, David Crane, Marta
  Kauffman, Ron Wolotzky
Story editors (1991 season): Jeff Greenstein, Jeff Strauss
Creators: David Crane & Marta Kauffman

---

12. "555-Hell" Sept. 23, 1990 11:30 p.m.-midnight

Martin's lonely weekend night is disrupted by a wrong number: a desperate woman trying to reach a suicide hotline. Director Thomas is a former cast-member of *Hill Street Blues*.
Gabrielle is the Dec. 1982 *Penthouse* Pet.

Announced cast includes: Catherine O'Hara, Monique Gabrielle

Director: Betty Thomas            Writer: Bernie Keating

13. "Doing the Bossa Nova" Sept. 30, 1990 11-11:30 p.m.

Martin is seduced by his new boss, who orders him to fire
Toby when she discovers their secret.

Director: Arlene Sanford
Writers: Jeff Greenstein & Jeff Strauss

14. "Premarital Ex" Oct. 7, 1990

Martin's ex-wife calls him to calm her premarital jitters -- per-
haps intimately.

Director: Arlene Sanford
Writers: David Crane & Marta Kauffman

**New cycle of first-run episodes begins July 7, 1991**

1. "The Second Greatest Story Ever Told"
   July 7, 1991 10-11 p.m.

When a film is being made of the life of Judith's new husband,
Dr. Stone, Martin falls for the actress (Rogers) playing Judith.

Announced cast includes:
Nick.....................................................................Tom Berenger
Film director Sir Roland.......................................David Bowie
Julia.....................................................................Mimi Rogers
And: Stephen Furst, Joey Travolta, Yvonne De Carlo, Eva
  Gabor, Ricardo Montalban

Director: John Landis
Writer: David Crane, Marta Kauffman

2. "And Your Little Dog, Too" July 14, 1991

A sleazy publisher (McKean) takes over the company, prompting Martin to commit the womanizing Eddie to a kiss-and-tell
autobiography. Director O'Hara is better known as an actress.

Announced cast includes:
Ben's boss.....................................................Michael McKean

Director: Catherine O'Hara
Writer: David Crane, Marta Kauffman

3. "The 37-Year Itch" July 21, 1991

Toby seems allergic to Martin's romantic cousin (Castellaneta).

Announced cast includes:
Phil........................................................Dan Castellaneta

Director: Betty Thomas            Writer: Dava Savel

4. "Calling the Kettle Black" July 28, 1991

A pot-smoking Martin faces his moral double-standard when
he confronts his son about smoking marijuana.

Director: Peter Baldwin
Writers: Jeff Greenstein, Jeff Strauss

5. "Futile Attraction" Aug. 4, 1991

While at a therapist's office for sexual dysfunction, Martin's attracted to a woman (Hecht) he later finds is violent during sex.

Announced cast includes:
Dr. Klein.................................................Martin Mull
Elaine.....................................................Gina Hecht

Director: Arlene Sanford
Writers: David Crane, Marta Kauffman

6. "No, I'm Just Happy to See You" Aug. 11, 1991

Martin buys a gun after he and Eddie are twice mugged.

Director: Arlene Sanford
Writers: Jeff Greenstein, Jeff Strauss

7. "What I Did for Lust" Aug. 18, 1991

Trying not to reject the bad manuscript of a prospective girlfriend, Martin gives it to his boss, who wants him to edit it.

Announced cast includes:
Chloe.....................................................Corinne Bohrer

Director: Bethany Rooney a.k.a. Bethany Rooney Hillshafer
Writer: Theresa Rebeck

8. "Play Melville for Me" Aug. 25, 1991

As host of a public-acces show on books, Martin must deal
with a psychotic fan (Kinney).

Announced cast includes: Kathy Kinney

Director: Arlene Sanford            Writer: Craig Hoffman

**New episodes scheduled through Oct. 6, followed by reruns
from Oct. 16-on; renewed for 1991-92.**

## E.A.R.T.H. Force

CBS            Saturdays, 9-10 p.m.

Series premiere: Sept. 16, 1990
Final telecast: Sept. 29, 1990

Adventure drama of a globe-trotting team of scientists funded
by the Earth Alert Foundation to fight threats to the ecology.
Filmed at Warner Roadshow Studios, Queensland, Australia.
Acronym stands for Earth Alert Research Tactical Headquarters. Working titles: *The Green Machine*, *The Elite*, *Eco-Force*.

Surgeon-geneticist Dr. John Harding.....................Gil Gerard
Administrator Diana Randall..........................Joanna Pacula

Nuclear physicist Carl Dana (orig. Adler)........Clayton Rohner
Pilot Charles Dillon...........................Stewart Finlay-McLennan
Marine biologist Catherine Romano......................Tiffany Lamb
Zoologist-anthropologist Peter Roland (ep. 1)....Robert Knepper

Chapman/Dial Productions in assoc. with Paramount
    Television
Executive producers: Richard Chapman, Bill Dial, Jeffrey M.
    Hayes
Producers: Arthur Fellows, Terry Keegan
Line Producer: Rod Allan (ep. 2-on)
Associate producer: Bernie Larramie (ep. 2-on)
Executive story consultant: Joe Shulkin
Director of photography: Martin McGrath (ep. 1): Barry
    Wilson
Environmental consultant: Teya Ryan
Music: Ken Harrison (ep. 1); Cory Lerios, John D'Andrea
Theme: Bill Conti
Creators: Richard Chapman and Bill Dial

------

1. "E.A.R.T.H. Force" Sunday, Sept. 16, 1990  9-11 p.m.;
    Tuesday, Sept. 25, 1990  11:30 p.m.-1:30 a.m.

When sabotage at a nuclear power plant triggers an alert, an
industrialist (Coleby) assembles a team to combat the crisis.

Frederick Mayer (orig. Winter)..............................Robert Coleby
Halloran.......................................................Lewis Fitz-Gerald
Bass..............................................................Stephen Leeder
Hunter...............................................................Alan Zitner

Director: Bill Corcoran
Writers: Richard Chapman & Bill Dial

2. "Not So Wild Kingdom"  Sept. 22, 1990

An animal broker for zoos (Russom) is discovered managing a
hunting range specializing in exotic endangered species.

Rucker....................................................................Leon Russom
Jim O'Brien...............................................................Scott Hoxby
Chappell................................................................Henk Johannes
Holland................................................................Harold Hopkins
La Pointe....................................................................Don Lane
Stillson...................................................................John O'Brien
Auctioneer.................................................................Jeff Wilken
Customs agent............................................................Rob Dator
Herrera......................................................................Nic Gazzana
Security guards......................Doug Meuller, Shaun Gibbons
And: Geoffrey Roberts (Pet store manager), Melitza Neill (Moth-
er), Joshua Jepperson (Boy), Arthur Skuthorpe (Hunter)

Director: Bill Corcoran
Writers: Richard Chapman & Bill Dial

3. Title NA  Sept. 29, 1990

A widow, whose son is dying of toxicity, asks the team to a
Kansas town that a big developer's landfill may be poisoning.

Mrs. McKenney.........................................Gwynyth Walsh
Sheriff Willard Hoyt....................................Dennis Grosvenor
Wooster..........................................................Steve Bisley
Robert Leckie.................................................John Larking
Warner.............................................................Paul Mason
David............................................Johnny Walker Jepperson

Director: Rod Hardy
Writers: Richard Chapman & Bill Dial

## Eddie Dodd

ABC      March 12-April 2   Tuesdays, 10-11 p.m.
          May 29-June 5     Wednesdays, 10-11 p.m.

Series premiere: March 12, 1991
Final telecast: June 5, 1991

Drama of a tough but idealistic "has-been" New York City attorney, a former radical activist, who champions lost causes.
Working title: *True Believer*, and for complicated rights purposes based, according to the producers, not on the 1989 theatrical film of that name, but on real-life San Francisco attorney J. Tony Serra, who inspired the film.

Edward J. (Eddie) Dodd......................................Treat Williams
Roger Bacon, his assistant.....................................Corey Parker
Private detective Kitty Greer..................................Sydney Walsh
Billie, Dodd's secretary..................................Anabelle Gurwitch

Lasker-Parkes Productions and Clyde Phillips Productions in
    assoc. with Columbia Pictures Television
Executive producers: Clyde Phillips, Walter F. Parkes,
    Lawrence Lasker
Co-executive producer: Peter Rosten
Supervising producer: R.W. Goodwin (orig. announced as:
    Producer: Bob Goodwin)
Executive story editors: P.K. Simonds, Jr., Christopher Keyser,
    Amy Lippman
Production consultant: Wesley Strick
Director of photography: Lloyd Ahern II
Music [and] Theme (instrumental): Dennis McCarthy
Creators: Walter F. Parkes & Wesley Strick & Lawrence Lasker

------

1. "Love and Death"  March 12, 1991

Eddie defends a former lover (Blakely), from ten years ago, on
charges she euthanized her critically ill husband.

Carolyn Sedgewick...............................................Susan Blakely
Prosecutor Jessica Tilden.................................Mary Cadorette
Lauren Sedgewick..............................................Lindsay Fisher
Dr. Garabedian.......................................................Ken Lerner
Mrs. Sedgewick..................................................Dorothy Dells
Judge.................................................................Pierre Epstein
Louise..................................................................
Punk...................................................................Roger Campo
Foreperson.........................................................Cynthia Frost
Sgt. Havisheim....................................................Russell Curry
Jessia's associate...........................................Peter Fitzsimmons

Director: Rob Cohen      Writer: Michael S. Chernuchin

2. "Solomon's Choice"  March 19, 1991

Eddie's mentor (Richardson), a judge suffering from Alzheimer's Disease, is assigned to a complex trial of Eddie's.

Judge Horn..........................................................Lee Richardson
Darryl Reed............................................................Keith Amos
D.A. Roth..........................................................Michael Durrell
Kaso....................................................................John Furlong
Bud Buxton....................................................David M. Parker
Judge Stuart....................................................Rudy Challenger
Rick Gamez........................................................Gino Cabanas
Benchlay.............................................................Johnny Silver
Zach Horn.............................................................David Wells
Seth Gustafson...............................................Danny de la Paz
Andy Malpaso.........................................................Mitch Hara

Arraignment Judge...................................................Helen Duffy
And: Patrik Balduff (Nolan), Pamela Gordon (Psychiatrist), Flo
Di Re (Woman), Susan Lentini (Asst. D.A.), Bo Sabato
(Jury foreperson), Brian Strauss (P.D.), Bo Zenga (Bailiff)

Director: Aaron Lipstadt
Writers: Matthew McDuffie and Christopher Keyser & Amy
Lippman

3. "Pound of Flesh" March 26, 1991

Eddie's defense of a white cop (Le May) accused of killing an
unarmed black youth is tempered by word of a police cover-
up. Taylor reprises her role from ep. 1.

Thomas Malcolm...................................................Bruce A. Young
Jack Flannery...................................................Bruce Kirby
Officer Sean Flannery...................................................John D. Le May
Corey's father...................................................Robert King
Judge...................................................Rhoda Gemignani
With: Adam Philipson
Dory Vine...................................................Shana Furlow
Chief McCullera...................................................Ric Mancini
Sharon Jackson...................................................Allison Dean
Kid...................................................Rich Battista
And: Scotty Brulee (Ike Robinson), Jerry Hauck (Doherty), Jodi
Taylor (Louise), Larry O. Williams, Jr. (Dwayne Benton)

Director: Ron Lagomarsino          Writer: Michael S. Chernuchin

4. "Unnecessary Losses" April 2, 1991

Eddie investigates after a tough reporter friend (Costanzo) is
mysteriously murdered while working on a major story. Cadorette reprises her role from ep. 1.

Prosecutor Jessica Tilden...................................................Mary Cadorette
Pauly Dibrio...................................................James Arone
Jake Spence...................................................Robert Costanzo
Charles Peck...................................................John Diehl
Agent Dwyer...................................................Joel Polis
Judge Harding...................................................Michael Fairman
With: James Borrelli, Tracey Walter
Shavian...................................................Don Stark
Morgue attendant...................................................Carlos Lacamara
Janet...................................................Marguerite DELAIN
And: Robert Nadder (Sturgis Unterford), Cedering Fox, Saida
Pagan (Reporters), Michael Petroni (Goon)

Director: Sandy Smolan          Writer: P.K. Simonds

**cancelled**

5. "Welcome Home" May 29, 1991

Eddie helps two radical-underground friends (Garfield, Snodgress) resurface after 20 years, unknowingly into a murder rap.

Benny Schaeffer...................................................Allen Garfield
Ellen Schaeffer...................................................Carrie Snodgress
Forst...................................................Thomas Ryan
Judge Oswald...................................................Richard Stahl
With: James Borrelli, Jim Doughan
Kasden...................................................Kent Williams
Carl Romney...................................................Earl Boen
Burt Finch...................................................Jimmie F. Skaggs
Garcia...................................Ismael Carlo a.k.a. Ismael (East) Carlo
And: Joseph Walter Davis (Claude Sanderson), Martin Azarow
(Officer), Loyda Ramos (Clerk), Anthony Russell (Foley)

Director: Larry Shaw

Writers: Amy Lippman & Christopher Keyser

6. "Excuses, Excuses" June 5, 1991

Eddie defends an allegedly corrupt senator whose daughter
(Bain) Roger defiantly dates. Orig. scheduled for April 2.

Julia Sprague...................................................Cynthia Bain
Senator Henry Sprague...................................................Stanley Kamel
Annandale...................................................Alan Feinstein
Judge Gilliam...................................................Abraham Alverez
With: Michael Holden, Michelle Moffett
Mitchell Tabori...................................................Brad Tatum
Alan Osbourne...................................................Rodney Saulsberry
Foreperson...................................................Naomi Serotoff
Reporters...............Al Sapienza, Nelson Mashita, Angela Moya

Director: David Carson
Writers: Christopher Keyser & Amy Lippman

## Empty Nest

NBC          Sept. 22-July 27     Saturdays, 9:30-10 p.m.
             Aug. 3-on            Saturdays, 9-9:30 p.m.

Series premiere: Oct. 8, 1988

Comedy of a widowed pediatrician at the Community Medical
Center in Miami, Fla., his two adult daughters living with him
(with an unseen third, Emily, away at college), and the friends
and women who want him to end his bachelorhood. Laverne's
hometown: Hickory. Bear's brother, Bodie, is a cast-member
of the USA Network afternoon series, *Dog House.*

Dr. Harry Weston...................................................Richard Mulligan
Barbara Weston...................................................Kristy McNichol
Carol Weston...................................................Dinah Manoff
Charley Dietz...................................................David Leisure
* Nurse Laverne Todd...................................................Park Overall
Dreyfuss (dog)...................................................Bear (uncredited)

* Given as "LaVerne" in *TV Guide*, but as "Laverne" in materials from NBC and the production company, Touchstone.

Witt Thomas Harris Productions in assoc. with Touchstone
Television
Executive producers: Paul Junger Witt, Tony Thomas, Gary
Jacobs
Supervising producers: Arnie Kogan, Susan Beavers
Producers: Roger Garrett, Rob LaZebnick, David Sacks, Harold
Kimmel, Gilbert Junger
Associate producer: Gwen McCracken
Executive story editor: Pat Dougherty
Story editors: Bill Braunstein, Sydney Blake
Bear trained by: Joel Silverman, Birds and Animals Unlimited
Music: George Aliceson Tipton
Theme: "Life Goes On" by George Aliceson Tipton and John
Bettis (words and music); performed by Billy Vera and
the Beaters
Director unless otherwise credited: Steve Zuckerman
Creator: Susan Harris

---

1. "A Flaw is Born" Sept. 22, 1990

Harry dates a world-famous brain surgeon (Thayer); Carol and
Barbara plot revenge on an inconsiderate man.

Dr. Lydia Gant...................................................Brynn Thayer

Monsieur Gerard...............................................Stanley Kamel
John Taylor...........................................................Tim Dunigan
Professor.......................................................Charles Stransky
Boy..................................................................Mitchell Allen

Writer: Susan Beavers

2. "Harry's Excellent Adventure"  Sept. 29, 1990

Harry joins a globe-trotting friend (Holliman) in Pamplona, Spain, for the running of the bulls.

Mike Bradovitch..............................................Earl Holliman
Lou..............................................................................Earl Boen
Gina..........................................................Debi A. Monahan
Russell....................................................................Robert Lesser
And: Billy Cohen (Stevie), Fred Sadoff (Mort)

Writer: Arnie Kogan

3. "There's No Accounting"  Oct. 6, 1990

Carol likes Barbara's new boyfriend (Terlesky), to whom Barbara's indifferent; Harry's great new beau (Carroll) bores him.

Bucky Barnes.....................................................John Terlesky
Leah...................................................................Janet Carroll
Gloria.................................................................Allison Mack

Writer: Gary Jacobs

4. "Barbara the Mom"  Oct. 13, 1990

Barbara babysits to try to determine if she has maternal instincts; Carol volunteers at the zoo.

Larry........................................................Christopher Castile
Annette.............................................................Sumer Stamper

Writer: Harold Kimmel

5. "The Tortoise & The Harry"  Oct. 20, 1990

Harry befriends a young patient (Bluhm) whose depression he can't seem to cure; Barbara tries taking Carol's art class.

Joey.......................................................................Brandon Bluhm
Mrs. Bierman...................................................Debra Mooney
Amanda.............................................................Jaclyn Bernstein

Writer: Roger Garrett

6. "Mad About the Boy"  Oct. 27, 1990

Harry grows concerned about Carol's dating despair when she brings home a mall cheese server (McKean). Orig. scheduled for Oct. 20.

Dennis....................................................................Michael McKean
Miss Bingham........................................Mary Catherine Wright
Russell.......................................................................Robert Lesser
Ian.............................................................Gregory Paul Martin

Writer: Pat Dougherty

7. "Honey, I Shrunk Laverne"  Nov. 3, 1990

Laverne quits when Harry complains she's making too many office decisions without consulting him.

Dr. Dawn Phelps.................................................Nana Visitor

Nurse Bradford.............................................Mary Pat Gleason
Art.........................................................................Art Metrano
John.................................................................John Apicella
Ed...........................................................................Ed Call

Writer: Miriam Trogdon

8. "The Boy Next Door"  Nov. 10, 1990

During a moment of mutual weakness, Carol and Charley have sex, and prepare to face the consequences.

Cindy..................................................................Candy Hutson
Mrs. Hill............................................................Gloria Dorson
Kids (orig. Ashley and Michael).....Ashley Bank, Michael Melby

Writer: Rob LaZebnick

9. "A Family Affair"  Nov. 17, 1990

Harry's instincts tell him Barbara's new boyfriend (Laurance) is married; Dreyfuss goes on a diet.

Scott...............................................................Mitchell Laurance
Mother...............................................................Cecelia Riddett

Writer: Susan Beavers

10. "Someone to Watch Over Me"  Nov. 24, 1990

Charley wants visitors during a hospital stay; a neighbor (Applegate) accuses Dreyfuss of fathering his dog's puppies.

Mr. Patrick.........................................................Fred Applegate
Fred.....................................................................Eddie Bracken
Ursula................................................................Dena Dietrich
Norman.............................................................Robert Gorman
Georgie...............................................................Brandon Adams
And: Marti Muller (Nurse), Susan Krebs (Norman's mom)

Writers: Bill Braunstein & Sydney Blake

11. "Harry Knows Best"  Dec. 8, 1990

Harry gives advice to Charley, who's contemplating a new career as a gigolo, and to a girl (Bialik) wanting rhinoplasty.

Laurie...................................................................Mayim Bialik
Paula........................................................Judith Marie Bergan
Woman.......................................................Kat Sawyer-Young
Photographer................................................................Stan Roth

Writer: David Sacks

12. "Whenever I Feel Afraid"  Dec. 15, 1990

Laverne is fearful after a mugging; Barbara and Carol compete for the attention of a handsome new neighbor (Carhart).

Billy...................................................................Timothy Carhart
Officer Hitner...................................................Aaron Lustig
Jimmy...........................................................Ben Ryan Ganger
Attendant.......................................................Jay Goldenberg
Customer.............................................................Robert Gould

Writer: Harold Kimmel

13. "A Shot in the Dark"  Jan. 5, 1991

Barbara mistakes Carol's new boyfriend (Sand) for a burglar, and shoots him in the leg; Laverne must overcome stage fright.

Avery................................................................Paul Sand
Emcee........................................................Channing Chase

Writer: Roger Garrett

**preempted Jan. 12**

14. "Sucking Up is Hard to Do"  Jan. 19, 1991

Carol advises Barbara to put on a flattering act to help achieve a promotion she's applied for; Laverne plays matchmaker.

Anne.............................................................Rebeccah Bush
Mrs. Moses...................................................Patricia Gaul
Hartman........................................................Paul Eiding
Michelle.........................................................Judy Baldwin
Woman...........................................................May Quigley
Secretary........................................................Shuko Akune
Timmy..........................................................Whitby Hertford

Writer: Pat Dougherty

15. "The Man That Got Away"  Jan. 26, 1991

Barbara tries to get a man she likes (Bierko) to ask her out; Laverne has to cast a deciding vote on a hometown issue.

Fred..............................................................Craig Bierko
Sam..............................................................Jeff Doucette
Lurlene.........................................................Jana Arnold

Director: Doug Smart             Writer: Susan Beavers

16. "The Mentor"  Feb. 2, 1991

Harry's mentor (Thomas, father of co-executive producer Tony Thomas and of actress Marlo Thomas) returns to Miami to practice, though he's far past his prime.

Dr. Leo Brewster.............................................Danny Thomas
Dr. Wakefield................................................Harvey Jason
Mrs. Lasko.....................................................Elise Ogden

Writer: Arnie Kogan

17. "The Dog Who Knew Too Much"  Feb. 9, 1991

When the girls decide it's time to move out, they and Harry individually pour their hearts out to Dreyfuss.

Mrs. Knox.....................................................Tina Johnson
Timmy.........................................................John Christian Graas

Writer: Gary Jacobs

18. "Guess Who's Coming to Dinner?"  Feb. 16, 1991

Harry dates a pretty 28-year-old (Kolis); in a quasi war-movie parody, drill sergeant Laverne shapes up a nurse trainee (Hartman, a cast-member of *Saturday Night Live*). Bernstein played a different character in ep. 5.

Tim Cornell....................................................Phil Hartman
Paige.............................................................Tracy Kolis
Pete, her father..............................................Kenneth Kimmins
Gayle, her mother..........................................Valorie Armstrong
And: Lance Davis (Waiter), Jaclyn Bernstein (Nancy)

Writer: Rob LaZebnick

**unscheduled preemption Feb. 23**

19. "All About Harry"  March 9, 1991

Harry gets uncomfortable when his journalist girlfriend (Ebersole) begins writing about their dates in her newspaper column. Orig. scheduled for Feb. 23.

Laura.............................................................Christine Ebersole

Writer: Meredith Siler

20. "'Drive,' He Said"  March 16, 1991

Birthday boy Charley takes Harry searching for an old girlfriend, while the girls try to keep a restless crowd from leaving the surprise party. Kramer is a cast-member of *Down Home*. Orig. scheduled for March 9.

Apartment manager.........................................Eric Allan Kramer
Salesperson....................................................Micole Mercurio
Airline clerk...................................................Kenneth Danziger
Party guests...................................Robert Gould, Don Sparks

Writer: David Sacks

21. "The Last Temptation of Laverne"  March 23, 1991

Laverne's aunt (Roberts) will lend a house down-payment if Laverne, though innocent, assumes blame for a car accident. Ogden reprises her role from ep 16.

Aunt Retha.....................................................Doris Roberts
Arnold...........................................................Henry Jones
Fire Marshall..................................................David Correia
Mrs. Lasko.....................................................Elise Ogden

Writers: Pat Dougherty & Harold Kimmel

**preempted April 6**

22. "What's Eating You?"  April 13, 1991

Harry and Carol counsel Barbara that the best way to cure her pre-ulcerous condition is to be open with her true feelings.

Tony.............................................................Michael Goldfinger
Davidson.......................................................Richard McKenzie
Secretary........................................................Lynne Marie Stewart

Director: Robert Berlinger
Writers: Sydney Blake & Bill Braunstein

23. "The Cruise"  May 4, 1991

On a cruise, Harry and Barbara have great times, and Carol gets a proposal from and loses her Mr. Right (Burgi).

Matthew Wright..............................................Richard Burgi
Myrna...........................................................Peggy Pope
Charlotte........................................................Pearl Shear
Simba Katzman...............................................Teresa Ganzel
M.C...............................................................David Jay Willis

Director: Doug Smart             Writer: Arnie Kogan

24. "The Way We Are"  May 11, 1991

Harry looks forward to a visit with a childhood sweetheart (Jones), until his childhood rival (Winter) also resurfaces.

Jean McDowell................................................Shirley Jones
Eric Lancaster.................................................Ed Winter

Little Harry..............................................Christopher Pettiet
Little Jean.................................................Robin Lynn Heath
And: Tom Henschel (Bartender), Cory Danziger (Little Eric)

Writers: Paul B. Price & Laura O'Hare

**renewed for 1991-92; new episodes begin Sept. 21, 1991**

## Equal Justice

ABC          Wednesdays, 10-11 p.m.

Series pr premiere: March 27, 1990
Final telecast: July 24, 1991

Drama of young lawyers in an urban District Attorney's office. Smith is married to *thirtysomething* cast-member Mel Harris.

D.A. Arnold Bach............................................George DiCenzo
Deputy D.A. Eugene Rogan...................................Cotter Smith
Julie Janovich.............................................Debrah Farentino
Sex Crimes Unit chief Linda Bauer................Jane Kaczmarek
Jesse Rogan, Eugene's wife..............................Kathleen Lloyd
Pete "Briggs" Brigman.......................................Barry Miller
Michael James..................................................Joe Morton
JoAnn Harris...........................................Sarah Jessica Parker
Peter Bauer.....................................................Jon Tenney
Christopher Searls.........................................James Wilder

*Recurring:*
Maggie Mayfield (ep. 3-4,6,10-11).......................Lynn Whitfield
• Detective Frank Mirelli (ep. 2,5,8)......................Stanley Tucci
Ellis Bernstein (ep. 6,9-10,12)...........................Jeff McCarthy
Kerry Lynn (ep. 6-7,11)......................................Colleen Flynn
Colin Baker (ep. 9,11-13).....................................George Coe
Sandra Hindell (ep. 9-11)....................................Meg Wittner
Lorene Basler (ep. 9-11)..................................Mariangela Pino

• First name erroneously given as John in *TV Guide.*

The Thomas Carter Co. in assoc. with Orion Television
Executive producers: Thomas Carter, David A. Simons, Christopher Knopf
Supervising producer: Frank Abatemarco
Producers: Ian Sander, David Rosenbloom
Executive story consultants: Deborah Joy LeVine, Bryce Zabel
Director of photography: Felix Alcala
Technical consultant: Frank Iannucci
Technical advisor: Leslie Brodsky
Disability consultants: Tari Susan Hartman, Barbara Faye Waxman, Diane Coleman, J.D.
Music: Joseph Vitarelli
Theme: David Bell & Susan Marder (words and music); performed by Carmen Carter & Carl Anderson
Creators: Christopher Knopf & David A. Simons and Thomas Carter

---

1. "Sleeping with the Enemy" Jan. 9, 1991

Micheal prosecutes a man who didn't tell his sex partner he had AIDS; Briggs's witness (Paymer) has multiple personalities. Hamilton is the daughter of comedian Carol Burnett.

Jillian.......................................................Carrie Hamilton
Stuey.........................................................David Paymer
Mary Ann.....................................................Dori Brenner
Charles.......................................................Linden Ashby
Dr. Yung.......................................................Floyd Levine

Judge Jamison................................................John C. Moskoff
Karen.........................................................Anne Gee Byrd
Public health officer.......................................Oz Tortora
Ed Bercik.....................................................John Welsh
Advocates............................Charles Dougherty, Sandy Martin
And: Lavelle Roby (Judge Myers), Lonnie Burr (Kozek), Andrew Craig (Wolfman), Joseph Hieu (Vietnamese man), Fred Pinkard (Clerk), Lee Mary Weilnau (Vietnamese woman)

Director: Michael Switzer          Writer: Deborah Joy LeVine

2. "End Game" Jan. 23, 1991

Searls confronts Bauer in a bid to win a death-sentence conviction against a 17-year-old (Harris); Julie contends with an obnoxious but attractive detective (new recurring guest Tucci); Linda faces a co-op board. Orig. scheduled for Jan. 16.

Martin Weiss.................................................Scott Marlowe
Antoine.......................................................David Harris
Dee Dee.....................................................Laverne Anderson
Judge Williams................................................Bill Morey
Dr. Hayes....................................................William Utay
Mrs. Skewes-Cox...........................................Margaret Muse
And: Jack Murdock (Spider), Judy Kain (Realtor), Brett Stimely (Porter), James Newell (Noble), Heather Lee (Grace), Torri Whitehead (Secretary), Roger La Page (Foreperson)

Director: Thomas Carter          Writer: Christopher Knopf

3. "Courting Disaster" Jan. 30, 1991

Michael believes his client (Durrell) is just as guilty as the man's ex-wife (Snodgress), who pled insanity after murdering the man's new wife; Searls tries to evade the seductress daughter (Bako) of a judge. Orig. scheduled for Jan. 23.

Jason Prentiss...............................................Michael Durrell
Sarah.........................................................Tricia O'Neil
Marla Prentiss.............................................Carrie Snodgress
Judge Wilcox................................................Will MacMillan
Georgine.....................................................Brigitte Bako
Judge Naisbett............................................Jacqueline Scott
Dr. Telander...............................................Nicholas Kepros
Katie Rogan, Eugene and Jesse's daughter......Tiffany Brissette
Elizabeth.....................................................Judith Jones
And: Richard Brestoff (Steinman), Susan Powell (Claire), Lahmard Tate (Rene), Duke Stroud (Farraday), Lamont Bentley (Childs), Yvette Freeman (Clerk)

Director: Dan Lerner          Writer: Francis Mahon

**preempted Feb. 6**

4. "In Confidence" Feb. 13, 1991

Bauer is the horrified confidant of his murderous sociopath client (Giuntoli); Michael must convince Maggie he is over his girlfriend's death. Brissette reprises her role from ep. 3. Orig. scheduled for Jan. 30.

Detective Al Perry.............................................Dan Hedaya
Jack...........................................................Neil Giuntoli
Jana Carlton...............................................Donna Bullock
Sam Raznick...................................................Allan Rich
Accosta....................................................Charles Walker
Dr. Weiss.......................................................Flo Di Re
Katie Rogan................................................Tiffany Brissette
Hennessey....................................................Jack Jozefson

Director: Thomas Carter          Writer: Deborah Joy LeVine

**preempted Feb. 20**

5. "Do No Harm"  Feb. 27, 1991

Rogan prosecutes a doctor (Elliott) accused of killing a terminally ill woman with her consent; Julie and Mirelli explore each other's worlds; Briggs dumps a messy case on JoAnn. Craig reprises his role from ep. 1.

Ms. Curtis.......................................Joan McMurtrey
Dr. Strathmore.................................Stephen Elliott
Paul Hauge......................................Wayne Tippit
Roberta..........................................Caroline Williams
Carla Siditsky..................................Bonnie Burroughs
Judge Constance Adler.........................Liz Sheridan
Wolfman...........................................Andrew Craig
Mary Beth........................................Lee Lawson
Catherine Abbot................................Susan Merson
Judge Keller.....................................Ryan MacDonald
Delvecchio.......................................Jimm Giannini
Puncione.........................................Doug Franklin
Little Eva........................................Lada Boder
Makela............................................Gregory J. Barnett
Clerk..............................................Douglas Koth
    Also orig. announced: Joely Fisher (Monica), John Finnegan (Crenshaw), Marco Hernandez (Trujillo)

Director: Michael Switzer          Writer: Bryce Zabel

6. "The Big Game and Other Crimes"  March 6, 1991
    10:20-11:20 p.m.

Mike and Chris negotiate rules to a basketball game versus the public defenders' team; Rogan uncovers possible misconduct in Bach's political past; Briggs faces an attractive, disabled lawyer (Flynn) in a case against an alleged crack-house arsonist (DeBroux). Delayed due to a presidential address.

Alex McCall......................................Lee DeBroux
Harold Shattuck.................................Robin Strand
Ida Bolton.......................................L. Scott Caldwell
With: Lois de Banzie
Judge Holly Billings.............................Jennifer Rhodes
Harold Barrett..................................Lawrence Tierney
Sgt. James Samuelson...........................Don Stark
Public Defender Reid............................Wren T. Brown
And: William Marquez (Judge Rodriguez), Nigel Miguel (Reggie), J. David Krassner (Director), Douglas Roth (Clerk)

Director: Kevin Hooks          Writer: Christopher Knopf

7. "Part of the Plan"  March 13, 1991

When Linda and Peter return home for their mother's funeral, Peter confronts their father (O'Loughlin), and Linda confronts a former flame (Gilliland); Briggs takes Kerry Lynn to dinner; JoAnn is held for contempt of court.

Robert Geller....................................Richard Gilliland
Dr. David Taylor................................Michael D. Roberts
Lieberthal........................................Paul Regina
Judge Boyd......................................Larry D. Mann
Judge Ernest Franklin...........................George Murdock
Pauline Bauer....................................Erica Yohn
Ted Bauer........................................Gerald S. O'Loughlin
Cantoli...........................................Paul Drake
Dee Dee Blue....................................Helaine Hunter
And: D. Paul Thomas (Dr. Strauss), Denny Salvaryn (Minister), John Gowan (Maitre d'), Patricia Hodges (Juror)

Director: Eric Laneuville          Writer: David A. Simons

8. "Who Speaks for the Children?"  March 20, 1991

JoAnn disagrees with Linda's argument for a conviction of a pregnant crack addict; Julie soul-searches about her romance with Mirelli; Briggs shares tips on working night court.

April Gibbons....................................Beverly Todd
Doris.............................................Melora Hardin
Maria Realle.....................................Roxann Biggs
Dr. Ruttenberg..................................Brian Markinson
Rivera............................................Charles Levin
Curcio............................................Joseph Carberry
Carbone..........................................Johnny Dark
James.............................................Brian Seemann
Rover.............................................John F. O'Donohue
And: Stephen Mendel (Judge Barron), Robert Levine (Justin), Roger Nolan (Howard), Edgar Small (Clerk), Kaylan Romero (Javiersito), Joe Farago (Spence)
    Also orig. announced: Jane Hallaren (Biglietta)

Director: Sandy Smolan          Writer: Frank Abatemarco

9. "Do the Wrong Thing"  March 27, 1991

Chris' undercover investigation goes awry when a key witness (Roccuzzo) is assaulted; Rogan faces a heavy price whether he runs against Bach or continues under him; JoAnn seeks a robbery conviction against a defendant claiming he's Jesus.

"Jesus of Nazareth".............................Douglas Roberts
George Basler....................................Mario Roccuzzo
Bobbie Finestra..................................Sue Giosa
Judge Heilbroner................................Philip Baker Hall
Claude Peterson.................................Alan Blumenfeld
Judith............................................Linda G. Miller
Savino............................................Rick Grassi
Claire Bach......................................Janis Flax
Dawkins..........................................Richard Zavaglia
Bussio............................................Eric Kohner
Persky............................................Laurence Haddon

Director: Dan Lerner          Writer: Bryce Zabel

**preempted April 3**

10. "Without Prejudice"  April 10, 1991

Mike tries to resolve whether a Korean grocer (Chi) killed a black man in self-defense; Searls agonizes over his failure to prevent the murder of a witness in an extortion case; Rogan decides to run for D.A.; Briggs helps Julie with her IRS audit.

Jameel Kimble...................................John Cothran, Jr.
Unah Yong.......................................Kim Miyori
Detective D'Alessio..............................Joe Marinelli
Mark Garnet....................................Joel Polis
Tyrone Reese....................................Lance Slaughter
Donald Holcomb.................................James O'Sullivan
Don Ming Sung.................................Chi Muoi Lo
Thornell Katz....................................Patrick Thomas O'Brien
Dunn.............................................Ryan Cutrona
John McKee......................................Lawrence Scott Maki
Young Ti.........................................Bill Cho Lee

Director: Barbara Amato          Writer: Frank Abatemarco

**on hiatus, then cancelled**

11. "Opening Farewell"  June 19, 1991

Rogan announces he's resigning to run against Bach; Searls'

murder case is thwarted by federal bigwigs; James' girlfriend's murderer is caught; Kerry takes part in a demonstration. O'Sullivan reprises his role from last episode.

Suzanne Garner.................................................Wanda De Jesus
Donald Holcomb.............................................James O'Sullivan
Detective Dankowski.............................................Steve Eastin
Jermaine Watkins..............................................Clifton Powell
Joe..........................................................................Alan Toy
Randa.......................................................Nancy Becker Kennedy
Willie...............................................................Eugene Williams
And: Thom Keane (Maitre d'), Carl T. Miller (Reporter), Fred Lerner (Officer), Kristen Wolfe (Caroline Bassler)

Director: Andy Wolk          Writer: Deborah Joy LeVine

12. "What Color Are My Eyes?" June 26, 1991

A homeless girl (Harrington) is too terrified to testify against her attacker; Rogan risks compromising his vision for politics; Harris wants to go on a TV dating show with Bauer. Guest Martindale is a game-show host.

Detective Monroe..................................................John Hancock
Trisha Jackson........................................Cheryl Francis Harrington
George Kirmen..................................................Steven Anderson
Cynthia.................................................................Cecily Adams
Judge Brown.......................................................Tom Dahlgren
Himself...........................................................Wink Martindale
Mrs. Thomason.....................................................Carol Bruce
Andrea..........................................................Christina Carlisi
Emergency Room physician................................Gayle Cohen
Defense attorney.........................................Catherine MacNeal
And: J. Downing (Producer), Charles R. Penland (Williams), Matt McKenzie (Attorney), Natasha Pearce (Vicki)

Director: Mark Sobel          Writer: Christopher Knopf

13. "The Devil His Due" July 3, 1991

JoAnn's nerves are shattered when a prisoner holding a gun on her is killed before her eyes; Rogan betrays his loved ones in an effort to revive his campaign; Michael prosecutes a popular basketball coach accused in his star player's death.

Frank Djakonski..................................................James Handy
Coach Nichols....................................................Chelcie Ross
Hazel McGee.................................................Starletta DuPois
George Kirmen..................................................Steven Anderson
Paul Milton.........................................................Jan Munroe
Judge Billings..................................................Jennifer Rhodes
Judge Max Bromberg..........................................Nathan Davis
Guido Escarrega..............................................Marco Rodriguez
And: Christine Avila (Mrs. Alvarez), William Marquez (Judge Rodriguez), Burton Collins (Greg Sterling), Greg Callahan (Moderator), Tom Middleton (Court officer)

Director: David Rosenbloom          Writer: Paris Qualles

**preempted July 31**

## Evening Shade

CBS        Sept. 21-Nov. 9          Fridays, 8-8:30 p.m.
           Nov. 19-June 3, July 15-on Mondays, 8-8:30 p.m.
           June 17-24                Mondays, 9:30-10 p.m.

Series premiere: Sept. 21, 1990

Comedy of a former Pittsburgh Steelers quarterback who re-turns to hometown Evening Shade, Ark. (a real town, though not Reynolds' hometown) to coach the Evening Shade High School Mules. Newton street address: 2102. Local paper: The Evening Shade Argus. Population: 11,248. Wood's old number: 22. Most episodes have no opening-theme sequence, but narration by Davis over the start of each story, with credits superimposed. Cast-member Wedgeworth was a guest ep. 1-5. Reynolds is married to actress Loni Anderson, Henner to Gabriel's Fire producer Robert Lieberman, Davis to actress Ruby Dee, and Holbrook to Designing Women co-star Dixie Carter; Thomason and Bloodworth-Thomason are husband and wife.

Woodrow (Wood) Newton.....................................Burt Reynolds
Ava Evans Newton, his wife...............................Marilu Henner
Taylor Newton (15)..............................................Jay R. Ferguson
Will Newton (4).....................................................Jacob Parker
Molly Newton (7)........................................Melissa Renee Martin
Assistant coach/math teacher Herman Stiles......Michael Jeter
Ava's Aunt Frieda Evans....................................Elizabeth Ashley
Blue's Barbecue cafe owner Ponder Blue................Ossie Davis
Dr. Harlan Elldridge..........................................Charles Durning
Merleen Elldridge, his wife...............................Ann Wedgeworth
Newspaper editor Evan Evans, Ava's father.........Hal Holbrook

*Recurring:*
Nub Oliver (ep. 1-3,8-12,14-16,18-19,21,23-24).....Charlie Dell
Stripper Fontana Beausoleil
    (ep. 1-2,5,9-11,14,16-19,24)....................Linda Gehringer
Principal Margaret Fouch (ep. 1,3,7-8,20-23)..........Ann Hearn
Virgil (ep. 1,5,8,11,13-16,18-20,23)....................Burton Gilliam
Dorothy (ep. 1,11,16,18,19,23)...........................Jane Abbott
Marion Mayfield (ep. 3-4,16,18-19)...............Michael O. Smith
Luther (ep. 6,8,14-15)......................................Brent Briscoe
Neal Heck (ep. 1,21,23)...................................Pepper Sweeney

CBS Entertainment Productions in assoc. with Bloodworth/ Thomason Mozark Productions and MTM Enterprises
Executive producers: Linda Bloodworth-Thomason, Harry Thomason, Burt Reynolds
Producers: Tommy Thompson, Douglas Jackson, David Nichols
Consulting producer: Stephen A. Miller
Associate producer: Lamar Jackson
Story editor: Sean Clark
Creative consultant (later in season): Don Rhymer
Director of photography: Nick McLean Sr.
Music (variously): Snuff Garrett
End-theme (instrumental): "The Evening Shade Closing Theme" by Sonny Curtis; performed by Hans Olson
Creator: Linda Bloodworth-Thomason

———————————————

1. "A Day in the Life of Wood Newton" Sept. 21, 8-9 p.m.; Monday, Sept. 24, 11:30 p.m.-12:30 a.m. (0601)

On his birthday/wedding anniversary, an innocent Wood is photographed with a stripper; Prosecuting Attorney candidate Ava discovers she's pregnant despite Wood's vasectomy.

Frances Blue, Ponder's wife..............................Virginia Capers
R.C. Blue....................................................Marlon Archey
Pauline Newton............................................Florence Schauffler
Ralph (orig. Jim Guy)...........................................Terry Wills

Director: Harry Thomason
Writer: Linda Bloodworth-Thomason

2. "There Once Was a Boy Named Wood" Sept. 28, 1990 (0603)

Frieda babysits, and fills in for Evan on poker night when he has a date with Miss Beausoleil. Wills reprises his role.

Vernon.........................................................Newell Alexander
Ralph....................................................................Terry Wills
Employee.......................................................Stacy Thomason
Florist.......................................................Billy Bob Thornton

Director: Harry Thomason
Writer: Linda Bloodworth-Thomason

3. "Whatever Happened to Clutch Newton?"
   Oct. 5, 1990  (0604)

On seeing an old game film, Wood discovers his most celebrated high school touchdown catch was actually out-of-bounds. Schauffler reprises her role from ep. 1.

Pauline Newton.........................................Florence Schauffler
Steve.................................................................Dan Gilvezan
Mike..............................................................George Parker
Tony......................................................................Dale Stern

Director: Harry Thomason            Writer: David Nichols

**preempted Oct. 19**

4. "Sadie Hawkins Dance"  Oct. 26, 1990  (0612)

During Sadie Hawkins week, the football team begins a seven-day series of pranks on Coach Newton.

Officer....................................................................Tom Kindle
Margie................................................................Tara Hutchins
Becky..........................................................Kristine Blackburn
Elmore..............................................................Bill Stevenson
Student (orig. Junior)...........................................Jon Hewitt

Director: David Steinberg            Writer: Stephen A. Miller

5. "Fast Women"  Monday, Oct. 29, 1990   8-8:30 p.m.  (0607)

Ava asks Wood to talk with both their son, Taylor, and her father about their choice in dates (Condra and Gehringer, repsectively).  Orig. scheduled for Oct. 12 and 26.

Michelle Marlin...................................................Julie Condra

Director: Frank Bonner    Writer: Linda Bloodworth-Thomason

6. "The Moustache Show"  Nov. 2, 1990  (0608)

Ava's high-school flame (McGinley) visits; Will shaves off half of Wood's mustache.  Star Reynolds' sitcom directing debut.

Kyle Hampton....................................................Ted McGinley
Frank..........................................................................Paul Meek
    Also originally announced: Michael O. Smith (Marion Mayfield), Alfie Wise (Voice of announcer)

Director: Burt Reynolds    Writer: Linda Bloodworth-Thomason

7. "All for Charity"  Nov. 9, 1990  (0610)

Hoping to win Wood's favor, Herman, at a fundraiser, bids for and wins a weekend with Wood and his family.

Director: Richard T. Kline            Writer: David Nichols

8. "Something to Hold Onto"  Nov. 19, 1990  (0605)

Wood and the rest of town tutor the football players in algebra so they won't fail their classes and be barred from a big game. Orig. scheduled for Nov. 16.

Chuck......................................................................S.A. Griffin
Nelson....................................................................Rick Hurst
"Big Ed" (Eddie) Satterfield................................Ed Beechner
Sam.....................................................................Steve Carlisle

Director: Burt Reynolds            Writer: Sean Clark

9. "Mr. Mom"  Nov. 26, 1990  (0614)

With Ava's prosecutorial work taking her away from her household duties, a miserable Wood has to take up the slack.

Director: David Steinberg
Writers: Sean Clark and David Nichols

**unscheduled hour-long rerun on Friday, Nov. 30, preempting the scheduled Uncle Buck and Bagdad Cafe**

10. "Hooray for Wood"  Dec. 10, 1990  (0609)

Wood gets a bit part  when a movie company and its temper-mental star (Kellerman) arrive to shoot a Civil War mini-series.

Shelley (orig. Lupe) Darling..............Sally Kellerman (orig. Rita Moreno)
Alan Roth.................................................Charles Nelson Reilly
Geoff.................................................................John Allsopp
Doug Jackson.....................................................Eddie Driscoll
Man.................................................................Brandon Meyer

Director: Burt Reynolds    Writer: Linda Bloodworth-Thomason

11. "The Wood Who Stole Christmas"  Dec. 17, 1990  (0616)

Tired of his kids' materialism, Wood gives their presents to a needy family.  Willis reprises his role from ep. 1.

Bobby................................................................Christian Hoff
Mayor...........................................................Michael Griswold
Ralph....................................................................Terry Willis
Soldiers....................................Terry Fitzgerald, Mimi Cagnetta

Director: Harry Thomason
Teleplay: Linda Bloodworth-Thomason
Story: Allen Crowe & Lyle Weldon

**preempted Dec. 31**

12. "Wood and Ava and Gil and Madeline"  Jan. 7, 1991  (0617)

Wood and Ava are asked to dinner by a married couple, who turn out to be swingers into spouse-swapping.

Gil (orig. Jay) Hall.............................................Murphy Dunne
Madeline (orig. Marilyn) Hall....................................Erin Gray

Director: David Steinberg
Writer: Linda Bloodworth-Thomason

13. "Wood's Thirtieth Reunion"  Jan. 21, 1991  (0613)

At his 30-year high school reunion, Wood hooks up with two old pals (Hampton, McClure) and one old flame (Taylor-Young).

Larry.......................................................................Leo Geter
Earl Mallory...................................................James Hampton
"Jaguar Johnny" Blanchard.............................Doug McClure
Becky Kincaid Winstead............................Leigh Taylor-Young
    Also orig. announced: Charlie Dell (Nub Oliver)

Director: Burt Reynolds            Writer: Stephen A. Miller

14. "Vote Early and Vote Often" Jan. 28, 1991  (0615)

Wood and Ava recall how friends rallied to help her get elected Prosecuting Attorney over her opponent (Applegate).

Jim Guy Puckett..........................................Royce D. Applegate
Dusty Parker.....................................................Alfie Wise

Director: David Steinberg            Writer: Stephen A. Miller

15. "Chip Off the Old Brick"  Feb. 4, 1991  (0618)

Herman's big, blustery father comes to visit, but talks football with Wood and chases after Frieda more than he sees his son.

Brick Stiles................................................Brian Keith
Bud......................................................Henry Gibson
       Also orig. announced:
       David White (Student), Patricia Rouleau (Waitress)

Director: Burt Reynolds              Story: Burt Reynolds
Teleplay: David Nichols and Sean Clark

16. "The Trials of Wood Newton"  Feb. 11, 1991  (0606)

Wood must testify against Evan, who's being defended by his daughter -- Ava. Griffin played a different role in ep. 8.

Attorney Rayford Taggart.............................Paul Dooley
Vernon Moody..........................................S.A. Griffin
Judge...................................................Ken Jenkins

Director: David Steinberg         Writer: David Nichols

17. "Into the Woods"  Feb. 18, 1991  (0619)

On Wood's annual deer-hunting trip, a local-legend deer drops dead in front of his cabin, outside official hunting grounds.

Big Mike...............................................Dennis Burkley
Dean....................................................Gary Grubbs
George.................................................Don Maxwell

Director: David Steinberg           Writer: Don Rhymer

18. "Nothing to Fear but Harvey Lujack"  Feb. 25, 1991  (0620)

A convict (Koch), who'd threatened prosecutor Ava when she had had him put away, escapes and heads toward town.

Mitch...................................................Matt Battaglia
Harvey Lujack...........................................Peter Koch

Director: Burt Reynolds              Writer: Bill Dial

19. "Gambler Anonymous"  March 4, 1991  (0621)

Wood tries to keep secret the presence of his guest, country-music singer Kenny Rogers, an old acquaintance. Ends with a conceptual music-video of Rogers' "20 Years Ago."

Himself................................................Kenny Rogers

Director: David Steinberg            Writer: Stephen A. Miller

20. "Sex Education"
     Sunday, March 24, 1991  8-8:30 p.m.  (0623)

An in-over-his-head Herman substitute-teaches a class in sex education, and calls in "expert" Wood. Orig. scheduled for March 18.

Mrs. Lindsey.........................................Bobbie Ferguson
Philpott.................................................David White
Karen.................................................Marla Bradley

Director: Harry Thomason            Writer: Don Rhymer

21. "I Am Wood, Hear Me Roar"  April 1, 1991  (0622)

Two female students (Grey, Holmquist) attempt to join the football team. Sweeney reprises his role from ep. 1, Carlisle from ep. 8, and White from last episode.

Yvonne................................................Kimberly Grey
Yvette...............................................Kristen Holmquist
Larry................................................Jimmy Burdette
Alvin....................................................Jake Price
Bill....................................................Mark Fauser
Jeff......................................................Rick Post
Sam...................................................Steve Carlisle
Reporters.........................Bill Schick, Patrick Mickler
Philpott................................................David White
       Also orig. announced: Burton Gilliam (Virgil)

Director: David Steinberg            Writer: Sean Clark

22. "Herman and Margaret Sitting in a Tree"
     April 8, 1991  (0627)

Herman's relationship with Margaret hits a snag when she refuses to be seen with Herman on a formal "date." Guest Henner is the brother of co-star Marilu Henner.

Ken...................................................Lorin Henner
Kelly.................................................Kaitlyn Walker
Daniel...............................................Ryan McWhorter
Daryl.................................................Daryl Siemer

Director: Harry Thomason
Writers: Sean Clark, Stephen A. Miller, David Nichols, Don Rhymer

23. "Far from the Madden Crowd"  April 29, 1991  (0625)

Ava goes into labor the night of the Booster Club Sports Banquet, to which Wood has invited his football archrival Terry Bradshaw (the NFL quarterback, as himself). Sweeney reprises his role from ep. 1 and 21. Part 1 of 2.

Himself...............................................Terry Bradshaw
       Also orig. announced: Burton Gilliam (Virgil), Wanda Jones (Waitress), Michael O. Smith (Marion Mayfield)

Director: Burt Reynolds
Writers: Sean Clark and Stephen A. Miller
(Orig. announced: Teleplay: Sean Clark and Stephen A. Miller; story: Jane Abbott & Linda Dew Kuti)

24. "The Baby Show"  Part 2   May 6, 1991  (0626)

Ava rides in the back of Ponder's catering truck on a chaotic ride to the hospital. Caroline Rhymer is the daughter of frequent series writer Don Rhymer and his wife Kate. Part 2 of 2.

Emily Frieda Newton (infant).......Caroline Rhymer (uncredited)
Note: Wanda Jones (Waitress) and recurring guests Hearn, Gilliam, Abbott, Sweeney and Smith had no apparent speaking roles.

Director: Burt Reynolds              Writer: Don Rhymer

**preempted May 20**

preempted June 10

preempted July 1 and July 8

renewed for 1991-92; new episodes begin Sept. 16, 1991;
Candace Hutson succeeds Melissa Renee Martin as Molly

## The Family Man

CBS Sept. 11-Dec. 1     Saturdays, 8-8:30 p.m.
    June 10-July 17     Mondays & Wednesdays, 8:30-9 p.m.

Series premiere: Sept. 11, 1990

Comedy of a recently widowed firefighter raising his four children with the help of his well-meaning, live-in father-in-law.
Co-stars Buchanan and Sterling are brother and sister; the
latter is also an *L.A. Law* recurring guest. Working title: *Four
Alarm Family.*

Jack Taylor.....................................................Gregory Harrison
Jeff Taylor (16).....................................................John Buchanan
Steve Taylor (14).................................................Scott Weinger
Brian Taylor (11)..............................................Matthew Brooks
Allison Taylor (6)...................................Ashleigh Blair Sterling
Joe Alberghetti.....................................................Al Molinaro

*Recurring:*
Patrick Kozak, Allison's friend
    (ep. 2-3,9,11-13,16-17,20).............................Josh Byrne
Hilary Kozak, his mother (ep. 3,12,20).................Gail Edwards
Gus Harbrook (ep. 6,8-9)........................................Ed Winter
Eddie Cooper (ep. 6,8-9,14)..................................Peter Parros
Ted Reinhard (ep. 6,8-9)......................................Adam Biesk
Jill Nichols (ep. 13-14,17,20-21)......................Nancy Everhard

Catalina Production Group and Miller • Boyett Productions in
    assoc. with Lorimar Television
Executive producers: Thomas L. Miller, Robert L. Boyett,
    William Bickley, Michael Warren
Co-executive producer: Ross Brown (ep. 2-on)
Supervising producers: Joe Fisch (later in season), Martha
    Williamson
Producers: Rich Correll, Deborah Oppenheimer (ep. 1); James
    O'Keefe (ep. 2-on)
Co-producers: Chuck Tately, Kevin White
Associate producer: Bonnie Bogard
Line producer: Shari Hearn (ep. 1)
Executive story editors: Pamela Wick, Susan Cridland Wick
Story editors: Geoff Gordon (early in season), Matt Ember
    (later in season), Julia Newton, Brian Bird, John Wierick
Creative consultant (early in season): John Steven Owen
Director of Photography: Monroe P. Askins., Jr., A.S.C.
Music [and] Theme (instrumental): Jesse Frederick & Bennett
    Salvay
Creators: William Bickley & Michael Warren
Developed by: Thomas L. Miller & Robert L. Boyett

———————————————

1. "The Family Man" Tuesday, Sept. 11, 1990  8:30-9 p.m.

The kids start school for the first time since their mother died.

Ms. Hickerson.................................................Melanie Wilson

Director: Rich Correll
Writers: William Bickley & Michael Warren

2. "Family Day" Sept. 15, 1990

Jack tries to initiate a regular "Family Day" with the kids.

Director: Richard Correll            Writer: Julia Newton

3. "Making Babies" Sept. 22, 1990

Jack reluctantly explains sex to Allison, who repeats it to a fellow kindergartner whose mother become furious.

Miss Campbell.........................................Francesca P. Roberts
Mrs. Korfinger.................................................Melissa Harrison
Kim.......................................................................Samantha Mills

Director: Richard Correll          Writer: Martha Williamson

4. "Roommates" Sept. 29, 1990

The boys switch rooms; Jack readies for a firehouse inspection.

Toad.....................................................................Chance Quinn

Director: Stewart Lyons        Writers: Brian Bird, John Wierick

preempted Oct. 6

5. "Tea for Two" Oct. 13, 1990

Allison talks Jack into co-hosting her school's mother-daughter tea. Roberts reprises her role from ep. 3.

Kate.......................................................................Cecile Callan
Miss Campbell.........................................Francesca P. Roberts
Whitney...................................................................Tasia Schutt

Director: Stewart A. Lyons          Writer: John Steven Owen

6. "Drive My Car" Oct. 27, 1990

After Steve and Jeff secretly borrow their dad's car, it turns up
with a dent.

Director: Stewart A. Lyons
Writers: Chuck Tately & Kevin White

7. "Torn Between Two Brothers" Nov. 3, 1990

The girl that Jeff likes prefers Steve.

Heather Lewis....................................................Marlee Shelton
Dr. Gordon...........................................................Garrison True
Brad................................................................Devine Kamienny
Dave....................................................Ladell "Tay" LeBaron

Director: Judy Pioli
Writers: Pamela Wick & Susan Cridland Wick

8. "Firebreak" Nov. 10, 1990

Fearing his firefighting work is too dangerous for a single parent, Jack tries taking a desk job.

Mr. Blair.................................................................John T. Olson
Students....................Grant Gelt, Nikki Cox, Cleandre Norman

Director: Judy Pioli                  Writer: Geoff Gordon

9. "The New Guy" Nov. 17, 1990  8:30-9 p.m.

Jack gets frustrated when both his firehouse colleagues and
his sons display sexual prejudice against a new and capable
female firefighter (Ulrich).

Pat........................Kim Ulrich a.k.a. Kim Johnston-Ulrich, Kim
    Johnston Ulrich (Maura Tierney orig. announced)
Firefighter................................................Tony Lucas

Director: Judy Pioli                Writer: Matt Ember

10. "The Coach" Dec. 1, 1990

Jack coaches Brian's basketball team, the Wildcats; Joe
brings his lady friend (Harout) home to meet the family.

Lillian......................................................Magda Harout
Dave Gilbert, Sr...................................Bruce Jarchow
Vicki Berkowitz.....................................Susan Cash
Mark Phelps.........................................Joseph Dammann
Rupert Phelps.......................................Steve Peterson
Dave Gilbert, Jr........................................Joe Kyle
And: Michael Monks (Referee), Nigel Gibbs (Bulldogs coach)

Director: James O'Keefe
Writers: Brian Bird & John Wierick

**on hiatus**

11. "Double Date" June 10, 1991

Steve commits to a prom date with a popular girl (Foster) after
having already invited a girl (Clayton) who'd pursued him.

Eve Green.............................................Melissa Clayton
Courtney..................................................Ami Foster
Mr. Green..................................................Rex Ryon
Rachel....................................................Devin Walker

Director: James O'Keefe
Writers: Pamela Wick & Susan Cridland Wick

12. "My Little Runaway" June 12, 1991

Allison's Buttercup cookie-drive money turns up missing; Joe
plans a romantic getaway with Lillian. Edwards reprises her
role from ep. 3; Quinn, from ep. 4. Orig. scheduled for Dec. 8.

Toad........................................................Chance Quinn

Director: Richard Correll         Writer: Martha Williamson

13. "Jack and Jill, Part I" June 17, 1991

When a TV reporter (new recurring guest Everhard) hooks up
with Jack for a week for a magazine-show story, a romance
develops. Part 2 follows in ep. 15.

Announced cast includes:
Casey.......................................................Ken Thorley
Carl Akers.................................................Carl Mueller

Director: James O'Keefe           Writer: Martha Williamson

14. "Trading Places" June 19, 1991

Jack agrees to trade places with Steve, who thinks being a
household head is much easier than being a typical teenager.

Lowell..................................................Christopher Castile
    Also orig. announced: Tony Lucas (Tony)

Director: James O' Keefe (Richard Correll orig. announced)
Writers: Chuck Tately & Kevin White

15. "Jack and Jill, Part II" June 24, 1991

Jack tries to pursue a relationship with Jill, but his family
responsibilities and her highbow friends get in the way.

Luke........................................................Justin Lord
Ted.......................................................Oliver Muirhead
Chip.........................................................Will Leskin
Diane......................................................Cherie Brown
Waiter...................................................Gordon Reinhart

Director: James O'Keefe           Writer: Julia Newton

16. "You Bet Your Life" June 26, 1991

Jeff and Steve may lose their shirts and their arms over a
football pool they set up; Allison wants to get her ears pierced.

Salesperson.............................................Diane Robin
Tiny......................................................Jaime Cardriche

Director: James O'Keefe           Writer: Matt Ember

17. "Scenes from a Marriage" July 1, 1991

Jack and his father-in-law see a marriage counselor when
their relationship gets strained over raising the kids.

Dr. Wendy Sterne....................................Alyson Reed

Director: James O'Keefe
Writers: Susan Sebastian & Diana M. Ayers

18. "A Tiny Advantage" July 3, 1991

Jack hires one of his sons' hefty friends (Cardiche, reprising
his role from ep. 16) in order to use him for tug-of-war at the
annual firehouse competition. Director Baio, cousin of former
child/teen actors Joey and Jimmy Baio, is a former cast-
member of *Happy Days*, *Charles in Charge* and other shows.

Director: Scott Vincent Baio a.k.a. Scott Baio
Writer: Matt Ember

Tiny.....................................................Jaime Cardriche
Dick Meecham.........................................Peter Jason

19. "Throw Momma from the House" July 8, 1991

Jack struggles for control of his home when his mother (Roberts) visits. Director Baker is a co-star of *Perfect Strangers*.

Peg Taylor..............................................Doris Roberts

Director: Mark Linn-Baker         Writer: Julia Newton

20. "Father Figure" July 10, 1991

Allison is jealous when Patrick spends a weekend visit male-
bonding with her brothers; Jack babysits Jill's goldfish.

Director: Tom Rickard
Writers: Chuck Tately & Kevin White

**preempted July 15**

21. "Thy Boss' Daughter" July 17, 1991

Jack finds himself dating his boss' daughter (Cross); Jill takes
cooking lessons from Joe. Orig. scheduled for July 15.

Glenn Morton.........................................Murphy Cross
Commissioner Morton...............................Arlen Dean Snyder

Director: James O'Keefe
Writers: Pamela Wick & Susan Cridland Wick

**renwed; announced as a replacement series for 1991-92**

Unaired

"Take My Dad, Please"

Orig. scheduled for July 17.

## Family Matters

ABC Sept. 21-April 19, May 31-Aug. 9    Fridays, 8:30-9 p.m.
    April 26-May 24    Fridays, 9-9:30 p.m.
    Aug. 16-on    Fridays, 8-8:30 p.m.

Series premiere: Sept. 22, 1989

Comedy of the extended Winslow household of Chicago, headed by a black police officer and his wife, the head of security at the fictitious *Chicago Chronicle* (the same newspaper employing Balki and Larry of *Perfect Strangers*, from which this series was spun-off).

Carl Winslow..........................................Reginald VelJohnson
Harriette Winslow...............................JoMarie Payton-France
Rachel Crawford, Harriette's sister...................Telma Hopkins
Grandma Winslow...........................................Rosetta LeNoire
Eddie Winslow.............................................Darius McCray
Laura Winslow...............................Kellie Shanygne Williams
Judy Winslow...................................Jaimee Foxworth
Richie Crawford, Rachel's son.........................Bryton McClure
Steve Urkel.................................................Jaleel White

*Recurring:*
Maxine (ep. 2,9,18,20)......................................Cherie Johnson
Lt. Murtagh (ep. 5-6,17,21,23)............................Barry Jenner

———————

Miller • Boyett Productions in assoc. with Lorimar Television
Executive producers: Thomas L. Miller, Robert L. Boyett, William Bickley, Michael Warren
Co-executive producer: David W. Duclon
Producers: Gary Menteer, Fred Fox, Jr.
Co-producers: Kelly Sandefur, Pamela Eells, Sally Lapiduss (latter two later in season)
Associate producer: Rebecca Misra
Executive script consultants: Pamela Eells, Sally Lapiduss (early in season)
Story editors: Sara V. Finney, Vida Spears, Stephen Langford, Janet Lynne Jackson
Creative consultant: Charlene Seeger (later in season)
Directors of photography (variously): Gregg Heschong; Richard A. Kelley, A.S.C.
Music (variously): Jesse Frederick & Bennett Salvay; Steven Chesne
Theme: "As Days Go By" by Jesse Frederick & Bennett Salvay (words and music); performed by Jesse Frederick
Creators: William Bickley & Michael Warren
Developed by: Thomas L. Miller & Robert L. Boyett

1. "Torn Between Two Lovers" Sept. 21, 1990 8:30-9:30 p.m.

Steve develops a crush on Rachel, who's dating her bank's loan officer (Hoffman).

Steve Webster..........................................Dominic Hoffman

Jolene................................................Brigid Coulter
    Also orig. announced: Deryl Carroll (Customer)

Director: Gary Menteer    Writer: Janet Lynne Jackson

2. "Marriage 101" Sept. 28, 1990

For a class project, Laura is "married" to Steve for a day.

Ms. Steuben..........................................Susan Krebs
Mark Healy..........................................Clint Hyson

Director: Richard Correll
Writers: Pamela Eells & Sally Lapiduss

3. "Flashpants" Oct. 5, 1990

Carl and Harriette practice for a dance contest.

Richie..........................................Bryton McClure
Charlie Carnelli..........................................Eddie Mekka
Ellen Carnelli.............Susan Pyles a.k.a. Kathy Susan Pyles
    a.k.a. Cathy Susan Pyles
Emcee..........................................Steve Vinovich

Director: Gerren Keith    Writer: Stephen Langford

4. "The Crash Course" Oct. 12, 1990

Steve insists on taking the blame when Eddie crashes the family car into the Winslow living room.

Jolene..........................................Brigid Coulter

Director: Gary Menteer    Writer: Manny Basanese

5. "Boxcar Blues" Oct. 19, 1990

Carl gets trapped inside a railroad boxcar with Steve and a cargo of cattle. TV-directing debut of Linn-Baker, a co-star of *Perfect Strangers*.

Robber..........................................Dan Siegel

Director: Mark Linn-Baker    Writer: Fred Fox, Jr.

6. "Dog Day Halloween" Oct. 26, 1990

Steve and Laura are held hostage during a Halloween bank robbery.

Rodney..........................................Randy Josselyn
Robber..........................................Mark Nassar
And: Doris Hess (Marcy), Dan Siegel (Clown)

Director: Gerren Keith
Writers: David W. Duclon & Fred Fox, Jr.

7. "Cousin Urkel" Nov. 2, 1990

Steve's cousin from Biloxi sets out to sweep Eddie off his feet.

Myrtle Urkel..........................................Jaleel White

Director: Gary Menteer
Writers: Pamela Eells & Sally Lapiduss

8. "Dedicated to the One I Love" Nov. 9, 1990

Laura is surprisingly jealous when Steve showers attention on another girl (Ward); a pretty neighbor (Beaubian) likes Carl.

Loretta McKay..................................................Susan Beaubian
Susie Crenshaw.................................................Caryn Ward

Director: Gary Menteer
Writers: Sara V. Finney & Vida Spears

9. "The Science Project"  Nov. 16, 1990

Steve and Laura team up for a science project -- an A-bomb.

Mr. Nagy [and] Reuben.............................................Joe Mays
Students..................Aaron Lohr, Sky Berdahl, Crystal Jenious
     Also orig. announced:
     Ian Abercrombie (Mr. Nagy), Cherie Johnson (Maxine)

Director: Gary Menteer
Writers: Pamela Eells & Sally Lapiduss

10. "Requiem for an Urkel"  Nov. 23, 1990

In the boxing ring, Steve stands up to a bully.

Willie Fuffner.................................................Larenz Tate
Coach Redding.................................................David Hayward
Fletcher (orig. Kevin) Thomas..........................Arnold Johnson
Greg............................................................Aaron Lohr
Waldo.......................................................Shawn Harrison
Students...................................Josh Waggoner, Salim Grant

Director: Joel Zwick              Writer: David W. Duclon

11. "Fast Eddie Winslow"  Nov. 30, 1990

Eddie is cornered by a tough pool hustler (Ryan). Josselyn
reprises his role from ep. 6. Dedication: "[T]o the loving
memory of John Andrew Franklin, Jr."

Rodney......................................................Randy Josselyn
Boyd Higins......................................................Tim Ryan
Chuckie...................................................Michael Rapposelli
Kevin.....................................................Irvin Mosley, Jr.

Director: Gerren Keith            Writer: Fred Fox, Jr.

12. "Rachel's Place"  Dec. 7, 1990

Rachel, feeling like a freeloader, decides to look for a career
beyond writing, and opens up a diner after Steve accidentally
burns down Leroy's. Orig. scheduled to be the first episode of
the season (Sept. 21) and chronologically occurs before the
episode that ran. Coulter reprises her role from ep. 4.

Leroy........................................................John Hancock
Steve Webster.............................................Dominic Hoffman
Jolene......................................................Brigid Coulter
Fire inspector............................................William Long, Jr.

Director: Richard Correll
Writers: David W. Duclon & Gary Menteer

13. "Have Yourself a Very Winslow Christmas"  Dec. 21, 1990

Steve is alone and fending for himself during the holidays;
Carl searches for a scarce toy for Richie.

Mrs. Ferguson...........................................Ellen Albertini Dow
And: Gabriel Pelino (Clerk), Peggy Mannix (Customer)

Director: Richard Correll          Writer: David W. Duclon

14. "Ice Station Winslow"  Jan. 4, 1991

Carl has a potentially critical accident while ice-fishing at Lake
Wannamuck with Eddie and Steve.

Director: Gary Menteer            Writer: Stephen Langford

15. "Son"  Jan. 11, 1991

After an escalating spat with his father, a grounded Eddie escapes from the house to keep a date.

Doctor.....................................................Lawrence Cook

Director: Gary Menteer            Writer: Jose Rivera

16. "Do the Right Thing"  Jan. 18, 1991

A jealous Steve wonders if he should tutor a basketball player
(Cameron) whom Laura likes; Carl finds a diamond bracelet.

Mrs. Peavy..................................................Natalie Core
Todd Helms................................................Keith Cameron
Mrs. Sniplitsky..........................................Neary Plummer
Teen.......................................................Josh Klausner

Director: Gary Menteer
Writer: Pamela Eells & Sally Lapiduss

**preempted Jan. 25**

17. "High Hopes"  Feb. 1, 1991

In a hot-air balloon, Carl tries es to overcome his fear of heights;
Harriette and Rachel clash over a car won in a contest.

Jimmy.......................................................Jim Doughan

Director: Gary Menteer            Teleplay: Fred Fox, Jr.
Writer: Dennis Snee

18. "Life of the Party"  Feb. 8, 1991

At a rooftop party, some kids spike Steve's punch. Tate reprises his role from ep. 10, Harrison from ep. 10.

Willie Fuffner.................................................Larenz Tate
Waldo.......................................................Shawn Harrison
And: Robert Balderson (Cop), Danny Kaye Hamilton (Harvey)

Song: "The Urkel Dance" by David W. Duclon, Fred Fox, Jr.,
     Pamela Eells, Sally Lapiduss (words), Kelly Sandefur
     (music)

Director: Gary Menteer            Writer: Janet Lynne Jackson

19. "Busted"  Feb. 15, 1991

When Eddie cracks up the family car, Steve suggests raising
repair money at an illegal gambling hangout.

Stickman.....................................................John Mariano
Mom.........................................................Georgy Paul
Guard....................................................Tom Milanovich
And: Ken Kerman (Cop), Felicia Bell (Woman)

Director: Richard Correll
Writers: David W. Duclon & Fred Fox, Jr.

20. "Fight the Good Fight"  Feb. 22, 1991

Laura launches a campaign to get a black history course
taught at her school. Krebs reprises her role from ep. 2.

Edgar Shimata...................................................Clyde Kusatsu
Ms. Steuben...........................................................Susan Krebs
And: Bobby Wynn (Buddy), Patrick Pieters (Gary), Jay Brad-
    ford (Mark), Antonio Todd (Fred), David Marcus (Darryl)

Director: Gary Menteer
Writers: Sara V. Finney & Vida Spears

21. "Taking Credit" March 15, 1991

Steve takes the credit due him for tutoring Eddie; Carl braves
gunfire on his job, but gives credit to Lt. Murtagh.

Reporters...........................Mary Ingersoll, Christopher Darga

Director: Richard Correll          Writer: David W. Duclon

22. "Finding the Words" March 22, 1991

A charming, mysterious figure (Winfield), claiming to be a family friend from the past, comes to visit.

Jimmy Baines (orig. Holmes)...............................Paul Winfield

Director: Richard Correll          Writer: Fred Fox, Jr.

23. "Skip to My Lieu" Monday, April 1, 1991 9-9:30 p.m.

Carl senses a promotion if he can help Lt. Murtagh get a date
with Rachel. Harrison reprises his role from ep. 10 and 18.

Waldo.......................................................Shawn Harrison

Director: Richard Correll          Writer: Charlene Seeger

24. "The Good, The Bad, and The Urkel" April 26, 1991

An argument over the Urkel family compost heap becomes an
Old West dream sequence: Carl vs. Two-Gun Urkel.

Cowboys.......................Tom Bishop, Victor Wilson, Steve Viall

Director: Richard Correll
Writers: Pamela Eells & Sally Lapiduss

25. "I Should Have Done Something" May 3, 1991

Steve schemes to take the reluctant Laura to a hot-ticket concert; Carl feels guilt in the aftermath of a hostage case.

Helen...............................................................Beah Richards
Karen Kosta.............................................................Tiiu Leek
Anchorperson.........................................................Ron Tank

Director: Richard Correll          Writer: David W. Duclon

**preempted Aug. 2**

**renewed for 1991-92; new episodes begin Sept. 20, 1991**

## The Fanelli Boys

NBC          Sept. 8-Nov. 14     Wednesdays, 9:30-10 p.m.
             Dec. 1-Feb. 16      Saturdays, 8:30-9 p.m.

Series Premiere: Sept. 8, 1990
Final telecast: Feb. 16, 1991

Comedy of a widowed Brooklyn matriarch who orders her four
troubled adult sons to move back home and straighten out

their lives. Working title: *The Boys Are Back.*

Theresa Fanelli....................................................Ann Guilbert
Dominic Fanelli...................................................Joe Pantoliano
Frankie Fanelli...............................................Christopher Meloni
Anthony Fanelli...................................................Ned Eisenberg
Ronnie Fanelli.........................................................Andy Hirsch
Father Angelo (Uncle Angelo)...........................Richard Libertini

*Recurring:*
Bartender/Pete (ep. 1,4-6,11,13).........................Nicholas Mele
Eddie DeTucci (ep. 3,11,13,16,18-19)...............Nick De Mauro
Moe (ep. 6,11,15,18-19)........................Anthony Russell •
Becky Goldblume, Ronnie's girlfriend
    (ep. 1)......................................................Melanie Chartoff
    (ep. 2,14)..................................................Wendie Malick
Philamena (ep. 1,4,15)......................................Vera Lockwood

• Additionally, credited as "Vinnie," ep. 7.

KTMB Productions in assoc. with Touchstone Television
Executive producers: Kathy Speer, Terry Grossman, Mort
    Nathan, Barry Fanaro
Supervising producers: Martin Weiss, Robert Bruce
Producer: Treva Silverman
Associate producer: Jill Andersen
Story editors: Don Woodard, Tom Maxwell, Michael Davidoff
Director of photography (variously): Richard Brown (ep. 1);
    Richard Hissong, William R. Davis, Vincent F. Contarino
Music: Thomas Pasatieri
First theme (instrumental): Thomas Pasatieri
Second theme: "Why Should I Worry" by Dan Hartman &
    Charlie Midnight (words), Scott Gale & Rich Eames
    (music); performer uncredited
Creators: Barry Fanaro, Mort Nathan, Kathy Speer, Terry
    Grossman

---

1. (pilot) Saturday, Sept. 8, 1990 9:27-10 p.m.

When her grown sons have seemingly insurmountable problems of the wallet and of the heart, Theresa has them come
back home to live. Odd timeslot due to the pilot running long.
Guest Chartoff is a cast-member of *Parker Lewis Can't Lose.*

Police officer.......................................................Shirley Prestia
Sicilians................................................Vito Scotti, Ralph Manza
Sandra.......................................................................Alix Elias

Director: James Burrows
Writers: Barry Fanaro, Mort Nathan, Kathy Speer, Terry
    Grossman

2. "You Can Go Home Again" Sept. 12, 1990

Ronnie announces his engagement, against Theresa's wishes,
and Dom offers to pay for the wedding with a planned windfall.

Mrs. Goldblume..............................................Shelley Morrison
Emily Bartlet...................................................Amzie Strickland
Rabbi Birnbaum..................................................Floyd Levine
Archbishop Mosconi.................................................Al Ruscio

Director: J.D. Lobue          Writers: Mort Nathan & Barry Fanaro

3. "Pursued" Sept. 19, 1990

Dom reunites with his high-school best friend (Palminteri).

Tommy Esposito...........................................Chazz Palminteri

Donna Fanucci.....................................................Susan Berman
Connie Fanucci...................................................Paddi Edwards
Joe Fanucci.......................................................John La Motta
Lloyd Fanucci..........................................................John Mese

Director: David Steinberg
Writers: Martin Weiss & Robert Bruce

4. "The Hex"  Sept. 26, 1990

The guys try to face the fact Mom is dating; Frankie suffers an apparent hex put on him by an irate girlfriend's grandmother.

Mickey..................................................................Louis Guss
Lisa.........................................................................Dani Klein
Grandmother.....................................................Harriet Medin
Luigi...................................................................Cleto Augusto
Women.........................................Kim Geraghty, Anita Gregory

Director: David Steinberg            Writer: Treva Silverman

5. "Heart Attack"  Oct. 3, 1990  9:05-9:35 p.m.

The boys reflect on their lives as their mother lies gravely ill during a blackout.  The unusual time-slot derived from an apparent NBC experiment in beginning shows at five minutes after the hour *a la* Superstation TBS; see also *Unsolved Mysteries*, *Dear John...* and *Hunter* for this date.

Young Dom.......................................................Raffi Di Blasio
Young Anthony.....................................................Benny Grant
Young Frank.......................................................Jacob Kenner

Director: J.D. Lobue    Writers: Kathy Speer & Terry Grossman

6. "Take My Ex-Wife, Please"  Oct. 10, 1990

Dominic tries to talk Anthony out of a love affair with a seductress (Heller) without informing anyone she's his ex-wife in search of overdue alimony.

Viva Fontaine...............Randee Heller (Leslie Easterbrook orig.
    announced)
Waitress.......................................................Donna Ponterotto
Eddie...................................................................Robert Gould
Bobby..................................................................Glen Mauro

Director: J.D. Lobue    Writers: Tom Maxwell & Don Woodard

**preempted Oct. 17**

7. "Poetic Justice"  Oct. 24, 1990

Frankie tags along to Ronnie's poetry class and plagiarizes one of his poems to impress the attractive teacher (Tyson).

Miss Hollister....................................................Barbara Tyson
Denise................................................................Gail Shapiro
Valentina..........................................................Catya Sassoon
Students...................................B.T. Taylor, Barbara de Santis

Director: Andrew D. Weyman
Writers: Kathy Speer & Terry Grossman

8. "Father Smoke"  Oct. 31, 1990  9:30-10 p.m.

Father Angelo considers leaving the clergy to play jazz; a shapely exchange student (Udenio) temporarily moves in.

Isabella..........................................................Fabiana Udenio
Holly..................................................................Bradni Burkett

Director: Gary Brown
Writers: Mort Nathan & Barry Fanaro

9. "Tarnished Angel"  Nov. 7, 1990

Dom is challenged to a test of his masculinity by the disapproving father (Stack) of his tony new girlfriend; Anthony goes in for a tonsillectomy. Stack had previously played a character named Kyle Hadley in the film *Written on the Wind* (1957).

Kyle Hadley.........................................................Robert Stack
Jennifer Hadley...............................................Michelle Abrams
Albert..................................................................Arthur Malet
Dr. O'Neal....................................................John Mallory Asher
Nurse.................................................................Annie Korzen
And: Christopher Castile (Timmy), Dan Tullis, Jr. (Boxer)

Director: Jim Drake        Writers: Robert Bruce & Martin Weiss

10. "The Two Doms"  Nov. 14, 1990

A high-school freshman neighbor (Hopper) has a crush on Frankie; Uncle Dom visits.

Uncle Dom..............................................................Bruce Kirby
Leslie...............................................................Heather Hopper
Margo...................................................................Tasha Scott
Winnie.............................................................Danielle Koenig

Director: Jack Shea        Writers: Tom Maxwell & Don Woodard

**preempted Nov. 21 and Nov. 28**

11. "Italian-American Gigolo"  Dec. 1, 1990

Frank's new job as assistant to a publisher (Mace) becomes a bit too intimate for him; Anthony is up for a business award.

Victoria Reid-Smith...............................................Cynthia Mace
Danielle............................................................Bren McKinley
Candy....................................................................Kelly Miller

Director: Jim Drake            Writer: Howard Gewirtz

12. "A Fanelli Christmas"  Dec. 8, 1990

On Christmas Eve, the clan reminisces via clips of past shows.

Kyle Hadley.......................................Robert Stack (from ep. 9)
Donna Fanucci...............................Susan Berman (from ep. 3)
Eddie DeTucci..................................Nick De Mauro (from ep. 3)
Becky Goldblume.........................Wendie Malick (from ep. 2)
Mrs. Goldblume.........................Shelley Morrison (from ep. 2)
Bartender/Pete.................Nicholas Mele (from a past episode)
Nina Donatelli................................................Shirley Prestia *
Denise..............................................Gail Shapiro (from ep. 7)
Isabella.....................................Fabiana Udenio (from ep. 8)

* No character by that name is listed in any previous episode credit, though Prestia had played a police officer in ep. 1.

Director: Jim Drake
Writers:  Barry Fanaro, Mort Nathan, Kathy Speer, Terry Grossman

13. "Oh My Papas"  Dec. 15, 1990

Theresa awaits a papal audience in Rome; Ronnie babysits his girlfriend's kids.  Orig. scheduled for Nov. 14 and Dec. 8.

Tina DeMarco...............................................Jana Marie Hupp

Alex..............................................................Billy Cohen
Sunshine Cadet.............................................Jaclyn Bernstein

Director: Jack Shea            Teleplay: Michael Davidoff
Story: Martin Pasko & Rebecca Parr

14. "Accidents Will Happen"  Jan. 5, 1991

Dom tries to have Frankie exaggerate an injury to collect a big settlement; Anthony asks Ronnie's girlfriend to his high-school reunion. Guest Elias played a different character in ep. 1.

Christina........................................................Alix Elias
LaCroix........................................................Daniel Riordan
Usher...........................................................Jimm Giannini
Emcee...........................................................Will Leskin
Steve Wild.....................................................James Arone
And: Don Marino (Mike), Lenny Citrano (Man)

Director: Gary Brown            Writer: Michael Davidoff

15. "Doctor, Doctor"  Jan. 12, 1991

The boys see a psychologist (Getty, a co-star of *The Golden Girls*) in an effort to get along better under one roof.

Dr. Newman....................................................Estelle Getty
Monica..........................................................Debra Engle
Ken Takaguchi..................................................Jim Ishida

Director: Andrew D. Wayman
Writers: Tom Maxell & Don Woodard

16. "Rope a Dope"  Jan. 19, 1991

Bunny...........................................................Gina Mastrogiacomo
Kid Comforte....................................................Art La Fleur
Mario...........................................................Robert Costanzo
And: Teddy Wilson (Butch), J.J. Johnston (Alfredo)

Director: Steve Zuckerman
Writer: Martin Weiss & Robert Bruce

17. "The Undergraduate"  Feb. 2, 1991

Ronnie fights off the advances of a new girlfriend's mom (Wilcox) while Dom, Frank and Father Angelo may be lost at sea.

Mrs. MacKenzie................................................Shannon Wilcox
Amanda MacKenzie..............................................Hannah Cutrona
Capt. Smith...................................................Jack Murdock
Widow.........................................................Lisa Alpert-Thames
Sarah.........................................................Meg Wyllie

Director: Steve Zuckerman            Writer: Michael Davidoff

18. "The Wedding, Part I"  Feb. 9, 1991

Theresa gets engaged to her beau (Windom), whose daughter sues the neighborhood Knights of Sicily club for sexual discrimination. Wilson reprises his role from ep. 16.

Ernie..........................................................William Windom
Lauren, his daughter..........................................Jessica Lundy
Butch..........................................................Teddy Wilson
Reporter.......................................................Richard Zobel
Joe............................................................Jeff Silverman

Director: James Burrows
Writers: Barry Fanaro, Mort Nathan, Kathy Speer, Terry Grossman

19. "The Wedding, Part II"  Feb. 16, 1991

While Theresa and Ernie are on their honeymoon, Lauren must turn to Dom for help when Ernie's diner burns down.

Ernie..........................................................William Windom
Lauren.........................................................Jessica Lundy
And: Teddy Wilson (Butch), Nancy Sheppard (Woman)

Director: James Burrows
Writers: Barry Fanaro, Mort Nathan, Kathy Speer, Terry Grossman

## Father Dowling Mysteries

ABC            Sept. 20-July 18    Thursdays 8-9 p.m.
               Aug. 1-22           Thursdays, 9-10 p.m.
               Aug. 29-Sept. 5     Thursdays, 8-9 p.m.

Premiere:
    As the NBC TV-movie *Fatal Confession: A Father Dowling Mystery*: Nov. 30, 1987
    As a series: Jan. 20, 1989
Final telecast: Sept. 5, 1991

Lighthearted mystery of a sleuthing Chicago priest (pastor, St. Michael's Church) and nun. Based upon characters in Ralph McInerny's "Father Dowling Mystery" novels. Series began on NBC, switched to ABC beginning Jan. 4, 1990. Title above is as appears onscreen. Co-star Nelson is the daughter of the late actor-singer Rick Nelson, the sister of singers Matthew and Gunnar Nelson, and the granddaughter of performers Ozzie and Harriet Nelson.

Father Frank Dowling..........................................Tom Bosley
Sister Stephanie (Steve)......................................Tracy Nelson
Father Phil Prestwick.........................................James Stephens
Marie Gillespie, the rectory housekeeper......................Mary Wickes

*Recurring:*
Sgt. Clancy
    (ep. 1,3,6,8-9,11-12,14-15,17-20,22)........Regina Krueger
Lt. Bob Foster (ep. 5,10,16)..................................Dick O'Neill

The Fred Silverman Co., Dean Hargrove Productions, and Viacom
Executive producers: Fred Silverman, Dean Hargrove
Supervising producer: Robert Schlitt
Producers: Joyce Burditt, Barry Steinberg, Gerry Conway (latter, later in season)
Co-producer: Victoria La Fortune
Executive story editor: Gerry Conway (early in season)
Executive story consultant: Brian Clemens
Creative consultant: Joel Steiger
Director of photography: Rick Anderson
Music (variously): Bruce Babcock; Peter Myers; Arthur Kempel
Theme (instrumental): Dick De Benedictis
Developed by: Dean Hargrove & Joel Steiger

---

1. "The Royal Mystery"  Sept. 20, 1990  (1927)

Sister Steve trades places with a lookalike Brit noble to infiltrate a trade delegation, one member of which may be a killer.

Lady Cara Winston.............................................Tracy Nelson
Gloria........................................................Francesca Buller
Mrs. Gibbons..................................................Sarah Douglas
Sir Robert....................................................David McCallum

Willie Lapinski..................................................Anthony Gioia
Sean McAlister.................................................Thomas Calabro
And: Tom Allard (Hustler), Brian Brophy (Fashion designer),
Camille Ameen (Fashion writer), William Raulerson (Battalion chief), Katie Mitchell (Sales manager), Sheila Scott
Wilkinson (Salesperson), Lew Saunders (Cop)

Director: Chris Hibler                 Writer: Gerry Conway

2. "The Medical Mystery" Sept. 27, 1990  (1928)

Father Prestwick's life is endangered at a hospital where a
murder conspiracy abounds.

Nurse Eunice................................................Carolyn Seymour
Dr. Dean (orig. Donald) Dixon.................Craig Richard Nelson
Dr. Carl Boxwell............................................James Staley
Dr. Brent (orig. Vincent) Riley.......................Steven Anderson
Father Garcia (orig. Jankowski)......................Daniel Faraldo
Scrub nurse................................................Belinda Balaski
Tony Newton (orig. Donatello)......................Robert V. Barron
Pathology intern................................................David Knell
Eddie Bell (orig. Corletto)....................................Bennie Grant
And: Greg Collins (Chip), Jack Jozefson (Leo), Shannon Beaty
(Candy striper), Gail Cameron (Nurse), Richard Grove, Patrick Lee James (Drivers), Pamela Roylance (Receptionist)

Director: James Frawley                Writer: Jeri Taylor

3. "The Devil and the Deep Blue Sea Mystery"
   Oct. 4, 1990  (1929)

To save her brother, Sister Steve apparently makes a deal with
the Devil (Champion), leading Dowling to try to outfox him.

Eddie Okowski................................................Steven Flynn
Harry Deil................................................Michael Champion
Ronald........................................................Jerry Rector
Roland..........................................................Jeff Rector
Dr. Randall (orig. Thomas) Pryer...........................Joe Dorsey
Floor nurse....................................................Beth Hogan
Janie Okowski............................................Michelle Little
Mrs. Blanchard............................................Anne T. Haney
ICU nurse......................................................Leilani Jones
Judge............................................................John Malloy

Director: Chris Hibler
Writers: Dean Hargrove & Joyce Burditt

**preempted Oct. 11**

4. "The Showgirl Mystery" Oct. 18, 1990

The wealthy fiance of Sister Steve's friend (Pouget) is murdered
on his wedding day, and the bride-to-be accused of the crime.
Buktenica is a recurring guest on *Life Goes On*.

Morgan............................................................Bill Macy
Dr. Palmer...............Mitchell Laurance (misspelled "Laurence"
in *TV Guide*)
Dupree......................................................Ray Buktenica
Trask........................................................Robin Strand
Claudia....................................................Brenda Bakke
Jillian McGuire................................................Ely Pouget
Olsen....................................................Robert Clotworthy
Horace Johnson......................Edwin Wallace Williams
Waiter....................................................Brian MacAndrew
And: Miguel Marcott (Croupier), Macka Foley (Lewis)

Director: Christopher Hibler
Writers: James Harmon Brown & Barbra Esensten

5. "The Movie Mystery" Oct. 25, 1990  (1930)

In a self-referential episode, odd accidents and a director's
(Portnow) murder disrupt the filming of a TV series about a
sleuthing priest and nun, using St. Michael's as its locale.

Brian Cahill..............................Philip Charles MacKenzie
Cameron Prince..............................Richard Portnow
Glenn Evert.......................................Mark Moses
Mark Tannen ("Father Patrick Flaugherty")...........John Furey
Sarah Soames ("Sister Eugenia").................Michele Scarabelli
Lex Armstrong..............................Patrick Dollaghan
Riki/costumer.................................Caroline Schlitt
Gofer.........................................Claude Knobler
Billy/editor.................................Peter Trencher
     Also orig. announced:
     Greg Allen Martin (Second assistant director)

Director: James Frawley           Story: William Conway
Teleplay: William Conway and Gerry Conway

6. "The Undercover Nun Mystery" Nov. 1, 1990  (1926)

During the Silver Jubilee celebration for the mother superior
of Sister Steve's old convent, an undercover cop is murdered.
Meaney is a recurring guest on *Star Trek: The Next Generation*.

Mother Margaret Edward...........................Fionnula Flanagan
Sam McCauley.......................................John Vernon
Mark Penn..........................................Mark Rolston
Ernie Simpkins....................................Colm Meaney
Murphy.............................................Amy Steel
Edward.............................................Don Hanmer
Man................................................Al Rossi
Nun...............................................Mimi Champlin
Charlie............................................Angelo DiMascio
John Morrow........................................Jason Edwards
Joe Fontaine.......................................Robert Gentili
Priest.............................................Andrew Herman

Director: James Frawley           Teleplay: Joyce Burditt
Story: Dean Hargrove & Joyce Burditt

7. "The Murder Weekend Mystery" Nov. 8, 1990 (1931)

The duo searches for a paid assassin who uses high-tech electronics to conceal his crime during a weekend retreat for mystery writers.

Sir Arthur Wedgeworth......................................David Warner
Lindsey Quinn.....................................Doran Clark
Drake.............................................Jim Beaver
Professor Clement Mitchell.........................Raymond Singer
Lt. Adams.........................................Greg Alan-Williams
Mystery author Jack Patton........................Scott Marlowe
Rental car agent..................................Lisa Marie Russell
Police officer....................................Richard Camphuis

Director: Harry Harris
Writer: Gerry Conway (Donald Paul Roos also orig. announced)

8. "The Reasonable Doubt Mystery" Nov. 15, 1990  (1934)

Citing reasonable doubt, Father Dowling deadlocks a murder
jury, then begins his own investigation into the case with Sister Steve before the retrial. Working title: "The Scam Mystery."

Lenny Rothstein...................................Robert Ginty
Gator Malloy......................................Dennis Burkley
Simon Putter......................................Roy Brocksmith
Defendant Karen Howard............................Katherine Moffat

Ruth Walenga.............................................Janet MacLachlan
D.A.............................................................David Selburg
And: Bill Kalmenson (Bank guard), David Wells (Wallace
    Grant), John Gowans (Kelsey), Bari K. Willerford (Eddie),
    Frank Novak (Judge), John David Conti (Foreperson),
    James R. Sweeney (Man)
    Also orig. announced: George McDaniel (Thomas Vilner)

Director: Robert Scheerer          Story: Brian Clemens
Teleplay: Brian Clemens and Gerry Conway

9. "The Renegade Priest Mystery" Nov. 22, 1990  8-10 p.m.

When Dowling suspects a young priest has been framed for
murder, the trail leads to the accused's own family. Frost is
the daughter of actor Warren Frost and the sister of producer
Mark Frost. Working title: "The Mafia Priest Mystery."

Guido Corabina.............................................Louis Guss
Peter Luciani.................................................John Aprea
Kathy Luciani...............................................Lindsay Frost
John Luciani................................................Martin Hewitt
Douglas.....................................................Andreas Katsulas
Cliff.........................................................Henry G. Sanders
Beth.........................................................Deborah Wakeham
Slick.........................................................J.W. Smith
Tom Fremont...............................................Joseph Whipp
Jerry Brooks...............................................Richard Yniguez
Chris Luciani...............................................Ramy Zada
And: Jimmy Stathis (Giulianio), Brick Karnes (Karnes), J.D.
    Hall (Mark), Dulcie Camp (Bernice), Sheila Traister
    (Marge), Harrison LeDuke (Solider)

Director: Charles S. Dubin         Writer: Robert Hamilton

10. "The Vanishing Victim Mystery" Nov. 29, 1990  (1933)

Sister Steve poses as a maid in the home of a mysteriously
vanished young root-beer heiress (Donald) whom Father Dowling befriended. Originally scheduled for Nov. 15 and 22.

Sybil Aspell.................................................Linda Kelsey
Aunt Em.....................................................Susan French
Paul Aspell.................................................Robert Nadir
Williams.....................................................Madison Mason
Lucy Aspell.................................................Juli Donald
Mr. Hakaido...............................................Robert Kino
Translator...................................................Yoshio Be
Goon.........................................................Sam Zap
Sumo bouncer...Glen Chin (Sebastian Massa orig. announced)
Geisha.......................................................Nancy Arnold
Massage girls.........................Rosa Chia-Hwai Li, Francine Lee

Director: Seymour Robbie           Writer: Robert Schlitt

11. "The Christmas Mystery" Dec. 13, 1990  (1935)

A murderous Santa Claus stalks a department store, as Sister
Steve attempts to protect the young son of the killer's victim.

Sam Pulver..................................................J.C. Quinn
Wendy Martin.............................................Anne Kerry Ford
Laura Bradshaw............................................Linda Carlson
Virginia.....................................................Frances Bay
Brian Martin.................................Christian/Joseph Cousins
Wilson.......................................................John Hostetter
Miller.........................................................David Pressman
Brewster.....................................................Robert Rothwell
Tully.........................................................James V. Christy
First Santa Claus............................................Joe Flood
Second Santa Claus........................................Pete Schrum

Director: James Frawley            Writer: Brian Clemens

**preempted Dec. 27**

12. "The Fugitive Priest Mystery" Jan. 3, 1991  (1938)

Father Dowling's criminal twin frames him for bank robbery.

Blaine Dowling.............................................Tom Bosley
Sly...........................................................Don Yesso
Lou...........................................................Tony Todd
Arnie.........................................................Ebbe Roe Smith
Ms. Hudson................................................Natalija Nogulich
Franco.....................................Kenneth John McGregor
Bud..........................................................Paul Benvictor
Randy.......................................................Peter Allas
Kimberly....................................................Michelle Forbes
Cop..........................................................Will MacMillan
Trainer.......................................................Pete Steinfeld
Card players....................Milton Murrill, Skip Ward
    Also orig. announced: Dean Wein (Security guard)

Director: James Frawley            Writer: Michael Reaves

13. "The Substitute Sister Mystery" Jan. 10, 1991  (1937)

The duo is caught amid a mobster, his kidnapped daughter, a
hired killer, and an ersatz nun (Lizer) impersonating Steve.

Lauren Gail.................................................Kari Lizer
Malcolm Rice...............................................Charles Cioffi
Grant Packer..............................Michael C. Gwynne
Bruno Olsen...............................................S.A. Griffin
Walker.......................................................A.C. Weary
Dr. Wallace.................................................Emily Yancy
And: Monique Salcido (Waitress), Oz Tortora (Kramer), Mitchell
    Group (Comedian), Laura Leigh Hughes (Vicky Rice),
    Kenny D'Aquila (Taxi driver), Don Knight (Heckler), An-
    thony Mangano (Man), Richard Assad (Guard), Arell
    Blanton (Uniformed cop), Sheldon Kurtz (Drunk)

Director: Charles S. Dubin         Teleplay: Gerry Conway
Story: Gerry Conway and Brian Clemens

**unscheduled preemption Jan. 17**

14. "The Missing Witness Mystery" Jan. 24, 1991  (1939)

To try to locate the sole witness to a murder for which a young
businessperson (Frank) has apparently been framed, Sister
Steve poses as a prostitute. Orig. scheduled for Jan. 17.

Tim Shanker................................................Peter Jurasik
Elliot Wagner.............................William Allen Young
Edith Monroe..............................................Jenny O'Hara
Don Bailey..................................................Charles Frank
Suzanne Preston..........................................Kerrie Keane
Walter Preston.............................H. Richard Greene
Michele......................................................Lycia Naff
Dawn.........................................................Christine Elise
Jake..........................................................Anthony Charnota
Newscaster..................................................Cynthia Bond
And: Gina Lamond (Rita), John T. Olsen (Man)

Director: Christopher Hibler        Teleplay: Lincoln Kibbee
Story: Lincoln Kibbee and Brian Clemens

15. "The Prodigal Son Mystery" Jan. 31, 1991  (1940)

A man (Rubinstein) accused of murdering his mistress turns
out to be the son Father Dowling never knew he had.

Tim Connell.....................................................John Rubinstein
Mike Malone.....................................................Michael MacRae
Rita Winters.....................................................Kate Vernon
Jimmy C..........................................................Vincent Guastaferro
Susan Connell..................................................Patricia Estrin
Bill Crawford...................................................Richard Bright
And: Angela Paton (Cleaning person), Walter Addison (Duane Bates), Pat Renella (Bartender), Dona Hardy (Old lady) Also orig. announced: Ellaraino (Mrs. Crowley)

Director: James Frawley          Teleplay: Jack Burditt
Story: Dean Hargrove & Joyce Burditt

16. "The Moving Target Mystery" Feb. 7, 1991 (1932)

After a hired killer refuses to assassinate Dowling, the priest learns he'd inadvertently taken incriminating photos. Orig. scheduled for Nov. 29 and Jan. 31.

Harold Berman...................................................Richard Kline
Martin Brill.....................................................Don Stroud
Munson...........................................................Anthony James
D.A. Brice Robeson..................Jack Ryland (orig. Tom Crowl)
Kelly.............................................................Michael David Lally
Reporters.........................Stephen Mendel, Marguerite DeLain
Judge John Allsberg (per his onscreen name-
    plate; misspelled "Allsburg" in credits)........Byron Morrow
Sen. McMillan...................................................John Christy Ewing
Broadcaster......................................................Mary Watson
Clerk............................................................Dale Swann
And: Brenda Varda (Secretary/Stella), Bruce Newbold (Brill's lawyer), Nick Ballo (Thug), Oscar Dillon (Officer)

Director: Robert Scheerer
Teleplay: Joyce Burditt
Story: Dean Hargrove & Joyce Burditt and Brian Clemens

17. "The Priest Killer Mystery" Feb. 14, 1991 (1941)

Sister Steve poses as a cabbie to try to locate a rooftop priest-sniper who almost makes Father Dowling his third victim. Guest Roche is a cast-member of *Lenny*.

Father MacElroy.............Eugene H. Roche a.k.a. Eugene Roche
Gun club manager...............................................John Astin
Father Crisp....................................................Mark Herrier
Father Pike.....................................................Roger Aaron Brown
Kane.............................................................Bill Moseley
Older cabbie....................................................Wynn Irwin
And: Marc Siegler (Father Baker), Alexander P. Enberg, Joanna Lipari (Cabbies), Katherine Henryk (Old woman)

Director: David Moessinger          Teleplay: Gerry Conway
Story: Gerry Conway and Brian Clemens

18. "The Mummy's Curse Mystery" Feb. 21, 1991 (1942)

When a pharaoh's burial chamber is exhibited at a museum, an ancient curse and modern science give clues to a treasure.

Kenneth Brubaker................................................David Hemmings
Helen Austin....................................................Frances Lee McCain
Amnon Bey.......................................................Aharon Ipale
Omar.............................................................Grant Heslov
Thomas (orig. Timothy) Douglas...................................Peter Donat
Wolfe............................................................Deryl Caitlyn
And: Duke Stroud (Carson), Jack Ross Obney (Sullivan)

Director: James Frawley          Writer: Michael Reaves

19. "The Monkey Business Mystery" March 7, 1991 (1943)

The duo faces arrest for harboring a murder suspect when Sister Steve protects a zoo chimp accused of killing an animal activist. Working title: "The Murderous Monkey Mystery."

Wendell Peck....................................................Dan O'Herlihy
Leonard Spaulding...............................................Ethan Phillips
Emily Stone.....................................................Vanessa Bell Calloway
MacReynolds.....................................................Tim Grimm
Bellino.........................................................John Apicella
Mrs. Julia Wiley...............................Mary Margaret Humes
Guard...........................................................Joseph Medalis
Mime (orig. announced as
    Kiki/man in monkey suit)........................Jody St. Michael
Chimp...........................................................Bubbles (uncredited)

Director: Peter Ellis          Writer: Doc Barnett

**preempted March 21**

20. "The Hardboiled Mystery" March 28, 1991 (1944)

A pal who's penned a 1930s detective novel (*Murder Cried the Padre*) with characters based on the duo is murdered, leaving clues to his killer in the manuscript. Westlake is the psuedonymous mystery author, who wrote the series' pilot; guest Frawley is the episode's director. Orig. scheduled for March 21.

Father Francis Xavier O'Downey (1930s)..................Tom Bosley
Sister Mary Katharine Ignatius (1930s)................Tracy Nelson
Gregory Laidlaw/Peter Stackpole (1930s).........Kevin McCarthy
Rich Vincent............................Donald E. Westlake
Nick Courtland/Big Ed Franklin (orig.
    Francisco) (1930s)...................................Robert Miranda
Joyce Morrison/Judith Carswell (1930s)............Laurie Holden
Howard Morrison/Anthony Carswell (1930s).............Tim Ryan
Det. Chet Lawson (1930s)........................Francis X. McCarthy
Psychiatrist....................................................James Frawley
Nurse...........................................................Jacky deHaviland
Thug............................................................Ron Gilbert

Director: James Frawley          Teleplay: Michael Reaves
Story: Robert Schlitt and Michael Reaves

21. "The Malibu Mystery" April 4, 1991

In Malibu, Calif., the duo tries to find the killer of a rock star's boyfriend.

Laurie Kidd.....................................................Patricia Charbonneau
Pete Garfield...................................................Robert Bauer
Moe Parker......................................................James Healy
Detective Miller/clown vendor...........................Richard Riehle
Choreographer...................................................Debi A. Monahan
Andy Garfield...................................David Anthony Marshall
Max Donovan.....................................................Rod McCary
Jennifer Donovan................................................Amy Lynne
Ron Baylor......................................................Stanley Kamel
Mrs. Connell....................................Beth Cloninger Mayo
And: Allen Rice (Security guard), Roman Cisneros (Cop)

Director: Christopher Hibler          Story: Wayne Berwick
Teleplay: Wayne Berwick & Gerry Conway

**preempted April 18**

22. "The Consulting Detective Mystery" April 25, 1991 (1945)

Dowling, witness to a theft that connects to multiple murders, is aided by fictional Sherlock Holmes, whom only he can see.

Sherlock Holmes................................................Rupert Frazer

Barone............................................Patrick Kilpatrick
Martin Kawecki.....................................Kevin Scannell
Larry Gable................................................Kurt Fuller
Maggie Eastland....................................Susan Krebs
George Eastland....................................Richard Roat
Auctioneer...............................................Emory Bass
Stu.........................................................Timothy Stack
Werner.....................................................Richie Allen
Security guard........................................Biff Yeager

Director: Sharron Miller          Teleplay: Gerry Conway
Story: Dean Hargrove and Gerry Conway
(Orig. announced:  Writer: Brian Clemens)

23. "The Joyful Noise Mystery"  May 2, 1991  (1936)

Tracking the death of a jazz musician, Father Dowling tries to
expose a hired killer before a bitter campaign for district attorney becomes bloody.  Orig. scheduled for Jan. 3 and 24.

Rev. Raymond Johnson..........................................Ivan Dixon
Brad Winfield (orig. Williams)...........................Richard Lawson
D.A. John Dalton................................................Jack Bannon
Detective Lt. Johnson.........................................J.A. Preston
Ray...............................................................Jeffrey Josephson
Gordon Powell.................................................Bruce A. Young
Cherie.............................................................Kelly Jo Minter
Keith Johnson.......................................................Keith Amos
Maurice Darnell......................................Billy "Sly" Williams
Boss.............................................................Richard Delmonte

Director: Robert Bralver
Teleplay: Joyce Burditt
Story: Dean Hargrove & Joyce Burditt

**preempted June 13**

**preempted July 11**

**preempted July 25**

**preempted Aug. 15**

## Ferris Bueller

NBC        Aug. 23            Thursday, 8:30-9 p.m.
           Sept. 10-Nov. 26   Mondays, 8:30-9 p.m.
           Dec. 9, Aug. 11-18 Sundays, 7-7:30 p.m.

Series premiere: Aug. 23, 1990
Final telecast: Aug. 18, 1991

Comic misadventures of a high-school junior and high-tech
schemer/operator, at Ocean Park High School. School team:
Vikings.  Based on the 1986 movie *Ferris Bueller's Day Off*.

Ferris Bueller................................................Charlie Schlatter
Bill Bueller, his father.............................................Sam Freed
Barbara Bueller, his mother..............................Cristine Rose
Principal Ed Rooney.......................................Richard Riehle
Jeannie Bueller.......................................Jennifer Aniston
Sloan..................................................................Ami Dolenz
Cameron Frye.........................................Brandon Douglas
School secretary Grace...................................Judith Kahan

*Recurring, virtually all episodes:*
Arthur Petrelli.....................................................Jeff Maynard

*Other recurring guests:*
History teacher Mr. Rickets (ep. 1-2,6)..................Jerry Tullos

Dork (ep. 4,6,11).................................................David Glasser
Wimp (ep. 4,6,11).................................................Brandon Rane

Maysh, Ltd. Productions in assoc. with Paramount Television
Executive producer: John Masius
Supervising producers: Lawrence Gay, Michael J. DiGaetano
Producer: Frank Pace (ep. 1); Pamela Grant
Associate producer: Steve Oster
Executive story consultant: Steve Pepoon
Executive story editors: Robert Ulin, Kathy Slevin
Director of photography: Marvin Rush (ep. 1); Steve Confer
Music [and] Theme (instrumental): Glenn Jordan
Developed by: John Masius
Based on characters created by: John Hughes

————————————

1. (pilot) Thursday, Aug. 23, 1990; Monday, Sept. 10, 1990

On the first day of school, Ferris becomes infatuated with
transfer student Sloan.  Rachins is an *L.A. Law* cast-member.

Alan Rachins lookalike/lawyer impersonator.......Alan Rachins
Greaser.........................................Bojesse Christopher Graham
Skinhead..............................................................Tony Nittoli
Jock.......................................................................Troy Shire
And: Gregory D. Smith (Cop), Suzanne Tara (Surfer girl)

Director: Jonathan Lynn          Writer: John Masius

2. "Behind Every Dirtbag"  Sept. 17, 1990  (002)

Ferris grooms a rebel (Walker) to oppose the principal's pre-
ferred candidate (Calvert) for school president.  Director Bixby
is also known as an actor.

Shred.................................................................Matthew Walker
Gary Hammerschmidt...........................................Jim Calvert
Librarian...................................................Melanie MacQueen

Director: Bill Bixby
Writers: Michael J. DiGaetano & Lawrence Gay

3. "Custodian of the People"  Sept. 24, 1990

Ferris has his janitor buddy impersonate the former Marine
drill sergeant Rooney hired as the new dean of students.

Announced cast includes:
Janitor/Lou...................................................Dennis Lipscomb
Mr. Prescott....................................................James Demarse
Student.....................................................................Tai Thai

Director: Bethany Rooney Hillshafer
Writer: Robert Ulin

4. "Without You I'm Nothing"  Oct. 1, 1990  (003)

Ferris tries to help Cameron with his identity crisis.  Orig.
scheduled for Sept. 24.

Director.................................................................Kent Minault
Algebra teacher.............................................Nicholas Shaffer
Alex....................................................................Kenny Eckman
Mike.....................................................................Randy Kaplan
Cindy.....................................................................Kelly Read
Student..............................................................Chris Claridge

Director: Steven Dubin          Writer: Steve Pepoon

5. "Between a Rock and Rooney's Place"  Oct. 8, 1990

Ferris throws a surprise birthday party for Cameron -- at the principal's house. Rap musician Tone-Loc lip-syncs portions of his #1 single, "Funky Cold Medina."

```
Himself.....................................................................Tone Loc
Tony...............................................................David Sheinkopf
Miss Connely.....................................................Myra Turley
Stacy..................................................................Linda Larkin
Noi.......................................................................Tai Thai
```
And: Chris Claridge (Surfer), Michael Ciotti (Stevie)

Director: James Whitmore, Jr.        Writer: Paul B. Price

6. "A Dog and His Boy"  Oct. 15, 1990

Sloan leaves Lucy, the campus canine, in Ferris' care.

```
Timmy.................................................................Micah Rowe
Mrs. Finch.......................................................Mary Gregory
Mr. Sugarbaker.............................................Chuck Sloan
Clerk.......................................................................Joe Lerer
```

Director: Victor Lobl        Writer: John Masius

7. "Ferris Bueller Can't Win"  Oct. 22, 1990

After a fortune teller sees a "black aura" around him, Ferris has a run of disastrously bad luck.

```
Marjorie Ganesha.........................................Karen Kondazian
Ms. Reynolds.....................................................Mary Portser
Mrs. Bickel..............................................................Dale Raoul
Geoffrey.........................................................Anthony Gordon
Himself (costumed character)...........The Famous Chicken/Ted
    Giannoulas
```

Director: Steven Dubin        Writer: Mary Conley

**preempted Oct. 29**

8. "Sloan Again, Naturally"  Nov. 5, 1990

Sloan, feeling smothered by Ferris, dates a dashing Italian exchange student whom Jeannie likes.

```
Himself.............................................Richard "Digger" Phelps
Ms. Behlman..........................................................Ellen Bry
Giancarlo...................................................................Marco Rufo
```
And: Frank Birney (Instructor), Karen Lombardo (Allison)

Director: Andy Tennant        Writer: Kathy Slevin

9. "Scenes from a Grandma"  Nov. 12, 1990

Ferris' nosy, know-it-all grandmother (Leachman) wants to turn her two-week visit into a permanent stay.

```
Grandma Margaret, Barbara's mother............Cloris Leachman
Tim................................................................Chris Claridge
Fast-food manager...............................................Sean Whalen
Man.................................................................David Powledge
```

Director: Arlene Sanford
Writers: Michael J. DiGaetano & Lawrence Gay & Steve Pepoon & Rob Ulin

**preempted Nov. 19**

10. "Stand-In Deliver"  Nov. 26, 1990

Ferris poses as the boyfriend of a girl (Gugino) whose gun-

toting father (Graf) forbids her to see real boyfriend Cameron. Orig. scheduled for Nov. 12.

```
Officer Peyson..................................................David Graf
Ann Peyson....................................................Carla Gugino
```

Director: Bethany Rooney Hillshafer        Writer: Andy Tennant

**preempted Dec. 9**

11. "Grace Under Pressure"  Dec. 16, 1990

Rooney tries to cancel the annual high school beach day when the superintendent's office schedules an inspection. Guest Hackett is a stand-up comic.

```
Emcee/himself.................................................Buddy Hackett
Phil Weldon....................................................Patrick Cronin
Mr. Tenser.....................................................James DeMarse
```
And: Michael Adler (Fred Worthman), David Chemel (Man)

Director: Victor Lobl        Writer: Rob Ulin

**cancelled**

12. "A Night in the Life"  Aug. 11, 1991

Ferris and Cameron survive an eventful night while trying to churn out an important class paper.

```
Mike.......................................................................Larron Tate
Mr. Carter.......................................................Roy Brocksmith
```
And: Al Ruscio (Tony), Steve Artiaga (Hector), Valente Rodriguez (Raoul), Arnold Johnson (Grandpa), Robert Schuch (Jimmy), Allen Covert (Steve)

Director: Christopher T. Welch        Writer: Evan Smith

Unaired

"Baby You Can't Drive My Car"

The 1962 Corvette that Ferris bought may be haunted. Orig. scheduled for Dec. 2, 1990.

```
Announced personnel:
Mr. McFarland.....................................................Dick Martin
Greg Knecht.........................................................Danny Nucci
```
And: Jack Kehler (Mr. Fusco), Paige Pengra (Annette)

Director: Bill Bixby        Writer: Steve Pepoon

# 1st & Ten

HBO        Wednesdays, 11-11:30 p.m.

Series premiere: Dec. 2, 1984

Comedy of the California Bulls NFL football team, owned by a beautiful woman (Tweed, the Nov. 1981 *Playboy* Playmate and 1982 Playmate of the Year). Information (incomplete) per HBO. Series subtitle (different each season): *In Your Face!*

```
Kristy Fulbright..............................................Shannon Tweed
General Manager T.D. Parker............................O.J. Simpson
Coach Ernie Denardo.........................................Reid Shelton
Lineman Bubba Kincaid....................................Prince Hughes
Jethro Snell.........................................................Cliff Frazier
Placekicker Zagreb Shkenusky...........................John Kassir
"Dr. Death" Crunchner.........................................Donald Gibb
```

Quarterback Mac Daniels..............................Jay Kerr
Linebacker Elvin Putts...............................Jeff Hochendonner
Receiver "Miracle Miles" Coolidge.....................Keith Amos

The Kushner-Locke Co.
Executive producers: Peter Locke, Donald Kushner
Supervising producer: Jonathan Debin
Producer: Dawn Tarnofsky
Line producer: Sylvia White
Director: Peter Bonerz

———————————

1. "Opening Night"  Oct. 3, 1990

Kristy falls for the new quarterback (Kerr).

Himself...........Los Angeles Raiders running back Marcus Allen
Himself......................Philadelphia Eagles quarterback Randall
    Cunningham

Writer: Bruce Kirschbaum

2. "Old Dogs...New Tricks"  Oct. 10, 1990

Dr. Death pulls a prank on hero-worshipping rookie Elvin.

Writer: Scott Spencer Gordon

3. "She's Ba-ack"  Oct. 17, 1990

The Bulls try to reunite coach Ernie with his ex-wife.

Writer: Richard Marcus

4. "Altared States"  Oct., 24, 1990

Kristy worries that Mac won't survive his bachelor party.

Writer: David Ehrman

5. "Going in Style"  Oct. 31, 1990

Bubba, thinking he's dying, becomes a philanthropist.

Writer: Maxwell Pitt

6. "Don't Powerburst My Bubble"  Nov. 7, 1990

Newlyweds Kristy and Mac clash over his endorsement offer;
Jethro and T.D. become involved with the same woman.

Writer: Tom O'Brien

7. "The Squeeze"  Nov. 14, 1990

Coolidge's girlfriend threatens a paternity suit; bookies want
Zagreb to throw a game.

FBI agent.................Houston Oilers quarterback Warren Moon

Writer: Jim Kearns

8. "Take My Wives...Please"  Nov. 21, 1990

In a *Lifestyles of the Rich and Famous* interview with host Robin Leach, Mac reveals he never divorced his first wife.

Himself.................................................Robin Leach

Writer: Nick Arnold

9. "Bull Day Afternoon"  Nov. 28, 1990

Putts and Dr. Death, held hostage by two deranged fans, must
escape before a deadline to claim a raffled Ferrari.

Tombstone Packer..........New York Giants linebacker Lawrence
    Taylor

Writer: Bruce Kirschbaum

10. "Sex, Bulls and Videotape"  Dec. 5, 1990

Jethro is conned into a fundraiser boxing match with former
heavyweight champ Larry Holmes (as himself); Kristy's niece
videotapes her lovemaking with players.  Guest Greene plays
for the Los Angeles Rams; Csonka is a former player for the
Miami Dolphins and the New York Giants.

With: Larry Holmes, Kevin Greene, Larry Csonka

Writer: Larry Balmagia

11. "Irma Za-Greb"  Dec. 12, 1990

When his old flame turns out to be a hooker, Zagreb buys up
all her time.

Writer: Richard Marcus

12. "If I Didn't Play Football"  Dec. 19, 1990

Practice rained out, the Bulls imagine life without football.
Hendricks is a former player for the Los Angeles Raiders.

With: Morey Amsterdam, Norman Fell, Ted Hendricks

Writer: Scott Spencer Gordon

13. "A Roast is a Roast"  Dec. 26, 1990

The Bulls throw a farewell roast for T.D.; a rival bar-owner
wants to buy Bubba and Jethro's place.

Writer: Richard Marcus

**preempted Jan. 2**

14. "Close Encounters of the Third Down"  Jan. 9, 1991

Tombstone thinks aliens want him to repopulate their planet.
Real-life player Taylor reprises his role from ep. 9.

Tombstone Packer..........................................Lawrence Taylor
And: Bubba Smith

Writer: Scott Spencer Gordon

15. "Flashbacks"  Jan. 16, 1991

The players recall their own close calls at marriage, including
Zagreb's appearance on *The Dating Connection*, a parody of the
syndicated TV program *The Love Connection*.

Writer: Bruce Kirschbaum

16. "Championship Game"  Jan. 23, 1991

The Bulls make the playoffs, and Jethro has yet another mon-
eymaking scheme.  Namath is a former New York Jets quarterback, Esiason an NFL quarterback, Kelly a real-life sports
announcer, and Sherman a former New York Giants coach.

Commentators/themselves..................Joe Namath, Tom Kelly
With: Boomer Esiason (Team doctor), Allie Sherman (Coach)

Writer: Larry Balmagia

**reruns continue to end of cycle; tentatively scheduled for renewal**

## The Flash

CBS          Sept. 20-Feb. 14     Thursdays, 8:30-9:30 p.m.
             Feb. 21-March 21     Thursdays, 9-10 p.m.
             March 30-June 1      Saturdays, 8-9 p.m.
             July 12-19           Fridays, 9-10 p.m.

Series premiere: Sept. 20, 1990
Final telecast: July 19, 1991

Adventure fantasy-drama of a forensic scientist in fictional Central City, who becomes a costumed crime-fighter after a lab accident endows him with superhuman speed. Based on the DC Comics character. Co-star Pays is the wife of actor Corbin Bernsen. Orig. scheduled for Thursdays, 8-9 p.m., but never occupied that time-period.

Barry Allen/The Flash................John Wesley Shipp
Tina McGee................................Amanda Pays
Julio Mendez................................Alex Desert

*Recurring:*
WCCN/Channel 6 reporter Joe Kline •
     (ep. 1,3,5,9,11,13,15-16,20,22)..............Richard Belzer
Officer Michael Francis Murphy
     (ep. 1,3-5,7,9-10,12-15,17,19-22)..............Biff Manard
Officer Bellows
     (ep. 1-5,7,9-10,12-15,17,19-22)..............Vito D'Ambrosio
Lt. Warren Garfield
     (ep. 1-3,5-6,8-12,14-18,20-22)..............Mike Genovese
Nora Allen, Barry's mother (ep. 1,6,14)............Priscilla Pointer
Fosnight (ep. 3,14,16-17,20-21)..............Dick Miller
Megan Lockhart (orig. Luckhan; ep. 3,12,22)........Joyce Hyser

• Initially spelled "Klein" onscreen, then changed to "Kline."

Pet Fly Productions in assoc. with Warner Bros. Television
Executive producers: Danny Bilson, Paul De Meo
Supervising producers: Stephen Hattman (early in season);
     Don Kurt (later in season)
Producers: Gail Morgan Hickman, Steven Long Mitchell, Craig
     W. Van Sickle, Don Kurt (latter three early in season)
Co-producers (later in season): Michael Lacoe, David L. Beanes
Associate producer: Frank Jiminez (ep. 2-on)
Story editors (early in season): Howard Chaykin, John Francis
     Moore
Executive story consultants (later in season): Howard
     Chaykin, John Francis Moore
Directors of photography (variously): Sandi Sissel (ep. 1);
     Francis Kenny; John C. Newby; Greg Gardiner
Flash suit designer-creator: Robert Short; conceptual
     designer: Dave Stevens
Music: Shirley Walker
Theme (instrumental): Danny Elfman
Developed for television by: Danny Bilson & Paul De Meo

---

1. "The Flash"  Sept. 20, 1990  8-10 p.m.;
     Friday, Sept. 28, 1990 11:30 p.m.-1:30 a.m.;
     Saturday, Oct. 13, 1990 9-11 p.m.

Barry Allen acquires super speed and becomes the Flash to

help combat a *Mad Max*-like motorcycle gang that's killed his brother (Thomerson). Da Re, the son of actor Aldo Ray, is a recurring guest on *Twin Peaks*.

Iris West................................Paula Marshall
Gang-leader Pike........................Michael Nader
Jay Allen, Barry's brother................Tim Thomerson
Lila..........................................Lycia Naff
Chief Arthur Cooper........................Robert Hooks
Henry Allen, Barry's father............M. Emmet Walsh
Eve Allen..................................Patrie-Allen
Rick.........................................Wayne Pere
Shawn Allen, Barry's nephew............Justin Burnette
Tyrone.......................................Eric Da Re
And:  Ricky Dean Logan (Scott), Mariko Tse (Linda Park), Sam
     Vlahos (Dr. Lawrence), Josh Cruze (Petrolli), David L.
     Crowley (SWAT Captain), Virginia Morris (Mother), Rich-
     ard Hoyt-Miller (Young father), Jan Stango (Young moth-
     er), Brad "Cat" Sevy a.k.a. J. Bradley Sevy (Waiter)

Director: Robert Iscove
Writers: Danny Bilson & Paul De Meo

2. "Out of Control"  Sept. 27, 1990

The Flash pursues a renegade geneticist killing the homeless, and finds himself in conflict with Tina's scientist friend (Ivar).

Dr. Carl Tanner............................Stan Ivar
Charlie.......................................Jeff Perry
Father Michael..........................John Toles-Bey
Dr. Mortimer..........................Robert Benedetti
Mickey..............................Michael Earl Reid
Sam........................................Mario Roccuzzo
Jack........................................Bill Dunnam
Cop........................................Macka Foley
     Also orig. announced:
     Biff Manard (Officer Michael Francis Murphy)

Director: Mario Azzopardi          Writer: Gail Morgan Hickman

**preempted Oct. 4 and Oct. 11**

3. "Watching the Detectives"  Oct. 18, 1990

A private investigator (recurring guest Hyser) retained by the crooked D.A. (Guastaferro) uncovers Barry's secret identity.

Thomas Castillo..............Vincent F. Guastaferro (misspelled
     "Gustaferro" onscreen)
Arthur Simonson............................Harris Laskawy
Sadie Grosso................................Helen Martin
Noble John Spanier........................Jordan Lund
Bartender..................................Hubert Braddock
Lounge lizard...............................Pat Cupo
Gillespie..................................Darrell Harris
Gordo............Manual Perry (Robert Apisa orig. announced)
Slinky dame..............................Brenda Swanson
Judith.......................................Frankie Thorn
Pat........................................Nicholas Trikonis

Director: Gus Trikonis
Writers: Howard Chaykin & John Francis Moore

4. "Honor Among Thieves"  Oct. 25, 1990

Criminals steal a priceless mask from a financially strapped museum, the curator of which is Barry's old mentor. Clemons is the former saxophonist for rock musician Bruce Spring-steen, Buchanan a recurring guest on *Twin Peaks*. Burnette reprises his role from ep. 1.

Stan Kovacs................................................Ian Buchanan
Mitch Lestrange.........................................Michael Green
Darrell Hennings....................................Clarence Clemons
Celia Wayne...........................................Elizabeth Gracen
Ted Preminger..............................................Paul Linke
Mark Bernhardt...............................................Rene Assa
Parry Johnson...............................................Jon Menick
Chu Lee............................................................Ping Wu
Shawn Allen, Barry's nephew...................Justin Burnette
Kate Tatting.................................................Lydie Denier
And: Sav Farrow (Franco Mortelli), Michael Wyle (Anderson)
    Also orig. announced: Shashawnee Hall (Cabbie)

Director: Aaron Lipstadt
Teleplay: Milo Bachman and Danny Bilson & Paul De Meo
(orig. announced: Teleplay: Paul De Meo & Danny Bilson and
    Tom Chehak)
Story: Howard Chaykin & John Francis Moore.

5. "Double Vision"  Nov. 1, 1990

As the Hispanic district's Day of the Dead festival gears up, a
drug czar (Fernandes) and a scientist (Hayward) plant an en-
thralling device in the Flash's brain. Orig. scheduled for Nov. 8.

Trachmann...............................................Charley Hayward
Paloma Tomarquin.......................................Karla Montana
Reuben Calderon.....................................Miguel Fernandes
Father Becerra........................................Ricardo Gutierrez
The Santero...................................................Zitto Kazann
Felix Tomarquin.......................................William Marquez
Peter Paul Aguilar....................................Richard Yniguez
Sofia Tomarquin.......................................Elisabeth Chavez
Official.....................................................Anne Gee Byrd
Javier O'Hara..............................Clifton Gonzalez Gonzalez

Day of the Dead Festival celebrated by: The Ventura County
    Multicultural Arts Council

Director: Gus Trikonis                    Writer: Jim Trombetta

6. "Sins of the Father"  Nov. 8, 1990

The Flash hunts a murderous escaped convict (Koslo) who
vows to kill Barry's ex-cop father (Walsh, reprising his role 1).
Guest Shayne played Inspector Henderson in the 1950s series
*The Adventures of Superman*. Orig. scheduled for Nov. 1.

Johnny Rax Hix..............................................Paul Koslo
Henry Allen...........................................M. Emmet Walsh
Pete Donello.................................................Richard Kuss
Gruber......................................................Michael James
Danny......................................................Ralph Seymour
Pool players.................................Cole McKay, Pete Antico
Prison guard..............Richard Camphuis (Nick Vallelonga orig.
    announced)
And:  Will Gill, Jr. (Security guard), Chuck Hicks (Senior offi-
    cer), Fred Lerner (Welles), Robert Shayne (News vendor
    Reggie), Wes Studi (Roller)
    Also orig. announced:
    Terrance James, Mario Roberts (Thugs)

Director: Jonathan Sanger             Writer: Stephen Hattman

7. "Child's Play"  Nov. 15, 1990

Two street urchins with stolen documents lead the Flash to a
cult-figure flower-child (Skaggs) with a plan to drug the city.

Terry.....................................................Jonathan Brandis
Pepper........................................................Perrey Reeves

Joan Sullivan..............................Michele Lamar Richards
Beauregarde Lesko....................................Jimmie F. Skaggs
Duvivier.......................................................Kirk Baltz
Carmen Hijuelos.............................................Ivonne Coll
Phillip Sullivan.........................................Freddie Dawson
Cory Cohan......................................................Remy Ryan
And: Mark Dacascos (Osako), Alec Murdock (Passenger), Awest
    (Male hippie), Lance Gilbert (Aliota)

Director: Danny Bilson
Teleplay: Howard Chaykin & John Francis Moore
Story: Stephen Hattman & Gail Morgan Hickman

8. "Shroud of Death"  Nov. 29, 1990

Barry must piece together a broken medallion to uncover the
reason a trained assassin is killing prominent citizens.

Mavis.....................................................Lenore Kasdorf
Callahan..............................................Walter Olkewicz
Angel............................................................Lora Zane
Frank DeJoy....................................................Don Hood
Judge Foster.............................................Fred Pinkard
Mrs. Foster.............................................Marguerite Ray
Reporter........................................................Dani Klein
Aide..................................................Randall Montgomery

Director: Mario Azzopardi         Teleplay: Michael Reaves
Story: Howard Chaykin & John Francis Moore

9. "Ghost in the Machine"  Dec. 13, 1990

Barry enlists the help of an old Central City superhero (Bernard) to help battle an evil computer genius (Starke) from 35
years before, who's just awakened from suspended animation.

Nightshade/Dr. Desmond Powell......................Jason Bernard
Belle Crocker.........................................Lois Nettleton
Skip......................................................Ian Abercrombie
The Ghost.............................................Anthony Starke
And: Floyd Raglin (Tex), Sherrie Rose (Young Belle)

Director: Bruce Bilson
Writers: John Francis Moore & Howard Chaykin

**preempted Dec. 27**

10. "Sight Unseen"  Jan. 10, 1991

Tina and her supervisor (May) are trapped in Star Labs with
deadly toxins planted by an invisible-man scientist (Neame).
Shayne reprises his role from ep. 6. Orig. scheduled for Jan. 3.

Quinn.................................................George Dickerson
Ruth Werneke........................................Deborah May
Brian Gideon.....................................Christopher Neame
Dr. Cartwright.....................................Francois Giroday
Edwards........................................................Sarah Daly
News vendor Reggie.................................Robert Shayne
Dr. Velinski...........................................James Tartan
    Also orig. announced: Sergio Lanza (Young man)

Director: Christopher Leitch        Teleplay: John Vorhaus
Story: Gail Morgan Hickman and John Vorhaus

**unscheduled preemption Jan. 17; preempted Jan. 24**

11. "Beat the Clock"  Jan. 31, 1991

Barry and Julio race to find new evidence that would prove a
jazz great (Jones) who faces imminent execution is innocent.

Elliott Cotrell................Thomas Mikal Ford a.k.a. Tommy Ford
Whisper.............................................................Ken Foree
Wayne Cotrell.............................................Jay Arlen Jones
Linda Lake, his wife.................................Angela Bassett
Dave Buell................Eugene Lee (Harry Gold orig. announced)
Father Michael........................................John Toles-Bey
Security guard...............................................Joe Bellan
Morgue attendant.........................................Dennis Vero

Director: Mario Azzopardi            Writer: Jim Trombetta

12. "The Trickster"  Feb. 7, 1991

A villainous magician (Hamill) tries to kill a detective (recurring guest Hyser) who knows the Flash's real identity, and to whom Barry is romantically attracted.

The Trickster/James Jesse...................................Mark Hamill
Sabrina.................................................Gloria Reuben
Jim Kline......................................................Tim Stack
Matthews............................................William Long, Jr.
Williams.........................................Christopher Murray

Director: Danny Bilson
Writers: Howard Chaykin & John Francis Moore

13. "Tina, Is That You?"  Feb. 14, 1991

A lab accident turns Tina -- who knows Barry is the Flash -- into a criminal member of the Black Rose Gang that's out to kill him.  Orig. scheduled for Jan 17.

Lisa March....................................................Yvette Nipar
Big Ed........................................................John Santucci
Shauna Duke.................................................Denise Dillard
Janie Jones..............................................Courtney Gebhart
Dr. Wilhite...............................................William Forward
Old woman.......................................................Ivy Bethune
Nurse Gladys.................................................Mary Gillis
        Also orig. announced: Bella Pollini (Harley Lyndon)

Director: William A. Fraker        Teleplay: David L. Newman
Story: Chad Hayes & Carey Hayes and David L. Newman

14. "Be My Baby"  Feb. 21, 1991

A woman (Neville) running from her child's father (Crantston) leaves her infant with Barry.

Philip Moses................................................Bryan Cranston
Stacy........................................................Kimberly Neville
Bodey Nuff...................................................Robert Z'Dar
Roy..........................................................David Chemel
Mills........................................................John Hostetter

Director: Bruce Bilson                Writer: Jule Selbo

15. "Fast Forward"  Wednesday, Feb. 27, 1991  8-9 p.m.

After his conviction for the murder of Barry's brother is overturned, an archvillain (Nader) propels the Flash 10 years into the future. Nader and Burnette reprise their roles from ep. 1, Reuben from ep. 12.

Nicholas Pike................................................Michael Nader
Victor Kelso..............................................Robert O'Reilly
Sabrina.....................................................Gloria Reuben
Monica.......................................................Beth Windsor
Shawn Allen.................................................Justin Burnette
Cop............................................................Hank Stone
Shawn Allen (age 17)......................................Paul Whitthorne

Director: Gus Trikonis            Writer: Gail Morgan Hickman

**preempted March 14 and March 21**

16. "Deadly Nightshade"  March 30, 1991  10:30-11:30 p.m.

Nightshade (Bernard, reprising his role from ep. 9) returns to help the Flash stop an imposter Nightshade (Burgi).  Orig. set for 10 p.m; late start due to a long-running sports event prior.

Nightshade/Dr. Desmond Powell......................Jason Bernard
Curtis Bohannan...........................................Richard Burgi
Dr. Rebecca Frost.........................................Denise Crosby
Keefe......................................................Will MacMillan
Pearl.........................................................Gloria LeRoy
Double Decker Johnny.................................Charles McDaniel
Felicia Kane................................................Jeri Lynn Ryan
Steve 4K (orig. Steve 3X)..............................Jonathan Fuller

Director: Bruce Bilson
Writers: John Francis Moore & Howard Chaykin

17. "Captain Cold"  April 6, 1991

Hired by a crime lord (Combs), the supervillain Capt. Cold begins freezing people to death, with the Flash next on his list.

Leonard Wynters/Capt. Cold......................Michael Champion
Reporter Terri Kronenberg.............................Lisa Darr
Jimmy Swain...............................................Jeffrey Combs
Johnny Choi...............................................Francois Chau
Nikolai Brown.................................Jeffrey Anderson-Gunter
And: Jerry O'Donnell (Ray McGill), Erni Vales (Luis Vega)

Director: Gilbert Shilton        Teleplay: Gail Morgan Hickman
Story: Paul De Meo & Gail Morgan Hickman

18. "Twin Streaks"  April 13, 1991

An obsessed young scientist (Lang) produces a faster clone of the Flash, who begins to take over Barry's identity and life. Orig. scheduled for March 30.

Pollux......................................................John Wesley Shipp
Ted Whitcomb...............................................Charley Lang
Jason Brassell.............................................Lenny Von Dohlen

Director: James A. Contner            Writer: Stephen Hattman

19. "Done with Mirrors"  April 27, 1991

Barry is duped by an old high school chum (Coleman) with a hologram-master partner (Cassidy) in a plot to raid Star Labs.

Sam Scudder................................................David Cassidy
Stasia Masters...........................................Signy Coleman
Serge Tallent..............................................Zack Norman
Jocelyn Weller, Tina's mother.......................Carolyn Seymour
Art buyer..................................................Richard Blackwell
Fletcher (orig. Bart Flesig)...........................William Hayes
        Also orig. announced: Gloria Reuben (Sabrina)

Director: Danny Bilson
Writers: Howard Chaykin & John Francis Moore

20. "Good Night, Central City"  May 4, 1991

A supposedly dead thief's cousin (Mumy) uses a sleep-inducer on the city to commit robberies and frame the Flash.

Roger Braintree.............................................Bill Mumy

Harry Milgrim......................................................Matt Landers
Stanley Morse......................................................Victor Rivers
Farrow................................................................Jeffrey King
Morgue attendant............................................Pamela Gordon

Director: Mario Azzopardi          Writer: Jim Trombetta

21. "Alpha"  May 11, 1991  10-11 p.m.

Barry helps an attractive android (Stansfield) escape from her
government creators, who want her as a programmable killer.

Col. Powers.....................................................Laura Robinson
Alpha...........................................................Claire Stansfield
Dr. Rossick....................................................Kenneth Tigar
Costigan.........................................................Jason Azikiwe
Joey C............................................................Anthony Powers
And: Sven-Ole Thorsen (Omega), Ross Partridge (Wiseguy)

Director: Bruce Bilson          Teleplay: Gail Morgan Hickman
Story: Gail Morgan Hickman & Denise Skinner

22. "Trial of the Trickster"  May 18, 1991  10-11 p.m.

The Trickster (Hamill) escapes from his courtroom and brain-
washes the Flash to turn him criminal.  Hammill reprises his
role from ep. 12, Reuben from ep. 12 and 15, Sevy from ep. 1.

The Trickster/James Jesse....................................Mark Hamill
Zoey.............................................................Corinne Bohrer
Denise Cowan.................................................Marsha Clark
Judge...............................................................Parley Baer
Sabrina.........................................................Gloria Reuben
Waiter..........Brad Sevy a.k.a. Brad "Cat" Sevy, J. Bradley Sevy

Director: Danny Bilson
Writers: Howard Chaykin & John Francis Moore

**preempted May 25**

**on hiatus after June 1 rerun; reruns begin again July 12;
reruns orig. scheduled to continue through Aug. 9, but
were replaced by rerun TV-movies on July 26 (*Spies, Lies
and Naked Thighs*), Aug. 2 (*The Secret Life of Archie's
Wife*) and Aug. 9 (*Pair of Aces*)**

## The Fresh Prince of Bel-Air

NBC          Mondays, 8-8:30 p.m.

Series Premiere: Sept. 10, 1990

Comedy of a street-smart West Philadelphia teen sent to live
with his wealthy relatives in Bel Air, Calif., and attend the all-
male Bel-Air Academy.  Smith is a Grammy-winning rap artist
who performs under the name the Fresh Prince alongside his
partner, recurring guest D.J. Jazzy Jeff [Townes]; co-producer
Medina is their manager. Title above is as appears on-screen.

Will Smith.........................................................Will Smith
* Attorney Philip Banks......................................James Avery
Vivian Banks, his wife.....................Janet Hubert-Whitten **
Carlton Banks, their son...................................Alfonso Ribeiro
Hilary Banks, their daughter............................Karyn Parsons
Ashley Banks, their daughter.........................Tatyana M. Ali
Butler Geoffrey.................................................Joseph Marcell

*Recurring:*
Henry Furth (ep. 1,3-4,6,15)................................John Petlock
Margaret Furth, his wife (ep. 1,4,6)................Helen Page Camp

Jazz (ep. 2,7,9-10,18,22,24)..........D.J. Jazzy Jeff [Jeff Townes]
Toni (ep. 3,7,12,18)..............................................Lisa Fuller
Edward (Ned) Fellows III (ep. 7,11,13)........Jonathan Emerson
Chadney Hunt (ep. 10,13-14,16).....................Michael Landes
Kellogg Lieberbaum (ep. 10,13-14,16)...............Michael Weiner
Jonathan Cartwell (ep. 10,13-14,16).....................Keith Bogart

* Occassionally listed as "Phillip" in some press materials.
** Listed as Janet Hubert in early press materials.

The Stuffed Dog Company and Quincy Jones Entertainment in
     assoc. with NBC Productions
Executive producers: Quincy Jones, Kevin Wendle, Susan
     Borowitz, Andy Borowitz
Producers: Joanne Curley Kerner (ep. 1); Samm-Art Williams,
     Werner Walian
Co-producer: Benny Medina, Jeff Pollack
Supervising producer: Cheryl Gard
Associate producer: Mara Lopez
Coordinating producers: Ilene Chaiken, Pamela Oas Williams
     (both ep. 1)
Executive story consultant: Rob Edwards, Lisa Rosenthal
Executive story editor: Sandy Frank
Story editor: Shannon Gaughan
West Philly homeboy consultants (variously, mostly early in
     season): Bennie "Boomps" Richburg, Jr.; Kenny "Scare-
     crow"; "Smooth Mikey B"; Charlie "Mack"; Miles "Midget"
Music: Quincy Jones III
Theme written and performed by: Will Smith (words and
     music; credited as The Fresh Prince)
Director unless otherwise noted: Jeff Melman
Based on a format by: Benny Medina & Jeff Pollack
Creators: Andy Borowitz & Susan Borowitz

------------------------

1. "The French Prince of Bel-Air"  Sept. 10, 1990

Aunt Vivian tries to mediate between her husband Philip and
the newly arrived Will.

Director: Debbie Allen
Writers: Andy Borowitz & Susan Borowitz

2. "Bang the Drum, Ashley"  Sept. 17, 1990

Will persuades Ashley to pawn her violin for a drum set.

Madame Chatchka....................................................Bette Ford

Director: Debbie Allen
Writer: Shannon Gaughan

3. "Clubba Hubba"  Sept. 24, 1990

To impress a girl (Rowell) and her tough father (Roundree),
Will gets tips from cousin Carlton on becoming preppie.

"Dr. No"/Mr. Mumford...............................Richard Roundtree
Mimi Mumford...................................................Victoria Rowell
Skip Nesbitt.......................................................Garon Grigsby
And: John Towey (Country club rep), Tatiana Thumbtzen (Girl)

Writer: Rob Edwards

4. "Not With My Pig, You Don't"  Oct. 1, 1990

Will tries to smooth things between Philip and his very rural
parents when they visit to see him receive an award.

Hattie Banks, Philip's mother...........................Virginia Capers

Joe Banks, Philip's father....................................Gilbert Lewis
Susan Klein.....................................................Kathy Griffin
Art....................................................................Jim Mapp
And: David Downing (Presenter), Jeffrey Hayenga (Waiter)

Writer: Lisa Rosenthal

5. "Homeboy, Sweet Homeboy"  Oct. 8, 1990

Hilary becomes infatuated with Will's visiting hometown friend (Cheadle).  Orig. scheduled for Sept. 17, 1990

Ice Tray.......................................................Don Cheadle

Writer: Samm-Art Williams

6. "Mistaken Identity"  Oct. 15, 1990

Will and Carlton are jailed while driving Furth's Mercedes to Palm Springs.  Azaria is a recurring guest on The Simpsons.

Sergeant.....................................................Dan Desmond
Police officer..................................................Hank Azaria
Bob........................................................Raymond McLeon
Newscaster.................................................Anthony Auer
Lawyer.......................................................Donald Grant

Writers: Susan Borowitz & Andy Borowitz

7. "Def Poet's Society"  Oct. 22, 1990

Will joins his prep school's poetry club.

Christina Johnson..............................................A.J. Johnson
Elizabeth.....................................................Laurel Moglen

Writer: John Bowman

8. "Someday Your Prince Will Be in Effect"
    Oct. 29, 1990  8-9 p.m.

When Will and Carlton compete for dates for a Halloween party, Will boasts of knowing famous people (seen in fantasy flashbacks).  Guest Williams is one of the series' producers.

Cindy.........................................................Tyler Collins
Melinda......................................................Paris Vaughn
Eugene..........................................................Tim Russ
Gadgets salesperson............................................Kelly Connell
Pen salesperson.............................................Patricia Clipper
Dancers.................Omarr Rambert, Jock Simmons, Mike Barr
Nina........................................................DeEdyre J. Burks
Shauna....................................................Kimberly Newberry
Cheryl.......................................................Gina Ravarra
Thug.....................................................Samm-Art Williams
Trick-or-treater............................................Anastasia N. Ali
Themselves..........football/baseball player Bo Jackson; record
        producer  Quincy Jones; actors Kadeem Hardison, Mal-
        colm-Jamal Warner; singers Al B. Sure! and Heavy D.

Teleplay: Cheryl Gard & Shannon Gaughn
Story: Bennie Richburg Jr.

9. "Kiss My Butler"  Nov. 5, 1990

Will and Carlton surprise Geoffrey on his birthday with a gorgeous date (Campbell).  When rerun together with ep. 18 on May 20, included the premiere of D.J. Jazzy Jeff and the Fresh Prince's music video for the song "Summertime."

Helen........................................................Naomi Campbell

Director: Rita Rogers Blye          Writer: Sandy Frank

10. "Courting Diaster"  Nov. 12, 1990

Carlton feels overshadowed by Will, who's become a basketball star at school. The Detroit Pistons' Isiah Thomas has a cameo.

Himself.....................................................Isiah Thomas
Wallace Thorvald................................................Bill Cort
Coach Smiley.................................................Dave Florek
O'Donnell....................................................Ron Perkins

Writers: Sandy Frank & Lisa Rosenthal

11. "Talking Turkey"  Nov. 19, 1990

Will's mom (Watson-Johnson, a different actress than that seen in the opening credits) visits for Thanksgiving.

Viola Smith.........................................Vernee Watson-Johnson
Jesse.......................................................Israel Juarbe

Writer: Cheryl Gard

12. "Knowledge is Power"  Nov. 26, 1990

Hilary becomes Will's personal maid when he threatens to disclose she's dropped out of UCLA.

Kimmy.......................................................Sarah Buxton
Cindy....................................................Beverly Jackson

Writer: Rob Edwards

13. "Day Damn One"  Dec. 3, 1990

Will tells Ashley's slumber-party guests a scary tale about his first day at Bel-Air Academy. Cort reprises his role from ep. 10.

Principal Dr. B. Langford Oates..........................James Tolkan
Wallace Thorvald................................................Bill Cort
Student Council Pres. Simon Stanhope.........Patrick Van Horn
Sasha......................................................Ashley Bank
Courtney...............................................Nichole Francois

Writer: Cheryl Gard

14. "Deck the Halls"  Dec. 10, 1990

Will inimitably dresses the mansion for the holidays, to the dismay of the neighbors, including heavyweight boxing champion Evander Holyfield (as himself).

Himself...................................................Evander Holyfield
Ronald Reagan.................................................John Roarke
Vic........................................................Taylor Negron
Mark Driscoll..........................................Michael Pniewski
Barton Grey.................................................Richard Roat
Mr. Uesato..............................................Rodney Kageyama
Mrs. Lang.................................................Shirley Mitchell
Kevin Driscoll..........................................Justin Shenkarow
Lisa.......................................................Valerie Jones
The Alligaroos: Brian Jay, Larry Jones, Mark Morales
Carolers: Brittany Levenbrown, Everett Wong, Nicholas Ruth-
        erford, Jamie Openden, Vicki Wauchope, Darneica Corley

Writer: Shannon Gaughan

**preempted Dec. 17**

**preempted Dec. 31**

15. "The Lucky Charm" Jan. 7, 1991

Philip may lose a superstitious client (O'Rourke) whom he advises not to make decisions based on Will's spontaneous remarks. Guest Frank is the series' executive story editor.

Jameson Whitworth..........................................Tom O'Rourke
Gladys...............................................................Diane Racine
Peter Leonard......................................................Sandy Frank

Writer: Samm-Art Williams

16. "The Ethnic Tip" Jan. 14, 1991

Will proposes a black-history class be instituted at Bel-Air Academy, and gets surpised when Aunt Viv arrives to teach it. Florek reprises his role from ep. 10.

Coach Smiley........................................................Dave Florek
Asst. Headmaster Armstrong.........................Edward Edwards
Cheerleaders.....................Monica Beavers, Kyausha Simpson

Writers: Benny Medina & Jeff Pollack

17. "The Young and the Restless" Jan. 21, 1991

Will sneaks Philip's elderly mother (Capers, reprising her role from ep. 4) out of the house for a night on the town.

Hattie Banks....................................................Virginia Capers
Security guard...............................................Greg Alan-Williams
And: Tom Holiday (Handsome man), Shaun Baker (Bystander)

Writer: Lisa Rosenthal

**preempted Jan. 28**

18. "It Had to Be You" Feb. 4, 1991

Will is fixed up with Jazz's beautiful but domineering sister (Fox). See ep. 9 for a note re: this episode's rerun.

Janet..................................................................Vivica A. Fox
Gia............................................................Carol-Ann Jeffers

Writer: Cheryl Gard

19. "Nice Lady" Feb. 11, 1991

The prim daughter (Krenn) of visiting royalty (Glover) turns out to be a secret hellion who favors bikers.

Otis........................................................................Tony Longo
Lady Penelope...................................................Sherrie Krenn
Lord Fowler....................................................William Glover
And: William Upton (Bouncer), Melvin Jones (Tough guy)

Writer: Sandy Frank

20. "Love at First Fight" Feb. 18, 1991

With romance distracting her, Will's new girlfriend (Guy, a cast-member of A Different World) risks losing her scholarship.

Taylor Samuels...................................................Jasmine Guy
Pamela..............................................................Carol Barbee
Dr. Kramer..........................................................Dell Yount

Writers: Lisa Rosenthal & Samm-Art Williams

21. "Banks Shot" Feb. 25, 1991

Philip tries to settle the score with pool sharks who've hustled Will; with Viv away, Hilary tries running the household.

Charlie Mack.........................................................J.D. Hall
Gloria..............................................................Angela Gordon
Louie.................................................................Jeff Chayette
Fred.....................................................................Hugh Dane
And: Michelle Simms (Michelle), Tanya Moore (Girl)

Writer: Bennie Richburg, Jr.

22. "72 Hours" March 11, 1991

Will challenges Carlton to "prove his ethnicity" by spending three days in Jazz's tough neighborhood.

Slick..................................................................Miguel Nunez
Tiny.............................................................."Tiny" Lister Jr.
Chuck.............................................................J'Vonne Pearson
The Alligators: Richard Gloria, Larry Jones, Rodney Knoll, Mark Moralez, Jamy Woodbury

Director: Rae Kraus              Writer: Rob Edwards

**preempted April 1**

23. "Just Infatuation" April 29, 1991

Will gets Ashley's teen idol (Campbell, a singer) to attend her birthday party, and intercedes when puppy love blooms.

Little T.............................................................Tevin Campbell
Lee Cohen..........................................................Ron Fassler
Girl at party...................................................Jaclyn Bernstein
Jason..................................................................Dax Biagas

Writers: Jeff Pollack & Benny Medina

24. "Working It Out" May 6, 1991

Hilary could lose her glam new job unless she can persuade Will to date her haughty movie-star boss (rap singer Queen Latifah). Orig. scheduled for March 18.

Marissa Redman..........................Queen Latifah (Dana Owens)

Director: Rita Rogers Blye         Writer: Shannon Gaughan

**renewed for 1991-92; new episodes begin Sept. 9, 1991**

## Full House

ABC         Sept. 21-Aug. 9   Fridays, 8-8:30 p.m.
            Aug. 13-on        Tuesdays, 8:30-9 p.m.

Series premiere: Sept. 22, 1987

Comedy of a widowed young San Francisco radio personality and TV sportscaster (Saget) raising three young daughters with the help of his rock musician brother-in-law (Stamos) and their comedian friend (Coulier), who run the small Double J Creative Services production company. Family dog: Comet.

Jesse Katsopolis...................................................John Stamos
Danny Tanner.......................................................Bob Saget
Joey Gladstone.....................................................Dave Coulier
Donna Jo (D.J.) Tanner...............................Candace Cameron
Stephanie Tanner.................................................Jodie Sweetin
Michelle Tanner (toddler)........Mary Kate & Ashley Fuller Olsen
Rebecca ("Becky") Donaldson .............................Lori Loughlin

*Recurring:*
Kimmy (ep. 2-6,8-9,11-15,18-21,23-16)............Andrea Barber
Cindy, Danny's girlfriend
    (ep. 10-11,13)........................................Debra Sandlund

Jeff Franklin Productions and Miller ● Boyett Productions in
    assoc. with Lorimar Television
Executive producers: Jeff Franklin, Thomas L. Miller, Robert
    L. Boyett
Producers: Don Van Atta, David Steven Simon a.k.a. David
    Simon
Co-producers: Leslie Ray, Mark Fink (later in season)
Supervising producers: Marc Warren, Dennis Rinsler, Ellen
    Guylas
Coordinating producer: Phyllis J. Nelson
Executive story editor: Scott Spencer Gorden
Story editor: Boyd Hale, Craig Heller, Guy Schulman (latter
    two later in season)
Director of photography: J. Bruce Nielsen
Creative consultant (some episodes): Lenny Ripps
Music: Jesse Frederick & Bennett Salvay
Theme: "Everywhere You Look" by Jesse Frederick & Bennett
    Salvay & Jeff Franklin; performed by Jesse Frederick
Director: Joel Zwick
Creator: Jeff Franklin

———————————

1. "Greek Week" Sept. 21, 1990

Jesse's Greek grandparents visit America, with Michele's twin
cousin Melina, and two young people for matchmaking.

Iorgos..................................................Jack Kruschen
Gina...................................................Vera Lockwood
Elena..................................................Jennifer Gatti
Sylvio.....................................................Josh Blake
Melina.....................................Mary Kate/Ashley Fuller Olsen

Writer: Jeff Franklin

2. "Crimes and Michelle's Demeanor" Sept. 28, 1990

No one has the heart to discipline prima donna Michelle.

Stu......................................................Paul Willson

Writer: Scott Spencer Gorden

3. "The I.Q. Man" Oct. 5, 1990

Jesse and Joey are hired to film a cologne commercial, but the
client wants a scantily dressed Jesse in the ad.

Ms. Garland.......................................Jeannie Wilson
Mr. Malatesta....................................James Hampton
And: Anne Marie McEvoy (Kathy Santoni), Kieta (Model)

Writers: Marc Warren and Dennis Rinsler

4. "Slumber Party" Oct. 12, 1990

Joey plays "mom" for Stephanie at her club's mother-daughter
slumber party.

Chris.................................................Mary Ann Pascal
Melissa.................................................Mayah McCoy
Lisa.......................................................Annie Barker
Mother................................................D'Bora Loggins

Writer: Martie Cook

5. "Good News, Bad News" Oct. 19, 1990

D.J., the new editor of the school paper, has to fire best friend
Kimmy, the sports editor.

Jake..................................................Christian Guzek

Writer: Ellen Guylas

6. "A Pinch for a Pinch" Oct. 26, 1990

Jesse is the parent volunteer at Michelle's pre-school when
she's bullied by a pinching classmate (Hughes).

Mrs. Manning....................................Rosanne Katon
Aaron.....................................................Miko Hughes

Writer: Charles A. Pratt, Jr.

7. "Viva Las Joey" Nov. 2, 1990

Joey's cold, estranged dad shows up when Joey opens for
singer Wayne Newton (appearing in a cameo).

Himself..............................................Wayne Newton
Major Gladstone....................Arlen Dean Snyder (uncredited)

Writers: Marc Warren & Dennis Rinsler

8. "Shape Up" Nov. 9, 1990

D.J. decides she's too heavy to wear a bathing suit at an upcoming swim party, and embarks on a dangerous crash diet.

Aerobics instructor.............................Brittan Taylor
Girl in class...........................................Lisa Melilli
Bodybuilder......................................Troy Zuccolotto

Writer: Jeff Franklin

9. "One Last Kiss" Nov. 16, 1990

When Jesse's high-school sweetheart (Eleniak) reappears,
Jesse has second thoughts about his engagement to Rebecca.
Eleniak is the July 1989 *Playboy* Playmate.

Carrie Fowler......................................Erika Eleniak
Hammer...............................................Ken Thorley
Roger....................................................Roger Lodge

Writers: Leslie Ray & David Steven Simon

10. "Terror in Tanner Town" Nov. 23, 1990

Danny's new girlfriend (Sandlund) has a havoc-wreaking 11-
year-old son (Michael).

Rusty.............................Jordan Christopher Michael

Writer: Boyd Hale

11. "Secret Admirer" Dec. 7, 1990

Everyone thinks a bogus love letter for D.J. is for them.

Rusty.............................Jordan Christopher Michael
Ricky....................................................R.J. Williams

Writer: Ellen Guylas

12. "Danny in Charge" Dec. 14, 1990

With Jesse and Joey off camping, Danny realizes how much he depends on his pals to keep the house running smoothly.

Teleplay: Boyd Hale & Scott Spencer Gorden
Story: Stacey Hur

13. "Happy New Year"  Dec. 28, 1990

Jesse and Danny secretly tape Joey for a video dating service, leading to a New Year's Eve date with his dream girl (Nipar). Michael and Williams repriser their roles from ep. 11.

Rusty..........................................Jordan Christopher Michael
Christine.................................................Yvette Nipar
Ricky.......................................................R.J. Williams
And: Robyn Donny (Ginger), Sherrie Rose (Darlene)

Writer: Jeff Franklin

14. "Working Girl"  Jan. 4, 1991

D.J., wanting to be independent, takes her first job, and the long hours affect her schoolwork.

Jack...................................................Andy Goldberg
Mother.............................................Donna Lynn Leavy
Anthony.............................................Marquis Nunley

Writers: Marc Warren & Dennis Rinsler

15. "Ol' Brown Eyes"  Jan. 11, 1991

Danny feels left out when D.J. asks only Jesse and Joey to perform at her school fund-raiser.

Writers: Ellen Guylas & Boyd Hale

16. "Stephanie Gets Framed"  Jan. 25, 1991

When Stephanie discovers she needs glasses, she's worried she'll be teased about them; Jesse picks a best man. White's character crosses over from *Family Matters*.

Steve Urkel.............................................Jaleel White
Julie...................................................Tasha Scott
Mrs. Claire...........................................Cynthia Steele
Classmate................................................Micah Rowe

Writer: Doug McIntyre

17. "A Fish Called Martin"  Feb. 1, 1991

Michelle wins a goldfish, and when it dies, the household has to try to explain death.

Bobby....................................................Jason Allen

Writers: Leslie Ray & David Steven Simon

18. "The Wedding" Part 1  Feb. 8, 1991

On the eve of his wedding, Jesse reacts to advice from Rebecca's father (Hood) by planning "one last adventure," skydiving.

Kenneth Donaldson.....................................Don Hood
Nedra Donaldson, his wife.................................Lois Nettleton
And: Michael John Nunes (Howie), Debbie Gregory (Connie)

Writer: Jeff Franklin

19. "The Wedding" Part 2  Feb. 15, 1991

Jesse turns up missing on his and Rebecca's wedding day.

Nick Katsopolis, Jesse's father...............................John Aprea
Irene Katsopolis, Jesse's mother.......................Yvonne Wilder
Kenneth Donaldson................................................Don Hood
Nedra Donaldson.................................................Lois Nettleton
Howie...........................................Michael John Nunes
And: Glenn Morshower (Farmer Bob), Debbie Gregory (Connie), Lenny Hicks (Driver), Robert Arthur (Minister)

Writer: Jeff Franklin

20. "Fuller House"  Feb. 22, 1991

Home from their Bora Bora honeymoon, the newlyweds prepare to move into Rebecca's apartment.

Writers: Leslie Ray & David Steven Simon

21. "The Hole-in-the-Wall Gang"  March 1, 1991

The attic undergoes remodeling to make room for Jesse and Rebecca after they decide to stay and save to buy a house.

Writers: Craig Heller & Guy Shulman

22. "Stephanie Plays the Field"  March 8, 1991

Ace pitcher Stephanie likes a boy (Fox) on a rival baseball team, who asks her to cheat and throw him easy pitches.

Rusty..........................................Jordan Christopher Michael
Brett.......................................................Sean Fox
Base umpire...............................................Jack Lightsy
Brett's dad............................................R. Todd Torok
Plate umpire..........................................James Clayton

Writer: Mark Fink

23. "Joey Goes Hollywood"  March 29, 1991

Joey signs to co-star in the TV pilot *Surf's Up*, starring 1960s teen idols Frankie Avalon and Annette Funicello. Guest Southwick is host of USA Network's *Hollywood Insider*.

Themselves.........................Frankie Avalon, Annette Funicello
Herself............................................Shawn Southwick
Himself/Audience warm-up person.......................Bob Perlow
Laker Girls......................................Michele Smith, Cyndi Pass

Writers: Leslie Ray & David Steven Simon

24. "Girls Just Wanna Have Fun"  Monday, April 1, 1991
8-8:30 p.m.

D.J. sneaks out of the house to meet a boy (Josselyn), getting her into trouble with her dad.

Ryan....................................................Randy Josselyn
Jake Bitterman...............................................Christian Guzek
Aaron....................................................Miko Hughes

Writers: Marc Warren & Dennis Rinsler

25. "The Graduates"  April 26, 1991

Jesse helps rock Michelle's pre-school graduation ceremony; D.J. graduates; Danny falls for a college student (Nash). Hughes reprises his role from last episode.

Kirsten.................................................Jennifer Nash

Mrs. Manning...................................................Rosanne Katon
And: Hank Garrett (Jerry), Miko Hughes (Aaron)

Writer: Ellen Guylas

26. "Rock the Cradle"   May 3, 1991

Jesse, distracted by the news his band has won a touring contract, doesn't pick up on Rebecca announcing she's pregnant.

Max Dobson.......................................................Keythe Farley

Writer: Boyd Hale

**renewed for 1991-92; new episodes begin Sept. 17, 1991**

## Gabriel's Fire

| ABC | Sept. 12-March 7 | Thursdays, 9-10 p.m. |
|---|---|---|
|  | April 17-May 1 | Wednesday, 10-11 p.m. |
|  | June 6-July 25 | Thursdays, 9-10 p.m. |
|  | Aug. 1-Aug. 22 | Thursdays, 8-9 p.m. |

Series premiere: Sept. 12, 1990
Final telecast: Aug. 22, 1991

Drama of a former Chicago cop, released from prison after serving 20 years for an arguably justifiable homicide, who becomes an investigator for the defense attorney whose discovery of suppressed data and trial inconsistencies led to his freedom. Producer Lieberman is married to actress Marilu Henner.

Gabriel Bird........................................................James Earl Jones
Attorney Victoria Heller.........................................Laila Robins
Jamil Duke..........................................................Brian Grant
Louis Klein..........................................................Dylan Walsh *
Cafe owner Empress Josephine Austin..............Madge Sinclair

*Recurring:*
Zoe (orig. Karen) Solomon
     (ep. 14-16,20-21)....Anne Bobby a.k.a. Anne Marie Bobby
Ted Duke (ep. 1,7,12)......................................Lincoln Kilpatrick
Hazel (ep. 12-14,16-17,20-21)......................Louisa Abernathy
** Harry (ep. 8-9,12,17,21).............................DeForest Covan
Jenny (ep. 15,20-21)...........................................Leesa Bryte

* Given as Charlie Walsh in early press materials.
** Character identified only as "Customer," ep. 8.

Crystal Beach Entertainment and Coleman Luck Productions
     in assoc. with Lorimar Television
Executive producers: Robert Lieberman, Coleman Luck
Co-executive producer (ep. 2-on): Stephen Zito
Supervising producer (ep. 2-on): Tom Towler
Producers: Carol Mendelsohn (ep. 2-on), Jacqueline
     Zambrano, Donald R. Boyle, Andrew A. Ackerman
Co-producer: Bobbie Edrick
Associate producer: Lisa A. Lewis
Executive story consultant: Charles Pratt, Jr. (later in season)
Director of photography: Tom Olgeirson (ep. 1), Victor Goss
Theme (instrumental) and music: William Olvis
Creators: Donald R. Boyle and Coleman Luck & Jacqueline
     Zambrano

-------------

1. "Gabriel's Fire"  Wednesday, Sept. 12, 1990, 10-11 p.m.;
     Sept. 13, 1990

After a series of dead-end jobs upon his release, Bird becomes

an investigator for Heller's firm, and finds himself threatened by those who set him up years ago.  Filmed partly in Chicago.

Capt. Jack O'Neil..................................................Chelcie Ross
Voice of Petroni..................................................Norman Bartold
And:  Jim Ortlieb (Fecky), Gary Houston (Judge), George Matthew (Asst. D.A), Ralph Foody (Hot dog vendor), Joe Liss (Waiter), David Reivers (Young Gabriel Bird)

Director: Robert Lieberman
Teleplay: Jacqueline Zambrano & Coleman Luck
Story: Coleman Luck & Jacqueline Zambrano and Don Boyle

2. "To Catch a Con" Part 1   Sept. 20, 1990

O'Neil sets a trap, convincing Bird a granddaughter he never knew was kidnapped by a child pornographer.

Capt. Jack O'Neil..................................................Chelcie Ross
Petroni.......................................................Peter Michael Goetz
"Celine," Bird's daughter/Dawn..........Michele Lamar Richards
Fitzgerald...............................................................Ketty Lester
Gustine...............................................................Clark Johnson

Director: Jack Sholder                    Writer: Tom Towler

3. "To Catch a Con" Part 2   Sept. 27, 1990

Bird discovers the woman posing as his daughter Celine was a prostitute hired by O'Neil to trap him.  Ross reprises his role from the two part ep. 1-2.

Capt. Jack O'Neil..................................................Chelcie Ross
Petroni.......................................................Peter Michael Goetz
"Celine"/Dawn.................................Michele Lamar Richards
Kathy Danube......................................................Laurie O'Brien
Carlo Musamina.................................................Marc Lawrence
Culp..................................................................Michael Cerveris
Gustine...............................................................Clark Johnson
Dr. Rayne..............................................................Susan Merson
Fitzgerald...............................................................Ketty Lester
And:  Jim Boeke (Roland), Berlinda Tolbert (Shelly), Rhonda Dotson (Bonnie), Tony Montero (Murry), Mark Phelan (Concierge). Don Maxwell (Cop), Kerry Michaels (Judge), Al Fann (Fosman), Robert Sorrells (Guard)

Director: Jack Sholder                    Writer: Tom Towler

4. "Louis' Date"  Oct. 4, 1990

After a smitten Louis is ripped off by a con artist (Hart, wife of star Jones), Bird enlists her talents to help catch an embezzler.

Harley Kovacs.......................................................Cecilia Hart
Jack Grimes.................................................H. Richard Greene
Sylvia (orig. Evelyn) Morris....................................Helen Brown
Agent Cooper.........................................................Hugh Holub
Parole board chairman.......................................James Mathers
Receptionist..........................................................Susan Savage
Asst. U.S. Attorney Towne................................J.P. Mullarkey
And: Corinne Kason (Manager), Armand Asselin (Desk clerk)
     Also orig. announced: Gail Hopkins (Judge Cameron)

Director: Stephen L. Posey          Writer: Carol Mendelsohn

**preempted Oct. 11**

5. "The Descent"  Oct. 18, 1990

When Heller's romance with a client (Zada) clouds her judgment, Bird investigates her lover's alleged triple murder.

Johnny Glass..............................................Ramy Zada
Inspector Axel Roark.....................Steven Gilborn (erroneously
    given as "Rourke: Steven Gilbrow" in *TV Guide*)
Abraham.................................................Mel Winkler
Laura Pickels...........................................Nita Talbot
Coleridge..............................................David Selkirk
And: Joe Palese (Lineup cop), Patrick Richwood (Desk clerk),
    Kaitlin Hopkins (Chanteuse), Leland Sun (Korean man-
    ager), Ellie Cornell (Student), Holly Wilkinson (Singer)
    Also orig. announced:
      D. Christopher Judge (George Washington)

Director: Dan Lerner                    Writer: Stephen Zito

6. "Money Walks"  Oct. 25, 1990

Bird investigates the murder of a teenager killed for his trendy
sneakers, after Heller defends the assailant (Perez).

Ernesto................................................George Perez
Mr. Frank...............................................Marty Davis
Mrs. Pena...............................................Ivonne Coll
Frank Benjamin.....................................Francois Giroday
Bobby "Smoke" Jackson............................Bentley K. Evans
Mr. Speculum..........................................Jack Kehler
Steven Thorn...................William Denis (misspelled "Dennis"
    in *TV Guide*)
Judge.................................................Victor Mohica
Caretaker..............................................Jerry Tullos
Shoe salesperson..........................................Jeb Brown
Basketball opponent................................Christopher Kirby
Mrs. Pena's brother......................................Jorge Tort
Passengers.............................Romeo DeLan, Jim Barcena
And: Eddie Frias (Driver) Nelson Lesmo (Kid), Bill Grant (Bail-
    iff), Barbara Lindsay (Foreperson), Charles Alvin Bell
    (1969 judge), W. Alex Clarke (1969 bailiff), Marty Zagon
    (1969 foreperson)
    Also orig. announced: Douglas Roberts (Lewiston), Wil-
    liam Edward Lewis (Dr. Stewart)

Director: Robert Lieberman              Writer: Grenville Case

7. "The Neighborhood"  Nov. 1, 1990

Jamil's accused of killing the deacon of a church, the minister
(Gunn) of which withholds evidence that could clear Jamil.

Bishop Cecil Dobbs..................................Moses Gunn
Sister Isabell.....................................Tremaine Hawkins
Patrice.......................................Clarence Williams III
Sugarman.............................................Felton Perry
Judge..................................................Liz Torres
Deacon Martin Jones.................................Teddy Wilson
Mr. Gonzalez..........................................Leon Singer
Jonas Rex............................................Paul Tuerpe
Trusty.............................................Jay Arlen Jones
And: Freeman King (Ned), Gregory Eugene Travis (Eight Ball),
    Craig Thomas (Bobby), Billy Kane (Teardrop), George C.
    Simms (Cop), Keenan B. Thomas (Secretary), The Greater
    Bethany Community Church Mass Choir

Director: Jesus S. Trevino              Writer: Jacqueline Zambrano

8. "I'm Nobody"  Nov. 8, 1990

Bird runs across a wino former colleague (Jenkins) while investigating the murder case against a homeless man (Cobbs)
who was once a famous 1950s doo-wop singer.

Walker Green............................................Bill Cobbs
Potter................................................Ken Jenkins

Miles Parker........................................Sy Richardson
Prosecuting attorney...............................Richard Fancy
Charlie Debs.................................Abdul Salaam El Razzac
Bernard Jackson..................................Wendell Wright
Annie...........................................Virginia Capers
Judge............................................Micole Mercurio
James..............................................Don Keefer
Buster..........................................Frank Collison
Young Walker Green.................................Lawrence Lowe
Young Charlie Debs...............................Dwight Donaldson
Young Miles Parker...............................Charles Penland
Young Bernard Jackson............................Kimble Jemison
Young Josephine...................................Nicole Niblack
Clay Austin........................................Donald Willis
And: Louis Winfield Bailey (Man on street), Byron Chung
    (Store owner), V.C. Dupree (Teen), Gretchen Palmer
    (Young lady), Clayton Martinez (Customer), Luis Con-
    treras, Santos Morales (Transients), Derrick Gumbus
    (Rap leader), Billy Davenport, Loren Chaney, Troy How-
    ard (Rap group)

Director: John Nicolella                Writer: Don Shroll

9. "The Wind Rancher"  Nov. 15, 1990

While held hostage with six others in Josephine's cafe, Bird
tries to calm an unstable young gunman (Frechette) who has
botched a robbery. Gilborn reprises his role from ep. 5, where
his title was given as Inspector, not Lieutenant; Capers reprises her role from last episode.

Dakota............................................Peter Frechette
Lt. Axel Roark.....................................Steven Gilborn
Stretch...........................................Scott Colomby
Annie...........................................Virginia Capers
Buggy...........................................Ricky Dean Logan
Reporter........................................Mary Ingersoll
Sgt. Glad.......................................Lance E. Nichols
Cop.................................................Mik Scriba
And: Jerry Hauck (Mr. Chicken), Marco Hernandez (Raoul),
    Patricia Matthew (Distraught mother), Raymond Mc-
    Queen (Kid), James Edson (Cop in Mr. Chicken), Kevin A.
    Duffis (Bus driver), Raymond Turner (Sniper)

Director: Victor Lobl                   Story: John L. Tracy
Teleplay: Carol Mendelsohn & Jacqueline Zambrano & Ste-
    phen Zito

**preempted Nov. 22**

10. "Windows"  Nov. 29, 1990

On a divorce-case surveillance, Bird and Duke witness a mob
killing; Heller, dressed as a prostitute for a costume party,
gets arrested and brutalized. Hargitay is the daughter of the
late actress Jayne Mansfield. Orig. scheduled for Nov. 22.

Carmen.........................................Mariska Hargitay
Connie DiFranco.................................Jennifer Rhodes
Nose...............................................Richard Assad
Attendant...........................................Shaun Toub
Superintendent................................Lereza Vinnichenko
Officers.............................Macka Foley, Orlando Bonner
Gang leader......................................Buddy Daniels
And: Gerry Black (Bartender) Lamont Bentley (Teen), Hubert
    Braddock, Angel Harper (Prositutes), Lyvingston Holmes
    (Bald woman), Frank Noon (Albino), Tim deZarn (Drunk)

Director: Vern Gillum                   Writer: Charles Pratt, Jr.

11. "Judgements"  Dec. 6, 1990

When Heller's respected judge father (Cariou) is accused of bribery, Bird's investigation suggests he may indeed be guilty. Guest Coll had played a different role, ep. 6.

Judge Norton Heller..............................................Len Cariou
Wallis Heller.........................................................Mary Carver
Alexandra Heller..........................................Michelle Joyner
Dr. Luisa Hernandez...........................................Ivonne Coll
Kyle Webster...........................................................Tim Grimm
Judge Stanley...............................................Stacey Keach, Sr.
Victoria Heller as a teen.....................................Tisha Putman
Florence Manners.........................................Pamela Roberts
Judge Kemper.................................................James Tartan
Clerk.......................................................................Lorna Scott
Victoria Heller as a child............................Candie Patterson

Director: George Kaczender      Writer: Carol Mendelsohn

12. " 'Tis the Season"  Dec. 20, 1990

Bird has a bittersweet holiday reunion with his ex-wife (Mac-Lachlan) after she sees him on *The Oprah Winfrey Show*. Syndicated discussion-show host Winfrey appears as herself.

Ellie Graves.............................................Janet MacLachlan
Herself...................................................................Oprah Winfrey
Thomas Graves........................................................John Wesley
Mrs. Graves..........................................................Royce Wallace
City official.............................................................Tom Dressen
Ace.........................................................................T. Rodgers
Jones................................................Tyrone Granderson Jones
Young Gabriel Bird.................................................Todd Davis
And:  Suzanne Carney (Woman in audience), Don Herion (Ex-con), Teron Stevenson (William Graves), Ogadae Evans (Phillip Graves), Marius Mazmanian (Waiter), Amy Tucker (Young Celine), Yvonne Farrow (Young Ellie), Bonnie Jean Brown (Pretty girl), Bob Stuart (Customer)

Director: Robert Lieberman
Writers: Steve Wasserman & Jessica Klein

**preempted Dec. 27**

13. "The Great Waldo"  Jan. 10, 1991

When a crack-addicted baby is abandoned in Josephine's cafe, Bird and Josephine journey through the child welfare system.

Ginny.......................................................................Amy O'Neill
Judge Helpman.......................................................John Lehne
McCord...................................................................Tim Ryan
Miss Richards.............................................Francesca P. Roberts
Boy...........................................................................Cylk Cozart
Mike Cangelosi........................................................Greg Rusin
Linda.........................................................Nicole Orth-Pallavinci
And:  Al Mancini (Cabbie), Donna Lynn Leavy (E.R. doctor), Stacy Ray (Foster mother), Michael Whaley (Bailiff), Clifton Powell (Admitting clerk), Robert Balderson (Bus driver), John H. Evans (Telephone repairperson), James Asher-Salt (Ticker seller), Robyn Faye Bookland, Douglas Tolbert (Foster children), Brandon LaRon Hammond (Tenement boy), John Rooney (Play-by-play announcer)

Director: Michael Switzer      Writer: Jacqueline Zambrano

**rerun preempted in progress by an unscheduled news report, Jan. 17**

14. "First Date"  Jan. 24, 1991

After Josephine begins dating a customer (Bailey), Bird asks her out and discovers how dating has changed in 20 years. Joyner reprises her role from ep. 11; Bailey was credited as "Man on street," ep. 8.

Alexandra Heller.........................................Michelle Joyner
Daniel Mosley............................................................Jeff Corey
Schlactman.............................................................Phil Leeds
Rollie Claiborne (orig. Perkins)................Louis Winfield Bailey
And:  Jordan Jacobson (Waiter), Neal Lerner (Maitre d'), Marchand Odette (Girl in record store), Jim Pirri (Lanny), James Schendel (Mort), Mimi Savage (Clara), Tina Belis, Alan Brooks (Couple in restaurant)

Director: George Kaczender      Writer: Ellen Herman

15. "Truth and Consequences"  Jan. 31, 1991

Heller defends a star football quarterback (Russ) suing a tabloid that has characterized him as gay.

Brad Fixx................................................................William Russ
Matthew Fixx, his son.....................................Jonathan Brandis
Jimmy Williams...................................................Clifton James
Walter Pinkay.......................................................Taurean Blaque
Kyle Ray.......................................................Christian Le Blanc
Judge Leah Mince..............................................Lillian Lehman
Scott Everett.................................................Alex Hyde-White
Michael McCorkindale.......................................Peter Bromilow
Betty Pinkay.........................................................B.J. Jefferson
And:  Leesa Bryte (Jenny), Marchand Odette (Girl in record store), Jacqi Bowe (Maruska De Leon), James R. Sweeney (Danny Dunne's partner), Jean Pflieger (Jury foreperson), David Snizek (Bailiff), Carol Bivins (Lynn Reynolds), Jonathan Palmer (Willis Wilkerson)

Director: Charles Braverman      Story: Stephen Zito
Teleplay: Carol Mendelsohn & Tom Towler & Jacqueline Zambrano

**preempted Feb. 7**

16. "Finger on the Trigger"  Feb. 14, 1991

Bird, hospitalized and near death after an accidental shooting, subconsciously reflects on the crime for which he was framed. Guest Davis reprises his role from ep. 12.

Stan Frankel......................................................Michael Madsen
Phil Mulavey.........................................................Robert Silver
Miss Mary.............................................................O-Lan Jones
Board of Review officer....................................Mark Bramhall
Paramedics.................Christopher Burgard, Patrick Johnston
Young Gabriel Bird.................................................Todd Davis
Detective Jorge....................................................Victor Gardell
And:  Gigi Groves (ER/ICU nurse), Michele Harrell (Admitting nurse), Michael McKenzie (ICU nurse), Michael Mitz (Doctor), Donald Nardini (Detective Alex), Vikki Powell (ER nurse), Peter Siiteri (O'Neil)

Director: James A. Contner      Writer: Christopher Canaan

17. "Postcards from the Faultline"  Feb. 21, 1991

In Hollywood, Bird and Louis find themselves entangled amid femmes fatales (Hunley, Sparks) and a screenwriter (Venton).

Gwen Kidder.......................................................Leann Hunley
Tawny....................................................................Dana Sparks
Jack Gordon.......................................................Harley Venton
Marshall Kidder................................................Bernard Kates
And:  Slavitza Jovan (Woman butler), Ruben Amavizca (Bell-

hop), Melissa Young (Starlet), David Stenstrom (Studio guard), John Harnagel (Hotel asst. manager), Mark Damon (Vendor), Chance Boyer, Jeff Bollow (Surfers), Sandra Nutt (Flight attendant)

Director: Fred Gerber                    Writer: Charles Pratt, Jr.

18. "A Prayer for the Goldsteins" March 7, 1991

A Holocaust survivor (Opatoshu) is arrested for stealing art he claims was stolen from his family in Poland during WWII. Bailey reprieses his role from ep. 14.

Max Goldstein.................................................David Opatoshu
Anton Vasylenko....................................................Jack Gwillim
Judge Wittenbauer.................................................David Sage
Evan Stahl........................................................Gregory Itzin
Rollie Claiborne........................................Louis Winfield Bailey
Young Max.....................................................Don Keith Opper
Mrs. Margaret Fairchild...............................Patricia Morison
Alan Lown....................................................Rodney Saulsberry
Alex Vasylenko...........................Charles James Kahlenberg
And: Manny Kleinmuntz (Sam), Maury Cooper (Waiter), Keythe Farley (Adam Bryce), Marc Grapey (David Klein), Sabina Weber (Maryasha Goldstein), Phillip Glasser (David Goldstein), Clara Bryant (Rachel Goldstein), Joe Toppe (S.S. Officer), Howard Mungo (Guard)

Director: Robert Lieberman              Writer: Julie Sayres

**on hiatus**

19. "One Flew Over the Bird's Nest" April 17, 1991

Bird goes undercover in a mental hospital to try to prove patients there are being abused and neglected. Orig. scheduled for March 21.

Dr. Jennings......................................................Caitlin Clarke
Dr. Stark..........................................................George Hearn
Moon Man...................................................Christopher Collet
Doc Fulton.......................................................Robert Harper
Liebowitz........................................................Sydney Lassick
Jackson..........................................................James McDaniel
Nurse Fuller.......................................................Sally Prager
Madame Butterfly (orig. Byron)..............................Stuart Bird
        Also orig. announced: Wesley Man (Buzzy)

Director: Mark Sobel                    Writer: Jacqueline Zambrano

20. "Kelly Green" April 24, 1991

Heller's defense of an alleged mobster (Furst) gets complicated when she falls for the cop (Tylo) who served his illegal warrant.

Daniel Kelly.......................................................Michael Tylo
Lawrence Daskell, III.........................................Stephen Furst
Alex Zapas..........................................................Kario Salem
Cherry Moran..................................................Deborah Richter
State's Attorney..................................................Fran Montano
Judge Karl Van Der Wyck..................................Robert Levine
Gun Pontine........................................................Gerry Vichi
Nonnan..............................................................Roger Kern
Detective Barks...................................................Robert Factor

Director: Michael Switzer              Writer: Carol Mendelsohn

21. "Birds Gotta Fly" May 1, 1991

Bird has a troubled reunion with a daughter (Cara) he hasn't seen in 20 years; and Josephine reunites with her son (Beach).

Celine Bird..........................................................Irene Cara
Michael Austin.................................................Michael Beach
Man..........................................................Christopher Michael
Woman...............................................................Rita Gomez
Young girls........Michelle Collins, Milan Dillard, Meagan Good, Melissa Negre

Director: Mario Van Peebles            Writer: Tom Towler

**on hiatus**

22. "Belly of the Beast" June 6, 1991

Bird returns to prison to question a serial killer (Russo) who may be able to identify a murderer-rapist (Scarfe) stalking a college campus. Tylo and Montano reprise their roles from ep. 20; Torres had previously played a judge in ep. 7.

Charles Crowley.................................................James Russo
Jackie Tate.....................................................Holly Robinson
Daniel Kelly.......................................................Michael Tylo
Prof. Dennison...................................................Alan Scarfe
Judge Trevino.......................................................Liz Torres
Doctor.........................................................Katherine Cortez
State's Attorney.................................................Fran Montano
And: Dierk Torsek (Baxter), Leland Orser (Edward), Mark Phelan (Officer Williams), Anne Leyden (College student), Frances Barrett (Bailiff), Stacey Adams (Yvonne Gordon), Dayton Callie (Uniformed officer)

Director: Mark Sobel                    Writer: Charles Pratt, Jr.

**preempted Aug. 15**

**cancelled; James Earl Jones and Madge Sinclair continue their characters in the 1991-92 series Pros & Cons (working title: Bird & Katt), debuting Sept. 26, 1991**

# Get a Life

Fox          Sundays, 8:30-9 p.m.

Series premiere: Sept. 23, 1990

Surreal comedy of a happy-go-lucky, 30-year-old paper boy who lives with his parents in Greenville, U.S.A. Child actors Bluhm and Fry departed the cast midway through the season. Chris Elliott is the son of co-star Bob Elliott, former half of the Bob & Ray comedy team; Robards is the son of performers Lauren Bacall and Jason Robards. Title is as onscreen.

Chris Peterson....................................................Chris Elliott
Larry Potter.......................................................Sam Robards
Sharon Potter, Larry's wife...................................Robin Riker
Fred Peterson, Chris' father....................................Bob Elliott
Gladys Peterson, Chris' mother.......................Elinor Donahue
Bobby Potter (ep. 1)......................................Zachary Benjamin
Bobby Potter (early in season).............................Brady Bluhm
Amy Potter (early in season)...................................Taylor Fry

*Recurring:*
Billy (ep. 3,5-7).................................................Bo Sharon
Eddie (ep. 3,5-7)..........................................Wesley Jonathan

Elliottland Productions and Mirkinvision in assoc. with New World Television
Executive producer: David Mirkin
Producers: Jason Shubb (ep. 1 only), Chris Elliott, David Latt, Marjorie Gross (latter ep. 2-on), Adam Resnick (later in season)

Co-producer: Adam Resnick (early in season) Steve Pepoon
    (later in season)
Associate producer: Jessie Ward (ep. 2-on)
Director of photography: Ronald W. Browne (pilot); Richard
    Hissong
Music: Stewart Levin, Tim Truman (pilot); Stewart Levin
Opening Theme: "Stand," music and lyrics by R.E.M.;
    performed by R.E.M.
End theme: Stewart Levin
Creators: Chris Elliott, Adam Resnick, David Mirkin

———————————

1. "Terror on the Hell Loop 2000 -- Pilot"   Sept. 23, 1990

Chris and Larry go to the unveiling of a new roller coaster.
Guest Brown is the singer-comedian, not the MTV veejay; Garlington is a cast-member of *Lenny*.

Connie Bristol......................................................Julie Brown
Mr. Simon........................................................Graham Jarvis
Angelica..........................................................Lee Garlington
Ride operator......................................................Tracy Walter
Engineer......................................Michael G. Hagerty
        Also orig. announced: Tim Eyster (Scott), Troy Davidson
        (Billy), Paul Tennen (Eddie)

Director: David Mirkin
Writers: Chris Elliott & Adam Resnick and David Mirkin

2. "The Prettiest Week of My Life"   Sept. 30, 1990

Despite a lack of qualifications, Chris becomes a male model.

Ted Baines..................................Brian Doyle Murray
Sapphire...............................................Tuc Watkins
Photographer...............................Duke Moosekian
And: Willie Leong (Stage manager), Darnell Rose (Assistant)
        Also orig. announced:
        John Walter Davis (Security guard), J.J. Miller (Sandy)

Director: David Mirkin
Writers: Adam Resnick & Chris Elliott

3. "Dadicus"   Oct. 7, 1990   (GL-102)

Chris convinces his retired dad to participate in a father-son
picnic, which turns out to have gladiator-style games. Director Dow co-starred in *Leave It to Beaver* (CBS, 1957-58; ABC,
1958-63), the TV-movie *Still the Beaver* (1983), and the cable
series *Still the Beaver* and *The New Leave It to Beaver*.

Dr. Kramer..........................................Earl Boen
Fletcher.........................................James Hampton
Otto.................................................David Tom
And: Clint Carmichael (Rick), Paul Coufos (Guy Henry)

Director: Tony Dow            Writer: Marjorie Gross

4. "A Family Affair"   Oct. 14, 1990   (GL-104)

Sharon gets hysterial when Chris starts dating her sister (Tefkin). Director Hickman is the former star of *The Many Loves
of Dobie Gillis* (CBS, 1959-63). Orig. scheduled for Oct. 21.

Charleen............................................Blair Tefkin
Morgan.............................................Tommy Hinkley
Ted...................................................Larry Cedar
And: Deborah Benson (Betty), Timothy Davis-Reed (Usher)

Director: Dwayne Hickman       Writer: Ian Gurvitz

5. "Pile of Death"   Oct. 21, 1990   (GL-103)

Chris raises money to save a playground by trying to break
the record for most things stacked atop a person.  Guest
Jones is a singer.  Orig. scheduled for Oct. 14.

Himself...............................................Jack Jones
Mr. Pipp..............................................Clive Revill
Dr. Kramer...........................................Earl Boen
Ben Spangler.................................Hal Landon, Jr.
And: Cathy Cahn (Spectator), Benjamin Diskin (Danny)

Director: Peter Baldwin
Writers: Chris Elliott & Adam Resnick

**preempted Oct. 28**

6. "Chris Peterson is a Steel Drivin' Man" a.k.a. "Paperboy
    2000" Nov. 4, 1990  (GL-105)

Chris fights for his livelihood when he's replaced by automa-
tion. Landon and Boen reprise their roles from last episode.

Dr. Kramer............................................Earl Boen
Mr. Martin, Chris' boss.....................Graham Jarvis
Ben Spangler.................................Hal Landon, Jr.
Mrs. Wilson...........................................Mink Stole
Mrs. Trogden......................................Marion Dugan

Director: Peter Baldwin
Writers: Adam Markowitz & Bill Freiberger

7. "Driver's License"  Nov. 11, 1990  (GL-106)

Despite failing his driver's license test, Chris borrows the family car for a date, and has a car chase with the police.

Jane...............................................Anastasia Barzee
Officer Hickox.....................................Don Sparks
Officer Gordon...............................Michael Leopard

Director-writer: David Mirkin

8. "The Sitting"  Nov. 18, 1990

Chris house-sits at an apparently haunted house, and winds
up barricading himself and a burglar.

Mrs. Cowan...............................Dorothy Patterson
Stacy.........................................Katherine Kamhi
Pizza person...................................Keith Anthony
Burglar........................................David Permenter
Louie the Demon Dog.................................Lulu

Director: David Steinberg
Writers: Miguel Furman and Marjorie Gross & Adam Resnick

9. "Bored Straight"  Dec. 2, 1990  (GL-108)

Chris starts a discussion group for the town's troubled teens.

Biff.....................................................Kirk Geiger
Snake................................................David Kriegel
Natalie...............................................Melissa Baum

Director: David Mirkin          Writer: Marjorie Gross

10. "Zoo Animals on Wheels"  Dec. 16, 1990

Chris annoys and amuses Sharon when he's cast opposite her
in a community-theater play she's directing.

Hastings..................................................Craig Richard Nelson
Jason...........................................................Martin Grey
Hyenas....................David Martel Bryant, Lloyd Tee Williams
Seal..........................................................Debi Derryberry
Giraffe.........................................................Robert Yacko
Police chief/lion.........................................Ken J. Letner

Director: Peter Baldwin              Writer: Adam Resnick

11. "Roots" Jan. 6, 1991 (GL-110)

Chris thinks he was adopted, and that his biological parents are Amish.

Jedidiah.....................................................Steven Gilborn
Marta...........................................................Elsa Raven

Director: Dwayne Hickman
Writers: Adam Markowitz & Bill Frieberger

12. "The Counterfeit Watch Story" Feb. 3, 1991 (GL-112)

Chris goes undercover for the police to sting a jeweler selling bogus goods. Moosekian had appeared in a different role in ep. 2. Orig. scheduled for Jan. 20.

Richardson.............................................J. Kevin Scannell
Tom..........................................................Richard Foronjy
Vic............................................................Dukeuke Moosekian
Salesperson................................................Bradley Mott
Owens.........................................................Charles Walker
Little girl in jewelry store.........................................(uncredited)

Director: David Mirkin              Writer: Adam Resnick

13. "Chris vs. Donald" Feb. 10, 1991 (GL-113)

At a family reunion, Chris feuds with his "perfect" cousin (Haley), who's upstaged him all his life.

Donald....................................................Jackie Earle Haley
Uncle Sid..........................................................Bill Cort
Uncle Milt...................................................James Keane
Uncle Brad...................................................David Wiley
And: Pat Crawford Brown (Aunt Molly), Bibi Osterwald (Aunt Tilly), Marte Boyle Slout (Aunt Kathy)

Director: Dwayne Hickman          Writer: Adam Resnick

14. "Chris Wins a Celebrity" Feb. 24, 1991 (GL-114)

Chris can't get rid of the initially obnoxious then super-friendly celebrity (Mull) he's won as a weekend guest.

Sandy Connors.....................................................Martin Mull

Director: Dean Parisot              Writer: Adam Resnick

15. "Houseboy 2000" March 10, 1991 (GL-111)

Chris becomes Larry and Sharon's househelper to repay them after inadvertently setting their kitchen on fire. Orig. scheduled for Feb. 3.

Mr. Hampton.....................................................Chuck Sloan
Betty..........................................................Deborah Benson
Woman...........................................................Jill Womack

Director: Peter Baldwin            Writer: Marjorie Gross

16. "Married" March 24, 1991 (GL-115)

A famous model (Shelton), in town to promote her perfume, meets Chris, falls in love, marries, and breaks up with him, all in one day. Garlington, a cast-member of *Lenny*, had appeared in a different role in ep. 1. Orig. scheduled for Feb. 17.

Nicolette Preston...........................................Deborah Shelton
Patti............................................................Lee Garlington
Justice of the Peace.........................................Lewis Arquette
Dr. Rand.......................................................Julie K. Payne

Writer-director: David Mirkin

17. "Camping 2000" March 31, 1991 (GL-117)

Chris and Larry go on a camping trip with Fred, and have homicidal delusions after eating hallucinogenic berries.

Beautiful woman.................................................Theresa Ring

Director: Dean Parisot              Writer: Steve Pepoon

18. "The Construction Worker Show" April 7, 1991 (GL-118)

Chris, a connoisseur of construction work, has his faith shaken when carpenters do a shoddy job on the kitchen. Guest Doty is a cast-member of the syndicated *What a Dummy*.

Dick..........................................................Ritch Brinkley
Ray............................................................Mickey Jones
Don...........................................................Peter Spellos
Priest..........................................................David Doty

Director: David Mirkin              Writer: Adam Resnick

19. "The Big City" April 21, 1991 (GL-116)

Chris embarrasses a city when a reporter writes how a stranger apparently drugged him and stole his wallet. Barzee had played a different role in ep. 7. Orig. scheduled for March 31.

Reporter May Evans......................................Anastasia Barzee
Officer O'Meara..............................................Gerry Gibson
J.D. Windell....................................................John T. Olson
Room service person.........................Robin Michael Cahall
Prostitute.........................................................d. Franki Horner
Mayor.............................................................Art Kassul
Shell guy.........................................................Eric Kohner
Fedora guy.......................................................Adam Stone
        Also orig. announced: Jason Turbin (Kid), Peter Spellos (Gangster), Adrian Drake (Conductor)

Director: Peter Baldwin            Writer: Marjorie Gross

20. "Neptune 2000'" April 28, 1991 (GL-120)

In their bathtub, Chris and Fred get stuck inside Chris' home-assembled submarine.

Young Chris.....................................................Brandon Crane

Director: David Mirkin              Writer: Steve Pepoon

21. "The One Where Chris and Larry Switch Lives"
      May 12, 1991 (GL-119)

...which happens after Chris uncovers an arrowhead at an Indian burial site. Bluhm and Fry are former cast-members.

Jackie............................................................Beth Broderick
Bobby Potter.....................................................Brady Bluhm
Amy Potter.........................................................Taylor Fry

Director: David Mirkin                    Writer: Edd Hall

22. "Psychic 2000"  May 19, 1991  (GL-121)

After a near-death experience, Chris has a vision of Sharon's impending doom.  Benson reprises her role from ep. 15.

Ted...........................................................................Larry Cedar
Betty....................................................................Deborah Benson
Abe Lincoln.......................................................Robert V. Barron
Guy...........................................................................Gary Bolen

Writer-director: David Mirkin

**preempted Aug. 25**

**renewed for 1991-92; return date unannounced at press time**

## Going Places

ABC   Sept. 21-March 8, May 31-July 5   Fridays, 9:30-10 p.m.

Series premiere: Sept. 21, 1990
Final telecast: July 5, 1991

Comedy of two writer brothers from Chicago and two women writers, all newly relocated to Los Angeles to work on the *Here's Looking at You* candid-video series, and compelled to share a house.  Series storyline and cast revamped beginning ep. 13, with the group becoming the production staff of a live, daily discussion program, *The Dick Roberts Show*.  Co-star Todd is the daughter of *The Fanelli Boys* star Ann Guilbert.

Charlie Davis...........................................................Alan Ruck
Alexandra (Alex) Burton...............................Heather Locklear
Kate Griffin............................................................Hallie Todd
Jack Davis..............................................................Jerry Levine
Dawn St. Claire, their first boss (ep. 1-13).........Holland Taylor
Producer Arnie Ross (ep. 13-on)........Philip Charles MacKenzie
Talk-show host Dick Roberts (ep. 13-on)............Steve Vinovich
Neighbor Lindsay Bowan....................................Staci Keanan
Nick Griffin (ep. 14-on).........................................J.D. Daniels

*Recurring:*
Sam Roberts, Dick's son (ep. 16-19)...........Christopher Castile

Miller • Boyett Productions in assoc. with Lorimar Telepictures
Executive producers: Thomas L. Miller, Robert L. Boyett,
    Robert Griffard, Howard Adler
Supervising producers: Robert Blair (early in season), Alan
    Eisenstock, Larry Mintz
Producers: Ronny Hallin (ep. 1), James O'Keefe (early in
    season), Deborah Oppenheimer, Shari Hearn, Valri
    Bromfield (latter two later in season)
Associate producers: Alan Plotkin (ep. 1), Myron Nash
Executive story editors: Sheree Guitar (early in season), Maiya
    Williams
Story editors: Michael B. Kaplan (early in season), Rob Bragin
Creative consultants: David Pollock, Elias Davis
Director of photography: Monroe P. Askins, Jr., A.S.C.
Music: Jesse Frederick & Bennett Salvay
Theme: "Going Places" by Jesse Frederick & Bennett Salvay;
    performed by Mark Lennon
Director unless otherwise noted: Richard Correll
Creators: Robert Griffard & Howard Adler
Developed by: Thomas L. Miller & Robert L. Boyett

———————————

1. "Welcome to L.A."  Sept. 21, 1990

Dawn informs her new writing staff that for efficiency's sake, she wants them to share a beautiful beach house she owns.

Woman...................................................Marianne Muellerleile
Cop.....................................................................Matt Landers
Bruno Dobson............................................Michael Rapposelli

Director: Joel Zwick
Writers: Robert Griffard & Howard Adler

2. "Born to Be Mild"  Sept. 28, 1990

To help improve Charlie's love life, Jack tries to spiff him up.

Brie, Dawn's receptionist.........................................Lisa Fuller
Victim.................................................................Ken Thorley
Rolf...................................................................Michael Hoit

Writer: Rob Bragin

3. "Another Saturday Night"  Oct. 5, 1990

Long-dateless Kate and Charlie each try the personals.

Larry..................................................................Ron Fassler
Suzi....................................................................Nancy Reed
Brad.......................................................................Doug Dale

Writers: Robert Griffard & Howard Adler

4. 'Clean Sweep'  Oct. 12, 1990

A spy may be in the writing team's midst.

Peenie.......................................................Kathryn Marcopulos
Gary....................................................................Aaron Lustig
Peterson.............................................................Bruce Jarchow

Writer: Robert Blair

**preempted Oct. 19**

5. "Married to the Mob"  Oct. 26, 1990

Charlie's blind date (Diol) is a mobster's (LaGrua) wife.

Joey "The Icepick" Montaine (orig. Malone)............Tom LaGrua
Donna Montaine (orig. Malone)................................Susan Diol
Michelle.............................................................Sherry Hursey

Writers: Alan Eisenstock & Larry Mintz

6. "Sex, Lies and Videotape"  Nov. 2, 1990

The writing team tries to retrieve from Dawn's bedroom a videocassette containing their unflattering impressions of her.  Director Baker is a co-star of *Perfect Strangers*.

Ronald.............................................................Craig Branham

Director: Mark Linn-Baker                    Writer: Rob Bragin

7. "Queen of Comedy"  Nov. 9, 1990

In her secret hobby -- stand-up comedy -- Kate makes Charlie the butt of her jokes.

Burns.................................................................John Di Santi
Howie Bonerz.....................................................Marty Schiff
Emcee/Bud........................................................Cleto Augusto
Man..................................................................Robert G. Lee

Director: Stewart A. Lyons          Writer: Maiya Williams

8. "Thanksgiving Show"  Nov. 16, 1990

On Thanksgiving, Charlie and Jack teach football to Kate while Alex insists on making dinner herself.  Working title: "The Bird's the Word"

Guest cast NA

Director: Lee Shallat              Writer: Robert Blair

9. "I Was a Teenage Bride"  Nov. 23, 1990

Lindsay develops a crush on Jack's 18-year-old brother (Ward), and the two decide to elope.

Jay Davis....................................................Jonathan Ward
Rev. King...................................................Peter Willcox
Clerk.........................................................Bonnie Urseth

Director: Lee Shallat
Writers: Alan Eisenstock & Larry Mintz

10. "Who's the Boss?"  Nov. 30, 1990

Jack gets a swelled head when Dawn makes him head writer.

Dick Marshall.............................................Patrick Cronin
Victim.......................................................Darlene Kardon
Troy...........................................................Jeff Nowinski

Director: Jack Shea
Writers: Alan Eisenstock & Larry Mintz

11. "Curse of the Video"  Dec. 7, 1990

After Jake makes fun of a woman (Moreno) claiming to be a witch, her curses disturbingly appear to work.

Madame Pushnik.........................................Belita Moreno
Woman.......................................................Christine Healy
Death.........................................................John Durbin

Director: John Pasquin
Writers: Robert Griffard & Howard Adler

**preempted Dec. 21**

12. "Feud Poisoning"  Jan. 4, 1991

Practical-jokeser Jack turns the house into a war zone of one-upmanship.

Burglar......................................................John Fleck
Police officer..............................................Tom Kindle
Reporter.....................................................Andrea Walters

Director: Lee Shallat              Writer: Robert Blair

13. "The New Job"  Jan. 11, 1991

Their series cancelled, the team finds work on a talk show with a manic host and a guest (Groh) targeted for murder.

Jerry Slaughter............................................David Groh
Production assistant Mortie Gallup............Christopher Gartin
Floor manager............................................Judd Laurance
Voice of announcer.....................................Grant Moran

Writers: Alan Eisenstock & Larry Mintz

14. "New Kid in Town"  Jan. 18, 1991

Kate's smart-aleck eight-year-old nephew (Daniels, joining the cast) comes to live with the group.

Michael.......................................................Ralph Bruneau
Garber........................................................I.M. Hobson
Nigel (orig. Ace).........................................Sav Farrow

Writers: Robert Griffard & Howard Adler

**preempted Jan. 25**

15. "Room to Move"  Feb. 1, 1991

In order to give Nick his own room, Kate tries bunking with Alex.

Krysten......................................................Kristen Cloke

Director: Lee Shallat  Writer: Rob Bragin

16. "Don't Go Changing"  Feb. 8, 1991

When the group baby-sits Dick's allergy-ridden son (new recurring guest Castile), Nick teaches him how to break rules.

Dr. Hughes.................................................Mary Portser
Bodybuilder................................................Eric Freeman
    Also orig. announced:
    Bernadette Bowman (Receptionist)

Writer: Maiya Williams

17. "Take My Girlfriend, Please"  Feb. 15, 1991

Nick's classmate Sam tutors him to prevent his cheating on a test; Alex and Kate argue over which of them has won $10,000.

Wendy Spencer............................................Darlene Vogel
Mrs. Umstead.............................................Margot Rose
George Farrell.............................................Edward Edwards

Director: Lee Shallat              Writer: Shari Hearn

18. "Mommy Dearest"  Feb. 22, 1991

Kate's visiting mother finds fault with how Nick is being raised, and wants to bring him to live with her in New York.

Claire (orig. Suzanne) Griffin, Kate's mother........Dena Dietrich
    Also orig. announced:
    Brett Miller (Brett)

Director: Lee Shallat
Writers: Robert Griffard & Howard Adler

19. "The Camping Trip"  March 8, 1991

Novice outdoorspersons Jack and Charlie chaperone Nick and a nervous Sam on an overnight camping trip.

Pam Stone...................................................Holly Gagnier
Max Stone...................................................Jacob Kenner
Joe.............................................................Christopher Babers
David.........................................................Rider Strong

Director: Lee Shallat
Writers: Alan Eisenstock & Larry Mintz

**on hiatus, then cancelled; reruns begin May 31**

## The Golden Girls

| NBC | Sept. 22-July 27 | Saturdays, 9-9:30 p.m. |
| | Aug. 3 | Saturdays, 8-8:30 p.m. |
| | Aug. 10-Sept. 14 | Saturdays, 8-9 p.m. * |

* Two rerun episodes each night; a one-hour rerun, Sept. 14.

Series premiere: Sept. 14, 1985

Comedy of four independent-minded woman housemates spending their golden years together in Miami, Fla. Sophia's late husband: Sal.

Dorothy Petrillo Zbornak..................................Beatrice Arthur
Sophia Petrillo, her mother..................................Estelle Getty
Rose Nylund.....................................................Betty White
Blanche Hollingsworth Devereaux.................Rue McClanahan

*Recurring:*
Stan Zbornak, Dorothy's ex-husband
    (ep. 3,7,16-17,23)..................................Herbert Edelman
Miles, Rose's beau/Nicholas Carbone
    (ep. 10,13,15,21).........................................Harold Gould

Witt Thomas Harris Productions in assoc. with Touchstone Television
Executive producers: Paul Junger Witt, Tony Thomas, Susan Harris, Marc Sotkin
Co-executive producers: Tom Whedon, Philip Jayson Lasker
Supervising producers: Gail Parent, Don Seigel, Jerry Perzigian, Richard Vaczy, Tracy Gamble
Co-producer: Nina Feinberg
Executive story editors: Marc Cherry, Jamie Wooten
Story editors: Jim Vallely, Mitchell Hurwitz
Music: George Aliceson Tipton
Theme: "Thank You for Being a Friend," by Andrew Gold (music and lyrics); performed by Cynthia Fee
Director unless otherwise noted: Matthew Diamond
Creator: Susan Harris

---

1. "Blanche Delivers"  Sept. 22, 1990

Blanche's pregnant daughter (Engle) wants to have her baby at a birthing center.

Rebecca...............................................................Debra Engle
Doctor.....................................................................Ken Lerner
Tamara..................................................................Leila Kenzle
And: John O'Leary (Ninervini), Marti Muller, Diane Racine

Writers: Gail Parent & Jim Vallely

2. "Once, in St. Olaf"  Sept. 29, 1990

At the hospital where she works as a candy striper, Rose accidentally meets her biological father -- a monk.

Brother Martin.....................................................Don Ameche
Dr. Warren..............................................................Scott Bryce
And: Michael Goldfiner (Attendant), Tom Henschell (Dr. Bob), Alicia Brandt (Dr. Tess), William Bumiller (Man)

Writer: Harold Apter

3. "If at Last You Do Succeed"  Oct. 6, 1990

Dorothy is wooed by the newly successful Stan; Rose finds

valuable war bonds among memorabilia she sold to Blanche.

Writer: Robert Spina

4. "Snap Out of It"  Oct. 13, 1990

Dorothy tries to get an aging hippie shut-in (Mull) to go out into the world; Rose plans a birthday party for Blanche.

Jimmy....................................................................Martin Mull
Emcee...................................................................Danny Breen
Mrs. Taylor.....................................................Lenore Woodward

Writer: Richard Vaczy & Tracy Gamble

5. "Wham, Bam, Thank You, Mammy"  Oct. 20, 1990

Blanche's long-vanished childhood nanny reappears.

Mammy Watkins.........................................................Ruby Dee
Mrs. Contini..............................................................Peggy Rea
Jack................................................................Richard McKenzie

Writers: Marc Cherry & Jamie Wooten

6. "Feelings"  Oct. 27, 1990

Dorothy resists pressure to pass a failing student-athlete (Barnes); Rose accuses her dentist of anesthesia hanky-panky. Orig. scheduled for Oct. 20.

Kevin.......................................Christopher Daniel Barnes
Dr. Norgan............................................................George Wyner
Coach Odlivak.................................................Robert Costanzo
Father O'Mara...................................................Frank Hamilton

Writer: Don Seigel & Jerry Perzigian

7. "Zborn Again"  Nov. 3, 1990

Sophia tries once again to dissuade Dorothy from reconciling with her ex-husband Stan.

Abby...................................................................Siobhan Fallon
Mr. Percy.........................................................Dion Anderson
Cop...........................................................................Stan Roth

Writer: Mitchell Hurwitz

8. "How Do You Solve a Problem Like Sophia"  Nov. 10, 1990

Sophia wants to join a convent after her favorite nun dies; Blanche has an accident with Rose's car.

Mother Superior...........................................Kathleen Freeman
Arthur Nivingston.................................................Paul Willson
Sister Claire.............................................................Lela Ivey
Sister Anne..............................................Lynne Marie Stewart

Writer: Marc Cherry & Jamie Wooten

9. "Mrs. George Devereaux"  Nov. 17, 1990

Blanche dreams of a visit by her deceased husband (Grizzard) and that Dorothy gets proposals from her celeb fantasy men.

George Devereaux...........................................George Grizzard
Themselves.....................................Sonny Bono, Lyle Waggoner
And: Todd Jeffries (Police officer), Brad Kepnick (Maitre d')

Writers: Tracy Gamble & Richard Vaczy

10. "Girls Just Wanna Have Fun...Before They Die"
    Nov. 24, 1990

Sophia turns into a seductress to try luring a man (Romero) to bed, while Rose takes a vow of celibacy. Gould reprises his role from three episodes last season.

Tony......................................................Cesar Romero

Writers: Gail Parent & Jim Vallely

11. "Stand By Your Man" Dec. 1, 1990

Blanche dates a physically disabled attorney (Farrington). Bear crosses over from *Empty Nest*. Orig. scheduled for Dec. 7.

Ted.......................................................Hugh Farrington
Librarian.................................................Tom Nibley
Butler Andy..............................................Andy Goldberg
Dreyfuss (dog)..........................................Bear (uncredited)

Writer: Tom Whedon

12. "Ebbtide's Revenge" Dec. 15, 1990

When Dorothy's brother unexpectedly dies, Dorothy tries to resolve a feud between their mother and his widow (Vaccaro).

Angela Petrillo........................................Brenda Vaccaro
Father Salerno.........................................Earl Boen

Writer: Marc Sotkin

13. "The Bloom is Off the Rose" Jan. 5, 1991

Rose makes her Miles feel like he's competing with her late husband; Blanche's beau (Ryan) treats her shabbily.

Rex......................................................Mitchell Ryan
Flight instructor.......................................Don Mirault

Writer: Philip Jayson Lasker

14. "Sister of the Bride" Jan. 12, 1991

Blanche confronts her mixed feelings when her gay brother (Markham) announces he plans to marry another man (Ayr).

Clayton................................................Monte Markham
Doug....................................................Michael Ayr
Irving..................................................Lou Cutell
Susan Dodd............................................Mimi Cozzens

Writers: Marc Cherry & Jamie Wooten

15. "Miles to Go" Jan. 19, 1991

Miles reveals he's a former mob accountant in the FBI's Witness Relocation Program, and must go underground anew.

Gladys................................................Mary Gillis

Writers: Don Seigel & Jerry Perzigian

16. "There Goes the Bride" Part 1 Feb. 2, 1991

Sophia threatens to cut Dorothy off from the family if she proceeds with her plan to remarry Stan.

Cop......................................................Jack Yates
Lois.....................................................Toni Sawyer

Teleplay: Mitchell Hurwitz
Story: Gail Parent, Jim Vallely, Mitchell Hurwitz

17. "There Goes the Bride" Part 2 Feb. 9, 1991

Dorothy continues her wedding plans (cancelling at the last minute); the housemates see a potential new roomie (Reynolds). Mitchelson is an attorney specializing in divorce cases.

Truby..................................................Debbie Reynolds
Himself................................................Marvin Mitchelson
Caterer................................................Raye Birk
And: Meg Wyllie (Myra), Jack Blessing (Father Monroe), Milt Oberman (Errol), Cleto Augusto (Photographer)

Writers: Gail Parent & Jim Vallely

18. "Older and Wiser" Feb. 16, 1991  8-8:30 p.m.

Sophia risks losing her new job as recreation director at a retirement home when the residents start having "too much" fun.

Mr. Porter.............................................Don Lake
Mr. Lewis..............................................Julius Harris
Lucille.................................................Carol Bruce
And: Bill Wiley (Smokey), Ellen Albertini Dow (Sarah)

Writers: Richard Vaczy & Tracy Gamble

19. "Melodrama" Feb. 16, 1991

Blanche tries to get a commitment from her on-again, off-again beau (King); Rose auditions for a local-TV reporting job.

Mel Bushman.........................................Alan King
Andy...................................................Tommy Hinkley
And: Jonathan Schmock (Robber), Phil Forman (Bill)

Writer: Robert Spina

**unscheduled preemption Feb. 23**

20. "Even Grandmas Get the Blues" March 2, 1991

Blanche tells her new beau (*L.A. Law* cast-member Rachins) that her grandchild is actually her own baby. Engle reprises her role from ep. 1; Schmock played a different role in ep. 19.

Jason...................................................Alan Rachins
Rebecca................................................Debra Engle
Actress................................................Allison Robinson
Director................................................Jonathan Schmock
Aurora (infant), Rebecca's daughter......................(uncredited)

Director: Robert Berlinger
Writers: Gail Parent & Jim Vallely

21. "Witness" March 9, 1991

Rose asks neighbor Barbara (McNichol's character from *Empty Nest*) to investigate a new man (Martin) in her life; Miles secretly visits; Blanche uncovers a Jewish grandparent. Orig. scheduled for Feb. 23.

Barbara Weston......................................Kristy McNichol
Karl/"The Cheese Man"...............................Barney Martin
Louise.................................................Beth Grant
Women................................................Marla Adams, Elise Ogden
Mrs. Ward.............................................Gloria Dorson

Director: Zane Buzby                    Writer: Mitchell Hurwitz

22. "What a Difference a Date Makes" March 23, 1991

When Dorothy's former teen flame (Linden) returns to reignite their romance, Sophia admits she'd sabotaged their prom date.

John......................................................Hal Linden
Don the Fool.........................................Sid Melton
Minstrel...............................................Nick Jameson

Director: Lex Passaris
Writers: Marc Cherry & Jamie Wooten

23. "Love for Sale" April 6, 1991

Dorothy's ex-husband Stan buys a date with Dorothy at a charity auction in hopes of a reconciliation.

Uncle Angelo, Sophia's brother.................Bill Dana
Terry.....................................................Lou Felder
Man......................................................Tom Seidman

Director: Peter D. Beyt
Writers: Don Seigel & Jerry Perzigian

24. "Never Yell Fire in a Crowded Retirement Home"
   April 27, 1991  9-10 p.m.

Sophia is the prime suspect in an old unsolved arson case at Shady Pines retirement home; the housemates reminisce.

Herb.....................................................Stanley Kamel
Detective Parres.....................................Richard Riehle
In past-show clips: Jeffrey Tambor, Herbert Edelman, McLean
   Stevenson, Tony Jay, Richard Herd

Teleplay: Tracy Gamble, Richard Vaczy, Tom Whedon, Mitchell
   Hurwitz (first part); Richard Vaczy, Tracy Gamble, Don
   Seigel, Jerry Perzigian (second part)
Story: Gail Parent (first part); Jim Vallely (second part)

25. "Henny Penny -- Straight, No Chaser" May 4, 1991

After Dorothy persuades her roommates to star in a school play, they and the first-graders get quarantined with measles.

Frank Nann............................................George Hearn
Deliveryperson.......................................David Jay Willis

Director: Judy Pioli          Writer: Tom Whedon

**renewed for 1991-92; new episodes begin Sept. 21, 1991**

## Good Grief

Fox          Sundays, 9:30-10 p.m.

Series premiere: Sept. 30, 1990
Final telecast: March 17, 1991

Comedy of two brothers-in-law in fictional Dacron, Ohio, who own and operate the Sincerity Mortuary.

Ernie Lapidus........................................Howie Mandel
Warren Pepper.......................................Joel Brooks
Debbie Pepper Lapidus, Ernie's wife.............Wendy Schaal
Raoul...................................................Sheldon Feldner
Ringo Prowley (ep. 2-on).........................Tom Poston

Triggerfish Productions & Morra, Brezner & Steinberg
   Entertainment in assoc. with 20th Century Fox Television

Executive producers: Larry Brezner, Stu Silver, David Steinberg
Supervising producer: Donald Todd
Producers: Marsha Posner Williams, Mark Masuoka, Ron Burla
Associate producer: Alan Padula
Story editor: Danny Kreitzberg (died Nov. 5, 1990)
Executive consultants: Phyllis Cohen, Sheryl Bernstein
Director of photography: Darryl Palagi
Music [and] Theme (instrumental): Steve Nelson
Director unless otherwise credited: Howard Storm
Creator: Stu Silver

---

1. "Ladies and Gentlemen...Ernie Lapidus!" Sept. 30, 1990

Ernie could be arrested when the Maserati he buried a woman in, then dug up for himself, turns out to be stolen.

Mrs. Hillendale.....................................Ruth Manning
Kid.....................................................Danny Silver
Cop....................................................Jack Yates
Clown.................................................Rene Edgardo
Puffy, the Lapidus dog......Ewok (from Hollywood Animal Stars)

Writer: Stu Silver

2. "Full Dress Burial" Oct. 7, 1990

Ernie heeds a male client's final wish to be buried in a dress.

Mrs. Whiteside......................................Dena Dietrich
Puffy (dog)...........................................Otis
Gretchen.............................................Dana Stevens
And: Noah Blake (Lars), Adam Keefe (Mourner)

Writer: Donald Todd

3. "Bury Me A Little" Oct. 14, 1990

Ernie helps a rock star fake his death, and inadvertently buries him alive.

Winston Payne.......................................Jeff Conaway

Writer: Ron Burla

4. "Warren Learns to Fly" Oct. 21, 1990

Raoul mistakenly cremates the late mayor. Orig. scheduled for Oct. 28.

Widow Blackwell.....................................Liz Sheridan
Emmie..................................................Jean Sincere
And: Herb Eden, Anne Marie Gillis, Angel Harper, Steven
   Schwartz-Hartley, Meg McCormick, Jack Ong

Writer: Stu Silver

5. "Mooses, Masons, and the Secret Life of Trees"
   Oct. 28, 1990

In order to give a lonely old drunk a festive send-off, Ernie cons a lodge into thinking he was a member.

Chip....................................................Pat Morita
Zumaya................................................Anita Morris
And: Whitman Mayo, Stack Pierce, Milton Murrill, Nick La-
   Tour, E.L. James, Murphy Bennett, Jolly Brown, Sandy
   Kenyon

Writer: Donald Todd

6. "Cub Scouts and Horses and Whiskers on Kittens"
   Nov. 4, 1990

Ernie fights with Warren over burying a kiddie-show cowboy with his horse; Debbie becomes den mother to a Cub Scout troop of old men. Originally scheduled for Oct. 21.

Chief Boom Boom.............................................Richard Stahl
Flipper.........................................................Ernie Sabella
Buckerette Helen..........Audrie Neenan a.k.a. Audrie J. Neenan
Buckaroo Bob...................................................Rick Hurst
Mrs. Haversham.....................................Marianne Muellerleile
Princess Warm Lea........................................Therese Kablan
Little girl.......................................................Marne Patterson
Beanie..........................................................Martin Garner
And:  Marty Brinton (Kippy), Don Perry (Doc), Armin Shimerman (Stinky), John Wheeler (Skippy), Bart Williams (Fatty), Christina Reguli (Newscaster)

Writer: Stu Silver

7. "The Good, the Bad and the Mariachis"  Nov. 11, 1990

Ernie learns that his competitor (Fell) has been lying about having a war hero buried in his cemetery.

Slezar.............................................................Norman Fell
Bruno...........................................................Wendel Wright
Waiter..........................................................Michael Chong
The Mariachis........................Javier Castaneda, Rafael Garcia, Guillermo Jimenez, Jose Trujillo
And: Adam Keefe

Writer: Ron Burla

8. "Viva Las Dacron"  Nov. 18, 1990

Ringo sets up a casino at the mortuary. Director Storm has a bit part. Dedication: "To the Memory of Our Friend and Colleague, Danny Kreitzberg, 1952-1990."

Goon...............................................................Rick Zumwalt
Cigarette person...............................................Ava Fabian
Patron............................................................Howard Storm
     Also orig. announced:
     Mrs. Heffner............................................Gloria Cromwell
     Piano player.................................................Stu Silver

Writer: Stu Silver

**preempted Nov. 25**

9. "Ringo Gets a Job"  Dec. 2, 1990

...as the counterperson in a local diner. Orig. scheduled for Nov. 25.

Guest cast NA

Writer: Donald Todd

10. "Birth of a Notion"  Dec. 16, 1990

Ernie fantasizes about parenthood when he thinks he's going to be a father.

Nudist leader.....................................................Gino Conforti

Writer: Mark Masuoka

**preempted Dec. 23**

11. "The Bear"  Jan. 6, 1991

When the town is terrorized by a bear, Ernie and his family must spend a Saturday night at home with no TV. Director Lewis, the movie comedian, has an uncredited cameo.

Director: Jerry Lewis                          Writer: Stu Silver

12. "The Big Bang Theory"  Jan. 13, 1991

Ernie is arrested after the fireworks for a traditional Chinese funeral explode prematurely and destroy a car. Guest Stahl played a different role in ep. 6, Fabian in ep. 8.

Tyrone...........................................................Ernie Sabella
District Attorney............................................Richard Stahl
Judge Connie................................................Virginia Capers
Alexander Hamilton..........................................John Lykes
Clarence Patterson...............................................E.L. James
"Touch Me Again and I'll Kill You".........................Ava Fabian
And: Andre Rosey Brown (Guard), Tom Milanovich (Bailiff)
     Also orig. announced:
     Pat Li (Helen Go)

Director: Stu Silver                            Writer: Ron Burla

13. "13th Episode Anniversary Special"  Feb. 3, 1991

Ernie, Warren and Ringo try to figure how they came to wake up inside a Latin American prison. Orig. scheduled for Jan. 20.

El Gallo.............................................................Pepe Serna
Elke...............................................................Tasia Valenza
Torchy........................................................Carlos Cervantes
Gomez............................................................Richard Coca
State Dept. official............................................Aaron Lustig
Customs agent..............................................Armando Molina
Gabriel Garcia Marquez.......................................Louie Novoa

Writer: Donald Todd

## Good Sports

| CBS | Jan. 10-Feb. 14 | Thursdays, 9:30-10 p.m. |
|---|---|---|
|  | Feb. 25, March 18, |  |
|  | May 27, June 3 | Mondays, various times |
|  | June 8-July 13 | Saturdays, 10:30-11 p.m. |

Series premiere: Jan. 10, 1991
Final telecast: July 13, 1991

Comedy of the love/hate relationship between an ex-supermodel and a former pro-football bad boy, the two anchors of the *SportsCentral* and *Sports Chat* shows on the Rappaport Broadcasting System's All Sports Cable Network (ASCN). Bobby's old team: The Green Bay Packers. Co-stars Fawcett and O'Neal are a longtime couple in real life.

Gayle Roberts...................................................Farrah Fawcett
"Downtown" Bobby Tannen..................................Ryan O'Neal
ASCN founder Rappaport.......................................Lane Smith
Producer John "Mac" MacKinney..............Brian Doyle-Murray
Field reporter Jeff Mussberger......................Cleavant Derricks
Leash (ep. 2-on)...................................................Paul Feig
Mrs. Tannen, Bobby's mother (ep. 1,3)....................Lois Smith
Missy Van Johnson (ep. 2,4-on)..................Christine Dunford

*Recurring:*
Nick Calder (ep. 10-12,14)....................................William Katt
Stage manager (ep. 1,2,10)............................Anthony Griffith *

* Listed as Anthony Van Griffin [cq] in early press materials.

Boom Productions, Silly Robin Productions and Brillstein-Grey Productions
Executive producers: Bernie Brillstein, Brad Grey, Alan Zweibel
Supervising producers: Monica Johnson, Larry Levin
Producers: Ron Zimmerman, Vic Kaplan
Coordinating producer: Terri Miller
Associate producer: Leo J. Clarke
Executive story consultant (ep. 1,3): Matt Wickline
Executive consultant: Sandy Wernick
Creative consultant: Russ Woody
Sports consultant: Michael Cohen
Director of photography: Ken Peach, Jr.
Opening credits choreographed by: Pat Birch
Music: uncredited/inapplicable
Theme: Andy Goldmark (words and music); performed by Al Green
Director: Stan Lathan
Creator: Alan Zweibel

---

1. "Pros and Ex-Cons"  Jan. 10, 1991

Bobby, given a one-week try-out after Gayle's co-anchor suddenly dies on-air, faces Gayle's intense dislike for him after she learns he has no memory of their weekend fling 20 years ago. Abdul-Jabbar is a former pro-basketball player; Alzado, a former football pro; Travalena, an impressionist.

Themselves...........Kareem Abdul-Jabbar, Fred Travalena, Lyle Alzado
Original co-anchor Stu Ramsey.....................Arthur Burghardt
Nina Logan...........................................................Molly Cheek
Risa Braun...........................................................Viveka Davis
Jeri Sabin...........................................................Noelle Wycoff
          Also orig. announced: Sherrie Rose (Yvonne Pamplona)

Writer: Alan Zweibel

**unscheduled preemption Jan. 17**

2. "Gayle Wouldn't Do That"
     Monday, Jan. 21, 1991  9:30-10 p.m.

The word about Gayle and Bobby's fling gets out. Guest Belzer is a stand-up comic, and a recurring guest on *The Flash*.

Himself...........................................................Richard Belzer

Writers: Larry Levin & Ron Zimmerman & Alan Zweibel

**preempted Jan. 24**

3. "Moving In"  Jan. 31, 1991

Bobby accidentally burns down Gayle's apartment complex. Feig's debut, though he appears in cast credits from ep. 2. Sweet is a former rock singer. Orig. scheduled for Jan. 17.

Himself.....Former Miami Dolphins quarterback Doug Williams
Mrs. Caldwell..............................................Susan Blommaert
Jay Newman.....................................................Michael Cole
Makeup person Donna Robbins...........................Rachel Sweet

Writers: Monica Johnson & Alan Zweibel

4. "The Bigger They Are, The Harder They Hit"  Feb. 7, 1991

An angry Gayle goes to interview Jim Brown after his rudeness makes Missy faint on air.  Orig. scheduled for Jan. 31.

Himself..........................Former pro-football player Jim Brown
Himself..........................Former Olympic athlete Bruce Jenner
Young Jim Brown...............................................Jahary Bennett

Writer: Ron Zimmerman

5. "John MacKinney is No Yes Man"  Feb. 14, 1991

George Steinbrenner has Bobby and then Gayle fired.

Himself...Ex-New York Yankees co-owner George Steinbrenner

Teleplay: Larry Levin & Ron Zimmerman
Story: Matt Wickline

6. "The Reviews Are In"  Feb. 25, 1991  10:40-11:10 p.m.

Mac tries to give Bobby a crash course in journalism.

Himself.........Los Angeles Laker basketball player Vlade Divac

Writer: Larry Levin

**on hiatus**

7. "A Kiss is Just a Kiss"  March 18, 1991  10-10:30 p.m.

Gayle, increasingly distracted by her conflicting feelings about Bobby, is dropped from *Sports Chat*.

Herself..........................Cincinnati Reds co-owner Marge Schott

Writer: Russ Woody

**on hiatus**

8. "A Book is Just a Book"  May 27, 1991  10-10:30 p.m.

Publishing lawyers pressure Bobby to deliver on a $50,000 advance, and he responds with a book of bad poetry.

Herself................Former Olympic athlete Velma Dunn Ploessel

Writer: Russ Woody

9. "The Cincinnati Kids"  May 27, 1991  10:30-11 p.m.

Former Cincinnati Reds player Pete Rose gives an exclusive live interview to Bobby, who interrupts it to propose to Gayle.

Himself....................................................................Pete Rose
          Also orig. announced: Julie Comins (Jill)

Writers: Larry Levin and Alan Zweibel

10. "Electricity"  June 3, 1991  10-10:30 p.m.

Bobby needs $1,800 to have his electricity turned back on; Gayle catches her boyfriend (new recurring guest Katt) with another woman.  Orig. scheduled for Feb. 21.

Barbara Kipnis.............................................Susan Blommaert

Writers: Larry Levin & Alaz Zweibel

11. "Moody Blues Swing"  June 8, 1991

When Gayle's beau (Katt, reprising his role from ep. 10) moves in, making her unexpectedly uneasy, Gail confides in Bobby.

Dr. Jay M'odsquad................................Michael Cole
Coroner Randi Hoover......................Joan Severance

Writer: Monica Johnson

12. "Love Means Never Having to Say You're Happy"
     June 15, 1991

Bobby notices continued discord at Gayle and Nick's.

Himself.....Former heavyweight boxing champ George Foreman

Writer: Ron Zimmerman

13. "Bobby & Gayle Go On a Date"  June 22, 1991

Gayle's father (Keel) urges her to give Bobby a chance.

Sonny Gordon......................................Howard Keel
Himself............Rev. Mark Holsinger of the Los Angeles Mission
Himself............Atlanta Braves baseball player Terry Pendleton

Writers: Ron Zimmerman and Alan Zweibel

**preempted June 29**

14. "The Return of Nick"  July 6, 1991

Gayle's ex-boyfriend Nick threatens to end Gayle and Bobby's
relationship at gunpoint.  Belzer previously appeared in ep. 2.

Himself.............................................Richard Belzer

Writer: Ron Zimmerman (Alan Zweibel orig. announced)

15. "A Class Act"  July 13, 1991

Gayle must decide whether or not to expose Bobby's old
teammate (Scheine) with a fraudulent claim to fame.

Andy Highgate....................................Raynor Scheine

Writer: Larry Levin

## Grand

NBC            Thursdays, 9:30-10 p.m.

Series premiere: Jan. 18, 1990
Final telecast: Dec. 27, 1990

Serialized comedy set in the fictional town of Grand, Penn.,
dominated by wealthy piano-factory patriarch Harris Weldon,
and focusing on former high school classmates Janice, now
Weldon's cleaning lady, and Carol Anne, Weldon's niece.

Janice Pasetti.....................................Pamela Reed
Edda Pasetti, her daughter........................Sara Rue
Carol Anne Smithson...........................Bonnie Hunt
Harris Weldon....................................John Randolph
Norris Weldon, his son...........................Joel Murray
Desmond, his butler.............................John Neville

*Recurring:*
Viva, Janice's mother (ep. 10-12)........................Carroll Baker
Richard Paton (ep. 10-12).....................................Mark Moses

Welladay in assoc. with The Carsey-Werner Co. and Bill Cosby
Executive producers: Michael Leeson, Caryn Mandabach, Tom
    Werner, Marcy Carsey

Supervising producer: Carol Gary
Producers: Henry Lange Jr., Nancy Haas
Executive story editor: Frank Mula
Story editors: David Richardson, Scott Rubenstein, Leonard
    Mlodinow
Consultants: Bill Cosby, Jerry Belson
Music: Tom Snow
Theme: "Play It Grand"  Michael Leeson (lyrics) and Tom Snow
    (music); performers uncredited
Director unless otherwise noted: Art Wolff
Creator: Michael Leeson

_____

1. "Janice Steals Home"  Oct. 4, 1990

After losing her mobile home to the tornado that struck at the
end of last season, Janice takes refuge in Weldon's house, as
does Carol Anne now that her husband Tom has disappeared.

Ray..................................................John Kapelos
Working girl.................................Deirdre Fitzpatrick
     Also orig. announced: Stephen Bowers (Repairperson)

Writer: Michael Leeson

2. "The Chickens Come Home to Roost"  Oct. 11, 1990

Carol Anne turns to a voodoo queen (Barnes) and a psychic
(Berkeley) to help find the missing Tom, while Janice uncovers
information about him when she visits a psychiatrist (Jones).

Dr. Frank............................................Eddie Jones
Wanda.........Annabella Price (Annie McEnroe orig. announced)
Jeffrey...........................................Xander Berkeley
And: Adilah Barnes (Jamaican lady), James Lefebvre (Agent)

Writer: Frank Mula

3. "The Healing"  Oct. 18, 1990

Janice takes Carol Anne to Norris' new club, where a bomb-
toting patron (Goodman, a co-star of *Roseanne*) demands a
dance.  Guest Florek is a cast-member of *Law & Order*.

Red....................................................John Goodman
Robert.................................................Dann Florek
Jimmy...................................................Tom Virtue
El Diablo......................................Micheal T. Rooney
And: Joe Costanza, Ron Dortch

Writer: Carol Gary

4. "The Return of Yale Pinhaus"  Oct. 25, 1990

Her 20-year reunion nigh, Janice dreads seeing the guy (Armstrong) she ditched at the prom in favor of her future ex-husband (Marinaro, reprising his role from the series premiere).

Eddie Pasetti.......................................Ed Marinaro
Yale Pinhaus................................Curtis Armstrong
And: Alberta Watson (Andrea), Kathleen McClellan (Misty)

Writers: Martin Braverman & Mike Langworthy

5. "Desmond's Mother"  Nov. 1, 1990

Desmond's "mother" (Christmas) arrives from England, and
announces he's a man who's been masquerading as a woman.

Maggie.............................................Eric Christmas

Writer: David Richardson

**preempted Nov. 8**

6. "Norris' Romance" Nov. 15, 1990

Norris dates a man-hating comedienne (Persky) at his club, blunting her edge; Carol Anne wants to have adventures.

Jenny.............................................................Lisa Jane Persky
Foley.......................................................Jeffrey Allan Chandler

Writer: Frank Mula

7. "Roamers and Rumors" Nov. 22, 1990

Edda and Janice are the victims of rumors; Carol Anne looks for a job; Weldon and Desmond try to recapture their youth.

Steven Ehrhardt...............................................Sam McMurray
Brad Ehrhardt.......................................................Blake Soper
Girl.......................................................................Rachel Bailit
Ex-cons.................................Milda Dacys, Audrey Pressman

Writers: Carol Gary & David Richardson

8. "Lady Luck" Nov. 29, 1990

Carol Anne, Janice and Edda share a lucky lima bean, and Norris and Desmond's failing bar institutes female wrestling.

Marge..................................................................Kathy Kinney
Father Reyes............................................................Craig Stepp
Ned Palmer.................................................................Sumant
Ruth Louise Henderson/female wrestler...........Spice Williams
Man.....................................................................James Pruitt
And: Cindy Gise, Roger Hewlitt, Ellen Martin, John Platt

Writer: Mike Scully

9. "One Way Out" Dec. 6, 1990

Carol Anne gets threats from a disturbed reader of her advice column; Weldon's secretary (Muellerleile) likes Desmond.

Colleen...................................................Marianne Muellerleile
Richard Paton.......................................................Mark Moses
And: Eddie Jones

Writer: David Richardson

10. "The Mother Load" Dec. 13, 1990

At a formal gala, the ex-con boyfriend (Bolger) of Janice's mother shoots Norris; Carol Anne wants motherhood.

Manny......................................................John Michael Bolger
And: Richard Roat (Stan Claus), Bruno Marcotulli (Detective)

Writer: Ron Bloomberg

11. "Wolf Boy" Dec. 20, 1990

Carol Anne adopts a son (Phelan) who was raised by wolves.

Timmy................................................................Shawn Phelan
And: Alice Hunt

Writer: Frank Mula

12. "The Well" Dec. 27, 1990

Carol Anne tries to keep her newly adopted son (Phelan, reprising his role from last episode) from being institutionalized; Janice is trapped in a well; Weldon, fighting a takeover bid, signs his company over to Norris; Desmond duels with Manny. Bolger reprises his role from ep. 10.

Timmy................................................................Shawn Phelan
Manny......................................................John Michael Bolger

Writer: Dale McRaven

Unaired

"The End of the World as We Know It"

Announced personnel:
Fire Chief Stanton.........................................Michael Pniewski
Boyd Dauber...................................................Dietrich Bader
And: Kelly Kincaid (Bill), Alan Curelop (Rene)

Writer: David Richardson

## Growing Pains

ABC Sept. 19-Aug. 14; Sept. 13-on    Wednesdays, 8:30-9 p.m.
    Aug. 23-Sept. 6                              Fridays, 8:30-9 p.m.

Series premiere: Sept. 24, 1985

Comedy of a Long Island family with a psychiatrist father working at home, and a local-TV newscaster mom. Ashley Johnson, 7, was the 1988 Little Miss America (home state: Michigan). Seaver home address: 15 Robin Hood Lane. Cameron and recurring guest Noble were married after the season ended.

Jason Seaver.........................................................Alan Thicke
Maggie Malone Seaver.........................................Joanna Kerns
Mike Seaver.......................................................Kirk Cameron
Carol Seaver............................................................Tracey Gold
Ben Seaver..........................................................Jeremy Miller
Chrissy Seaver....................................................Ashley Johnson

*Recurring:*
Kate McDonnell, Mike's girlfriend
    (ep. 2,13,18,20,23).....................................Chelsea Noble
Ed Malone, Maggie's dad (ep. 2-3,8,16)...............Gordon Jump
Kate Malone, Maggie's mom (ep. 2-3,8-10).........Betty McGuire
Eddie, Mike's friend (ep. 4,13,23)...........................K.C. Martel
Stinky Sullivan (ep. 2-3,5,15)...............................Jamie Abbott

Guntzelman Sullivan Marshall (a.k.a. GSM) Productions in
    assoc. with Warner Bros. Television
Executive producers: Dan Guntzelman, Mike Sullivan, Steve
    Marshall
Co-executive producer: David Kendall
Producers: Joey Scott, Rich Reinhart, Nick LeRose, Michael
    Ware, Bob Burris (latter two later in season)
Associate producer: Laura Lynn
Executive script consultants: Jay Abramowitz (early in
    season), Shelly Landau
Executive story consultants: Jake Weinberger, Mike Wein-
    berger
Executive story editors: Michael Ware, Bob Burris (both early
    in season)
Story editor: Leilani Downer (later in season)
Director of photography: George Spiro Dibie
Music: Steve Dorff
Theme: "As Long As We Got Each Other" by Steve Dorff
    (music), John Betts (lyrics); performed by B.J. Thomas
    and Jennifer Warnes

Director: John Tracy
Creator: Neal Marlens

---

1. "Mike's Choice"  Sept. 19, 1990

When Mike lands a role in an off-off-Broadway play, he leaves college to pursue acting full-time in New York City.  Guest Marshall is a cast-member of *Twin Peaks*.

Maurice........................................................Neil Elliot
Actor..........................................................James Marshall

Writer: David Kendall

2. "Midnight Cowboy"  Sept. 26, 1990

Mike is broke and homeless in New York City. Vale is a singer.

Sophie.......................................................Kathleen Freeman
Liz.............................................................Keely Christian
Himself......................................................Jerry Vale

Writer: Nick LeRose

3. "Roommates"  Oct. 3, 1990

Mike becomes roommates with sis Carol, a Columbia University student.  Freeman reprises her role from ep. 2.

Sophie.......................................................Kathleen Freeman
Agnes........................................................Ann Nelson
Modesto.....................................................Lou Richards
Karl...........................................................Eliott Harold
Cop............................................................Michael Chieffo
Seedy Guy..................................................William Blair II
       Also orig. announced: Neil Elliot (Maurice)

Writers: Bob Burris & Michael Ware

4. "Daddy Mike"  Oct. 10, 1990

Mike and his friend Eddie (recurring guest Martel) schemingly join "Parents Without Mates" to meet women.

Rachel.......................................................Kelly Rowan
Marsha (orig. Giselle)..................................Susan Krebs
Betty.........................................................Sandra de Bruin
Natalie......................................................Angel Tompkins
And: Kate Romero (Jeanie), Jessie Gold (Judith)

Writers: Elias Davis & David Pollock

5. "Ben's Sure Thing"  Oct. 17, 1990

At the school's Parents Night, the Seavers learn Ben's been telling his friends that the girl he's dating is promiscuous.

Rhonda Green.............................................Andrea Barber
Moe Green..................................................Johnny Dark
Vito...........................................................Kenny Morrison
Gary..........................................................Jason Horst
Mr. Sullivan...............................................Mickey Morton
And: Cherie Franklin (Mrs. Krupmeyer), Ted Pitsis (Father)

Writer: Shelly Landau

6. "Jason Flirts, Maggie Hurts"  Oct. 24, 1990

A flirty Jason gets jealous when Maggie turns the tables.

Gretchen....................................................Jeannine Renshaw
Marcus.......................................................Duke Moosekian
Trainer......................................................Tuc Watkins

Writers: Jake Weinberger & Mike Weinberger

7. "Happy Halloween"  Oct. 31, 1990  8-9 p.m.

The Seavers spend a rainy Halloween night telling ghost stories.  Dedication: "To Rick Hoskins, 1948-1990."

Kara Daye...................................................Jamie Lunder
Officer Krumpkey.........................................Matt Landers
And: Susan Griffiths (Marilyn Monroe), Leslie Morris (Babe Ruth), Van Epperson (Truman Capote), Stuart Nisbet (George Washington), Jan Rabson (Rod Serling), Charles L. Brame (Abraham Lincoln), Bob Tremaine (Col. Sanders), Jerome Patrick Hoban (Ed Sullivan), Zachary Prather (Jimi Hendrix), Maxine Elliott (Elderly woman), Daryl Wagner (Liberace), Jeffrey Briar (Stan Laurel), Bevis Faversham (Oliver Hardy), Timothy Scott Bennett (Fool), Beau Richardson (Kid), Larry Coven (Lecherous man), Kate Randolph Burns (Token vendor), Joe Banks (Frank), Joseph Weinberger (Dwayne)

Writers:  Jay Abramowitz and Nick LeRose and Dan Guntzelman

8. "Let's Go Europe" Part 1   Nov. 7, 1990

Jason buys an anniversary trip to Paris from travel agent Mike, who himself wins a European tour that falls apart; Maggie, in Paris, is struck with appendicitis.

Amy Boutilier..............................................Heather Langenkamp
Hotel clerk.................................................Raoul N. Rizik
French cab driver........................................Joseph Lennon McCord
And: Alli Brown (Dee Dee), Judith Jones (Martha)

Writer: David Kendall

9. "Let's Go Europe" Part 2   Nov. 14, 1990

Maggie is hospitalized in Paris, while Mike finds himself stuck on the road with an angry customer (Langenkamp).

Amy Boutilier..............................................Heather Langenkamp
Hotel clerk.................................................Raoul N. Rizik
Doctor.......................................................Regina Leeds
Father of the bride......................................J.J. Paladino
Spanish motorist.........................................Noe Montoya
French ambulance driver...............................Phil Stellar

Writers: Bob Burris & Michael Ware

**preempted Nov. 21**

10. "Let's Go Europe" Part 3   Nov. 28, 1990

Mike and Amy continue to bicker their way toward Paris.

Amy Boutilier..............................................Heather Langenkamp
Doctor.......................................................Regina Leeds
Henri.........................................................Marius Mazmanian
Policia.......................................................Ernesto Ravetto, Timothy Miranda
       Also orig. announced: Scot Van Der Horst (Maurice)

Teleplay: Michael Ware & Bob Burris
Story: David Kendall & Dan Guntzelman

11. "Divorce Story"  Dec. 5, 1990

Jason, happy to see his mother's (Powell) second marriage crumbling, doesn't want to provide her with professional help. Singer Vale previously appeared as himself in ep. 2.

Irma Seaver Overmier..............................................Jane Powell
Wally Overmier...................................................Robert Rockwell
Margo..............................................................Jennifer Nash
Himself...............................................................Jerry Vale
Waiter...............................................................J.P. Hubbell

Writer: David Pollock & Elias Davis

**preempted Dec. 12**

12. "The World According to Chrissy"  Dec. 19, 1990

Chrissy starts spending much time with her imaginary friend, a six-foot-tall mouse named Ike.

Sally Garner.........................................................Joely Fisher
Norman.............................................................David Gail
"Ike".................................................................Kirk Cameron

Writer: Leilani Downer

13. "How Could I Leave Her Behind?"  Jan. 2, 1991

Mike's friend Eddie shows up for a double date with Mike's ex-girl (recurring guest Noble). Orig. scheduled for Dec. 5.

Tina..................................................................Melissa Young
Joan..............................................................Christine Kendrick
Jill.....................................................................Jill Pierce

Writer: Jake & Mike Weinberger

14. "Like Father, Like Son"  Jan. 9, 1990

At an intrafamily communications seminar, Mike and Jason discover just how alike they are.

Dr. Frankovich...................................................Nicholas Pryor
Dr. Miller.........................................................Susan Barnes
Hank............................................................Michael A. Goorjian
T.C...............................................................Ross Chamberlain
Dr. Bales...........................................................Dan Schaffer
Dr. Danvers..............................William Hubbard Knight
And: Peter Spellos (Lloyd), Perla Walter (Mrs. Sierra)

Writer: Vince Cheung & Ben Montanio

**preempted Jan. 16**

15. "Ben's Rap Group"  Jan. 23, 1991

Jason becomes Ben's business partner in the management of a rap group, but uses the money he's invested to control Ben.

Bernie...............................................................Dan Schaffer
Laura Lynn........................................................Jodi Peterson

Writer: Todd Thicke

16. "Eddie, We Hardly Knew Ye"  Jan. 30, 1991

Maggie's dad (recurring guest Jump) drops in for an unexpected visit, with news of his imminent death.

Young Ed Malone................................................Larry Marks
Young Maggie.....................................................Alexis Greig
Cabbie..................................................................Beano

Writer: Rich Reinhart

17. "Maggie Seaver's ' The Meaning of Life ' "  Feb. 6, 1991

Jason takes Maggie on a tropical getaway to lift her spirits after her father's death, trusting Chrissy to Mike and Carol.

Cabbie................................................................Richie Allen
Flight attendant.....................................Siobhan E. McCafferty
Swapping passenger..............................................Jack Stauffer
Concerned passenger.............................................Brian Peck

Writer: Jay Abramowitz

18. "All the World is a Stage"  Feb. 13, 1991

Mike competes with a well-established actor (Smith) for a role in a soap opera, learning how tenuous an acting career can be. Guest Peck had played a different role last episode.

Eric Douglas.......................................................Forry Smith
Wardrobe woman/Kathleen....................Pat Crawford Brown *
Mimi..............................................................Trisha McNerney
Receptionists..........................Nicole Renee Tracy, Kathy Tracy
Mike as adult.....................................................Robert Cameron
Audition doofus....................................................Brian Peck
Security guard/Dave...................................David John Hayes
Bettina............................................................Barbara Wilder
       Also orig. announced:
       Richard Minchenberg (Gordie), Scott Geyer (Ryan Kilgor)

* erroneously listed onscreen as Pat Crawford.

Writer: David Kendall

19. "Not With My Carol You Don't"  Feb. 20, 1991

Though Jason had an insensitive Carol pitch in at the clinic, he objects to her dating an ex-con (Lawrence) she meets there. Barnes reprises her role from ep. 14.

Webster Winslow.................................................Scott Lawrence
Dr. Miller.........................................................Susan Barnes
Diner owner (orig. announced as Sen. Pat Geary)......Al Checco
T.C...............................................................Ross Chamberlain
Officer Mills......................................................Joseph Reale

Writer: Leilani Downer

20. "Meet the Seavers"  March 6, 1991

In an homage to *The Twilight Zone*, Ben awakens to discover he's Jeremy Miller, an actor on the set of *Meet the Seavers*. Guest Ashley Kerns is the daughter of co-star Joanna Kerns; Harris is the series' script supervisor; Stellar had played a different role in ep. 9, Peck different roles in ep. 17 and 18.

Stage manager...................................................James L. Marshall
Chauffeur............................................................John LaMotta
Bub....................................................................Bill Erwin
Director............................................................Brian Backer
Voice of director..................................................Ray Willes
Herself...............................................................Ashley Kerns
Script supervisor Susan......................Susan Straughn Harris
Audience warm-up person.......................................Phil Stellar
Special effects guy.................................................Brian Peck
Hans..................................................................Neil Farrell

Teleplay: Bob Burris & Michael Ware
Story: Dan Guntzelman & Steve Marshall, David Kendall, Nick
       LeRose and Mike Sullivan

## 21. "Carol's Carnival" March 27, 1991

On a blind date shaping up as a disaster, Carol goes to the carnival, and finds unexpected fun and excitement.

Jake...............................................................Jay Acovone
Brad............................................................Manfred Melcher
Trish...........................................................Shonda Whipple
Kvetch-O the Clown (orig. Harry).........................Jack Angeles
        Also orig. announced: Earl Johnson (Sammy)

Writer: Rich Reinhart

**preempted April 3**

## 22. "Home Schooling" April 17, 1991

When Ben is suspended from school for a few days, Maggie tries teaching him herself.

Willis DeWitt...............................................Sam Anderson

Teleplay: Nick LeRose
Story: Dan Guntzelman & Mike Sullivan

## 23. "Viva Las Vegas" April 24, 1991

Mike and Kate accompany the eloping Eddie and a hat-check bimbette to Las Vegas, giving Mike and Carol the wrong idea. Young reprises her role from ep. 13.

Tina..............................................................Melissa Young
Edgar.................................................................Bill Erwin
Miriam.........................................Jacalyn O'Shaughnessy
Stan (man on plane)...........................................Jim Jansen
Elderly woman on plane (orig. Maxine)...............Maxine Elliott
        Also orig. announced: Elizabeth Lambert (Stewardess)

Writer: Shelly Landau

**preempted July 3; Sept. 6 rerun, 9:30-10 p.m.**

**renewed for 1991-92; new episodes begin Sept. 18, 1991**

## Guns of Paradise

CBS               Fridays, 8-9 p.m.

Series premiere: Oct. 27, 1988
Final telecast: June 14, 1991

Western drama of a reluctant gunfighter in the 1890s boom-town of Paradise, who unexpectedly inherits responsibility for his sister's four children. Recurring guests Crittenden and Bloom reprise their roles from last season. Formerly titled *Paradise* (1988-1990).

Ethan Allen Cord.................................................Lee Horsley
Amelia Lawson, his fiancee.............................Sigrid Thornton
Claire Carroll.......................................................Jenny Beck
Joseph Carroll...........................................Matthew Newmark
Benjamin Carroll..................................................Brian Lando
George Carroll...............M.P. (a.k.a. Michael Patrick) Carter
John Taylor............................................................Dehl Berti
Dakota.............................................................John Terlesky

*Recurring:*
Deputy Charlie (ep. 1,5-7,10-12)..............James Crittenden
Tiny (ep. 1,5-6,9,12)..................................John Bloom
Carl (ep. 1-2,6-7,10)......................................Will Hunt

Axelrod (ep. 1,5,12)..........................................Michael Ensign
Baxter (ep. 1,9,12)................................................John Miranda
Martin (ep. 2,6,12)..................................................Aeryk Egan
Jackie (ep. 2,9,12)..........................................Marcia Solomon
William (ep. 6,9,12)...........................................Louis R. Plante
Swenson (ep. 6-7,9)................................................Pat Skipper
Suzie (ep. 6,8-9).....................................................Janet Gunn

Roundelay Productions in assoc. with Lorimar Television
Executive producer: David Jacobs
Supervising producer: James L. Conway
Producers: James H. Brown, Robert Porter, Joel J.
      Feigenbaum
Associate producer: Avery C. Drewe
Director of photography: Richard M. Rawlings, Jr., A.S.C.
Music (variously): Jerrold Immel; Richard Warren; Christopher
      Klatman
Theme (instrumental): Jerrold Immel
Creators: David Jacobs & Robert Porter

---

## 1. "Out of the Ashes" Jan. 4, 1991

Ethan befriends a hot-headed gambler (new cast-member Ter-lesky) and becomes the new marshal after a gunfight with the crooked present one; George struggles with a reading disorder.

Marshal Blake...................................................Robert Fuller
Stark...........................................................H. Richard Greene
Garret...............................................................Bruce Wright
Butler...........................................................Christopher Crabb
And: Leah Remini (Rose), Jim Burke (Otto), Buddy Jo Hooker
      (Jackson), Zachary Benjamin (Emmet)

Director: Cliff Bole                    Writer: James L. Conway

## 2. "The Bounty" Jan. 11, 1991

When Dakota needs the reward money to pay off gambling debts, he competes with new marshal Ethan to catch a gang; George is discovered to be what we now know of as dyslexic. Stark reprises his role from last episode.

Stark...........................................................H. Richard Greene
Gang-leader Jack Donner.............................Patrick Kilpatrick
Marshal Pike......................................................Tom O'Rourke
And: Peter Vogt (Scratch) Joshua Harris (Robby), Chuck Sloan
      (Roberts), Peg Stewart (Rae Miller), Jan Merlin (Joe Mill-
      er), Ben Scott (Hogg), Walker Edmiston (Doc Thomas),
      David James Alexander (Croupier), Jack Forbes (Luke)

Director: Michael Caffey               Writer: Joel J. Feigenbaum

**preempted Jan. 18**

## 3. "The Women" Jan. 25, 1991

While Ethan and Dakota pursue a gang of bank robbers, they must protect three women whose men were slain by the out-laws. Guest Podewell is a cast-member of *Dallas*.

Laura............................................................Cathy Podewell
Martha.............................................................Carol Huston
Hodges......................................................Jeffrey Josephson
Esther..............................................................Betsy Randle
Slatter.............................................................Buck Taylor
And: Billy Ray Sharkey (Miller), Michael Medeiros (Hicks),
      John C. Meier (Dewitt), Jim Raymond (Seth), Richard
      Epcar (Novak)

Director: Cliff Bole                Writer: Thomas C. Chapman

4. "Bad Blood"  Feb. 1, 1991

Ethan voluntarily goes to Texas to stand trial for a gunfight killing five years ago, but faces a mockery of a court.

Patricia Forrester.................................Barbara Rush
Samantha Forrester Sweeney........................Kristen Meadows
Calvin Forrester......................................Joe Dorsey
Tuck Sweeney......................................Christopher Curry
Paul Forrester.......................................Todd Allen
Judge Sweeney.......................................Hoke Howell
Eddy the lamplighter................................Ed Hooks
Sisk..........................................Gregory Scott Cummins
And: Milt Tarver (Conductor), Tom Reese (Farmer), Melissa
     Young (Daughter), Kim Waltrip (Tess)

Director: Harry Harris              Writer: Joel J. Feigenbaum

5. "The Valley of Death"  Feb. 8, 1991

Ethan interrupts his wedding ceremony to deal with bank robbers, then learns a vengeance-seeking Dakota believes Ethan killed his father.  O'Rourke reprises his role from ep. 2.

Morgan..........................................Brooks Gardner
Lisa................................................Susan Diol
Dodd........................................F. William Parker
Marshal Pike....................................Tom O'Rourke
Margaret...........................................Julie Payne
Rafe..............................................Mitch Pileggi
Minister..........................................Ben Kronen
     Also orig. announced: John Lyons (Frank Walker)

Director: Michael Caffey            Writer: James L. Conway

6. "A Bullet Through the Heart"  Feb. 15, 1991

When a murderer's (DiCenzo) alibi compels his release from jail, the townsfolk turn into a lynch mob; Claire sends Dakota love notes. Guest Harris reprises his role from ep. 2. Orig. scheduled for Jan. 18 and Feb. 15.

Ned Wick.........................................George DiCenzo
Beckie............................................Kim Lankford
Robby...........................................Joshua Harris
Noah...............................................Doug Sloan
Kate..............................................Benita Andre
And: Betsy Soo (Belle), Jim Nickerson (Wagon driver)

Director: Harry Harris              Writer: Robert Porter

7. "See No Evil"  Feb. 22, 1991

During a mysterious epidemic, Ethan reluctantly joins forces with Amelia's new suitor (Burleigh), a doctor, to find the cause.

Dr. Kenneth Winthrop...............................Stephen Burleigh
Marsh..............................................Brett Porter
Callaway.......................................Richardson Morse
Wade............................................Randy Crowder
Gus..............................................Graham Jarvis
And: Laurence Haddon (Bass), Robert S. Telford (Dietrick)

Director: Cliff Bole               Writer: Robert Porter

8. "Birthright"  March 8, 1991

The kids' disreputable, presumed-dead father (Albert, the son of actor Eddie Albert) rides in to try to reclaim them.

Robert Carroll.....................................Edward Albert
Bartender/James.....................................Dell Yount
Pearl..............................................Gay Hagen

Director: Harry Harris             Writer: Joel J. Feigenbaum

**preempted March 15 and March 22**

9. "A Study in Fear"  March 29, 1991

Ethan accepts the help of a by-the-book detective (Pollard) to find a serial murderer preying on the town's young women. Guest Payne had played a different character in ep. 5; Yount reprises his role from last episode, Crowder from ep. 7.

Lester Barr.......................................Michael J. Pollard
Bartender/James.....................................Dell Yount
Jesse..............................................Jack Kehler
Hattie.............................................Julie Payne
And: Randy Crowder (Wade), Lisa Toothman (Hillary)

Director: Nick Havinga             Writer: Robert Porter

10. "The Search for K.C. Cavanaugh"  April 5, 1991

After Ethan captures a female outlaw (Crosby), she plans her escape with Ben and Claire, who believe she's innocent. Mary Crosby a.k.a. Mary Francis Crosby is the daughter of singer Bing Crosby and his second wife, Katherine Grant.

K.C. Cavanaugh.....................................Mary Crosby
Marshal Bartlet.....................................David Graf
Man................................................Dean Smith

Director: Harry Harris             Writer: Theresa G. Corigliano

11. "Shield of Gold"  April 12, 1991

Ethan reluctantly arrests Taylor for stealing a gold shield, which he discovers holds a key to Taylor's tribe's massacre.

John Wolcott.......................................Rod Arrants
Marshal Gordon.................................Will MacMillan
Chester........................................Michael Milhoan
And: Randy Boffman (Bill), Russ McCubbin (Brody)

Director: Cliff Bole               Writer: Joel J. Feigenbaum

**preempted April 26**

12. "Twenty-Four Hours"  May 3, 1991

A prostitute (Sheridan, a cast-member of *Knots Landing*), an overly amorous teacher (Arranga), Dakota's gambling, and a friend's (Bloom) near-death keep Ethan working 24 straight hours. Director Rawlings is the series' director of photography.

Lily...............................................Nicollette Sheridan
Miss Jenner........................................Irene Arranga
Caroline Dryer...................................Maggie Roswell
Bellamy............................................Greg Collins
Theodore...........................................Patrick Wright
Croupier......................................David James Alexander
And: Paul Michael Brennan (Jake), Gregory Cassel (Cowboy)

Director: Richard M. Rawlings, Jr.   Writer: Robert Porter

13. "Unfinished Business"  May 10, 1991

Ethan recalls his life (via clips from past episodes) as he prepares for a showdown with an old nemesis (Libby).

Dan Bridges.................................................Brian Libby
Stagecoach driver....................................Bob Swain
    Also orig. announced:
      Rex Linn (Grant Page), Kathryn Leigh Scott (Lucy)

Director: Harry Harris
Writers: James L. Conway & Joel J. Feigenbaum

## Head of the Class

ABC
Sept. 11-Jan. 15, May 28-June 25     Tuesdays, 8:30-9 p.m.

Series premiere: Sept. 17, 1986
Final telecast: June 25, 1991

Ensemble comedy of the gifted children in the Individual Honors Program (IHP) of fictional Millard Fillmore High School in New York City, and of their eccentric, Scottish history-teacher (Connolly, succeeding Howard Hesseman, who played teacher Charlie Moore through last season). Rain Pryor is the daughter of comedian Richard Pryor.

Billy MacGregor.................................................Billy Connolly
Principal Dr. Samuels...............................William G. Schilling
Asst. Principal Bernadette Meara.................Jeannetta Arnette
Alex Torres................................................Michael DeLorenzo
Arvid Engen.....................................................Dan Frischman
Darlene Merriman.................................................Robin Givens
Simone Foster..................................................Khrystyne Haje
Jasper Kwong.............................................Jonathan Ke Quan
Alan Pinkard.......................................................Tony O'Dell
Viki Amory............................................................Lara Piper
T.J..................................................................Rain Pryor
Eric Mardian....................................................Brian Robbins
Sarah Russell................................................Kimberly Russell
Dennis Blunden.............................................Daniel Schneider
Aristotle McKenzie........................................De'Voreaux White

Eustis Elias Productions in assoc. with Warner Bros.
    Television
Executive producers: Michael Elias, Rich Eustis
Supervising producers (orig. announced as producers): Frank
    Pace, Ray Jessel, Andy Guerdat, Steve Kreinberg
Co-producer: Jeffrey Duteil
Associate producer: Bari Halle
Executive story editors: David Hurwitz, Bill Rosenthal, Noah
    Taft
Story editors: Danny Smith, Carol Corwen
Creative consultant: Jonathan Roberts
Director of photography: Richard Brown
Theme (instrumental) and music: Ed Alton
Creators: Rich Eustis & Michael Elias

———————————————

1. "Where's Charlie" Sept. 11, 1990

Now that their teacher, Charlie, has left to pursue acting, the class puts his Oxford-educated successor through tests.

Director: Howard Storm
Writers: Rich Eustis & Michael Elias

2. "Twelve Angry Nerds" Sept. 18, 1990

When Alan is caught cheating, Billy has the class act as a jury to decide his punishment.

Miss Coleman, the librarian............................Laura Waterbury

Director: Alan Rosen
Writers: Rich Eustis & Michael Elias

3. "The Heartbreak Nerd" Sept. 25, 1990

Arvid goes out with gorgeous Viki. Orig. scheduled for Oct. 2.

Director: Lee Shallat
Writers: Ursula Ziegler & Steve Sullivan

4. "And Then There Were None" Oct. 2, 1990

Arvid's infectious flu may keep the class from performing in a Shakespeare competition. Director Bonner is better known as an actor. Orig. scheduled for Sept. 25.

Director: Frank Bonner
Writers: Michael Elias & Rich Eustis

5. "Getting Personal" Oct. 9, 1990

Billy tries the personals ads.

Director: Alan Rosen          Writer: Danny Smith

6. "Napoleon Blown Apart" Oct. 16, 1990

Eric, inspired by French class, goes to "find himself" in Paris.

Student..............................................................Alison Brooks

Director: Alan Rosen          Writer: Carol Corwen

7. "Billy's Big One" Oct. 23, 1990

Billy fakes a heart attack to circumvent a health-insurance bureaucracy; the IHP girls try writing a romance novel.

Dr. Hayes...........................................................Rosalind Cash
Nurse Lemas.....................................................Carol Ann Susi

Director: Lee Shallat
Writers: Ursula Ziegler & Steve Sullivan

8. "Dead Men Don't Wear Pocket Protectors" Part 1
    Oct. 30, 1990

After Billy is robbed, he has the class write papers on gun control, leading Arvid to a harrowing experience when he buys a gun for the assignment. Per ABC, the series' 100th episode.

Zach Butler.......................................................Jason Kristofer
Customer with handgun......................Gregory Scott Cummins
Store owner..........................................................Lance Davis
Customer with rifle............................................Dominic Oliver

Director: Lee Shallat
Writers: Andy Guerdat & Steve Kreinberg

9. "Dead Men Don't Wear Pocket Protectors" Part 2
    Nov. 6, 1990

The bullying Zach may have Arvid's missing gun.

Zach Butler.......................................................Jason Kristofer
Police detective.....................................................(uncredited)

Director: Lee Shallat
Writers: Andy Guerdat & Steve Kreinberg

10. "Fillmore vs. Billy Jean's" Nov. 13, 1990

The IHP class behaves obnoxiously when its bus breaks down at a rural truck stop.

Lucas.................................................Howard Morris
Betty Jean..........................................Mary Lou Childs
And: Tracy Fraim (Lee), Ron Frazier (Ed), Virginia Watson (Lucille), Christopher Wynn (Dwight)

Director: Art Dielhenn                Writer: Jeffrey Duteil

11. "Be My Baby...Sitter"  Nov. 20, 1990

When Jasper's overprotective parents hire a babysitter for him one evening, it turns out to be Sarah, from his class.

Mrs. Kwong..........................................Denice Kumagai
Mr. Kwong...........................................Tzi Ma

Director: Art Dielhenn
Writers: Tom Chapman & Jonathan Torp

12. "Dancing Fools"  Nov. 27, 1990

Billy and Bernadette take dance lessons at the studio where Alex teaches, and where he's pursued by a woman (Kent).

Maureen Foster......................................Enid Kent
Warren Waxman.....................................Barry Vigon

Director: Art Dielhenn
Writers: Andy Guerdat & Steve Kreinberg

13. "My Son, the Primate"  Dec. 4, 1990

Arvid trains a chimp at his part-time pet store job, and rather than let it be sold, hides it in the classroom.

Mr. Birch...........................................Stephen Root
Mr. Finneman.......................................H. Richard Greene
Herself.............................................Maisy (chimp)

Director: Howard Storm              Writer: David Hurwitz

14. "The Importance of Being Alex"  Dec. 11, 1990

Simone's reputation suffers when Alex lies to his friends about a romance with her.

Mrs. Torres, Alex's mother..........................Liz Torres

Director: Howard Storm              Writer: Carol Corwen

15. "Viki's Torn Genes"  Dec. 18, 1990

At Christmas, Billy helps Viki find her birth mother, but the woman doesn't want to see her.

Greta Amory, Viki's adoptive mother.................June Gable
Rose Gibson, Viki's birth mother....................Cynthia Mace

Director: Buzz Sapien
Writers: Bill Rosenthal & Noah Taft

**preempted Jan. 1**

16. "The Last Waltz"  Jan. 8, 1991

T.J. turns down Aristotle's invitation to the senior prom.

Bobby Pace..........................................T.E. Russell
Colleen.............................................Michelle Boudreau

Director: Bill Davis
Writers: Bill Rosenthal & Noah Taft

17. "Most Likely to Be Forgotten"  Jan. 15, 1991

The kids work on their yearbook, with Eric beginning to regret not having participated more extracurricularly.

Director: Howard Storm
Writers: Ursula Ziegler & Steve Sullivan and David Hurwitz

**on hiatus**

18. "The Strange Case of Randy McNally"  May 28, 1991

To save Dennis after a prank, Billy creates a fictional student, who apparently gets the M.I.T. scholarship Dennis wanted. Director Hickman is the former star of *The Many Loves of Dobie Gillis* (CBS, 1959-63).

Mrs. Samuel.........................................Karen Ragan

Director: Dwayne Hickman           Teleplay: Jeffrey Duteil
Story: Tom Chapman & Jonathan Torp

19. "My Dinner with Darlene"  June 4, 1991

Darlene promises to treat the class to an elaborate farewell dinner, but then finds her credit card revoked.

Waiter..............................................Dell Yount

Director: Renny Temple             Writer: Danny Smith

20. "The Phantom of the Glee Club"  June 11, 1991

The class learns T.J. is more than just a contemporary-style musician when Billy discovers her operatic talent.

Monica..............................................Kirsten Holmquist
Nancy...............................................Jodee Williger
Juilliard representative............................Marie Pollara

Director: Robin Saek              Writer: David Hurwitz

21. "It Couldn't Last Forever" Part 1   June 18, 1991

With a wrecking ball ready to demolish the school, the IHP class waits to find out who's to be valedictorian.  Christie is a recurring guest from past seasons; Vallely a former cast-member; and Sapien, the series' associate director.

Dorfman.............................................Peter Vogt
Lori Applebaum......................................Marcia Christie
Worker..............................................Buzz Sapien
    Also orig. announced:
    Tannis Vallely (Janice Lazarotto), Ray Jessel (Wafting)

Director: Howard Storm
Writers: Ray Jessel and Jeffrey Duteil

22. "It Couldn't Last Forever" Part 2   June 25, 1991

The IHP class graduates, with T.J. as valedictorian.

Dorfman.............................................Peter Vogt
Lori Applebaum......................................Marcia Christie
Foreperson..........................................Charles Noland
And: Buzz Sapien (Worker), Kellie Overbey (Jackie)
    Also orig. announced:
    Tannis Vallely (Janice Lazarotto), Ray Jessel (Wafting)

Director: Howard Storm
Writers: Ray Jessel and Jeffrey Duteil and Andy Guerdat & Steve Kreinberg

## Hi Honey, I'm Home!

ABC              Fridays, 9:30-10 p.m.

Series premiere: July 19, 1991
Final network telecast: Aug. 23, 1991

Surrealistic comedy of next-door neighbors in suburban New Jersey: a divorced, politically active, telephone-repairperson mother (Cella) and her two sons, and a family of fictional characters from a cancelled 1950s TV show, placed there by the Sitcom Relocation Program. Title punctuation is as appears onscreen. Produced by the cable service Nickelodeon, the first time a cable service has produced a primetime network series. Each episode is rerun on Nickelodeon's "Nick at Nite" schedule the weekend following its network airing. Taped in Orlando, Fla.

Honey Nielsen.................................................Charlotte Booker
Lloyd Ralph Nielsen.....................................Stephen Bradbury
Mike Duff.............................................................Pete Benson
Babs Nielsen............................................................Julie Benz
Sidney "Skunk" Duff...........................................Eric Kushnick
Chucky Nielsen.....................................................Danny Gura
Elaine Duff..............................................................Susan Cella

RiPe Productions and Nick at Nite / MTV Networks
Executive producer: Rick Mitz
Producers: Penny Stallings, Angelika Bartenbach
Supervising producer: Barry Secunda
Associate producer: Maureen Badger Schultz
Consultants (not all episodes): Tom Leopold, Suzanne Collins
Music: Rupert Holmes
Theme: composer/lyricist uncredited; performed by Rupert
    Holmes; end-theme is a synthesized, dissonant, mostly
    instrumental version of the opening theme
Director: Doug Rogers
Creators: Rick Mitz & Penny Stallings

---

1. "Meet the Nielsens"  July 19, 1991

Mike discovers the new neighbors' secret, and vows to keep it and to help them learn to cope with the '90s. Gordon played the character Mr. Mooney from 1963-68 on *The Lucy Show*.

Mr. Mooney, Lloyd's boss (cameo)........................Gale Gordon
Malcolm................................................................Barry Cutler

Writers: Rick Mitz & Penny Stallings

2. "Make My Bed"  July 26, 1991

Honey takes measures after she's robbed at home. Billingsley's character crosses over from *Leave It to Beaver* (CBS, 1957-58; ABC, 1958-63), the TV-movie *Still the Beaver* (1983) and the cable series *Still the Beaver* and *The New Leave It to Beaver*.

June Cleaver.......................................Barbara Billingsley
Burglar..........................................James Michael Detmar
Mrs. Naughton..............................................................Ilse Earl
And:  Danny Dillon, Conrad Goode, Bill Lorenz, Filmore, Allen
    Penney, Tommy Mack Turvey

Writers: Rick Mitz & Penny Stallings

3. "Fur Flies"  Aug. 2, 1991

Lloyd tries to break up Honey's and Elaine's friendship after the women are arrested at an anti-fur protest. Meadows' and Randolph's characters cross over from *The Honeymooners*.

Alice Kramden...................................................Audrey Meadows
Trixie Norton.....................................................Joyce Randolph
And: Carolyn Casanave

Writers: Rick Mitz & Penny Stallings

4. "Hi Mom, I'm Not ot Home"  Aug. 9, 1991

Elaine's upset when Mike wants to celebrate his birthday with the Nielsens. Nabors' character crosses over from *Gomer Pyle, U.S.M.C.* (CBS 1964-70). Orig. scheduled for Aug. 2.

Gomer Pyle...........................................................Jim Nabors
Pianist..............John Rangell (Rupert Holmes orig. announced)

Writer: Lee Kalcheim

5. "Grey Skies"  Aug. 16, 1991

Jobless Lloyd feels he's losing his manhood. Lewis' character crosses over from *The Munsters* (CBS, 1964-66).

Grandpa Munster.....................................................Al Lewis
Dr. Stanley Siegel.................................................Barry Cutler

Writer: Suzanne Collins

6. "SRP"  Aug. 23, 1991

Mike jeopardizes the Nielsen's chance to return to TV land. Davis' character crosses over from *The Brady Bunch* (ABC, 1969-74) and its spinoff TV-movies and series.

Alice Nelson.........................................................Ann B. Davis
And: James Michael Detmar

Writer: Michael Patrick King

## The Hitchhiker

USA July 27, 1990-June 28, 1991  Fridays, 10-10:30 p.m.
      July 5-on                              Fridays, 10:30-11 p.m.

Series premiere: Nov. 23, 1983
USA Network premiere: Jan. 6, 1989

Horror-suspense anthology, with prologue and epilogue soliloquy by the metaphoric Hitchhiker. First nine episodes filmed in Toronto, the remainder in Paris. Series began on HBO, which telecast 39 editions, then switched to USA Network.

The Hitchhiker.................................................Page Fletcher

Quintina Productions and Atlantique Productions in
    affiliation with Markowtiz/Chesler/Rothstein Producing,
    in cooperation with USA Network and La Cinq
Executive producers: Lewis Chesler, David Perlmutter,
    Boudjemaa Dafimane, Jacques Methe
Supervising producers: Wendy Grean (ep. 1 only); Tab Baird
Producer: Barbara Shrier
Creative producer: Jeremy Lipp
Executive story editor: Gail Glaze
Director of photography includes (variously): Richard Wincenty, Cyril Lathus, Robert Jaffray, Reginald H. Morris

Music: Jack Procher, generally with Anthony Lancett
Theme (instrumental): Paul Hoffert
Creators: Riff Markowitz, Lewis Chesler, Richard Rothstein

———————————

1. "Fading Away"  Sept. 21, 1990

A paranoid ex-Marine (Mancuso) believes himself abandoned on a dangerous, clandestine mission.

Mitchell.....................................................Nick Mancuso
String lady...............................................Helen Hughes
And: Angelo Rizacos (Freak), Brenda Bazinet (Mary), Michael Tait (Major), Conrad Coates (Frank)

Director: Gerard Ciccoritti          Story: Gail Glaze
Teleplay: Lawrence G. DiTillio a.k.a. Larry DiTillio

2. "Tough Guys Don't Whine"  Sept. 28, 1990

An arrogant director steals the girlfriend of a young hood, and when he accidentally kills her tries to buy his way out.  Thicke is a cast-member of *Growing Pains*.

Mickey Black....................................................Alan Thicke
James.........................................................Raoul Trujillo
Penny.........................................................Krista Bridhes
Bowie......................................................Frank Pellegrino
Tiny.................................................................Peter Cox
And: Joseph Griffin (Tug), Heidi Von Palleske (Interviewer), Larry McLean (Charlie), Tim Burd (Dealer)

Director: Jorge Montesti          Teleplay: Bradley R. Swirnoff
Story: Gail Glaze

3. "Riding the Nightmare"  Oct. 5, 1990

A wealthy careerist (Hutton) uses the power of a recurring nightmare to eliminate obstacles to her adulturous affair. Based on a short story by Lisa Tuttle.

Tess.........................................................Lauren Hutton
Gordon...................................................Garwin Sanford
Jude...........................................................Victoria Snow
Karen....................................................Rachel Blanchard
And: Katherine Trowell (Dorothy), Peter Langley (Jim Voth)

Director: Christian Duguay          Teleplay: Naomi Janzen

4. "Strate Shooter"  Oct. 12, 1990

A boy (Rydell) tries to emulate his TV-show hero, and rescue a young woman from her mobster father.

Johnny Mattell...........................................Chris Rydell
Young woman..............................................Andrea Roth
Matt Strate..................................................Matt Cooke
Richard Mattel.........................................Andrew Gillies
Buzz...........................................................Phil Morrison
And: Chandra West (Woman at club), Gigi DeLeon (Asian)

Director: Mark Rezyka          Teleplay: Naomi Janzen
Story: Lawrence Levy

5. "Hard Rhyme"  Oct. 19, 1990

A failed writer (Foxworth), teaching poetry in a prison, steals a convicted murderer's journal to achieve literary success.

Lee Greavy.........................................Robert Foxworth

Louella Stone.................................Heidi Von Palleske
Margaret Cabot..................................Charmion King
Jesse............................................Silvio Oliviero
And: Daniel Kash (Killer), Gene Mack (Manny)

Director: Leon Marr          Story: David Nevens
Teleplay: Michael J. Murray III and Jeremy Lipp

6. "Toxic Shock"  Oct. 26, 1990

Toxic wastes destroy a man's memory.

Raskin.......................................................Zach Galligan
Bobby..........................................................Kevin Hicks
Sally.............................................................Tracey Cook
Sheriff.....................................................John Stoneham

Director: Gerard Ciccoritti          Writer: Jeremy Lipp

7. "New Dawn"  Nov. 2, 1991

A woman (McKeon) goes to desperate measures to keep her straying husband, a lawyer trying to become an artist.

Dawn Wilder................................................Nancy McKeon
Ken Wilder.................................................Barclay Hope
Sherri...........................................................Lori Hallier
Mimi Rasmussen........................................Jill Frappier
Mark Wallengreen................................Victor Ertmanis
And: Kaye Tremplay (Art critic), Doug Lennox (Sheriff)

Director: Mitch Gabourie   Teleplay: Max Bloom & Jeremy Lipp
Story: Jeremy Lipp

8. "A Function of Control"  Nov. 9, 1991

A prim, efficent secretary (Dale) has erotic dreams of her boss (Gillies, who'd appeared in a different role in ep. 4).

Laura Perry..............................................Jennifer Dale
Warren Harrison......................................Andrew Gillies
Mandy........................................................Nadia Capone
Karen........................................................Kaya McGregor
And: Ferne Downey (Helen), Sandy Crawley (Detective)

Director: Leon Marr
Teleplay: M.C. Varley and Bradley R. Swirnoff
Story: Gail Glaze and Sarah Timberman

9. "Trust Me"  Nov. 16, 1990

A con artist (Lamas) who romances and swindles elderly women finds himself blackmailed by a sexy young one.

Tom Astor.................................................Lorenzo Lamas
Michelle.....................................................Carolyn Dunn
Teddy......................................................Lawrence Bayne
Helen Masters.....................................Maruska Stankova
And: Larissa Lapchinski (Gina), Burns Proudfoot (Butler)

Director: Tab Baird          Writer: Ed Redlich

10. "Windows"  Nov. 23, 1990

A frustrated artist (Grant) finds that scenes he paints appear to come true.

Jake......David Marshall Grant (David Morant orig. announced)
Sophie....................................................Annabelle Mouloudji
Monique.........................................................Claude Jade
Victor..................................................Jean-Claude Bouillon

Director: Rene Manzor    Writer: Elizabeth Baxter

11. "Working Girl" Nov. 30, 190

A rich wife (Lipton) falls under the control of the mistress/witness she spared when killing her adulterous husband.

Helen.................................................................Peggy Lipton
Lucille.............................................................Marine Delterme
Roger...............................................................Gilles Millinaire
Detective........................................................Denys Fouqueray

Director: Miguel Courtois
Teleplay: Larry DiTillio a.k.a. Lawrence G. DiTillio

12. "White Slaves" Dec. 7, 1991

Two American college students in their last Parisian semester kidnap a woman for sex. Working title: "The Lovers."

Gerald.........................................................C. Thomas Howell
Eric.............................................................Gerard Watkins
Adrienne.........................................................Mapi Galan
Georges............................................................Yan Epstein
And: Vincent Grass (Cop), Alexandra Fierro (Albertine)

Director: Robin Davis    Story: Jeremy Lipp
Teleplay: Naomi Janzen and Jeremy Lipp

13. "Tourist Trap" Dec. 14, 1991

A thief and con-artist (Benson) separates a tourist from an apparently valuable box.

Bart...............................................................Robby Benson
Adara..............................................................Hodan Siad
Samantha.......................................................Veronike Ryke
Ahmed..............................................................Karim Salah

Director: Frank Apprederis    Teleplay: Martin Brossollet
Story: Martin Brossollet & Elizabeth Baxter

14. "The Homecoming" Jan. 11, 1991

A neofascist's (Howard) rise to power is undermined by his growing paranoia his past will be exposed.

Dubois...............................................................Ken Howard
Jeanne.............................................................Laura Favali
And: Jean-Pierre Stewart (Derval), Jean Descanvelle (Julien), Valerie LAGRANGE (Claire), Christian VAN Acker (Claude), Patrick Bresson (Groundskeeper)

Director: Bruno Gantillon    Writer: Jean-Vincent Fournier

15. "Living a Lie" Jan. 18, 1991

A bartender (Valentine) goes on a shopping spree with a credit card stolen from a patron.

Joe..............................................................Scott Valentine
Catherine/Agnes..................................................Ingrid Held
Ted Bruce........................................................Bradley Cole
Paul..............................................................Yves Collignon

Director: Bruno Gantillon    Writer: Elizabeth Baxter

16. "Made in Paris" Jan. 25, 1991

A sweat-shop manager (Knox) suffers supernatural revenge by his Asian workers. Working title: "Bad to the Bone."

Leon...............................................................Terence Knox
Mai Jan.........................................................Yumi Fujimoro
Sylvie.............................................................Cecile Paoli
And: Jim Adhi Limas (Sam), Jean-Claude Tran (Yong)

Director: Rene Manzor    Teleplay: Etienne Strubel
Story: Martin Brossollet & Elizabeth Baxter

17. "A Whole New You" Feb. 1, 1991

A crime witness (Gould) undergoes plastic surgery to protect his identity.

Augie.............................................................Elliott Gould
Denis..........................................................Olivier Rabourdin
Dr. Renaud.....................................................Judith Burnett
Carrie.........................................................Micky Sebastian
And: Herve Geandel (Thug), Bernard Nissile (Patient)

Director: Patricia Mazuy    Teleplay: Naomi Janzen
Story: Gail Glaze

18. "Offspring" Feb. 8, 1991

A grown son (Roche) tries to leave his suffocating mother.

Mother..........................................................Louise Fletcher
Glenn..........................................................Sebastian Roche
Alice.............................................................Laura Favali
And: Florence Haziot (Woman), Christine B. Dawson (Hooker)

Director: Robin Davis    Writer: Jeremy Lipp

19. "Secrets" Feb. 15, 1991

A murderous wife and her lover are visited by the husband they "killed," who wants a piece of his insurance money.

Veronica...........................................................Mary Frann
Roger...........................................................Daniel Briquet
Bernard........................................................Frederic Norbert
M. Cluet.........................................................Michel Voletti

Director: Jacques Richard    Teleplay: Naomi Janzen
Story: Elizabeth Baxter

20. "New Blood" Feb. 22, 1991

A struggling actress puts her life and blood on the line.

Leesa...........................................................Rae Dawn Chong
Varsig.........................................................Didier Sauvegran
Consuela.........................................................Joanna Pavlis
Thierry........................................................Jerry Di Giacomo
And: Jean-Philippe Chartier (Stephane), Geoffrey Carey (Alec)

Director: Joel Farges    Teleplay: Jean-Vincent Fournier
Story: Elizabeth Baxter

**preempted March 29**

**preempted April 12 and April 19**

**renwed; reruns, mostly from past years, continue into fall season**

## The Hogan Family

| | | |
|---|---|---|
| CBS | Sept. 15-Dec. 1 | Saturdays 8:30-9 p.m. |
| | July 10-20 | Various |

Series premiere: March 1, 1986
Final telecast: July 20, 1991

Comedy of an Oak Park, Ill. airline pilot's sons, overseen primarily by their aunt, a high school vice principal. Formerly on NBC as *Valerie* (March 1986-Sept. 1987), starring Valerie Harper, and *Valerie's Family* (to June 1988) after Harper's departure and her character's death. Sole season on CBS.

Sandy Hogan.......................................................Sandy Duncan
Northwestern U. student David Hogan (20).......Jason Bateman
Mark Hogan (17)..................................................Jeremy Licht
Willie Hogan (17), his twin...............................Danny Ponce
Patty Poole...........................................................Edie McClurg
Burt Weems.........................................................Steve Witting
Cara, Mark's girlfriend........................................Josie Bissett
Brenda, Willie's girlfriend.........................................Angela Lee
Michael Hogan, the boys' father..............................Josh Taylor
Lloyd Hogan, his and Sandy's father...............John Hillerman

Miller • Boyett Productions in assoc. with Lorimar Television
Executive producers: Thomas L. Miller, Robert L. Boyett, Irma Kalish
Supervising producer: Larry Spencer
Producer: Ronny Hallin, Shari Hearn, Michael Loman
Consulting producer: Richard Correll
Associate producer: Karen Kirchner
Executive story consultants: Steve Granat, Mel Sherer, Richard Albrecht, Casey Keller
Story editor: Daryl Busby
Director of photography (variously): Richard A. Kelley, A.S.C.; Robert F. Sparks
Music: Bruce Miller
Theme: "Together Through the Years" by Charles Fox (music), Stephen Geyer (lyrics); performed by Roberta Flack
Creator: Charlie Hauck

------------------------------

1. "California Dreamin' Part I" Sept. 15, 1990

The Hogans go to Los Angeles to visit boatsman Grandpa Lloyd, worried at how he's handling his recent divorce, and then fearing he's lost at sea. Part 1 of 2.

Jennifer Seift...........................................................Liz Keifer
Brooke..................................................Tiffani-Amber Thiessen
Ashley.............................................................Elizabeth Berkley
Director..................................................................Grant Heslov
Sergio.............................................................John David Conti
And: Eric Freeman (Harbor officer), Aldo Billingslea (Security), Bill Stevenson (Crew member), Chance Boyer (Mad Dawg)

Director: Stewart A. Lyons
Writers: Larry Spencer & Michael Loman

2. "California Dreamin' Part II" Sept. 22, 1990

The missing Grandpa Lloyd turns up safe; David finds work on a movie set; Cara shows up to surprise Mark. Part 2 of 2.

Jennifer Seift...........................................................Liz Keifer
Brooke..................................................Tiffani-Amber Thiessen
Ashley.............................................................Elizabeth Berkley
And: Grant Heslov (Director), Toni Attell (Mime)

Director: Stewart A. Lyons          Writer: Shari Hearn

3. "The Baby Stops Here" Sept. 29, 1990

The babysitting kids misplace Mrs. Poole's infant niece.

Mrs. Gordon.................................................Valorie Armstrong
Mr. Reynolds.......................................................Steve Carlisle
Sally.......................................................................Candy Huston
Mr. Reynolds...............................................Jocelyn Seagrave
Police officer...............................................................Rif Hutton

Director: Judy Pioli
Writers: Richard Albrecht, Casey Keller

**preempted Oct. 6**

4. "The Play's the Thing" Oct. 13, 1990

Willie wins the lead in a school play opposite Cara; Michael and Lloyd test their friendship on the golf course. The series' 100th episode.

Ms. Palmer.......................................................Lucy Lee Flippen
Arnold.........................................................Patrick McDonald
Stagehand..............................................................Seth Howard
And: Danielle McGovern (Erica), Kendra Booth (Suzanne)

Director: Stewart A. Lyons          Writer: Daryl Busby

**preempted Oct. 20**

5. "From Russia with Fries" Oct. 27, 1990

Sandy and Mrs. Poole entertain a group of Russian dignitaries at Bossy Burger; David accidentally destroys an heirloom.

Mr. Brooks.........................................................Peter Isacksen
Nicholai.......................................................Savely Kramarov
Rick.......................................................................Dale JaRosz
Voice of DiFranco brother................................David Kaufman

Director: Garren Keith
Writers: Steve Granat, Mel Sherer

6. "Ex Marks the Spot" Nov. 3, 1990

A dismayed Sandy finds David in her ex-husband's (Vinovich) wedding party; Lloyd buys the twins a motorcycle without consulting Michael.

Director: Garren Keith          Writer: Alicia Marie Schudt

Richard.................................................................Steve Vinovich
Mrs. Laughton.......................................................Susan Brown
Pam.............................................................Elizabeth Baldwin
And: Rick Scarry (Minister), Tim Neil (Rider)

7. "Come Fly With Me" Nov. 10, 1990

Michael becomes furious when David borrows his pilot's uniform to help him meet girls.

Nanette...........................................................Whitney Kershaw
Honey.....................................................Mary-Margaret Humes
Dawn.........................................................................Ria Pavia

Director: Jack Shea
Writers: Richard Albrecht & Casey Keller

8. "It Happened One Night -- Or Did It?"
   Nov. 17, 1990  9-9:30 p.m.

The family becomes suspicious when Cara spends the night in Mark's room; David takes over Burt's campaign for Treasurer.

Steven Eisenberg.................................................Stanley Kamel

Director: Jason Bateman                Writer: R.J. Colleary

9. "Best of Friends, Worst of Times" Dec. 1, 1990

While shooting a hospital documentary for class, David finds an old friend has AIDS. Guest/co-writer Hodges reprises his recurring role from last season. Orig. scheduled for Nov. 17.

Rich........................................................Tom Hodges
Mr. Pfeiffer...............................................Al Fann
Stacy Hanover...........................................Karen Mistal

Director: Jack Shea                    Teleplay: Michael Loman
Story: Tom Hodges

**cancelled**

10. "A Sneaking Suspicion" Wednesday, July 10, 1991  8-8:30 p.m.

David plans revenge on Mark and Willie when he loses his latest girlfriend (Remini) because the twins beat her to a new job. Orig. scheduled for July 3.

Shop teacher Phil Morton...............................Don Amendolia
Joanne....................................................Leah Remini
Grace Alsop...............................................Marianne Muellerleile
Shannon...................................................Maria Bradley

Director: Jack Shea
Writers: Larry Spencer & Michael Loman

11. "Ho Ho Hogan" Wednesday, July 17, 1991  8-8:30 p.m.

The family suffers Christmastime stress; David becomes a department-store Santa Claus. Orig. scheduled for July 20, 8:30-9 p.m.

Mrs. Umstead.............................................Betsy Randle
Benjamin Umstead........................................Jarrett Lennon
Denise's Mother..........................................Kathy Connell
Storeperson..............................................Judd Laurance
Denise....................................................Tina Hart
Karen.....................................................Sabrina Wiener
Randy.....................................................Thomas Hobson

Director: Garren Keith                  Writer: Shari Hearn

12. "Isn't It Romantic?" Saturday, July 20, 1991  8-8:30 p.m.

Lloyd, set to rendezvous with his old first love, gives Willie some romantic advice when he and Brenda are on the outs.

Arnie.....................................................Tim Neil
Gary Thompson............................................Barry Jenner
Dishwasher repairperson/Raymond.........................James Hampton
Melissa Gordon...........................................Amy L. Taylor
Sally.....................................................Candy Hutson

Director: Kent Bateman                  Writer: Daryl Busby

13. "A Family Affair" Saturday, July 20, 1991  8:30-9 p.m.

Dad's young new girlfriend (Gagnier) turns out to be David and Burt's college classmate; the boys babysit a pedigree dog. Orig. scheduled for July 17.

Elizabeth.................................................Holly Gagnier
Mrs. Walker..............................................Dale Raoul

Director: Gerren Keith                  Writer: Ann Marcus

## Hull High

NBC          Sundays, 7-8 p.m.

Series premiere: Aug. 20, 1990
Final telecast: Dec. 30, 1990

Musical seriocomedy of the students and teachers at Cordell Hull High School. School team: Devils. Cast-member Belafsky was a guest in ep. 1. The episode title-designations treat the pilot as episode number zero. Working titles: *Hell Street High*, *Hull Street High*, *Hull St. High*, *Be True to Your School*.

History teacher John Deerborn...........................Will Lyman
English teacher Donna Breedlove.........................Nancy Valen
Principal Amery Dobosh (ep. 2-on).......................George Martin
Cody Rome (ep. 2-on)....................................Harold Pruett
Mark......................................................Mark Ballou
Louis Plumb (ep. 2-on)..................................Marty Belafsky
Mr. Fancher..............................................Marshall Bell
D.J.......................................................Kristin Dattilo
Camilla..................................................Cheryl Pollak
Rappers (ep. 1): Trey Parker, Phillip DeMarks, Carl Anthony
    Payne*, Lawrence "G. Love E." Edwards
Rappers/The Hull High Devils (ep. 2-on): Trey Parker, Phillip
    DeMarks, Carl Anthony Payne*, Bryan Anthony

*Recurring:*
Joe Brawley (ep. 1-2,4)................................Gary Grubbs
** Straight girl (ep. 1-4,6)..........................Jennifer Blanc
** Hip girl (ep. 1-4,6)...............................April Dawn
Michelle (ep. 1-3,5-6).................................Holly Fields
Randy (ep. 1-6).......................................Rowdy Metzger

\* Listed as Carl A. Payne II on an early press release.
\*\* Character given as one of two "Morning announcers," ep. 1.

Gil Grant Productions in assoc. with Touchstone Television
Executive producers: Kenny Ortega (ep. 2-on), Gil Grant
Supervising producer: Peter Dunne (ep. 2-on)
Producers: Peter Dunne (pilot); Steven Hollander
Associate producer: Howard Taksen (ep. 2-on)
Executive story editor: David Babcock
Director of photography: Charles Minsky (ep. 1); Dennis T.
    Matsuda
Music supervisor: Maureen Crowe
Music: Stanley Clarke (ep. 1); Richard Gibbs
Music consultant: Brock Walsh
Choreographers: Kenny Ortega, Peggy Holmes
Theme: "Once in a Lifetime" by Lawrence "G. Love
    E." Edwards (lyrics); Kenny Ortega & Peggy Holmes
    (chant lyrics); Stanley Clarke (music); produced by
    Stanley Clarke
Creator: Gil Grant

---

1. (pilot)  Monday, Aug. 20, 1990 8-9 p.m.; Sunday,
   Sept. 16, 1990 8-9 p.m.

Donna asks John to observe her class; Mark tries to find out why Camilla is so aloof. Guest Imperio is the series' assistant choreographer. Dedication: "Thank you, Jim Henson."

Mr. Kelm.................................................Roy Brocksmith
Amanda...................................................Deonca Brown
Louis Plumb..............................................Marty Belafsky
Rudy......................................................Tony Perez
Janitor..................................................Mavis Vegas Davis
Coach Davis..............................................Stogie Harrison
And: Adrian Richards (Mrs. Hawes), Alejandro Quezada (Alfre-

do), Tyren Perry (Gail), Liz Imperio (Daphne), Michael Bower (Big boy), Mark David (Student), George Perez (Boy), Ezra Sutton (Derek), Frank W. Vega (Byron)

Director: Kenny Ortega          Writer: Gil Grant

2. "Episode 1"  Sept. 30, 1990

A practical joke may have killed a visiting Russian teacher; Mr. Brawley's driver's-education class takes a wild ride.

Mr. Slovak..............................................Joe Ruskin
Richard Stoltz.....................................Rodney Eastman
Michael..............................................Carl Steven
Old lady............................................Janet Brandt
Mrs. Cross........................................Anne Gee Byrd
And: Nancy Fish (Miss Hollander), Adrian Ricard (Mrs. Hawes), Charles Walker (Mr. Stubbs), Mary Valena Broussard (Girl), Lee Maddox (Cute boy), Michael McNab (Paradmedic), D.A. Pawley (Young man)

Director: Kenny Ortega          Writer: Gil Grant

3. "Episode 2"  Oct. 7, 1990  7:43-8:43 p.m.

A tough student (Fromin) challenges John to a fight; D.J., now on the boys wrestling team, prepares for a match. Late start due to a long-running sports event prior. Brocksmith and Fish reprise their roles from ep. 1.

Mr. Kelm...........................................Roy Brocksmith
Coach Henke.......................................Marvin Elkins
Good cop.........................................Joseph Malone
Mr. Nukbaum......................................Phil Rubenstein
Miss Hollander......................................Nancy Fish
Stan Foley...........................................Troy Fromin
Mrs. Gompers..................................Mary Pat Gleason
Bad cop.............................................Bruce Scott
And: Hue Anthony (Dennis), Michael Cudlitz (Schwartz), Lindsay Fisher (Cute girl), Brandon McNaughton (Palmquist), Patrick J. Pieters (Recruit), Derek Stefan (Henderson)

Director: Bryan Spicer          Writer: David Babcock

4. "Episode 3"  Oct. 14, 1990

Camilla and a young science teacher (Matthews) grapple with mutual attraction; John and Donna are each nominated for most popular teacher; D.J. tries to upgrade the cafeteria fare.

Dr. Mackey........................................Brian Matthews
Mrs. Hawes.......................................Adrian Richards
Priscilla.............................................Lucy Vargas
And: Mark David (Mark), Micki Duran (Micki)

Director: Steven Robman          Writer: Steven Hollander

**cancelled**

5. "Episode 4"  Dec. 23, 1990

The bus breaks down during a school ski trip, leaving class and teachers stranded at a desert hotel; Mark falls victim to a practical joke. Eastman reprises his role from ep. 2, Davis from ep. 1 (where listed as playing "Janitor").

Richard Stoltz....................................Rodney Eastman
Bus driver/Gus...................................Hal Landon, Jr.
Mavis............................................Mavis Vegas Davis
Mindy Wellington....................................Dorit Sauer
And: Andrea Paige Wilson (Dana Cleeter), Mary Broussard (Girl)

Director: Kenny Ortega          Writer: Shawn Schepps

6. "Episode 5"  Dec. 30, 1990

Fourth-string quarterback Mark is set to start in a big game; Donna frets over John's former flame (Wittner); Randy steals the rival school's pig mascot. Enberg is an NBC sportscaster.

Himself.............................................Dick Enberg
Coach Barkley......................................Alan Weeks
Catherine Manning................................Meg Wittner
Wansley.............................................Bruce Kirby
Eddie Thomas.............................Christopher M. Brown
Carpenter.............................Christopher Carter-Hooks
And: Michael Cudlitz (Schwartz), Christie Clark (Shannon)

Director: Bruce Bilson          Writer: Dennis Leoni

## Hunter

NBC     Sept. 19-Feb. 27                Wednesdays, 10-11 p.m.
        March 8-April 26, May 31-June 28   Fridays, 9-10 p.m.
        Aug. 9-30                       Fridays, 10-11 p.m.

Series premiere: Sept. 18, 1984
Final telecast: Aug. 30, 1991

Action-drama of a tough plainclothes police detective and his female partner in the Los Angeles Police Deptartment's Metro investigative unit. Star Dryer was a 13-year NFL football player and two-time NFL All-Pro. Cast-members Lane and Barilla were guest players, ep. 12. The name of Fluegel's character is "Molenski" (per her badge, seen onscreen); it was misspelled "Molinski" and "Molinsky" in *TV Guide* and "Molinski" in initial NBC press materials. Bit player Cis Rundle is the wife of theme co-arranger Nils Lofgren.

Sgt. Rick Hunter.....................................Fred Dryer
Officer Joann Molenski (ep. 1-12)..............Darlanne Fluegel
Sgt. Christine (Chris) Novak (ep. 12-on)...........Lauren Lane
Allison Novak (ep. 12-on)........................Courtney Barilla
Capt. Charles Devane.............................Charles Hallahan

*Recurring:*
Commander Clayton (ep. 1-2,9,12,20)................Paul Mantee
Len Dorsey
    (ep. 7,9,11-12,14-17,19)..........Ronald William Lawrence
Ossie Dunbar, M.E (1,3,6,9-10,14-15)...........Anthony Winters

*Bit players*
● Officer Righetti (ep. 3-4,6,8-9,12-20)...............Joe Bucci
Forensic officer/technician (ep. 7,12-23)...........Carrie Hall
Uniformed officer (ep. 2,10,12,21).................Cis Rundle

● As an unnamed officer, ep. 3-4,6,8-9.

Stephen J. Cannell Productions
Executive producers: Fred Dryer, Larry Kubik
Co-executive producers: David H. Balkan, Mark Lisson
Supervising producers: Jo Swerling, Jr., Terry D. Nelson
Producers: Victor A. Schiro, Robert Hargrove
Associate producer: Marianne Canepa
Story editors: Deborah R. Baron (early in season), Daniel Chodos
Creative consultant (later in season): Simon Muntner
Director of photography: Fredrick V. Murphy II
Music: Walter Murphy
Theme: Mike Post and Pete Carpenter; arranged by Nils Lofgren and Walter Murphy
Creator: Frank Lupo

1. "Deadly Encounters, Part I"  Sept. 19, 1990

While pursuing a rural family that murdered a restaurateur, Hunter crosses paths with a woman police detective whose partner (O'Reilly) is killed.  Combined with ep. 2 as a two-hour episode, "Angel on My Shoulder," when rerun March 22, 1991.

Nicolae Janosch.............................................Andreas Katsulas
Harlan Pinder........................................................Bill McKinney
Lyle Pinder..................................................Ramsey Midwood
Duane Pinder................................................Brad Tatum
Dottie Pinder.........................................................Beth Grant
Leroy Banes...........................................Dennis Moynahan
Petra......................................................................Pamela Gien
George Malitza...........................................................Jan Triska
Michael Saccio.............................................Cyril O'Reilly
Mirov Janosch, Nicolae's brother.....................Apollo Dukakis
And: Steve Jason Oliver (Illia Brancus), Anthony Watson (Kid), Hugh Dane (Father), Paul Anthony Weber (Officer)

Director: Winrich Kolbe            Writer: Mark Lisson

2. "Deadly Encounters, Part II"  Sept. 26, 1990

Hunter and Molenski investigate a series of murders involving a deranged rural family, Romanian immigrants and the black market; Devane is appointed Captain of the Metro Division.

Nicolae Janosch.............................................Andreas Katsulas
Harlan Pinder........................................................Bill McKinney
Lyle Pinder..................................................Ramsey Midwood
Duane Pinder................................................Brad Tatum
Petra......................................................................Pamela Gien
Etta Daniels...........................................Robin Braxton
Bank clerk...................................................Anita Ortega
Officers.................Phillip Troy, Philip Sheppard, Don Brunner
Officer Haines.............................................Raymond D. Turner

Director: Winrich Kolbe            Writer: Terry D. Nelson

3. "Where Echoes End"  Oct. 3, 1990  10:05-11 p.m.

The new partners investigate a murder in which the key witness (Starr), Hunter's former partner, suffers from Alzheimer's disease.  The unusual running time derived from an apparent NBC experiment in beginning shows at five minutes after the hour/half-hour *a la* Superstation TBS; see also *Unsolved Mysteries*, *The Fanelli Boys* and *Dear John...* for this date.

Marilyn Fowler.............................................Lynne Thigpen
Gibbs...................................................Asher Brauner
Allison Janowitz...............................................Kim Walker
Jake Janowitz........................................................Beau Starr
Torres.........................Ismael Carlo a.k.a. Ismael (East) Carlo
Matson..................................................Shawn Thompson
Hired killer...............................................Edward Bunker
Security guard.................................................William S. Taylor
Ernie Delvecchio...........T.J. Castronovo a.k.a. T.J. Castronova
And: Joanna Sanchez (Movie ticket seller), Jon Greene (Treasury agent), Bruno Acalinas (Hal)

Director: James Darren            Writer: Walter Brough

4. "Kill Zone"  Oct. 10, 1990

Molenski's ability to track a serial rapist-killer may be affected by her traumatic childhood memories of a friend's murder.

Jack Cody.............................................David Ledingham

Laurie Peterson.....................................Mary Kohnert
Officer Karen Palmer...........................................Andi Chapman
Martin Heller.............................................Richard Grove
Wenders....................................................Al Pugliese
Major Cody.............................................William Smithers
Pathologist...............................................Rob Narita
Man in restaurant...............................................Clint Howard
And: Baoan Coleman (Mr. Tai), Brian Haymond (John Herman), Tom Van Hoof (Prison guard), My-Ngoc Tran (Le Ny-Diem Kuano), Jacqueline Huynh (Mai Lie), Sadie Kratzig (Young girl)

Director: Corey Allen            Writer: Kevin Droney

**preempted Oct. 17**

5. "The Incident"  Oct. 24, 1990

Molenski confronts an old acquaintance (Primus) whose biased newspaper stories support the neighborhood watch group that assaulted an innocent youth.

Andrew McBride.................................................Barry Primus
Sam Miller...............................................Al Ruscio
Danko.................................................Mitch Pileggi
Randy Ellis.............................................Rugg Williams
Joe Baker.............................................Cort McCown
Lisa Baker.............................................Devon Odessa
Ann Baker.............................................Anne Gee Byrd
David Alden Walker.............................................David Heavener
Ray Snyder.............................................Charles R. Penland
Fitch..................................................Peter Wise
Mrs. Ellis.............................................Gloria Hendry
And: Michael Barker (Jack), Tricia Long (Gloria), Jack Capece (Bob), Alma Beltran (Screaming woman)

Director: Fred Dryer            Writer: Kathy McCormick

6. "A Snitch'll Break Your Heart"  Oct. 31, 1990

Molenski tries to get police protection for her longtime informant; Hunter reopens a 17-year-old case of apparent infanticide by a now-respected judge.

Albie Wayne.................................................Seth Isler
Karen Brandt.............................................Katherine Cannon
Lt. Horton.............................................Jeff McCarthy
Tun Duk.............................................Steven Leigh
Judge Donald Graber.............................................Peter White
Alisa Graber.............................................Christina Carlisi
Inga Hanson.............................................Gloria Cromwell
Galvez.................................................Javi Mulero
D.A. Peter Danson.............................................Stephen Carver
Tun Roh.............................................Timothy Dang
Coniff.................................................Bruce Hermann
Sam Woo.............................................Byron Chung
Uniformed officers.........................Phillip Troy, Kim Hedrick
And: Frank Rossi (Cop), Deasa Turner (Sheila Webber)

Director: Tony Mordente            Writer: Jeff Benjamin

7. "Oh, the Shark Bites!"  Nov. 7, 1990

Capt. Devane appears to have corrupt connections to a loan-shark operation, and refuses to cooperate with investigators.

Harold Goodman.............................................Nehemiah Persoff
Paul Miller.............................................Carmine Caridi
Thomas Barnett.............................................Geof Prysirr
Harry Prima.............................................John Capodice
David Garner.............................................Richard Yniguez

Barbara Doyle.................................................Marcia Rodd
Oscar...............................................John Haynes Walker
And: Sarah Simmons (Eileen Miller), Eugene Choy (Takoto)

Director: Peter Crane          Writer: Simon Muntner

8. "The Usual Suspects"  Nov. 14, 1990

A murder may be linked to the computer-hacker release of
small-time criminals from the county jail.  Ventura is a professional wrestler and occasional actor.

Phil Slade.........................Jessie Ventura a.k.a Jesse Ventura
Ginny Bertolian...................................Rebecca Stanley
Peter Hawkins.............................Gregory Alan-Williams
Ernie Lydell............................................Tuck Milligan
Alice Lydell...........................................Cecile Callan
Amanda Lydell..........................................Taylor Fry
Bert Bertolian........................................Mark Voland
Sgt. Bobby Haines............................Raymond D. Turner
Off. Jim Rivera......................................Mario Marcelino
Ramon Gonzales......................................Robert Gallo
And: Valerie Reynolds (Rita Herman) Charles Noland (Elmer
    Bickie), Annette Quinn (Carol), Harvey Fisher (Mustang
    owner), Phillip Troy (Metro officer)

Director: Alan Myerson          Writer: Deborah Baron

**preempted Nov. 21**

9. "This is My Gun"  Nov. 28, 1990

Molenski's gun is stolen and used as a murder weapon. Capozzola is star Dryer's real-life attorney.

Armand...............................................Lewis Van Bergen
Odell..................................................Charles Boswell
Leon............................................John Michael Bolger
Denise Sanders......................................Breon Gorman
Skully...............................................Scott Burkholder
Shannon..............................................Paul Benvictor
Himself...............................................Tony Capozzola
Frank....................................................Monty Bane
Allistair.............................................Beverly Johnson
Ted Holmby...........................................Paul Napier
And: Megan Butler (Sally), Claudia Bloom (Wendy), William T.
    Amos (Pronzoni), Cheryl Janecky, Tom Baumgartner
    (People at meeting), Sally Champlin (Concerned woman),
    James Bontempo (Sgt. Vincent), Jeffrey Anderson-Gunter
    (Cab driver),

Director: Winrich Kolbe          Writer: Robert Vincent O'Neill

10. "La Familia"  Dec. 5, 1990

Hunter becomes embroiled in gang warfare while trying to
help a young ex-con break from his family's gang tradition.

Ernesto Delgado.......................................Joe Santos
Carlos Delgado......................................Luis Guzman
Tomas Delgado......................................Raymond Cruz
Henry Lopez..........................................Michael Wren
Lester Smith.......................................Leonard Lightfoot
Maria Delgado.......................................Teresa Di Spina
Sloan.................................................George Gerdes
Devon Lewis.......................................Andre Rosey Brown
Blade Jenkins.........................................Grand L. Bush
And: Eddie Frias (Paco), Cora Lee Day (Elderly woman), Pete
    Leal (Priest)

Director: Tony Mordente          Writer: Walter Brough

11. "Acapulco Holiday"  Dec. 12, 1990

A lawyer (Walker) accuses Hunter of false arrest during an
investigation of robberies at automatic bank-teller machines.

Gloria Morrell...........................................Nina Foch
Leslie Maynard......................................Kasey Walker
Elliott Rogers........................................Dick Christie
Dale Shawn............................................Paul Linke
Jack Roland...........................................Scott Getlin
Willie Pratt..........................................David Neidorf
Amos Cassidy..........................................Kevin Hagan
Julia Sanchez........................................Yolanda Lloyd
Father Willis.........................................Virgil Wilson
Marybelle Adams.....................................Homeselle Joy
Andy Crewes.........................................David Glassner
And: Nancy Sheeber (Woman at ATM), Philip Sheppard (Officer
    Beacon), Mark Hattan (Hickox), Patty Toy (Stanley), Fer-
    nando Ponce (Sketch artist)

Director: Tony Mordente          Writer: Jeff Benjamin

**preempted Dec. 19**

12. "Fatal Obsession"  Jan. 9, 1991  9-11 p.m.

Hunter reunites with a former colleague (new cast-member
Lane) to investigate a series of campus murders; Molenski is
shot and killed when she stops a suspicious driver.

Bill Gleason...........................................Ken Marshall
Jim Wilkens.........................................Jeffrey Combs
Mickey Welch.........................................Kevin Wixted
Jack Kane.........................................Marcus Giamatti
Selma Lansky.........................................Frances Bay
Spencer.................................................Seth Jaffe
Carl Garber...........................................Alex Kubik
Segalla..............................................Jack Jozefson
Red Ellison..............................................Red West
Himself.......................Los Angeles Police Chief Daryl Gates
Loreen...............................................Ellen Wheeler
Joyce Gleason.......................................Alice Barden
Jill Hayward......................................Anderson Tappe
Nancy..........................................Mary-Beth Manning
Paskin..........................................Robert M. Steinberg
Dirk Lawson.......................................Matt Borlenghi
Mr. Molenski, Joann's father.......................Gene Dynarski
And:  Freddie Dawson (Officer Donald Jackson), Clinton All-
    mon (Jewelry salesperson), Kerry Stein (Laundry manag-
    er), Tabby Hansen (Abbie Sloan), Richard Livingston
    (Loreen's father), Weldon Bleiler (Grocer)

Directors: Corey Allen (first half); Winrich Kolbe (second half)
Writers:  David H. Balkan (first half); Terry D. Nelson  (second
    half)

**preempted Jan. 16**

13. "Under Suspicion"  Jan. 23, 1991

Hunter competes with an ex-cop bounty hunter (James) for a
bail jumper (Silverman); Novak teams with a police computer
researcher (Alan-Williams, reprising his role from ep. 8). Orig.
scheduled for Jan. 16.

Peter Hawkins.............................Gregory Alan-Williams
Lois Lord.............................................Teresa Ganzel
Ken Lord............................................Jeff Silverman
Bud Crawford......................................Danny Woodburn
John McArthur........................................Robert Schuch
Jean..............................................Christopher Morley

Bill Stevens..................................................Barry Doe
Thomas Duffy.............................................Brion James
Secretary.................................................Vivian Paxton
And: Rick Prieto (Ruiz), Alex Zonn (Bartender), Clint Carmichael (Hank), David Snizek, Adele Malis-Morey (Bar customers), Robert Dowdell (Motel manager), Philip Sheppard (Officer Beacon)

Director: Gus Trikonis          Writer: Daniel Chodos

14. "The Reporter"  Jan. 30, 1991

A robbery investigation is impeded by Novak's friend (Curtis), a cocaine-using reporter who gets too close to a suspect.

Amy........................................................Kelly Curtis
John Griffin.........................................Arlen Dean Snyder
Dave Jordan...........................................Joey Aresco
Mike Bell............................................David A. Kimball
Roy Hamilton..........................................Don Fischer
Jake Flam..............................................Danny Wells
Lyle Trickle...........................................Joe E. Tata
Officer Rivera.......................................Mario Marcelino
Ben Green.............................................Murray Rubin
Ida Green..............................................Fritzi Burr
Dooley..................................................Ed Hooks
Ellen Novak, Chris's mother..........................Sue Casey
And: Jean Pflieger (Mary Connors), Robert Kino (Domo), Michael Yama (Iko) Harold Wayne Jones (Hal), Royden Clark (Davis), Dick Butler (Howe), Chuck Hicks (Foster)

Director: Corey Allen            Writer: Simon Muntner

**preempted Feb. 6**

15. "Room Service"  Feb. 13, 1991

On a case involving a bunko couple mugging and killing tourists, Hunter is teamed with Novak's ex-husband (Thomas). Dedication: "In Memory of Richard Lee Schultz."

Al Novak...............................................Robin Thomas
Steve Abbott..........................................Kevin Page
Paula Allen............................................Cindy Morgan
Scott Nichols........................................Jeremy Roberts
Ahmed Farid..........................................Brian George
Henry Olson...........................................Biff Manard
Jack Doyle............................................Stephen Rowe
Joy Daniels...........................................Saxon Trainor
And: Dean Stuart (Spence Martin), Sheila Caan (Gina), Cynthia Lee Neyland (Andrea), Danna Hansen (Alice), Kelly Zapp (Waiter), Helen Faraday (Waitress)

Director: Peter Crane            Writer: Terry D. Nelson

16. "Shadows of the Past"  Feb. 20, 1991

Novak, trying to reconcile with her estranged dad (Ryan), discovers he's the hub of a right-wing drugs-and-arms conspiracy.

Tom Novak.............................................Mitchell Ryan
Mickey Dolan..........................................Joe Marinelli
Campos..................................................Alex Colon
Ray Cassidy...........................................Carl Strano
Evan Michaels.........................................Jeff Austin
Dolan's wife.........................................Annie Grindlay
Polisi....................................................Ron Max
Jim Matolla..........................................Antony Ponzini
D.A. Ramon Diaz.......................................Ruben Pla
Arnie Johnson........................................Steven Field
Lisa Dolan (infant)...................................(uncredited)

Director: Tony Mordente          Writer: Mark Lisson

17. "The Grab"  Feb. 27, 1991  10:18-11:18 p.m.

Hunter and Novak search for the kidnapped Allison, a pawn in a scheme involving Novak's ex (Thomas, reprising his role from ep. 15). Late start due to an NBC News report at 9 p.m.

Al Novak...............................................Robin Thomas
Morrison...........................................Vincent Guastaferro
Hayworth.............................................Joris Stuyck
Hendrix...............................................Greg Collins
Puckett...............................................Casey Sander
Juarez..................................................Edith Diaz
"The Dutchman".....................................Christopher Neame
Chong..................................................Francois Chau
And: Rif Hutton (George Richard), Antony Carbone (Peterson)

Director: Corey Allen             Writer: Morgan Gendel

18. "All That Glitters"  March 8, 1991

While Hunter pursues a killer (St. Esprit) with a lust for gold coins, Novak hunts the mugger (DeLuise) of a friend (Crosby, granddaughter of singer Bing Crosby). DeLuise is the son of comedian Dom, and the brother of actors Michael and Peter. Guest Pla reprises his role from ep. 16.

Pam Sutton...........................................Denise Crosby
Jack Colfax........................................Patrick St. Esprit
Councilperson Howard Prescott..........................Alan Fudge
Jodie Prescott, his daughter.......................Kimberly Neville
Sam Olin...............................................Sal Viscuso
Sandra.................................................Cindy Brooks
Randy Morton.........................................David DeLuise
Liz Morton............................................Lee Kessler
Adele Hauser.........................................Patricia Barry
Phillip Dawes.......................................Peter J. Saputo
D.A. Ramon Diaz.......................................Ruben Pla
And: Ron Dortch (Judge), Lesli Kay Pushkin (Colleen), Barbara London (Sylvia Weaver), William C. Burch (Conventioneer), Peggy Lane O'Rourke (Nurse)

Director: Tony Mordente           Writer: Daniel Chodos

19. "Cries of Silence"  March 15, 1991

Novak helps a deaf mom (Frelich) search for her runaway child (Grace); a murder investigation uncovers a weapons cartel.

Barbara Collins.....................................Phyllis Frelich
Carlos Griego.....................................Michael Fernandes
Dani Collins.........................................Pierrette Grace
Bill August...........................................Greg Mullavey
Meg Harris...........................................Melissa Hayden
Tonio De Perez.......................................Victor Rivers
Luiz Mendoza.........................................Tony Vatsula
Jean Wells.............................................Jodi Benson
And: Marc Riffon (Woody), Tony Montero (Jonathan Brady), Chad Hayward (Titus/Hall), Tracy Vaccaro (Linda), Robert Curtin (Leo Styles), Don Bexley (Alf)

Director: Peter Crane             Writer: David H. Balkan

**preempted March 29**

20. "Ex Marks the Spot"  April 5, 1991

A dry-cleaning kingpin (Rickles), money-laundering for a mobster (Karabatsos), is being robbed by a gang made up of his secretary (Burroughs), mistress (Copley), and ex (Easterbrook).

Harold Schwan...................................Don Rickles
June...................................Leslie Easterbrook
Laura...................................Bonnie Burroughs
Traci...................................Teri Copley
Monk...................................Ron Karabatsos
Breech...................................Tony Longo
Barbara...................................Stacey Nelkin
Digby...................................Michael Tomlinson
And: Lou Beatty, Jr. (Tom Bolan), La Rita Shelby (Angie), Teresa Truesdale (Doreen), Jeffrey Jena (Director), Tracy Vaccaro (Linda), Wesley Leong (Wu Fong), Galen Thompson (Waiter), Jack Capece (Officer Webb)

Director: Gus Trikonis          Writer: Simon Muntner

21. "Little Man with a Big Reputation" April 26, 1991

A truck hijacking operation may involve an ex-con (Mordente), being framed for murder, who wants Devane as his best man.

Jake Hutton...................................Tony Mordente
Wanda...................................Jean Kasam
Snake Harris...................................Ted Markland
Sanders...................................Thom McFadden
Otis Wood...................................Gary Wood
Nadell...................................Art Metrano
Bud McCrae...................................Peter Sherayko
Lonny Frost...................................Otto Felix
With: John Anthony Williams
And: Cathy Susan Pyles a.k. Kathy Susan Pyles a.k.a. Susan Pyles (Bridesmaid), Helen Faraday (Maid of Honor), Andrew Herman (Priest), Jack E. Miller (Bernie), Nigel Gibbs (Security guard)

Director: James Darren          Writer: Tom Blomquist

**on hiatus; reruns begin May 31; on hiatus again after June 28 rerun; reruns begin again Aug. 9**

**preempted Aug. 23**

# In the Heat of the Night

NBC          Tuesdays, 9-10 p.m.

Series premiere: March 6, 1988

Drama of the Sparta, Miss., police chief and his black chief of detectives. Supporting actor Hugh O'Connor is the son of co-star Carroll O'Connor. Series based on the novel by John Ball and on the 1967 movie. Occasional writer Matt Harris is the pseudonymous Carroll O'Connor; occasional director Leo Penn is the father of actor Sean Penn. Filmed partly in Covington, Ga. NOTE: Though the onscreen credits spell the name of recurring guest Denise Nicholas' character as "De Long," onscreen artifacts (campaign posters, etc.) spell it "DeLong"; Nicholas reprises her role from three episodes last season.

Chief William O. (Bill) Gillespie...................Carroll O'Connor
Chief of Detectives Virgil Tibbs...................Howard Rollins
Althea Tibbs, his wife...................Anne-Marie Johnson
Lt. Bubba Skinner...................................Alan Autry
Parker Williams...................................David Hart
Willson Sweet...................................Geoffrey Thorne
Lonnie Jamison...................................Hugh O'Connor

*Recurring:*
Councilperson Harriet DeLong
     (ep. 7,8,12,16,20)...................Denise Nicholas
Eugene Glendon, her son (ep. 7-8,20)...................Rugg Williams

D.A. Darnelle (ep. 4,6,8,13-15,17,20)...................Wilbur Fitzgerald
LuAnn (ep. 4-5,7-10,12-18,20-21)...................Crystal Fox
Aunt Etta (ep. 6-10,12,17,20-21)...................Tonea Stewart
Dr. Robb (ep. 4-6,13,15,18)...................Dan Biggers
Officer Dee (ep. 9-10,14,18,21)...................Dee Shaw

The Fred Silverman Co. and Juanita Bartlett Productions in assoc. with MGM/UA Television
Executive producers: Carroll O'Connor, Fred Silverman
Supervising producer: Ed Ledding
Producers: Robert Bielak
Co-producers: Walton Dornisch, Herb Adelman
Story editors: William Royce, Cynthia Deming
Executive story consultant: Joe Gannon (later in season)
Director of photography (variously): Peter Salim; Jim Blanford
Music (variously): David Bell; Nan Schwartz; Larry Blank
Theme: "In the Heat of the Night" by Quincy Jones (music) and Alan and Marilyn Bergman (lyrics); arranged by Chris Page; performed by Bill Champlin
Developed for television by: James Lee Barrett

1. "Brotherly Love" Sept. 18, 1990 9-11 p.m.

In Philadelphia, Tibbs is charged with the killing of a former partner; in Sparta, Althea prepares to give birth to twins.

Calvin Petersen...................................Mel Stewart
Charles Ryan...................................Andy Romano
Lou D'Agostino...................................Peter Van Norden
Brian Kasch...................................Jeffrey Hayenga
Harlan Cassidy...................................Bruce Kirby
Capt. Jenkins...................................Geoffrey Lewis
Dwight Walker...................................J.D. Hall
Ceclia Walker...................................Olivia Virgil Harper
Ruth Peterson...................................Ellen Holly
Ray Nuguchi...................................Jesse Dizon
Michael Edwards...................................Anthony Auer
And: Larry Gelman (Desk cop), Penny Santon (Mama Cimino), Connie Sawyer (Hannah), Bob Larkin (Officer Roberts)

Director: Harry Harris
Writers: William Royce (first hour); Cynthia Deming (second hour)

2. "Lessons Learned" Sept. 25, 1990

Gillespie investigates the murder of a teenage prostitute, whose father is indifferent to the crime. Stewart reprises his role from last episode.

Calvin Petersen...................................Mel Stewart
Charlene...................................Deborah Strang
Raylynn...................................Tammy Amerson
Rocky...................................Bruce McKinnon
And: Stuart Culpepper (Judd), Ken Strong (J.W.)

Director: Mario Azzopardi          Writer: Cynthia Deming

3. "Perversions of Justice" Oct. 2, 1990 9:17-10:15 p.m.

Mob hysteria mounts when a science teacher (Vince) is charged with molesting a fifth-grade student. Late start due to a Presidential address.

Announced cast includes:
Leonard Grissom...................................Pruitt Taylor Vince
Jeff Dillard...................................Wynn Hollingsworth
Jimmy Dillard...................................Brian Lando
Lorraine Reeves...................................Ronnie Claire Edwards
Puller...................................Ray McKinnon
Elroy Baines...................................Hudson Adams

Director: Harry Harris                Writer: Robert Bielak

**preempted Oct. 9 and Oct. 16**

4. "And Justice for Some"  Oct. 23, 1990

The FBI gives immunity to an out-of-state drug dealer (Shockley) involved in a hit-and-run of Tibbs' young neighbor.

Troy Caldwell...................................................William Shockley
Duwayne............................................................Kevin Corrigan
Margaret..............................................................Esther Huston
Kevin...................................................................Ryan Marshall
Angent Donnelly.............................................Marc Macaulay
And: Ron Culbreth (Sheriff McComb), Bob Penny (Mr. Epp)

Director: Harry Harris                Teleplay: William Royce
Story: William Royce & Michael Thurman

5. "Heart of Gold"  Oct. 30, 1990

Bubba romances his high-school flame (Keane), now a wealthy widow who may have murdered a local attorney (Galloway).

Christine Millings.................................................Kerrie Keane
Sam Dortland.....................................................Don Galloway
Ramsey Morgan................................................Gary Williams
Officer Randy..................................................Randall Franks

Director: Russ Mayberry               Writer: Mitchell Schneider

6. "Quick Fix"  Nov. 6, 1990  9:01-9:55 p.m.

Evidence points to a young retarded woman (Larsian) as the mother of a dead infant found in a shallow grave.  Unusual time-slot due to insertion of election-news segments.

Kitty........................................................................Amy Lynne
Willa.....................................................................Tara Larsian
George Mastin...............................................William Lucking
Tucker........................................................................Tim Black
Dr. Jennings....................................................John Patricks
Mrs. Phibbs...................................................Joanne Daniels
Mrs. Dunbar...............................................Joanne F. Pankow
And: Tommy Chappelle (Jasper), Debra Duke (Melody)

Director: Winrich Kolbe                Writer: Julie Friedgen

7. "Homecoming"  Nov. 13, 1990

The town blames Gillespie and a lawyer (Carlson) for helping obtain parole for a convict (Perea) -- who is later murdered.

Sheila Meredith................................................Karen Carlson
Hubie Meredith..................................................Greg Mullavey
Emory Tanner.................................................Sonny Shroyer
Niles Maitland........................................................Larry Black
Walt Tanner...................................................Collin Alexander
Rachel Tanner.................................................Kathryn Firago
Ted Marcus.........................................................Thom Gossom
Prosper Hoag..........................................................Pierre Perea
And: Mary Holloway (Ellen), Paige Trewhitt (Bessie)

Director: Russ Mayberry               Writer: Robert Bielak

8. "A Problem Too Personal"  Nov. 20, 1990

DeLong's ex (Wesley) faces a murder charge unless his burglary partner alibis him.  Gossom reprises his role from ep. 7.

* Dick DeLong.......................................................John Wesley

Lambert.............................................................Dabbs Greer
Sheriff McComb.................................................Ron Culbreth
Ted Marcus.......................................................Thom Gossom
Mitch Nellin.........................................................Gerald Brown
And: Clennon King (Priest), Sharon Anderson (Sue)

* erroneously listed as "Vic Glendon" in NBC press materials.

Director: Winrich Kolbe
Writer: Matt Harris (Carroll O'Connor)

9. "A Final Arrangement"  Nov. 27, 1990

The sweet-tempered husband (Schallert) of a book-store owner is accused of her shooting death.

Carl Tibbets....................................................William Schallert
Cleve Rumford....................................................Randal Patrick
Rusty...................................................................Benji Wilhoite
Grace Keeshan.......................................................Sally Drew
Donna Jean........................................................Karen Thomas
Chery....................................................................Leslie Rhodes
And: Rand Hopkins, C.C. Taylor

Director: Leo Penn
Writers: David F. Hamilton & Peter W. Telep

10. "Family Matters"  Dec. 4, 1990

The son (Burgess) of Virgil's feuding, ostracized aunt (Bennett) is a prime suspect in a murder-robbery.

Ruta Gibson.......................................................Fran Bennett
Wade Baxley.......................................................Don Stallings
Tyrell Gibson...................................................Michael Burgess
Mrs. Johnson....................................................Donna Biscoe
Austin........................................................................Scott Kerr
And: Adrian Roberts (Jeb), Ronn Leggett (Neville), Scott Paxton
        (Manager), M.J. Coveny (Clerk)

Director: Vincent McEveety            Writer: Mitchell Schneider

11. "Bounty Hunter"  Dec. 11, 1990

A bounty hunter (Ware) is out to bring in or kill a Sparta man (Meadows) wanted for questioning in a Houston murder case.

Jack Whearty...............................................Stephen Meadows
Kathleen Whearty...............................................Romy Walthal
Tiny Randall.................................................................Tim Ware
R.J. Kincaide...........................................................Bob Hannah
Ed..............................................................................Bill Steis
Randy Calhoun.......................................................Scott Higgs
Mimi Kincaide...................................................Marilyn Martin
And: Ellen Wall (Rita Sue), Beth Burns (Pizza person)

Director: Russ Mayberry
Writer: Cynthia Deming & William Royce

12. "Blessings"  Dec. 18, 1990

Gillespie is the unwilling subject of a newspaper article by a local reporter (Robinson) whose motives the Chief suspects.

Millie Tornby......................................................Judith Robinson
Mel Levis............................................................Johnny Popwell
"With thanks for appearances by": Deborah Atkinson, Paul
        Benjamin, Peter Gabb, Thom Gossom, Kathy Payne,
        Sherly Lynn Piland, Alice Sneed

Director: David Soul                   Writer: Walton Dornisch

**preempted Dec. 25 and Jan. 1**

13. "Shine On Sparta Moon"  Jan. 8, 1991

Bad moonshine leaves a high school football star (Goggins) blind and his girlfriend dead.

Greg Casdan............................................Jeff Hochendoner
Dean Harbin...............................................Paul Gonsoulin
Lane Jeffries................................................William Cort
Robbie.......................................................Walt Goggins
Vern Tolliver.............................................Fred Covington
Joan Tolliver...............................................Laura Whyte
Marci Jeffries...............................................Randy Martin
Marci Werner..............................................Joan Croker
And: Heather Jones (Becky), Bill Whitworth (Goody), Terrence Gibney (Doctor), Terry Hobbs (Boy)

Director: Leo Penn                  Writer: Robert Bielak

14. "An Execution of Trust"  Jan. 15, 1991

A psychiatrist (Pickles) asserts that her patient (Walker), a convicted killer set for execution, is innocent. Pankow played a different role, ep. 6.

Dr. Laureen Alcott.......................................Christina Pickles
Ray Garrett...................Robert Walker a.k.a. Robert Walker Jr.
Osley......................................Steven Schwartz-Hartley
Ramey.........................................................Danny Nelson
Lucy............................................................Robby Preddy
Rita............................................................Judy McDowell
Vester............................................................Bill Crabb
Mrs. Abercrombie......Joanne Pankow a.k.a. Joanne F. Pankow

Director: Leo Penn                  Writer: Mitchell Schneider

**preempted Jan. 29**

15. "A Child of Promise"  Feb. 5, 1991

Virgil arrests a young alleged drug dealer (Edwards), the brother of one of Althea's honor students (Baker).

Terry...........................................................Shaun Baker
Mrs. Johnson.............................................Kim Hamilton
Derek Johnson...........................................Kenneth Edwards
Bobby...................................................Christopher Lobban
Semple.......................................................Randall Taylor
Nathan...........................................................Jeff Rose
Teri.............................................................Temi Epstein
Young.....................................................Maury Covington
Bob Phillips.................................................Kent Whiple
And: Rosemary Newcott (Darlene), Tyler King (Jimmy)

Director: Vincent McEveety          Writer: Cynthia Deming

16. "Paper Castles"  Feb. 12, 1991

The building-development partner of Tibbs' friend (Leon) dies suspiciously in an auto accident. Orig. scheduled for Feb. 19.

Bree...........................................................Sharon Wyatt
Lawrence..................................................Stephen Young
Abe Tucker....................................................Steve Boles
Thomas Spier.................................................Kenny Leon
And: Ellen Heard (Gracie), Jen Harper (Samantha), Tom Deardorff (Seth), Michael H. Moss (Rob)

Director: Vincent McEveety          Teleplay: Joe Gannon
Story: Arthur Bernard Lewis

17. "Laid to Waste"  Feb. 19, 1991

The authorities, finding no body, won't prosecute when a blind woman (Snyder) IDs an alleged killer (Nowicki) by his voice.

Julie Lofton...............................................Suzanne Snyder
Donner....................................................Richard McKenzie
Ned Conklin..................................................Tom Nowicki
Lester...........................................................Tom Even
Taylor............................................................Jeff Lewis
      Also orig. announced: David Hart (Parker)

Director: Vincent McEveety
Writers: William Royce & Cynthia Deming

18. "First Deadly Sin"  Feb. 26, 1991

An affluent father (Lambie) forbids his witness son (Dattilo) from reporting a rapist, fearing it'd uncover the boy's illiteracy.

Elliot Gardner............................................Joseph Lambie
Marcella....................................................Sally Spencer
Boyd Gardner...............................................Bryan Dattilo
Jake Cruthers...................................................Eddie King
Vivian Nolley...........................................Stacia Fernandez
Elmer..........................................................Ted Manson
Lydia.......................................................Maureen Dowdell

Director: Peter Salim                  Writer: Julie Friedgen

**preempted March 12**

19. "Just a Country Boy"  March 19, 1991

In Los Angeles, unwordly Bubba and an insurance investigator (Sandlund) hunt a bail-jumper (Forchion) from Sparta.

Pat Day....................................................Debra Sandlund
Kid..............................................................Chi-Muoi Lo
Tommy Vincent...........................................Franklin Cover
Wallace Fannoy..........................................Raymond Forchion
Stanley L. Garish.............................................Will Leskin
Judge Clint....................................................Bill Zuckert
Benny Torres................................................Jose Rosario
Detective Walden........................................William Flatley
Bob Fannoy.................................................Daryl Wilcher
FBI Agent James...........................................(uncredited)
Mississippi Asst. Attorney General Emmett Tully...(uncredited)
And: Mary Pat Gleason (Hostess), Julie Inouye (Nurse), Jay Arlen Jones (Ticket person), Frank Lugo (Cesar), Greg McKinney (Allie Jones), Bob Penny (Eppy)
      Also orig. announced: Brett Porter (Locky)

Director: Carroll O'Connor
Writer: Matt Harris (Carroll O'Connor)

20. "No Other Road"  March 26, 1991

Virgil and Lonnie try to help Eugene deal with his father's facing the death penalty. Wesley reprises his role from ep. 8.

Dick DeLong....................................................John Wesley
Frank Kloot...........................................Randall "Tex" Cobb
Ted Marcus..................................................Thom Gossom
And: Michael Genevie (Glenn Wottle), Ruth Moore (Mrs. Bernie), Chris Kayser (Judge), C.C. Taylor (Officer Peake)

Director: Paul Chavez
Writer: Matt Harris (Carroll O'Connor)

**preempted April 16**

21. "A Turning" April 30, 1991

During the hunt for those responsible for killing two drug dealers, Althea urges Tibbs to rethink his dangerous career.

Davy.....................................................................Craig Thomas
Dr. Cameron.........................................................Ed Grady
Winnie.................................................................Challen Cages
Jimmy Dawed......................................................Afemo Omilami
Beau....................................................................Haynes Brooke
Sissy Walton........................................................Myrna White
Judge Emory Walton............................................Bob Banks
And: Judy Langford (Thelma), Ed Corbin (Ronnie Price), Phillip Roper (Calvin), Leslie Rhoades (Cheryl)

Director: Paul Chavez
Writers: Matt Harris (Carroll O'Connor) & Joe Gannon

**preempted May 14**

**preempted June 18 and June 25**

**preempted July 9**

**renewed for 1991-92; new episodes begin Oct. 1, 1991**

# In Living Color

Fox                    Sundays, 8-8:30 p.m.

Series premiere: April 15, 1990

Satirical sketch comedy with a black perspective. Regular skits and characters include: the belligerent Homey the Clown, bum Anton and loquacious convict Oswald (all D. Wayans); Velma Mulholland (Coffield), a woman with a Joan Crawford complex; and the "Men on [insert subject]!" critics, Blaine Edwards (D. Wayans) and Antoine Merriweather (Grier), a parody of Siskel & Ebert-style movie reviewers with an exaggeratedly effeminate gay duo. Most musical guests are end-credit cameos only. Damon, Shawn and Kim Wayans are two brothers and a sister of Keenen Ivory Wayans; oldest brother Dwayne is a production assistant and occasional extra.

Host-performer: Keenen Ivory Wayans
Ensemble: James Carrey, Kelly Coffield, Tommy Davidson, David Alan Grier, T'Keyah "Crystal" Keymah, Damon Wayans, Kim Wayans
Dancers: The Fly Girls (Cari French, Carrie Ann Inaba, Deidre Lang, Lisa Marie Todd, Michelle Whitney-Morrison and [ep. 14-on] Carla Garrido)
D.J.: Shawn Wayans

Bit players (generally one per episode, ep. 1-13; several per episode ep. 14-on): Al Chalk (multiple episodes), Jimmy Aleck, Russell Alexander, Phyllis Applegate, Richard Arvay, Billy Bastiani, Alan Berman, Eugene Twyman Berry, Joe Blake, Thomas Booth, Alison Brooks, Alex Brown, Beecey Carlson, Rosemarie Castaland, Lenny Citrano, Michael Clarke, Ellen Cleghorn, Johnny Cocktails, Troy Curvey Jr., Maurice Davis, Michael Durrette, Greg Elam, John Escobar, Carmen Fleming, Ray Forchion, Alan Gelfant, Archie Gibson, Rick Goldman, Garon Grigsby, Harriett Guiar, Trevant Hardson, Jameel Hasan, Ted W. Henning, Michael James, Doug Jones, Tanu Kiel, Randy Kirby, Jennifer Lane, Colin Lawrence, T.J. MacInturf, Eric Mansker, Madison Mason, William McDonald, Rich Nice, Raymond Oliver, John Quigley, Devika Parikh, Michael Phenicie, Stephanie Pope, Gary Price, Gina Ravarra, Lysa Regina, Romye Robinson, Annette Robyns, John Sakahian, Hal Shafer, Robin Skye, Wonderful Smith, Elena Statheros,

Tenee Tenison, Robert Vinson, E. Imani R. Wilcox, Eugene Williams, Gerald Winn, Alma Yvonne.

Ivory Way Productions in assoc. with 20th Century Fox Television
Executive producer: Keenen Ivory Wayans
Producers: Tamara Rawitt
Co-producer: Michael Petok
Associate producer: Kevin A. Berg
Writers: John Bowman, Buddy Sheffield (supervisors); Fax Bahr, Kim Bass, Greg Fields, Les Firestein, Becky Hartman, Paul Mooney, J.J. Paulsen, Adam Small, Steve Tompkins, Pam Veasey, Damon Wayans, Keenen Ivory Wayans (variously, most on each episode)
Choreographer: Rosie Perez
Music: Tom Rizzo
Theme: Heavy D & the Boyz
Director: Paul Miller
Creator: Keenen Ivory Wayans

1. Sept. 23, 1990 (LC-201)

"Men on Film" review the summer's movies; Jamaican-family sitcom "Hey Mon" in the hospital; TV-detective drama, "Sidekick." Musical guest: Queen Latifah (Dana Owens).

2. Sept. 30, 1990 (LC-202)

"Anton Volunteers" for the Army; "Roseanne Barr Sings American's Favorites"; "Training Men the Wodehouse Way"; "When Homey Met Sally."

3. Oct. 7, 1990

Post-Emmy story meeting; beauty secrets of female bodybuilder "Vera De Milo" (Carrey); "Cephus and Reesie" in a third-rate gospel musical. Musical guests: Sandra Crouch and the Andrae Crouch Singers.

4. Oct. 14, 1990 (LC-204)

Gossipy "Benita Butrell [K. Wayans]: Uninvited Guest"; uptight teacher "Al Macafee [Grier]: Hall Monitor." Musical guest: Monie Love.

5. Oct. 21, 1990 (LC-205)

Tom and Tom Brothers host "Black Like You"; women's talk show "Go On Girl"; prison phone calls; "Miss Black Person USA Pageant."

6. Oct. 28, 1990 (LC-206)

"Hey Mon" in the courthouse ("Hedley Court"); "Shahrazad Ali's Video," a how-to on abusing black women; the "Snackin' Shack" soul-food diner; seventies holdover Frenchie at a black-tie affair. Musical guests: Heavy D and the Boyz.

7. Nov. 4, 1990 (LC-207)

Inept promoters the B.S. Brothers -- Howard (Davidson) and Clavell (Grier) -- backstage at a Madonna show; Iraqi fashions on "Style Minute: Elsa Klutch"; "Li'l Miss Trouble: The School Play" (Coffield as Edna Louise); "Buffed, Beautiful and Bitchin' with Vera De Milo"; "Hollywood Homeboys" Ice and Whiz.

8. Nov. 11, 1990

"Magenta Thompson's Acting School"; "The Foundation for Golf Heritage"; I Love Lucy parody, "I Love Laquita," featuring guest Billy Dee Williams.

**9. Nov. 18, 1990 (LC-209)**

"Lassie '90"; "Rocky VI"; "PMS Defense Box"; "Men on Vacation" review European locales. Musical guests: Karl Jamal Taylor (uncredited), 3rd Bass.

**10. Nov. 25, 1990 (LC-210)**

Tom and Tom Brothers meet "Two Sisters for Two Brothers"; "Read in Jail" with Barbara Bush (Coffield); "Cherub of Justice" Dickie Peterson at the convenience store; "Anton's Thanksgiving." Musical guest: D. Nice.

**11. Dec. 16, 1990 (LC-211)**

"Three Champs and a Little Lady"; parody of *The Newlywed Game*; "The Good Behavior Show"; "The Justice Legion of America" gets integrated. Musical guest: Nikki D.

**12. Dec. 23, 1990 (LC-212)**

"Afro-Phone"; mock blooper reel; Vera DeMilo as "Veracosa, Mistress of Destruction"; Cephus and Reesie's Christmas album; Edna Louise (Coffield) and Parnell (Carrey) go to the museum (originally announced as "Little Miss Trouble and Her Twin Skippy," featuring Coffield in dual roles); "Homey Claus."

**13. Jan. 13, 1991 (LC-213)**

"Tom and Tom for the Arizona Tourism Commission"; "Johnny Abdul's Greatest Hits"; a 35-year-old waiting to be adopted; Velma Mulholland; the B.S. Brothers court a Japanese investor; "The Head Detective."

**14. Feb. 3, 1991**

"Mr. Squeegee"; the B.S. Brothers' Funky Finger Productions takes a meeting; tampon fashions; pyromaniac Fire Marshall Bill (Carrey); the Home E. Cheese restaurant.

Remote segment directed by: Matthew Wickline

**15. Feb. 10, 1991 (LC-215)**

Benita Butrell at the projects; Vanilla Ice parody, "White, White Baby"; "Al Macafee, Prom Chaperone"; "Oswald Meets the Parole Board"; anti-apartheid movie "My Dark Conscience"; famous boxers for boxer shorts. Whoopi Goldberg also orig. announced, in a skit entitled "Anton and Fontaine."

**16. Feb. 17, 1991 (LC-216)**

"The Ejector Bed"; Frenchy at a bachelor party; ambulance-chaser Lonnie Parker; Siamese-twin standup comics "Les and Wes [Rawls], Twin Stars"; With John Tesh, Leeza Gibbons (*Entertainment Tonight* co-hosts, as themselves). Musical guest: Leaders of the New School.

**17. Feb. 24, 1991 (LC-217)**

"Win, Lose or Draw" in prison; "Marsha Warfield Milk Commercial"; "War in the Gulf" parody of a Gen. Colin Powell press briefing; blues singer "Calhoun Tubbs on the Campaign Trail" for Sen. Helmsley; "The Great Sperm Bank Robbery"; Andrea Dice Clay on *Love Connection*.

**18. March 3, 1991 (LC-218)**

Tom and Tom Brothers join an all-white country club; Oprah Winfrey anti-drug spot; touchdown choreographer; "Please, Mama, Don't Eat the Government Cheese"; "Classroom Safety

with Fire Marshall Bill." Musical guest: Another Bad Creation.

Remote segment director: Matthew Wickline

**19. March 17, 1991**

Velma Mulholland gets a ticket; Ceephus and Reesie at a prison execution; Dirty Ha Ha Harry gameshow, "Do You Feel Lucky?"; the Church of Discount Sin; Vera DeMilo in "Pretty Buffed Woman." Musical guest: KRS-One.

**20. March 31, 1991**

"B.S. Brothers and Sisters," the fabulous Falanas (K. Wayans, Keymah); Summer's Dawn salad dressing/douche; Edna Louise considers running away; "The Superfly"; white waitress Rose at the Snackin' Shack.

**21. April 28, 1991 (LC-223)**

"The Comedy Wheel of Race"; "Detective Head Goes Bowling"; "Handi Man's Evil Twin";"The Arsenio Hall of Justice." Musical guests: Public Enemy, Ice Cube.

**22. May 12, 1991 (LC-224)**

"Li'l Magic: The Audition"; "Oprah's Restaurant"; "Homey the Sellout" hawks sugary Homey Wheats cereal; Blaine, on "Men on Television," gets hit on the head and turns straight (latter two segments to be continued next season).

**23. Aug. 11, 1991**

Cherub of Justice at a Vice Presidential appearance; "A New 911 Message Service"; Frenchie at an opera benefit; "Clear Conscience Fur Farm"; Velma Mulholland at an ice-cream shop; Oswald explains the birds and bees.

**preempted Aug. 25**

Rerun-compilation editions

April 14, 1991

Compilation from past episodes, including from last season. Scheduled: "Men on Film II"; "Anton Volunteers"; "Spike's Joint"; "Ejector Bed"; "The Head Detective."

May 5, 1991 (LC-227)

Compilation from past episodes. Scheduled: "White, White Baby"; "Black Like You"; "Three Champs and a Little Lady."

**renewed for 1991-92; new episodes begin Sept. 22, 1991**

## Jake and the Fatman

CBS            Wednesdays, 9-10 p.m.

Series premiere: Sept. 26, 1987

Mystery-drama of prosecutor McCabe and investigative partner Styles. Dog performer Buford is the third in the role, following Winston and Sebastian. Series filmed and set in Hawaii until ep. 9, when the locale switched to Los Angeles.

| | |
|---|---|
| Jason L. "Fatman" McCabe | William Conrad |
| Jake Styles | Joe Penny |
| Asst. prosecutor Derek Mitchell | Alan Campbell |
| Max (bulldog) | Buford (uncredited) |

*Recurring:*
Lisbeth Berkeley-Smythe, McCabe's secretary
    (ep. 2-3,7,9-12,14,17,20-23)..........................Olga Russell

The Fred Silverman Co. and Dean Hargrove Productions in
    assoc. with Viacom
Executive producers: Dean Hargrove, Fred Silverman, Joel
    Steiger
Co-executive producer: Bernard L. Kowalski
Producers: Kimmer Ringwald, David Abramowitz, Robin
    Madden
Co-producer: Bruce L. Shurley
Executive story consultant: William Conway
Associate producer: Todd Powers a.k.a. Todd Thomas Powers
Director of photography (variously): John C. Flinn III, A.S.C.;
    Ronald M. Vargas, A.S.C.
Music (variously): Joel Rosenbaum, Peter Myers, Steven
    Bramson
Theme: Dick De Benedictis
Creator: Dean Hargrove, Joel Steiger
Creative consultant and developed by: Douglas Stefen Borghi

1. "God Bless the Child" Sept. 12, 1990 (3601)

McCabe's friends, a wealthy businessperson and his wife, are
murdered execution-style by their two children.

Frank Bronski.......................................................Richard Herd
John Bronski........................................................Doug Savant
Julia Bronski......................................................Romy Walthall
Herb Rossner.........................................................Ramy Zada
Ruth Bronski.............................................Lynne Ellen Hollinger
Charlie Dee.......................................................Michael Cowell
Dennis Freeman........................................................Tom Triggs
Coat check clerk....................................................Robin Stille
Waiter...............................................................Ron Genta
Maitre d'..........................................................Glenn Pinho
Judge Smithwood......................................................Jack Hogan

Director: E.W. Swackhamer       Writer: David Abramowitz

2. "The Tender Trap" Sept. 19, 1990 (3604)

Derek's uncle (Ryan) is found dead, shortly after his marriage
to an attractive young woman (Ulrich). Working title: "The
Spider and the Fly."

Ethan Mitchell.....................................................Mitchell Ryan
Tessa Carmichael...................Kim Johnston Ulrich a.k.a. Kim
    Johnston-Ulrich a.k.a. Kim Ulrich
Bartender..........................................................Hank George

Director: Michael Lange         Writer: Michele Val Jean

3. "Exactly Like You" Sept. 26, 1990 (3603)

A bank official is slain execution-style, and the confession by a
mild-mannered man doesn't ring true. Hogan reprises his role
from ep. 1. Working title: "The Man in the Mirror."

Morgan Steele.......................................................Kerrie Keane
Lyle Wicks/Jason Miller.............................Bryan Cranston
Jeannie Wicks.....................................................Mary Cadorette
Marcie Thompson....................................................Maria O'Brien
Lt. Kamalani (orig. Lt. Marshall)...................Danny Kamekona
Sam Howard.........................................................Jimmy Borges
Justine Gordon...........................................................Ektara
Judge Smithwood.......................................................Jack Hogan
Detective..........................................................Howard Bishop
Tanned man...........................................................Mike Ebner
Barmaid............................................................Katie Ralson

Knuckles..............................................Kimo Wilder McVay
And: Ben Wong (Suit), Bob Whiting (Official), Deana Karas
    (Manager), Toby Lael (Todd Wickes)

Director: Ron Satlof            Writer: William Conway

4. " 'Round Midnight" Oct. 3, 1990 (3605)

A world-class car thief steals Jake's borrowed Porsche.

Marion "Slick" Leach.........................................Robert Miranda
Lincoln Hart.......................................................Reiner Schone
Alexis...............................................................Cec Verrell
Manny.............................................................Richard Zobel
Cecil Tolson.......................................................Bill Ogilvie
Bartender..........................................................Lee Woodd
And: Chuck Picerni, Jr. (Parking valet), Bob Silva (H.P.D. cop)

Director: Ron Satlof           Teleplay: Kimmer Ringwald
Story: Robert Hamilton

**preempted Oct. 10 and Oct. 17**

5. "Only You" Oct. 24, 1990 (3607)

Jake's troubled, jealous, high-school flame (Sibbett) blows his
cover when she observes him with the attractive prime suspect
(Burroughs) in an industrial-espionage sting operation.

Halsey Reed.........................................................Martin Sacks
Marilyn Murphy..................................................Bonnie Burroughs
Dana Ashford........................................................Jane Sibbett
And: Tom Fujiwara (Masuda), Steven Perry (Cop), Bob Apisa
    (Leo), James Roache (Waiter)

Directed: Ron Satlof            Writer: Carol Saraceno

6. "My Boy Bill" Oct. 31, 1990 (3606)

The partners of a man (Gwynne) arrested for trying to fence
stolen jewelry kidnap the young son of one of McCabe's prosecutors (Humes). Hogan reprises his role from ep. 1 and 3.

Frank Compton.................................................Michael C. Gwynne
Janet Fromer.............................................Mary-Margaret Humes
Billy Fromer................................Glenn Walker Harris, Jr.
Charles Tyler.....................................................Stanley Kamel
Commander Joseph Riker............................William Lucking
Judge Smithwood......................................................Jack Hogan
Lt. Pete Simpris....................................................Joe Moore
Reg Wilson.....................................................Rod Gilman Aiu
And: Bill Holland (Emmanuel Sosa), Gil Combs (Michaels)

Director: Reza Badiyi           Writer: David Abramowitz

7. "More Than You Know" Nov. 7, 1990 (3602)

A woman (Johnson), spurned by her married lover (Hatch),
kills his wife and frames him for murder. Perry appeared in
ep. 5 credited only as "Cop." Originally scheduled for Oct. 24.

Amelia St. John....................................................Laura Johnson
Dr. Richard Davis.................................................Richard Hatch
Vic Fargo...........................................................Tobin Bell
Rafferty.....................................................George O'Hanlon, Jr.
Nurse Okani.........................................................Susan Park
Lulu..............................................................Elissa Dulce
Elaine Davis.....................................................Kathleen Furey
Joanne.............................................................Devon Guard
Valet-parking attendant..............................................Tony Fair
Sgt. Frank Scardino.................................................Steven Perry

TV reporter................................................Garrett R. Sprinkle
Amd: John Rickley (Officer London), Simone Boisseree (Patty Kalama), Marcy Peck (Lani), Remi Abellira (Bellhop)

Director: Bernard L. Kowalski          Writer: Paul Robert Coyle

8. "Night and Day" Nov. 14, 1990 (3608)

A private investigator (Garber) with a vendetta against a crime boss (Sattels) may blow a complex undercover operation.

Casey Quinn..............................................Terri Garber
Jerry Malik..............................................Mark Rolston
Peter LaMotta...........................................Barry Sattels
Phil Chandler...........................................Glenn Cannon
Mick Taylor.............................................Norm Compton
Sally....................................................Karen Iboshi
Miller...................................................Peter Clark
Hal Culver.............................................Scott Oughterson
Harvey Woodman.........................................Ted Sackett
Maggie...............................................Stephanie Reynolds
Businessperson..........................................Tricia Rowley
Woman....................................................Shari Lynn
Husband..................................................Tom Jerke
Hoods.............................................Billy Burton, Louie Elias
Police officers.......Martha Fontana, Chaz Mann, Glen Cancino, George Smith
    Also orig. announced: Leighton Kaonohi (Police officer), Harland Reed (H.P.D. officer Frank)

Director: Michael Lange          Teleplay: Joyce Burditt
Story: Dean Hargrove & Joel Steiger

**preempted Nov. 21**

9. "Goodbye" Nov. 28, 1990 9-11 p.m. (3609)

A cover-up of the hijacking and murder of Colombian drug runners brings the duo to Los Angeles, where the Mayor asks McCabe to return as D.A., and Jake is framed for murder.

Asst. D.A. Kathy Jameson.....................................Lise Cutter
Netter.....................................................Richard Grove
Pete.......................................................Bill Kohne
Mayor Brandon Sims................................Francis X. McCarthy
Lee Milkin................................................Eric Menyuk
Marcus Packard.............................................Ed Nelson
Strega...................................................Geoffrey Rivas
Sennett (orig. Sanborne; Simpson)..................Jeremy Roberts
Latham (orig. Laymon).......................................Forry Smith
Jordan Lee..................................................Tony Todd
Sharon Lee...............................................Berlinda Tolbert
Waiter..................James Stellos (George Kee Cheung also orig. announced)
And: Nick Angotti (Doctor), Stogie Harrison (Prison guard), Candace Mack (Allie Lee), Julio Oscar Mechoso (Desk clerk), Tom Allard, Bob Minor (Prisoners), Kathleen O' Malley (Mrs. Milkin), Frank Atienza (Attendant), Steve Barbro (Detective), Ted Neale, Jeff Cadiente (Crew members), Joe Fanene, Leighton Kaonohi (Cops), Norman Howell (Biker), Henry Kingi (Pilot), Grace Morley (Clerk), Josie Over (H.P.D. sketch artist), Tom Rosales (Carlos), Marc Siciliani (Paramedic), Tamar Tibbs (Leeanne)

Director: Bernard L. Kowalski     Story: J. Michael Straczynski
Teleplay: J. Michael Straczynski and William Conway

10. "I Know That You Know" Dec. 12, 1990 (3610)

A burglar (Anthony) may have been framed for killing the wife of a rich art collector (Frank). New opening sequence begins.

Tommy Malone.............................................Gerald Anthony
Michael Wilton..........................................Charles R. Frank
Jill Crockett.............................................Erin Gray
Abigail Stevens........................................Diane McBain
Leon Bittman............................................Joe Bratcher
Abernathy................................................Steven Hack
Judge..................................................Laurence Haddon
Bruno..................................................John Hostetter
Blonde.....................................................Kelly Jones
Caroline Wilton..................................Nicole Orth-Pallavicini
And: Arlene Sterne (Tommy's lawyer), Steve Tschudy (Clerk), Caroline Cornell (Customer), Jack Ong (Proprietor), Tom Regan (Medical examiner), Vivian Tann (Jury foreperson)

Director: Russ Mayberry          Writer: Robin Madden

11. "Let's Call the Whole Thing Off" Jan. 2, 1991 (3611)

Jake seeks a mobster's (Groh) mistress (Vernon) after a hired killer murders a key witness against the mobster.

Sara Fairchild........................................Jennifer Bassey
Robert (orig. Roger) Burgess..............................David Groh
Johnny Burgess.............................................Jay Pickett
Rachel Garraty...........................................Kate Vernon
Clerk.....................................................Beth Hogan
Teacher................................................Richard Jamison
Mechanic.................................................Raf Mauro
Joey (orig. Keith) Burgess................................Barry O'Neil
Truckers.................Arell Blanton, Ray Young (Jim Boeke orig. announced)
And: Albert Owens (Burgess' lawyer), Gregg Watkins (Bailiff), Jack Younger (Sol), Laurel Schaefer, Stephen Poletti (Reporters), John Wyler (Guide), Ken Zavayna (Captain)
    Also orig. announced: Bruce French (Judge)

Director: Daniel Attais          Writer: Robert Brennan

12. "I May Be Wrong" Jan. 9, 1991 (3612)

The beautiful leader (Byron) of a South African racist group is accused of murder. Working title: "When Irish Eyes Are Smiling" (orig. about a British intelligence agent who believes an I.R.A. spokesperson is behind the murder of a member of Parliament). Guest Over appeared in ep. 9 in a different role. Director Penn is the father of actor Sean Penn.

Benjamin Tatsa....................................Clarence Williams III
Vanessa Kruger.......................................Antoinette Byron
Bergstrom............................................Jonathan Farwell
Serge.................................................Patrick Kilpatrick
Dante Vorster...........................................Mike Preston
Andrea (orig. Audrey) Durrant............................Erica Rogers
Jordan Lee................................................Tony Todd
Arlo..............................................David Wells (orig. Jon Menick)
And: Ryan MacDonald (Col. Van Der Merwe), Josie Over (Cop)

Director: Leo Penn          Writer: Robert Brennan

**unscheduled preemption Jan. 16; preempted Jan. 23 and Jan. 30**

13. "Daddy's Home" Feb. 6, 1991 (3614)

Jake's wandering dad resurfaces after 27 years, with his old bookie boss (Scott) out to kill him. Angie's address: 147 Angel Terrace, Costa Del Mar, CA 54313 [sic]. The character of Sonny Rosetti was played by Jay Acovone one episode last season.

Bartender/Big Jake Styles............................Harry Guardino
Angie Rosetti, Jake's sister.........................Cassandra Byram

Carla Styles, Jake's mother............................Rhoda Gemignani
Hugo.................................................................Mike Moroff
Prince...............................................................Judson Scott
Wanda Lee......................................................Anjanette Comer
Felcher..............................................................Monty Bane
Sonny Rosetti, Angie's husband....................Richard Molinare
And: Frank Noon (Sticky), Maria Rangel (Nurse), Darwyn
    Swalve (Patch), Mike Masters (Tinker), Gerry Okuneff
    (Officer), Father Albert M. Vazquez (Priest)

Director: Bernard L. Kowalski          Writer: Kimmer Ringwald

14. "I'm Gonna Live Till I Die" Feb. 13, 1991 (3615)

When a bookkeeper (Paymer) finds he has two days to live, he
becomes fearless in trying to track down the person responsible for his and his boss' deaths. Working title: "That's Life."

Henry Stocker.................................................David Paymer
Ron Destry.................................................Bradford English
Janice.........................................................Caryn Richman
Rogers..........................................................Tim Rossovich
Hugh Lawson...................................................Wayne Tippit
And: Scott Layne (Cal), John Moskoff (Max Green), Lisa Robins
    (Waitress), Kimber Sissons (Terry)

Director: Alexander Singer             Writer: William Conway

15. "Pretty Baby" Feb. 27, 1991 (3616) 9:30-10:30 p.m.

The duo guard the infant daughter of a waitress (Snyder) who
disappeared after witnessing a mob-style execution. Director
Flinn is one of the series' directors of photography. Working
title: "Yessir, That's My Baby."

Ruben (orig. Carlos) Aragon...............................Casey Biggs
Darlene........................................................Lenore Kasdorf
Manny Pachinko.............................................Robert Miano
Art..................................................................Robert Pine
Cindy O'Malley.............................................Suzanne Snyder
Mrs. Johnson......................................................Jan D'Arcy
Surgeon................................................................
Caitlin O'Malley (infant)...................................(uncredited)
And: Lou Elias (Surgeon), Min Lee, Ruth Peebles (Paramedics),
    Gary-Michael Davies, Victor Leigh (Cops), Ed McCready
    (Merchant), Zuleika (Registrar), Greg Thirloway (Biggs),
    Nelson Mashita (Medical examiner), Grant Owens (Doc-
    tor), Kate Finlayson (Admitting nurse),

Director: John C. Flinn III             Writer: Robin Madden

16. "I Cover the Waterfront" March 6, 1991 10-11 p.m. (3613)

On the docks, Derek investigates to try to prove an old friend
was murdered and the death made to look like a suicide.
Working title: "Friendship." Orig. scheduled for Jan. 16.

Dennis Morgan..................................................Jason Beghe
Alisa.............................................................Roxann Biggs
Larry Renco.........................................................Joe Flood
Tommy.................................................Kenneth David Gilman
Bernie (orig. Charley) Moffit..............................Scott Marlowe
Marcus Stone.......................................................Beau Starr
Peter Romer.....................................................Bruce Wright
Watson...........................................................Larry Gelman
Hector Rivera.................................................Tonyo Melendez
Sebastian Kelley.................................................John Petlock
And: Danielle Zuckerman (Becky), Steve Barbro (Dectective),
    Janice Ehrlich (Paramedic), Kevin Hagan (Dock worker),
    Jack Kaufman (Patron), Michael Ray Miller (Bartender)
    Also orig. announced: Bruce French (Judge)

Director: Harry Harris          Writer: David Abramowitz

17. "You Don't Know Me" March 13, 1991 (3618)

A socialite (Cannon) may have murdered her boyfriend, and
her jilted husband (Coster) asks his pal McCabe for help.

Vicky Blane (orig. Cain)...............................Katherine Cannon
Marci Terrel.......................................................Marcia Cross
Bernard (orig. Barnett) Guterman....................Charles Dennis
Greg Hatten.........................................................Robin Sachs
Jordan Lee............................................................Tony Todd
Arlo.................................................................David Wells
Judge.............................................................Carmen Zapata
Andrew Blane (orig. Arthur Cain)....................Nicholas Coster
Tom Johnson..............................................Robert J. Bernard
Soprano (orig. Tenor)..........................................Laurel James
And: Vachik Mangassarian (Maitre d'), Perla Walter (Maid)

Director: Reza Badiyi     Writers: Eric Estrin & Michael Berlin

18. "It Never Entered My Mind" March 20, 1991 (3617)

McCabe's free-spirited doctor friend (Van Dyke) is charged
with killing a hospital administrator (Cromwell) who'd accused
him of malfeasance.

Dr. Mark Sloan (orig. Stone)............................Dick Van Dyke
Mrs. Clark............................................................Carol Bruce
Russell (orig. Robert) Havilland.....................James Cromwell
Richard Bates (orig. Geary)..........................Stephen Eckholdt
Dr. Howard Locke (orig. Kennedy).....................Sam Hennings
Dr. Michael Sommers..........................................Gregory Itzin
Carol Blair (orig. Blake)....................................Margaret Reed
Thad Wilcox.................................................Kristoff St. John
Tyler Morgan....................................................Mark L. Taylor
Josie Arnold........................................................Ally Walker
Mrs. Murphy................................................Elisabeth Brooks
Alice Williams................................................Ellen Dunning
And: Una Kim (Betsy), Mary-Margaret Lewis (Mrs. Rollins),
    Peter Slutsker (Anesthesiologist), Dierk Torsek (Baker),
    Virginia Watson (Nurse), Jeff Witzeman (Student)

Director: Bernard L. Kowalski          Writer: Joyce Burditt

19. "Second Time Around" April 3, 1991
    10:10-11:10 p.m. approx. (3619)

A man (Kilner), supposedly murdered five years ago, resurfaces after his alleged killer has been executed. Tabori is the
son of director Don Siegel and actress Viveca Lindfors. Working title: "Since I Found You." Orig. scheduled for March 27.
Late start due to a long-running live event previous to it.

Donovan Bruce..............................................Kristoffer Tabori
Carolyn Loy.........................................................Lori Hallier
Jack Carpentier..................................................Kevin Kilner
Billy Nickel..................................................Hector Mercado
Cookie............................................................Richard Bright
And: Pamela Kosh (Mrs. Teewhistle), Audrey Lowell (Salesper-
    son), Harris Shore (Father), Frank Collison (Wino)

Director: Michael Lange
Writers: Paul Schiffer, Kimmer Ringwald

20. "I'd Do Anything" April 10, 1991 (3620)

A psychiatrist (Culea) manipulates her teenage lover (Lucas)
into murdering her wealthy husband.

Dr. Ellen Webster (orig. Helen Warner)...............Melinda Culea

Dr. Marcus Webster (orig. Warner)..................Michael Durrell
Jeffrey Boyce.................................................Joshua Lucas
Sifu.....................................................George Kee Cheung
And: Nelson Mashita (Medical Examiner), Ted Neale (Ted), Enrique Renaldo (Gardener), Dana Stein (Barbara)

Director: Ronald Gary Stein
Writers: David Abramowitz and William Conway

21. "We'll Meet Again" April 24, 1991

A man (Culp) whom McCabe once convicted of murder may be the one who, in clown disguise, just attempted to shoot him. Neale reprises his role from last episode. Working title: "Who Would've Dreamed?"

Harrison Gregg.........................................Robert Culp
Ray Powell.............................................Ron Karabatsos
Harriet.............................................Catherine MacNeal
Ted......................................................Ted Neale
Jerry..................................................Frank Pesce
Mrs. Swarthmore........................................Karon Wright
Amanda..................................................Shay Astar
Reporters.........................Mark Ritter, Daryle Ann Lindley

Director: Bernard L. Kowalski          Writer: William Conway

22. "It's a Sin to Tell a Lie" May 1, 1991  (3622)

Jake and an attractive female cop try to clear a pastor (Weary), suspected of killing two young congregation women with whom he was romantically involved. Working title: "Amazing Grace."

Carol Delaney.......................................Elizabeth Gracen
Darcy Warren........................................Julie McCullough
Martha Rowe...........................................Joan McMurtrey
John Rowe................................................A.C. Weary
Cindy Warren........................................Marilyn McIntyre
Robert Warren.........................................Tom Urich
Paul..................................................Brenden Boone
Joe....................................................Brian Doughty
Kevin Barlow...........................................Jim Jansen
Kim Warren.........................................Samantha Jordan
And: Jack Jozefson (Rudi), Jack Kaufman (Officer), Tony Rayner (Ray), Connie Sawyer (Helen)

Director: George Fenady          Writer: David Abramowitz

23. "Nevertheless" May 8, 1991  (3623)

The young husband (Burgi) of a socialite (Meriwether) is the prime suspect in her murder, despite his claims a burglar did it. Wells reprises his role from ep. 12 and 17.

Ellen Kurtin..........................................Lee Meriwether
Det. Dennis Morgan.....................................Jason Beghe
Todd Kurtin..........................................Richard Burgi
Alan Tremaine/Voice/Fence.............................Warren Burton
Franklin Patterson................................Mitchell Laurance
Meredith Toomey........................................Nancy Sorel
Arlo....................................................David Wells
Viktor................................................J. Downing
Maid/Lydia...........................................Monica Ferren
Director..............................................Clifton Powell
     Also orig. announced: Burton Smith (Judge)

Director: Alexander Singer          Writer: Robert Brennan

**preempted May 22**

**preempted July 3**

**preempted July 31**

**preempted Aug. 28**

**renewed for 1991-92; new episodes begin Sept. 18, 1991**

## Knots Landing

CBS          Thursdays, 10-11 p.m.

Series premiere: Dec. 27, 1979

Prime-time soap opera of family and business intrigue in the affluent, fictitious California community of the title, particularly the homes in a cul-de-sac on Seaview Circle. A spin-off of *Dallas*. Lee, Peterson, Shackelford and Van Ark are the remaining original cast-members. Phillips is a former member of the 1960s rock-pop group The Mamas and the Papas. Val's novels: *Capricorn Crude, Nashville Junction.*

Greg Sumner.........................................William Devane
Marion Patrick (Mack) MacKenzie,
     Karen's second husband..........................Kevin Dobson
Karen Fairgate MacKenzie, his wife...................Michele Lee
Paige Matheson, Mack's daughter...............Nicollette Sheridan
Michael Fairgate, Karen's son.........................Patrick Petersen
Anne Matheson, Paige's mother...................Michelle Phillips
Frank Williams.........................................Larry Riley
Valene (Val) Gibson Ewing Waleska....................Joan Van Ark
Gary Ewing, her ex-husband..........................Ted Shackelford

*Recurring, all or virtually all episodes:*
Claudia Whittaker, Sumner's sister.................Kathleen Noone
Kate Whittaker, her daughter.........................Stacy Galina
Julie Williams, Frank's daughter.................Kent Masters-King

*Other significant recurring characters:*
Linda Fairgate (ep. 1-2,5,8-16)........................Lar Park Lincoln
Nick Schillace a.k.a. Dimitri Pappas
     (ep. 5-12,17-23,25)........................Lorenzo Caccialanza
Jason Lochner (ep. 9-26)......................Thomas Wilson Brown
Dick Lochner, his father
     (ep. 12-18; voice only, ep. 11)...........................Guy Boyd
Steve Brewer (ep. 15-26)...............................Lance Guest
Charlotte Anderson
     (ep. 11,13-16,19-20,22,24-26)........................Tracy Reed
Danny Waleska,
     Val's new husband (ep. 1-5,8).....................Sam Behrens
Tom Ryan (eps 1-6,9-10,26)............................Joseph Gian
Jeff Cameron (ep. 1,3-4)...................................Chris Lemmon
Peggy (1-2,7,12-17,20,22-23,25-26)...........Victoria Ann-Lewis
Bobby Ewing, Gary and Val's son (ep. 1-9,
     11-13,15-19,22,24,26).............Christian/Joseph Cousins
Betsy Ewing, Gary and Val's daughter
     (ep. 1-4).............................................Jennifer/Jessica Aaron
     (ep. 6-9,11-13,15-19, 22-26)...................Emily Ann Lloyd
Meg MacKenzie, Karen and Mack's daughter
     (ep. 1-6,8-12,14-16).....................Kara/Kimberly Albright
     (ep. 17,20-26)...................Rhianna Janette [Tompkinson]

*Minor recurring characters, more than one storyline:*
Mort Tubor (ep. 1-8,10-15,18,21-26)....................Mark Haining
Bob Phillips (eps 1-8,10-16,18,24-26)...................Zane Lasky
Dr. Herrara (ep. 1-2,4,10-12).............................Gerald Castillo
Dr. Stanovich (ep. 11,15-16,18-19,21-23)...........Mary Gregory
Butler/Carlos (ep. 1-3,7,9,12,15,22,25)...........Carlos Cantu
Harvey (ep. 2-3,9-10)........................................Robert M. Koch
Receptionist (ep. 2,6,10,12)..............................Rande Leaman

Roundelay-MF Productions in assoc. with Lorimar Television

Executive producers: Michael Filerman, David Jacobs
Co-executive producer: Lawrence Kasha
Producers: Mary-Catherine Harold, Lynn Marie Latham,
    Bernard Lechowick
Coordinating producer: Joel Okmin (later in season)
Associate producer: Joel Okmin (early in season)
Executive script consultant: James Stanley
Executive story editor: Dianne Messina
Story editor: Mimi Kennedy, Scott M. Hamner (both later in
    season)
Director of photography (variously): Lowell Peterson; Craig
    Denault
Music (variously, sometimes in combination): Jerrold Immel;
    Craig Huxley; Bruce Miller; Al Kasha; Joel Hirschhorn;
    Christopher Klatman; Larry Riley; Joel Rosenbaum; Doug
    Walter; Ron Grant
Theme: Jerrold Immel
Creator: David Jacobs

1. "Return Engagement"  Sept. 13, 1990    (446201)

Discussion-show host Karen agrees to a promo trip with her
producer (Lemmon); Danny returns from jail; Paige searches
for clues to Tom's disappearance on the day they were to be
married; Greg is apparently dying of poisoning; Frank and his
young-teen daughter Julie try to adjust to his wife's death.

Kimmy.................................................................Kerry Noonan
Waiter.............................................................Steve Greenstein

Director: Lorraine S. Ferrara         Writer: Bernard Lechowick

2. "Blind Side" Sept. 20, 1990    (446202)

Karen and Mack mourn the apparent death of Cameron; Gary
and Val look for a home in Texas; Tom visits Paige as she considers a cruise offer from Greg, who notices Kate resembles his
late daughter; Michael decides to stay with Linda.

Aunt Virginia...................................................Betsy Palmer
Ranch hand/Pete.................................................Jack Yates
Marvin Woods...................................................Hal England
Sales clerks..............Gwen Van Dam, Ed Morgan, Georgie Paul
Steward........................................................Geoffrey R. Smith
Office workers.........................Dianna Patton, Patrick Fischler
    Also orig. announced: Jennifer Rhodes (Attorney)

Director: Nicholas Sgarro         Writer: Lynn Marie Latham

3. "God Will" Sept. 27, 1990    (446203)

Val's husband Danny takes violent revenge on Gary; Karen
becomes trapped at the studio; Tom tries to win back Paige;
Claudia checks on Anne's credit; Julie rebels at home.

Kimmy.................................................................Kerry Noonan
Attorney.............................................................Jennifer Rhodes
Guests...................................Maria Serrao, Joseph Cardinale

Director: Jerome Courtland         Writer: Bernard Lechowick

**preempted Oct. 4**

4. "Dead But Not Buried" Oct. 18, 1990    (446204)

The alive and psychotic Cameron traps Karen in the studio;
Danny's body is discovered in the pool; Val organizes a search
for Gary; Paige throws Anne out of her apartment; Greg resists
Claudia's overture of friendship.

Aunt Virginia....................................................Betsy Palmer

Dianne Kirkwood.................................................Robin Strasser
Sgt. Levine.......................................................Herbert Edelman
Lt. Guthrie............................................................Pam Grier
Attorney...............................................................Jennifer Rhodes
And: Cindy Riegel (Realtor), Michelle Davison (Secretary),
    James Reeder (Officer), Wallace J. Duffy (Security guard)

Director: Nicholas Sgarro   Writer: Dianne Messina

5. "What If"  Oct. 25, 1990    (446205)

Mack tries to help Karen recover from her post-traumatic depression; police suspect Frank killed Danny; Paige, now living
with Tom, looks for a new job so she can leave Sumner Corp.;
Anne receives a blackmail letter.

Aunt Virginia.......................................................Betsy Palmer
Sgt. Levine.......................................................Herbert Edelman
Lt. Guthrie.............................................................Pam Grier
Marco Conti......................................................Reiner Schone
Ed Boyer................................................................Paul Comi
And: Michael Mitz (Reynolds), Terrence Beasor (Alan Long)

Director: Jerome Courtland         Writer: Parke Perine

6. "You Can Call Me Nick"  Nov. 1, 1990    (446206)

Anne becomes frightened when Nick, the emissary Marco sent
to uncover the blackmailer, moves into her apartment; Karen,
back at work, tries to end her feud with producer Kirkwood;
Paige confronts Greg; the police begin concentrating on Frank.

Sgt. Levine.......................................................Herbert Edelman
Aunt Virginia.......................................................Betsy Palmer
Dianne Kirkwood.................................................Robin Strasser
Sue.........................................................................Sue Bugden
Banker.....................................................................Rod Britt
Woman in bank.................................................Karen Hensel
Salesperson......................................................Susanne Tegman
Delivery person....................................................Don Mueller
Bank teller.........................................................Claudia Bloom

Director: Nicholas Sgarro         Writer: Lynn Marie Latham

7. "Do Not Attempt to Remove"  Nov. 8, 1990    (446207)

Val and Gary continue their wedding plans; Anne's blackmail
plot threatens to backfire; Paige threatens to leave perpetually
jealous Tom; Levine says he has a witness to Danny's murder;
Frank discovers Julie has been frequently absent from school.

Sgt. Levine.......................................................Herbert Edelman
Security guard.....................................................Richie Allan
Shoppers..........................................Shirley Prestia, Judith Burke,
        Cyndi Strittmatter, Jeanne Sakata
Clerk.................................................................Paul Nakauchi
Ranch hand/Pete.................................................Jack Yates
Salesperson.........................................................Lavelle Roby
Matt Calloway....................................................Don Stewart
Counselor............................................................Janni Brenn
Salesclerk.........................................................Louise DeCarlo
        Also orig. announced: Joseph Gian (Tom Ryan)

Director: Bernard Lechowick         Writer: Joseph L. Scanlan

8. "The Best Laid Plans"  Nov. 15, 1990    (446208)

Julie speaks to the police about Danny; Karen and Mack
throw a party for a bickering Val and Gary; a tabloid prints a
lurid photo of Anne; Paige spends the night with Greg; Michael
and Linda prepare to meet Karen again; Claudia house-hunts.

Sgt. Levine...................................................Herbert Edelman
Barbara...........................................................Ronne Troup
Realtor............................................................Cindy Riegel

Director: Michele Lee            Writer: James Stanley

9. "Side by Side"  Nov. 29, 1990  (446209)

Claudia attempts to bar Paige from visiting Greg at the hospital; an astonished Gary announces Val has cancelled the wedding; Linda accepts a lunch invitation from Karen; Nick discovers Anne has tried to steal the blackmail money, and the two face choosing a briefcase with either the money or a bomb.

Barbara...........................................................Ronne Troup
Janitor..........................................................Nathan Karras
Carla............................................................Melissa Baum
Paul............................................................Marco Sanchez
Waitress..........................................................Udana Power
And: Don Mueller (Security guard), Synthia L. Hardy (Nurse)

Director: Lorraine Senna Ferrara   Writer: Bernard Lechowick

10. "The Lady or the Tiger"  Dec. 6, 1990  (446210)

Claudia arranges a liver transplant for Greg; Nick and Anne agonize over the briefcases, and Anne proposes; Mack finds Julie illegally buying beer; Gary is disturbed by Val's increasingly strange behavior; Paige again confronts Tom.

Alex Georgi........................................................Kevin Kilner
Matt Callaway...................................................Don Stewart
Ranch hand/Pete..................................................Jack Yates
Mary Stevens....................................................Shannon Holt
Clerk.........................................................Michael Morrison
Nurse..........................................................Synthia L. Hardy
Wino............................................................Jack Jozefson
And: Tony Ralph-Wilson (Administrator), Susan Mackin (Ticket seller), Mika Quintard (Maitre d'), Doug Kaback (Harry)

Director: Nicholas Sgarro
Writer: Lynn Marie Latham and James Stanley

11. "Asked to Rise"  Dec. 13, 1990  (446211)

Greg's surgery done, Claudia finds he might marry Paige; Gary speaks with a doctor about Val; Anne and Nick get married; Frank spies on Julie; Linda strikes a side deal with Callaway Industries, which Sumner Corp. is acquiring; Mack wants to help a troubled 15-year-old (new recurring guest Brown).

Alex Georgi........................................................Kevin Kilner
Minister.........................................................Jack Orend
Paul............................................................Marco Sanchez
Carla............................................................Melissa Baum
Miss Barbara..........................................Barbara Kaye Minster
And: Hope Levy (Student), Myrna Niles (Woman), Angelo Orefice (Bus driver), Geoffrey Smith (Police officer)

Director: Kevin Dobson            Writer: Bernard Lechowick

12. "A Merry Little Christmas"  Dec. 20, 1990  (446212)

Paige accepts Greg's marriage proposal, making Claudia nervous about his will; Anne and Nick return from Las Vegas; Val's mental problems endanger the twins; Mack tries to shield Jason from his abusive father; Frank and Julie argue over how to spend their first Christmas after her mother's death.

Alex Georgi........................................................Kevin Kilner
Owen Buchanan...................................................David Gale

Eric Thomas.......................................................John DeMita
Helen Young......................................................Yolanda Lloyd
Sean McAllister.................................................Bob Margitich
And: Michael Ashe (Police officer), Ben Kronen (Man), Marla Fries (Secretary), Malcolm Mazer (Delivery person)

"Have Yourself a Merry Little Christmas" sung by Michele Lee

Director: William Devane         Writer: James Stanley

**preempted Dec. 27**

13. "The Unknown"  Jan. 3, 1991  (446213)

Greg returns to work; Paige calls off the engagement when Greg wants a prenuptial agreement and reveals his vasectomy; Gary tries to get medical help for Val; Jason rebuffs Mack's efforts to help him; Anne has news of Greg's fraudulent wills; Frank finds himself nervous around Julie's teacher (Reed). Guest Lloyd was listed as a different character last episode.

Woman...........................................................Patricia Barry
Miss Martinez...................................................Yolanda Lloyd
Paul............................................................Marco Sanchez
Bartender........................................................Tom Finnegan

Director: Nicholas Sgarro        Writer: Dianne Messina

14. "Simmer"  Jan. 10, 1991  (446214)

Greg is increasingly taken with Linda after he and Paige announce their engagement is off; Mack and Karen take Jason into their home, but later he runs away; Anne plots to seduce Gary.  Director Pleshette is a former series regular.

Attendant...................................................Julio Oscar Mechoso
Pizza delivery person............................................Brent Briscoe
Bruce Coe........................................................Lance Roberts

Director: John Pleshette         Writer: Bernard Lechowick

**unscheduled preemption Jan. 17; preempted Jan. 24**

15. "A Sense of Urgency"  Jan. 31, 1991  (446215)

As Mack recalls being an abused child himself, he and Karen search for Jason; Gary finds Val hasn't been taking her medication; Paige moves to sabotage Linda as Sumner Corp. prepares a merger; Frank breaks a date with Charlotte; Kate is drawn to a photographer (Guest).  Orig. scheduled for Jan. 17.

Mrs. Richfield....................................................Ann Nelson
Susie Richfield, her niece...............................Jana Marie Hupp
Restaurant host.....................................................Tony Brafa
Employees..............................Dianna Patton, Richard Herkert
Receptionists.......................................Avi Simon, Edith Varon

Director: Lorraine Senna Ferrara
Writers: Dianne Messina & Jim Stanley

16. "Always On Your Side"  Feb. 7, 1991  (446216)

Mack and Karen agonize over whether to become Jason's foster parents; Gary gets bad news from Val's doctor; Mrs. Richfield's niece (Hupp) joins Sumner Corp; Paige has a run-in with Steve; Frank attempts another date with Charlotte; Mack is arrested for shielding the missing Jason.  Guest Lloyd played different characters in ep. 12 and ep. 13.

Mendoza.........................................................Geoffrey Rivas
Susie Richfield................................................Jana Marie Hupp

Ms. Ramirez..............................................Yolanda Lloyd
Mr. Thomas.............................................Michael O'Guinne
And: Matt Roe (Harris), Patricia Hodges (Deputy Sheriff)

Director: Jerome Courtland          Writer: Lynn Marie Latham

17. "In the Dog House" Feb. 14, 1991   (446217)

Mack is held in contempt for not revealing Jason's where-
abouts, and Karen feels the repercussions on her talk show;
Val accuses Gary of having an affair; Claudia infuriates Paige
with talk of an inheritance due Paige upon marriage; Steve
tells Claudia he's the son she gave away as an infant.

Judge Percal.............................................Joseph Campanella
Demby....................................................Wortham Krimmer
Gil.......................................................Charles Boswell
Sue........................................................Sue Bugden
Ed.........................................................Lindsey Ginter
Doris......................................................Myra Turley
Nancy Muller..............................................Dale Raoul
Hotel clerk...............................................Rolanda Mendel
Harris..................................................Matt Roe (in teaser only)
Mendoza...............................................Geoffrey Rivas (in teaser only)

Director: Joseph L. Scanlan
Writers: James Stanley & Dianne Messina

18. "Call Me Dimitri" Feb. 21, 1991   (446218)

Mack is released from jail after Jason returns to his abusive
dad; Anne's delight at again seeing Nick (now a.k.a. Dimitri) is
short-lived when she finds a dead woman named Betty in his
room; Claudia shocks Kate with her revelation about Steve;
Val tries to turn the twins against Gary. Guest Lloyd, here
listed as "Mrs. Ramirez," was "Ms. Ramirez" in ep. 16.

Supervisor................................................Rosalind Cash
Mrs. Ramirez.............................................Yolanda Lloyd
Linda Takashi............................................Elizabeth Sung
Alexander................................................Bruno Alexander
Chrissy...................................................Paige Pengra
Stan......................................................Michael Kearns
Maid.....................................................Irene Olga Lopez
Mrs. Hale................................................Anita Ortega
Relatives............Barbara Schillaci, Jack Ragotzy, Renata Scott
Deputy sheriff...........................................Jim Townsend
Guard....................................................Aaron Seville

Director: Nicholas Sgarro           Writer: Lynn Marie Latham

19. "Bad Dog" Feb. 28, 1991   (446219)

Mack and Karen learn Jason is hospitalized; Nick and Anne
try to sell a mysterious doll intended for Betty, but Val's puppy swallows the contents; Michael and Linda split up after she
sleeps with Greg; Frank is upset Julie has a date; Claudia
continues to shun her out-of-wedlock son, Steve.

Man.......................................................Ivan G'Vera
Appraiser.................................................Gene Dynarski
Ms. Kotler................................................Marie Thomas
And: Keith Cameron (Horace), David Farentino (Student), Noor
    Shic (Jeweler), John F. O'Donohue (Armed guard)

Director: Joseph L. Scanlan
Writers: James Stanley & Dianne Messina

20. "Gone Microfiching" March 7, 1991   (446220)

Mack and Karen again take in foster-child Jason; Anne and

Nick, threatened by a gunman, try to find the puppy; Linda
again upstages Paige in front of Greg; Frank decides he can no
longer date Charlotte; Val agrees to return to the hospital.

Toya......................................................May Quigley
Alexander................................................Bruno Alexander
Howard...................................................Jack King
Appraiser................................................Gene Dynarski
Judith....................................................Claudette Roach
And: Eddie Frias (Clerk), Theresa Karanik (Waitress), Michael
    G. Booten (Panhandler)

Director: Kevin Dobson              Writer: Mimi Kennedy

**preempted March 14 and March 21**

21. "Upwardly Mobile" March 28, 1991   (446221)

A judge wants to disbar Mack over Jason; Anne and Nick, having been duped by counterfeit money, try to start over in legit
jobs; Steve becomes Paige's assistant; Linda continues her affair with Greg; Val vows to become sane.

Supervisor................................................Rosalind Cash
Mendoza..................................................Geoffrey Rivas
State Bar investigator.....................................Rick Podell
Walsh/landlord...........................................William Bronder
Restaurant owner.........................................Magda Harout
Officer worker...........................................Christopher Durmick
Passengers...Marion Kodama Yue, Don Perry, Darnell Harrison
Customers.....................Bernadette Bowman, Jack L. Harrell,
    Anthony S. Johnson
Shoppers...........................Marcy Goldman, Sheryl Samuels

Director: Neal Ahern, Jr.
Writers: Lynn Marie Latham & Dianne Messina

22. "An American Hero" April 4, 1991   (446222)

Mack is suspended; Jason is torn by feelings toward his fa-
ther; Greg makes Claudia head of the Sumner Foundation
when she threatens to move with Kate across the country;
Paige plots against Linda; Steve snoops around Sumner Corp.;
Anne pressures Claudia into a job. Dedication: "We remember
Steve Shaw who was Eric Fairgate on *Knots Landing*."

Susie Richfield...........................................Jana Marie Hupp
Paul......................................................Marco Sanchez

Director: Joseph L. Scanlan
Writers: James Stanley & Dianne Messina

23. "Where There's a Will, There's a Way" April 11, 1991
    (446223)

Mack tries holding his firm together during his three-month
suspension; Greg makes Paige and Linda work together; Anne
joins the board of the charitable Sumner Foundation; Val returns from the hospital; Gary accidentally injures Kate, possibly ending her tennis career.

Doris.....................................................Mimi Kennedy
Mrs. Richfield............................................Ann Nelson
Susie Richfield...........................................Jana Marie Hupp
Mr. Leland...............................................Steve Gilborn
Prof. Manning............................................John Ingle
Leland's secretary........................................Judith Jordan
And: Anna Miller (Salesclerk), Robert Burnett (Driving teacher)

Director: Michele Lee
Writers: James Stanley & Dianne Messina

**preempted April 18**

24. "The Last One Out" April 25, 1991   (446224)

Val and Gary's rehearsal is delayed when a fire traps guests at Sumner, and the couple, ahead of schedule, marry for the third time; Paige becomes more attracted to Steve; Frank begins to resent Charlotte's seeing other boyfriends; Jason and Julie kiss. Per CBS, the series' 300th episode.

Scott...........................................................Willie C. Carpenter
Monica..............................................................Stephanie Pope
Monica's husband.............................................George C. Simms
Security guards..........Reid Smith, Loyda Ramos, Rick Cramer,
   Vance Valencia
And: Dianna Patton (Employee), Ed Evanko (Judge)

Director: Nicholas Sgarro          Writer: Bernard Lechowick

25. "A Horse is a Horse"  May 2, 1991   (446225)

Anne and Nick plan to steal from Greg's art collection; Paige is attracted to an architect (P. Brown) designing the Sumner Plaza; Kate wants to work at Gary's ranch for the summer; Linda confronts Michael; Frank hollers at Mack about Jason; Claudia names Paul Galveston as Steve's father.

Brian Johnston........................................................Philip Brown
Mr. Leland..............................................................Steve Gilborn
Leland's secretary.................................................Judith Jordan
Waiter.....................................................................Jesse Garrett
Co-workers.................................Jean Montanti, Phil Poulos

Director: Anita W. Addison          Writer: Scott M. Hamner

26. "Play, Pause, Search"  May 9, 1991   9-11 p.m.   (446226)

Paige and Linda are threatened by incriminating sex videos made by Johnston; Claudia fires Anne, who becomes homeless; Jason is found in the wreckage of a car that fired a rifle at Karen; Paige is arrested. Dedication: "This season is dedicated to the memory of Lawrence Kasha, 1932-1990."

Brian Johnston........................................................Philip Brown
Walsh/landlord..................................................William Bronder
Mrs. Richfield............................................................Ann Nelson
Paul......................................................................Marco Sanchez
Woman................................................................Coleen Maloney
Maitre d'..............................................................James Raymond
Gun shop dealer..............................................Michael O'Dwyer
Detective Linton.......................................................Donald Willis
Police officers..........Mik Scriba, Drew Smith, Kathryn Danielle
And: T.C. Warner (Teenager), Emily Kuroda (Cleaning person),
   Frank Novak (Guest), Perry Scott, Frank Noon (Gang
   members), Graham Galloway (Parking attendant), Sal
   Blydenburgh (Shop owner), Jerry Boyd (John), Kathy
   Christopherson (Waitress)

Director (first hour): William Devane
Director (second hour): Lorraine Senna Ferrara
Writers: James Stanley and Dianne Messina

**renewed for 1991-92; new episodes begin Sept. 12, 1991; Petersen departs the cast**

# L.A. Law

NBC          Thursdays, 10-11 p.m.

Series premiere: Sept. 15, 1986

Ensemble drama set at the high-profile Los Angeles law firm McKenzie, Brackman, Chaney, Kuzak and Becker. New cast-member Donohoe was a guest ep. 4-8; Spencer, ep. 6-8; and Hoffman, ep. 12-14 and 16. Bernsen is the son of soap opera actress Jeanne Cooper, and the husband of actress Amanda Pays. Tucker and Eikenberry, married on the show, are also married in real life. Their infant son on the show: Matthew. Recurring guest Sterling is a cast-member of *The Family Man*, as Ashleigh Blair Sterling; Sheila Kelley is not related to the series' executive producer, David E. Kelley.

Michael Kuzak...........................................................Harry Hamlin
Grace Van Owen.............................................................Susan Dey
Arnold Becker.........................................................Corbin Bernsen
Ann Kelsey...............................................................Jill Eikenberry
Douglas Brackman, Jr................................................Alan Rachins
Abby Perkins..........................................................Michele Greene
Victor Sifuentes.........................................................Jimmy Smits
Stuart Markowitz.....................................................Michael Tucker
Roxanne Melman........................................................Susan Ruttan
Jonathan Rollins.................................................Blair Underwood
Benny Stulwicz.............................................................Larry Drake
Leland McKenzie....................................................Richard Dysart
Cara Jean (C.J.) Lamb (ep. 4-on)...................Amanda Donohoe
• Tommy Mullaney (ep. 6-on)...............................John Spencer
Asst. D.A. Zoey Clemmons, his ex-wife (ep.
   12-14,16-on)........Cecil (rhymes with "wrestle") Hoffmann

*Recurring characters, more than one storyline:*
Rosalind Shays (ep. 1-3,8,10,12,15,16).............Diana Muldaur
Murray Melman, Roxanne's father
   (ep. 1-2,5,7-8).........................................Vincent Gardenia
Corrinne Hammond Becker, Arnie's wife
   (ep. 1,3,7-8,10-12).......................................Jennifer Hetrick
Chloe, her daughter (ep. 1,11-12)...................Ashleigh Sterling
Attorney Jack Sollers (ep. 1-5,16,18,19-22)...........Denis Arndt
   (consistently misspelled "Dennis" in *TV Guide*)
Judge Richard Armand (ep. 3-4,16,22)...............John Hancock
Secretary Gwen Taylor (ep. 2-3,6-7,13,17)............Sheila Kelley
D.A. Bruce Rogoff (ep. 1,3,12)..................................Bruce Kirby

Voiceovers (variously, several per episode, uncredited): Edwin
   Cook, Linda Overlin Cook, Wendy E. Cutler, Tim Dorn-
   berg, Starr Gillard, Rod Gist a.k.a. Rod L. Gist, Andy
   Goldberg, Malcolm Groome, Marabina Jaimes, Nick Jame-
   son, Donna Lynn Leavy, DeVera Marcus, Gracie Moore,
   Vahan Moosekian, Kimberly S. Newberry, Tina Panella-
   Hart, Bert Rosario, Claudette Sutherland, Gail Youngs

• Also given as Tommy Hamline in initial NBC press materials.

Twentieth Century Fox Television
Executive producers: David E. Kelly, Rick Wallace
Supervising producer: Patricia Green (William M. Finkelstein
   orig. announced)
Coordinating producer: Alice West
Producers: John Hill (early in season), Robert Breech, James
   C. Hart, Elodie Keene, Alan Brennert (later in season)
   (Michael M. Robin also orig. announced)
Associate producer: Monica Wyatt
Story editors: Barry M. Schkolnick (early in season); Judith
   Feldman, Sarah Woodwise Gallagher (both later)
Director of photography (variously): David J. Plenn; Timothy
   E. Wade
Executive consultant: Steven Bochco
Theme (instrumental) and music: Mike Post
Creators: Steven Bochco & Terry Louise Fisher

1. "The Bitch is Back"  Oct. 18, 1990   (7L01)

Ex-partner Rosalind claims sexual discrimination and engages Sollers to sue the firm; a civil-rights activist (Winfield) orchestrates the media as Kuzak defends a white cop (Guinee) who shot a black youth. Gardenia and Muldaur begin reprising their roles from the previous season.

Derron Holloway.....................................................Paul Winfield
Off. Brian Chisolm.....................................................Tim Guinee
Asst. D.A. Marcia Fusco.....................................Jordan Baker
Judge Walter Stone.............................J. Kenneth Campbell
Judge Marilyn J. Travelini.................................Anne Haney
Dr. Jeffrie Wolin.....................................Francois Giroday
Kenny Adler...........................................................Hiram Kasten
Police officer...........................................................Dan Moseley
Reporters........Tina Panella-Hart, Alec Murdock, Orin Kennedy
Eric Perkins.............................................Chauncey Leopardi
Foreperson.............................................Charles Bazaldua
    Also orig. announced: George Pentecost (Dan Nystrom)

Director: Elodie Keene          Writer: David E. Kelley

2. "Happy Trails" Oct. 25, 1990  (7L02)

Van Owen combats Shays with a surprise witness, but the firm loses the case; Kuzak confronts a biased judge (Campbell), and he and Rollins are jailed for contempt; Kelsey and Markowitz agree to a sex moratorium; Brackman bids adieu to his sex-surrogate lover (Peterson) after a man dies in her bed. Guest Finkelstein is the producer of *Cop Rock*.

Derron Holloway.....................................................Paul Winfield
Diana Moses.............................................................Renee Jones
Off. Brian Chisolm.....................................................Tim Guinee
Asst. D.A. Marcia Fusco.....................................Jordan Baker
Judge Marilyn J. Travelini.................................Anne Haney
Judge Walter Stone.............................J. Kenneth Campbell
Marilyn Hopkins.............................................Robyn Peterson
Susan Shays Raab, Rosalind's daughter........Kristina Coggins
Rudy Lewis.............................................Hector Maisonette
Arthur Pryor...........................................................Duane Davis
Anchorperson...........................................................Barry Pintar
Reporters.............Monica Horan, Randy Broad, Jonathan Doll,
    Kate Finlayson
Foreperson.............................................Charles Bazaldua
And: Steve Small (Bailiff), Bill Finkelstein (Howard Hulce), Tim
    Hart (Waiter)
    Also orig. announced: Darwyn Carson (Bailiff #2)

Director: Win Phelps          Writer: Barry M. Schkolnick

3. "Lie Harder" Nov. 1, 1990  (7L03)

Abby represents a couple (Jansen, Eiding) trying to return a violent, adopted six-year-old (Graas); the secretary (Kelley) Becker seduced on his wedding eve comes to work at the firm; Van Owen has a cop-shooting case with racial overtones.

Derron Holloway.....................................................Paul Winfield
Off. Brian Chisolm.....................................................Tim Guinee
Asst. D.A. Marcia Fusco.....................................Jordan Baker
Judge Roseann Robin.............................C.C.H. Pounder *
Judge Michael Conover.....................................James Avery
Judge Marilyn J. Travelini.................................Anne Haney
Jaime Rodriguez.............................................Castulo Guerra
Carol Slaeffer.............................................Christine Jansen
Dr. Sarah Evans...........................................................Jenny O'Hara
Ben Slaeffer...........................................................Paul Eiding
Billy Slaeffer.............................................John Christian Graas
Jerome Bailey...........................................................Tommy Morgan
And: Dan Cashman (Lowry), Marian E. Green (Amy Lewis),
    Chauncey Leopardi (Perkins), Gay Hagen (Foreperson)

* This actress' initials are usually given as "CCH," without periods, though periods appeared onscreen here.

Director: David Carson
Writers: Judith Feldman & Sarah Woodside Gallagher

4. "Armand's Hammer" Nov. 8, 1990  (7L04)

Rollins defends a white cop accused of killing a black youth, challenging Holloway; a sharp young attorney (new cast-member Donohoe) outmaneuvers the firm, and is rewarded with a job offer; Sifuentes romances Van Owen, and defends a humiliated professor (Harkins) suing a candid-video TV show.

Derron Holloway.....................................................Paul Winfield
Martin Lowens.....................................................John Harkins
Off. Brian Chisolm.....................................................Tim Guinee
Asst. D.A. Marcia Fusco.....................................Jordan Baker
Judge Steven Lang.....................................................Raye Birk
Wilma Russ.............................Vernee Watson-Johnson
August Oberzan.............................................Barry Snider
Kenneth Clipner...........................................................John Vickery
Gail Egan.............................................Kandis Chappell
Jerome Bailey...........................................................Tommy Morgan
Forepersons.........................Gay Hagen, Redmond M. Gleeson

Director: Menachem Binetski          Writer: John Hill

5. "Smoke Gets In Your Thighs" Nov. 15, 1990  (7L05)

Kelsey tries to get Markowitz removed from a stressful case, and represents a gay man (Kilner) denied visitation rights to his terminally ill lover; Becker and Abby try to retrieve money Benny gave to a questionable religious order.

Marcia Schwartz.....................................................Nina Foch
Ames Campbell.....................................................Kevin Kilner
Duncan Young...........................................................Mitchell Ryan
Dr. Laura Ortiz.............................................Katherine Cortez
Lawrence Bradley.............................................Albert Owens
Thomas Young...........................................................Frank Beddor
Judge Harlan Shubow (orig. Theresa Hayden)......Stan Kamber
Judge Richard Lobel.............................................Stanley Grover
And: Bonnie Hellman (Elaine), Virginia Watson (Paramedic)

Director: Richard Compton          Writer: Patricia Green

6. "Vowel Play" Nov. 29, 1990

Brackman appears on the game show *Wheel of Fortune* (with the show's Vanna White, Bob Goen and others appearing as themselves); C.J. and an old lawyer friend (new cast-member Spencer, beginning his recurring role) fight a tobacco company in a cancer suit; Sifuentes argues for a murder victim's family whose doctor did not report her repeated spousal beatings; Stuart's affection for his assistant (Kelley) turns romantic.

Herself/Letter-turner.............................................Vanna White
Himself/Daytime-version host.....................................Bob Goen
Meg Duffy.............................................Cheryl Giannini
Terrance Flaherty (orig. Richard Neeland).............Alan Fudge
Ellen Klein.............................................Mary-Joan Negro
Dr. Stephen Harbaugh.............................................David Groh
Michael McGery.............................................Arlen Dean Snyder
Dr. Kenneth Cahill.............................................Byrne Piven
Ferret...........................................................Stephen Root
Edna Girth.............................................Mary Pat Gleason
Judge Matthew Saucier (orig. Judge Green).....Warren Munson
David Sheppard.............................................Kent Williams
Milton Stadler.............................................Jeff Pomerantz
Foreperson.............................................David Michael Myers

Himself/Announcer..............................................Charlie O'Donnell
Herself/FCC observer...........................................Debbie McGee
Herself/Makeup artist.........................................Leigh Mitchell
Jeffrey Wolin.....................................................Robert J. Wallace

Director: Ed Sherin
Writers: David E. Kelley & Patricia Green

7. "New Kidney on the Block"  Dec. 6, 1990  (7L07)

Van Owen represents a badly diabetic friend (Strang) in need
of a kidney going to a rich patient suddenly on the waiting list;
Kuzak argues for a flag-burning Vietnam vet (Gunton); new
roommates Murray and Benny pose as lawyers to get dates.
Guest Frost is a cast-member of *Twin Peaks.*

Robert Weston....................................................Bob Gunton
Dam Ramel.......................................................Adam Storke
Felix Echeverria (orig. Barry Arthur).....................Paul Regina
Carol Graf........................................................Deborah Strang
Judge Douglas McGrath....................................Michael Fairman
Crystal.............................................................Julie Garfield
Aurora...............................Candice Azzara (orig. Susan Tyrell)
Mitch Stafford...................................................Paul Collins
George Maltin....................................................Warren Frost
Maura Fitzgerald...............................................Leann Hunley
Dr. Kevin Greggory.......................................Robert Schenkkan
Judge Walter Green..............................................Keith Mills
Judge Harlan Shubow.........................................Stan Kamber
Frank Royko......................................................John Nesci
Helena Washington.............................................Leigh Kilton
Joseph Fielding..................................................Carl Strano
Asst. D.A. Peters (orig. Minnis)...................Robin Pearson Rose
And: Shelly Lipkin (Dr. Kendall), David McKnight (Foreperson),
    David Welch (Joe), Allan Graf (Dick), Tom Baumgartner
    (Psychiatrist), Kurt Reichenbach (Waston), Karen Barcus
    (Nurse), Joe Staton (Clerk), Alan G. Ross (Alfred)
    Also orig. announced: Stephen Held (Police officer)

Director: Steven Robman    Writers: John Hill & Stephen Katz

8. "God Rest Ye Murray Gentlemen"  Dec. 13, 1990  (7L08)

Murray fatally suffers from his Alzheimer's; McKenzie wants to
defend Shays on an S&L fraud charge; Sifuentes opposes a
doctor (Glover) fired because of his disfigurement; Brackman
and Rollins use hypnosis to help a client (Wolpe) with Tou-
rette's Syndrome; C.J. arranges the office holiday party; Kelsey
wants a divorce; Leland beds Rosalind. White reprises her role
from ep. 6, Azzara and Garfield from last episode.

Dr. Paul Kohler..................................................John Glover
Susan Hauber..................................................Concetta Tomei
Herself...............................................................Vanna White
Dr. George Westbrook.........................................George Hearn
Noah Cowan......................................................Lenny Wolpe
Judge Mary Barcourt.........................................Lillian Lehman
Ellen Andriosi.....................................................Julie Ariola
James Markos..................................................Dennis Creaghan
Scott Wexler...................................................Scott Williamson
Crystal..............................................................Julie Garfield
Aurora.............................................................Candice Azzara
Coroner.............................................................Frank Novak
Foreperson.......................................................Corinne Kason
Singers (uncredited): Kathy Hazzard, Louis Price, Alfie Silas
    (plus Alice Echols, off-camera)
    Also orig. announced: Bruce Kirby (D.A. Bruce Rogoff),
    Jaime Cardriche (Big man)

Director: Tom Moore
Writer: David E. Kelley & Stephen B. Katz

9. "Splatoon"  Jan. 3, 1991  (TL09)

Sifuentes is named a partner, and he and Van Owen embark
on a relationship; Abby appears on the *Donahue* TV discussion show; Brackman, Markowitz and Rollins go on a paint-
gun war game; Mullaney represents the wife (Calloway) of a
brain-damaged boxer (Love); Markowitz and Kelsey reconcile.
Donahue makes his episodic-TV debut.

Mitchell Dune.............................................William Allen Young
Larry Edwards.....................................................Victor Love
Robyn Edwards.......................................Vanessa Bell Calloway
Russell Spitzer...................................................Don Sparks
Donnie Lott.......................................................George Rogan
Judge Kevin Apler............................................Pierre Epstein
Richard Fliegel..................................................Rod Arrants
Dr. William Harris..............................................Erick Avari
Walter..........................................................Douglas MacHugh
Prof. Henry Bennett..............................................Jay Bell
Himself...........................................................Phil Donahue
And: Kevin Page, Jeff Heston (Bookworms), Gary McGurk (Ref-
    eree), Philip Brown, Mike Jolly (Raiders), Joyce Meadows
    (Foreperson), Christopher J. Keene, Frank S. Palmer
    (Wildcats)

Director: Elodie Keene
Writers: John Hill & Barry M. Schkolnick

10. "Pump It Up"  Jan. 10, 1991  (7L10)

Markowitz and Kelsey discover Leland and Rosalind's relationship; Kuzak and Van Owen clash; Sifuentes is compelled by
the court to defend an alleged sociopathic murderer; the firm
throws a surprise birthday party for an adulterous Becker.

Leonard Bey......................................................Steve Forrest
Lionel Sanders...................................................M.K. Harris
Christina Shepherd...............................................Ally Walker
Mark Cleland.................................................Steven Eckholdt
Asst. D.A. Ellen Kennedy....................................Joanna Merlin
Wendy Brussell............................................Jacqueline Schultz
Judge Paul Hansen............................................Leonard Stone
Dr. James Felder................................................Joseph Ragno
Detective Thomas Saleno.....................................Frank Stoeger
Reporters............Cal Gibson, Tina Panella-Hart, Alec Murdock
And: Cynthia Sanders (Foreperson), Bill Majik (Bailiff)

Director: Mervin Dayan
Writers: David E. Kelley & Judith Feldman & Sarah  Woodside
    Gallagher

**unscheduled preemption Jan. 17**

11. "Rest in Pieces"  Jan. 31, 1991  (7L11)

Brackman takes temporary charge of the firm; Van Owen goes
before a military tribunal to co-represent a solider (Collet);
Corrinne throws Becker out after Roxanne is indiscreet about
his infidelities; Becker fires Roxanne, in turn hired by Brackman; C.J. argues for a couple who bought a "haunted" house.

Maj. Charles Rainero.......................................James McDaniel
2nd Lt. Richard Braden..............................Christopher Collet
Pres. Kenners......................................................Dale Dye
Judge Janice L. Neiman......................................Annie Abbott
Col. Barney Massien.........................................Will MacMillan
Marsha Shaw..................................................Maggie Roswell
Capt. Paul Jaworski............................................Noah Blake
Kenneth Clipner................................................John Vickery
Joan Dawson......................................................Alyson Reed
Dr. Mitchell Lewen............................................Adrian Sparks

Capt. Sam Danowitz....................................John Rensenhouse
Stephan Gendler...............................................John Apicella
And: Tyde Kierney (Braden), Lawrence McNeal III (M.P.)

Director: Win Phelps
Writers: Patricia Green & John Robert Bensink

12. "He's a Crowd"  Feb. 7, 1991  (7L12)

Kuzak defends a murder suspect (Robinson) with multiple personalities; McKenzie seeks Rosalind's help in keeping a big client; Becker attends family court, with Roxanne subpoenaed in his divorce case; C.J. and Abby share a romantic kiss.

Gregory Edmonson........................................Andrew Robinson
Judge Mary Harcourt.........................................Lillian Lehman
Dr. Donald Carlson..........................................Stanley Anderson
Kyle Santars.................................................Stephen Nichols
Tom Baker....................................................Philip Baker Hall
And: Peter Vogt (Wendle), Daniel Kern (Kevin Wilkes)

Director: Elodie Keene          Writer: David E. Kelley

13. "Dances with Sharks"  Feb. 14, 1991  (7L13)

Rollins is brutalized by police for "not fitting the profile" of a white neighborhood; a divorced Navajo father kidnaps his half-Caucasian son, and seeks a Native American court ruling to raise him on a reservation.  Guest Greene is not the author.

David Wauneka..............................................Graham Greene
Judge William Gainser...................Floyd Red Crow Westerman
James Long............................................Sheldon Peters Wolfchild
Janice Long, his ex-wife....................................Annalee Jefferies
Asst. D.A. Bill Graphia.........................................Sam Anderson
John Barkley................................................Jonathan Prince
Officer Jansen.................................................Carl Mueller
Dr. William Landale................................Branscombe Richmond
Judge Harlan Shubow...........................................Stan Kamber
Judge Richard Lobel...........................................Stanley Grover
Sgt. Cobb...................................................Stephen Quadros
And: Kym Douglas (Sarah Douglas), Bruce Newbold (Anchor-person), Christian McCabe (Joshua), Joyce Guy (Clerk)

Director: David Carson
Teleplay: Patricia Green & Alan Brennert
Story: Patricia Green, Alan Brennert, Melinda M. Snodgrass

14. "The Gods Must Be Lawyers"  Feb. 21, 1991  (7L14)

Victor has Grace to dinner with his family, and later must have the life-support removed from his critically hurt brother (Sandoval); Kuzak and Mullaney defend a woman (Kozak) and her lover charged with murdering her much older husband; Zoey opposes a sleazy attorney (Newton, a singer) representing a wealthy executive accused of raping a 16-year-old girl (Lee).

Brian Byrd ....................................................Wayne Newton
Rikki Davis..............................................Harley Jane Kozak
Joseph Sifuentes, Victor's father.........................Tomas Milian
Gaby Sifuentes, Victor's mother..........................Miriam Colon
Judge Douglas McGrath................................Michael Fairman
Orin Baldwin.................................................Thomas Callaway
Laurie Penn..................................................Alexondra Lee
Charlie Sifuentes, Victor's brother.....................Lou Sandoval
Judge Paul Hansen............................................Leonard Stone
Marsha Henderson.............................................Debra Mooney
Dr. Alice Nyberg..............................................Melody Ryane
Shirley Penn, Laurie's mother.........................Kathleen Doyle
Walt Shipman.................................................Charles Parks
Anna Sifuentes, Victor's sister.....................Margarita Franco

Reporters..........Joyce Kurtz, Ted Baader, Janice Ryan, Robina Suwol, Joel Swetow (uncredited), John Towey (uncredited)
Foreperson......................................................Joe Staton
Also orig. announced: Paul Regina (Felix Echeverria)

Director: Tom Moore          Writer: David E. Kelley

**preempted Feb. 28**

15. "The Beverly Hills Hangers"  March 14, 1991  (7L15)

Kuzak and Mullaney, gearing up for their big case, are dealt a blow when the murder suspect's (Kozak) lover (Caffrey) testifies against her; Rosalind proposes to McKenzie, who declines.

Rikki Davis..............................................Harley Jane Kozak
Judge Gary Gates..............................................Gerry Bamman
Mark Chelios...............................................John de Lancie
Asst. D.A. Newell Cook........................................Francis Guinan
Detective John Foley......Charles Napier (orig. Richard Jaeckel)
David Schaeffer...........................................Stephen Caffrey
Joyce Kulhewic.............................................Claudia Cron
Reporters...................John Towey, Robina Suwol, Joyce Kurtz, Ted Baader, Janice Ryan, Stephen Howard
Foreperson....................................................Marie Thomas
Photographer.........................................Ned Hall (uncredited)

Director: Gabrielle Beaumont   Writer: David E. Kelley

16. "Good to the Last Drop"  March 21, 1991  (7L16)

Rosalind fatally falls down an elevator shaft; Victor counsels a couple (Gorman and Gehringer, a recurring *Evening Shade* guest) to spurn a settlement that'd keep a hospital's malpractice secret; Stuart represents a tax rebel (Brewster); Clemmons tries to prosecute two drive-by shooters; Grace is pregnant.

Noreen Carter.............................................Elizabeth Van Dyke
Jimmy Hoffs...............................................Michael Chiklis
Judge Saul Edelstein..........................................Larry Dobkin
Judge Donald Phillips......................................Daniel Benzali
Edward Johnson.........................[Sir] James Randolph
Kate Recklaw...............................................Linda Gehringer
William Lowell..............................................Robert Walker
Dr. Everett Kyle..............................................James Karen
Upton Weeks..................................................Niles Brewster
Lyman Hatcher.............................................James Sutorious
IRS agent Marv Fletcher....................................Roy Brocksmith
Brenda Lunsford.............................................Susan Berman
Nicholas Klein..............................................Mark La Mura
Billy Michaels............................................Mitch David Carter
Ed Recklaw.................................................Andrew Gorman
Asst. D.A. John Stephans....................................Philip Moon
Ralph Waring.........................................Milo Kevin Floeter (uncredited)
And: Karen Radcliffe (Joanne Byers), Clement Von Francken-stein (Krug), Ron House (Schmidt), Bernard Rehhaut (Krieger), Carl Held (West), Michael Kinney (Funeral director), Jeanne Sakata, Bob Farley (Forepersons), Joe Banks (Clerk), Merry Lee Traum, Steve Tietsort (Reporters)

Director: Menachem Binetski
Writers: David E. Kelley, Patricia Green, Alan Brennert

17. "Mutinies on the Banzai"  March 28, 1991  (7L17)

McKenzie keeps Brackman as senior partner; Kuzak mounts a revolt and is fired; Rollins opposes a firm that replaced its U.S. executives with Japanese; Becker is tormented.  Walker reprises her role from ep. 10. Per NBC, the series' 100th episode.

Christina Shepherd.............................................Ally Walker

Bruce Fairchild..............................................Robert Pine
Yoshi Nakajima..............................Danny Kamekona
Russell Spitzer....................................Don Sparks
Judge Walter Green..............................Keith Mills
Patrick Phillips..................................Tom Everett
Page Lockhart................................Diane Salinger
John Ordover.......................................Tom Isbell
Harriet Ordover................................Susan Angelo
Donald Schwartz...................................Joe Farago
And: Cliff Howard (Guard), Marga Chavez (Foreperson)

Director: Win Phelps
Writers: David E. Kelley, Patricia Green, Alan Brennert

18. "As God Is My Co-Defendant"  April 4, 1991  (7L18)

Victor and Grace agree to join Kuzak's firm; Abby and Rollins
resign; Kuzak (leaving after 14 years) sues the firm, which
hires Sollers to litigate a suit alleging sabotage; the court appoints a temporary receiver (Florek, a cast-member of *Law &
Order*); Mullaney defends a Christian Science couple (Morrison
and Hofmann, a cast-member of *Dear John...*) charged with
involuntary manslaughter in their son's death.

Dave Meyer.......................................Dann Florek
Asst. D.A. Malcolm Gold........................Jerry Hardin
Karen Morrison...............................Isabella Hofmann
Greg Morrison...................................Mark Metcalf
Judge Walter L. Swanson..........................Earl Boen
Dr. James Rissler..........................Don R. McManus
Dr. Robert Lebb...................................Ray Stewart
Judge Kent Watson................................Ken Tobey
Lee Chang.........................................Evan C. Kim
Prof. Thomas Wadkins.....................Jerome Courtland
Judge Esposito..................................Jo de Winter
Judge Wirt.....................................Harvey Vernon
Judge Kennedy....................................Neal Vipond
And: Gene Chronopolous (Jerzy Rowalski), George C. Simms,
    Mark D. Friedman (Office guards), Joyce Guy (Clerk),
    Ginger Rose Fox (Foreperson), Karen Corso-Plitt, R. Leo
    Schreiber, J. Christopher Sullivan, Catherine M. Cum-
    mings (Jurors), John E. Thompson (Kuzak's guard)
    Also orig. announced: Sheila Kelley (Gwen Taylor)

Director: Miles Watkins
Writers: David E. Kelley, Judith Feldman, Sarah Woodside
    Gallagher

19. "Speak, Lawyers for Me"  April 25, 1991  (7L19)

Meyer has dire recommendations; Kuzak gives up his dissolu-
tion motion after Benny has a depression-related breakdown;
Brackman defends a transsexual model (Christian) fired when
her operation was discovered; Mullaney represents the family
of a college football player who took steroids and became suicidal; Abby and Rollins return; Abby asks C.J. for a date. Florek reprises his role from last episode, Regina from ep. 7.

Dave Meyer.......................................Dann Florek
Susan Convers...............................Claudia Christian
Coach John Lungren.............................Paul Gleason
Judge Douglas McGrath.......................Michael Fairman
Felix Echeveria..................................Paul Regina
Christina Leong......................................Jodi Long
Kenny Webster..................................Eriq LaSalle
Bruce Ingalls.....................................John Calvin
Dr. Michael Lattimer..........................Michael O'Hare
Dennis Rhodes...................................Geof Prysirr
Judge Matthew Saucier.......................Warren Munson
Judge Kent Watson................................Ken Tobey
Arthur Webster..............................Gene Whittington

Dr. Kyle Waits.................................John Harnagel
Forepersons....................Marty Brinton, Anne Etue

Director: Paul Lazarus
Writers: David E. Kelley, Patricia Green, Alan Brennert

20. "There Goes the Judge"  May 2, 1991  (7L20)

Clemmons' old professor (Wallach), a judge, is going mad; Rollins defends a fearful motorist (Derricks) who led police on a
chase after having seen a news video of a police beating; Becker helps Benny recover; Abby seeks Kelsey's advice; MacKenzie
reassumes his position; the firm is renamed, minus Kuzak.

Judge Adam Biel....................................Eli Wallach
Asst. D.A Kari Simms...........................Lonette McKee
Billy Castroverti.................................Tom Verica
Mark Wright..................................Cleavant Derricks
Dr. Louis Birch................................Nicholas Pryor
Officer Gary Katleman.............................Scott Kraft
Judge Robert L. Daytona..........................Paul Bartel
Stephen Chekles..................................Peter Zapp
Clay Jones..................................William Bumiller
Dr. Bradley Michaelson.........................Ivar Brogger
Walt Johnston.................................William Flatley
And: Claudia Bloom (Foreperson), Charles Emmett (Clarence)

Director: Elodie Keene
Writers: David E. Kelley, Patricia Green, Alan Brennert

21. "On the Toad Again"  May 9, 1991  (7L21)

Kelsey and Sollers represent an obsessive (Farr) charged with
murdering her married lover; C.J. argues for a retiree (Greer)
accused of licking his Cane toads to get high; part-time arbi-
tration judge McKenzie rules on a blues singer's (Taylor) suit.

Elliot "The Wompman" Miller.....................Ron Taylor
Hester Mead.......................................Dabbs Greer
Suzanne Hamil....................................Michele Farr
Jeanette Walker.................................Elaine Kagan
Asst. D.A. Anthony Blake.......................Tony Spiridakis
Corey Walker, Jeanette's son.................Christopher Pettiet
• Meredith Korngold.................Lora Staley (orig. Tricia O'Neill)
Mark Kumpel.....................................John Pleshette
Hawks team owner Brian Harden....................John Considine
Judge Donald T. Phillips......................Daniel Benzali
Judge Sidney Schroeder..........................Bernie Hern
Alex Wayne........................................Bruce Gray
Wendel Mueller..................................Peter Elbling
Detective Douglas French..........................Paul Comi
Newscaster.....................................Bruce Newbold
And: M. Scott Wilkinson (Foreperson), Eric Fleeks (Cop),
    Joyce Kurtz, Orin Kennedy, Merry Lee Traum (Reporters)

• Role combines the previously separate character of Lisa
  Maynard.

Director: Michael Katleman          Writer: David E. Kelley

22. "Since I Fell for You"  May 16, 1991  (7L22)

Kelsey, held by client-attorney privilege from saying who murdered her client, acquitted last episode, is disbarred for three
months for revealing the killer; Sifuentes and Van Owen marry, and he represents an AIDS-stricken lawyer (Kamel) against
an insurer; Becker falls through the ceiling having sex with
Roxanne; Abby's made a partner. Verica reprises his role from
ep. 20, Coggins from ep. 2, Kagan and Comi from last episode.

Mark Gilliam...................................Stanley Kamel

Billy Castroverti..............................................Tom Verica
Jeanette Walker................................................Elaine Kagan
Susan Shays Raab.........................................Kristina Coggins
Cashman.........................................................Milt Tarver
Judge Whitney Baldwin...........................Macon McCalman
Judge Richard Lobel....................................Stanley Grover
Judge Donald Tyrell.....................................Mort Sertner
Detective Douglas French.............................Paul Comi
And: Julia Vera (Margarita Sanchez), Michael Eristu Sams
      (Judge Armand's clerk), Orin Kennedy, Merry Lee Traum
      (Reporters), Fred Kronenberg (State Bar clerk)

Director: Win Phelps
Writers: David E. Kelley, Patricia Green, Alan Brennert

**preempted May 30**

**preempted June 20 and June 27**

**preempted Sept. 12**

**renewed for 1991-92; new episodes begin Oct. 10, 1991;
Hamlin, Smits and Greene depart cast**

## Law & Order

NBC        Sept. 13-Oct. 11              Thursdays, 10-11 p.m.
           Oct. 23-April 22, June 19-on Tuesdays, 10-11 p.m.

Series premiere: Sept. 13, 1990

New York City police drama, the first half focusing on the detectives of the 36th precinct in mid-Manhattan, the second on
the courts that try their cases. Working title: *Law and Order.*
Filmed in New York City.

Detective Sgt. Max Greevey...........................George Dzundza
Asst. D.A. Ben Stone....................................Michael Moriarty
Detective Mike Logan.................................................Chris Noth
Capt. Donald Cragen.....................................Dann Florek
Asst. D.A. Paul Robinette................................Richard Brooks
D.A. Adam Schiff..............................................Steven Hill

*Recurring:*
Shambala Green (ep. 2,9,18)......................Lorraine Toussaint
Profaci (ep. 3,8,11,13,19)......................................John Fiore

Wolf Films and Universal Television, an MCA Co.
Executive producers: Dick Wolf
Co-executive producer: Joseph Stern
Supervising producers: Michael Duggan, David Black
Producers: Robert Palm, Daniel Sackheim (latter co-producer
      ep. 1)
Co-producers (generally on different episodes): Judith Stevens,
      Jeffrey Hayes
Coordinating producer (pilot): Peter A. Runfolo
Associate producer: Anthony Mazzei (early in season); Arthur
      W. Forney (later in season)
Executive story editor (later in season): Robert Stuart Nathan
Story editor (early in season): Ed Zuckerman
Directors of photography (variously): Ernest Dickerson;
      Constantine Makris
Technical advisor (police): Michael Struk
Technical advisor (D.A): William N. Fordes
Theme (instrumental) and music: Mike Post
Creator: Dick Wolf

-----

1. "Prescription for Death" Sept. 13, 1990 (66209)

An emergency room chief resident (Sparer) is brought to trial
when his possible alcoholism may have led to a death.

Dr. Edward Auster ................................................Paul Sparer
Howard Morton ...............................................John Spencer
Philip Nevins ...................................................Ron Rifkin
Dr. Raza...........................................................Erick Avari
Dr. Chester......................................................Alvin Epstein
Jean Mills.....................................................Maryann Urbano
Simonson........................................................Bruce McCarty
Hoffman..............................................................Ed Setrakian
Dr. Thomas Lignell.............................................W.T. Martin
And: Daniel Benzali (Medical Examiner), Frederica Meister
      (Melanie Stivic), Annie Corley (Stewart), Rocky Carroll
      (Davids), William Roerick (Dr. Abraham), Russell Horton
      (Markowitz), Tom Kubiak (Rasmussen), Harry S. Murphy
      (Don), Maeve McGuire (Dr. Walters), Stephanie Gordon,
      Joan Kaye (Nurses), Kate Wilkinson (Gray-haired lady),
      Shona Tucker (Records clerk), Nick Damici (Dubuque),
      Leslie Goldman (Judge), Chaz McCormack (McInerry),
      Lee Tergesen (Clemens), Sean Whitesell (Intern)
      Also orig. announced:
      Alvin Epstein (Dr. Chester), Orderly (Reggie Bythewood),
      Ebony Jo-Ann (Receptionist)

Director: John P. Whitesell II          Teleplay: Ed Zuckerman
Story: David Black & Ed Zuckerman

2. "Subterranean Homeboy Blues" Sept. 20, 1990 (66205)

The cops and courts wrestle with an apparent self-defense
subway shooting.

Laura di Biasi.....................................................Cynthia Nixon
Judge Manuel Leon.................................................Sam Gray
Darnell Shenault...................................................Akili Prince
Nurses.......................Phyllis Somerville, Stephanie Berry
Abby Diamond...............................................Alexandra Gersten
Woman.............................................................Tonya Pinkins
Hastings..........................................................Barbara Caruso
Hones............................................................Dwayne McClary
Aimee...............................................................Wanda Richert
And: Jose Ramon Rosario (Administrator), Shirl Bernheim
      (Landlady), Cynthia Belgrave (Librarian), David E. Wein-
      berg, Kevin Eshelman (Police officers), Mark Werheim
      (Stevenson; orig. Williamson), Tim Kelleher (Intern), Mimi
      Weddell (Homeless person), Gerald M. Kline (Paramedic),
      Phil Parolisi (Orderly), Cedric Turner (Transit police offi-
      cer), Damon Pooser (Angel)
      Also orig. announced: Dan Desmond (Reporter)

Director: E.W. Swackhamer              Writer: Robert Palm

3. "The Reaper's Helper" Oct. 4, 1990 (66215)

A gay man undertakes "assisted suicides" of AIDS sufferers.
The character "Cioran" is played by a different actor in ep. 4
and 10, and yet another in ep. 12.

Jack Curry...........................................................Peter Frechette
Richard (orig. Anthony) Holland........................Tom Signorelli
Patricia Holland................................................Barbara Andres
Suarez.....................................................................Jesse Corti
Julia DeBakey...................................................Charlotte Moore
Hamilton..................................................................Tony Hoty
Brownell/Stillman.......................................Michael Cunningham
Dixon....................................................................Jay Spadaro
Carl Gordon.........................................................Neal Ben-Ari
Terry Roland.................................................Richard Steinmetz
Lois Rivera...........................................................Millie Tirelli
Trial judge...........................................................Steven Gilborn

Jed Coles........................................................Francis Guinan
Allison McGill.................................................Susan Knight
And: Suzanne Shepherd (Arraignment judge), Jack Laufer (Wellman), Frank Girardeau (Massacio), Tommy A. Ford (Harry Pincher), Merrill Holtzman (Hurley), Josh Pais (Cioran), Roger Rignack (Irate man), Matthew Locricchio (Court officer), Olinda Turturro (Jury foreperson), Christopher Rubin (Reporter), Daniel Kenney (Bradley)
  Also orig. announced:
  Richard Poe (Gruen), Helen Breed (Bernice)

Director: Vern Gillum
Writers: Thomas Francis McElroy and David Black & Robert Stuart Nathan

4. "Kiss the Girls and Make Them Die"  Oct. 11, 1990  (66210)

A golden-boy Ivy Leaguer who apparently murdered his preppie girlfriend looks like he may avoid conviction.

Berkley...........................................................Dennis Boutsikaris
Rebecca..........................................................Marita Geraghty
Ned................................................................Thomas Calabro
Polly..............................................................Haviland Morris
Packard..........................................................Priscilla Lopez
Judge Larkin...................................................Jacqueline Brookes
And: Troy Ruptash (Steve Feinstein), Sarah Fleming (Libby), Lori Alan (Martha), Nandrea Lin-Courts (Elise Brody), Matthew Penn (Alex Brody), Janet Zarish (Phipps), David Cromwell (Jesse), David Edward Jones (Belknap), Adam LeFevre (Bartender), Kellie Overbey (Cheryl), Baxter Harris (Bartlett), Lolita Lesheim (Carol), Anthony Fusco (Epstein), James Murtaugh (Christianson), Colleen Quinn (Linda), Stephen deFluiter a.k.a. Stephen DeFluiter (Cioran), Jack Ryland (Arraignment judge), John Battle, Matt Tomasino (Police officers), Marcell Rosenblatt (Louise), Jed Krascella, Melinda Wade (Yuppie couple), Rodolfo Diaz (Jury foreperson)
  Also orig. announced:
  Jennifer Harmon (Worthington), Marnie Cooper (Nurse), Edythe Davis (Secretary)

Director: Charles Correll       Teleplay: Robert Stuart Nathan
Story: Dick Wolf

5. "Happily Ever After"  Oct. 23, 1990  (66216)

Greevey and Logan, suspicious of a woman's testimony regarding her husband's murder, uncover her adultery with the couple's business manager, prompting Stone to pit the two lovers against each other on the stand.  Guest Vanessa Williams is not the dethroned Miss America 1984.

Janet Ralston..................................................Roxanne Hart
Bob Himes......................................................Bob Gunton
Norris.............................................................Barton Heyman
Willie Timmons................................................Kelly Neal
Helen Ralston..................................................Meg Mundy
Bozak.............................................................Chip Zien
Strickland........................................................Cari S. Corfman
Hurley............................................................Richard Poe
Shell (orig. Gordon Shaeffer)...............................Philip Bosco
Arraignment judge............................................Doris Belack
Ellen Kirst.......................................................Joyce Reehling
Tracy Stark......................................................Faith Prince
Matt Luck.......................................................David Little
Dorothy Luck...................................................Mary Elaine Monti
Vera...............................................................Vanessa Williams
And: Aida Turturro (Carmen), Joseph Palmas (Bill Liu), Joe Lisi (Morrel), Nancy Fichman (Magnani), Edward Seamon (Conrad), Steven Gilborn (Judge Marton), David Brisbin

(Dr. Bennett), Linda Atkinson (Jill Vitello), F.X. Vitolo (Plainclothes officer Rick Fenton), Louis Cantarina (Bank guard), Gregory Chase (Alan Ralston), Chester A. Sims (Jury foreperson), Gilbert Cruz (Paramedic Faber)
  Also orig. announced:
  Arthur French (Bucky Carson), Tim Mardirosian (Osborn)

Director: Vern Gillum        Story: Dick Wolf & David Black
Teleplay: David Black & Robert Stuart Nathan

6. "Everybody's Favorite Bagman" (pilot)  Oct. 30, 1990

The mugging of a councilperson uncovers corruption involving him, a mobster (Guilfoyle) and the parking violations bureau.

Wentworth.......................................................Roy Thinnes
Cosmatos........................................................Trey Wilson
Conti..............................................................Dick Latessa
Lasco..............................................................Michael Wikes
Alice Halsey.....................................................Marica Jean Kurtz
Alicia Heslin....................................................Debra Stricklin
Jefferson.........................................................Ron Foster
McCormack......................................................W.H. Macy
Tremaine.........................................................Leo O'Brien
With: Paul Guilfoyle
And: Ronald Guttman (Father), Stuart Burney (Wentzel), Sully Boyar (Swersky), David Chandler (Goldberg), Mark Boone, Jr. (Garage manager), Anthony K. Means (Simonize), Audrey Matson (Maggie), Stephen Pearlman (Rosen)

Director: John Patterson           Writer: Dick Wolf

**preempted Nov. 6**

7. "By Hooker, By Crook"  Nov. 13, 1990  (66203)

The detectives uncover a call-girl ring for the rich and powerful, run by a politically well-connected madam (Clarkson) with an MBA.

Sarah Winthrop.................................................Patricia Clarkson
Jolene.............................................................Jenny Robertson
Folger.............................................................Bernie Barrow
Au Clair..........................................................Addison Powell
Mrs. Stringfellow...............................................Patricia Barry
Jasmine...........................................................Kelle Kerr
Kurtz..............................................................Robert Lupone
Stanko.......Paul Austin (per onscreen), Ray Xifo (per Universal)
With: Courtney B. Vance
And: Steven Marcus (Sheets), Thomas Anderson (Emile Lucy), Bernice Massi (Mrs. Diamond), Martin Shakar (Doctor), Christine Dunford (Reporter), Lillias White (Streetwalker), Byron Utley (Cookie Molina), Dana Morosini (Call girl Camilla), Joe Pentangelo (Macaulay), Yvette Edelhart (Sadie), Beth Hirsch (Elisabeth Roth), Kathryn Meisle (Catherine Moody), Carol Goodheart (Juror), Ralph Buckley (Bailiff), Sandra Beall (Jogger), Terry Burstein (Medical examiner), Gregory Burke (Birthday boy), Leslie Goldman (Trial judge), Nick Muglia (Trevelyn), Prianga Pieris (Lakshmi)
  Also orig. announced: Brian Smiar (Judge Harper)

Director: Martin Davidson          Writer: David Black

8. "Poison Ivy"  Nov. 20, 1991  (66211)

When a black Ivy League student is killed by a cop (Finn), Greevy and Logan suspect a gun was planted on the victim, while Robinette discovers cracks in the student's sterling image.  Alexander is a cast-member of The Cosby Show.  Orig. scheduled for Oct. 11.

Officer Fredo...................................................John Finn
Reverend......................................................Al Freeman, Jr.
Doris...........................................................Erika Alexander
Officer Davis................................................Jack Gwaltney
Hillary........................................................Stuart Burney
Abel...........................................................Richard Habersham
Bernie........................................................John Capodice
Silky Ford....................................................Erik King
Gowdy.......................................................Gregg Almquist
Mrs. Richardson..........................................Saundra McClain
Corey.........................................................Christopher Wynkoop
Wesley Parker.............................................Jake Weber
Mrs. Rodriguez............................................Graciela Lecube
William Harriman, Jr.....................................Barry Sherman
Medical Examiner Borak.................................Josh Pais
And: Daryl Edwards (Richard), Dayton Callie (Monaghan), David Sharp (Hurley), Lawrence Weber (Judge Sirkin), Joe Pentangelo (Sergeant), Minnie Gentry (Bernice), Martha Guilarte (Adela), Karen Myrie (Claudia), Shirley Rumierk (Cissy), Damien Leake (Guard), Dan Moran, David E. Weinberg (Police officers), Michele Wagner (Laurie), Howard Wesson (Baker)
  Also orig. announced:
  Juney Smith, Kitty Crooks (reporters), Suzanne O'Malley (Deputy Mayor), L. Kenneth Richardson (Black leader), George Vlachos (TV anchor)

Director: E.W. Swackhamer          Teleplay: Jacob Brackman
Story: Jack Richardson & Jacob Brackman

9. "Indifference"  Nov. 27, 1991  (66207)

The young daughter of a well-to-do couple dies after continuous child-abuse by seemingly respectable parents, and indifference by school and neighbors. Concludes with a disclaimer regarding similarities to New York City's Steinberg case.

Carla..........................................................Marcia Jean Kurtz
Principal Babcock.........................................John Seitz
Lowenstein/Father........................................David Groh
Redding.......................................................Paul Geier
Eugenia Rawlings..........................................Diane Salinger
Rudy Scelza.................................................Gordon Joseph Weiss
Medical Examiner..........................................Eugene Troobnick
Dobrinski....................................................Mary Joy
Teacher Miss Perez........................................Blanca Camacho
With: Louis Zorich
And: Sarah Rowland Doroff (Deidre "Didi" Lowenstein), Brian Smiar (Judge Harper), Amanda Carlin (Doctor) John Rothman (Internist), Richard M. Davidson (Court clerk)
  Also orig. announced:
  Bruce Nokick (Paramedic), Mary Joy (Dobinski), Shami Chaikin (Crone), George Bartenieff (Professor), Sandra Kazan (Clerk), Cathie Bauer (Reporter)

Director: James Quinn                 Writer: Robert Palm

10. "Prisoner of Love"  Dec. 4, 1990  (66208)

When an artist famous for his depictions of sadomasochism dies under S&M circumstances, an arts commissioner (Keith) and a socialite (Conroy) are among the murder suspects.

Hendrick......................................................Frances Conroy
Rothman.......................................................Larry Keith
Stohlmeyer...................................................Amy Aquino
Cathy...........................................................Marjorie Monaghan
Sondra.........................................................Fran Brill
Jordan..........................................................Don R. McManus
Lab technician Hurley.....................................Sam Schact
Hoexter........................................................Jay Patterson

Celine..........................................................Anthony Crivello
Judge Fadenhecht.........................................Sidney Armus
Johnson........................................................Edye Byrde
Arita Swenson...............................................Valerie Kingston
Dr. Gray (orig. Dr. Gregg)...............................Marjorie Lovett
And: Richard Seff (Hoffer), Brad Greenquist (Bartender), Ted Marcoux (Brian), Stephen DeFluiter a.k.a. Stephen de-Fluiter (Cioran), Harry O'Reilly (McCarry), Antone Pagan (Ubillez), Wayne Maugans (Gary), Jack Ryland (Arraignment Judge), Cecilia Wilde (Sintra), Rudy Hornish (Sterling/Hendrick's lawyer), Marc Plastrik (Investigator)

Director: Michael Fresco       Teleplay: Robert Stuart Nathan
Story: David Black & Robert Stuart Nathan

11. "Out of the Half-Light"  Dec. 11, 1990

When a young black woman (Miller) claims to have been raped by white cops, and an opportunistic black politician (Preston) then creates a media circus, the D.A.'s office suspects a hoax. Faison is a co-star of *True Colors*.

Eaton...........................................................J.A. Preston
Angela Wilkes................................................Billie Neal
Lester Twiggs................................................Frankie R. Faison
Mrs. Crawford...............................................Sandra Reaves-Phillips
Judge Crutcher..............................................Novella Nelson
And: Charles Weldon (Westbrook), Graham Brown (Minister/Louis Warren), Kisha Miller (Astrea), Kelly Cinnante (Police officer), Ruben Santaigo-Hudson (Marvin Gaines), Harold Perrineau, Jr. (Jordan Hill), Verna Hampton (Mrs. Evans), Tichina Arnold (Leona), Adina Porter (Neighbor), Murray Rubinstein (Resident), David L. King, Elizabeth Swackhamer, Juney Smith (Reporters), Rosanna Carter (Mrs. Jackson)
  Also orig. announced:
  Sean Weil (Attendant), Louise Stubbs (Nurse), John Di-Benedetto (Security guard

Director: E.W. Swackhamer             Writer: Michael Duggan

**preempted Dec. 18**

**preempted Jan. 1**

12. "Life Choices"  Jan. 8, 1991  (66213)

When an anti-abortion zealot is killed in an abortion-clinic bombing, police find a second radical linked to the bombing, and that the victim was actually there for an abortion.

Schwimmer...................................................Caroline Kava
Ballard.........................................................Paul Hecht
Molloy.........................................................Pat McNamara
Patrick.........................................................Clark Gregg
Olivera.........................................................Jaime Tirelli
McClure........................................................Bridget Ryan
George.........................................................Kevin Cooney
Barbara........................................................Laurie Kennedy
With: Paul Butler, Kevin O'Rourke
Fogarty.........Frank Anderson (per onscreen), Lenny Loftin (per Universal; see immediately below also)
Man.............................................................Frank Anderson (per Universal)
And: Johann Carlo (Colman), Jonathan Hogan (Corcoran), LaTanya Richardson (Lorraine), Sully Boyar (Arraignment judge), Jim Fyfe (Cleary), Julie Halston (Jane), Isa Thomas (Gwen Matson), Rafael Ferrer (Clerk), Steve Itkin (O'Hare), Howard Spiegel (Bernstein), Timothy Britten Parker (Cioran), Latty Attile (Foreperson), Richard M. Davidson (Court clerk), Camryn Manheim (Leila), Lynn Anderson, Jane Sanders (Women)

Also orig. announced:
Cynthia L. Raftus, Ilana Levine (Women)

Director: Aaron Lipstadt                    Story: Dick Wolf
Teleplay: David Black & Robert Stuart Nathan

13. "A Death in the Family" Jan. 15, 1991

A crooked cop is shot dead and thrown from the window of a
tenement.

Sandoval........................................................Wendy Makkena
Simpson.........................................................David Margulies
Yost..............................................................Louis Guss
Cassie...........................................................Nan-Lynn Nelson
Mavis Bell......................................................Susan Batson
Sgt. Duff........................................................Thomas A. Carlin
Bridges..........................................................Madison Arnold
And: Jerry Mayer (Car salesperson Quinn), Ron Ryan (Ross),
Judson Camp (Harding Cistal), Leah Maddrie (Officer
Trent), Fracaswell Hyman (Laneer), Ellis Williams (Ray
Bell), Sharon Ernster (Doris Rennick), Jerome Preston
Bates (Brutus Walker), Jinsey Dauk (Louisa Birken), Leo
O'Brien (Red), Beatrice Winde (Miss Perry), Karina Arro-
yave (Revina), Mordecai Lawner (Leon March), Ariane
Brandt (Police officer), James Reno (Rennick)

Director: Gwen Arner                        Story: Joe Viola
Teleplay: Joe Viola and David Black

**preempted Jan. 22 and Jan. 29**

14. "The Violence of Summer" Feb. 5, 1991  (66219)

When prosecutors drop a gang-rape case after the victim (Gallagher) can't identify her attackers, the police re-investigate.
Randy Danson is the first wife of actor Ted Danson; the end-
credits give Philip Hoffman and Phil Hoffman in separate roles,
though the latter is not listed on a Wolf Films cast sheet.

TV reporter Monica Devries............................Megan Gallagher
Louise Taggert................................................Samuel L. Jackson
Diane Manso...................................................Randy Danson
Mike Lucia.....................................................Sandy Baron
Tim Pruiting...................................................Al Shannon
Howard Metzler...............................................Gil Bellows
Steven Hanauer...............................................Philip Hoffman
Ryan Cutrona.................................................Ken Johnston
And: Mike Hodge (Judge), David Green (Dr. Kornfeld), Robert
Heller (Thomas Silva), Phil Hoffman (Hypnotherapist),
Marie Barrientos (Mimi Varella), Jean Taylor (Mrs.
Hollis), Phil Stein (Technician), James Pyduck (Bailiff)

Director: Don Scardino                      Writer: Michael Duggan

15. "The Torrents of Greed" Part 1  Feb. 12, 1991

An assault on a candy store owner mushrooms into a disastrous investigation into the powerful Masucci mob family.

Harv Beigel....................................................Bruce Altman
Katherine......................................................Christine Baranski
Frank Masucci.................................................Charles Cioffi
Zuckert.........................................................Steven Keats
Pilefsky.........................................................Stephen McHattie
Le Claire.......................................................Lee Richardson
Elena............................................................Anna Katarina
With: Robert Fields, Steven Keats, Ronald Hunter, Philip R.
Allen, Hy Anzell, Doris Belack
And: Lyn Greene (Meg Hennessy), Jacques Sandulescu (Skol-
nick), Christopher McCann (Hoover), Janis Dardaris

(Mrs. Mackey), Rick Zieff (Dr. Cohen), Joe Lisi (Mahoney),
Dean Iandou (Finkie), Eric Payne (Boswell), Luis Ramos
(Valdez), James Noah (Arraignment judge), Nancy Addi-
son, Jim Gillis (Reporters), Coco Barat (Hotel manager)
Also orig. announced: Michele Tauber (Joanne Melton)

Director: E.W. Swackhamer
Teleplay: Michael S. Chernuchin
Story: Michael Duggan & Michael S. Chernuchin

16. "The Torrents of Greed" Part 2  Feb. 19, 1991

Stone, burned by false testimony, may get vengeance when a
bribery charge brings a Masucci-family mobster to court.

Harv Beigel....................................................Bruce Altman
Katherine......................................................Christine Baranski
Frank Masucci.................................................Charles Cioffi
Pilefsky.........................................................Stephen McHattie
Le Claire.......................................................Lee Richardson
Elena............................................................Anna Katarina
With: Robert Fields, Steven Keats, Ronald Hunter, Philip R.
Allen, Sidney Armus
And: Rex Everhart (Fire inspector), Michael P. Moran (Limo
driver), Michael Heintzman (Lonner), Victoria Christian
(McGinty), Maria Cellario (Connie Masucci), Linda Atkin-
son (Vitello), F.X. Vitolo a.k.a. Francis X. Vitolo (Fenton),
Jacques Sandeulescu (Skolnick), David Cryer (Arraign-
ment judge), Marvin A. Chatinover (Housing judge), Gene
Canfield (D'Agostino), John Anthony Williams (Varone),
Julie White (Waitress), Mike O'Malley (New York police
officer), Bruce Kirkpatrick (New Jersey trooper)

Director: E.W. Swackhamer   Teleplay: Michael S. Chernuchin
Story: Michael Duggan & Michael S. Chernuchin

17. "Mushrooms" Feb. 26, 1991  (66218)

After two children are accidentally shot, one killed, by a 14-
year-old assassin (Cozier) in a botched hit, Stone and Robinette follow the trail to a drug dealer and a real-estate agent.

Joe Anson......................................................Brad Sullivan
Edward Kay....................................................Michael Mantel
Denise Winters................................................S. Epatha Merkerson
Judge Real.....................................................Malachi Throne
Brian Doxsee..................................................Tom Mardirosian
Harold Morton................................................Victor Raider-Wexler
Ingrams.........................................................James McDaniel
And: Justin Cozier (T-Ball Howard), Terrance Telfair (Dizz Wil-
liam), Merlin Santana (Roneld Griggs), Eugene Byrd
(Tonel Otten), Rhetta Hughes (Grandmother), Laurie
Heineman (Janice Kay), Regina Taylor (Evelyn [orig. Alice]
Griggs, Richard Ziman (Alex Cassini), Merwin Goldsmith
(Judge Gollub), Barbara Spiegel (Judge Doremus), Tom
Kopache (Sam Drucker), David Wolos-Fonteno (Coach
Dan Lucas), Edwina Lewis (Angela Otten), Alex Bess
(Gregory Winters), Helmar Augustus Cooper (Herb Wil-
liams), Laduane Allen (Calin), Michele Ann Wagner (Bal-
listics technician), Brian Williams (Burnham), Donna
Haley (Reporter), Michael Saposnick, James Pyduck
(Bailiffs)
Also orig. announced:
Daniel Benzali (Medical examiner), Josh Pais (Asst. M.E.),
Donna Haley (Reporter)

Director: Daniel Sackheim                    Writer: Robert Palm

**preempted March 5**

18. "The Secret Sharers" March 12, 1991  (66227)

A community rallies to cover up the details behind a teenager's shooting of a convicted drug dealer and known felon.

Chet Burton.................................................J.D. Cannon
Father Torres...........................................Paul Calderon
Judge Markham.....................................Stephen Elliott
Mrs. Rivers.................................................Miriam Colon
Anita Urbano.................................Cordelia Gonzalez
Judge Durren..............................................Diane Kagan
Alicia (orig. Maria) Rivers..............................Sully Diaz
Nicky......................................................Enrique Munoz
And: Hazel J. Medina (Nurse Rita), Stephen Mendillo (Harmon), Jack Hallett (Morton), Saoul Mamby (Luis Cartagena), Duke Stroud (Hurley), Ron Faber (Santmyer), Ray Gill (Officer Binns), Anthony Ruiz (Officer Lopez), Rafael Baez (Nunez), Adriana Sananes (Julie Reyes), Sixto Ramos (Angel), Minerva Scelza (Rosa), Hector Colicchio (Urbano), Paula Garces (Lucy [orig. Elena] Rivers), Susan Browning (Jury foreperson), Brian Williams (Asst. D.A. Dickey), Sal Trapani (Jail guard), Frank Anderson, Joseph Dobish (Bailiffs), Daniel Kenney (Forensics expert), Blas Hernandez (Herrera), Giselle Liberatore (Avila)
Also orig. announced:
Gloria Irizarry (Woman in crowd), Billy Van (Cop)

Director: E.W. Swackhamer    Writer: Robert Stuart Nathan

19. "The Serpent's Tooth" March 19, 1991 (66224)

A wealthy businessperson and his wife are gunned down in their home, apparently by their teen sons (Mailer, Hofherr).

Margaret.......................................Francis Sternhagen
Greg Jarmon.....................................Stephen Mailer
Nick Jarmon.......................................Matt Hofherr
Eli Schwab........................................Lewis Stadlen
Osinksi...................................................Olek Krupa
Anderson.....................................George Morfogen
Epstein.....................................................Lee Wilkof
Edmonds...............................................Norman Rose
Petrovich.......................................Jonathan Hadary
And: Elaine Bromka (Secretary), Bernie McInerney (Judge Michael Callahan), Don Peoples (Hecht), John Christy Ewing (Dean), Ted Sorel (Doctor), Robert Riesel (Zarovic), John Henry Kurtz (Pelletier), Mary Barbara Alexander (Ruta), Duke Stroud (Technician), Johnny Dapolito (Palone), Alberto Vasquez (Block), Anthony Alessandro (Carpetperson), Richard M. Ticktin (Judge Rosenblum), Edward D. Murphy (Foreperson)
Also orig. announced:
Richard Backus (Gill), Vasek C. Simek (Rostov), Spike Finnerty (CSU cop), Christopher Rubin (Police officer)

Director: Don Scardino
Teleplay: Rene Balger & Robert Stuart Nathan
Story: I.C. Rapoport & Joshua Stern

20. "The Troubles" March 26, 1991 (66214)

Logan faces his cultural biases when a Lebanese gun smuggler and an Irish Republican Army solider are both suspected in the killing of a drug dealer. Orig. scheduled for Jan. 22.

Announced cast includes:
O'Connell............................................Anthony Heald
McCarter.......................................Kevin J. O'Connor
Axelrod..................................................Robert Silver
Mallahan..........................................Donal Donnelly
Reilly.......................................................Alan North
Fenwick........................................Paxton Whitehead
Mrs. McDiarmid.......................................Betty Miller

And: Michael Cullen (Roberts), Ray Iannicelli (D'Amato), James Canning (Pringle), Harriet Sansom Harris (Sheila), William Severs (Judge), Paul-Felix Montez (Montez), Richard Russell Ramos (Coroner), Gy Mirano (Interpreter/Santamaria), Parvin Farhoody (Mrs. Mustafa), Brendan Burke, Walter Flanagan (Old men), Mike Alpert (Driver), John McLoughlin (Court clerk), Manny Silverio (Mustafa), Bill Nelson (Shelby), Arch Johnson (Judge O'Brien), Mike Sergio (Guard), Valentina Fratti, Spike Finnerty (Reporters), John Ring (Bartender)

Director: NA   Writer: NA

21. "Sonata for Solo Organ" April 2, 1991 (66226)

A millionaire (Weaver) goes to illegal extremes with a surgeon (Roebling) to get a kidney for his transplant-needing daughter.

Woodleigh................................................Fritz Weaver
Dr. Reberty.............................................Paul Roebling
Ellen Hale.........................................Deborah Hedwall
Rubell................................................Dominic Chianese
Patton.......................................................Bill Moor
MacDaniel...........................................Chuck Cooper
Dr. Lieber.................................................Lonny Price
Dr. Kershan.............................................Randy Graff
Judge Lenz............................................Tanya Berezin
Judge Pursley....................................Fred J. Scollay
Barsky...................................................Ralph Byers
Teresa Franz...........................................Ann Dowd
And: Kayla Black (Nurse Davis), Jennifer Van Dyck (Joanna Woodleigh), Zach Grenier (Lemish), Kevin O'Morrison (Judge Boyack), Leslie Lyles (Kern/Reberty's ex-wife), Peter McRobbie (Manager), Robert Robinson (Dr. Ames), Rose Arrick (Mrs. Birnbaum), John MacKay (Nevins), Olga Merediz (Rosaria Mendez), Brian Burke (Hospital clerk), Marcella Lowery (Nurse), Jonathan Teague Cook (Bum), Joe Pentangelo (Curran), Nick Muglia (Schull), Garreth Williams (Technician), John Santamaria (Bailiff)
Also orig. announced:
Bill Anton (Dr. Backus)

Director: Fred Gerber
Teleplay: Joe Morgenstern & Michael S. Chernuchin
Story: Joe Morgenstern & Michael Duggan

**on hiatus**

22. "The Blue Wall" Sunday, June 9, 1991  9:39-10:39 p.m. (66220)

When Cragen becomes linked to a corruption scandal, Greevey, Logan and Stone suspect he may indeed be guilty. Orig. scheduled for June 11. Odd timeslot due to a late-running sports event prior. On the West Coast, ran 8:09-9:09 p.m.

Chief of Operations Peter O'Farrell...................Robert Lansing
Dennis Shearer.................................John Christopher Jones
Kimball....................................................Gerry Bamman
Mulvehill...............................................Michael Ingram
Albert McCrory..................................William Andrews
Gowdy (orig. McElwaine)......................Gregg Almquist
Saunders.........................................Robert Hirschfeld
Judge Caffey...........................................John Newton
Congressperson William Wilson.....................Pirie MacDonald
John Ryder...........................................George Guidall
Donnelly (orig. Hillery)..........................Michael Hirsch
Bettyann Waller (orig. Wallach).....................Dolores Sutton
Cassidy.............................................Stephen Prutting
With: David Leary, Donald Billett
And: John Ramsey (Judge Dowling), Dylan Price (Sgt. Buscal-

era), Catherine Wolf (Judge Harris), Ellen Tobie (Marge Cragen, Donald's wife), Donna Haley, Keith Glover (Reporters), Anthony DeRiso (McCrory's lawyer), Michael C. Mahon, Joel Leffert (Police officers), Jerry Matz, Stephaney Lloyd (Jury forepersons), John Doman (Bailiff)
Also orig. announced:
Gary Goodrow (Patterson), Anthony DeRiso (Horton), Michael C. Mahon, Joel Leffert (Cops)

Director: Vern Gillum          Teleplay: Robert Stuart Nathan
Story: Dick Wolf & Robert Stuart Nathan

**preempted July 9**

**renewed for 1991-92; new episodes begin Sept. 17, 1991; Dzundza departs the cast**

# Lenny

CBS          Sept. 10-Oct. 3      Wednesdays, 8-8:30 p.m.
             Dec. 15-March 9      Saturdays, 8:30-9 p.m.

Series premiere: Sept. 10, 1990
Final telecast: March 9, 1991

Comedy of a blue-collar worker in Boston who moonlights as a hotel doorperson, and wryly confronts the day-to-day crises of family life.

Lenny Callahan..................................................Lenny Clarke
Shelly Callahan, his wife..................................Lee Garlington
Eddie Callahan, his brother................................Peter Dobson
Pat Callahan, his dad.....Eugene Roche a.k.a Eugene H. Roche
Mary Callahan, his mom................................Alice Drummond
Kelly (orig. Trisha) Callahan (13).........................Jenna Von Oy
Tracy Callahan (10)........................................Alexis Caldwell
Elizabeth Callahan (infant)
    (ep. 1)....................................................The Hall Twins
    (ep. 2-on)............................................The Farmer Twins

Impact Zone Productions and Witt/Thomas Productions in
    assoc. with Touchstone Television
Executive producers: Paul Junger Witt, Tony Thomas, Don
    Reo
Supervising producers: Judith D. Allison, Bill Richmond (both
    ep. 2-on)
Producers: Gilbert Junger (ep. 1-on), Rachelle Rosett Schaefer,
    David Landsberg, Josh Goldsten, Jonathan Prince (latter
    four ep. 2-on)
Associate producer (variously): Janet Grushow, Laura L.
    Garcia
Executive script consultants: William C. Kenny, Brenda
    Hampton-Cain
Music: Mike Post (ep. 1); Frank Denson
Theme: Dion & Bill Tuohy (words and lyrics); performed by
    Dion
Director unless otherwise noted: Andy Cadiff
Creator: Don Reo

————————

1. "Lenny"  Sept. 10, 1990; Thursday, Sept. 27, 1990
    11:30 p.m.-midnight

Lenny has to come up with money for his dad's operation.

Dr. Thomas......................................................Ken Kimmins
Mrs. Luby..........................................................Martha Jane

Director: Terry Hughes          Writer: Don Reo

2. "Three Men and Three Babies"  Sept. 19, 1990

When Shelly and Mary wind up in the hospital, Lenny, Eddie and Pat are left to take care of the house and the girls.

Writer: Judith D. Allison

3. "Opportunity Knocks Out"  Sept. 26, 1990

At a formal party, Lenny's hotel boss makes a pass at Shelly. Scripter and co-producer Landsberg plays the veterinarian.

Mr. Evans..........................................................Steve Vinovich
Veterinarian..................................................David Landsberg
Ms. Green........................................................Audree Chapman
And: John Drayman (Waiter), James Eakle (Man with cat)

Writer: David Landsberg

4. "The Loan Ranger"  Oct. 3, 1990

Lenny finds himself lending money to too many people.  Scripter Richmond has a cameo.

Detective Joey Gannon.......................................Kevin Scannell
Bernie Weintraub/Beverly Glenn...........David Shawn Michaels
Bartender..................J.J. Wall (James Vallely orig. announced)
And: Bill Richmond

Writer: Bill Richmond

5. "Yes, Virginity, There Is a God"  Dec. 15, 1990

On Lenny's day off, Kelly needs to discuss sex, Tracy announces her atheism, and Eddie breaks the TV set.

Father...................................................................Art Metrano
Little girl..........................................................Bonnie Morgan
Ant'ny...............................................................Chance Quinn
Mother.....................................................................Eda Zahl

Writer: Racelle Rosett Schaefer

6. "Career Day"  Dec. 22, 1990

Lenny goes to a mortified Kelly's "Career Day" at school.

Sister Mary George...............................................Anne Haney
Sister Theresa..................................................Bonnie Urseth
Dr. Anthony Scala...............................................Tony Simotes
Betty McGruder..........................................Donna Lynn Leavy
Glen Nowell.......................................................William Utay

Writers: William C. Kenny & Brenda Hampton-Cain

7. "New York Stories"  Dec. 29, 1990

Stuck in a New York blizzard after his Uncle Shamus' funeral, the Callahan men may miss Tracy's dance recital. Kassir is a cast-member of *1st & Ten*.

Clerk...................................................................Mandy Ingber
Man in airport.................................................Furley Lumpkin
Bum..................................................................John Delgado
Max...................................................................John Kassir
And: Melissa Lechner (Shanda), Rick Scarry (Priest)

Writer: Don Reo

8. "My Boyfriend's Black and There's Gonna Be Trouble"
    Jan. 5, 1991

Lenny's sister (Hoag) announces she's marrying a black lawyer (Lawrence).  Guest Jane reprises her role from ep. 1

Megan Callahan....................................................Judith Hoag
Richard Johnson.............................................Scott Lawrence
Jim Johnson........................................................Henry Harris
Sarah Johnson....................................................Ann Weldon
And: Martha Jane (Mrs. Luby), John Ingle (Priest)

Writer: Racelle Rosett Schaefer

9. "G.I. Joe" Jan. 12, 1991

Lenny's doctor conducts a series of gastriointestinal tests on him when a potentially life-threatening problem crops up.

Dr. Randall..........................................................Don Lake
Nurse....................................................................Lauren Tom

Writer: David Landsberg

**preempted Jan. 19**

10. "Lenny Get Your Gun" Jan. 26, 1991

After Pat and Mary are is burglarized, they buy a gun and expect Lenny to do the same.  Orig. scheduled for Jan. 19.

Miles Swanson (orig. Niles Brewster).................Fred Applegate

Writer: David Landsberg

11. "The Gas Man Cometh" Feb. 2, 1991

An explosion on a gas line leaves Lenny trapped 10 feet below the street with an engineer (Cho), Eddie, and one sandwich.

Nick Harimoto (orig. Watanabe)..............................Henry Cho
Charlie..................................................................Lou Bonacki

Writer: Josh Goldstein and Jonathan Prince

12. "A Fine Romance"  Feb. 9, 1991

Lenny's romantic interlude with Shelly is soured by his worry over a boxing match on which Eddie bet their vacation money.

Bobby.................................................................Fred Stollier

Writer: Bill Richmond

13. "Cold" Feb. 16, 1991  9:30-10 p.m.

When Lenny tries fixing the furnace himself, the family ends up bunking at his parents' house for heat.  Scripter Wall appeared as an actor, ep. 4.

Furnace repairperson...........................Shabaka/Barry Henley

Director: Patrick Maloney              Writer: J.J. Wall

**unscheduled preemption Feb. 23**

14. "Family Matters" March 2, 1991

The Callahans gather for a loud family dinner at Pat and Mary's house.  Dedication: "In memory of Bobby Brooks."

Agility Tortorici................................................Fabiana Udenio

Writer: Don Reo

15. "It Ain't the Heat"  March 9, 1991

Fed up with winter, Pat flies off to Florida to stay with a pal (Dana), while Mary insists on staying home.  Orig. scheduled for Feb. 23.

Charlie Gold.............................................................Bill Dana

Writer: Josh Goldstein & Jonathan Prince

<u>Unaired</u>

Kelly babysits a terror (Von Oy) who disappears during hide-and-seek, while both sets of parents bowl a grudge match.  Orig. scheduled for March 9.

Announced cast:
Mrs. Luby...........................................................Martha Jane
Larry Luby.............................................................Jack McGee
Lester "The Terror" Luby.....................................Tyler Von Oy
Waitress...........................................................Brenda Klemne
Sgt. Murphy.........................................................Ron Canada

Writer: Bill Richmond

# Life Goes On

ABC            Sundays, 7-8 p.m.

Series premiere: Sept. 24, 1989

Drama of a suburban Chicago family whose adult son (Burke) is a high-level Down syndrome sufferer.  Recurring guest Needham succeeds cast-member Monique Lanier, who left the show after last season.  Diner: Glen Brook Grill.  Becca's school: Marshall High.

Diner-owner Drew Thacher.................................Bill Smitrovich
Ad copywriter Libby Giordano Thacher.................Patti LuPone
Corky Thacher......................................................Chris Burke
Becca Thacher.....................................................Kellie Martin
Tyler Benchfield...................................................Tommy Puett
Arnold "the Semi-Wonder Dog".....Bullet (uncredited onscreen)

*Recurring:*
Paige Thacher, Drew's daughter
       (ep. 7,9-15,17-20,22)...............................Tracey Needham
Gina Giordano, Libby's sister
       (ep. 10-16,21-22)..............................Mary Page Keller
Zoe (9), her daughter (ep. 10-14,16,21-22)........Leigh Ann Orsi
Hans the cook (ep. 1,7-9,11,13,15,19)....................David Byrd
Maxie (ep. 1-2,4,6,8,10,15-16,18,22)...............Tanya Fenmore
Ad agency head Jerry Berkson
       (ep. 4-7,10,13,18,21).............................Ray Buktenica
Doreen (ep. 8,11,13,15,18)...............................Elyssa Davalos
Paul (ep. 7,11,18-20)..............................................Steve Jerro •
Brian Russo (ep. 8,18,21)......................................Eric Welch
Eddie (ep. 9,11,13,18,19)........................................John Welsh
Matt (ep. 13,15-16)..................................................Adam Carl

• Character identified only as "Customer," ep. 8.

Toots Productions in assoc. with Warner Bros. Television
Executive producer: Michael Braverman
Co-executive producer: Rick Rosenthal
Producers: Phillips Wylly, Sr., Michael Nankin, Jule Selbo
       (latter early in season)
Co-producer: William O. Cairncross
Supervising producer: Liz Coe
Associate producer: Lorenzo DeStefano

Creative consultant: David Wolf
Executive story editor: Brad Markowitz
Director of photography: Joe Pennella
Arnold's trainer: Richard Calkins
Music: William Olvis
Theme: "Ob-La-Di, Ob-La-Da" by John Lennon & Paul
     McCartney, written for the Beatles' 1968 album *The Bea-
     tles* a.k.a. "The White Album"; performed by the
     series cast; end-theme by Craig Safan
Creator: Michael Braverman

---

1. "Honeymoon from Hell" Sept. 16, 1990

The Thachers win a problem-plagued, church-raffle trip to
Hawaii. Guest Ho is a singer; announced guest Rosenthal is
the series' co-executive producer. Filmed in Hawaii. Part 1 of 2.

Father McMichaels..............................Patrick Thomas O'Brian
Ticket-taker................................................Ray Bumatai
Earl.........................................................Denis Arndt
Mr. Leighton..............................................Oliver Clark
Mrs. Kneffer.............................................Gloria Gifford
Himself.........................................................Don Ho
Mrs. Schiller................................................Lisa Zebro
          Also orig. announced: Rick Rosenthal (Uncle Richard)

Director: Rick Rosenthal          Writer: Michael Braverman

2. "Corky and the Dolphins" Sept. 23, 1990

On vacation, Corky goes dolphin-riding and Becca falls for a
surfer (Cain). Filmed in Hawaii. Part 2 of 2.

Earl..........................................................Denis Arndt
Kimo..........................................................Dean Cain
Elaine Oslot..............................................Janet Carroll
Wayne Oslot...............................................Robert Pine
Joleen.................................................Elizabeth Lindsey
Stevie.................................................Evan Murakami
Emcee................................................Moku Young, Jr.

Director: Rick Rosenthal          Writer: Jule Selbo

3. "The Visitor" Sept. 30, 1990

Libby discovers she's expecting again, and the the family fears
the consequences of a pregnancy at her age.

Boy..................................................Bradley Michael Pierce
Mr. Leighton..............................................Oliver Clark
Shelley...............................................Stephanie Dicker
Dr. Tabouri.............................................Lynn Milgrim
Milo.................................................J.G. Buzanowski
Radiologist..............................................Gregory White
Pigtails..................................................Kara Dennis
Japanese girl.........................................Nasslynne Mama-o
And: Kevin Mockrin (Kid), Jake Price (Loudmouth)

Writer-director: Michael Nankin

4. "Becca and the Band" Oct. 7, 1990

Becca becomes manager of Tyler's band; Libby contemplates
returning to work at the ad agency.

Shelley...............................................Stephanie Dicker
Rona.................................................Michelle Matheson
Frank Zifkin...........................................Jeff Silverman
Jim..................................................G. Adam Gifford

Director: Kim Friedman             Writer: Susan Wald

5. "The Banquet Room Renovation" Oct. 14, 1990

Corky's jealous of his dad's friendship with a boy (Leitch) helping add a room to the diner; Libby gets a dog-food account.

Everett Nichols..........................................George Furth
Farmer Jack...............................................Paul Koslo
Teddy.................................................Donovan Leitch
Lucy..................................................Susan Merson
Mrs. Fitzwater.........................................Paddi Edwards
Plumber/Pete........................................Charles Champion
And: Gary Grossman (Director), Gary McGurk (Patron), Andi
     Matheny (Owner), Tiny Ron (Tall man)

Director: E.W. Swackhamer          Writer: Wesley Bishop

**preempted Oct. 21**

6. "Halloween" Oct. 28, 1990

Corky doesn't want to remove his mask and reveal his Down
syndrome to a girl (Lawrence) he meets at a Halloween party.

Molly................................................Lisa Lawrence
Teacher/Mr. Schirmer...................................Danny Goldman
D.J...................................................Jon Melichar
Bartender..............................................Aaron Seville
Witch.................................................Bonnie Morgan
Partygoers................Dennis Nishi, Ben Pfeiffer, Masami Saito
Desk clerk..............................................James Schendel
And: Adam Wylie (Trick or treater), Stephanie Block (Sarah)

Director: Kim Friedman             Writer: Liz Coe

7. "Chicken Pox" Nov. 4, 1990

The kids and Drew contract chicken pox, putting stress on
Libby, who becomes bedridden on doctor's orders; eldest
daughter Paige (Needham, debuting in her recurring role) visits with the news her beau, Oliver, is marrying someone else.

Finicky man..............................................Robert Arthur
Pregnant woman.........................................Melora Marshall
And: Howard Mungo (Repairperson), Debra Sullivan (Nurse)

Director: Chuck (a.k.a. Charles) Braverman
Writer: David M. Wolf

8. "La Dolce Becca" Nov. 11, 1990

Becca becomes fascinated with a group of students who use
alcohol and drugs; Drew saves a woman choking in his diner.

Ms. Stricker..............................................Anna Berger
Selena.................................................Elizabeth Berkley
Marina Maxwell...........................................Julie Cobb
Midori.................................................Terri Ivens
Dylan.................................................Joshua Lucas
And: Nick De Mauro (Ricco), Freeman King (Jamal), Barry Lee
     (Michael Hauser), Jordan Ligget (Pin), Susan Varon (Pin-
     gatore), Claudia Bloom (Woman)

Director: Miles Watkins            Writer: Star Frohman

9. "A Thacher Thanksgiving" Nov. 18, 1990

Corky dreams his family is at the first Thanksgiving celebration, in 1621; Drew meets a homeless former classmate. Ruscio and Santon reprise their recurring roles from last season.

Bea..................................................................Diane Bellamy
Benjy................................................................John Calvin
John..................................................................Robert Costanzo
Samoset.............................................................Sam Vlahos
Lucy.................................................................Susan Merson
Sal Giordano, Libby and Gina's father.......................Al Ruscio
Teresa Giordano, Libby and Gina's mother.........Penny Santon
And: Dan Desmond (Hanson), Tony Salome (Larry), Joe Starka (Wiry guy), Parker Whitman (Father)

Director: Charles (a.k.a. Chuck) Braverman
Writers: Michael Nankin & Michael Braverman

10. "Libby's Sister" Nov. 25, 1990

Libby's free-spirited sister and her daughter visit, and stay to help after Libby is ordered to remain bedridden through her pregnancy. Keller and Orsi debut in their recurring roles; Milgrim reprises her role from ep. 3.

Young Becca.......................................................Heather Lind
Dr. Tabouri........................................................Lynn Milgrim

Director: Rick Rosenthal                          Writer: Liz Coe

**preempted Dec. 2**

11. "The Buddy" Dec. 9, 1990

A former buddy (Blankfield) advises Drew on how to make a quick buck; Becca has difficulty sharing a room with Zoe.

Roy Hergenroeder..................................................Nick Angotti
John Khatchadorian...........................................Alan Blumenfeld
Paintz Kutner....................................................Peter Van Norden
Charlie.............................................................Mark Blankfield
Harper.............................................................Julian Dyer
And: Rhomeyn Johnson (Delivery person), Ken Kliban (Sereda), Hamilton Mitchell (Reporter), Don Stewart (Dalrymple), Carlease Burke (Diner regular), Oscar Dillon (Football player), Tony Pandolfo (Customer), Michael A. Williams (Poker player)

Director: Roy Campanella II                      Writer: Brad Markowitz

12. "The Bicycle Thief" Dec. 16, 1990

Corky is determined to compete in a 50-kilometer bicycle race.

Brian................................................................Anthony Addabbo
Police officers....................................................Peter Iacangelo
Mark.................................................................Dylan Kussman
Ted Wilson........................................................Will Jeffries
Official.............................................................Robert Rothwell
      Also orig. announced:
      David Byrd (Hans), Ken Kliban (Sereda)

Director: Mel Damski                               Writer: David M. Wolf

13. "Isn't It Romantic?" Jan. 6, 1990

Cupid literally visits Becca and classmate Matt (new recurring guest Carl); Paige and her biker-beau Kent; Gina and Jerry; and Hans the cook. Bellamy reprises her role from ep. 9.

Bea..................................................................Diane Bellamy
Kent.................................................................Craig Hurley
Rona................................................................Michele Matheson
Mr. Seedling.....................................................Michael Alldredge
Gordon.............................................................Frank Miller
Businessperson..................................................Wilfred Lavoie

Deliverypersons..................Ken Thorley, Katherine Armstrong
Cupid...............................................................John Wolford
And: Grant Gelt (Aaron), Tiffany Sue Muxlow (Mary Margaret), Lou Briseno (Violinist)

Director: Michael Lange                           Writer: Michael Nankin

14. "The Bigger Picture" Jan. 13, 1990

Corky has a hard time accepting that his teacher (Chapman) plans to move on; Gina fights with her folks (Ruscio, Santon, reprising their roles from ep. 9).

Mrs. Kneffer......................................................Gloria Gifford
Sal Giordano......................................................Al Ruscio
Teresa Giordano..................................................Penny Santon
Amanda.............................................................Andi Chapman
Dasarian...........................................................Christopher Carroll
George Washington..............................................Pierre La John
Angel...............................................................David Lupash
Sharon Gallaway.................................................Nancy Stephens
Lisa Gallaway.....................................................Karen Rauch
And: Tai Thai (Ven), Christi Allen (Gum chomper), Robin Buck (Singing waiter), David Bursin (Hallway teacher)

Director: Jerry Jameson                           Writer: Star Frohman

**preempted Jan. 20 and Jan. 27**

15. "Last Stand in Glen Brook" Feb. 3, 1991

Becca stages a free-speech rally supporting a store record-owner (Jones, a real-life record producer) arrested for selling allegedly obscene music. Alldredge and Hurley reprise their roles from ep. 13.

Dan Webster.......................................................Quincy Jones
Mr. Seedling......................................................Michael Alldredge
Cousin Angela.....................................................Gina Hecht
Kent.................................................................Craig Hurley
Harried woman....................................................Judy Kain
Roxy................................................................Lara Lyon
Wally...............................................................Robert Machray
And: Brandi Chrisman (Girl), Michael Ciotti (Boy), George Ede (Tweedy man), Dawn Landon (Teen), Matt McKenzie (Cop), John T. Olsen (Meek man), Jimmy Staszkiel (Man), Neil Vipond (Waiter), Jerry Winsett (Customer)

Director: Larry Shaw                              Writer: Marti M. Noxon

16. "Head Over Heels" Feb. 10, 1991

Becca falls for her gym teacher (Hubley); Gina decides to leave when Drew objects to her dating a younger man (St. Gerard).

Coach Eric Bradford.............................................Whip Hubley
Jed Chandler......................................................Michael St. Gerard
Miss Watkins......................................................Anne Gee Byrd
Alison O'Malley..................................................Julie Ann Gourson
Photographer......................................................Andrew Tarr

Director: Dick Rogers                             Writer: Liz Coe

**preempted Feb. 17; unscheduled preemption Feb. 24**

17. "Corky's Travels" March 10, 1991

Corky takes his first solo bus trip into Chicago, to meet Paige, but when her car breaks down on the way, he's left stranded and finds himself guided by a mystical spirit (Redbone, a blues and folk musician). Orig. scheduled for Feb. 24.

22. "Proms and Prams" May 5, 1991

Libby reflects on how life might have been with her former love (Murphy); Becca goes to the prom; Libby gives birth to a boy.

Jordan Parnell..............................................Ben Murphy
Dr. Ettinger..............................................Jonathan Prince
And: John Apicella, Zack Phifernd (Men), Vali Ashton (Singer), Montrose Hagins (Nurse), Annie Korzen (Woman)

"More Than You Know" sung by: Patti LuPone

Director: Kim Friedman              Writer: Liz Coe

**preempted May 12 and May 19**

**preempted June 9**

**renewed for 1991-92; new episodes begin Sept. 22, 1991**

## LifeStories

NBC        Aug. 20-Dec. 2    Sundays, 8-9 p.m.
           Dec. 18           Tuesday, 10-11 p.m.

Series Premiere: Aug. 20, 1990
Final telecast: July 14, 1991

Medical anthology series, hosted/narrated by a symbolic "Storyteller" (Robert Prosky). Aside from regular series consultants Steiner and Blaney, each episode has (an) additional medical consultant(s). Blaney appears as a bit player, virtually all episodes. Title is as appears onscreen. Working titles: *Life and Death, Signs of Life.* After the Dec. 2 episode, six more were orig. scheduled to run as a series of specials.

Ohlmeyer Communications and Jeffrey Lewis Productions in assoc. with Orion Television
Executive producers: Jeff Bleckner (ep. 2-on), Jeffrey Lewis, Don Ohlmeyer
Supervising producer: Linda Jonsson (ep. 1); Jacob Epstein, Christian Williams
Producers: Lee Miller (ep. 1); Ken Solarz, Paul Rabwin, Nick Anderson (all ep. 2-on), Marjorie David (added later)
Director of photography: Paul Onorato, A.C.S. (ep. 1); Judy Irola
Series medical advisor: Jerrold H. Steiner, M.D., F.A.C.S.
Series technical consultant: Donna Blaney, B.S.R.N.
Music: Brad Fiedel (ep. 1); Dennis McCarthy
Theme (instrumental with voiceover by narrator Prosky): Brad Fiedel
Creator: Jeffrey Lewis

————————————

1. (Pilot) Aug. 20, 1990 10-11 p.m.; Thursday, Sept. 27. 1990 11:30 p.m.-12:30 a.m.

A family man develops colon cancer.

Don Chapin..............................................Richard Masur
Mrs. Chapin..............................................Lisa Banes
Their son..............................................Kieran Mulroney
Their daughter..............................................Christine Healy
Dr. Bronstein..............................................George Wyner
Dr. Koosman..............................................Will Nye
Eileen Chapin..............................................Angela Paton
Stanley..............................................Frank Hamilton
Harold..............................................Abdul Salaam El Razzac
Dr. Friendly..............................................Rob Miller

Leon Turner..............................................Leon Redbone
Pug..............................................Edward Carnevale
Perry..............................................Bernie Coulson
And: Robin Tunney (Mary), Sip Culler (Wino), Troy Frumin (Gang member), Jerome Front (Usher)

Songs: Mark Mueller (words) and Craig Safan (music)

Director: Rick Rosenthal              Writer: David M. Wolf

18. "Thanks a Bunch, Dr. Lamaze" March 17, 1991

Drew has personality changes as he awaits the new baby; an article by Becca gets Tyler dropped from the basketball team. Orig. scheduled for March 10.

Ms. Roberts..............................................Georgann Johnson
Paintz Kutner..............................................Peter Van Norden
Mr. Simon..............................................Bradford English
Fig..............................................Leeza Vinnichenko
And: Patricia Ayame Thomson (Mon), James Boyce (Dad), Jan Devereaux (Woman at shower), Marc Marosi (Orderly)

Director: Michael Lange              Writer: Brad Markowitz

**preempted March 24**

19. "Ghost of Grandpa Past" March 31, 1991

Drew, anxious about the pending sale of his diner, gets advice from the ghost of his restaurateur grandfather (Remsen). Hecht reprises her role from ep. 15; Balsam is the daughter of performers Martin Balsam and Joyce Van Patten.

Cousin Angela..............................................Gina Hecht
Melanie Karlsen..............................................Talia Balsam
Gramps..............................................Bert Remsen
Paramedic..............................................James Edgcomb
Serviceperson..............................................Johnny Lage

Director: Kim Friedman              Writer: Michael Braverman

20. "Arthur" April 7, 1991

Corky befriends a Down syndrome man (McFarlane, a Canadian actor with Down syndrome, who had worked with series creator Braverman on *Quincy*, which Braverman co-produced).

Lester..............................................Ryan Bollman
Mrs. Schiller..............................................Lisa Zebro
Eleanor..............................................Frances Bay
Arthur..............................................David McFarlane
Nathan..............................................Walter Olkewicz
And: Annabelle Weenick (Receptionist), Greg Alper (Adam), Andrew William Chamberlain (Steve), Bruce Prescott (Bob)

Writer-director: Michael Nankin

21. "Lighter Than Air" April 28, 1991

Libby seeks a better position at the ad agency; Corky and Zoe play detective to find out who Tyler is dating besides Becca.

Shanna..............................................Ana-Alicia
Ron..............................................Tom O'Rourke
Miller..............................................Alfred Dennis
Sonia..............................................Christine Kendrick
Dream dance partner..............................................James P. Hogan
Dancer..............................................Caitlin McLean

Director: Michael Braverman          Writer: Dick Lochie

Dr. Weld............................................................Kelly Connell
Malkovich...............................................William Frankfather
Andriotti.......................................................Joe d'Angerio
And: Emily Kuroda (Room nurse), Lance Crouther, Harry Frazier, Arnold Johnson, Drasha Meyer (Homeless people), Michael Chieffo (Minister), Scott Williams (Reporter), Jennifer Hughes, Michael Lundberg, Joelle Jacobi (Kids), Jay Ingram, Wynn Reichert (Golfers), Brian Joseph Moore (Street person), Jerrold Steiner, M.D. (Anesthesiologist), Peter Kwon, M.D. (Assistant surgeon), Mary J. Split, R.N. (Circulating nurse)

Director: John Patterson        Writer: Jeffrey Lewis

2. "Rebecca McManus and Steve Arnold"  Sept. 30, 1990

A childless, fortyish couple try in-vitro fertilization. Crouse is the wife of playwright David Mamet.

Rebecca McManus...........................................Lindsay Crouse
Steve Arnold...................................................Dwight Schultz
Dr. Dolores Washington..........................................Jane Daly
Dr. Cohen...............................................Robert Schenkkan
Hillary..............................................................Susan Krebs
Edna............................................................Suzanne Dunn
Erika.............................................................Emily Kuroda
Joe...................................................................Rob Narita
Sue..........................................................Evelyn Guerrero
Maria.....................................................Judy Jean Berns
And: Gerald Burns (Dr. Houseman), Michelle Davison (Jane), Darwyn Carson (Dr. Blair), Denis Latella (Nurse), Kathryn Graf (Hostess), Anita Ortega (Receptionist), Claudia Larson (Ultrasound doctor), Alexandra Cooper (Kid), Jacqueline Asfall (Ultrasound nurse)

Director: Jeff Bleckner        Writer: Marjorie David

3. "Frank Brody"  Oct. 7, 1990  8:43-9:43 p.m.

Real-time depiction of the first 47 minutes of a man's heart attack. Late start due to a long-running sports event prior.

Frank Brody...................................................Michael Murphy
Mrs. Brody......................................................Susan Blakely
Mr. Haden...........................................................Al Ruscio
Enrique........................................................Raymond Cruz
Dr. Duran....................................................Wanda De Jesus
Ed Nielson......................................................Casey Sander
Dr. Protech...........................................Richard Minchenberg
Gross.............................................................Nigel Gibbs
Yamato....................................................Rodney Kageyama
Nurse Short...................................................Charles Walker
And: Norma Donaldson (Michelle), Gloria Dorson (Margaret), Chuck Walling (Bill), Gina Ravarra (Triage Nurse), Ken Smolka (Sgt. Holloway), James Tartan (Peter), Bill Shick (Technician), Tina Chappel (Nurse Spivak), Bethany Richards (Rebecca), T.J. Hynd (Bobby), Christopher Pettiet (Jason), Huck Liggett (Medic)

Director: Jeff Bleckner        Writer: Christian Williams

4. "Beverly Whitestone, Dan Drabowski, Sadie Maxwell, Lois Barnes"  Oct. 14, 1990

Four case studies in plastic surgery.

Beverly Whitestone.......................................Natalija Nogulich
Dan Drabowski.................................................Robert Pine
Sadie Maxwell.................................................Debra Sandlund
Lois Barnes.....................................................Micole Mecurio
Tommy........................................................Carl Weintraub

Dr. Elaine Holmes (erroneously listed as "Ellen" in end-credits)..................................Joan Welles
With: Cynthia Bain
And: Harrison Page (Gus), James O'Connell (Earl), Jennifer Rhodes (Jeanine), Alan Haufrect (Dr. Walter Paley), James Ingersoll (Dr. Robert Fischer), Mik Scriba (Bartender), Richard Fullerton (Nail gun), Diane Charles (Amy), Trish Garland (Brenda), Terry McQueen (Annie), Peter Stelzer (Bev's husband), Roger Hampton (Andy), Terri Semper (Technician), Robin Skye (Priscilla), Karen Barcus (Aide), Cris Capen (Carmine), Jamies Openden, Vanessa deVeritch, Jamie Lynn Grenham (Girls), Serena Viharo (Lois at 15), Mike Jerrick (Newscaster)

Director: Jefferson Kibbee        Writer: Kat Smith

**preempted Oct. 21**

5. "Jerry Forchette"  Nov. 4, 1990  (1004)

A small-time gambler and wheeler-dealer uses the fact of his terminal brain tumor to try to scheme one last good deed.

Announced cast includes:
Jerry Forchette...............................................Louis Giambalvo
Julio...................................................Giancarlo Esposito
Helen Forchette.................................................Jennifer Salt
Jane....................................................................Lisa Kudrow
Earl.......................................................................Al Fann
Mr. Pearl.......................................................Thomas Ryan
Nancy Grimes...................................................Kate Zentall
Gardner Epps...................................................Milt Tarver
Dr. Labiner...................................................Mark L. Taylor
Dr. Glussman...................................................Richard Fancy
Boss.........................................................H. Cannon Lopez

Director: Bruce Seth Green        Writer: Jacob Epstein

6. "Art Conforti"  Nov. 11, 1990  (1003)

A high-school teacher (Tucci) and his wife (Carter) confront her alcoholism through a tough "family dynamic intervention."

Art Conforti.....................................................Stanley Tucci
Sally Conforti....................................................Finn Carter
Josh Gidding..............................................Stephen Tobolowsky
Jennifer Conforti (10)......................................Vicki Wauchope
Dr. Ronald Lewinski.......................................Michael Laskin
June Weinberg.....................................................Kitty Swink
Allen Pressman............................................Matthew Faison
Luke Conforti.....................................................Shawn Levy
Russ Buzby..............................................Michael Pniewski
Averill Weissman..............................................William Utay
Judge Verschbow (orig. Flores)............................Donald Hotton
And: James F. Dean, Michele Harrell, Maura Soden (Teachers), Robert Ruth (Bartender), Pamela Roberts (Foster), Nicholas Shaffer (Tweedy), Glenn Morshower (Desk cop), Barry Wiggins (Cop), Timothy Davis Reed (Waiter)

Director: Don Ohlmeyer        Writer: Ken Solarz

7. "The Hawkings Family"  Dec. 2, 1990  (1010)

The parents of a child (Lawrence) needing a bone-marrow donor search for a son they gave up for adoption 15 years before.

Bill Hawkings....................................................Chris Cooper
Maggie Hawkings...........................................Wendy Phillips
Chris Hawkings...........................................Matthew Lawrence
Ray Albertson...............................................Nicholas Pryor
Ann Albertson....................................................Joanna Miles

Dr. Chandler..........................................................Margot Rose
Paul Albertson.......................................................Nicholas Katt
Sister Marie................................................................Linda Hoy
Dr. Goldman........................................................Terry Boseman
And: Marilyn Rockafellow (Dr. Grosshaus), Suanne Spoke
      (Patty), Gene Wolande (Marv), John Thomas Turk (Class
      president), Jack Cleland (Jake), Kim Murdock (Reception-
      ist), Jan Hoag, Cynthia Dale Scott, Gwynne Rhynedance
      (Cheerleaders), Jonathan Fong (Tommy), Heather Olson
      (Alex), Doug Kerzner (Parking attendant)

Director: Charles Siebert          Writer: Mark St. Germain

8. "Steve Burdick" Tuesday, Dec. 18, 1990 10-11 p.m. (1002)

A TV news anchor (Moffett) goes public with the news he has
tested positive for the HIV virus. Guest Rutledge is a real-life
co-anchor of KCOP/Los Angeles.

Steve Burdick.......................................................D.W. Moffett
Barbara Hudson........................................................Joyce Hyser
Laverne Williamson............................................Juanita Jennings
Lisa Harkin (orig. Gonzales)..............................Wendy Rutledge
With: Wayne Tippit, Mitchell Laurance, Kirk Baily, Jon May-
      nard Pennell, Ryan MacDonald
And: Peter Schuck (Giordano), Camille Ameen (Susan White),
      H. Stephen Day (Nelson Everette), Scott Segall (Matthew),
      Paul Ivy (Thomas), Frantz Turner (Technical director), Ed
      Crick (Floor director), Faith Quabius (Nancy), Nora Mas-
      terson (Receptionist), Michael Leopard, Gene Gutierrez
      (Camerapersons)

Director: Aaron Lipstadt          Writer: Richard Gollance

9. "Darryl Tevis" July 14, 1991

A high-school basketball star (Barnes) suffers a mild stroke,
yet riskily continues to pursue a college athletic scholarship.

Roxanne Tevis, Darryl's mother..........................CCH Pounder
K.C....................................................................Tim Russ
Darryl Tevis.........................................................Don Barnes
Coach Staggerhorn................................J. Kenneth Campbell
Dr. Loudon.....................................................Nancy Youngblut
With: Leslie Morris, Ron Orbach, Mark Lowenthal
And: Julialian Gamble (Athletic director), Herb Mitchell (Princi-
      pal), Granville Aames (Dr. Krauss), Joe Howard (Dr.
      Abrams), Richard Hoyt-Miller (E.R. doctor), Tommy Mor-
      gan (Edwin), Nigel Gibbs (Nichols), Montrose Hagins
      (Grandmother), Carol Ann Jeffers (Toni), Glen Walker
      (Reporter), Abdul Salaam El Razzac (Lloyd), Mary Garrip-
      oli (Nurse Kitty), Angela Moya (Physical therapist), Russ
      Bolinger (Recruiter), Karen Constantine (Nurse), Martin
      Davis (Rapper), Joseph Romeo (Teacher), Michael E.
      Lekawa (Assistant surgeon), Holly Brothers (Surgical
      nurse), James W. Futrell Jr. (Anesthesiologist), Jerrold
      Steiner (Doctor), Philip R. Hidey (Paramedic)

Director: Jesus Trevino          Writer: Ken Solarz

## Love & Curses

Quasi-syndicated*   One-hour

* Initially, only on the MCA-owned stations KCOP/Los Angeles and WWOR/New York City. In New York, primetime
  airings were Mondays, 8-9 p.m.

New York City premiere: March 4, 1991
Final New York City telecast: April 8, 1991

Lighthearted fantasy-drama of a reluctant female lycanthrope
living with her British parapsychologist boyfriend in Southern
California while they investigate possible cures for her periodic
transformations into a wolf-being. Retitled, reformatted version of She-Wolf of London (see that entry).

Randi Wallace.....................................................Kate Hodge
Prof. Ian Matheson...........................................Neil Dickson

*Recurring:*
Producer Skip Seville (ep. 1-2,4-6).......................Dan Gilvezan

Finnegan-Pinchuk, MTE, Hollywood Premiere Network in
      assoc. with HTV International
Executive producers: Sheldon Pinchuk, Pat Finnegan, Bill
      Finnegan
Producer: Chuck Murray
Supervising producers: Tom McLoughlin, Lee Goldberg,
      William Rabkin
Executive consultant: Mick Garris
Director of photography (variously): Brian Morgan; Howard
      Block
Theme (instrumental) and music: Steve Levine
Creators: Mick Garris & Tom McLoughlin

———————————

SW 0715. "Curiosity Killed the Cravitz" March 4, 1991

When Randi's California friend (Dunbar) is killed by a troll in
league with aliens, Ian and Randi go the U.S. to investigate,
and decide to stay when Ian becomes host of his own talk
show about the supernatural, *How Strange*, on station KBLA.

Julian Matheson, Ian's teenaged nephew.................Scott Fults
Mum Matheson...................................................Jean Challis
Dad Matheson.........................................................Arthur Cox
Aunt Elsa.......................................................Dorothea Phillips
Harvey the Troll....................................................Paul Williams
Cathy Brady.........................................................Eileen Seeley
Ellen Cravitz..................................................Mary-Ellen Dunbar
Randi as she-wolf............................................Diane Youdale
And: Milton Selzer, David Alan Brooks

Director: Brian Grant
Writers: William Rabkin & Lee Goldberg

SW 0716. "Habeas Corpses" March 11, 1991

Searching for a female vampire (Kerns) who may have killed
her own husband, Randi and Ian infiltrate a law firm.

Alan Decker........................................................Barry Van Dyke
Nancy Chambers...................................................Marta DuBois
And: Sandra Kerns, Robert Dorfman, David Sage, Lela Ivey,
      Robert Roitblatt

Director: Chuck Bowman
Writers: William Rabkin & Lee Goldberg

SW 0717. "Bride of the Wolfman" March 18, 1991

Randi and Ian, investigating strange goings-on at a movie
theater, mystically become part of an old horror film.

Dr. Pretorius......................................................Tony Amendola
Elizabeth..............................................................Gayle Cohen
Oscar......................................................................Joe Bova
George.............................................................Howard George
Boris..................................................................Tracey Walter
And: Roy Abramsohn, Michael Berryman

Director: Bruce Seth Green          Writer: Kate Boutilier

SW 0718. "Heart Attack" March 25, 1991

The duo confronts a legion of crazed cupids wielding cross-bows that fire homicide-inducing rays into people in love.

Head female cupid.......................................Kim Morgan Greene
And: Todd Susman, Denise Miller, Robert Torti, Ben Slack, Leah Lail, Thomas Bridgett, Sherry Williams, Burke Reynolds

Director: Chuck Bowman
Writers: William Rabkin & Lee Goldberg

SW 0719. "Mystical Pizza" April 1, 1991

Randi goes undercover at the Three Gals from Salem pizza shop after people start turning into animals upon eating there.

With: Kim Lankford, Lynn Llewelyn, Brenda Varda, Heather Haase, Matt E. Levin, Kim Newberry, R.C. Everbeck, Dan Sachoff

Director: Bruce Seth Green
Writers: William Rabkin & Lee Goldberg

SW 0720. "Eclipse" April 8, 1991

A lunar eclipse affects Randi's curse, leading her to try find help at an institute for the "supernaturally gifted."

Dr. Alana Horton...........................................Barbara Tarbuck
Agent Thompson......................................Jan Munroe
Dirk..........................................................Gregg Berger
And: Merle Kennedy

Director: Gary Walkow
Writers: Richard Manning & Hans Beimler

## MacGyver

ABC           Mondays, 8-9 p.m.

Series premiere: Sept. 29, 1985

Lighthearted adventure-drama of an ingeniously resourceful do-gooder (with no revealed first name) traveling the globe for the Phoenix Foundation, accompanied by its Director of Field Operations. MacGyver's family nickname: "Bud" (see ep. 7, below). Co-star Elcar's real-life glaucoma and surgery were incorporated as a running storyline for his character. Story editor Considine is better known as an actor, and appeared as such in ep. 16. Filmed in Vancouver, British Columbia.

MacGyver..........................................Richard Dean Anderson
Pete Thornton........................................................Dana Elcar

Henry Winkler/John Rich Productions in assoc. with Paramount Television
Executive producers: Henry Winkler, John Rich, Stephen Downing
Supervising producer: Michael Greenburg
Co-producer: John B. Moranville
Line producer: Robert Frederick
Associate producer: Thomas R. Polizzi
Executive story editor: John Sheppard
Story editor: Lincoln Kibbee (early in season); John Considine, Art Washington (both later in season)
Creative consultant: Rick Mittleman

Director of photography (variously): Tony Westman, Rob McLachlan
Music (variously): Ken Harrison; William Ross; Dennis McCarthy (latter on flashback episode, ep. 21)
Theme (instrumental): Randy Edelman
Creator: Lee David Zlotoff

———————————

1. "Tough Boys" Sept. 17, 1990   (106)

MacGyver and a new Challenge Center instructor (Roundtree) team to stop a druglord's retaliation against a vigilante gang.

Rutherford (R.T.) Hines...............................Richard Roundtree
Manny Lopez..................................................Richard Chaves
Coco Hubbard....................................................Garvin Funches
Angel Rojas.............................................................Jason Scott
Sinclair Dokes.................................................Danny Wattley
Hector Gonzales.....................................................Gabe Khouth
Leland Dennis.......................................................Dale Wilson
And: Don Thompson (Myron), Gerry Bean (Harris)

Director: Michael Vejar          Writer: Art Washington

2. "Humanity" Sept. 24, 1990   (105)

In Bucharest, Romania, MacGyver and Pete are among a delegation assessing the archives of deposed dictator Ceausescu.

Victor...................................................................Brooks Gardner
Cuzo......................................................................Larry D. Mann
Krik............................................................................Alan Scarfe
K-Man..............................................................Andrew Kavadas
French delegates..........................Serge Houde, Liduin Currell
English delegate...........................................Maureen Sheridan
Young Victor...................................................Jonathan Sedman
Young Nicholae.............................................Jonathan Pedlow
Police officer.........................................................George Josef

Director: William Gereghty          Writer: Lincoln Kibbee

3. "The Gun" Oct. 1, 1990   (107)

MacGyver traces a weapon's history when a Challenge Center member (Payne) is implicated in the fatal shooting of a cop.

Breeze.................................................Charles Andrew Payne
Todd Fowler.......................................................Zachary Ansley
Laura Fowler.........................................................Julie Downing
J.D. Maddox.......................................................Jerry Wasserman
Raschid Zamora........................................................Jay Brazeau
Wyatt.....................................................................Dan Muldoon
Evers........................................................................Anthony Ulc
Sgt. Crawley.....................................................Peter Blackwood
Dr. Fisher.................................................................Alec Burden
Bernie Green.............................................................Terry King
Chief Cooke.......................................................Campbell Lane
And: Troy Christopher Mallory (Rudy Gibbs) Vincent Gale (Dyke Lyman), Paul McLean (Guard), Vanessa Okuma (Club member), Jim Szekeres, Paul Bittante (Cops)

Director: William Gereghty          Writer: Robert Sherman

4. "Twenty Questions" Oct. 8, 1990

MacGyver's teenaged friend (Bialik) has developed a drinking problem and become the dupe of an upscale burglary ring.

Lisa......................................................................Mayim Bialik
Eric Woodman...................................................Joseph Lambie

Katherine Woodman...............................................Patrie Allen
Brett Reynolds.......................................................Linden Ashby
Holly....................................................................Kimberly Defrees
Jonathan..............................................................Cavan Cunningham
Adam...................................................................Allan Grant
And: Jackson Davies (Kiley), Robin Mossley (Wilt Bozer), Claire
    Brown (Betty), Dawn Stofer-Rupp (Maid)

Director: Michael Caffey            Writer: Rick Mittleman

5. "The Wall"  Oct. 22, 1990

An elderly toy-shop owner (Selzer) and his granddaughter
(Stenburg) are imperiled by former East German secret police.

Otto Romburg......................................................Milton Selzer
Maria Romburg....................................................Brigitta Stenburg
Weise..................................................................Reiner Schoene
Kurt....................................................................Oliver Becker
Huber..................................................................John Horn
Lt. Kiley..............................................................Jackson Davies
Eric Romburg.......................................................Vince Deadrick, Jr.
And: Bruce Harwood (Willis), Johanna Stange (Young Maria)

Director: Michael Preece            Writer: Rick Drew

6. "Lesson in Evil"  Oct. 29, 1990

An old MacGyver nemesis (Sheppard, reprising his previous-
season role) plots to kill the police officer (Zimmer) who arrested him and the therapist (Moody) who pronounced him cured.

Dr. Marion Skinner...............................................Lynne Moody
Lt. Kate Murphy....................................................Kim Zimmer
Dr. Zito...............................................................W. Morgan Sheppard
Judge Ruth O'Dell................................................Karen Elizabeth Austin
D.A. Howard.........................................................Michael Rogers
Zito's lawyer.........................................................Ken Kramer
Charles................................................................Alvin Sanders
Orderly................................................................Douglas Stewart
Paramedic............................................................William MacDonald
Security chief........................................................Paul Stafford
Legal secretary......................................................Andrea Brown
Kids.....................................................John Kirkconnell, Tony Ail
        Also orig. announced: Jackson Davies (Capt. Mike Kiley)

Director: William Gereghty         Writer: John Sheppard

7. "Harry's Will"  Nov. 5, 1990

MacGyver encounters eccentric characters out to find a supposed treasure related to his grandfather's will. Guest Winkler
is one of the series' executive producers; Alzado and Butkus,
former pro football players; and Williams, a rock singer. John
Anderson reprises his role from a previous season. Note:
Though his grandfather's codicil twice refers to MacGyver as
"Bud," as does a flashback, this apparently is a nickname and
not a given name, as the attorney (Winkler) had previously
noted he could find no first name for MacGyver.

Cody...................................................................Abe Vigoda
Tiny....................................................................Lyle Alzado
Harry Jackson.......................................................John Anderson
Big Earl Dent........................................................Dick Butkus
Speedy................................................................James Doohan
Man in station wagon.............................................Henry Gibson
Old woman...........................................................Sandra Gould
Biff Arnold...........................................................Rich Little
Police officer........................................................Marion Ramsey
Sister Robin..........................................................Marion Ross
Mel.....................................................................Jesse White

Big Mama..............................................................Wendy O. Williams
Wilton Newberry..............................Henry Winkler (uncredited)
Young MacGyver....................................................Shane Meier
Drive-thru girl.......................................................Celia Martin
Kids....................................Jenny Jickles, Jessica Jickles

Director: William Gereghty          Writer: Lincoln Kibbee

8. "MacGyver's Women"  Nov. 12, 1990

A dream takes MacGyver to the Old West, where he rescues
three women with strange resemblances to his romantic object
Maria, his friend (Zimmer), and a runaway (Lords, the Sept.
1984 Penthouse Pet and former adult-video performer). Stenburg and Zimmer reprise their roles from ep. 5 and ep. 6, respectively. Co-star Elcar portrays Mr. Destiny in the dream.

Lt. Kate Murphy....................................................Kim Zimmer
Maria Romburg....................................................Brigitta Stenburg
Jenny..................................................................Traci Lords
Milt Bozer............................................................Robert Donner
Wilt Bozer............................................................Robin Mossley
Harvey Logan/Kid Curry.........................................Marshall Teague
Sam "News" Carver................................................Frank C. Turner
The Sundance Kid..................................................Dale Wilson
Jesse James..........................................................Wil Calhoun
Billy the Kid.........................................................Russell Hamilton
And: John Bear Curtis (Barney Butterfield), Bill Croft (Tansey)

Director: Michael Preece
Writers: Stephen Kandel and Lincoln Kibbee

9. "Bitter Harvest"  Nov. 19, 1990

A labor-organizer friend (Ontiveros) is murdered by grape-
growers suspected of using illegal pesticides.

Alex Silva.............................................................James Medina
Caspar Kasabian....................................................Richard Sarafina
Nick Kasabian.......................................................Joey Aresco
Carmen Garcia.......................................................Yvette Cruise
Hector Lopez.........................................................Anthony Pena
Chief of Police Kyle Davis........................................Allan Lysell
Tony Garcia...........................................................Bill Ontiveros
Felix Mendoza.......................................................David Efron
Natalie Garcia........................................................Giann Goncalves
Police officers...................................David Symons, Charles Andre
Laborer................................................................Betty Hansen

Director: Michael Vejar             Writer: Michael Kane

10. "The Visitor"  Dec. 3, 1990

Apparent space aliens promise to sell a farmer (Musser) and
his sick wife (Payne) a trip to a happier, healthier realm.
Working title: "Trip to Another World."

Sheriff Kellog.......................................................Ken Pogue
"Alien"/Dawn Rigel................................................Beth Toussaint
Phil Sternweis.......................................................Christopher Gaze
"Alien"/Ray Rigel...................................................Ryan Michael
John Wiley............................................................Larry Musser
Tommy Wiley.........................................................Kaj-Erik Eriksen
Sarah Wiley...........................................................Suzie Payne
And: Bruce Harwood (Willis), Ian Black (Parnell)

Director: William Gereghty          Writer: Brad Radnitz

11. "Squeeze Play"  Dec. 17, 1990

A girl (Zak) tries to free her baseball-star dad (McCord) from a blackmailing collectibles counterfeiter (Stewart). Jackson is a former New York Yankees and Oakland A's player; Reese is a jazz singer.

Mama Colton................................................Della Reese
Himself.....................................................Reggie Jackson
Norvus Reilly...............................................Kent McCord
Clayton Marsh..............................................Malcolm Stewart
Willard.....................................................Tim Rossovich
Wendy Reilly...............................................Catherine Zak
And: William Samples (Eli), Brock Johnson (Store manager), Whitney Stewart (T.J. Mitchel), Jeff McLeod (Ricky)

Director: Michael Preece            Writer: Art Washington

**preempted Dec. 31**

12. "Jerico Games"  Jan. 7, 1991

MacGyver's high school flame (Pascal) is being abused by her spouse, a media mogul televising an international competition.

Ellen Jerico...............................................Mary Ann Pascal
Mikolai Rostov.............................................Paul Haddad
Dan Reese.................................................Madison Mason
Coach Litminov............................................Adam Gregor
Ralph Jerrico..............................................Robert Pine
Vince King.................................................Kevin Hayes
Officer Barnes.............................................Pat Mermel
Lorraine Anderson.........................................Kimberly Sheppard
And: Peter Hanlon (Norton), Ken Kirzinger (Bodyguard), Nyree Roy (Receptionist), James West (Security guard)

Director: William Gereghty          Writer: Robert Sherman

**preempted Jan. 14**

13. "The Wasteland"  Jan. 21, 1991

A despoiling land developer (McMullan) and his ambitious children (Pyper-Ferguson, Kapture) mark MacGyver for death. Orig. scheduled for Jan. 14.

Andrew Bartlett...........................................Jim McMullan
Laura Bartlett.............................................Mitzi Kapture
Scott Barlett..............................................John Pyper-Ferguson
Willis......................................................Bruce Harwood
Reporter...................................................Kevin Hayes
Big Hefty..................................................Rick Pearce
Lenny......................................................Michael Gall
        Also orig. announced: Michael Puttonen (Simon Rogolf)

Director: Michael Caffey            Story: Robert Hamner
Teleplay: Robert Hamner and Grant Rosenberg

**preempted Jan. 28**

14. "Eye of Osiris"  Feb. 4, 1991

MacGyver helps an archaeologist (Haworth) and his assistant (Foreman) outwit raiders of Alexander the Great's lost tomb.

Beth Webb................................................Deborah Foreman
Nikolaus von Leer.........................................Kai Wulff
Achmed Hakim.............................................Antony Stamboulieh
Prof. Axford...............................................Peter Haworth
And: Mark Acheson (Kurush), Raimund Stamm (Worker)

Director: Michael Vejar             Writer: John Sheppard

15. "High Control"  Feb. 11, 1991

An innocent parolee (Butkus, reprising his role from ep. 7) faces blackmail from a gang of thieving bikers.

Big Earl Dent.............................................Dick Butkus
R.J. Montana..............................................Gwynyth Walsh
Kluge.....................................................Don Stroud
Rote......................................................Bill Croft
Ed Travis.................................................Howard Storey
Blue-collar man...........................................Bill Murdoch
Derrick....................................................Scott Owen
And: Anthony Schmidt (Hawkins), Sonny Surowiec (Dock-worker), Tony Dakota (Boy), Jennifer Griffin (Bartender), Richard Lautsch (Wally), Brian Warren (Ex-con)

Director: Michael Caffey            Writer: Lincoln Kibbee

16. "There But for the Grace"  Feb. 18, 1991

MacGyver's friend (Murdoch), a priest ministering to the homeless, is found murdered amid a patient-care-home scam.

Doc.......................................................Nicolas Coster
Rachel....................................................Marie Stillin
A.R. Sandler..............................................John Considine
Danny.....................................................Scott Bellis
Riker.....................................................Todd Duckworth
Lt. Rhome.................................................Blu Mankuma
Mooney...................................................David McLeod
Father Jim................................................Laurie Murdoch
And: Paul Bittante (Guard), Garrison Chrisjohn (Paul Landau), Rebecca Toolan (Chairperson), Randall Wong (Doctor), Amanda O'Leary (Homeless girl), Becky Maynes (Allison)

Director: William Gereghty          Writer: John Considine

**preempted Feb. 25**

17. "Blind Faith"  March 4, 1991

A death squad tries to prevent MacGyver from getting a slain Latin-American leader's daughter (De Bari) back to her land.

Samantha Lora............................................Irene DE BARI
Paul Stams................................................Michael MACRAE
Col. Cardoso..............................................Ed Trotta
Ramos.....................................................Hector Mercado
Nelson Richardson.........................................Andrew Rhodes
And: Kevin Hayes (Vince King), Beverly Hendry (Production assistant), Judith Berlin (Busybody), Ron Halder (Cop)

Director: Michael Caffey            Writer: John Considine

18. "Faith, Hope & Charity"  March 18, 1991

Two feisty old sisters help extricate MacGyver, on the trail of the endangered gray wolf, from mobsters seeking stolen loot.

Faith Lacey...............................................Natalie Core
Hope Lacey...............................................Helen Page Camp
Leo Burns.................................................Antony Holland
Bobby.....................................................Paul Boretski
Abe.......................................................Barry Greene
Gorman...................................................Herb Edelman

Director: William Gereghty          Writer: Brad Radnitz

**preempted April 1**

19. "Strictly Business"  April 8, 1991

A desperate single mother (Meadows) and her daughter, hiding from the woman's ex, help MacGyver battle his arch-nemesis (Des Barres, reprising his role from a previous season).

Murdoc..................................................Michael Des Barres
Suzanne..................................................Kristen Meadows
Amy, her daughter.....................................Rochelle Greenwood
Men...............................Michael Puttonen, Long John Baldry
And: Judith Maxie (Woman), Larry Hill (Sheriff)

Director: Michael Vejar          Writer: John Sheppard

20. "Trail of Tears"  April 29, 1991

A utilities company and a Native American tribe clash over the rights to sacred land.  Gregory had played star Anderson's brother in the daytime serial *General Hospital* in the 1970s.

Larry Whitecloud............................................Michael Gregory
Standing Wolf..................................................Nick Ramus
Everett Johnson................................................Jack Bannon
Dick Russell.....................................................Gerry Bean
Broom........................................................R. Nelson Brown
Willis.......................................................Bruce Harwood
Judd Samuels.............................................Joe-Norman Shaw
Phil Crow..................................................Gordon Tootoosis
Plant manger................................................Gordon White
Boy...........................................................Cory Douglas
And: William B. Davis (Judge), Sandra Ferens (Foreperson)

Director: Michael Preece          Writer: Lincoln Kibbee

21. "Hind-Sight"  May 6, 1991

On the eve of Pete's eye surgery, Pete and MacGyver recall some adventures (via flashbacks to previous episodes), and Pete's ex-wife appears.  Star Anderson apppeared post-episode in a brief spot about obtaining information about glaucoma.

Betty Thornton..................................................Linda Darlow
Willis.......................................................Bruce Harwood
Nurse Krandall.........................................Barbara E. Russell
Surgeon...........................................................Forbes Angus

Director: Michael Preece    Writer: Rick Mittleman

Unaired

"The Coltons"

A family of bounty hunters aids a young Amerasian woman (Morison) on the run after witnessing the slaying of a China-town gang lord.  Pilot for a spinoff series.  Reese reprises her role from ep. 11.  Orig. scheduled for May 20, 10-11 p.m.

Announced cast includes:
Frank Colton....................................................Cleavon Little
Jesse Colton...................................................Richard Lawson
Billt Colton....................................................Cuba Gooding
Mama Colton.........................................................Della Reese
Patricia Fielding...............................................Akiko Morison
John Denmark....................................................Richard Gant
G. Irwin Fielding..........................................Christopher Thomas
Loretta Fielding.........................................Irene Yah-Ling Sun
Chi.............................................................Francois Chau
And: Richard Yee (Chan), Bill Dow (Danko), Michael Sicoly (Quilla), Michael Crestejo (Wing), Derek Lowe (Hsi), Mari-lyn Chin (Suzi), Lesley Ewen (Maid), Terry King (Garden-er), Martin Evans (Maitre d'), Andrew Johnston (Egan), James Hong (Kuang), Mitchell Kosterman (Wyatt)

Director: NA   Writer: NA

**preempted Aug. 5, Aug. 12, Aug. 19**

**preempted Sept. 2**

**renewed for 1991-92; new episodes begin Sept. 16, 1991**

## Major Dad

CBS         Sept. 17-June 3    Mondays, 8:30-9 p.m.
            June 10-July 8     Mondays, 8-8:30 p.m.
            July 15-on         Mondays, 8:30-9 p.m.

Series premiere: Sept. 18, 1989

Comedy of a career Marine officer (Staff Secretary to the Commanding General of fictitious Camp Hollister in Virginia) married to a widowed reporter with three daughters. Made with the cooperation of the U.S. Marine Corps.  Cast-member Cypher was a guest ep. 1-3.  The family's street-address number: 485.

Major John D. (Mac) MacGillis.........................Gerald McRaney
Polly Cooper....................................................Shanna Reed
Elizabeth Cooper....................................................Marisa Ryan
Robin Cooper....................................................Nicole Dubuc
Casey Cooper................................................Chelsea Hertford
Lt. Gene Holowachuk.........................................Matt Mulhern
Gunnery Sgt. Alva "Gunny" Bricker...................Beverly Archer
Commanding General Marcus Craig.......................Jon Cypher

*Recurring:*
Jeffrey Craig, Marcus' grandson (ep. 1-2,4)..................Chance
          Michael Corbitt (Robert Gorman orig. announced)
Jesse Menlow (ep. 8,12,15,17)....................Lance Wilson White
Pvt. Harris (orig. Herndon; ep. 20,23-24)................Matt Nolan

SBB Productions and Spanish Trail Productions in assoc. with Universal Television, an MCA Co.
Executive producers: Rick Hawkins, Earl Pomerantz, Gerald McRaney
Supervising producer: Jim Evering
Coordinating producer: Abby Singer
Producer: Todd Stevens
Co-producers: Miriam Trogdon, Barry Gold
Executive story consultants: Carrie Honiglbum, Renee Phillips
Production consultant: Richard C. Okie
Director of photography: Vincent A. Martinelli, A.S.C.
Music: Steve Dorff (occasionally with John Bettis)
Theme (instrumental): Roger Steinman
Director: Michael Lembeck
Creators: John G. Stephens & Richard C. Okie
Developed by: Earl Pomerantz

———————————————

1. "Safe at First Base"  Sept. 17, 1990

The family relocates to Camp Hollister, where the General's grandson snaps provocative pictures of Polly.

Writers: Rick Hawkins, Earl Pomerantz

2. "Welcome to Hollister"  Sept. 24, 1990

The General enlists Mac to make a major event out of the Vice President's stopping at the base for plane refueling.

Writer: Jim Evering

3. "Get a Job"  Oct. 1, 1990

After Polly is hired by the camp newspaper, *The Bulldog*, as editor of the human interest section, "At Ease," Mac fears her first article will offend the General.

Lenny Franklin.....................................................Mark Howell

Writer: Barry Gold

4. "The Goat"  Oct. 8, 1990

A newspaper story falsely blames Robin for the camp's base-ball team's loss against Quantico in the finals.

Writer: Earl Pomerantz

5. "First Anniversary" Oct. 15, 1990

Take-charge Bricker baby-sits the kids when Mac and Polly go out to celebrate their one-year anniversary.

Deliveryperson...........................................................Jim Piper
Bellhop..................................................................Paul Eiding
    Also orig. announced: Peter Jolly (Maintenance person)

Writers: Carrie Honigblum & Renee Phillips

6. "Wetting Down"  Oct. 22, 1990

Teetotaler Holowachuk throws a party to celebrate making 1st Lieutenant.

2nd Lt. Ned Nicholas..........................................Don Fullilove
Capt. Ron Baylor............................................Matthew Nelson
1st Lt. Huck Green.........................................William J. Woff
Bartender....................................................Mike Rauseo

Writer: Miriam Trogdon

7. "Infant-ry"  Oct. 29, 1990

Casey emulates Mac by becoming a mini Marine.

Pvt. LaBonte...................................................Christian Jacobs
    Also orig. announced: Wren T. Brown (Sgt. Truesdale)

Writers: Rick Parks & Peter Garcia

8. "Birthday Ball"  Nov. 5, 1990

On Elizabeth's 16th birthday, Vice President Quayle (filmed in his real-life office) responds to Mac's invitation to attend a Ma-rine Corps 215th-anniversary celebration.

Himself...........................................Vice President Dan Quayle
Himself..........Marine Corps Commandant Gen. Alfred M. Gray

Writer: Rick Hawkins

9. "Wish You Were Here"  Nov. 12, 1990

Mac tries to be spontaneous by taking the family on a last-minute trip to Hawaii.

Sgt. Whitfield.............................................Olivia Virgil Harper
Capt. Sommer...................................................David Cowgill

Writer: Barry Gold

10. "Love on the Run"  Nov. 19, 1990

After a wonderful blind date, Holowachuk and his newfound girlfriend (Donald) decide to get married immediately.  Rauseo reprises his role from ep. 6.

Gail Callaghan.....................................................Julie Donald
Bartender...........................................................Mike Rauseo

Writer: Janet Leahy

11. "Operation: Fun Run"  Nov. 26, 1990

Bricker and Holowachuk must carry on after Mac is hospital-ized while organizing a "fun run" Navy Relief fundraiser.

Nurse Collins.....................................................Pamela Dunlap

Writer: Jim Evering

**preempted Dec. 10**

12. "Gift of the Major"  Dec. 17, 1990

Mac tries to preserve Casey's belief in Santa Claus by tracking down a special toy she knows Santa will bring her.  Guest Archey reprises his cast-member role from last season.

Staff Sgt. Byron James......................................Marlon Archey
Sam.................................................................Sam Lembeck

Writer: Rick Hawkins

13. "Flying Solo"  Jan. 7, 1991

Mac anticipates savoring some quiet time when Polly takes the girls out shopping for the day.

Anita.........................................................Cynthia Stevenson

Writer: Leslie Rieder-Rasmussen

14. "A Bird in the Hand"  Jan. 14, 1991

Mac accidentally destroys Bricker's prize possession, a ceram-ic  eagle once owned by the Corps' most decorated Marine.

Writers: Carrie Honigblum & Renee Phillips

15. "Learning to Drive"  Jan. 21, 1991

New driver Elizabeth hits the General's parked MG.

Writer: Lisa Albert

16. "Over Here"  Feb. 4, 1991

On Jan. 15, 1991, with the camp anxious over the impending Persian Gulf war, Mac settles a territorial dispute at home.

Sgt. Lonigan.........................................................Parley Baer
Sgt. Willis..............................................................Sid Melton
Sgt. Goodman..............................................Reid Cruickshanks

Writer: Rick Hawkins

17. "Valentine's Day  Feb. 11, 1991

Polly writes a Valentine's Day tribute to Mac in the base pa-per, embarrassing him; Elizabeth finally goes out with Jesse.

Writer: Jim Evering

18. "Sins of the Father"  Feb. 18, 1991

A guilt-stricken Mac tries to return a Zorro watch he stole from a store in his youth. Orig. scheduled for Feb. 4 and 25.

Peavy..............................................................Eric Christmas
Marvin.............................................................Merlin Santana

Writer: Barry L. Gold

19. "The Possible Dream"  Feb. 25, 1991

The camp staff readies their annual talent show; Robin runs for student-council president. Orig. scheduled for Feb. 18.

Marvin.............................................................Merlin Santana
Sergeant..........................................................Nathan Stein

"The Impossible Dream" sung by: Jon Cypher

Writer: Manny Basanese

20. "Private Affair"  March 11, 1991

Elizabeth's dream date (new recurring guest Nolan) turns out to be the practical-joking Marine who's been testing Mac's patience.

Writers: Carrie Honigblum & Renee Phillips

21. "Polly's Choice"  March 18, 1991

Polly's playful, spirited old photographer boyfriend, Mac's total opposite, works on a book with Polly. Guest Parker co-starred with McRaney on Simon & Simon (CBS, 1981-1988).

Evan Charters...................................................Jameson Parker

Writer: Miriam Trogdon

**preempted April 1**

22. "The Silent Drill Team"  April 8, 1991

Mac fulfills his lifelong dream of performing with the U.S. Marine Corps Silent Drill Team.

Themselves........................U.S. Marine Corps Silent Drill Team

Writer: Barry Gold

23. "Elmo Come Home"  April 29, 1991

Bricker becomes attached to a homeless pup she's dog-sitting while Mac tries to convince Polly to adopt it for Casey.

Elmo (dog)............................................................Jimmie

Writer: Jim Evering

24. "Together"  May 13, 1991

While writing a speech for a Desert Storm troop-welcoming ceremony, Mac asks for the girls' consent to adopt them. Episode includes footage of real-life Operation Desert Storm Marines returning to, according to CBS, Camp Pendleton, Calif. and Quantico, Va.

Writer: Rick Hawkins

**preempted May 20**

**renewed for 1991-92; new episodes begin Sept. 16, 1991**

## The Man in the Family

ABC                    Wednesdays, 9:30-10 p.m.

Series premiere: June 19, 1991
Final telecast: July 31, 1991

Comedy of an Italian-American ne'er-do-well who moves back in with his family in his old Brooklyn neighborhood after promising his dying father that he'll run the family grocery, Carmine's Deli. Working titles: When You're Smiling; The Ray Sharkey Show.

Sal Bavasso.......................................................Ray Sharkey
Angie Bavasso, his mother.................................Julie Bovasso
Annie, his divorced sister...................................Anne De Salvo
Tina, his teen sister..............................................Leah Remini
Uncle Bennie..........................................................Louis Guss
Cha Cha................................................................Don Stark
Robby, Annie's son.........................................Billy L. Sullivan

Columbia Pictures Television / The Weinberger Co.
Executive producer: Ed. Weinberger
Co-executive producer: Alan Kirschenbaum
Supervising producer: Ron Clark
Producers: Tracey Ormandy, Dennis Gallegos
Consulting producer: John Rich
Co-producers: Herb Nanas, Peter Golden
Associate producer: Kim Rozenfeld
Executive story editors: Oliver Goldstick, Phil Rosenthal
Creative consultants: Mark Reisman, Jeremy Stevens
Special consultant (ep. 3-on): Johnny "Cha Cha" Ciarcia
Director of photography: Daniel Flannery
Music: uncredited; only a "music supervisor" listed
Theme: "When You're Smiling," a pop standard by Mark
       Fisher, Joe Goodwin and Larry Shay (words and music);
       performed (vintage recording) by Louis Prima
Director: John Rich
Creators: Ed. Weinberger & Gina Wendkos

_____

1. "Honor Bound"  June 19, 1991

Sal tries to fulfill his promise to his father, but Vinnie and Cha Cha comes up with a tempting wild business scheme.

Mrs. Panetta.......................................................Sylvia Sidney
Vinnie...................................................................Joe Cortese
Carmine Bavasso, Sal's father...................................Al Ruscio
Visitor.............................................................Sylvia Harman
Salesperson.....................................Lenny Wolpe (uncredited)

Teleplay: Ed. Weinberger
Story: Ed. Weinberger & Gina Wendkos

2. "Once Bitten..."  June 26, 1991

Sal faces suspicious police and an angry family in his valiant attempt to reconcile with the woman (Parks) he left at the altar.

Mrs. Minetti..........Rose Marie (Morgana King orig. announced)
Christina Minetti..............................................Catherine Parks
Mr. Minetti......................................................John Capodice
Mrs. Parisi.........................................................Gloria Manos
Detectives.........................................Ric Mancini, Steve Kavner
Police officer.......................................................Frank Novak

Writer: Ron Clark

3. "Sal Falls In Love"  July 3, 1991

Sal turns down first-date sex with an attractive woman.

Jenny Solino................................................Constance Marie
Bellhop..........................................................David Auerbach

Writer: Alan Daniels

4. "Uncle Sal"  July 10, 1991

To impress a woman, Sal pretends nephew Robby is his son; Angie dates a cobbler. Auerbach reprises his role from ep. 3.

Paula.................................................................Teresa Ganzel
Albert (orig. Dominick)........................................Ralph Manza
Bellhop..........................................................David Auerbach

Writer: Ron Wullner

5. "Date with a Don"  July 17, 1991

Sal arranges a date with Annie for a mobster, then has to explain why she doesn't like him or his marriage proposal.

Frank D'Angelo...................................................Charlies Cioffi
Bodyguard Paulie............................Johnny "Cha Cha" Ciarcia
Customers.....................Marsha McClelland, John David Conti
Bandleader........................................................Tony DeBruno
Musicians.......................Tino DeBruno, Anthony Ciaramitaro,
     Michael Macchia

Writer: Oliver Goldstick & Phil Rosenthal

6. "Real News"  July 24, 1991

The Bavassos make some hindsight adjustments when they reenact an attempted burglary for a "reality TV" show.

Lori Whitt..........................................Anne Elizabeth Ramsay
Mr. Mitchell..............................................................Lee Weaver
And:  Gary Berner (Cameraperson), Bruce Herman, Brent Williams (Burglars), Andrew Philpot (Stage manager), Robert Yacko (Boom person)

Writers: Ron Clark & Alan Daniels

7. "Pal Joey"  July 31, 1991

Sal doesn't want an old pal (Prozzo) dating his niece Tina.

Joey Capra.....................................................Michael Prozzo

Writers: Ron Clark & Alan Daniels

## Married People

ABC          Sept. 18-Jan. 30   Wednesdays, 9:30-10 p.m.
             March 16           Saturdays, 9:30-10 p.m.
             Aug. 7-Sept. 11    Wednesdays, 10:30-11 p.m.

Series premiere: Sept. 18, 1990
Final telecast: Sept. 11, 1991

Comedy of three couples in a Harlem brownstone: landlords and grocery-store owners Nick and Olivia, married 37 years; baby-boomers Elizabeth, an attorney, and Russell, a freelance writer; and transplanted Midwestern newlyweds Allen, a Columbia University freshman, and aspiring dancer Cindy. Co-creators Sternin and Fraser are husband and wife.

Nick Williams......................................................Ray Aranha

Olivia Williams....................................Barbara Montgomery
Elizabeth................................................Bess Armstrong
Russell Meyers..............................................Jay Thomas
Cindy Campbell...............................................Megan Gallivan
Allen Campbell.................................................Chris Young
*Recurring:*
Max Meyers (infant)
     (ep. 9)............................Jonathan/Matthew Lester
     (ep. 10-11,14-16)...........................(uncredited)

Sternin & Fraser Ink in assoc. with Columbia Pictures Television / ELP Communications
Executive producers: Robert Sternin, Prudence Fraser
Co-executive producer (later in season): Lissa Levin
Producers: Jan Siegelman (ep. 1); Asaad Kelada, Kathy Landsberg, Gina Wendkos, Robert Rabinowitz
Co-producers (later in season): Daphne Pollon, David Castro
Executive story editors (early in season): Daphne Pollon, David Castro
Director of photography (variously): Mark Levin (ep. 1); Mikel Neiers; James Jensen
Music: Bob Boykin
Theme: Bob Boykin (words and music); performers uncredited
Director unless otherwise noted: Asaad Kelada
Creators: Robert Sternin & Prudence Fraser

————————————

1. "Married People"  Tuesday, Sept. 18, 1990

As Cindy and Allen move in, building owners Nick and Olivia marvel at seeing their neighborhood become trendy.

Writers: Robert Sternin & Prudence Fraser

2. "The Truth, the Whole Truth...."  Sept. 19, 1990

Elizabeth disinvites Russell from dinner with her boss; a fellow student flirts with Allen; Nick tries to save an old pool hall.

Dr. Thomas....................................................Vincent Howard
Tracy................................................................Darcy Marta

Writer: Robert Rabinowitz

3. "First Impressions"  Sept. 26, 1990

Allen's all nerves at dinner when Cindy's father visits.

Paul..................................................................Paul Gleason

Writers: Daphne Pollon & David Castro

4. "Once More, With Passion"  Oct. 3, 1990

Allen's attractive lab partner (Berkley) rooms with him and Cindy; Elizabeth and Olivia have beauty makeovers.

Isabel.........................................................Elizabeth Berkley
Gloria...........................................................Carol Ann Susi

Writer: Eric Gilliland

5. "Money Changes Everything"  Oct. 10, 1990

Russell loans Allen and Cindy $50; Nick's friend (Cobbs) is moving away.  Orig. scheduled for Sept. 26.

Willis..................................................................Bill Cobbs
Sarah...............................................................Lillian Lehman
And: Mike Jacobs, Jr.

Writer: Debra Fasciano

6. "Live and Let Go"   Oct. 17, 1990

Allen fears Cindy is "going New York"; Nick and Olivia discuss plans for their son to take over the store.

Evelyn...............................................Florence Stanley
Joey Williams, Nick and Olivia's son.........J.J. a.k.a. J.J. Jones

Writers: Lynne Kadish & Barry Bleach

7. "Room for One More"   Oct. 24, 1990

Russell and a very pregnant Elizabeth plan a night out.   Orig. scheduled for Oct. 17.

Delivery person........................................G. Smokey Campbell

Writer: Kermit Frazier

8. Title NA   Oct. 31, 1990

Up in the attic, Cindy meets a ghost from Olivia's past.

With: Vincent Schiavelli, Gilbert Lewis, Furley Lumpkin,  Lawrence Mandley

Writers: Debra Fasciano & Robert Rabinowitz & Gina Wendkos

9. "Term Paper"   Nov. 7, 1990

Russell pays a rosy-eyed visit to his alma mater.

Dr. Cashin...................................David Ogden Stiers
Plumber.......................................Timothy Williams
Plasterer......................................Chris Anastasio
And: Eric Champnella (Ted), Gregory Cooke (Steve Lerman), John Walter Davis (Plasterer's assistant), Matthew Walker (Ed), Karen Mistal

Writer: Craig Hoffman

10. "The Baby Cometh"   Nov. 14, 1990

While the couples plan on having Thanksgiving dinner together, Elizabeth goes into labor and delivers a boy.

Stuie..........................................Ian Patrick Williams
Nurse..........................................Gwen Shepherd

Writers: Daphne Pollon & David Castro

**preempted Nov. 21**

11. "Four Neighbors and a Baby"   Nov. 28, 1990

Everybody in the building wants to mother baby Max.  Greene is a cast-member of *The Days and Nights of Molly Dodd*.

Waiter Max........................................James Greene

Writer: Debra Fasciano

12. "Partners"   Dec. 5, 1990

A working Elizabeth must decide whether to stay home with Max, or at her practice with a long-coveted partnership.

Delia.............................................Jenny O'Hara
And: Doug Ballard (Larry Fields), John Ingle (Michaelson)

Writers: Jim Fisher & Jim Staahl

13. "Compromise"   Dec. 19, 1990

Elizabeth gets Allen a part-time job at her firm, and finds he doesn't get along with her partners.  Orig. scheduled for Dec. 12.  Ballard and Ingle reprise their roles from last episode.

Larry Fields....................................Doug Ballard
Michaelson......................................John Ingle
And: Julian Christopher, Montrose Hagins

Director: Will Mackenzie          Writer: Kermit Frazier

14. "To Live and Drive and New York"   Dec. 26, 1990

To try making a better life for Max, Russell gets a driver's leaning permit, and Elizabeth tries becoming a better homemaker.

Ned, Elizabeth's brother.................................Christopher Rich
Janie, his wife..............................................Lela Ivey
Brian, their son...........................................Brian Bonsall
Emily, their daughter.......................................Thora

Director: Will Mackenzie
Writers: Daphne Pollon & David Castro

15. "The Nanny"   Jan. 9, 1991

Russell interviews a streetwise New Yorker (Raggio) for a job as nanny for Max; Cindy inadvertently gets hired as a stripper.

Rosie...............................................Lisa Raggio
Miss Graham......................................Natalie Core
Terri................................................Pamela Anderson
Joyce..............................................Debi A. Monahan

Director: Will Mackenzie     Teleplay: Jim Fisher & Jim Staahl
Story: Debra Fasciano and Jim Fisher & Jim Staahl

16. "Mommy and Me"   Jan. 23, 1991

Russell takes Max to a "Mommy and Me" parent-infant bonding class.  Orig. scheduled for Jan. 16.

With: Carol Huston, John Bennett Perry, Christopher Birt, Moosie Drier, Richard Horvitz, Zig Roberts, Virginia Bingham, Mary Garripoli

Director: Will Mackenzie          Writer: Timothy Williams

17. "Dance Ten, Friends Zero"   Jan. 30, 1991

Cindy thinks she got a part in a Broadway show only because of Russell's influence; choir soloist Olivia faces tough competition (Reese, the jazz singer, not playing herself).  Orig. scheduled for Jan. 23.

With: Della Reese, Andrea Elson, Frantz Turner, Michael Kubala, Billy Palmieri, Sindy Fox

Director: Will Mackenzie          Writer: Eric Gilliland

**off the schedule, then cancelled**

18. "You Were Right and I Was..."   March 16, 1991

Russell's story about building inspectors results in Allen and Cindy being ordered out of their "uninhabitable" apartment. Raggio reprises her role from ep. 15. Working title: "Sorry, Honey, I Was Wrong."  Orig. scheduled for Oct. 30.

Rosie..................................................Lisa Raggio
Mike Beiderman...............................Sam Anderson

Director: Will Mackenzie
Teleplay: Lissa Levin and Daphne Pollon & David Castro
Story: Robert Sternin & Prudence Fraser

## Married With Children

Fox            Sundays, 9-9:30 p.m.

Series premiere: April 5, 1987

Surreally farcical comedy of an oafish Chicago shoe salesperson and his family. Series title usually printed as *Married... With Children*, though no elipses appear on-screen. Kids' school and team: The Polk High School Panthers. Recurring guest McGinley had appeared as a different character in the Dec. 17, 1989 episode, "It's a Bundyful Life."

Al Bundy........................................................Ed O'Neill
Peg Bundy....................................................Katey Sagal
Bud Bundy.................................................David Faustino
Kelly Bundy..........................................Christina Applegate
Marcy Rhoades D'Arcy..................................Amanda Bearse
Buck (dog)...(uncredited; variously given as Buck and Michael)

*Recurring:*
Jefferson D'Arcy (ep. 12-14,16-19,21-23,25)........Ted McGinley

Columbia Pictures Television/ELP Communications
Executive producers: Michael G. Moye, Ron Leavitt, Katherine Green, Arthur Silver
Supervising producers: Ralph R. Farquhar, Ellen L. Fogle
Producers: Kevin Curran, Barbara Blachut Cramer, Harriette Ames-Regan (latter, later in season)
Director of photographer: Thomas W. Markle
Buck trained by: Steven Ritt
Music: uncredited/inapplicable
Theme: "Love and Marriage" by Sammy Cahn and Jimmy Van Heusen; performed by Frank Sinatra (1955 recording)
Director: Gerry Cohen
Creators: Ron Leavitt and Michael G. Moye

---

1. "We'll Follow the Sun" Sept. 23, 1990 (MC-502)

The Bundys get caught in a Labor Day traffic jam.

Gerry....................................................Eric Menyuk
Kitty......................................................Maria Fries
Motorists...............................Frank Lloyd, Gita Isak, Eddie Rio

Writers: Ron Leavitt & Michael G. Moye

2. "Al...With Kelly"' Sept. 30, 1990 (MC-501)

Al and Kelly feign illness to avoid going to Peg's mother's.

Yvette.............................................Pamela Anderson
Yvonne.............................................Beckie Mullen
And: Jay Anthony Franke (Pizza person), Teresa Frost (Nurse)

Teleplay: Stacie Lipp    Story: Gabrielle Topping

3. "Sue Casa, His Casa" Oct. 7, 1990 (MW-503)

A litigious Al sees a chance for a big settlement when Bud has an accident with the family car.

Judge..............................................Dr. Joyce Brothers
Mr. Lincoln.........................................Mark L. Taylor
Bailiff....................................................Rif Hutton

Writer: Kevin Curran

4. "The Unnatural" Oct. 14, 1990

Al, benched by his softball team in favor of a young rival (Blom), is called on to save a game when the guy is injured. Guest Ziering is a cast-member of *Beverly Hills, 90210*.

Roy....................................................Reid Shelton
Barney...............................................Steve Susskind
Norris....................................................Frank Lloyd
Sven Hunkstrom.........................................Dan Blom
And: Greg Lewis (Old codger), Ian Ziering (Kid), Ray J. Templin (Announcer), Derek Sellers (Hardy)

Writer: Katherine Green

5. "Dance Show" Oct. 21, 1990 (MC-505)

A highly domestic gay man (Castellaneta) feeds a grateful Al while complaining that his lover is out dancing with Peg.

Pete..............................................Dan Castellaneta
Andy.............................................Sam McMurray
Trixie.................................................Dorit Sauer

Writer: Arthur Silver

6. "Kelly Bounces Back" Oct. 28, 1990 (MC-506)

Kelly goes to modeling school and competes for a car-show job with a move called "the Bundy Bounce."

Piper....................................................Tia Carrere
Miss Beck..............................................Tina Louise
Incense.........Joanna Goode (Randi Ingerman orig. announced)
And: Debbie Dunning (Rochelle), Wendy Nichols (Girl)

Writer: Al Aidekman

7. "Married...With Aliens" Nov. 4, 1990 (MC-507)

Al encounters space-beings, who need his socks for fuel. Silla had played Cousin Itt on *The Addams Family* (ABC 1964-66).

Oliver.............................................Leonard Lightfoot
Aliens...........Phil Fondacaro, Debbie Lee Carington, Tony Cox, Patty Maloney, Felix Silla, Susie Rossitto

Writer: Ellen L. Fogle

8. "Wabbit Season" Nov. 11, 1990 (MC-508)

Al's attempt at gardening to lower his blood pressure leads to all-out war against an invading rabbit.

Writers: Michael G. Moye & Ron Leavitt

9. "Don't You Think I'm Sexy?" Nov. 18, 1990 (MC-509)

When Al moves a sexy neighbor's couch and gets hailed as a neighborhood hunk, he temporarily develops self-confidence.

Brenda................................................Rhonda Shear
Jade....................................................Teri Weigel
Mandi..................................................Sherrie Rose
And: Lucy Filippone (Athena), Rhonda Britten (Donna)

Writer: Kevin Curran

10. "One Down, Two to Go"  Nov. 25, 1990   (MC-510)

After Kelly storms out to find her own place, Al thinks she's become a mistress and goes after her apparent sugar daddy.

Sam....................................................Stewart J. Zully
Brooke...........................................................Julie Gray
And: Charles Howerton (Older man), Rick Waugh (Jake)

Writer: Ralph R. Farquhar

11. "And Baby Makes Money"  Dec. 16, 1990

Al wants to have another child when he learns he'll inherit a fortune if he names the baby after a distant relative.

Miss Penza.............................................Beth Broderick
Eugene Bundy............................................Charlie Brill

Song: "She Works Hard for the Money" performed by Monalisa Young

Writer: Art Everett

12. "Married...With Who?"  Jan. 6, 1991   (MW-512)

Marcy wakes up after a raucous night married to a man in her bed, and hires the Bundys to throw a backyard wedding.

Voice of Cap'n Hank.............................................(uncredited)

Writer: Ellen L. Fogle

13. "The Godfather"  Feb. 3, 1991   (MC-514)

Al becomes a self-styled neighborhood godfather when Kelly dates an alderman (Davies) who gets him political favors.

Harry Ashland..............................................Lane Davies
Newspaper deliverer.......................................Scott Ferguson
And: Angel Broadhurst (Salt Water), Annie Marie Gillis

Writer: Ralph R. Farquhar

14. "Look Who's Barking"  Feb. 10, 1991

Buck brings home a bitch.  Orig. scheduled for Jan. 20.

Voice of Buck.................................................Cheech Marin
Street musician.....................................................B.B. King
Chef................................................................Brian George
Restaurant owner..........................................Rodney Kageyama
Hans..............................................................Kort Falkenberg
Voice of female dog..(uncredited; evidently cast-member Sagal)

Song: "Buck's Lament" written and performed by B.B. King

Writer: Katherine Green

15. "A Man's Castle"  Feb. 17, 1991   (MC-515)

Peg redecorates Al's bathroom

Mick................................................................Dave Florek
And: Fitzhugh G. Houston (Rich), Deryl Carroll (Prof. Lavar)

Writer: Stacie Lipp

16. "All-Nite Security Dude"  Feb. 24, 1991   (MC-516)

Al, working as a security guard at his old Polk High School, has to retrieve a trophy from his gridiron days, stolen by his former football rival (Smith, the former pro football player).

Spare Tire Dixon......................................Bubba Smith
Trixie...........................................................Dorit Sauer
Principal.................................................Carol Gustafson

Writers: Glenn Eichler & Peter Gaffney

17. "Oldies But Young 'Uns"  March 17, 1991   (MC-518)

Al becomes obsessed with finding the title and performer of an oldies song.

Charlie Verducci.......................................Joseph Bologna
Vinnie Verducci............................................Matt LeBlanc
Dave.......................................................Suli McCullough
Customers..........................Michael Stanton, Ron Litman
Voice of Rick Cool.........................................Bean Baxter

Writer: Bill Prady

18. "Weenie Tot Lovers & Other Strangers"  March 24, 1991   (MC-517)

Kelly enters the "Miss Weenie Tot" contest, a beauty competition sponsored by the factory of the quasi-food.

Mr. Shnick....................................................Ray Girardin
Flopsie, his secretary..................Heather Elizabeth Parkhurst
Johnson...................................................F. Richard Ford
IRS agent......................................................Milt Tarver
Butter Lefkowitz.......................................Helena Apothaker
Rhonda Rose...............................................Jennifer Braff
Police officer................................................Dan Tullis, Jr.

Writer: Kevin Curran

19. "Kids! Wadaya Gonna Do?"  April 7, 1991   (MC-521)

When Al refuses to give Bud and Kelly money for concert tickets and a modeling field trip, respectively, they seek work.

Crystal.....................................................Helena Apothaker
Agatha............................................................Edith Varon
June Hubbard..............................................Irina Cashen
March Hubbard...........................................Joey Simmrin
January Hubbard..........................................Matt Leavitt
December Hubbard.......................................Kristen Semon
July Hubbard.................................................Cheri Semon
April Hubbard.........................................Samantha Leavitt
Voice of Buck..............................................(uncredited)

Director: Linda Day                    Writer: Ellen L. Fogle

20. "Top of the Heap"  April 7, 1991   9:30-10 p.m.

Al loses his TV set on a boxing bet involving his friend Charlie's son; Charlie and Vinnie crash a society party.  Bologna and LeBlanc, reprising their roles from ep. 17, spin off into the series Top of the Heap; though presented as the second half of a Married With Children hour, only O'Neill appears, in a supporting role.  Orig. scheduled for March 24, 9:30-10 p.m.

Charlie Verducci.......................................Joseph Bologna
Vinnie Verducci...........................................Matt LeBlanc
Kathleen Morgan.......................................Diana Bellamy
Mona Mullins..................................................Joey Adams
Tyler Cameron...........................................Rebecca Cross
Roger Bonderly..........................................John Mansfield

Nelson.............................................................Charles Howerton
And: Dennis Holahan (Man), Kathryn O'Reilly (Woman), Tim Hill (Security guard), Jill Pierce (Mary Ann)
Also orig. announced:
Candice Azzara (Rosie Mullins, Mona's mother)

Writers: Arthur Silver & Ron Leavitt

21. "You Better Shop Around" Part 1  April 14, 1991 (MC-519)

When the house gets too hot, Al moves the family into a supermarket, where he becomes the store's one-millionth customer. Orig. scheduled for March 31.

Manager.................................................................Bruce Jarchow
Stockperson/Bob........................................John Mallory Asher
Cashier....................................................................Jodi Mann
Nibbles...............................................................Bobbie Brown
Cheese lady............................................................Regina Leeds
Mrs. Gillis..............................Louise Pellegrino Rapport
Butter Lefkowitz.....................................Helena Apothaker
Voice of D.J..........................................................Kevin Ryder

Director: Linda Day
Writers: J.D. Brancato & Michael Ferris

22. "You Better Shop Around" Part 2  April 21, 1991 (MC-520)

The store owner makes the Bundys and the D'Arcys compete in a run-off. Mathers is the former star of *Leave it to Beaver*.

Himself/emcee.....................................................Jerry Mathers
Mr. Foodie......................................................Alan Oppenheimer
Manager.................................................................Bruce Jarchow
Nibbles...............................................................Bobbie Brown
And: Brent Corman (Boy), Jodi Mann (Cashier)

Director: Linda Day   Writer: Stacie Lipp

23. "Route 666" Part 1   April 28, 1991  (MC-522)

In Lucifer, New Mexico, en route to a shoe convention, the Bundys find a strange prospector (Byner) and a gold mine. Guest Moye is the series co-creator.

Prospector............................................................John Byner
Codgers.............................................Carmen Filpi, Owen Bush
Young Zeke.................................................Michael G. Moye
Banjo player.......................................................Buddy Matlock

Writer: Katherine Green

24. "Route 666" Part 2   May 5, 1991  (MC-523)

It's everyone for him/herself as the Bundys and the D'Arcys work their jointly owned gold mine.

Demerson............................................................Earl Billings
Yetta....................................................................Sharyn Leavitt
Macadamia........................................................Renee Tenison
Cashew..............................................................Pamela Anderson
Honey Roasted........................................................Ava Fabian
Pecan...............................................................Bobbie Brown
Almond.......................................Heather Elizabeth Parkhurst
Fantasy men......Derek Sellers, Richard Hanson, David Nelson, Alex Walters, Steve Henneberry
Announcer.......................................................Edd Hall (uncredited)

Writer: Ralph R. Farquhar

25. "Buck the Stud" May 19, 1991 (MC-524)

A dog expert (Shimerman) declares Buck is a rare breed (a briard) and offers $10,000 to use the canine as a stud.

Lovejoy..............Armin Shimerman (misspelled "Shimmerman" onscreen)
Bubbles...............................................................Debbie Dunning
And: Jennifer Blanc (Margie), Trea Shields (Bridgett)

Writers: Chip Johannessen & John Rinker

**preempted Aug. 25**

**renewed for 1991-92; new episodes begin Sept. 8, 1991**

# Matlock

NBC          Tuesdays, 8-9 p.m.

Series premiere: March 3, 1986

Lighthearted drama of a canny Atlanta defense attorney who takes on headline-making murder cases. Frequent director Leo Penn is the father of actor Sean Penn.

Benjamin L. (Ben) Matlock................................Andy Griffith
Junior partner Michelle Thomas........................Nancy Stafford
Asst. D.A. Julie March....................................Julie Sommars
Conrad McMasters....................................Clarence Gilyard, Jr.

*Recurring:*
Les Calhoun (ep. 8,12,20)....................................Don Knotts
Lt. Bob Brooks
     (ep. 1,3,5-6,8,11-12,14-20).......................David Froman
Judge Richard Cooksey
     (ep. 3,5,7,10-11,13,16,18,20)..................Richard Newton
Judge Leo Harrington (ep. 8,17,20)................Arthur Eckdahl
Judge Michael Alden (ep. 12,14,19)................Alexander Zale
Mrs. Hawkins (ep. 1-3).........................................Diane Shalet

Dean Hargrove Productions, the Fred Silverman Co., and Viacom
Executive producers: Fred Silverman, Dean Hargrove, Joel Steiger
Supervising producer: Jeff Peters
Producers: Richard Collins, Joyce Burditt
Co-producer: William S. Kerr
Associate producer: John M. McLean
Executive story supervisor: Andy Griffith
Executive story consultant: Anne Collins
Story editor: Gerald Sanoff
Director of photography (variously): Frank Thackery, Jiggs Garcia
Creative consultant: Aaron Ruben
Music (variously): Bruce Babcock; Artie Kane; John Cacavas
Theme (instrumental): Dick DeBenedictis
Creator: Dean Hargrove

---

1. "The Mother" Sept. 18, 1990  (1853)

A client (Knight) may be falsely confessing to murder in order to protect her daughter (Toussaint).

Frank Larson.................................................James O'Sullivan
Andrea Todd.....................................................Beth Toussaint
Phyllis Todd.......................................................Shirley Knight
Secretary/Sarah Richards (orig. Reed)...............Anita Corsaut
Young Woman/Carol.........................................Kathy Karges
Laura Larson....................................................Eileen Barnett

And: Gregg Daniel (Bartender), Philip Baker Hall (Judge)

Director: Robert Scheerer          Writer: Michael Marks

2. "Nowhere to Turn: A Matlock Movie Mystery"
   Sept. 25, 1990  8-10 p.m.  (1851)

A bad day in the life of Matlock, from losing his luggage to being framed for murder. Working title: "The Lawyer."

Arthur Prescott.....................................Joe Regalbuto
Gilbert Lehman......................................Charles Siebert
Daryl Wilson........................................Roger Aaron Brown
Scott Walker........................................J. Kenneth Campbell
Andrew Sloan........................................Don Calfa
Lt. Meyerson........................................David Hayward
Judge George Clayton................................Earl Boen
Bartender...........................................Walter Olkewicz
Driver/Tommy........................................John Mese
Assistant D.A. Nelson...............................Robert Clotworthy
Ticket agent........................................Una Kim
Stewardess..........................................Kim Brant
Middle-aged woman...................................Karon Wright
And:  Murray Rose (Baggage attendant), Gregory Millar (Cab-
      bie), Bennett Liss (Desk clerk), Ron Mokwena (Singing em
      ployee), Rodrigo Obregon (Hotel employee), James Crom-
      well (Judge Raymond Price), Gene Steichen (Cellmate),
      David G. Thomas (Security guard), Robert Martin Stein-
      berg (Asst. D.A. Richard O'Connor), Alberto Isaac (Pro-
      prietor), Rebecca Patterson (Secretary/Linda), Sal Lopez
      (Lucinda Bartender), Miguel Sandoval (Carlos Berman),
      Shohreh (Saleslady), Shaun Toub (Rahmad Hussein),
      Richard Assad (Heavy), Jerry Giles (Patrolman), Nigel
      Gibbs (Police officer), Duchess Dale (Foreperson), Arell
      Blanton (Man at bar), Laura Bassett (Witness), Will Jef-
      fries (Asst. D.A. William Ferber), Rudy Gaines (Client)

Director: Harvey Laidman
Writers: Dean Hargrove & Joel Singer

3. "The Madam"  Oct. 2, 1990  (1852)

Matlock defends a bordello owner (Arthur) accused of killing an ex-employee (Gracen) who was blackmailing famous clients. Ferber reprises his role from last episode.

Ann Rawls...........................................Maureen Arthur
Dr. David Campbell..................................Kenneth David Gilman
Janie Ladd..........................................Elizabeth Gracen
Sen. Jeffrey Paul...................................Robert Pine
Rev. Morley Phelps..................................Noble Willingham
Roger Chapman.......................................Lewis Dauber
Tom Marshall........................................Kevin E. West
Bert Ginsberg.......................................John Apicella
Dominick Sinclair...................................Jonathan Palmer
Asst. D.A. William Ferber...........................Will Jeffries
Foreperson..........................................Janis Ward

Director: Leo Penn                 Writer: Gerald Sanoff

4. "The Personal Trainer"  Oct. 9, 1990

Matlock's roofing contractor (DiCenzo) is accused of killing his wife's amorous personal trainer (Marc).

Betty Harding.......................................Fran Bennett
Morrie..............................................Phil Brock
George Wilton.......................................George DiCenzo
Joanna Wilton.......................................Leslie Easterbrook
Brigitte Laird......................................Mary-Margaret Humes
Harry Slade.........................................Peter Marc

Bobbie Baxter.......................................Rosa Nevin
Deedee Lambert......................................Romy Walthall
Judge Katz..........................................Everett Greenbaum
Asst. D.A...........................................George Ne Jame
Doorperson..........................................John O'Leary
And: Sebastian Anzaldo (Boy), Michael Consoldane (Stenogra-
     pher), Gordon Lett (Alex), David Wyler (Jury foreperson)

Director: Burt Brinckerhoff        Writer: Lincoln Kibbee

**preempted Oct. 16**

5. "The Narc"  Oct. 23, 1990  (1856)

Matlock exposes corruption when he defends an undercover narcotics cop (Welliver) accused of murdering a fellow officer.

Charlie Orbach......................................David Beecroft
Harlan Fondy..............Robert Clohessy a.k.a. Robert Clohesse
Frank Tobias........................................Robert Ginty
Holly Tobias........................................Gail Ramsey
Billy (orig. George) Pierce.........................Tony Todd
Johnny Bauer........................................Titus Welliver
Eileen Fondy........................................Marguerite Hickey
TV newscaster.......................................Sharon Wyatt
Narcs...............................James Arone, Jeff Langton
Commissioners..............Dusty Rhoads, Lewis Arquette
Thug................................................Andrew Castillo
Arresting officer...................................Thor Edgell
Drug dealer.........................................Anthony Gioia
Parking attendant...................................Ashley Smock
Bobby Chan (orig. Angel Ruiz).......................Galen Yuen
Ballplayers (children)............Daniel Laidman, Matthew Roveto,
     Vanessa Roveto

Director: Harvey Laidman           Writer: Phil Mishkin

6. "The Secret" Part 1  Oct. 30, 1990  (1855)

Matlock is high on a hit list when he investigates the case against his client (Taylor), a musician and gambler accused of murdering his bookmaker boss (Porter).

Ty Mullins..........................................Ron Taylor
Tom Hermanski.......................................James McDonnell
Eric Gaston.........................................Brett Porter
Sherry Brown........................................Jacqueline Schultz
John Delaney........................................Forry Smith
Roy Stevens.........................................William Allen Young
Patrick Gilbert.....................................Gerald Berns
Martin Kravetz......................................John McCann
Man in crowd........................................Jeffrey Concklin
Sally Harrison/Secretary............................Doreene L. Hamilton
Auctioneer..........................................Glynn Williams, Jr.
Davey/Janitor.......................................Dan Zukovic
     Also orig. announced: Clay Boss (Stablehand)

Director: Leo Penn                 Writer: Gerald Sanoff

7. "The Secret" Part 2  Nov. 6, 1990  8:01-8:55 p.m.  (1855)

After a blackmailer's (Schultz) apparent death, Conrad finds and confronts her. Guest Blackwell is a fashion maven. Per NBC, the 100th episode (counting parts 1 and 2 separately). Unusual time-slot due to insertion of election-news segments.

Ty Mullins..........................................Ron Taylor
Don Davis...........................................Lorry Goldman
Tom Hermanski.......................................James McDonnell
Sherry Brown........................................Jacqueline Schultz
John Delaney........................................Forry Smith

Roy Stevens................................William Allen Young
And: Mr. Blackwell (Art dealer), Randy Brown (Bellhop), Fil Formicola (Card player), Robert Gentili (Frankie Lance), Sally Hughes (Foreperson), John McCann (Martin Kravetz), Stefanos Miltsakakis (Joey), Gunnar Peterson (Mail carrier), Eric Server (Sheriff), Edmund L. Shaff (Henry Macklin), Chuck Sloan (Asst. D.A. McGrath)

Director: Leo Penn                     Writer: Gerald Sanoff

## 8. "The Brothers" Nov. 13, 1990 (1857)

Matlock is tempted to throw the case when he suspects both his client (Tabori) and the man's twin brother may be guilty of murdering the client's partner, then framing a patient. Tabori is the son of director Don Siegel and actress Vivica Lindfors.

Dr. Lowell Carr................................Kristoffer Tabori
Dr. Scott Weston................................David Haskell
Ellie Stanford................................Patricia Heaton
Lori Atwood................................Ann Marie Lee
Doreen Ferguson................................Barbara Whinnery
Dr. Alvin Prescott................................Peter Boyden
Ken Groman/William Hodges................Robert Miano

Director: Christopher Hibler           Teleplay: Anne Collins
Story: Gerald Sanoff

## 9. "The Cover Girl" Nov. 20, 1990 (1859)

Conrad's fashion-model girlfriend (Headley) is suspected in the murder of an agent killed in a photographer's darkroom.

Harry Samuels (orig. Sorrell, then Saxon)..............M.K. Harris
Carla Royce (orig. Rhodes)................................Shari Headley
Agent Bobby Michaelson (orig. Michaels)................Paul Lieber
Agency head Jackie Whitman (orig. Wheeler)........Tricia O'Neill
Frannie Morrisey (orig. Morrison)................Lisa Waltz
Judge Arthur Beaumont................................Jason Wingreen
Lauren Chadwick (orig. Chapman)................Amy Yasbeck
Deliveryperson................................Richard Speight, Jr.
Assistant................................Jonathan Gorman

Director: Christopher Hibler            Writer: Max Eisenberg

## 10. "The Biker" Nov. 27, 1990 (1858)

The uncooperative and menacing motorcyclist son (Nichols) of a judge is accused of murdering a film star (Meadows).

Cliff Lockwood (orig. Clete Coulter)................Stephen Nichols
Steve Miller................................Steve Eastin
Sherman Lockwood................................Paul Lambert
Nicky Tower................................Stephen Meadows
Gary Benton................................Joel Polis
Newscaster................................Craig Shoemaker
Renee Williams................................Ally Walker
Charlie................................Nick De Mauro
State Highway Patrol officer................Donald Nardini
And: Willy Parsons (Sonny), Jerry Potter (Joseph Bonzer), Gene Ross (Drunk), Holly Sampson (Vicky Miller)

Director: Harvey Laidman
Writers: Reed Shelly & Bruce Shelly

## 11. "The Broker" Dec. 4, 1990 (1860)

When March won't abandon a closed case in which a suspect (Hardin) apparently killed himself, she's targeted for death.

Taylor Sinclair................................Signy Coleman

John Randall................................Edward Edwards
Avery "A.C." Campbell................................Jerry Hardin
Stanley Hayden................................Andrew Robinson
Richard Wagner................................Robert Sampson
Betty Cole................................Lorinne Vozoff
Paul Campbell................................Ted W. Henning
Celeste Wagner................................Deborah Hobart
And: Ted Lehmann (Custodian), Gregg Watkins (Bailiff)

Director: Robert Scheerer          Writer: Diana Kopald Marcus

## 12. "The Fighter" Dec. 11, 1990 (1861)

A boxing champ (Foree) with a violent temper is accused of killing a journalist (Allport) who wrote a negative article on him.

Nick Underwood................................Christopher Allport
Asst. D.A. Hawkins................................Steven Anderson
Mickey Callahan................................Dick Bakalyan
Alana Leon................................Wanda De Jesus
Billy Leon................................Ken Foree
Clayton Ross................................Stanley Kamel
Monroe Weber................................Tom Ruben
Freddy Romano................................James V. Christy
Doctor................................John Petlock
And: Aurelia Sweeney (Maid), Garth Wilton (Hotel manager)

Director: Christopher Hibler
Teleplay: David Hoffman & Leslie Daryl Zerg
Story: David Hoffman & Leslie Daryl Zerg and Phil Combest

**preempted Jan. 1**

## 13. "The Critic" Jan. 8, 1991 (1862)

The playwright (Blake) of a Broadway-bound musical about attorneys is accused of murdering a tough theater critic (Jay).

Tommy Deluca................................Joel Grey
Guy Palmer................................Tony Roberts
Steven Spelvin................................Geoffrey Blake
John Bosley Hackett................................Tony Jay
Sidney Falco................................Ken Michelman
Sally Ayn White................Lauren Mitchell (uncredited)
Brian................................Kim Strauss
"Asst. D.A. Moran"................................Chuck Wagner
"Miss Snyder"................................Janeen Best
Lead dancers................Raymond Del Barrio, Melissa Hurley
And: Mark Ritter (Announcer), Paul Thorpe ("Judge")

Director: Robert Scheerer            Writer: Phil Mishkin

## 14. "The Parents" Jan. 15, 1991 (1863)

A couple (Dusenberry, Royal) is accused of killing a surrogate mom (Elise) who changed her mind about giving up her child.

Chris Miller................................Paul de Souza
Amy Boggs................................Ann Dusenberry
Jill Lambert................................Christine Elise
Matt Grayson................................John Furey
Asst. D.A. Carl Stephens................................Gregory Itzin
Harry Neiman................................Cliff Potts
Mrs. McArdle................................Marge Redmond
Howard Boggs................................Allan Royal
John Franklin................................John Saxon
Punk................................Chad Bell
Painter/Harvey Lang................................Anthony Charnota
Barbara Dewitt Grayson................................Melinda Fee
And: Curt Lowens (Hotel clerk), Pete Steinfeld (Attendant)
    Also orig. announced: Earlene Davis (Foreperson)

Director: Harvey Laidman          Writer: Michael Marks

**15. "The Man of the Year"  Jan. 29, 1991  (1864)**

On the night Matlock is to be honored as Atlanta's Man of the Year, he gets lost, robbed, arrested, and stranded miles away.

Arthur Saxon...............................................................S.A. Griffin
Sheriff................................................................................Bo Hopkins
Mrs. McArdle............................................Marge Redmond
Mrs. Burnett.........................................Pat Crawford Brown
Desk clerk.......................................................Wayne Duvall
Young man.........................................................Micah Grant
Deputy Terwillinger.................................Glenn Morshower
          Also orig. announced: Diane Shalet (Mrs. Hawkins)

Director: Burt Brinckerhoff          Teleplay: Anne Collins
Story: Gerald Sanoff

**16. "The Arsonist"  Feb. 5, 1991  (1865)**

The co-owner (Dobkin) of a clothing store is murdered after arguing with his partner (Macy) over hiring an arsonist.

Sid Franklin.......................................................Bill Macy
Tailor/Enrico.......................................................Wil Albert
Ross Gordon..................................................Jeffrey Byron
Al Brown/Melvin Latham.......................Michael Cavanaugh
Cheryl Houston....................................Marietta De Prima
Marv Shea........................................Lawrence Dobkin
Asst. D.A. Lloyd Burgess..........................Michael Durrell
Mrs. McArdle.......................................Marge Redmond
And: Sis Greenspon (Foreperson), Kevin Hagan (Fire Marshall), Hariet S. Miller (Mrs. Shea), Howard Mungo (Guard), Tony Pierce (Pete), James Tartan George Clancy)

Director: Robert Scheerer          Writer: Jim McGrath

**17. "The Formula"  Feb. 12, 1991  (1866)**

The protege (Stratton) of a chemical company executive with a possible cure for baldness is accused of killing his mentor.

Dr. Tim Crider.......................................Christian Clemenson
Dr. Doris Massler..............................Carol Mayo Jenkins
Ed Billings (orig. Fred Billington)...............James Karen
Jerry (orig. Gary) Hughes......................................Joe Mays
Jeff (orig. Jonathan) Duvall....................Charlie Stratton
Security guard...................................................Steve Archer
Dr. Julian Ingersol.....................................Morgan Hunter
And: Patricia Daniels (Denise), Earlene Davis (Foreperson) Pamela Kosh (Housekeeper), Nancy Sullivan (Mrs. Crider)

Director: Christopher Hibler          Teleplay: Anne Collins
Story: Gerald Sanoff (orig. announced as sole writer)

**18. "The Trial" Part 1  Feb. 19, 1991  (1867)**

The Attorney General appoints Matlock the Special Prosecutor on a case involving the death of an assistant D.A. (Carter).

Judge David Bennett.......................................Mike Farrell
Judge Donna Levin.....................................Diana Muldaur
Tom O'Hare.....................................Carmen Argenziano
Jimmy Giles.......................................................Ned Bellamy
Attorney General Stewart Roberts...............Terry Bozeman
Asst. D.A. Howard (orig. Harvey) Wright............John Carter
Jean (orig. Joann) Wright......................Marilyn McIntyre
Glen Connor (orig. John Woodman).............Rick Podell
John (orig. Jack) McLean...............................Thom Sharp
Maxwell Toys Vice President..................Robert J. Bernard

Giles' lawyer................................Michael Bryan French
Informant/clerk/Terry Lasher...........................Sean Gavigan
Detective Doug (orig. Paul) Savage.............Vincent Howard *
Security guard/DeCarlo...............................Clifton Powell

* Listed as Vincent Howard House in early press materials.

Director: Frank Thackery          Teleplay: Anne Collins
Story: Gerald Sanoff

**19. "The Trial" Part 2  Feb. 26, 1991  (1867)**

After his investigation uncovers a judicial conspiracy involving two judges, Matlock must face a top defense attorney (Coster) in the courtroom.  Guest Penn is a frequent *Matlock* director.

Judge David Bennett.......................................Mike Farrell
Judge Donna Levin.....................................Diana Muldaur
Tom O'Hare.....................................Carmen Argenziano
Jean (orig. Joann) Wright......................Marilyn McIntyre
Sidney Spaulding..................................................Leo Penn
Sam Bergstrom.....................................................Frances Bay
Chester Gaddis....................................Nicolas Coster
Jim Sullivan.....................................................Beans Morocco
Receptionists.....................Leesa Bryte, Lori Ashton
Foreperson...........................................................Ann Shalla

Director: Frank Thackery          Teleplay: Anne Collins
Story: Gerald Sanoff

**20. "The Accident"  March 26, 1991  (1868)**

The evidence trail behind the murder of a shady personal-injury attorney leads to an amusement park.  Wingreen reprises his role from ep. 9.  Orig. scheduled for March 19.

Mrs. Amanda Dobbs...................................Pamela Brull
Diane Radovich.......................................Judith Chapman
Asst. D.A.......................................................Michael Durrell
Al Demont..................Charlie Frank a.k.a. Charles R. Frank
Joe Kramer.......................................................Richard Grove
Eugene Dobbs..................................................Tom Henschel
Norman Wheeler...............................................Ken Lerner
Dr. Eldon McNeeley...........................Richard McGonagle
Judge Arthur Beaumont...............................Jason Wingreen
Nick (orig. Rick) Burnett.......................Richard Molinare
Injured worker/Clayton Sudowsky.................Chris Anastasio
And: Bruce Wright (Janitor), Edward Paul Allen (Director), Ed McCready (Foreperson), Heather Lind (Elizabeth), Julie Lloyd (Masseuse), Clifford H. Turknett (Officer)
Also orig. announced:
Wesley Mann, Carole Ita White (Patients), Michael J. Shea (Park attendant)

Director: Christopher Hibler
Writers: Max Eisenberg & Lonon Smith

**preempted April 9**

**21. "The Celebrity"  April 30, 1991  (1869)**

A cosmetics executive and former actress (Keane) is a suspect in the murder of her former lover and would-be blackmailer.

Jackie Flemming.............................................Arlene Golonka
Edgar Welden (orig. Wells)..............................Peter Hansen
Catherine Welden (orig. Wells)...........................Kerrie Keane
Homicide detective Stoner.................................David Morin
Peter Bates.......................................................Barry Sattels
Gil (orig. Henry) Altman...............................James Sutorius
Jeremy Conway.......................................Scott Williamson

And: Walter Addison (Judge), Anita Finlay (Diane Berliner), Rod Loomis (Ron), Michael J. Shea (Waiter), Nancy Sorel (Faith Gamson), Greg Thirloway (Asst. D.A.)
   Also orig. announced: Maurice Hill (Card player)

Director: Leo Penn                    Writer: Gerald Sanoff

**preempted May 7, May 14, May 21; rerun May 10, 8-9 p.m.**

**preempted June 18**

**Reruns continue to Sept. 10; announced as a midseason replacement series for the 1991-92 season**

## Midnight Caller

NBC               Fridays, 10-11 p.m.

Series premiere: Oct. 25, 1988
Final telecast: Aug. 2, 1991

Drama of an outspoken ex-cop turned controversial host of the titular late-night radio call-in show on San Francisco FM station KJCM. New cast-member Eilbacher was a guest, ep. 5. Jack's hangout bar: Carmen's. Filmed in San Francisco.

Jack Killian ("The Nighthawk").....................Gary Cole
Station owner Devon King (ep. 1-5).............Wendy Kilbourne
Station manager Nicolette "Nicky" Molloy
   (ep. 5-on)...........................................Lisa Eilbacher
Producer-engineer Billy Po......................Dennis Dun
Reporter Deacon Bridges........................Mykel T. Williamson
Lt. Carl Zymak....................................Arthur Taxier

*Recurring:*
Inspector Martin Slocum
   (ep. 1-2,4,9-14,17,19-20,22)..........Steven Anthony Jones
Bar-owner Jerado (ep. 1-5,8,9,12,16,19-22)....Jerado Carmona
Inspector Jerry Larkin (ep. 1,3,6,10).....................Denny Delk
Father Joe Di Maggio of St. Mike's
   (ep. 2,13,21-22)...........................................Reni Santoni

December 3rd Productions in assoc. with Lorimar Television
Executive producer: Robert Singer
Co-executive producer: David Israel
Producers: James Kramer, Randall Zisk, Eric Laneuville, Penny Adams
Supervising producer: John Schulian
Associate producer: Jim Michaels
Executive story editor: Michael Marks (later in season)
Executive consultant: Robert Butler
Director of photography (variously): Gordon M. Paschal; Bradley B. Six, A.S.C.
Music: Ross Levinson (occasionally with Peter Kaye)
Theme (instrumental): Brad Fiedel
Creator and creative consultant: Richard DiLello

---

1. "The Class of '80" a.k.a. "Burned Beyond Recognition" Sept. 28, 1990

Jack, delighted that Devon's seductive former college classmate (Phillips) has won a date with him at a charity auction, gets suspicious when fellow classmates are murdered.

Dani Hopkins.....................................Julianne Phillips
Alix Albright......................................Felicity La Fortune
Z.B. Burlingam...................................Amy Resnick
Susan Dunne......................................Susan Anne Matthews

Samuel Albright...............................Jay Jacobus
And: Adele Proom (Betty), Leigh French (Sunny Farina), Debi Gould (Lynn), Stu Klitsner (Minister)

Director: Eric Laneuville
Writers: David Israel & Robert Singer

2. "The Language Barrier" Oct. 5, 1990

After Billy is harrassed by neighborhood toughs for being Asian, Jack takes an on-air stand.

Augie Busico.......................................Michael Constantine
Jimmy................................................Neill Barry
Chang.................................................Tzi Ma
Mike Scarpelli.....................................Joe Maruzzo
Phil Wong...........................................Victor Wong
Wu Tsing............................................Willard Chin
Sharon Caputo.....................................Elissa Misner
Linda..................................................Michele Maika
And: Doreen Chou Croft (Amy Wong), Priscilla Alden (Elderly woman), Alec Jason (Grady), James Jack Duane (Mover)

Director: James A. Contner         Writer: John Schulian

3. "Old Friends" Oct. 12, 1990

Jack places his surrogate father (Balsam) in a nursing home, and finds residents dying through a network of mercy killers.

Gil Stolarski.......................................Martin Balsam
Jeanne Dansby.....................................Teddi Siddall
Ambrose McGee....................................Jeffrey Lynn
Henry Corday.......................................Scott Lincoln
Estelle Zymack, Carl's mother................Ruth Kobart
Guz Zymack, Carl's father......................Sydney Walker
Young Jack..........................................Chad Harden
Rusty.................................................Edward Markmann
Slick dude...........................................Ken Newman
Mason Kiley.........................................W. Allen Taylor
Stan Hildebrand....................................Anthony St. Martin
And: Pat Everett (Duke Bishop), Yvonne O'Reilly (Lonella), Jack Tucker (Ferdy), David J. Piel (Barney), Ella Johnson (Lucille Kiley), Gregory Proops (Cabbie), Charles Queary (Dr. Alan Farago), Robert "Bob" Hirsch (Character)

Director: Robert Singer            Writer: James Kramer

4. "Ain't Too Proud to Beg" Oct. 19, 1990

Jack proposes to the very pregnant Devon, just as her child's missing biological father (Lawford) returns. Part 1 of 2.

Hilary Townsend King, Wendy's mother...........Bonnie Bartlett
Richard Clark..........................................Christopher Lawford
Gossip columnist Becca Nicholson..........Eugenie Ross-Leming
Sunny...................................................Leigh French
Malcom "Flash" Gordon.............................Bill Bonham
Ava Brown.............................................Jacqueline Chappell
And: Dick Bright (Doorperson), James Gamble (Dock worker)

Director: James Quinn            Writer: John Schulian

5. "Sale Away" Oct. 26, 1990

Jack, Devon's Lamaze partner, is split between financial offers from KJCM's new owner (Meredith) and a rival station. Part 2 of 2.

Hilary Townsend King...............................Bonnie Bartlett
Foster Castleman....................................Don Meredith

Richard Clark...........................................Christopher Lawford
Richmond Waters.....................................Alex Hyde-White
Judge DeKoven..............................................Timothy Wise
Todd Billings................................................Mitchell Lester
Henry Niland...................................Mujahid Abdul Rashid
And: Liz Rolpe (Secretary), Kay E. Elizabeth (Nurse), Tom
    McGraw (Maitre d'), Kevin McGuire (Dr. Jenkins), Jerry
    Motta (Waiter), James Tripp (Man)

Director: Rob Bowman
Writer: Randall Zisk & Robert Singer

6. "Life Without Possibility" Part 1   Nov. 2, 1990

Jack agrees to rioting convicts' demands that he broadcast
their grievances from a live show within their prison -- where,
unknown to Jack, waits a killer (Knox) he once put away. Portions filmed at Alcatraz Penitentiary.

Luther Krock............................................Stan Shaw
Reno Thrift..............................................Terence Knox
Carlos Valenzuela....................................Robert Beltran
J.D. Stillwell...........................................Alan Rosenberg
William Buchanan........................................J.A. Preston
Nicholas Pierce...........................................Paul Lieber
Jeep Moseby.........................................Michael Whaley
Luis Ruiz.............................................Carlos Gonzalez
"Lone Ranger".........................................Nick Granado
Felix "Gato" Alvarez.....................................Noe Montoya
Joseph McDermott..................................Christopher Doyle
Rev. Darian Hayes........................................J.P. Phillips
Dickie Vaught.............................................Scott Rankin
Capt. Thomas Falcone..................................Charles Hoyes
And: Jack Shearer (Chesleigh Brant), Mary Dilts (TV newsper-
    son), Regina Saisi (Joan Slater), Susan D. Anderson (He-
    len Moseby), Fred D. Coleman, Jr. (Hostage)

Director: Eric Laneuville          Writer: David Israel

7. "Life Without Possibility" Part 2   Nov. 9, 1990

The convict that ex-cop Jack had had put away stalks him inside the prison as riot conditions deteriorate.

With: Shaw, Knox, Beltran, Rosenberg, Preston, Lieber, Wha-
    ley, Gonzalez, Granado, Montoya, Phillips, Rankin, Hoyes
    and Shearer from last episode
And: Darryl Scott (Kelvin Murray)

Director: Eric Laneuville          Writer: David Israel

8. "Ryder on the Storm"   Nov. 16, 1990

Jack run across his iconoclastic, boyhood radio hero (Klein),
and tries to find the troubled ex-DJ a job at the station.

Paul Ryder.............................................Robert Klein
Tom Barlow...............................................Jim Beaver
Kristen Barlow.............................Tracy O'Neil Heffernan
Ralph Gardina......................................Kenneth Grantham
Vincent Vincent.....................................Marcos Estebez
Noah Barlow..........................................Ryan Ashford
Beth Barlow.............................................Katie Sowell
Doctor...................................................Susan Emerson
Construction worker........................Charles Anthony Ganim

Director: Fred Gerber              Writer: John Schulian

**preempted Nov. 23 and Nov. 30**

9. "Home to Roost"   Wednesday, Dec. 5, 1990  9-10 p.m.

A grownup Vietnam War orphan (Okumoto) kidnaps an ex-cop
(Thomas) he believes guilty of war atrocities, and uses Jack's
audience as a "jury." Dilts reprises her role from ep. 6.

Jessick...................................................Robin Thomas
Le Minh..................................................Yuji Okumoto
Le Hong...................................................Alice Carter
Mary Jessick..............................................Ayn Ruymen
Nguyen...........................................Williams Ellis Hammond
Capt. John Danbury..................................Richard Butterfield
Col. William Taylor........................................Paul Henri
Ramirez..................................................Miguel Perez
Young Le Minh...........................................Justin Haroon
Cops....John X. Heart, Robert James Fairless, Donald Clyburn
Vietnamese man..........................................Sonyy Huynh
And: Bill Starr (Driver), Mary Dilts (TV newscaster), Wayne A.
    Morse (Security guard), June Melby (Catering boss)

Director: Robert Singer            Writer: Michael Marks

10. "With Malice Towards One"   Dec. 14, 1990

A homicidal ex-con (Levine) whom Jack sent to prison seeks
revenge. Former cast-member Kilbourne returns as a guest.

Devon King...........................................Wendy Kilbourne
Frank Brewer.............................................Ted Levine
Roy (orig. Dean) Brewer...................................S.A Griffin
Dean (orig. Roy) Brewer.........................Christopher Bradley
Amiko...................................................Diana Lee-Hsu
Harris Grimes......................................Drew Letchworth
Al Rambar..........................................Chuck L. Hilbert
Twitchy Sauerwein.................................Michael Bellino
And: John Balma (Blatchley), Allison Chase (Cathy), Viola
    Lucero (Dr. Bryant), Robert J. Fairless (Officer Tollier)

Director: James Quinn              Writer: John Schulian

11. "That's Amore"   Jan. 4, 1991

An old-world chef (Novello) for a criminal kingpin (Lipscomb) is
kidnapped by a rival crime boss. Guest Vale is a singer.

Aldo Marino...............................................Don Novello
Nick Clemente......................................Dennis Lipscomb
Ricky Roses............................................Scott Colomby
Rudolfo Scorza......................................John Del Regno
Catherine Marino..................................Heather McComb
Himself...................................................Jerry Vale
Sully..................................................Mark Amarotico
Jason Jordan..........................................Charles Aups
Baby John................................................Jeff Bryant
Bells.................................................Vincent Duvall
Frank................................................Michael Nicolosi
And: Gina Ferrall (Marla Martino), Richard Devon (Martin
    Longo), Brandan Andres (Boy on street), Al Cingolanti
    (Vito), Everett Y. Lee (Kim), Nicholas Romm (Bartender)

Director: James A. Contner         Writer: Peter Bonventre

**preempted Jan. 11 and Jan. 18**

12. "Her Dirty Little Secret"   Jan. 25, 1991

Jack thinks he spotted the long-missing wife (Austin) of a cop
friend (Marinaro), who beat her. Marinaro and director
Thomas were cast-members together on *Hill Street Blues* (NBC,
1981-87). Orig. scheduled for Jan. 18.

Joe Holloway...........................................Ed Marinaro
Jenna..................................................Karen Austin

Molly Jacobs..............................................Robin Frates
Lorraine Tilden..........................................Sharon Moore
Charlotte Coburn.......................................Nellie Cravens
Gun salesperson........................................Will Marchetti
Janitor/Cecil.......................................William McKereghan
Roy McMillan....................................Robert G. Fuentes

Director: Betty Thomas      Writer: Karen Clark

13. "Uninvited Guests" Feb. 1, 1991

Zymack has apparently fallen for an Immigration agent (Severance) whom Jack suspects is a murderer and extortionist.

Nora Cheever............................................Joan Severance
Benny Fuentes...........................................Eddie Velez
Cliff Bain.................................................Jon Van Ness
Father Rogelio Miramontes...................Richard Yniguez
Alicia Flores.............................................Maria Diaz
Miguel Torres..........................................Ramon Franco
Fernando Rojas.......................................Andrew Castillo
Deputy Coroner Bernie Slivka..........Michael Richard O'Rourke
Frank Rodriguez.......................................Carlos Baron
Felipe Salazar...........................................Luis Saguar
Hispanic woman...................................Christabel Savalas
And: Pepe Arteaba (Recruiter), Leonard Parnell (INS officer)

Director: James Quinn      Writer: James Kramer

14. "Play Blotto...and Die" Feb. 8, 1991

A protected witness (Carey) risks a gangster's vengeance when he must appear in person to claim a $46 million lottery prize.

Harry Flowers............................................Ron Carey
Crystal....................................................Crystal Carson
Nathan Dread..........................................Miguel Sandoval
Debbie Blye.............................................Valerie Curtin
Ducky Fenstermaker..................................Robert Dinner
Customer.................................................Joe Weatherby
And: Nathaniel Roberts (Blue), Erika Phillips (Teenaged girl)

Director: Eric Laneuville      Writer: John Schulian

15. "Can't Say N-N-No" Feb. 15, 1991

Nicky is nervous and concerned about the reappearance of her drug-addicted, musician ex-boyfriend (Rock and Roll Hall of Famer Daltrey, of The Who, who sings "Feel So Alive").

Danny Bingham.......................................Roger Daltrey
Joey Nolan................................................Jack McGee
Simon Potter...........................................Victor Talmadge
Officer Cal McGuane..................................Michael E. Stone
Buddy....................................................Craig Oldfather
And: Mark Petrakis (Nelson), James Friedman (Ben Margules), Darold Ross (Doctor), Sue Trigg (Chelsea)

Director: Randall Zisk      Writer: James Kramer

**preempted Feb. 22**

16. "Blood Ties" March 1, 1991

The long-gone, alcoholic father (Frank) of a boy to whom Jack is a Big Brother wants to return to his family. Guest Craig is a San Francisco 49ers player. Orig. scheduled for Feb. 22.

Hank Scanlon............................................Gary Frank
Brian Scanlon..........................................Barrett Brown
Teri Scanlon............................................Jayne Atkinson

Nancy Wiley............................................Joan Mankin
Speaker...................................................Bob Scott
Himself.........................................Roger Craig (uncredited)

Director: Win Phelps      Writer: Michael Marks

**on hiatus**

17. "The Added Starter" April 5, 1991

After a political aide (Caffey) walks in on the apparent corpses of a state senator (Albert) and a call girl, the bodies vanish.

State Sen. Jordan Pearl.........................Edward Albert
Callie Lodge............................................Colleen Caffey
Allison Pratt..................................Allison Rutledge-Parisi
Meredith Gaynor.....................................Phyllis Coates
Richard Hasburgh....................................Marshall Bell
Nina Wolfe.............................................Richel Kompst
Leo Stanky.............................................Charles Dean
Rigby.......................................................John Bellucci
Benjamin Laird..........................................Jay Morse
Cecil Sandberg........................................James L. Kelly
Dorothy...............................................Teresa R. Roberts
Crime technician.........................................Bill Starr
Homeless persons..........................Jack Halton, Russ Davison

Director: Eric Laneuville      Writer: David Braff

18. "The Loneliest Number" April 12, 1991

Jack disapproves when his bubbly but man-dependent kid sister (Garber) shows up after ten years, and falls for Deacon.

Katie......................................................Terri Garber
Dr. Lee Cartmell.......................................Victor Bevine
Chesleigh Brant.......................................Jack Shearer
And: Khadijah (Receptionist), Bonnie Steiger (Ora Lee), Cheryl Wilson (Jill Fielder), Albert McCarthy (Driver)

Director: Peter Levin      Teleplay: James Kramer
Story: Teddi Siddall and James Kramer

19. "A Cry in the Night" April 19, 1991

The building's security guard (Evans) accidentally kills his drug-crazed son, and blames it on Jack's on-air advice. Director Sgriccia is one of the series' film editors.

Garland....................................................Art Evans
Lola Atkins......................................Stephanie E. Williams
Rey Atkins..............................................Calvin Levels
Byron Walsh............................................Squire Fridell
Irving Pappas.........................................Chris Lemmon
Donald Pell..............................................Chris Clark
Pamela Mossman.......................................Vilma Silva
Judge....................................................Patricia Kane
Dr. Sheila Rayner.....................................Judith Moreland
And: Merv Maruyama (Doctor), Taylor Brock (Nurse), Jonathan Wafer (Young man), Darren (infant; uncredited)

Director: Philip J. Sgriccia
Writers: Chris Carter and Michael Marks

20. "The Leopard" April 26, 1991

Jack is shaken down by mobsters to whom his absent, con-artist/gambler father owes $50,000. Boyle reprises his role from April 3, 1990 and a 1989 episode, Bryant from ep. 11.

J.J. Killian..............................................Peter Boyle

"Terrible" Tommy Bombacelli....................................Alex Rocco
Nick Clemente................................................Dennis Lipscomb
Tony "Gloves" D'Arco...........................................Joe Marinelli
Johnny "The Nose" Roti.....................................Michael Rogen
Filomena Clemente....................Amelia Martinez Schumacher
Baby John.........................................................Jeff Bryant
Tough guy....................................................Ernesto Ravetto
And: Maria Fortuna (Opera diva), Ed Pansullo (High roller),
    Rudy Paige (Bustout player), Greg Lucey (Weirdo)

Director: James Quinn          Writer: Charles Robert Carner

**preempted May 3**

21. "City of Lost Souls" Part 1  Tuesday, May 7, 1991

A teen (Furlow) claims Jack is her father, prompting him to
canvass the city's homeless for her real dad (Chase), Jack's
former high-school classmate.

Travis Quarry.....................................................Jerry Hardin
Andrew France...................................................John Hancock
Lori Winrow.....................................................Shana Furlow
Sonny Rote.......................................................David Chase
Stephanie Corbridge.........................................Kathryn Knotts
Ezra Bates.......................................................Bruce Mackey
Clare Winrow, Lori's mother.........................Delia MacDougall
Ned..............................................................Russ Davison
Coach "Buck" Schalbuck.......................................Edward Ivory
And: Michael McFall (Grady Hatton), Melody Cole (Bag lady)

Director: Eric Laneuville          Teleplay: John Schulian
Story: David Israel & John Schulian

22. "City of Lost Souls" Part 2  May 10, 1991  9-11 p.m.

Jack unsettles politicians and the police when he attacks the
lukewarm investigation into his homeless friend's murder.
Liddy is the convicted Watergate conspirator.

Fredrik Van Woerkom.....................................G. Gordon Liddy
Travis Quarry.....................................................Jerry Hardin
Cassie Douglas................................................Judie Aronson
Nelson Briles.......................................................Blake Clark
Gene Calder...................................................Charles R. Frank
Lori Winrow.....................................................Shana Furlow
Denton Medwick...............................................Nicholas Guest
Andrew France...................................................John Hancock
Dallas Castleman.................................................Stan Ivar
Patrick Squier....................................................Scott Freeman
Stephanie Corbridge.........................................Kathryn Knotts
Clare Winrow, Lori's mother.........................Delia MacDougall
Al Haynie.........................................................C.W. Morgan
And: Bruce Mackey (Ezra Bates), Michael Ray Wisely (Uni-
    formed officer), Allen Bebhardt (Cabbie), Melody Cole
    (Bag lady), James K. Lewis (Cop), Matt Silverman (Home-
    less man), Joseph Metzgar (Captain), Mary-Margaret Lew-
    is (Emcee), Michael L. Ching (Florist), Andrea Yee (His
    wife), David Maier (Flunky), Frank Widman (Gardener),
    Mary Elizabeth Uhland (Secretary), Jessica Myerson

Director: James Quinn
Teleplay (first hour): Michael Marks and David Israel & Robert
    Singer
Story (first hour): David Israel & John Schulian & Michael
    Marks
Teleplay (second hour): John Schulian and James Kramer &
    Michael Marks
Story (second hour): John Schulian

**preempted May 17 and May 24**

**preempted June 28 and July 5**

## Morton & Hayes

CBS          Wednesdays, 8:30-9 p.m.

Series premiere: July 24, 1991
Final telecast: Aug. 28, 1991

Parody of, and homage to, old-Hollywood comedy teams, with
host Rob Reiner introducing "newly unearthed" black-and-
white comedy shorts from the vault of fictitious producer Max
King, starring straight-man Morton and foil/patsy Hayes.
Working title: *Partners in Life*. The series title above is as given
by CBS in press materials and in onscreen promos; no actual
series logo appears on the show itself.  Logo for the faux film-
lets: *Max King Presents Chick Morton & Eddie Hayes*. Produc-
er-director Guest is married to actress Jamie Lee Curtis.

Chick Morton/Albert Mosburg.............................Kevin Pollak
Eddie Hayes/Vincenzo Jacomelli...........................Bob Amaral

Castle Rock Entertainment
Executive producers: Rob Reiner, Dick Blausucci, Christopher
    Guest
Supervising producers: Tom Gammill, Max Pross
Producer: Steven Ecclesine
Associate producer: Tim Kaiser
Director of photography: Jeffrey Jur
Music: Hummie Mann
Theme: Hummie Mann & Christopher Guest
Director unless otherwise noted: Christopher Guest
Creators: Rob Reiner & Phil Mishkin

---

1. "Daffy Dicks"  July 24, 1991

As private eyes, Morton and Hayes are hired by a rich woman
(O'Hara) who suspects her husband of having an affair.

Mimi Vib Astor/Amelia Von Astor..................Catherine O'Hara
Reginald.............................................................Raye Birk
And: Monte Landis (Ambassador), Dale Raoul (His wife), Henry
    Polic, II (Maitre d'), Clive Rosengren (Cop), Molly Cleator
    (Miss Abercrombie), Christopher Guest (Dr. Von Astor)

Writer: Phil Mishkin

2. "The Bride of Mummula"  July 31, 1991

Chick and Eddie are stranded in a Bavarian village until they
receive an invitation to stay at a mad doctor's castle.

Jody......................................................Penelope Ann Miller
Dr. Mummenschvantz....................................Michael McKean
Hunchback/Steve............................................Hamilton Camp
And: Wil Albert (Old man), Peter Zapp (Villager)

Writers: Christopher Guest & Michael McKean
(Orig. announced: Michael McKean)

3. "Society Saps"  Aug. 7, 1991

Waiters Eddie and Chick are mistaken for society gents at a
party, and win the affection of the rich, homely hostesses.

Abigail Caldicott............................................Maria Parkinson
Beatrice Caldicott..............................................Allison Janney
Mr. Caldicott....................................................Lewis Arquette

Mr. Franklin.................................................Bradley Mott
And: Jacob Kenner (Aldo), Nick Toth (Subway passenger), Linda Hoy (Party guest), Mimi Cozzens, Jennifer Rhodes (Hunt guests), Barry Dennen (Waiter), John O'Leary (Minister), Christopher Guest (Crooner)

Song: "Cold Potatoes" by Christopher Guest & Michael McKean (words and music)

Writers: Christopher Guest & Dick Blasucci

4. "Oafs Overboard" Aug. 14, 1991

Stowaways Chick and Eddie walk the plank and wind up on an island where they're to become human sacrifices.

Princess Lucy....................................................Courteney Cox
Ooloo the Giant................................................Jack O'Halloran
Hong Kong theater manager..............James Hong (uncredited)
And: Hamilton Camp (Smitty), Clarence Felder (Dock worker), Dale Ishimoto (Native Chief), Tui Letuli (Native), Dennis Drake (Wally), Christopher Guest (El Supremo)

Songs: "Friends" and "Ooloo," lyrics by Tom Gammill & Max Pross

Writers: Tom Gammill & Max Pross

5. "The Vase Shop" Aug. 21, 1991

The boys are left in charge of an antique vase shop.

Mr. Nicolides....................................................Paul Benedict
Rollo.................................................................Michael Ciotti
Officer Rafferty................................................Clive Rosengren
Rose of Sharon.................................................Molly Hagan
Mrs. Shubb.......................................................Marianne Muellerleile
John D. Rockenfuss...........................................George O. Petrie
And: Jackie Sloan (Betty Nicolides), Rick Floyd (Spats), Bradley Mott (Mr. Shubb), Joe Flaherty (Thug)

Writers: Dick Blasucci & Joe Flaherty

6. "Home Buddies" Aug. 28, 1991   9:30-10 p.m.

While their overbearing wives are visiting their mothers, Chick and Eddie become millionaires as winners of a radio contest.

Mrs. Morton.....................................................Allison Janney
Mrs. Hayes.......................................................Maria Parkinson
Mr. Franklin....................................................Bradley Mott
French maid......................................................Fabiana Udenio
And: Raye Birk (Butler), Clive Rosengren (Cop), Jeff Doucette (Crook), Michael Lee Gogin (Messenger)

Director: Michael McKean
Writers: Tom Gammill & Max Pross

## Murder, She Wrote

CBS          Sept. 16-June 2, July 14-on   Sundays, 8-9 p.m.
             June 9-July 7                 Sundays, 9-10 p.m.

Series premiere: Sept. 30, 1984

Lighthearted mystery-drama of a crime novelist in Cabot Cove, Maine, who finds herself solving real murders. Star Lansbury appears only in framing sequences in the five episodes this season featuring insurance investigator Dennis Stanton. Recurring guest Todd is a cast-member of Going Places.

Jessica (J.B.) Fletcher......................................Angela Lansbury

*Recurring:*
Dennis Stanton (ep. 3,8,10,12,18).......................Keith Michell
Sheriff Mort Metzger (ep. 2,6,13,17,23)...................Ron Masak
Deputy Floyd (ep. 6,13,17,23)..............................Will Nye
Lt. Catalano (ep. 3,8,10,12,18)............................Ken Swofford
Rhoda (ep. 3,8,10,12,18)....................................Hallie Todd

Universal Television, an MCA Co.
Executive producer: Peter S. Fischer
Supervising producer: Robert F. O'Neill
Producers: Robert E. Swanson, Robert Van Scoyk
Associate producer: Anthony J. Magro
Director of photography: John Elsenbach, A.S.C.
Music (variously): Richard Markowitz; David Bell
Theme (instrumental): John Addison
Creators: Peter S. Fischer and Richard Levinson & William Link

_____

1. "Trials and Tribulations" Sept. 16, 1990

Jessica is accused of bribery and lying when a convicted murderer is killed in an attempted jailbreak. Director McEveety has a cameo; Hamilton is the daughter of Carol Burnett.

Beatrice Vitello..............................................Kim Hunter
Von Steuben....................................................George Hearn
Geraldine.......................................................Carrie Hamilton
Justin Fields...................................................Michael Beck
Anne Stevenson.................................................Molly Cheek
Sgt. Paulsen....................................................Stephen Furst
Charlie Cosmo..................................................George Maharis
Ray Dandridge..................................................Ben Masters
Lady.............................................................Molly McClure
Mrs. Torgeson..................................................Darlene Kardon
Driver...........................................................Ron Tron
Waiters............Richard Hoyt-Miller, Jerry Tullos, Thom Keane
And: Gerry Okuneff (Eddie Stone), Joe Nesnow (Cab driver), Richard Campluis, Vincent J. McEveety (Guard), Lance E. Nichols (Police officer), Mary Angela Shea (Secretary)

Director: Vincent McEveety          Writer: Peter S. Fischer

2. "Deadly Misunderstanding" Sept. 23, 1990

Jessica breaks her arm in a bicycle accident and hires a typist (Cutter) who becomes a suspect when her spouse is murdered.

Melissa Maddox.................................................Lise Cutter
Ben Devlin......................................................Joe Dorsey
Hank Crenshaw...................................................Geoffrey Lewis
Rita Garrison...................................................Janet Margolin
Garrison........................................................David McCallum
Jeff Ogden......................................................David Oliver
Trudy...........................................................Mary Ann Pascal
Ralph Maddox....................................................Cliff Potts

Director: Anthony Shaw          Writer: Robert F. Swanson

3. "See You in Court, Baby" Sept. 30, 1990

Dennis Stanton investigates when a disputed divorce settlement over a car leads to the murder of a flashy lawyer (Reed).

Amy Sue..........................................................Heidi Bohay
Karen...........................................................Judith Chapman
Joe Briscoe.....................................................Charles Haid
Ed Kriegler.....................................................Tom Isbell

Jason....................................................................Peter Kowanko
Charmaine...........................................................Vera Miles
Calloway..............................................................Robert Reed
Marcia McPhee....................................................Nana Visitor

Director: Vincent McEveety          Writer: Peter S. Fischer

**preempted Oct. 7**

4. "Hannigan's Wake" Oct. 28, 1990

At the request of a dying, Pulitzer Prize-winning author (Johnson), Jessica investigates a 16-year-old miscarriage of justice.

Hannigan...........................................................Van Johnson
Grant.................................................Efrem Zimbalist, Jr.
Commissioner Folkes.................................Bradford Dillman
Eric Grant.........................................................Anthony Geary
Phyllis Thurlow.................................................Cynthia Harris
Dorothy Folkes...................................................Mala Powers
Stephen Thurlow.............................................Raphael Sbarge
Bert Kravitz.....................................................Guy Stockwell
Ernie Dolan....................................................Stephen Young
Jonathan Barish...................................................Emory Bass
Madeline.......................................................Le Reine Chabut
Victor Impelleteri...............................................Johnny Crear
Madge.......................................Kate Randolph Burns
Eddie Folkes....................................................Isaac Turner

Director: Vincent McEveety          Writer: Peter S. Fischer

5. "The Family Jewels" Nov. 4, 1990

While at a Manhattan fundraiser for a friend (Farrell) running for D.A., Jessica finds a kleptomaniacal socialite (Vaccaro), a dead chauffeur, and a social-climbing detective (Rocket).

Drew Borden....................................................Mike Farrell
Sheila Kowalski Finley......................................Brenda Vaccaro
Police Lt. Stuyvesant........................................Charles Rocket
Rocco Pastolino....................................................Joey Aresco
Porter Finley III..............................................John Considine
Sid Staples.....................................................Stanley Kamel
Margaret Gable..................................................Jonna Lee
Charles Laurence...........................................Howard McGillin
D.L. Beaumont..............................................Richard Davalos
Arthur Morris.....................................................Doug Mears
Barbara Loring.............................................Deborah Benson
Secretary/Olivia...........................................Pamela Roylance
Reporters.........................Forrest Witt, Marcy Goldman
And: Diana Lewis (Newscaster), Michael Halpin (Technician)

Director: Jerry Jameson          Writer: Tom Sawyer

6. "A Body to Die For" Nov. 11, 1990

The handsome new workout instructor (Beghe), over whom the townswomen swoon, has a shady past linking him to a murder.

Nancy.............................................................Sally Struthers
Fred Keppard..................................................Hugh O'Brian
Eve Simpson......................................................Julie Adams
Wayne Bennett.................................................Jason Beghe
Ben Devlin..........................................................Joe Dorsey
Lil Hardin.............................................................Alix Elias
Renee...................................................................Ruta Lee
And: Ernie Lively (Joe Hardin), Patricia McPherson (Betty),
    James Olson (Clarence), Katharine Durish (Receptionist),
    Michele Bernath (Woman), Paul Lueken (Paramedic)

Director: Anthony Shaw          Writer: Donald Ross

7. "The Return of Preston Giles" Nov. 18, 1990

Jessica is concerned when her former publisher, paroled after her investigation led to his murder conviction, returns to Sutton Place Publishing. Hill reprises his role from the pilot.

Preston Giles.........................................................Arthur Hill
Sutton Place owner Ross McKay.....................Michael McKean
Linette McKay, his wife.......................................Brynn Thayer
Millie Stafford.......................................................Lois Chiles
Martin Bergman...................................................George Coe
Gloria Winslow................................................Arlene Golonka
Detective Sgt. Jack Slocum..............................Todd Susman
Kendall Stafford.........................................Gordon Thompson
And: Regina Leeds (Dorothy), Kriss Turner (Secretary), Michael
    Eugene Fairman (Cabbie), Steven Connor (Asst. Manager)

Director: Walter Grauman          Writer: Tom Sawyer

8. "The Great Twain Roberry" Nov. 25, 1990

Dennis Stanton investigates a "newly found" Mark Twain manuscript insured for $5 million, then destroyed in a fire.

Anna Louise.......................................................Diane Baker
Lawrence Erlich...................................................David Birney
Fitzpatrick............................................................Roy Dotrice
Lindsey Barlow................................................Holly Gagnier
Stavros...........................................................Nehemiah Persoff
Robert Butler...................................................James Sloyan
Sgt. Oliver....................................................Stephen Prutting
Authenticator........................................................Russ Marin
Book lover.............................................................Jan Hoag
Duke of Nonesuch.............................................Lewis Dauber
Reporters........................Freddie Dawson, Delana Michaels
And: Daniel Namath (Maitre d'), Susan Ware (Newscaster)

Director: Jerry Jameson          Writer: Steve Brown

9. "Ballad for a Blue Lady" Dec. 2, 1990

On a Nashville vacation, Jessica visits country music-star friends, but feudin' and fightin' lead to murder. Guests Dean, Gilley and Wolley are real-life country performers.

Patti Sue Diamond.....................................Florence Henderson
Bobby Diamond...................................................Jimmy Dean
Alice Diamond, Bobby's daughter................Daphne Ashbrook
Brittany Brown.......................................................Jeri Gaile
Conrad Booker..................................................Mickey Gilley
Garth................................................................Blake Gibbons
Preston Wardell...................................................Tom Hallick
Mark Berringer..................................................Gary Grubbs
Lt. Jackson.....................................................Brandon Maggart
Billy Ray Hawkins.............................................Sheb Wolley
And: John Christy Ewing (Dr. Benson), Bob Swain (Forensic
    person), Cary Pitts (Guard), Marji Martin (Mirabelle)

Director: Jerry Jameson          Writer: William Bigelow

10. "Murder in F Sharp" Dec. 16, 1990  8:05-9:05 p.m.

Dennis Stanton investigates when the insured hands of a famous pianist (Montalban) are severly burned, and his wife is murdered. Late start due to a long-running sports event prior.

Vaclav Maryska..............................................Ricardo Montalban
Milena Maryska..................................................Patricia Neal
Alex Seletz...................................................Stephen Caffrey
Nicole...............................................................Melinda Culea
Ben Devlin............................................................Joe Dorsey

Robert Butler...................................................James Sloyan
And: Dean R. Miller (Charlie), Anne Gee Byrd (Widow), Aaron Heyman (Mr. Morris), John Kerry (Security guard)

Director: Kevin G. Cremin          Writer: William Bigelow

11. "Family Doctor" Jan. 6, 1990 8:21-9:21 p.m.

When a mobster's killed at a restaurant, Jessica and Seth are held as pawns until she can uncover the assassin. Windom reprises his recurring role from past seasons. Orig. scheduled for Dec. 16. Late start due to a long-running sports event prior.

Dr. Seth Hazlitt................................................William Windom
Carmine Abruzzi..................................................Tige Andrews
Denise Abruzzi...................................................Cynthia Bain
Sal...............................................................David Ciminello
Jerry Marino....................................................Joseph Cortese
Freddie..........................................................Robert Costanzo
Phyllis Chase....................................................Diane Franklin
Rose Abruzzi......................................................Rose Gregorio
Michael Abruzzi.................................................Vincent Irizarry
Andrew Chase.....................................................Monte Markham
Connie Canzanaro.....................................................Amy Yasbeck
Agent Milson (orig. Wilks).....................................William Utay
Agent Zweibeck (orig. Thompson)...................Newell Alexander
Desk Sergeant.....................................................Howard George
Cops.........................................Michael Blue, Jay Hill
And: Linda Larkin (Waitress), Randall James Jeffries (Bellhop)

Director: Walter Grauman          Writer: Robert Van Scoyk

12. "Suspicion of Murder" Jan. 20, 1991 8:36-9:36 p.m.

Dennis Stanton rekindles a relationshsip with a former flame (Blakely) and finds himself a suspect in her husband's murder. Late start due to a long-running sports event prior.

Christina Hellinger.............................................Susan Blakely
Joey Hellinger.....................................................Sam Bottoms
Ryan Donovan......................................................Dennis Cole
Robert Butler.....................................................James Sloyan
Danny Hellinger....................................................Robin Strand
Clerk..............................................................Adam Silber
Police officers.......Ed Beechner, Dennis O'Sullivan, John Arndt
And: Paul Keith (Cashier), Lenny Citrano (Doorperson), Robert Donovan (Man), Judy Kerr (Housekeeper)

Director: Vincent McEveety          Writer: Peter S. Fischer

13. "Moving Violation" Feb. 3, 1991

The sheriff defies political pressure by arresting an ambassador's drunk-driving son, then is accused of the son's murder.

Meredith Hellman.................................................Susan Clark
Ambassador Chandler Hellman..............................Jack Colvin
Lt. Avery Powell..................................................Robert Ginty
Haskell Drake....................................................Harry Guardino
Ed Costner......................................................Philip Baker Hall
Bradley Hellman, the ambassador's son...........David Lansbury
Jason Farrell....................................................Stephen Macht
Mayor Sam Booth.................................................Richard Paul
Morgan.............................................................Suzanne Snyder
Phyllis Costner...................................................Lois de Banzie
And: Barbara C. Adside (Janet Costner), Phyllis Franklin (Mabel), Daniel Ben Wilson (Mickey), Jason Bo Sharon (Billy)

Director: Anthony Shaw          Writer: Robert E. Swanson

14. "Who Killed J.B. Fletcher?" Feb. 10, 1991

Members of her fan club help Jessica when one of their own (Withers), posing as Jessica, is arrested and mysteriously dies. Guest Machado is a real-life newscaster.

Boone Willoughby..................................................Max Baer
Bertie.............................................................Janet Blair
Kit Parkins.......................................................Betty Garrett
Sheriff Tanner....................................................Earl Holliman
Florence..........................................................Terry Moore
Jane.............................................................Margaret O'Brien
Lisa McCauley......................................................Jamie Rose
Rick.............................................................Tom Schanley
Mitchell Lawrence.................................................Lyman Ward
Caroline..........................................................Marie Windsor
Marge Allen.......................................................Jane Withers
And: David Cowgill (Deputy), Jon Menick (Kennel clerk), Mario Machado (Anchorperson), Rod Britt (Clerk), Marvyn Byrkett (Technician), Marc Marosi (Waiter), Michael Leopard (Cabbie), Curt Booker (Security guard)

Director: Walter Grauman          Writer: Lynn Kelsey

15. "The Taxman Cometh" Feb. 17, 1991

Jessica's bakery-magnate friend (Newman) is accused of killing her ex-husband, and stealing $2 million in tax payments.

Gail Curtis........................................................Robin Dearden
Richard Wellstood..................................................Gregg Henry
Noel Hayes......................................................Macon McCalman
George Arus.......................................................Kent McCord
Edna Hayes.......................................................Phyllis Newman
J.K. Davern........................................................Roy Thinnes
Lt. Phillips.......................................................Fred Willard
IRS agent George Yelverton........................................Max Wright
Maid.............................................................Joan Crosby
And: Dominic Oliver (Pizza person), Greg Allan Martin, John Christopher (Officers), Annie O'Donnell (Mrs. Leeman), Larry Eisenberg (Clerk)

Director: Anthony Shaw          Writer: Donald Ross

16. "From the Horse's Mouth" Feb. 24, 1991

In Kentucky, Jessica and (Orbach, reprising his role from previous seasons) find a thoroughbred owner (McCarthy) killed apparently over a rivalry. Guest Belli is a real-life lawyer.

Harry McGraw......................................................Jerry Orbach
Judge Harley B. Prescott...................................Melvin M. Belli
Derek Padley...................................................Maxwell Caulfield
Diana Snowcroft.....................................Patricia Charbonneau
Sheriff McKenna...................................................Robert Donner
Emmaline Bristow.................................................Nanette Fabray
Randolph Sterling...........................................Kevin McCarthy
Althea Mayberry...................................................Tricia O'Neil
Tod Sterling.................................................John Allen Nelson
Christie Morgan.................................................Debra Sandland
Lamar Walcott...................................................Gregory Walcott
Martha Jane Stokes...............................................Helena Carroll
Justin King.......................................................James Bartz
And: Michael Ayr (Mark Mason), Patricia Huston (Edie), Kathy Hartsell (Young woman), Richard Balin (Coroner)

Director: Jerry Jameson          Writer: Gerry Day

17. "The Prodigal Father" March 10, 1991

A suspected bank robber (Rhodes) is killed upon resurfacing after 20 years to reunite with his child (Christian). Guest Paul reprises his role from ep. 13. Orig. scheduled for March 24.

Bonnie Hastings............................................Claudia Christian
Elton Summers................................................Don Galloway
Herb Walsh.....................................................Robert Lansing
Maxine Molloy...............................................Kathleen Nolan
Mayor Sam Booth.............................................Richard Paul
Gil Blocker......................................................Andrew Prine
Ned Jencks..................................................Donnelly Rhodes
George, owner of the Lighthouse Motel...................Abe Vigoda
Dave Hastings, Bonnie's husband......................Larry Wilcox
Dr. Lyle Rush.....................................................Mark Roberts
Linda.................................................................Robin Gordon
Sally, Dave and Bonnie's daughter...............Mindy Ann Martin
And: Sarah Simmons (Woman), Gary Hollis (Man)

Director: Anthony Shaw
Writers: Maryann Kasica & Michael Scheff

18. "Where Have You Gone, Billy Boy?"
    March 17, 1991  8:29-9:29 p.m.

Dennis Stanton investigates when a shy ventriloquist (Shaud, a cast-member of *Murphy Brown*) becomes the prime suspect in the murder of a comedy club's ruthless owner (Brown). Orig. scheduled for March 10. Late start due to a long-running sports event previous.

Woody Perkins....................................................Grant Shaud
Kate Kelley......................................................Georgia Brown
Brenda McCoy........................................................Teri Copley
Sally..........................................................Leslie Easterbrook
Joe Gelardi...........................................................Marty Ingels
Tom Benzinger, Woody's manager........................Jim Metzler
Robert Butler, Dennis' boss..............................James Sloyan
Vic DiMarco.....................................................Lyle Waggoner
Elmo.....................................................................Mike Jolly
Budding comic.............................................David Stenstrom
Comic..................................................................Jeffrey Jena
Insurance co-workers.............Kevin McCoy, Jana Grant, Matt
    McCarter, Susan Welby

Director: John Llewellyn Moxey        Writer: Peter S. Fischer

**preempted March 24**

19. "Thursday's Child"  April 7, 1991

A woman (Miles), accused of murder, says her architect son (Gilliland) was fathered by Jessica's late husband, Frank. Frost is the daughter of actor Warren Frost and the brother of producer Mark Frost, both of *Twin Peaks*.

Nancy Landon.........................................................Vera Miles
Andrew Dixon...................................................John Anderson
Ben Olston................................................................John Beck
Dawn Bickford...................................................Lindsay Frost
Axelrod................................................................Alan Fudge
Steve............................................................Richard Gilliland
Lt. Barney Claymore............................................Paul Gleason
Clint Phelps.......................................................Martin Milner
Cynthia Olston..............................................Jennifer Warren
Crocket.................................................................Jim Boeke
And: Fredric Cook (Aarsonson), Scott Bullock (Cabbie), Steven
    Novak (Roy Temple), Elven Havard (Duty patrol officer)

Director: Anthony Shaw          Writer: Robert E. Swanson

20. "Murder, Plain and Simple"  April 28, 1991

Jessica's assistant (Block), her escort to Amish country, is the prime suspect when their host (Sarrazin) is found murdered. Orig. scheduled for March 24.

Ethan Kaufmann.......................................Todd Eric Andrews
Reuben Stoltz...................................................Hunt Block
Sarah Lapp.......................................................Martha Byrne
Sheriff Haines......................................................John Ireland
Bishop Burkhart..................................................Jay Robinson
Rebecca Beiler.............................................Jennifer Runyon
Jacob Beiler....................................................Michael Sarrazin
Samuel Kaufmann.....................................Arlen Dean Snyder
Driver.................................................................Ed McCready

Director: Vincent McEveety          Writer: Chris Manheim

21. "Tainted Lady"  May 5, 1991

When three townspeople die of arsenic poisoning, Jessica's diner-owner friend (Stone) is unfairly accused and ostracized. Orig. scheduled for April 14.

Ellen Wicker..................................................Dee Wallace Stone
Ross Corman.......................................................Marshall Colt
Laura Corman.......................................................Mary Crosby
Katie Emhardt.........................................................Nina Foch
Herb Apple............................................................Sam Freed
Dr. John Logan.................................................Jack Kruschen
Sheriff Deloy Hays...........................................Gary Lockwood
Doris Gerringer..................................................Laurie Prange
Edge Potter..........................................................Don Swayze
Deputy Ray Gomez.................................................Javi Mulero
Deputy Mary Jo Rush..........................................Karen Hensel
Young man........................................................Peter Gregory

Director: Vincent McEveety          Writer: Robert Van Scoyk

22. "The Skinny According to Nick Cullhane"  May 12, 1991

A writer (Harrington) is killed because his manuscript, which Jessica was critiquing, is actually an expose of a kidnap scam. Orbach reprises his role from ep. 16; Easterbrook played a different role in ep. 18. Frank is the U.S. Postmaster General. Orig. scheduled for May 5.

Harry McGraw.......................................................Jerry Orbach
Vikki Palumbo.............................................Leslie Easterbrook
Nick Cullhane.................................................Pat Harrington
Ogden Schmesser......................................Alex Hyde-White
Phil Mannix.......................................................Tony Lo Bianco
Richard..........................................................Michael McGrady
Gordon Forbes..............................................Jameson Parker
Florence................................................................Tricia Long
Letter-carrier Finnerty................................Anthony M. Frank

Director: Walter Grauman          Writer: Tom Sawyer

**preempted June 2**

**renewed for 1991-92; new episodes begin Sept. 15, 1991**

# Murphy Brown

CBS          Mondays, 9-9:30 p.m.

Series Premiere: Nov. 14, 1988

Comedy about the *FYI* ("For Your Information") TV news-magazine, and its temperamental co-anchor. Set in Washington, D.C. The variable opening theme is an excerpt from a (generally Motown) pop/soul song, loosely tied to the episode. A running gag, impacting on the guest cast, involves Murphy's inability to keep a secretary. Recurring guests Carroll, Hostetter and Brinkley reprise their roles from past seasons.

Murphy Brown...............................................Candice Bergen
Corky Sherwood-Forrest...............................Faith Ford
Jim Dial...........................................Charles Kimbrough
Frank Fontana...............................................Joe Regalbuto
News director Miles Silverberg............................Grant Shaud
Bar-restaurant owner Phil..............................Pat Corley
Housepainter-artist Eldin Bernecky...............Robert Pastorelli

*Recurring:*
Doris Dial, Jim's wife (ep. 7,10,16).....................Janet Carroll
Stage manager John (ep. 1-2,4-5,7,14,20-21)....John Hostetter
Cameraperson Carl (ep. 2,4-5,9,17)....................Ritch Brinkley

Shukovsky/English Productions in assoc. with Warner Bros. Television
Executive producers: Diane English, Joel Shukovsky
Supervising producers: Gary Dontzig, Steven Peterman
Co-supervising producer: Tom Palmer
Producer: Barnet Kellman
Co-producer: Deborah Smith
Consulting producer: Korby Siamis
Executive story editors: Sy Dukane, Denise Moss
Director of photography: Gil Hubbs
End-theme (instrumental) and music: Steve Dorff
Director unless otherwise noted: Barnet Kelman
Creator: Diane English

---

1. "The 390th Broadcast"  Sept. 17, 1990  (186851)

Miles hires an image consultant (Shearer) to make *FYI* more "viewer-friendly."

Chris Bishop.............................................Harry Shearer
Secretary #37...........................................Peter Slutsker
Greta......................................................Felicity La Fortune
Mrs. Hooley.............................................Jessie Jones
And: Zar Acayan (Pizza deliverer), Laverne Anderson (Teenager), Channing Chase (Housewife), Jordan Lund (Construction worker), Peggy Mannix (Woman in loud outfit), Cliff Medaugh (Older man), Kerry Stein (Nerdy man)

Writer: Diane English

2. "Brown and Blue"  Sept. 24, 1990  (186852)

Murphy tests her journalistic integrity when interviewing a sexist, racist shock-comic (Chiklis).

Tony Rocket.............................................Michael Chiklis
Newswriter.............................................Denise Dennison
Secretary #38...........................................Laura Waterbury
Orderlies..................Zack Phifer, Charles Champion

Writers: Denise Moss & Sy Dukane

3. "Loco Hero"  Oct. 1, 1990  (186853)

Frank panics when he has to entertain his visiting parents and throw their golden anniversary party -- at Murphy's home.

Rose Fontana...........................................Rose Marie
Dominic Fontana.....................................Barney Martin
Caterer...................................................James Lashly
Pat Fontana, Frank's sister................................Gracie Moore
Mary Fontana, Frank's sister.........................Sara Ballantine
Uncle Sal................................................Richard Zavaglia
Cousin Maria...........................................Karen Hensel
Stycek....................................................Jordan Myers
Office worker...........................................Ernest Frank-Taylor

Writers: Gary Dontzig & Steve Peterman

**preempted Oct. 8**

4. "Strike Two"  Oct. 15, 1990  (186854)

When *FYI*s anchors go on strike, Miles, network boss Kinsella and scab reporter Redfield try to do the show.  Guests Oppenheimer and Rich reprise their roles from previous seasons.

Miller Redfield.......................................Christopher Rich
Network head Eugene Kinsella.....................Alan Oppenheimer
James Chandler......................................Paul Collins

Writer: Scott Kaufer

5. "The Gold Rush"  Oct. 22, 1990  (186855)

Tabloid-TV king Jerry Gold (*Married People* co-star Thomas, reprising his role from last season) joins *FYI* in a new segment, "Nose to Nose," and rekindles a romance with Murphy.

Jerry Gold.............................................Jay Thomas

Writers: Steven Peterman & Gary Dontzig

6. "Bob and Murphy and Ted and Avery"  Nov. 5, 1990  (186856)

Murphy's mother (Dewhurst, reprising her role from last season) moves in with Murphy, and takes over their social lives.

Avery Brown...........................................Colleen Dewhurst
Bob Wilkes.............................................John Getz
Theodore Wilkes.....................................George Coe

Writer: Diane English

7. "The Last Laugh"  Nov. 12, 1990  (186857)

After an uncontrollable giggle-fit on the air leaves him professionally humiliated, Jim goes into hiding.

Secretary #39.........................................Barbara Perry

Writer: Tom Palmer

8. "Rootless People"  Nov. 19, 1990  (186858)

After Murphy plays series of practical jokes, no one believes she has really been kidnapped by a trio of ecological fanatics. Guest King is a radio and CNN interviewer.

Elliot....................................................Curtis Armstrong
Alex.....................................................Craig Bierko
Marhshal..............................................Andrew Hill Newman
Himself (on TV).....................................Larry King

Teleplay: Sy Dukane & Denise Moss
Story: Lisa Chernin and Sy Dukane & Denise Moss

9. "The Bummer of 42"  Nov. 26, 1990  (186859)

On Murphy's 42nd birthday, Frank hires an actress (Ebersole) to spend 12 hours playing the sister Murphy always wanted.

Maddy..................................................Christine Ebersole

Writer: Tom Palmer

10. "Trouble at Sherwood-Forrest"  Dec. 10, 1990  (186860)

Their marriage strained, Corky and Will throw a disatrous dinner party. Bryce and Leeves reprise their recurring roles from last season.

Will Forrest................................................Scott Bryce
Audrey, Miles' girlfriend........................Janes Leeves
    Also orig. announced: Lauren Mitchell (Secretary #40)

Writers: Sy Dukane & Denise Moss

11. "Jingle Hell, Jingle Hell, Jingle All the Way"
    Dec. 17, 1990 (186861)

Murphy breaks the *FYI* pact of donating to charity instead of exchanging holiday presents, setting off a buying frenzy. Frank-Taylor appeared in ep. 3, credited as "Officer worker."

Salespeople..........................Jennifer Lewis, Jane A. Johnston
Lynne............................................Gael Shipstad
Marv............................................Ernest Frank-Taylor
    Also orig. announced:
    June Gable (Secretary #41), Peter Chew (Bobby)

Writers: Gary Dontzig & Steven Peterman

12. "Retreat"  Jan. 7, 1991  (186862)

The *FYI* anchors and Miles attend a weekend retreat program called "Yes We Can" to try to rekindle their team spirit.

Justin..........................................Doug Ballard
Trish............................................Lisa Darr
Laura..........................................Jeanine Jackson
Dick............................................Lance Davis
Esther..........................................Gloria Dorson

Writer: Tom Palmer

13. "Eldin Imitates Life"  Jan. 14, 1991  (186863)

When a famous artist (Langton) discovers Eldin and hails him as a major new talent, Eldin sells a mural for $1.2 million.

Nathan David Weis.....................................Basil Langton
Chet............................................Murphy Dunne
Bartender.......................................Peter Iacangelo
Holly Hastings...................................Cheryl Giannini
Brian............................................Patrick Massett
Janine..........................................Brenda Strong
People in gallery..................Roger Guenveur Smith, Claudette
    Sutherland
Secretary #40 [cq] (no lines)....................Sheila Shaw

Writer: Peter Tolan

14. "Contractions"  Jan. 21, 1991  (186864)

Murphy uses interest from the aggressive new Wolf Television Network for leverage during contract renegotiations.

Wolf president Barry Tartiledge.....................Robert Desiderio
Secretary #41 [cq].............................Patti Yasutake
Messenger.......................................Aaron Seville

Writer: Scott Kaufer

15. "Hoarse Play"  Feb. 4, 1991  (186865)

While needing to crash a presidential press conference, Murphy loses her voice. Pres. George Bush "appears" through edited footage of a real press conference.

Dr. Bishop........................................David Paymer
Allen............................................Robert Clotworthy
Secretary #42 [cq]................................Nick Ullett
Dan..............................................Erick Avari
Bill..............................................Stephen Burks
Maureen.........................................Sally Champlin
Ted..............................................David A. Kimball
Security guard....................................Sana Craig
Telephone repairperson..........................John Medici
Voice of Pres. George Bush.....................Bill Farmer
Reporter.........................................Charles Hutchins

Writers: Steven Peterman & Gary Dontzig

16. "The Novel"  Feb. 11, 1991  (186866)

Jim's unpublished spy novel reveals a secret passion for Murphy. The performer playing Murphy's secretary, with no speaking lines (as on ep. 13) is uncredited (unlike ep. 13).

Secretary #43 [cq] (no lines)...................(uncredited)

Writer: Korby Siamis

17. "Terror on the 17th Floor"  Feb. 18, 1991  (186867)

After American Industrial Enterprises buys the network, a budget shark (Youngblut) makes devastating cuts. Oppenheimer reprises his role from ep. 4.

Network head Eugene Kinsella....................Alan Oppenheimer
Barbara Boyle...................................Nancy Youngblut
AIE VP Roger Harris.............................Kevin Conroy
AIE VP Ted......................................Martin Grey
AIE VP Neil.....................................John Hillner
AIE VP Tom......................................Will Jeffries
AIE VP Mike.....................................Gary Lazer
AIE VP Dave.....................................Drew Smith
And: Glen Vernon (Eddie), Frank Novak (Worker)

Writers: Denise Moss & Sy Dukane

18. "On Another Plane"  Feb. 25, 1991  9-10 p.m.  (186868)

When their plane develops engine trouble and starts to plummet, Murphy and Frank review their lives (via flashbacks, including to past episodes), and hallucinate about their deaths. Marie and Martin reprise their roles from ep. 3.

Rose Fontana....................................Rose Marie
Dominic Fontana................................Barney Martin
Flight attendant.................................Nancy Mette
Secretary #44 [cq].............................Susan J. Blommaert
Little Murphy...................................Meghann Haldeman
Little Frank....................................Sean Baca
Pretty girl.....................................Nikki Cox
Brian...........................................Ben Gregory
Frank's sisters [Pat and Mary] as children.....Brittany Murphy,
    Shanelle Workman
Bob.............................................Darrell Harris
And: Michael Kaufman (Al), Callan White (Mourner)

Writer: Diane English

19. "Driving Miss Crazy"  March 4, 1991  (186870)

The *FYI*ers drive each other crazy on their car-pool ride to work in Corky's new car. Leeves reprises her role. from ep. 10.

Audrey..........................................Jane Leeves
Garage attendant/Carmello......................John Del Regno

Writer: Tom Palmer

**preempted March 11**

20. "Every Time It Rains...You Get Wet" March 18, 1991
(186871)

After a series of downbeat news stories, Miles sends the team in a near-fruitless search for a heart-warming report. A rerun of ep. 4 played the same night, 10:30-11 p.m.

Richard Cooper.................................................Ethan Phillips
Gunzenhauser.....................................................David Brisbin
Sister Cecile........................................................Laurel Cronin
Mrs. Beale.......................................................Elmarie Wendel

Writers: Gary Dontzig & Steven Peterman

**preempted April 1**

21. "Corky's Place" April 8, 1991 (186872)

Corky, hosting her first special, *Corky's Place*, tries to prove she's not a soft interviewer by nailing her first guest: Murphy.

Woman in Phil's.....................................................Sandra Nutt
      Also orig. announced:
      Lauren Mitchell (Secretary #45 [cq])

Writer: Tom Palmer

22. "Small" April 29, 1991 (186873)

At a ceremony when Phil donates his historic men's-room door to the Smithsonian, Murphy's joke is taken as a slur against short men. Zahn and McEwen, in a fictional *CBS This Morning* segment, are real-life newspersons on that show. Previous newspersons appearing as themselves: Connie Chung, Walter Cronkite, Irving R. Levine, Linda Ellerbee, and Larry King.

Themselves.................Paula Zahn, Mark McEwen (uncredited)
John J. Edwards..............................................Jonathan Prince
Ron......................................................................Gary Grossman
Howard....................................................................Kyle Heffner
Reporter Jeff..................................................Geoffrey Nauffts
Julian...................................................................Ernie Sabella
Charlie.......................................................................Bill Saluga
Richard Hutchins (orig. Thornton)..................Charles Bartlett
Roland Petrie..............................................Dennis Creaghan
Reporter Bill...................................................Stephen Burks
Maureen................................................................Sally Champlin
Hank.............................................................Mark Zimmerman

Director: Peter Bonerz
Writers: Sy Dukane & Denise Moss

23. "The Usual Suspects" May 6, 1991 (186874)

Murphy suspects everyone everywhere when information about her private life is leaked to a sleazy national tabloid. Other *FYI* newsworkers named this episode: Marv (probably an uncredited Ernest Frank-Taylor) and Dave.

Mailroom person Ray/Bob.................................Chuck Clayton
Men in Phil's..............................Harry Murphy, Johnny Heller
Woman in Phil's...................................................J. Teddy Davis

Director: Peter Bonerz
Writer: Sam Austin (Scott Kaufer orig. announced)

24. "Q & A & F.Y.I." May 13, 1991 (186875)

To benefit charity, the *FYI* gang goes up against Yale students on the *Collegiate Q&A* TV quiz show.

Host Dr. Wade Benoit...........................................Tony Jay
Ben Lawson.....................................................Phillip LaMarr
Pizza deliverer.......................................................David Knell
Alexis Dewar....................................................Penny Balfour
Melissa Denton.....................................................Rebecca Cross
And: Sam King (Paul Hatfield), Adam Goldberg (Donald Klein)

Writer: Peter Tolan

25. "Uh-Oh, Part I" May 20, 1991 (186876)

Murphy has to choose between her poltical activist ex-husband Jake, to whom she was married for five days in 1968, or talk-show host Jerry, back from L.A. and his failed late-night show. Robin Thomas reprises his role from the Dec. 5, 1988 episode; Jay Thomas (no relation) reprises his role from ep. 5 and last season. Part 2 scheduled to be telecast next season.

Jerry Gold............................................................Jay Thomas
Jake Lowenstein..............................................Robin Thomas
Security guard Scotty.............................................Cal Gibson
Violinist Albert............................Joseph Shamaa (uncredited)

Teleplay: Diane English
Story: Korby Siamis & Diane English

**preempted Aug. 19**

**renewed for 1991-92; new episodes begin Sept. 16, 1991**

## My Life and Times

| ABC | April 21-May 1 | Wednesdays, 9:30-10 p.m. |
| | May 23-30 | Thursdays, various times |

Series premiere: April 24, 1991
Final episode: May 30, 1991

Seriocomedy of a philosophical 85-year-old in A.D. 2035, living in the Briars Retirement Retreat, reflecting on his life as a copywriter, journalist and family man in the halcyon 20th century. May 23-30, two episodes ran back-to-back each night.

Ben Miller.................................................................Tom Irwin
Susan, a retirement-home aid...........................Megan Mullally
Rebecca Eastman Miller, Ben's wife.......................Helen Hunt

*Recurring:*
Robert Miller, Ben's grandson (ep. 1,4,6)............Matt McGrath

Sea Change Productions in assoc. with ABC Productions / a.k.a.
      Productions
Executive producer: Ron Koslow
Producer: Kenneth R. Koch
Co-producer: Patricia Livingston
Associate producer (ep. 2-on): Anthony Mazzei
Directors of photography (variously): Andrew Dintenfass
      (ep. 1); James Glennon; Robert Primes, A.S.C.
Special make-up designer: Greg Cannom
Music (variously): Lee Holdridge, Alf Clausen, Don Davis
Theme (instrumental with voiceover by star Irwin): Lee
      Holdridge
Creator: Ron Koslow

1. "My Life and Times" April 24, 1991

Ben recalls being trapped with his boss in the 1989 San Francisco earthquake, while his first child was about to be born.

Joe Morton, Ben's ad-agency boss..............Lawrence Monoson
Secretary.................................................................Carla Belver
Police officer...........................................Fitzhugh G. Houston
Jessie (1978; momentary flashback;
      no lines)...............................................Claudia Christian
Paramedic............................................................Johnny Judkins
Firefighter............................................................Michael McNab
Jessie (2035; no lines).........................................Harriet Medin

Director: Michael Apted          Writer: Ron Koslow

2. "Jessie"  May 1, 1991

Ben meets his lost love (Christian) from 1978, and recalls with her a passionate but heartbreaking Fourth of July.

Jessie (1978)...................................................Claudia Christian
Jane........................................................................Cynthia Mace
Jessie (2035)........................................................Harriet Medin
Waitress..............................................................Bok Yun Chon
And: George O'Hanlon (Mr. Ellis), Edward Will (Man)

Director: Michael Apted          Writer: Ron Koslow

**preempted May 8 and May 15**

3. "Our Wedding"  May 23, 1991  9-9:30 p.m.

A humorous look back at Ben and Rebecca's nontraditional wedding ceremony, in 1985.  Orig. scheduled for May 8.

Announced cast includes:
Martin....................................................................John McLiam
Rev. Evans.........................................................Hansford Rowe
Phyllis.............................................................Priscilla Pointer
Jack Miller, Ben's father.......................................Paul Dooley

Director: John Pasquin          Teleplay: Evan Katz
Story: Ron Koslow and Evan Katz

4. "Millennium"  May 23, 1991  9:30-10 p.m.

Widowed Ben and his boys celebrate New Year's Eve, 1999 in a festive train station, where Ben meets a new woman (Zane). Orig. scheduled for May 15.

Announced cast includes:
Daniel Miller, Ben's son (2035)..................................Tim Stack
Lilly.........................................................................Lisa Zane

Director: NA    Writer: NA

5. "Fare on Park Avenue"  May 30, 1991  9-9:30 p.m.

Ben recalls his 1980s days as a cab driver/struggling novelist, and his stock-market speculation just before Black Monday. Stack reprises his role from last episode.

Daniel Miller...........................................................Tim Stack
Pete Hagerty.....................................................Spencer Garrett
Merlino...............................................................Geoffrey Lower
Broker......................................................................Jim Holmes
Doorperson..............................................................Jiggs Ryan
Yuppie woman....................................................Jeremy Green
Men.........................................Ryan Cutrona, Anthony Russell

Director: Michael Tuchner          Story: Ron Koslow
Teleplay: Hugh O'Neill and Jerry Rigg

6. "The Collapse of '98"  May 30, 1991  9:30-10 p.m.

Ben recalls factory work and violent, black-marketing co-workers during a 1990s economic depression.

With: Thomas Duffy, John Jackon
Daniel, Ben and Helen's son (1998)..........................Sean Baca
Melanie, Ben and Helen's daughter (1998)......Emily Ann Lloyd
Michael Miller, Ben's grandson (2035).........Christopher Pettiet
Workers....................Pat Asanti, Orlando Bonner, Otto Coelho

Director: Christopher Leitch
Teleplay: Jerry Rigg and Hugh O'Neill
Story: Bill Levinson and Jerry Rigg

## Night Court

NBC          Sept. 28-Jan. 11    Fridays, 9-9:30 p.m.
             Jan. 23-on          Wednesdays, 9-9:30 p.m.

Series premiere: Jan. 4, 1984

Surreally farcical comedy of a Manhattan night court presided over by an irreverent judge and amateur magician.  Formerly produced by Starry Night Productions.

Judge Harry T. Stone.......................................Harry Anderson
Asst. D.A. Dan Fielding..................................John Larroquette
Public defender Christine Sullivan Giuliano...........Markie Post
Court clerk Mac Robinson...........................Charles Robinson
Bailiff Bull Shannon............................................Richard Moll
Court matron Roz Russell..............................Marsha Warfield

*Recurring, all or virtually all episodes:*
Court stenographer Lisette Hocheiser....................Joleen Lutz
News vendor Jack Griffin.................................S. Marc Jordan

*Other recurring guests:*
Quon Le, Mac's wife (ep. 3,16,20)....................Denice Kumagai
Tony Giuliano, Christine's husband
      (ep. 7,22-23).............................................Ray Abruzzo
Building maintenance-person Art
      (ep. 5,8,11,13,17-18,21)............................Mike Finneran
Reporter Margaret Turner (ep. 3-4,8,16)...........Mary Cadorette
Phillip (Phil) Sanders (ep. 4,8,13,18)..........................Will Utay
Will Sanders, his twin brother (ep. 22-23)..................Will Utay

Warner Bros. Television
Executive producers: Stuart Kreisman, Chris Cluess
Supervising producers: Fred Rubin, Bob Underwood
Producer: Tim Steele
Associate producer: Christine Reedy
Executive story consultant: Kevin Kelton (Bill Bryan also orig.
      announced as executive script consultant)
Executive story editors: Bill Fuller, Jim Pond, Elaine Aronson
      (later in season)
Story editor: Elaine Aronson (early in season); Nancylee Myatt
      (later in season)
Director of photography: Charles L. Barbee
Theme (instrumental): Jack Elliott
Director unless otherwise noted: Jim Drake
Creator: Reinhold Weege

1. "A Family Affair" Part 1  Sept. 28, 1990

Christine returns from maternity leave; Dan enlists Bull's help when the beautiful sister he hasn't seen in 20 years visits.

Donna....................................................................Susan Diol
Miss Crombie...........................................................Fran Ryan

And: Pete Schrum (Dock worker), Christina Whitaker (Angelica), Dein Wein (McCutty), Robert Bendall (Ted)

Writers: Chris Cluess & Stuart Kreisman

2. "A Family Affair" Part 2   Oct. 5, 1990

After Dan accuses Bull of taking advantage of his sister, who'd seduced him, Bull decides he must propose.

Donna.................................................Susan Diol
Miss Crombie.....................................Fran Ryan
Mr. Ketover.......................................Larry Gelman
Mr. Austin..........................................Ben Slack

Writers: Chris Cluess & Stuart Kreisman

3. "When Harry Met Margaret"   Oct. 12, 1990

Hard-hitting court reporter Margaret Turner (new recurring guest Cadorette) falls for the romantically naive Harry.  Kumagai begins reprising her recurring role from past seasons.

Maitre d'...........................................Nick Ullett
Waiter...............................................Greg Allen Johnson
And: Carlos Lacamara (Busperson), Cristi Conaway (Woman)

Writer: Benjy Compson

4. "Can't Buy Me Love"   Oct. 19, 1990

A lecherous dowager (Core) successfully bids on Dan at a bachelor's auction, where Christine is stood up by her husband.  Guest McCoo is a singer.

Mrs. Fostmulleur................................Natalie Core
Sonia Blair.........................................Louan Gideon
Emcee................................................Marilyn McCoo
Roxanne "Roxy" Reynolds.................Debi A. Monahan
Woman...............................................Candi Milo
    Also orig. announced: Ray Abruzzo (Tony Giuliano)

Writer: Elaine Aronson

5. "Death Takes a Halloween"   Oct. 26, 1990

When a man in the holding pen claims to be the Spirit of Death, Dan's obituary inexplicably appears in the newspaper.

Spirit of Death.................................Stephen Root
Hooker..............................................Melba Englander
Werewolf............................................Brian Kaiser
Dracula..............................................Douglas MacHugh
And: Raf Mauro (Bum), Steven Jason Oliver (Burglar), Blanche Rubin (Muriel Brown), Matt Love (Clown)

Writer: Harry Anderson

6. "Crossroads"   Nov. 2, 1990  9-10 p.m.

When quarantined in the courtroom after an apparent deadly virus is unleashed, the staff recall turning points in their lives: Harry as a fledgling magician, Roz as a stewardess (on Paramus Air), Christine as a 19-year-old Miss North Tonawanda in the Miss Buffalo (NY) competition (measurements: 37-23-35), Dan as a naive young Louisiana attorney, and Mac as an Army sergeant in Viet Nam, with Bull befuddled by fantasy.

Deyoung.............................................Phil Proctor
Foley..................................................Jack Bannon
Evangeline..........................................Theresa Bell

Marty Melman......................................Stanley Brock
Kid in Viet Nam...................................Chi-Muoi Lo
Ventriloquist.......................................Ronn Lucas
And: Rod McCary (Emcee), Charles McDaniel (Gil-Ray), Michael McManus (Harris), Craig Richard Nelson (Steward), Dorothy Parke (Miss Mahapac), Sandy Ward (Senior partner), David Wiley (Partner #2)

Writer: Bob Underwood

7. "Day Court"   Nov. 9, 1990

The staff switches temporarily to day session; Christine's husband (Abruzzo, reprising his recurring role from last season) wants to end their marriage.  Guest Jones is a singer.

Norm..................................................Phil Leeds
Angelo................................................Ralph Manza
And: I.M. Hobson (Maitre d'), Bill Boyett (Arresting officer), Stanley Ullman (Douglas), Jack Jones (Himself)

Writer: Kevin Kelton

8. "A Night Court at the Opera"   Nov. 16, 1990

As an exercise, Dan tries to woo Margaret from Harry; Bull is mistaken for an ancient god by religious cultists.

Matilda...............................................Meg Wyllie
Zealots..............................Robert Trebor, Melanie MacQueen
Matron................................................Mary Pat Gleason
    Also orig. announced:
    Milton James (Rossi), Nancy Marlow (Mrs. Aronson)

Writers: Jim Pond & Bill Fuller

9. "Nobody Says Rat Fink Anymore"   Nov. 23, 1990

The schoolyard bully (Gibb) from Harry's childhood shows up in court, more vicious than ever and out to settle a score.

Terry Benoon......................................Don Gibb
Rose Minnik........................................Chris Weatherhead
Lenny..................................................Rick Zumwalt
And: Mary Dean (Beatrice Williker), Logan McKarra (Woman)

Director: Howard Ritter          Writer: Fred Rubin

**preempted Nov. 30**

10. "Jail Bait"   Dec. 7, 1990

Christine impulsively throws herself into the arms of a 24-year-old street artist (Calvert) whom she's defending.  Mauro reprises his role from ep. 5.

Ian McKee...........................................Bill Calvert
Pam....................................................Terri Hendrickson
And: Ken Myles (Con-Ed worker), Raf Mauro (Bum)

Director: Christine Ballard          Writer: Nancylee Myatt

11. "It's Just a Joke"   Dec. 14, 1990

A grandstanding conservative minister (James) makes a citizen's arrest of a shock comic (Mustillo).

Monte Potter.......................................Louis Mustillo
Rev. Lester Sinclair.............................Clifton James
Reporters............................................Beth Robbins, Kenney Dee
Working guy.........................................Perry Wayne

Director: Howard Ritter                    Writer: Lee Maddux

**preempted Dec. 28**

12. "Bringing Down Baby"  Jan. 4, 1991

An obnoxious child star (Cohen), who plays a 10-year-old lawyer on TV, comes to observe the court. Orig. scheduled for
Jan. 16.

Head Bailiff Reedy...................................Hal Williams
Billy MacDonald.....................................Billy Cohen
Victoria Fillmore...................................Katie Layman
And: Barbara Brownell (Mrs. MacDonald), Jeri Gaile (Miranda)

Directors: Charles Robinson, Howard Ritter
Writer: Elaine Aronson

**unscheduled preemption Jan. 16, when series was orig.
scheduled to begin airing on Wednesdays**

13. "Presumed Insolvent"  Jan. 23, 1991

An old man (Christmas), wiped out by a savings-and-loan failure, breaks into the bank president's (Ingle) home; Phil the
bum, killed by a falling piano, is revealed as a rich eccentric.
Orig. scheduled for Jan. 16.

Olmeyer...........................................Eric Christmas
Kitteridge.............................................John Ingle
And: Stuart Pankin (Shoope), Ron Ross (Dirk)

Writer: Kevin Kelton

14. "Mama Was a Rollin' Stone"  Jan. 30, 1991

Bull tries to talk his seafaring mother into retirement; Dan is
the beneficiary of Phil's estate, and executor of the philan-
thropic Phil Foundation. Orig. scheduled for Jan. 23.

Henrietta "Hank" Shannon.....................Paddi Edwards
Clarence Egan..................................Edward Winter
Doyle.........................................Walter Olkewicz
And: Nicholas Worth (Birnbach), Biff Manard (Dane)

Writers: Bill Fuller & Jim Pond

15. "Attachments Included"  Feb. 6, 1991

Bull goes to a matchmaker (McAuley), whom he starts dating;
Christine is served divorce papers; Harry prepares to move in
with Margaret. Guest Brothers is a psychologist-author.

Wanda Flinn....................................Cathy McAuley
Claire Lee.....................................Cynthia Steele
Herself......................................Dr. Joyce Brothers

Writer: Fred Rubin

16. "Alone Again, Naturally"  Feb. 13, 1991

Harry, heartbroken, thinks Margaret is about to propose, and
she explains instead she's leaving as a protected witness.

J. Anthony......................................Murphy Dunne
Spring....................................Jacalyn O'Shaughnessy
And: Carolyn Grieg (Yolanda Wells), Steve Jones (FBI agent)

Director: Tim Steele         Writer: Alison Rosenfeld-Desmarais

**preempted Feb. 20**

17. "Hey, Harry, F'Cryin' Out Loud -- It's a Wonderful
Life...Sorta"  Feb. 27, 1991  9:18-9:48 p.m.

A guardian angel (singer Torme, who performs "Pick Yourself
Up") shows a despondent Harry what the world might have
been like without him (in black-and-white segments). Late
start due to an NBC News report; followed by a *Night Court*
rerun preempting the scheduled *Seinfeld*.

Himself [and] Guardian angel Herb.........................Mel Torme
Miss Wagner.......................................Sharon Lee Jones
Bailiffs..........................Candi Brough, Randi Brough
DeShicken (erroneously listed as Arnovitz in credits).......Thom
     Rachford
Shifty guy............................................Richard Morof

Writers: Stuart Kreisman & Chris Cluess

18. "To Sleep, No More"  March 6, 1991  9:49-10:19 p.m.

Insomnia-stricken Dan, troubled by a guilt, hallucinates and
sees dead Phil. Guest Parks is the former longtime Miss America pageant host. Delayed due to a presidential address.

Jim Wimberly...........................................Jack Riley
Dr. Nagelson (orig. Byrnes)..........................Larry Linville
Wendy.............................................Melinda McGraw
Boring man..........................................Brian Kaiser
Mr. Hampton.........................................Milton James
Frosted Neon Nuggets spokesperson/himself...........Bert Parks

Teleplay: Bob Underwood
Story: Tom Abraham & Mike Underwood

19. "With a Little Help from My Friends"  March 13, 1991

Christine coaxes Roz to try her Happy Alone Healthy Adults
(HAHA) support group. Dunne and O'Shaughnessy reprise
their roles from ep. 16.

Marty Griffin, Jack's son.........................Marty Pollio
J. Anthony.......................................Murphy Dunne
And:  Bruce Jarchow (Marcus), Jacalyn O'Shaughnessy
     (Spring), Kamella Tate (Cecily), Delia Sheppard (Monique)

Director: Kevin Sullivan              Writer: Nancylee Myatt

20. "Mac Takes a Vocation"  March 20, 1991

New college graduate Mac is courted for a clerkship by a state
Supreme Court justice; Dan hires a English butler (Ullett).

Justice Welch......................................Larry Dobkin
Kimmel..........................................George O. Petrie
Jerome...............................................Nick Ullett

Writer: Fred Rubin

21. "Harry's Fifteen Minutes"  April 3, 1991

After a magazine names him one of New York's 10 Most Inter-
esting Men, Harry becomes too busy to date Christine.

David Sachs........................................Rod McCary
Mrs. Fyborg....................................Valorie Armstrong
Curtis..........................................Tommy Hinkley
And: Joel Swetow (Producer), Stevie Sterling (Twinkie)

Writers: Bill Fuller & Jim Pond

**preempted April 24**

22. "Fools Rush In" Part 1   May 1, 1991

Harry and Christine's platonic romance is complicated by the return of her ex; the late Phil's twin (recurring guest Utay) arrives, offering to help the Foundation.  McAuley reprises her role from ep. 15; Englander played a different role, ep. 5.

Wanda Flinn.............................................Cathy McAuley
Kitty.....................................................Melba Englander

Writer: Elaine Aronson

23. "Fools Rush In" Part 2   May 8, 1991

A distraught Harry trails Christine and Tony as they try to figure out their relationship; Dan is broke after Will skips with his and the Foundation's money.  Wahl, the 1983 *Penthouse* Pet of the Year, is the estranged wife of actor Ken Wahl.  James reprises his role from ep. 18, Mauro from ep. 5 and 10.

Mugger....................................................Gregory Itzin
Mr. Hampton................................................Milton James
Voluptuous woman (orig. Kelly)....Corinne Wahl a.k.a. Corinne Alphen
Bum............................................................Raf Mauro

Writer: Kevin Kelton

**preempted May 15**

**preempted June 5 and June 12**

**preempted July 10**

**unscheduled preemption Aug. 21**

**preempted Sept. 4**

**renewed for 1991-92; new episodes begin Sept. 18, 1991**

## Northern Exposure

CBS          Mondays, 10-11 p.m.

Series premiere: July 12, 1990

Seriocomedy about the denizens of the Alaskan outback town of Cicely, population 815 *, and of a New York City doctor facing culture shock upon discovering his Columbia University medical school grant must be repaid by a four-year stint there.  Holling's diner/bar: The Brick.  Moose in opening sequence: Morty, a male living at Washington State University. Director of photography Hayman is the husband of *Designing Women* co-star Annie Potts.  Filmed in Bellevue and Roslyn, Wash.

* As per dialog; erroneously given as 839 in press accounts.

Dr. Joel Fleischman.........................................Rob Morrow
Maurice Minnifield.............................................Barry Corbin
Maggie O'Connell...............................................Janine Turner
Holling Vincoeur.................................................John Cullum
Ed Chigliak......................................................Darren E. Burrows
KBHR radio DJ Chris Stevens.............................John Corbett
Shelly Tambo.....................................................Cynthia Geary
*Recurring, all episodes:*
Marilyn Whirlwind, Joel's assistant......................Elaine Miles
Shopkeeper Ruth-Anne..........................................Peg Phillips

Finnegan • Pinchuk and Falahey/Austin Street Productions from Universal Television, an MCA Co.

Executive producers: Joshua Brand, John Falsey
Co-executive producer: Andrew Schneider
Supervising producers: Robin Green, Diane Frolov
Producers: Cheryl Bloch, Matthew Nodella
Associate producers: Martin Bruestle, Alan Brent Connell
Story editor: Henry Bromell
Director of photography (variously): James Hayman; James Lebovitz
Theme (instrumental) and music: David Schwartz
Creators: Joshua Brand & John Falsey

---

1. "Goodbye to All That"  Monday, April 8, 1991   10-11 p.m.

When his fiancee, Elaine, dumps him, the townsfolk try to help the depressed Joel; Shelly gets addicted to TV.  Goodeve reprises his role from last season.

Tory Gould.......................................................Beverly Leech
Rick Pederson, Maggie's boyfriend.....................Grant Goodeve
Joel as a child....................................................Grant Gelt
Alison................................................Therese Xavier Tinling
Proprietor........................................................Margaret Mason

Director: Stuart Margolin          Writer: Robin Green

2. "The Big Kiss"  April 15, 1991

An Indian spirit (Westerman) helps Ed try to trace his parents; Chris tries to overcome laryngitis by sleeping with Maggie.  Film excerpt seen in episode: *Boys Town* (1938).

One-Who-Waits...........................Floyd Red Crow Westerman
Smith..............................................................Eloy Casados
Great Aunt....................................................Geraldine Keams
Girl...............................................................Jessika Cardinahl
Bingo caller....................................................Albert J. Hood
Mrs. Emerson.....................................................Carolyn Byrne
Townspeople..........................David J. Guppy, Don Eastman
Bingo players........Rosetta Pintado, Katherine Davis, Susan Morales, Oscar Kawagley

Director: Sandy Smolan          Writer: Henry Bromell

3. "All is Vanity"  April 22, 1991

Maggie cons her father into believing Joel is her doctor-boyfriend; Holling wants to get circumcised to please Shelly; the town gets attached to an unidentified stranger who died there.

Frank O'Connell, Maggie's father.......................John McCann
Martin...............................................................Rex Linn
Husband...................................O.C. "Mac" McCallum
And: Sharon Collar (Wife), Cathy Bryan (Patient #10), Peter Bradshaw, Charles Russo (Men)

Director: Nick Marck
Writers: Diane Frolov and Andrew Schneider

4. "What I Did for Love"  April 29, 1991

Maggie foresees Joel's death on his upcoming New York visit; Maurice renews a fling with an astronaut groupie (Huddle).

Ingrid Klochner..............................................Elizabeth Huddle
Dr. David Ginsberg.............................................Leo Geter
Streisand/Death-figure........................................Paul Fleming
Women......................Pamela Abas-Ross, Dorothy Hanlin
And:  Phil Lucas (Man), David A. Hrdlicka (Little boy), Laura Kenny (Mrs. Streisand/Death-figure)

Director: Steven Robman          Writer: Ellen Herman

5. "Spring Break"  May 6, 1991

Spring fever: Holling tries to pick fights, Ed tracks a thief, Maggie fantasizes about Joel, Maurice falls for a tough female state trooper, and the men run naked through the streets.

State Police Officer Sgt. Barbara Semanski..........Diane Delano
Gary McClelland....................................................John Mese
Knockouts [in Robert Palmer music-
      video parody]............................Jill Pierce, Mary Anderson
Lumberjack....................................................Gregg Loughridge
Logger.................................................................Gary Taylor

Director: Rob Thompson          Writer: David Assael

6. "War and Peace"  May 13, 1991

The town welcomes a famous Russian singer (Baskin) on his annual getaway, though his yearly chess match with Maurice escalates into a duel; Ed finds love, using Chris' words.

Nikolai Ivanovich Appolanov.................................Elya Baskin
Lightfeather..........................................................Dana Andersen
Father Duncan..........................................................Alan Fudge
Dave, Hollings' cook.......................William James White Eagle

Director: Bill D'Elia      Writers: Henry Bromell & Robin Green

7. "Slow Dance"  May 20, 1991

When Maggie's boyfriend (Goodeve, reprising his role from ep. 1) is killed by a falling satellite, everyone blames a curse that's claimed four previous beaux; a gay couple (Ballard, McManus) buys a house from Maurice; Shelly wants to be older.

Ron.....................................................................Doug Ballard
Erick..................................................................Don McManus
Rick Pederson......................................................Grant Goodeve
And: Pat Millicano (Gary), Megan Cole (Anita), Kit McDonough
      (Valerie), J.R. Clarke (Customer)

Director: David Carson (Jim Hayman orig. announced)
Writers: Diane Frolov & Andrew Schneider

**preempted May 27 and June 3; reruns began June 10**

**preempted Aug. 19**

**preempted Sept. 16**

**renewed for 1991-92; new episodes begin Sept. 23, 1991**

## Over My Dead Body

CBS          Oct. 26-Dec. 21      Fridays, 9-10 p.m.
             June 6-20           Thursdays, 10-11 p.m.

Series premiere: Oct. 26, 1990
Final telecast: June 20, 1991

Lighthearted mystery-drama of a burnt-out crime novelist with an enigmatic Scotland Yard background, who pairs himself with a fledgling reporter and obit-writer for the *San Francisco Union* to solve (and then write about) crimes. Filmed partly in San Francisco.

Inspector Maxwell Beckett.........................Edward Woodward
Nikki Page.................................................................Jessica Lundy

*Recurring*:
Wendy (ep. 1-6,8)..........................................................Jill Tracy
Cosby (ep. 1-2,4).....................................................Gregory Itzin
Detective Mueller (ep. 3-4,10)..............................Peter Looney

Universal Television, an MCA Co.
Executive producers: David Chisholm, William Link (ep. 1);
      Richard C. Okie, Bradford May (ep. 2-on)
Supervising producer: Scott Shepherd
Producer: Ken Topolsky (ep. 1); Mark A. Burley (ep. 2-on)
Co-producer: Robin Jill Bernheim
Coordinating producer: Paul Cajero
Associate producer: Daniel Cahn
Executive story editor: Peter Tilden
Executive story consultant: William Link
Director of photography: Eric Van Haren Noman
Music (variously): Lee Holdridge (ep. 1); David Bell; Peter
      Bernstein; Jeff Sturges
Theme (instrumental): Lee Holdridge
Creators: William Link & David Chisholm

1. (pilot)  Oct. 26, 1990  9-11 p.m.

Obit columnist Page witnesses a murder, but can find no body nor convince the police a crime occurred, and seeks out Beckett to help solve the crime and get herself a front-page story.

Announced cast and crew include:
Detective Shirer.................................................Edward Winter
Tony Rialdo...............................................................Dan Ferro
Erdman..................................................................David Wells
Lacy.............................................................Brenda Thompson
Braynard.................................................................Ivory Ocean
Doris (orig. Jessie)..........................Vernee Watson-Johnson
Building manager......................................................Fran Ryan
Wife.............................................................Carolyn Seymour
Sister Margolin.............................................Mary Jo Catlett
Sister Dempsey....................................................Frances Bay
And: Mike Genovese (Mr. Page), Richard McGonagle (Hargrove)

Director: Bradford May          Teleplay: David Chisholm
Story: William Link, David Chisholm

2. "No Ifs, Ands...or Butlers"  Nov. 2, 1990

Nikki persuades Max to play butler for her wealthy friend Patty's family after the current one (Glover) is accused of murder.

Rose Haversham.......................................................Nan Martin
Brandon..............................................................Jay Underwood
Mary Haversham...............................................Shannon Wilcox
Patty Haversham.................................................Diana Barton
Henry Lodge......................................................William Glover
Debra Latham................................................Clare Kirkconnell
John Stanton.........................................................Ken Marshall
Ethel Hallingby....................................................Diana Hansen
Enrique.............................................................Carlos Lacamara
Det. Mueller...........................................................Peter Looney
Shopper............................................................Bonnie Snyder
Voice of publisher Derek........................................(uncredited)

Director: Bradford May          Writer: Richard C. Okie

3. "Dad and Buried"  Nov. 9, 1990

A young con-artist and Beckett fan (Curtis) persuades Max to search for his long-lost ex-boxer father, who had mob links.

Chris Shaw...............................................................Scott Curtis
Frank Moraza.........................................................Gianni Russo
Jesse Moraza........................................................Scott Colomby

Curly...............................................................Tony Burton
Roger Price....................................................Nicolas Surovy
Byron Bond...................................................Scott Lawrence
Douglass...........................................................
And: Rick Marzan (Pedro), Skip O'Brien (Cop), Patricia Johnson (Receptionist), James DiStefano (Douglass)
Also orig. announced: Wayne Dvorak (Waiter)

Director: Bruce Seth Green          Writer: Mark A. Burley

4. "Obits and Pieces" Nov. 16, 1990

Nikki becomes the prime suspect when her obnoxious new boss (Furey) is murdered immediately after they dine together.

Dane Chalmers..................................................John Furey
Lila Chalmers.................................................Caitlin O'Heaney
Joey Templeton................................................Forry Smith
Seth Hershfeld................................................Jack Shearer
Sandra Alucard................................................Cec Verrell
Karl Garrett..................................................Michael Gates
Claudine Moliere Hershfeld.....................................Lydie Denier
And: Taylor Fry (Lorelei), David Maier (Travis)

Director: James Quinn
Writers: Sylvia Stoddard & Steven Smith and Scott Shepherd

5. "If Looks Could Kill" Nov. 23, 1990

Max agrees to write the biography of a famous model-turned-businessperson (Taylor-Young) who was acquitted of murdering her husband, but whom Nikki suspects is guilty.

Announced cast and crew include:
Linda Talmadge................................................Leigh Taylor-Young
David Lehrman.................................................James O'Sullivan
Julie Talmadge................................................Martha Byrne
Chelsea Winters...............................................Michelle Brin
Elliot Richards..............................................Daniel Bardol
Murray........................................................John D. LeMay
Westin Talmadge...............................................Taldo Kenyon
Photographer..................................................Michael DeMartini
And: Brian Degan Scott (Waiter), Mike Girardin (Cop), Luis Oropeza (Stage manager), Kitty Swink (Prosecutor), Floyd Foster, Jr. (Foreperson), John Mallory Asher (Messenger)

Director: Richard Compton          Teleplay: Robin Jill Bernheim
Story: Tom Sawyer

6. "Dead Air" Nov. 30, 1990

While Max is promoting his book on a local radio station, his deejay friend (Oppenheimer) is murdered.

Curt Raney....................................................Alan Rosenberg
Dave Baker....................................................Alan Oppenheimer
Louis.........................................................Tom Isbell
George Moore..................................................H. Richard Greene
Jack Biston (orig. Bittner)...................................Will Nye
Brian Burton..................................................Lightfield Lewis
Susan Baker...................................................Shelby Leverington
Morgue attendant (orig. Attorney).............................Madison Monk
And: David Hall (Darren Cole), Rick Fitts (Detective Rittner)

Director: Bradford May             Writer: Peter Tilden

7. "A Passing Inspection" Dec. 7, 1990

Max is afraid his old rival (Ogilvy), in town for the investigation, may reveal Max's real, lowly Scotland Yard job to an entranced Nikki. Watson-Johnson reprises her role from ep. 1.

Inspector Miles Cottrell......................................Ian Ogilvy
Paul Emerson..................................................Alan Feinstein
Clarice.......................................................Jennifer Bassey
Ralph.........................................................Craig Hurley
Jonathan Tapply...............................................Brad Jeffries
Doris.........................................................Vernee Watson-Johnson
And: Will Utay (Daly), Ron Recasner (Manners), Leila Kenzle (Hooker), Patience Cleveland (Matron), Rob Narita (Uniformed cop), Bernard McDonald (Webster), James Matthew Campbell (Waiter), Scott Allyn (Airport clerk)

Director: Bradford May             Writer: Scott Shepherd

8. "Carrie Christmas and a Nappie New Year" Dec. 21, 1990

While Christmas shopping, Nikki is left with an abandoned baby whose vanished mother she and Max must locate. Fitts reprises his role from ep. 6.

Announced cast and crew include:
Leon Geary....................................................Joseph Campanella
Carrie Grant..................................................Lea Floden
Rustakovich...................................................Alex Rodine
Fender........................................................Kevin McCorkle
Woman.........................................................Lisa Kaminir
Vincent Morris................................................Patrick Massett
And: Harry Frazier (Santa), Rick Fitts (Detective Rittner), Yvette Freeman (Nurse Hunter), Joseph Malone (Ozzie), David Proval (Adam), Elena Stiteler (Francesca Morris)

Director: Timothy Bond             Writer: Walter Brough

**cancelled**

9. "Naked Brunch" June 6, 1991

A framed Max tries to act like all's normal when the hidden corpse of his agent (Jason) keeps popping up at a publishing party for Max's new novel, Hooker by Crook. Fitts played a different detective, ep. 6 and 8.

Metro Editor Perry Wright (orig. Harry White)..Alex Hyde-White
Raymond.......................................................John Bennett Perry
Valerie.......................................................Judith-Marie Bergan
Gus Arnheim...................................................Harvey Jason
Briggs........................................................Richard Riehle
May...........................................................Susan Cash
Bud Eckles....................................................Paul Eiding
With: Debbie McLeod
And: Carolyn Seymour (Diane Beckett), Rick Fitts (Detective Robbins), Ricardo Gutierrez (Officer Joe)

Director: Charles Correll          Writer: Jim McGrath

**preempted June 13**

10. "An Actor Prepares" June 20, 1991

The actor (Bloom) playing Max in a film from one of his novels trails him and Nikki on a case of a murdered journalist. LeMay reprises his role from ep. 5. Orig. scheduled for June 13.

Johnny Mason..................................................Brian Bloom
Diane Beckett.................................................Carolyn Seymour
Sen. Ronald Caldwell..........................................Michael Goodwin
Cheryl Caldwell...............................................Eileen Barnett
Sam Heinson...................................................Jeff Lester
Murray........................................................John D. LeMay
And: Andi Chapman (Pharmacist), Lindsey Ginter (Gustav Hoffman), Danny Ray (Metallica man)
Also orig. announced: Barney McFadden (Capt. Heath)

Director: Janet Greek      Teleplay: Jim McGrath
Story: Violet Pullbrook

Unaired

Max reluctantly investigates the murders of three private detectives, fearing that Nikki may be next on the killer's list. Orig. scheduled for June 20.

Announced cast and crew:
Wendy........................................................Jill Tracy
Pete Columbus.......................................John Gavigan
Detective Loraine McBride............................Barbara Rhoades
Violet Stoddard.......................................Amy Van Nostrand
Mouse.......................................................Ted Markland
Larry Chadway.........................................David James Elliott
Suzi Skinner..............................................Lisa Melilli
Hildy Windham........................................Nancy Lenehan
Cosby.......................................................Gregory Itzin
And: Mike Worth (Hired killer), Paul Ghiringhelli (Orderly), Charles C. Meshack (Bartender), David Garrison (Burly guy), Jake Jacobs (Waiter), Gary Berner (Police officer)

Director: Noel Black      Writer: Robin Jill Bernheim

## Parenthood

| NBC | Aug. 20-Nov. 19 | Saturdays, 8-8:30 p.m. |
| | Dec. 16 | Sunday 10:30-11 p.m. |
| | Aug. 11-18 | Sundays, 7:30-8 p.m. |

Series premiere: Aug. 20, 1990
Final telecast: Aug. 18, 1991

Comedy of four diverse, related households and generations in San Jose, Calif. Based on the 1989 movie, from which Slade, Schwan and LaVoy reprise their roles. David Arquette is of the Arquette family of actors (Rosanna, etc.)

Gil Buckman..............................................Ed Begley, Jr.
Karen Buckman.............................................Jayne Atkinson
Frank Buckman, Gil's father..........................William Windom
Marilyn Buckman, Gil's mother........................Sheila MacRae
Helen Buckman, Gil's sister...........................Maryedith Burrell
Susan Buckman-Merrick, Gil's sister.......Susan Gayle Norman
Nathan Merrick, Susan's husband............................Ken Ober
Great Grandma Greenwell................................Mary Jackson
Julie Buckman-Hawks, Helen's daughter................Bess Meyer
Tod Hawks, her husband................................David Arquette
Garry Buckman (14).................................Leonardo DiCaprio
Kevin Buckman (10).....................................Max Elliott Slade
Taylor Buckman (8)...........................................Thora
Justin Buckman (4)..........................................Zachary LaVoy
Patty Merrick (4)...............................................Ivyann Schwan

Imagine Television
Executive producers: Ron Howard, Brian Grazer (both ep. 1-on), Babaloo Mandel, Lowell Ganz (both ep. 1 only), David Tyron King (ep. 2-on)
Co-executive producers (ep. 2-on): Lowell Ganz, Babaloo Mandel, Allan Arkush
Supervising producer: Sascha Schneider (ep. 1); Russ Woody
Producer: Allan Arkush (ep. 1); Sascha Schneider, April Smith (Trish Soodik also orig. announced)
Co-producer (ep. 2-on): Joss Whedon
Associate producers: Scott Citron, Walter Von Huene (ep. 1); Gary Chandler, Walter Von Huene
Executive story editor: Glen Merzer
Director of photography: Gordon G. Lonsdale (ep. 1); Gerald Perry Finnerman, A.S.C.

Music: Mason Daring
Theme: Randy Newman, performed by Randy Newman
Based on characters created by Lowell Ganz & Babaloo Mandel & Ron Howard

————————————

1. (pilot)
Monday, Aug. 20, 1990, 9-10 p.m.; Thursday, Sept. 6, 1990

Gil and Karen try to reassure Kevin on his first day back at school; Helen has a disastrous date; the clan celebrates Great Grandma Greenwell's birthday.

With: Lyman Ward, Doug Ballard, John Hostetter, Kathy Motter, Isabel Cooley, David Ducommun, Joe Lerer, Billy O. Sullivan, Janne Peters, Tritia Setoguchi, Tamara Steffen

Director: Allan Arkush
Writers: Lowell Ganz & Babaloo Mandel

2. "My Dad Can Beat Up Your BMW" Sept. 22, 1990

Garry hopes his dad will appear at his baseball team's championship game, but Helen doubts her indifferent ex will show up; Marilyn gives Susan's childhood stewardess doll to Patty.

With: Gerrit Graham

Director: Allan Arkush      Writer: David Tyron King

3. "The Plague" Sept. 29, 1990

The kids get chicken pox.

With: Lyman Ward

Director: Alan Myerson      Writer: Joss Whedon

4. "I Never Invested for My Father" Oct. 6, 1990

Gil volunteers to help untangle his father's finances; Patty freezes during a ballet recital. Director Thomas is a former co-star of Hill Street Blues.

With: Nancy Fish

Director: Betty Thomas      Writer: David Tyron King

5. "The Marriage" Oct. 13, 1990

Julie walks out on Tod when she discovers he's planning the formal wedding they never had.

With: Frank Owen Smith

Director: Allan Arkush      Writer: Russ Woody

6. "Cards and Cars" Oct. 20, 1990

Gil's jealous when Max prefers to spend time with Grandpa; Helen is attracted to a housepainter who's like an older Tod.

Wiley.......................................................James McDonnell

Director: Alan Myerson      Writer: Glen Merzer

7. "Hollow Halloween" Oct. 27, 1990

Gil and Karen's plans for an old-fashioned Halloween make the kids feel dowdy next to their Ninja Turtled friends.

With: Ryan Bollman, Stephen Cadigan, Toby Scott Granger, Tina Hart a.k.a. Tina Panella-Hart, Tobey Maguire, Kelly Wellman

Director: Allan Arkush                    Writer: Jerry Lacy

8. "Small Surprises"  Nov. 3, 1990

Helen finds Garry kissing a girl (Leeds) in his room; Gil and Karen try to get rid of a pesky raccoon.

Casey..........................................Marcie Leeds
And: Arnold Turner

Director: Matia Karrell                    Writer: Joss Whedon

9. "Take My Parents, Please"  Nov. 10, 1990

With the kids away, Gil and Karen anticipate a romantic 11th anniversary, until Gil's mom shows up on their doorstep.

Director: NA  Writer: NA

10. "Thanksgiving with a ' T,' and That Rhymes with 'B,' and That Stands for Basketball"  Nov. 19, 1990

Thanksgiving at the Buckmans'.  Director Thomas is a former cast-member of *Hill Street Blues*.

Director: Betty Thomas                    Writer: David Tyron King

**off the schedule, then cancelled**

11. "Gil vs. the Deck"  Sunday, Dec. 16, 1990  10:30-11 p.m.

Building an outdoor deck makes Gil a hero to Kevin, making it difficult for Gil to quit as he'd like. Orig. scheduled for Dec. 1.

Director: NA  Writer: NA

**off the schedule**

12. "Fun for Kids"  Aug. 11, 1991

Tod's stripper mother (Peterson) visits; Frank locks horns with Nathan over child-rearing.  Orig. scheduled for Dec. 29, 10:30-11 p.m., and preempted by an unscheduled *Dear John...* rerun.

With: Robyn Peterson

Director: Allan Arkush
Writers: David Tyron King & Joss Whedon

## Parker Lewis Can't Lose

Fox            Sundays, 7:30-8 p.m.

Series premiere: Sept. 2, 1990

Surrealistic comedy of a con-artist high-school junior and his hench-students at Santo Domingo High (team: Flamingoes). Cast-members Benrubi and Johnson were guests in ep. 1.

Parker Lewis..........................................Corin Nemec
Michael Patrick (Mikey) Randall.....................William Jayne
Jerry Steiner..........................................Troy Slaten
Principal Grace Musso................................Melanie Chartoff
Shelly Lewis, Parker's sister........................Maia Brewton
* Larry Kubiac........................................Abraham Benrubi
Marty Lewis, Parker's dad (ep. 2-on)................Timothy Stack

Judy Lewis, Parker's mom (ep. 2-on)...................Anne Bloom
Student Obedience Helper Frank Lemmer............Taj Johnson

*Recurring:*
Dr. Norman Pankow (ep. 8,12,18,22)................Gerrit Graham
Conrad Fleck (ep. 4,6,9,19,24,26)................Lawrence Spinak
Badge (ep. 4,7,9,14,16,19,22)...................................B.J. Barie
Mr. Loopman (ep. 5,8,11,17)......................Robett Greenberg **

* Also spelled "Kubiak" in some initial Fox press materials.
** One of three actors in this minor role; credited only as "Teacher," ep. 5

Clyde Phillips Productions in assoc. with Columbia Pictures Television / CPT Holdings
Executive producer: Clyde Phillips
Co-executive producer (ep. 2-on): Tom Straw
Supervising producer: Robert Lloyd Lewis, Lon Diamond
Producer: John Ziffren (ep. 1); Russell Marcus
Line Producer: Robert Rolsky (later in season)
Associate producer: Russell Denove
Story editors: Alan Cross, Tom Spezialy, Peter Ocko, Adam Barr (latter two later in season)
Director of photography (variously): Robert Seaman (ep. 1); Arnie Sirlin; Chuck Arnold; Paul Maibaum
Music [and] Theme (instrumental): Dennis McCarthy
Creators: Clyde Phillips & Lon Diamond

---

1. "Pilot"  Sunday, Sept. 2, 9:30-10 p.m.; Thursday, Sept. 6, 8:30-9 p.m.

When Parker kisses Mikey's heartthrob, the pals' relationship is strained, until both are threatened by monstrous Kubiac.

Robin Fecknowitz.............................................Milla Jovovich
Larry Kubiac................................................Abraham Benrubi
Frank Lemmer..................................................Taj Johnson
History teacher Mr. Loopman............................Clyde Kusatsu
Mr. Kornstein...............................................Scott Thomson
Andrea Russell...............................................Lisa Canning
Bobby Kubiac, Larry's younger brother.........Zachary Bostrom
Grad school genius......................................Christopher Faulk
Registrar..................................................Evelina Fernandez
And: Mary Ellen Trainor, Sherman Howard

Director: Thom Eberhardt
Writers: Lon Diamond & Clyde Phillips

2. "Operation Kubiak" (sic)   Sept. 9, 1990

Lemmer exposes Kubiac's math illiteracy before some college football recruiters, prompting Parker into tutorial action.

Mr. Kubiac................................................Patrick T. O'Brien
Mrs. Kubiac..............................................Melanie MacQueen
Scouts.....................................Stephen Burrell, Jack Jozefson
Reporters............................Steven Whiteford, Susan Angelo
Teen babe......................................................Deborah Stern

Director: Andy Tennant
Writers: Clyde Phillips & Lon Diamond

3. "Power Play"  Sept. 16, 1990

A slick transfer student (Wixted) tries to out-Parker Parker.  A different actor plays Mr. Loopman than in ep. 1.

Matt Stiles...........................................Kevin Wixted
Donna Sue Horton......................................Julia Condra

And: Keith Williams (Gordy), Vernon Weddle (Mr. Loopman)

Director: Max Tash        Writers: Alan Cross & Tom Spezialy

4. "Parker Lewis Must Lose"  Sept. 23, 1990

Parker's attempts to throw his own election for Student Body President inadvertently keep making him more popular.

Candidate Becky Grant.....................................Kim Valentine
Jamie.................................................................Torri Whitehead
And: Scott Egan (Jock), Tiffanie Poston (Cheerleader), Scott Jensen (Man in body cast)

Director: Andy Tennant           Writer: Tom Straw

5. "Close, But No Guitar"  Sept. 30, 1990

After a particularly humiliating day, Mikey wants to drop out of school to become a guitarist. Ziggy Marley is the reggae-musician son of Bob Marley; Kool Moe Dee is a rap singer.

Mary Lou.................................................................Alla Korot
Uncle Paul.............................................................Wynn Irwin
Aunt Celia................................................................Mina Kolb
Gym coach............................................................Macka Foley
Student........................................................Rodney Allan Rippy
Little girl..............................................................Trina Cashen
Themselves (cameos).....................Ziggy Marley, Kool Moe Dee

Director: Bryan Spicer
Writers: Lon Diamond & Clyde Phillips

6. "G.A.G. Dance"  Oct. 7, 1990  (PL-106)

Parker's dating seminar backfires. Korot reprises her role from last episode.

Tracy Lee Summers.............................................Robin Lively
Mary Lou.................................................................Alla Korot
Bonnie Bubka....................................................Penina Segall
And: Laurie Plaxen (Stacy), Caroline Gilshian (Girl)

Director: Lyndall Hobbs
Writers: Clyde Phillips & Lon Diamond

7. "Love's a Beast"  Oct. 14, 1990  (PL-107)

Mikey becomes the desired of a secret admirer -- apparently, Parker's sister. Plaxen reprises her role from last episode.

Kristen.............................................................Keely Christian
Stacy.................................................................Laurie Plaxen

Director: Max Tash        Writers: Peter Ocko & Adam Barr

8. "Saving Grace"  Oct. 21, 1990  (PL-108)

When an even more dictatorial principal (new recurring guest Graham) succeeds the suspended Musso, Parker connives to get her back. Poston reprises her role from ep. 4.

Men................................................Ron Canada, Wesley Mann
Cook.....................................................................Monty Bane
And: Phyllis Flax (Librarian), Tiffanie Poston (Cheerleader)

Director: Bryan Spicer           Writer: Russell Marcus

9. "Musso & Frank"  Oct. 28, 1990  (PL-109)

Parker unknowingly sets Lemmer up with Musso's niece (El-

son). Faustino is a cast-member of *Married With Children*.

Confused student (cameo)................................David Faustino
Denise......................................................................Andrea Elson
Audrey......................................................................Paige French

Director: Max Tash      Writers: Clyde Phillips & Lon Diamond

10. "Deja Dudes"  Nov. 4, 1990  (PL-110)

Before the opening of a time capsule at the school's 20-year reunion, Parker must try to remove incriminating evidence from a humiliating prank his dad played on Musso in 1970.

Vic............................................................................David Morin
Gary.....................................................................Gary Grossman
Bronc Adelson.......................................................R.A. Mihailoff
George...............................................................J. Frank Stewart
And: Michele Buffone (Tina), Joel Swetow (Rod)

Director: Bryan Spicer           Writer: Tom Straw

11. "Radio Free Flamingo"  Thursday, Nov. 15, 1990
     8:30-9 p.m.  (PC-111)

Parker and his gang start a pirate radio station. Condra reprises her role from ep. 3.

Donna Sue Horton...............................................Julia Condra

Director: Jeff Melman
Writers: David Caplan & Brian LAPAN

12. "Science Fair"  Nov. 18, 1990

In a science-fair contest, the pressure is on Jerry to beat rival school El Corrado, led by Musso's enemy, Principal Pankow.

Young Jerry............................................................Luke Edwards
Judge...........................................................................Jack Tice
Sam........................................................................Kevin Krakower

Director: Max Tash          Writer: John DeBellis

13. "Teacher, Teacher"  Dec. 2, 1990

When Parker's pranks make a favorite teacher (Johnson) decide to retire, he earns the enmity of his schoolmates.

Ms. Donnelly.......................................................Penny Johnson
Luke MacDonald.............................................Jamie Cardriche
Mr. Krantz....................................................................John Horn
Mothers...............................Delana Michaels, Lyndsey Fields
Fathers.......................................Parker Whitman, Lee Anthony

Director: Bryan Spicer
Writers: Clyde Phillips & Lon Diamond

14. "Rent-a-Kube"  Dec. 16, 1990  (PL-114)

Parker's parents hire Kubiac as a security guard at their Mondo Video store, but find he scares away customers. Guest Osbourne is rock musician. Rippy reprises his role from ep. 5.

Himself....................................................................Ozzy Osbourne
Officer Donovon..................................................Gary McGurk
Gina Lang........................................................................Dani Lee
Rev. Rafferty.............................................................Paul Wiley
Pretty girl..................................................Kymberleigh St. Peter
Rodney.........................................................Rodney Allen Rippy
Tim..................................................................Robert Cavanaugh

Director: Andy Tennant                 Writer: Tom Straw

15. "Heather the Class" Jan. 13, 1990 (PL-113)

Shelly joins the bitchy "Vogues" clique of girls, who trick Kubiac into targeting Jerry. Foley reprises his role from ep. 5.

Jamie.................................................Michele Abrams
Annie Ricker.......................................Tiffany Brissette
Gym coach........................................Macka Foley
And: Malaika (Merlene), Randy Murzynski (Sports reporter)

Director: Max Tash          Writers: Tom Spezialy & Alan Cross

16. "Jerry: Portrait of a Video Junkie" Feb. 3, 1991 (PL-116)

Jerry's school work and personal life begin to suffer when he gets addicted to video games.

Mom Musso, Ms. Musso's mother..............Barbara Billingsley
Theodore Musso, Ms. Musso's younger brother...Jerry Mathers
Group leader.....................................Bruce Jarchow
Todd..................................................Jeffrey Arbaugh
Steven................................................Aron Eisenberg
And: Donna Eskra (Darla), Ken Exner (Alan)

Director: Bryan Spicer
Writers: Lon Diamond & Clyde Phillips

17. "Splendor in the Class" Feb. 10, 1991 (PL-118)

Parker begins dating a girl (Lerman) who wants to break up his friendships with Mikey and Jerry.

Hayley................................................April Lerman

Director: Larry (a.k.a. Lawrence) Jay Lipton
Writer: Michael Swerdlick

18. "The Human Grace" Feb. 17, 1991 (PL-117)

Parker tries igniting romantic sparks between Musso and her rival Pankow. Yankovic is a pop-music parodist.

Chairperson.......................................Takayo Fischer
Randy................................................Charles Wahleheim
Himself.............................................."Weird Al" Yankovic

Director: Max Tash                   Writer: Tom Straw

19. "Citizen Kube" Feb. 24, 1991 (PL-121)

Kubiac rapidly gives away the $2 million he's won in a publisher's sweepstakes; Musso wants to replace Lemmer. Guest Wolf is an entertainment reporter.

Young bum/rock star...........................Taime Downe
Man...................................................Wesley Mann
Yuppie...............................................William Lester Collins
Herself..............................................Jeanne Wolf
    Also orig. announced:
    Ryan Stiles (Man), Dennis Fimple (Hillbilly dad)

Director: Max Tash       Teleplay: Alan Cross & Tom Spezialy
Story: Clyde Phillips & Lon Diamond

20. "Randall Without a Cause" March 10, 1991 (PL-119)

After Mikey joins a motorcycle gang and takes the fall for a crime they commit, Parker gets help from a cool cop (Rocket). Orig. scheduled for Feb. 17.

Jake.................................................Charles Rocket
Sammy..............................................Brad Tatum
And: Dennis C. Stewart (Mean guy), Ron Dortch (Officer)

Director: Max Tash       Writers: Lon Diamond & Clyde Phillips

21. "Jerry's First Date" March 24, 1991 (PL-120)

With the assitance of Parker and Mikey, Jerry goes out with a highly intelligent girl (Langer) taking college-level courses.

Melissa..............................................A.J. Langer
Future Jerry.......................................Jan Rabson
Evan.................................................Joshua Lucas
And: Bob Tzudiker (Doctor), Noni White (Questioner)

Director: Bryan Spicer       Writers: Peter Ocko & Adam Barr

22. "Against the Norm" April 7, 1991

Musso's tricky nemesis Pankow withdraws from the Federal Education Forum to beg Musso for a job. St. Peter played a different role, ep. 14.

Waitress............................................Kymberleigh St. Peter

Director: Bryan Spicer               Writer: Tom Straw

23. "King Kube" April 28, 1991 (PL-125)

When Jerry gets Kubiac elected Prom King as a prank, Parker and Mikey rescue Jerry by creating an "It's a Wonderful Life"-type video of Kube. Guest Osmond is a singer.

Himself..............................................Donny Osmond
Eileen Larson......................................Yohanna Yonas
Amber................................................Joe Crell
And: Leanna Crell (Kandy), Monica Crell (Barbie)

Director: Bryan Spicer       Writers: Tom Spezialy & Alan Cross

24. "Teens from a Mall" May 5, 1991

With a mall as the thematic thread, Parker girl-chases, Jerry helms an information booth, and Musso tries to curb her shopping. Jarchow played a different role, ep. 16.

Sarah...............................................Josie Bissett
Ira Lefko...........................................Don Lake
Dr. Carroll.........................................Bruce Jarchow
Credit officer.....................................Wesley Mann
Grodnik Griddle person........................Cynthia Mann
Lady.................................................Rusty Schwimmer
Store manager David............................Simon Hart
Clerk................................................Venus Thomas

Director: Andy Tennant
Writers: Clyde Phillips & Lon Diamond

25. "My Fair Shelly" May 12, 1991 (PL-126)

When Parker's sister wants him and his friends to find her a date for a big party, they attempt a *Pygmalion* number on her. Malaika plays a different role than in ep. 15.

Brad.................................................Jonathan Ward
Melinda.............................................Brooke Theiss
Caroline............................................Malaika
And: Sharon Case (Joanne), Todd Shawn (Dude)

Director: Andy Tennant       Writers: Peter Ocko & Adam Barr

26. "Parker Lewis Can't Win" May 19, 1991 (PL-122)

On the last day of school, everything, incredibly, goes wrong for Parker. Valentine reprises her role from ep. 4.

Augie.........................................................Ray Walston
Becky Grant.............................................Kim Valentine
Silhouettes ("Ferris" and friend).....Robert Cavanaugh, Richard Feldman
Host.................................................................Jim Lange

Director: Bryan Spicer          Writer: Tom Straw

**renewed; begins its 1991-92 season Aug. 11; Mary Ellen Trainor succeeds Anne Bloom in the role of Judy Lewis.**

## Perfect Strangers

ABC          Sept. 28-April 19    Fridays, 9-9:30 p.m.
             April 26-on          Fridays, 9:30-10 p.m.

Series premiere: March 25, 1986

Comedy of mismatched Chicago roommates -- a photojournalist (Linn-Baker) and his odd immigrant cousin (Pinchot) from the fictional Mediterranean island of Mypos -- who both work at the fictitious *Chicago Chronicle* (the same newspaper employing Harriette Winslow of *Family Matters*).

Balki Bartokomous......................................Bronson Pinchot
Larry Appleton..............................................Mark Linn-Baker
Flight attendant Jennifer Lyons.......................Melanie Wilson
Mary Anne......................................................Rebeca Arthur
Advice columnist Lydia Markham.......................Belita Moreno
Sam Gorpley, Balki's mailroom boss..................Sam Anderson
Tess Holland (ep. 2-on)........................................Alisan Porter

*Recurring:*
Wainwright, Larry's boss (ep. 2,9,12,21,23)..............F.J. O'Neil

Miller • Boyett Productions in assoc. with Lorimar Television
Executive producers: Thomas L. Miller, Robert L. Boyett, William Bickley, Michael Warren
Co-executive producer: Paula A. Roth
Supervising producer: Terry Hart
Consulting producer: James O'Keefe
Producers: John B. Collins, Tom Devanney, Bill Daley
Co-producers: Alan Plotkin, Barry O'Brien, Cheryl Alu (latter two later in season)
Associate producer: Michael J. Morris
Executive story editors: Barry O'Brien, Cheryl Alu (early in season)
Story editors: Tom Amundsen, Thomas R. Nance
Creative consultant: Judy Pioli
Directors of photography (variously): Gregg Heschong; Tony Askins, A.S.C.; David Nowell
Theme: "Nothing's Gonna Stop Me Now" by Jesse Frederick & Bennett Salvay; performed by David Pomeranz
Music (variously): Steven Chesne; Jesse Frederick & Bennett Salvay
Creator and executive consultant: Dale McRaven

---

1. "Safe at Home" Sept. 28, 1990

Larry accidentally sets off their new high-tech burglar alarm, and then forgets how to turn it off.

McNulty.........................................................Raye Birk

Voice of alarm.................................................Mitch Carter

Director: Richard Correll
Writers: Barry O'Brien & Cheryl Alu

2. "New Kid on the Block" Oct. 5, 1990

Larry can't concentrate on his writing when Balki babysits the new seven-year-old neighbor.

Mrs. Holland..................................................Andrea Walters

Director: Greg Antonacci          Writer: Bill Daley

3. "The Breakup" Oct. 12, 1990

Larry, crushed when Jennifer goes out with an old flame, proposes marriage. According to ABC, the series' 100th episode.

Bill Madden...................................................David Sederholm
Maitre d'.......................................................Brian Carpenter

Director: James O'Keefe          Writer: Terry Hart

4. "A Horse is a Horse" Oct. 19, 1990

Balki tries to treat a diseased racehorse, inside the apartment.

Dr. Tierney...................................................William Denis
     Also orig. announced:
     Dennis Tufano (Man), Alan Buchdahl (Track announcer)

Director: Greg Antonocci          Writer: Tom Devanney

5. "Family Feud" Oct. 26, 1990

Larry inadvertently steps into a centuries-old Myposian feud.

Zoltan.........................................................Nicholas Kadi

Director: Judy Pioli          Writer: John B. Collins

6. "Call Me Indestructible" Nov. 2, 1990

The guys take a plane ride with a daredevil pilot (Mars) who puts the single-engine airplane into a tailspin.

"Ace" Atkins...................................................Kenneth Mars
Radio voice.....................................Dennis Tufano (uncredited)

Director: James O'Keefe          Writer: Paula A. Roth

7. "The Men Who Knew Too Much" Part 1   Nov. 9, 1990

While in L.A. with Larry, who's covering the wedding of a soap-opera star (Bowman), Balki inadvertently videotapes a mob hit.

Marco Madison...................................................Scott Marlowe
Herb............................................................Steven Gilborn
Sheila...........................................................Jessie Jones
Darla Wayne....................................................Teresa Bowman
Thugs.........John Lee, Michael Hungerford, Matt Johnston
Drug agent.....................................................Chris Hendrie
Salesperson...................................................Donald Willis
Customer....................................................Elaine Bartolone
Waiter........................................................Michael Caldwell
Guests...............................Renee Wedel, Timothy Noyes

Director: Richard Correll          Writer: Terry Hart

8. "The Men Who Knew Too Much" Part 2   Nov. 16, 1990

The guys are chased by murderers whose crime they witnessed, and police who think Larry and Balki are the killers.

With: Marlowe, Gilborn, Jones, Bowman, Lee, Hungerford, Caldwell, Willis, Bartolone, Caldwell, Wedel and Noyes from last episode
Newscaster......................................................Dale Harimoto
Roy..........................................................................Amy Hill
Mugger.............................................................Michael Stanton
Vendor.....................................................................Joe Bellan

Director: Richard Correll               Writer: Terry Hart

9. "The Ring"  Nov. 23, 1990

When Larry finds out the engagement ring he bought Jennifer is fake, he and Balki try to engineer a switch.

Director: Richard Correll
Writer: Harriet Helberg & Sandy Helberg

10. "Black Widow"  Nov. 30, 1990

Larry fears Mary Anne may be a serial killer.

Director: Judy Pioli                 Writer: Tom Amundsen

11. "The Sunshine Boys"  Dec. 7, 1990

The guys get badly burned by sunlamps, but are determined to attend an important party regardless.

Bunky.....................................................................Mark Neely

Director: Judy Pioli                 Writer: John B. Collins

**preempted Dec. 14 & 21**

12. "Hocus Pocus"  Dec. 28, 1990

At a charity show, Larry's chance to interview British Prime Minister Margaret Thatcher (who had recently resigned by the time this aired) hinges on Larry filling-in for a magician.

Secret Service agent............................................Tony Montero
Mrs. O'Neil........................................................Gloria McMillan
The Amazing Timmy......................Nick Lewin (orig. Kip King)
Steve/Woody.......................................................Bruce Lanoil

Director: Judy Pioli                 Writer: Tom Devanney

13. "Finders Keepers"  Jan. 4, 1991

A deceased man's suit contains the key to a safe-deposit box with money enough to keep an orphanage from closing.

Father Killion....................................................Bryan O'Byrne
Minister...............................................................John Petlock
    Also orig. announced: Dona Hardy (Old lady)

Director: Judy Pioli                 Writer: Tom Amundsen

14. "Grandpa"  Jan. 11, 1991

The guys try to reenergize Larry's 76-year-old Grandpa Appleton after he's dumped by his younger girlfriend (Thomson). Orig. scheduled for Jan. 4.

Grandpa Appleton..........................................John Anderson
George...............................................................George Poulos
Sam...............................................................Brenda Thomson

And: Helen Lambros (Sophia), Marianne Muellerleile (Athena)

Director: Joel Zwick
Writers: Barry O'Brien & Cheryl Alu

15. "Little Apartment of Horrors"  Jan. 18, 1991

Larry overfeeds a special Myposian plant with medicinal powers, creating a weird, monstrous vegetation.

Deliveryperson.....................................................Robert G. Lee

Director: Judy Pioli                 Writer: Terry Hart

16. "I Saw This on TV"  Feb. 1, 1991

In an homage to *The Honeymooners*, Balki tells a tale demonstrating how Larry's tiny lie to Jennifer will create trouble.

Director: Joel Zwick                 Writer: Paula A. Roth

17. "Speak, Memory"  Feb. 8, 1991

A bump on the head gives Larry intermittent amnesia, adding to his anxiety as he's about to meet Jennifer's mother.

Mrs. Lyons...........................................................Marla Adams
Waiter.................................................................John Drayman

Director: Judy Pioli                 Writer: John B. Collins

18. "Out of Sync"  Feb. 15, 1991

Balki seems headed for stardom as rap singer Fresh Young Balki B., but discovers a dubbed singing voice on his video.

Manager Clive Enright................................Ian Patrick Williams
Director...............................................................Gene Wolande

Dancers (uncredited): Connie Chambers, Jodie McDonald, Fumi Shishino, Paula Brown, Eliana Alexander, Sybil Avur

Director: Judy Pioli
Writers: Barry O'Brien & Cheryl Alu

19. "See How They Run"  Feb. 22, 1991

Balki runs for college student body president, with Larry going overboard as his campaign manager.

Moderator.....................................................Marte Boyle Slout
Students......................................Rhonda Britten, Troy Fromin

Director: Judy Pioli               Writer: Thomas R. Nance

**preempted March 8**

20. "Climb Every Billboard"  March 15, 1991

Larry tricks Balki into living on a billboard until the Chicago Bulls basketball team starts winning.

Announcer.....................................Tom Amundsen (uncredited)

Director: Judy Pioli                 Writer: Tom Devanney

21. "A Catered Affair"  March 22, 1991

Larry inadvertently overbooks part-time caterer Balki's already tight schedule.

Betty.................................................Mary Pat Gleason
Gunther................................................Alfred Dennis
Billy Joe Bob....................................Newell Alexander
Cowgirl..............................................Noreen Reardon

Director: Judy Pioli                 Writer: Tom Amundsen

22. "Duck Soup" April 5, 1991

Larry and Balki go duck hunting with Larry's boss.

Director: Judy Pioli                 Writer: Terry Hart

23. "Great Balls of Fire" April 26, 1991

Larry and Balki take volunteer-firefighter training, and start a
fire in the firehouse.

Fire Chief Newton.......................................Ron Dean

Director: Bill Petty         Writers: Barry O'Brien & Cheryl Alu

24. "See You in September" May 3, 1991

With no wedding plans made six months after their engagement, Larry and Jennifer take a Myposian compatibility test.

Director: Judy Pioli                 Writer: Paula A. Roth

**preempted July 5**

**renewed for 1991-92; new episodes begin Sept. 20, 1991**

# Perry Mason

NBC          Sundays, various

Courtroom drama of a seemingly invincible defense attorney.
Continuation of 1957-1966 CBS series also starring Burr and
Hale; series revived 1973-74 with a different cast (*The New
Perry Mason*), then as a series of TV-movies following the suc-
cessful NBC telefilm *Perry Mason Returns* (December 1, 1985).

Perry Mason.......................................Raymond Burr
Della Street..........................................Barbara Hale
Ken Malansky................................William R. Moses

Dean Hargrove Productions, The Fred Silverman Co., Viacom
Executive producers: Fred Silverman, Dean Hargrove
Co-executive producer: Joel Steiger
Producers: Billy Ray Smith, David Solomon
Director of photography: Daniel McKinny (ep. 1), Robert
    Seaman (ep. 2-4)
Original *Perry Mason* theme: Fred Steiner
Music: Dick De Benedictis
Legal advisor: Dennis Smith
Based on characters created by: Erle Stanley Gardner

---

1. "The Case of the Defiant Daughter"
   Sept. 30, 1990 9-11 p.m. (2513)

While in Las Vegas to see a boxing match, Mason is called on
to defend an accused killer (Posey) at the behest of the man's
daughter (Lewis). Working title: "The Case of the Deadly Deal."

Richard Stuart.........................................Robert Culp
Jay Corelli............................................Robert Vaughn
L.D. Ryan............................................Ken Kercheval

Cliff Bartell.................................................Jere Burns
Steven Elliot.............................................Kevin Tighe
David Benson.............................................John Posey
Melanie Benson (13)...................................Jenny Lewis
Hotel clerk...............................................Lynne Hart
Elaine Hochman....................................LuAnn Buckstein
Martin Hochman.......................................John Apicella
Ms. Young.........................................Michele Scarabelli
Sgt. Hollenbeck......................................Don Galloway
Sarah Andrews......................................Lois de Banzie
And: Tricia Springer (Reporter), J. Bryan Morse (Police officer),
    Harry J. Lennix (Prosecutor Keith Warner), Ron Pinkard
    (Judge Thomas McElvy), Valerie Karasek (Belinda
    Foster), Joe Horvath (Hood), Colin Ward, Lucinda Dickey
    (Employees), Denise Galik (Alice Sherman), Jack O'Hallo-
    ran (Big man), Michael Leopard (Mr. Sherman), Jamie
    Horton (Bailiff), Dulcie Camp (Court clerk)

Director: Christian I. Nyby II         Teleplay: Anne Collins
Story: Dean Hargrove & Joel Steiger

2. "The Case of the Ruthless Reporter"
   Jan. 6, 1991 9-11 p.m. (2514)

Mason defends a TV-news anchor (Keane) suspected of killing
her universally disliked co-anchor (James). Working title:
"The Case of the Late Newsman."

Brett Huston...........................................John James
Vic St. John..........................................Jerry Orbach
Twyla Cooper........................................Susan Sullivan
Chuck Gilmore...............................Philip Michael Thomas
Al Shockley...........................................Earl Billings
Sam Garza...............................................Gary Giem
Judge Phyllis Markham........................Betsy Jones-Moreland
Gary Slate.............................................Peter Jurasik
Gillian Pope...........................................Kerrie Keane
Cassie Woodfield..............................Mary Page Keller
Lt. Ed Brock.......................................James McEachin
Asst. D.A. Jack LaRusso....................................Andy Romano
Dave Franco..............................................Beau Starr
And: Una Kim (Brenda), Susan Lentini (Elise Franco), Ed O'-
    Brien (Fred Davidson), Dwayne Carrington (Detective
    Peters), Ron Headlee (Detective Jackson), Brad Leland
    (Fire Captain), Doug Lenzini (Technician/Mr. Jenner),
    Bev Newcomb, Cecile Walker (Landladies), Owen O'Far-
    rell (Officer Paretti), Roger Pancake (Hank Rossiter), Terry
    Rhoades (Lance), Jeff Valdez (Standup comic)
Also orig. announced:
    Tracy Smith (Floor director), John Nance (Director), Wil-
    liam Hahn (Engineer), Cornelia Van Esso (Court re-
    porter), Enoch Jackson (Man in apartment), Jennifer
    Cooke-Siegel (Heather)

Director: Christian I. Nyby II
Writer: Sean Cholodenko (George Eckstein orig. announced)

3. "The Case of the Maligned Mobster"
   Monday, Feb. 11, 1991 9-11 p.m. (2515)

With frameups and counter-plots directed against his once-
violent client, Mason defends a former mobster (Nader)
charged with murdering his wife (Walsh). Jones-Moreland had
played a different judge, ep. 2; guest Anka is a singer. Filmed
in Denver. Orig. scheduled for Feb. 24.

Frank Halloran........................................Mason Adams
Johnny Sorrento....................................Michael Nader
Paula Barrett........................................Anne Schedeen
Nick Angel...............................................Paul Anka
Joanna Calder......................................Pamela Bowen

Judge Elinor Harrelson (orig. Phyllis Markham)...............Betsy
   Jones-Moreland
Jeff Sorrento.................................................Sean Kanan
Janice Kirk (orig. Kirkwood)..............................Mitzi Kapture
Karen Thatcher.............................................Beverly Leech
Mike Calder.................................................Howard McGillin
Dave Barrett...............................................Richard Portnow
Sgt. Phil Baranski.....................................Stephen Tobolowsky
Maria Sorrento............................................Gwynyth Walsh
And: Rich Beall (Albert Faro), Kevin Gray (Valet), Dan Kop-
   per (Man in supermarket), Leigh Rayburn (Charlene),
   Eric Server (Asst. D.A. Phil Stuart), Rosie Waters (Connie
   Angel), Walker Williams (Bartender #1/Halstead), Jeff
   Austin (Pool hall manager), Gary Cupp (Bartender #2),
   Prince Havely, Annette Marin, Katy Whelan (Reporters)
   Also orig. announced:
     James McEachin (Lt. Ed Brock), Gil Colon (Cop)

Director: Ron Satlof
Writer: Sean Cholodenko (George Eckstein orig. announced)

4. "The Case of the Glass Coffin"
   Monday, May 13, 1991  9-11 p.m. (2516)

An illusionist (Scolari) is accused of murder when his mis-
tress/stage-assistant (Grahn) is killed during a futuristic levi-
tation trick.  McEachin reprises his role from ep. 2; Jones-
Moreland had played differently named judges in ep. 2-3.
Filmed in Denver.

David Katz...................................................Peter Scolari
Kate Ford...............................................Nancy Lee Grahn
Jake Morrison................................................John Karlen
Max Lemar...............................................Dennis Lipscomb
Betty Farmer...............................................Julie Sommars
Judy Katz, David's wife.....................................Kim Braden
Asst. D.A. Scott Willard.....................................Bob Gunton
Judge.............................................Betsy Jones-Moreland
Lt. Ed Brock...........................................James McEachin
Paul Torrence..........................................Conor O'Farrell
Terry Weidner...............................................Kate Vernon
Ann Morrison.............................................Romy Walthall
Henry Eiseman.............................................Richard Jury
Casey........................................................Vern Porter
Gordon Cosgrove.............................Joseph Gwin McDonald
   Also orig. announced:
     Lise Simms, Gil Colon, Paul Reinertson (Reporters), Jo-
     hanna Morrison (Ticket clerk), Annette Marin (Reception-
     ist), Robert Himber (Sheriff), David Richards (Gus)

Director: Christian I. Nyby II          Writer: Brian Clemens

## Quantum Leap

NBC           Sept. 28-Jan. 4      Fridays, 8-9 p.m.
          March 6-on           Wednesdays, 10-11 p.m.

NOTE: Aired daily, Monday, June 24 to Friday, June 28 (10-
    11 p.m. each day except Monday, 9-11 p.m.)

Series premiere: March 31, 1989

Semi-anthological science-fiction drama of a physicist whose
flawed time-travel experiment in 1999 hurls his essence un-
predictably into the bodies of individuals from the 1950s to
the 1980s, with no knowledge of his temporary identity, but
with aid from the hologram of the charmingly roguish project
leader (Stockwell).  Sam's original research headquarters: The
Quantum Leap Control Center.  The project supercomputer:
Ziggy.  Creator Bellisario and co-executive producer Pratt are

husband and wife; assistant director Kevin Corcoran is a former actor, and the sibling of performers Brian Corcoran and
Noreen Corcoran.  "Mirror" below refers to the silent bit player,
seen in a reflection, showing the body Sam's persona inhabits.

Sam Beckett.................................................Scott Bakula
Admiral Albert (Al) Calavicci............................Dean Stockwell

Belisarius Productions in assoc. with Universal Television,
   an MCA Co.
Executive producer: Donald P. Bellisario
Co-executive producers: Deborah Pratt, Michael Zinberg
Supervising producer: Harker Wade
Producer: Chris Ruppenthal
Co-producers: Paul Brown, Jeff Gourson
Associate producer: James S. Giritlian
Executive story editor: Tommy Thompson
Director of photography (variously): Michael Watkins; Bradley
   B. Six, A.S.C.
Special effects: Whitey Krumm
Music: Velton Ray Bunch
Theme: Mike Post; instrumental with voiceover narration by
   Deborah Pratt (uncredited)
Creator: Donald P. Bellisario

1. "The Leap Home: November 25, 1969"  Sept. 28, 1990

Sam leaps into his own life at age 16 on the family farm in Elk
Ridge, Indiana, and tries to alter history to postpone the
deaths of his 55-year-old father and Vietnam-bound brother.

John Beckett, Sam's father...................................Scott Bakula
Thelma Beckett, Sam's mother...........................Caroline Kava
Tom Beckett, Sam's brother.............................David Newsom
Katey Beckett, Sam's sister.............................Olivia Burnette
Coach Donnelly.................................................Mik Scriba
Mary Lou.................................................Hannah Cutrona
Lisa.......................................................Mai-Lis Kuniholm
And: Niles Brewster (Dr. Berger), Ethan Wilson (Sibby), Mat-
   thew John Graeser (Herky), John L. Tuell (No Nose Pru-
   itt), Adam Affonso (Young Sam/mirror)

Director: Joe Napolitano          Writer: Donald P. Bellisario

2. "The Leap Home Part II -- Vietnam: April 7, 1970"
   Oct. 5, 1990

Sam gets a second chance to save his brother, a Navy SEAL,
when he leaps into the life of a 'Nam grunt.  Supporting actor
Whiteside was the technical advisor on this episode.

Tom Beckett.................................................David Newsom
Maggie Dawson..........................................Andrea Thompsom
Col. Deke.....................................................Ernie Lively
Dempsey..................................................David Hayward
Titi...........................................................Tia Carrere
Preacher.....................................................Adam Nelson
Blaster...................................................Patrick Warburton
Shamoo.......................................................Ryan Reed
Doc.......................................................Rich Whiteside
Signalman Second Class "Magic"
   Williams/mirror...................................Christopher Kirby

Director: Michael Zinberg          Writer: Donald P. Bellisario

3. "Leap of Faith: August 19, 1963"  Oct. 12, 1990

As a Philadelphia priest, Sam intervenes between a murderous
youth (Nucci) and a vengeful fellow cleric to prevent a killing.

Father John "Mack" McRobert...........................Sandy McPeak

Tony Pronti.............................................Danny Nucci
Joey Pronti...........................................Davey Roberts
Rose Montocelli.........................................Erica Yohn
Rita Montocelli.......................................Penny Santon
Young man............................................Kane Picoy
Young boxer.......................................Todd Raderman
Woman........................................Pat Crawford Brown
Allen.............................................Robert Bleecher
Police officer............................................Bo Sabato
Cabbie..........................................Dominic Oliver
Mrs. Dellisio...........................................Lisa Passero
Father Pistano.......................................Bud Sabatino
Tony's girlfriend.......................................Amy Tritico

Director: James Whitmore, Jr.    Teleplay: Tommy Thompson
Story: Nick Harding & Karen Hall and Tommy Thompson

4. "One Strobe Over the Line: March 15, 1963" Oct. 19, 1990

As a fashion photographer, Sam tries to save a model (Mona-ghan) from OD'ing on amphetamines given her by her agent.

Agent/Helen..........................................Susan Anton
Byron...............................................Kristoffer Tabori
Edie..........................................Marjorie Monaghan
Mike.............................................David Sheinkopf
Frank.............................................Robert Trumbull
Irv....................................................John Achorn
Waiter................................................Nigel Gibbs
Karl Stone............................................Dan McCoy
Nubian guard.............................Lawrence McNeal III

Director: Michael Zinberg        Writer: Chris Ruppenthal

5. "The Boogieman: October 31, 1964" Oct. 26, 1990

Sam leaps into the life of a horror novelist in Salem, Mass.
Producer and episode writer Ruppenthal has a cameo.

Mary..............................................Valerie Mahaffey
Sheriff..................................................Paul Linke
Stevie..............................................David Kriegel
Tully..............................................Donald Horton
Dorothy.................................................Fran Ryan
Nurse................................................Jan Stratton
Joshua Rey/mirror............................Chris Ruppenthal

Director: Joe Napolitano        Writer: Chris Ruppenthal

6. "Miss Deep South: June 7, 1958" Nov. 2, 1990

In his third leap into a woman's body, Sam, as a beauty-pag-eant contestant, must prevent a sleazy photographer (Brooks) from selling nude photos of another girl (McAdam). Guest Stafford was Miss Florida in the 1976 Miss America Pageant.

Peg Myers........................................Nancy Stafford
Connie Duncan, Miss Corn Muffin.............Heather McAdam
Clint Beaumont...................................David A. Brooks
Victoria Jenkins.................................Julie Ann Lowery
Judge...................................................Hugh Gillin
Arlene.................................................Linda Hoy
Judge.........................................Marte Boyle Slout
Emcee................................................Martin Clark
Cheryl Lynn Birch...............................Karen L. Moore
Contestant/Sawyer.........................Janeen Ray Heller
Darlene Monty, Miss Sugar Belle/mirror.............Theresa Ring

Director: Christopher T. Welch    Writer: Tommy Thompson

7. "Black on White on Fire: August 11, 1965" Nov. 9, 1990

Amid the Watts riots, Sam as a black medical student is torn between community loyalty and his white fiancee (Henninger).

Nita Jordan (orig. Mama Harper).........................CCH Pounder
Lonnie Jordan (orig. Harper), her son.............Gregory Millar
Susan Bond..................................Corie Henninger
B.B...............................................Sami Chester
Papa Dee.............................................Ron Taylor
Capt. Paul Bond.................................Marc Alaimo
Shari Hill......................................Laverne Anderson
Matty...........................................Montrose Hagins
Young woman.........................Cheryl Francis Harrington
Police sniper............................................Jon Berry
Ray Jordan (orig. Harper), Nita's son/mirror......Garon Grigsby

Director: Joe Napolitano        Writer: Deborah Pratt

8. "The Great Spontini: May 9, 1974" Nov. 16, 1990

Sam leaps into the life of a second-rate magician whose ex-wife (Steel) demands custody of their daughter (Woodland).

Maggie Spontini....................................Amy F. Steel
Steve Slater.............................Erich Anderson (erroneously
    given as Erich Slater in TV Guide)
Jamie Spontini (12)...........................Lauren Woodland
Judge Mulhern.................................Michael Fairman
Elaine.................................................Robin Greer
Mrs. Futre.............................................Jean Adams
Harry Spontini/mirror....................................Dan Birch

**preempted Nov. 23**

9. "Rebel Without a Clue: September 1, 1958" Nov. 30, 1990

As a 1950s biker in the Cobras gang, Sam befriends an en-dangered young woman (Bissett) who digs real-life beat author Jack Kerouac. Working title: "On the Road."

Becky.................................................Josie Bissett
Dillon...........................................Dietrich Bader
Diner owner Ernie Tyler..........................Teddy Wilson
Jack Kerouac.............................Michael Bryan French
Ice.....................................................Scott Kraft
Mad Dog.................................Mark Boone Junior
Kraut..............................................Joshua Cadman
Shane "Funnybone"("Bone") Thomas/mirror..Kristopher Logan

Director: James Whitmore, Jr.
Teleplay: Randy Holland and Paul Brown
Story: Nick Harding and Paul Brown

10. "A Little Miracle: December 24, 1962" Dec. 21, 1990

On Christmas Eve, Sam, as valet to a heartless land developer (Rocket), uses Dickensian tactics to enlighten the man. Orig. scheduled for Dec. 14.

Blake..............................................Charles Rocket
Laura..........................................Melinda McGraw
Max...............................................Robert Lesser
Jason Calloway.....................................Tom McTigue
Lt. Porterman.............................Michael Dan Wagner
Tiny boy...........................................Jarrett Lennon
Newscaster........................................Dale Harimoto
Mickey.........................................Christopher Fleming
Charlie.......................................Dylan Day Brown
Maintenance person...........................Duane Whitaker
Pearson/mirror......................................Milan Micksic

Director: Michael Watkins        Story: Sandy Fries

Teleplay: Sandy Fries and Robert A. Wolterstorff

11. "The Runaway: July 3, 1964" Jan. 4, 1991

As a gangly 13-year-old on a family vacation, Sam tries to keep his mom (Faison) from deserting her husband and kids.

Norma Rickett............................................Sandy Faison
Hank Rickett............................................Sherman Howard
Billl........................................................Joseph Hacker
Alex........................................................Ami Foster
Beth........................................................Amber Susa
Lew.........................................................Jason Logan
Butchie Rickett/mirror...............................Buff Borin

Director: Michael Katleman          Writer: Paul Brown

### on hiatus

12. "8 1/2 Months: November 15, 1955" March 6, 1991
    10:19-11:19 p.m.

Sam leaps into the body of an unwed 16-year-old about to deliver a child, and who suffers the scorn of her father (Whitmore, Jr., the actor-director son of actor James Whitmore). Late start due to a presidential address.

Dotty......................................................Lana Schwab
Bob Crockett............................................James Whitmore, Jr.
Keeter.....................................................Hunter von Leer
Effy........................................................Tasha Scott
Mrs. Thailer.............................................Anne Haney
Dr. Rogers...............................................Parley Baer
Leola......................................................Ann Walker
Willis.......................................................Philip Linton
Nurse Denton...........................................Peggy Walton-Walker
Mrs. Suffy...............................................Molly McClure
Billy Jean Crockett/mirror.........................Priscilla Weems

Director: James Whitmore, Jr.        Writer: Deborah Pratt

13. "Future Boy: October 6, 1957" March 13, 1991

As a live-TV teen actor, Sam must help the troubled, time-traveling Captain Galaxy (Herd) from being committed.

Moe Stein/Captain Galaxy............................Richard Herd
Irene Kiner, his daughter............................Debra Stricklin
Ben Harris...............................................George Wyner
Dr. Sandler (orig. Scanlan)..........................Alan Fudge
Production assistant..................................David Sage
Caped Futurite..........................................Jason Kincaid
Small boy................................................John Christian Graas
Kid.........................................................Jesse Switzer
Kenny Sharp/Future Boy/mirror....................Matt Marfoglia

Director: Michael Switzer          Writer: Tommy Thompson

14. "Private Dancer: October 6, 1979" March 20, 1991

As a Chippendale's dancer, Sam must steer a young deaf dancer (real-life deaf actress-dancer Beriault) toward auditioning for a noted choreographer (Allen, the episode's director).

Alana (orig. Joanne)...................................Debbie Allen
Mario......................................................Louis Mustillo
Valerie....................................................Heidi Swedberg
Otto........................................................Robert Schuch
Gina.......................................................Marguerite Pomerhn-Derricks
Diana......................................................Rhondee Beriault
Martin.....................................................Henry Woronicz

Winnie....................................................Melinda Cordell
Officer Arden...........................................Charles Emmett
Lou.........................................................Frank Novak
Louie.......................................................Harry Cohn
Rod the Bod/mirror...................................Christopher Solari

Consultant: Terrylene Saccehetti

Director-choreographer: Debbie Allen      Writer: Paul Brown

15. "Piano Man: November 10, l985" March 27, 1991

A killer stalks both the tacky lounge pianist whom Sam leaps into, and the musician's ex-partner/girlfriend.

Lorraine..................................................Marietta DePrima
Carl........................................................Angelo Tiffe
Frank......................................................John Oldach
Jenelle....................................................Denise Gentile
Hector.....................................................Frank Roman
Thelma....................................................Cherry Davis
Chuck/Joey/mirror.....................................Sam Clay

"Somewhere in the Night" by Scott Bakula and Velton Ray Bunch; performed by Bakula

Director: James Whitmore, Jr.        Writer: Ed Scharlach

16. "Southern Comforts: August 4, 1961" April 3, 1991

Engaged to a New Orleans brothel madam (Taggart), Sam's pimp persona must prevent the murder of a woman (Emelin) living there. No "mirror" performer this episode; a portrait used instead. Working title: "Love for Sale: August 4, 1961."

Marsha....................................................Rita Taggart
Sheriff....................................................David Graf
Gina........................................................Georgia Emelin
Jake........................................................Dan Butler
Sophie.....................................................Lauren Tom
Ruby.......................................................Minnie Summers Lindsey
Rhonda....................................................Diane Delano
Luther.....................................................David Powledge
Warren....................................................Walter Sylvest
Sailor......................................................J. Marvin Campbell
Paulette...................................................Stacey Cortez
And: Monica McMurtry (Abby), Jeffrey Concklin (Reese), David Alan Graf (Carl), Richard White (Gilbert)

Director: Chris Ruppenthal          Writer: Tommy Thompson

17. "Glitter Rock: April 12, 1974" April 10, 1991

As glitter-rock star King Thunder, Sam is stalked by an obsessed fan. Guest Noone was lead singer of Herman's Hermits.

Flash......................................................Jonathan Gries
Dwayne...................................................Peter Noone
Philip......................................................Christian Hoff
Cavin......................................................Michael Cerveris
Nick........................................................Robert Bauer
Sandy......................................................Liza Whitcraft
Whittler...................................................Jan Eddy
Blonde....................................................Sharon Martin
Heather...................................................Dorrie Krum
And: Bob Cady (Chase), Bruce Michael Paine (Tonic/mirror)

"Rock the Redhead" and "Mystic Traveler" by Scott Bakula and Chris Ruppenthal; performed by Bakula.

Director: Andy Cadiff          Writer: Chris Ruppenthal

18. "A Hunting We Will Go: June 18, 1976" April 17, 1991

Sam leaps into a bounty hunter handcuffed to a beautiful con-artist and alleged embezzler (Sibbett) who enraptures him.

Diane......................................................................Jane Sibbett
Rodney...............................................................Ken Marshall
Sheriff Michaels....................................................Cliff Bemis
Jack............................................................Michael McCarty
Bill...............................................................................Dale Swann
Luke...............................................................Jeffrey King
Clive...............................................................Warren Harrington
Edwine...............................................................Maxine Elliott
Cashier...............................................................Dorothy Blass
Gordon...............................................................Ken Kells

Director: Andy Cadiff              Writer: Beverly Bridges

**preempted April 24**

19. "Last Dance Before an Execution: May 12, 1971"
    May 1, 1991

With a 48-hour stay of execution, Sam, as a Cuban immigrant convicted of murdering a priest, must discover if he and his alleged accomplice (Mechoso) are guilty. Gago is a cast-member of *DEA: Special Task Force*.

Tearsa Marguerita LaReya...............................Jenny Gago
Raul...............................................................Julio Oscar Mechoso
Alan Ripley...............................................Christopher Allport
D.A. Theodore Wallace (Theo) Moody..................James Sloyan
Officer Little...............................................Leonard C. Lightfoot
Officer Hudson...............................................Jack Jozefson
Herb Stein...............................................Michael Holden
Maria...............................................................Krista Muscare
Father Rafferty...............................................Charles Woolf
Tia...............................................................Irene Olga Lopez
Bart Manners...............................................A.J. Freeman
Reporters.....................Wendy Jill Gordon, Andrew Amador
Older man in jail...............................................Harry Fleer
Black man in jail...............................................Neil Barton
Jesus Ortega/mirror...............................................Stephen Domingas

Director: Michael Watkins         Teleplay: Deborah Pratt
Story: Bill Bigelow & Donald P. Bellisario & Deborah Pratt

20. "Heart of a Champion: July 23, 1955" May 8, 1991

With a brother (Bossard) during the Cold War, Sam is one of two American wrestlers performing as The Battling Russkies.

Ronnie...............................................................Jerry Bossard
Lamar...............................................................Don Hood
Sherry...............................................................Deborah Wakeham
Lotty...............................................................Angela Paton
Dr. Griggs...............................................................Rance Howard
Myra...............................................................Susan Isaacs
Stan...............................................................Tim deZarn
Referee...............................................................Don Dolan
Carl...............................................................Terry Funk
Terry/mirror...............................................Jeff Hochendoner
The Executioner...............................................Jay S. York
Hank...............................................................John Kidwell

Director: Joe Napolitano          Writer: Tommy Thompson

21. "Nuclear Family: October 26, 1962" May 15, 1991

During the Cuban missile crisis, Sam's persona, selling bomb shelters, tries not to add to his niece and nephew's terror.

Mac Ellroy...............................................Timothy Carhart
Burt...............................................................Kurt Fuller
Kate Ellroy, Mac's wife...............................Kim Flowers
Stevie Ellroy, Mac and Kate's son...............Robert Hy Gorman
Kimberly Ellroy,
    their daughter........Candy Hutson a.k.a. Candace Hutson
Mrs. Klingman...............................................Della Salvi
Eddie Ellroy, Mac's brother/mirror...........Patrick M. Bruneau

Director: James Whitmore, Jr.     Writer: Paul Brown

22. "Shock Theater: October 3, 1954" May 22, 1991

Sam receives electro-shocks as mental patient Sam Bieder-man, calling forth multiple personalities from his previous personae and leaving him unable to recognize a horrified Al.

Nurse Chatam...............................................Lee Garlington
Dr. Masters...............................................David Proval
Butcher...............................................................Bruce A. Young
Tibby...............................................................Scott Lawrence
Dr. Wickless...............................................Robert Symonds
Dr. Beaks of the Quantum Leap project.......Candy Ann Brown
Freddy...............................................................Nick Brooks
Mortimer...............................................................Frank Collison
Oswald...............................................................Ralph Marrero
Young doctor...............................................Kevin Page
Older doctor...............................................Harry Pugh
Jesse Tyler/mirror.........................Howard Matthew Johnson
Samantha Stormer/mirror...........................Le Reine Chabut
Jimmy/mirror...............................................Brad Silverman

Director: Joe Napolitano          Writer: Deobrah Pratt

**preempted June 5 and June 12**

**preempted July 10**

**renewed for 1991-92; new episodes begin Sept. 18, 1991**

## The Ray Bradbury Theater

USA              Fridays, 9:30-10 p.m.

Series premiere: May 21, 1985
USA Network premiere: Oct. 17, 1987

Fantasy/science-fiction suspense anthology, based on short stories and overseen by noted author Bradbury, who appears in the stock opening credits sequence each episode. Series began on HBO, then switched to USA Network, which initially telecast six HBO reruns; original made-for-USA editions began Jan. 23, 1988. The series' cycle of 12 first-run episodes was in progress when the fall season began Sept. 17, 1990; the first episode within the new season aired Oct. 12 (following reruns Sept. 21-Oct. 5). A Canada/New Zealand co-production.

Atlantis Films Ltd., Avalon Television Centre [and Bradshaw, MacLeod & Associates, at least one episode] in assoc. with Wilcox Productions and Allarcom, in cooperation with USA Network, with the participation of the Alberta Motion Picture Development Corp., and in assoc. with First Choice Canadian Communications Corp., The Global Television Network, Superchannel, and Super Ecran / RBT V Productions and Allarcom Pay Television Ltd.

Executive producers: Peter Sussman, Larry Wilcox, Ray Bradbury
Supervising producers (variously, in combination): Tom Cotter, Seaton McLean, Jonathan Goodwill

Producers: Jonathan Goodwill, Pamela Meckings-Stewart (both early in season); Doug MacLeod, Tom Dent-Cox, Pamela Meckings-Stewart (all later in season)
Director of photography (variously): Warrick Attewell; Alun Bollinger; Jim Jeffrey; John Spooner
Music includes (variously): Amin Bhatia; Charles Cozens; Lou Natale, Donald Quan
Theme (instrumental with Bradbury voiceover): uncredited
Creator: inapplicable

---

6. "Touch of Petulance" Oct. 12, 1990

A man encounters another claiming to be his future self.

Future Jonathan Hughes......................................Eddie Albert
Present Jonathan Hughes...................................Jesse Collins
Alice Hughes.....................................................Dulcie Smart

Director: John Laing                    Writer: Ray Bradbury

7. "And the Moon Be Still as Bright" Oct. 19, 1990

Astronauts exploring Mars find one of their number taken over by the deadly spirit of a long-dead Martian.

With: David Carradine, Kenneth Welsh, James Purcell, Ben Cardinal, Brian Jensen, Warren Perkins

Director: Randy Bradshaw                 Writer: Ray Bradbury

8. "The Toynbee Convector" Oct. 26, 1990

Newscasters gather 'round the arrival of a famous time traveler (Whitmore).

Craig Bennett Stiles.......................................James Whitmore
And: Michael Hurst, Perry Piercy, Michael Galvin

Director: John Lang                       Writer: Ray Bradbury

9. "Exorcism" Nov. 2, 1990

A housewife (Eastwood) brews a potion to combat a supposed witch (Kellerman) who's kept her from their club presidency.

Clara Goodwater.............................................Sally Kellerman
Elmira Brown..................................................Jayne Eastwood
And: Bartley Bard, Jordan Singer

10. "The Day It Rained Forever" Nov. 9, 1990

Three old men sit at a desert hotel, waiting for the rain.

With: Vincent Gardenia, Gerard Parkes, Robert Clothier, Sheila Moore (Miss Blanche Hillgood)

Director: NA   Writer: NA

11. "The Long Years" Nov. 16, 1990

On Mars, astronauts find a scientist (Culp) living with his family, despite the departure of Earth colonists 20 years before.

John Hathwaway................................................Robert Culp
Capt. Wilder.....................................................George Touliatos
And: Judith Buchan, Donna Larson, Bruce Mitchell, Jason Wolff

Director: Paul Lynch                       Writer: Ray Bradbury

12. "Here There Be Tygers" Nov. 30, 1990

An idealistic space explorer (Bottoms) finds a beautiful yet deceptively deadly new world.

With: Timothy Bottoms (Driscoll), Peter Elliott, George Henare, Lorae Parry

Director: John Laing                      Writer: Ray Bradbury

**reruns, mostly from past years, continue into fall season; new episodes ordered**

## Roseanne

ABC                    Tuesdays, 9-9:30 p.m.

Series premiere: Oct. 18, 1988

Comedy of a blue-collar family with three kids in Lanford, Ill. Barr and co-producer Arnold are husband and wife; she and executive consultant Pentland are divorced. Barr changed her last name to Arnold following this season. Recurring guest Bonnie Sheridan, listed in early press materials as Bonnie Bramlett Sheridan, was half of the late 1960s-early 1970s pop-soul duo Delaney and Bonnie.

Roseanne Harris Conner....................................Roseanne Barr
Dan Conner....................................................John Goodman
Jackie Harris, Roseanne's sister........................Laurie Metcalf
D.J. Conner....................................................Michael Fishman
Darlene Conner................................................Sara Gilbert
Becky Conner....................................................Lecy Goranson
Crystal Anderson..................................................Natalie West

*Recurring:*
* Arnie Thomas (orig. Arnie Merchant)
   (ep. 2,7-8,14,17,22,24)...................................Tom Arnold
Bonnie (ep. 17,19,23-24)................................Bonnie Sheridan
Coffe-shop manger Leon Carp (ep. 17,19,23)..........Martin Mull
Anne Marie (ep. 9,14,24)....................................Adilah Barnes

* Given as Arnie Merchant in NBC press materials for all but ep. 14, and not specified within the episodes themselves; according to Carsey-Werner, "Arnie's name changed from Merchant to Thomas and is currently Thomas."

The Carsey-Werner Co.
Executive producers: Tom Werner, Marcy Carsey, Jay Daniel, Bob Myer
Supervising producer: Chuck Lorre
Senior producer: Jeff Abugov (later in season)
Producers: Al Lowenstein Roseanne Barr, Tom Arnold, Jeff Abugov (early in season), Brad Isaacs
Co-producer: Maxine Lapiduss (later in season)
Associate producer: Barbara Stoll
Story editors (later in season): Joel Madison, Don Foster, Jennifer Heath, Amy Sherman
Executive consultant: Bill Pentland
Theme (instrumental) and music: Dan Foliart & Howard Pearl
Director unless otherwise noted: John Whitesell
Creator: Matt Williams
Based upon a character created by: Roseanne Barr

---

1. "The Test" Sept. 18, 1990

The family nervously awaits the results of Roseanne's home-pregnancy test. Orig. scheduled for Sept. 25.

Writer: Bob Myer

2. "Friends and Relatives"  Sept. 25, 1990

Dan refuses to accept money from Jackie to pay back his buddy Arnie.  Originally scheduled for Sept. 18.

Willie, bartender at the Lobo...............................Don Maxwell

Writer: Chuck Lorre

3. "Like a Virgin"  Oct. 2, 1990   9:15-9:44 p.m.

Roseanne and Dan decide to speak with Becky about birth control.  Late start due to a Presidential address.

Gary Hall, Jackie's boyfriend...............................Brian Kerwin
Brian...................................................................Matt Norero

Writer: Brad Isaacs

4. "Like, A New Job"  Oct. 9, 1990

Despite her misgivings, Roseanne, working late as a coffee-shop waitress, leaves Dan in charge of their kids.

Kelly.................................................................Katsy Chappell
Dana................................................................Lindsay Fisher
Jan.................................................................Alyson Hannigan
Customers........Gina Kaufman, Parker Whitman, Greta Brown
Kids............................................Jake McLaine, Johnny Sunset

Writer: Jeff Abugov

5. "Good-bye, Mr. Right"  Oct. 16, 1990

Police officer Jackie and a disraught Gary break up after she's slightly injured in the line of duty.

Gary Hall..........................................................Brian Kerwin
Nurse...............................................................Louisa Abernathy

Writer: Bruce Graham

6. "Becky, Beds and Boys"  Oct. 23, 1990

Becky's folks pressure her to stop dating a boy (Quinn).

Mark Healy........................................................Glenn Quinn
Salesperson.......................................................Oz Tortora

Writers: Jennifer Heath & Amy Sherman

7. "Trick or Treat"  Oct. 30, 1990

Roseanne, mistaken for a guy in her lumberjack Halloween costume, plays along.  Maxwell reprises his role from ep. 2.

Pat....................................................................Guy Boyd
Andy..................................................................Robert Miranda
Davey................................................................James Pickens, Jr.
Pete..................................................................Steve Carlisle
And: Don Maxwell (Bartender/Willie), Duane Whitaker (Mike),
     Michael Leopard (Richard), R. Lee Telford (Bill), Delana
     Michaels (Woman), Ken Kells (Monster)

Teleplay: Chuck Lorre & Jeff Abugov     Story: Chuck Lorre

8. "PMS, I Love You"  Nov. 6, 1990

On Dan's birthday, Roseanne has pre-menstrual syndrome.

Telegram woman....................................................Stevie Sterling

Writer: Tom Arnold

9. "Bird Is the Word"  Nov. 13, 1990

Becky is suspended for apparently making an obscene gesture in her class photo.  Florek is a cast-member of *Law & Order*.

Principal Hiller...................................................Dann Florek
Secretary...........................................................Judith Jordan

Writers: Joel Madison & Don Foster

**preempted Nov. 20**

10. "Dream Lover"  Nov. 27, 1990

Dan ill-advisedly tells Roseanne he's having dreams of a mysterious, and oddly homely, other woman (Darbo).

Carl...................................................................Ritch Shydner
Marge Holman.....................................................Patrika Darbo

Writer: Chuck Lorre

11. "Do You Know Where Your Parents Are?"  Dec. 4, 1990

The girls continually break curfew; Dan and Roseanne celebrate the anniversary of their first lovemaking.

Writers: David A. Caplan & Brian LaPan

12. "Confessions"  Dec. 18, 1990

An angry and deflated Roseanne discovers that her mother (Parsons) always thought sister Jackie had more potential.

Bev Harris..........................................................Estelle Parsons

Writer: Brad Isaacs

**preempted Jan. 1**

13. "The Courtship of Eddie, Dan's Father"  Jan. 8, 1991

Dan's visiting father (Beatty, reprising his guest role from last season) announces plans to marry Crystal.  Part 1 of 2.

Ed Conner...........................................................Ned Beatty
David................................................Stephen Wesley Bridgewater
Woman in coffee shop.....D'Anne Avner a.k.a. D'Anne Jo Avner

Teleplay: Don Foster & Joel Madison     Story: Bob Myer

14. "The Wedding"  Jan. 15, 1991

Roseanne forges ahead with wedding preparations, with Crystal revealing she's pregnant with Ed's child.  Part 2 of 2.

Ed Conner...........................................................Ned Beatty
Lonnie Anderson, Crystal's son.................Kristopher Kent Hill
Pastor McCabe.....................................................Don Took
And: Marla Fries (Alice), Lynn Anne Leveridge (Lucy)

Writer: Jeff Abugov

15. "Becky Doesn't Live Here Anymore"  Jan. 22, 1991

Becky runs away from home to live with Jackie.  Director Cordray is normally the series' associate director.

Jonathan......................................................Timothy Carhart

Director: Gail Mancuso Cordray
Writers: Amy Sherman & Jennifer Heath

**preempted Jan. 29**

16. "Home-Ec"  Feb. 5, 1991

Roseanne gives Darlene's home economics class a lesson in real-life family budgeting; D.J. has to deal with a bully.

Jack Morgan............................................................Vic Polizos
Mrs. Hamilton.............................................Marilyn Rockafellow
Checkout clerk.......................................................David Greenlee
Meryl......................................................................Yunoka Doyle
And: Jenny Beck (Tanya), Cynthia Marie King (Suzy)

Writer: Mark Lloyd Rappaport

17. "Valentine's Day"  Feb. 12, 1991

Roseanne is mad at Dan for forgetting Valentine's Day, and Darlene's upset when a boy she likes asks out Becky.

With: Shawn Phelan
Jennifer...............................................................Gracie Harrison
Barry.........................................................................Tristan Tait
Amy...........................................................................Judy Gold
Little old lady...........................................................Molly David
And: Tobey Maguire, Jason Horst

Writer: Bob Myer

18. "Communicable Theater"  Feb. 19, 1991

Jackie tries acting in community theater, Dan's ill, and D.J.'s getting a merit badge.  Working title: "Community Theater."

Cyrano de Bergerac/Phil.....................................Jack Blessing
Christian....................Robert Clohessy a.k.a. Robert Clohesse
And: John David Conti (Lou), Bradley Mott (Ragueneau)

Writers: Jennifer Heath & Amy Sherman

19. "Vegas Interruptus"  Feb. 26, 1991

Roseanne may lose her job if she and Dan go on their long-awaited trip to see Wayne Newton perform in Las Vegas.  Tait reprises his role from ep. 17.

Barry.........................................................................Tristan Tait
Eric.........................................................................David Lascher
Ladies..................................Annie Abbott, Susan Quick
Frank.........................................................................Gary McGurk
Girl...........................................................................Rachel Hunt
Voice of airplane Captain...........................................Nick Toth
Men................................................Allen Covert, Rick Spector
Brian...................................................................(uncredited)

Teleplay: Chuck Lorre & Jeff Abugov        Story: Bob Myer

20. "Her Boyfriend's Back"  March 12, 1991

Becky and her boyfriend (Quinn, reprising his role from ep. 6) borrow Dan's treasured motorcycle against his orders.

Mark Healy...........................................................Glenn Quinn

Teleplay: Brad Isaacs & Maxine Lapiduss
Story: Sheldon Krasner & David Saling

21. "Trouble With the Rubbles"  March 26, 1991

The new wife next-door (Faye) looks down on Roseanne and complains D.J. is a bad influence on her son (Davidson).

Kathy Bowman.......................................................Meagen Faye
Jerry Bowman...........................................................Danton Stone
Todd Bowman...........................................................Troy Davidson

Writer: Joel Madison

22. "Second Time Around"  April 2, 1991  8-8:30 p.m.

Roseanne helps Crystal with her Lamaze classes; Dan's near-fatal accident at work makes D.J. follow him obsessively.

Woman....................................................................Bonnie Urseth
Instructor.....................................................................Eileen Davis

Writer: Maxine Lapiduss

23. "Dances With Darlene"  April 30, 1991

Roseanne tries to convince Darlene to wear something feminine to a big school dance.  Working title: "Prom Night."

Linda Wagner............................................................Amy Aquino
Jerry, Leon's lover.........Michael Des Barres (orig. Fred Willard)

Director: Gail Mancuso Cordray        Writer: Brad Isaacs

24. "Scenes From a Barbecue"  May 7, 1991

The Connors celebrate Mother's Day with a barbecue with Roseanne's feisty grandmother (Winters).  Sheridan sings "You Really Got a Hold On Me." Hill reprises his role from ep. 14.

Grandma Mary..................................................Shelley Winters
Chuck, her husband.....................................James Pickens, Jr.
Lonnie Anderson [no lines].........................Kristopher Kent Hill
Chuck, Jr.....................................................Jojo Smollett, Jr.

Writers: Bob Myer & Chuck Lorre

25. "The Pied Piper of Lanford"  May 14, 1991

Dan and Roseanne commit to opening a motorcycle shop with a free-spirited old friend (Sanders, reprising his role from last season), who gets cold feet at the last minute.

Norbert ("Ziggy")...............................................Jay O. Sanders
Loan officer/Doug...................................................Brad Garrett

Writer: Jeff Abugov

**renewed for 1991-92; new episodes begin Sept. 17, 1991**

## Seinfeld

NBC        Jan. 23-Feb. 27    Wednesdays, 9:30-10 p.m.
           April 4-June 13    Thursdays, 9:30-10 p.m.
           June 26-on         Wednesdays, 9:30-10 p.m.

Series premiere:  May 31, 1990

Semiautobiographical comedy of a middlingly successful stand-up comic and single guy in Manhattan, punctuated by his observations on stage.

Jerry Seinfeld..................................................Jerry Seinfeld

George Costanza.............................................Jason Alexander
Elaine Benes..............................................Julia Louis-Dreyfus
Kramer.....................................................Michael Richards

West/Shapiro Productions in assoc. with Castle Rock
    Entertainment
Executive producers: Andrew Scheinman, Larry David, George
    Shapiro, Howard West
Producer: Jerry Seinfeld
Supervising producer: Tom Cherones
Line producer: Joan Van Horn (title added later to existing
    Unit production manager/first asst. director)
Associate producer: Tim Kaiser
Executive story editor: Larry Charles
Story editor: Matt Goldman (early episodes)
Program consultant: Marc Jaffe (early episodes)
Director of photography (variously): Jerry Good, S.O.C.;
    Charles W. Short
Music: Jonathan Wolff
Director unless otherwise noted: Tom Cherones
Creators: Larry David & Jerry Seinfeld

---

1. "The Ex-Girlfriend"  Jan. 23, 1991

George breaks up with an overbearing girlfriend (Kolis) by
pawning her off on Jerry.  Orig. scheduled for Jan. 16.

Marlene.................................................Tracy Kolis
Receptionist.........................................Karen Barcus

Writers: Larry David & Jerry Seinfeld

2. "The Pony Remark"  Jan. 30, 1991

Jerry fears his inadvertently upsetting joke at a family-reunion
dinner may have killed an elderly relative.

Helen Seinfeld, Jerry's mother.............................Liz Sheridan
Morty Seinfeld, Jerry's father.............................Barney Martin
Manya.......................................................Rozsika Halmos
Uncle Leo....................................................Len Lesser
Isaac........................................................David Fresco
And: Scott N. Stevens (Intern), Earl Boen (Eulogist)

Writers: Larry David & Jerry Seinfeld

3. "The Jacket"  Feb. 6, 1991

Jerry is disillusioned after buying the pricey suede jacket of
his dreams.  Orig. scheduled for Jan. 23.

Alton Benes, Elaine's novelist father..............Lawrence Tierney
Salesperson....................................................Frantz Turner
And: Suanne Spoke (Customer), Harry Hart-Browne (Manager)

Writers: Larry David & Jerry Seinfeld

4. "The Phone Message"  Feb. 13, 1991

George is a wreck over angry, idiotic messages he left on a
potential girlfriend's (Polone) answering machine.

Carol.......................................................Tory Polone
Donna....................................................Gretchen German

Writers: Larry David & Jerry Seinfeld

**preempted Feb. 20; unscheduled preemption Feb. 27, then
on hiatus**

5. "The Apartment"  April 4, 1991

Jerry regrets encouraging Elaine to try to take an apartment
that's become vacant directly above him.

Co-landlord Manny...............................................Tony Plana
Co-landlord Harold.............................................Glenn Shadix
Roxanne......................................................Jeanine Jackson
Rita..........................................................Leslie Neale
And: Theresa Randle (Janice), Patricia Amaye Thomson (Susi),
    Melody Ryane (Joanne), David Blackwood (Stan)

Writer: Peter Mehlman

6. "The Statue"  April 11, 1991

Jerry suspects a student (Conway) he hired to clean his
apartment swiped a statue of his.  Orig. scheduled for Feb. 27.

Ray..............................................................Michael D. Conway
Rava............................................................Nurit Koppel
Non-smoker in elevator.........................................(uncredited)

Writer: Larry Charles

7. "The Revenge"  April 18, 1991

George seeks revenge on his realty-firm boss (Applegate), and
Jerry, on a laundromat owner (Capodice).

Levitan...........................................................Fred Applegate
Vic..............................................................John Capodice
Ava, George's co-worker.........................................Teri Austin
Glenda, George's co-worker...................................Patrika Darbo
Dan, George's co-worker.................................Marcus Smythe
Greeny, George's co-worker.................................John Hillner
Bill, George's co-worker.................................Deck McKenzie

Writer: Larry David

8. "The Heart Attack"  April 25, 1991

George, whose "heart attack" turns out to be tonsilitis, takes
Kramer's advice to see a holistic healer (Tobolowsky).

Tor.............................................................Stephen Tobolowsky
Dr. Fein.......................................................John Posey
Paramedic attendant............................................John Fleck
Paramedic driver...............................................Jimmy Woodard
Voice of man in other bed......................................Pat Hazell
Nurse..........................................................Sharon McNight
Cook...........................................................Thomas Wagner
Waitress.......................................................Heather James
Man in TV science-fiction movie............................(uncredited)

Writer: Larry Charles

9. "The Deal"  May 2, 1991

Jerry and ex-girlfriend Elaine try to have sex and remain just
friends.

Tina, Elaine's roomate....................................Siobhan Fallon
    In end-credits but no speaking role:
    Norman Brenner (Clerk)

Writer: Larry David

10. "The Baby Shower"  May 16, 1991

The installer for Jerry's pirated cable-TV arrives the day Elaine throws a baby shower for an arrogant friend (Dunford, a cast-member of *Good Sports*), whom George wants to tell off.

Leslie............................................Christine Dunford
Tabachnick.........................................Vic Polizos
Assistant...........................................James Lashly
Mary............................................Margaret Reed
FBI agent.....................................George C. Simms
Flight attendant...................................Marla Fries
Passenger..........................................Don Perry
Party guests................................Kate Mulligan, Audrey Frantz

Writer: Larry Charles

11. "The Chinese Restaurant" May 23, 1991

Jerry, Elaine and George try to get a table at a crowded Chinese restaurant. Orig. scheduled for May 2.

Maitre d'/Bruce..................................James Hong
Cohen.............................................David Tress
Lorraine............................................Judy Kain
Persons on phone.......................Kate Benton, Michael Mitz
Man............................................Kendall McCarthy

Writers: Larry David & Jerry Seinfeld

**preempted May 30**

**preempted June 19**

12. "The Busboy" June 26, 1991

George feels guilty over getting a busperson (LaBiosa) fired; Elaine regrets having a boyfriend (Ballard) visit for a week.

Antonio............................................David LaBiosa
Eddie.............................................Doug Ballard
Restaurant manager.............................John Del Regno

Writers: Larry David & Jerry Seinfeld

**preempted July 10**

**unscheduled preemption Aug. 21**

**preempted Sept. 11**

Unaired

"The Stranded"

Jerry feels guilty for keeping the host of a party up late while he and Elaine wait for Kramer to pick them up. Orig. scheduled for July 17.

Director: NA   Writer: NA

**renewed for 1991-92; new episodes begin Sept. 18, 1991**

## Shades of LA

Quasi-syndicated*   One hour

* Initially, only on the MCA-owned stations KCOP/Los Angeles and WWOR/New York City. In New York, primetime airings were Wednesdays, 8-9 p.m. from Oct. 10-Dec. 12, 1990; Dec. 26, 1990 to March 6, 1991, and sporadically, Wednesdays, March 20 to Sept. 18, 1991. Airdate order different in New York than in Los Angeles. Episodes listed inor-

der of production number.

New York City premiere: Oct. 10, 1990

Light adventure-drama of a Los Angeles police detective, shot and nearly killed on duty, who returns from a near-dead state with knowledge of, and intervention from, ghostly spirits in limbo. Recurring guest Mayron is the sister of *thirtysomething* co-star Melanie Mayron. Working title: *Rest in Peace*.

Michael Burton...................................John DiAquino
Lt. James Wesley...............................Warren Berlinger

*Recurring:*
Uncle Louie (ep. 0601,3,6,9,11,17,19)............Kenneth Mars
Annie Brighton (ep. 0601,3,5,
    8,10-13,16,19)............Gale Mayron a.k.a. Gail Mayron
Jack Monaghan (ep. 0601,3,6,10-13,15,17)........David Crowley
Nick Santini (ep. 0601,4,6,8,10-11,15,17).............Brian Libby
Luis Cardeno (ep. 0601-2,5,11)........................Daniel Faraldo
Mark Hobson (ep. 0601,8,11).................David Michael O'Neill
Detective Liz Homoly (ep. 0606,11,17)................Beverly Leech

Papazian-Hirsch Entertainment, MCA TV
Executive producers: Robert A. Papazian, James G. Hirsch
Supervising producer: William Bleich
Producer: Richard L. O'Connor, Bruce Cervi (later in season)
Associate producer: Deborah Edell
Executive story editor: Bruce Cervi (early in season)
Story editors: Brenda Lilly, Renee Palyo
Director of photography: Brianne Murphy, A.S.C.
Creative consultant: Tom Blonquist (later in season)
Theme (instrumental, with voiceover by star DiAquino) and
    music: Dana Kaproff
Creator: William Bleich

---

SLA 0601. "Shades of L.A."

After nearly being killed by gunfire, Michael's contacted by the spirit of an astronaut dead before his time, possibly murdered.

Chuck Yellin.....................................Ben Murphy
Frank Gregson.................................Greg Mullavey
Cowboy..............................John Dennis Johnston
Hank in Limbo.............................Anthony Charnota
Chief engineer............................Conrad Bachmann
Technician.....................................Szu-Ming Wang
Accountant...................................Nicholas Shaffer
Dr. Jameson..................................Augustine Lam

Director: Bob Sweeney          Writer: William Bleich

SLA 0602. "The Wrong Man"

A dead thief (Winslow) feels guilty over having framed an innocent man (Dawson), now on death row for murder.

Lewis Delgado..............................Michael Winslow
D.A. Connors.......................................Ron Glass
Janine Sutton................................Beverly Johnson
Old man.........................................Bob Sweeney
Robbie.........................................Christopher Birt
Vinnie.........................................E. Danny Murphy
Young Robbie...............................Nicholas Phillips
Hector Williams..............................Freddie Dawson

Director: Jack Shea          Writer: Bill Taub

SLA 0603. "Dead Dogs Tell No Tails"

Michael helps Trudy, a dog accidentally killed while being used in a bank robbery, save her four pups from similar fates. Guests Schiavelli and Beasley are husband and wife.

Rooney Wilson..................................................Geoffrey Lewis
Boyd Hoagland.......................................................Casey Biggs
Psychologist..........................................................Allyce Beasley
Dr. Greenstreet.............................................Vincent Schiavelli
Charlie Bracker...................................................Marvin Kaplan
Frank Mitchell..........................................................H. Ray Huff
Trudy (dog)..............................................................(uncredited)

Director: Jerry Jameson          Writer: Bruce Cervi

SLA 0604. "Where There's No Will, There's a Weigh-In"

The greedy nephew (Conaway) of a recently deceased retired woman (Paige) plans to keep the portion of her estate that she'd willed to her financially strapped senior center.

Ruth Lockwood...........................................................Janis Paige
Richard..................................................................Jeff Conaway
Jessica Pope..........................................................Mary Crosby
Evan Hendricks........................................................Ronnie Schell
And: Juanita Moore (Clara), Dorothy Neumann (Gertrude), Ray
     Walston (Charlie), Toni O'Grady (Amy)

Director: Bob Sweeney          Writer: Randy Holland

SLA 0605. "Concrete Evidence"

The ghost of a mob-involved musicians-union leader (Winter) asks Burton to locate his missing corpse.

Frankie Mannis............................................................Ed Winter
Carl Spina.............................................................Frank Gorshin
Pressman................................................................Conrad Janis
Shawna..............................................................Kimberley Kates
With: Nicky Blair
And: Suzanne Gabrielle (Security guard)

Director: Nancy Malone          Writer: Ed Scharlach

SLA 0606. "Cooper's Coroner"

A baseball announcer wants to make peace with the grown-up son (Hershberger) of a former rival he'd framed for gambling.

"Hammerin' Hank" Cooper...............................Chuck McCann
Doyle Reese...........................................................James Parks
Dennis Pickford...............................................Gary Hershberger
Bartender..............................................................Zelda Rubinstein

Director: Jim Johnston          Writer: Jim Brecher

SLA 0607. "Some Like It Cold"

A tough, attractive lawyer (Purcell), on whom Michael had a crush, falls in love with him only after she's murdered.

Alex Taylor.................................................................Lee Purcell
Detective Roscoe Phillips.........................Clarence Williams III
Jack Dymond...........Jeff East (Troy Donahue orig. announced)
Lawrence Parish..................................................Barry Kinyon
Hermila Garcia.......................................................Alma Beltran
Candy........................................................................Susan Ware
And: Gustave Rex (Roberto Garcia), Betty Lynn (Sister Clara)
     Also orig. announced:
     Tom Ritter (Jury foreperson), Charles McDaniel (Judge)

Director: Bob Sweeney          Writers: Renee Palyo & Brenda Lilly

SLA 0608. "Big Brother is Watching"

The murdered, ventriloquist sibling (Naughton), of one of Michael's friends (Garber) returns to point out his killer.

Neil....................................................................David Naughton
Julie.......................................................................Terri Garber
Fred "Evil" Smitts.......................................................Don Most
Pool player.......................................................Preston Maybank
And: Holly Wilkinson (Waitress), Susan Ware (Voice of Bobby)

Director: Nancy Malone          Story: Bruce Jacobs
Teleplay: Brenda Lilly & Renee Palyo and Bruce Jacobs

SLA 0609. "Pointers from Paz"

Prodded by a dead detective (Murzik) framed for corruption, Michael goes after the true crooked cop (Argenziano). Working title: "El Mordita."

Detective Ed Pazahosky......................................Peter Murzik
Lt. Walsh......................................................Carmen Argenziano
With: David Harris
Lt. Armacost......................................................Carrie Snodgress
Detective Barnes............................................Kenneth Edwards
And: Sal Lopez (Molina), Gina Spellman (Officer Chaves), Dan
     Sturdivant (Detective), Kristopher Logan (Cat thief), Bill
     Dearth (Duty Sergeant), Lisa Marie Soble (Glenda)

Director: David Jackson   Writers: Jerry Stahl and Bruce Cervi

SLA 0610. "The Teacher from Hell"

The shade of Michael's old high school science teacher (Stricklyn) helps him solve the case of a reporter's apparent suicide.

Dagle........................................................................Ray Stricklyn
Russ Barger.......................................................Lonny Chapman
Melissa.............................................................Marilyn Hassett
Detective Nitz..........................................................Jim Antonio
Jughead.......................................................................Will Nye
Dr. Ernest Lindstrom...................................Leigh J. McCloskey
And: Mark Fauser (Leech), Michael Blakely (Uniformed cop)

Director: Judith Vogelsang          Writers: Bruce Cervi, Tom
                                        Blomquist, Renee Palyo, Brenda Lilly

SLA 0611. "Dreams"

Michael must find a dead woman's (Jones) missing son, whose bone marrow may save his dying brother. Beasley reprises her role from ep. 0603, where her character name was not given.

Announced cast includes:
Louise Morley...................................................Marilyn Jones
Mitch/Christopher............................................Nicholas Sadler
Dr. Johnson..........................................................Allyce Beasley
Candy........................................................................Susan Ware
And: Carmine Caridi (Keith Welch), Christie Alvarez (Little boy)

Director: NA   Writer: NA

SLA 0612. "Send Up the Clowns"

Michael goes undercover at a circus to investigate the murder of two miming clowns, possibly by their ringmaster (Sierra).

Raul........................................................................Gregory Sierra
Olga, his wife.....................................................Melody Rogers
Sebastian.......................................................Miguel Fernandes
Rita...........................................................................Susan Tyrell

Holly..................................................................Lisa Rinna
And: Chip Reynolds (Nutsy), Scott Land (Jocko), Dick Monday
(Bongo the Clown), April Tatro (Contortionist)

Director: Dennis Donnelly              Writer: Ed Scharlach

SLA 0613. "Last Laugh"

A standup comic (Lazer) is killed, along with the trashy blonde
(Monahan) who half-unwittingly led him to his death.

Alan Gafkin........................................................Stephen Furst
Comedy-club owner Brenda................................Cassie Yates
Danny Houdeen..................................................Gary Lazer
Sherry.............................................................Debi A. Monahan
Martin Hollenbeck...............................................John McCann
Jeff Barrett.......................................................Coleby Lombardo
Murray Banning, Danny's agent................Joseph Della Sorta
Frank Barton.........................................................Roger Rook

Director: Kevin Cremin              Writer: William Bleich

SLA 0614. "Burial Ground"

While returning a suspect to L.A., Michael helps a Nevada cop
(Beltran) killed trying to stop an Indian Payroll Service robbery.

Russell Thorn.....................................................Robert Beltran
Bobbi Murdoch.......................................................Dana Hill
Walt....................................................................Stephen Nichols
Larry..............................................................Michael J. Pollard
Sheriff's Dept. Chief Davis.......................................L.Q. Jones
        Also orig. announced: Don Fox Greene (Don)

Director: Sutton Roley    Writers: John Lansing & Bruce Cervi

SLA 0615. "Cross the Center Line"

While Lt. Wesley is investigated for shooting a fleeing suspect,
Michael encounters two '50s-biker ghosts (Nash, Naff).

Rod.....................................................................Chris Nash
Cherry.................................................................Lycia Naff
Steve Rohrback....................................................Ritch Brinkley
Duke Masters......................................................William Smith
Mark Vogler...........................................................Vonte Sweet
Capt. Lannon....................................................Michael McGuire

Director: Jim Johnston              Writer: Tom Blomquist

SLA 0616. "Till Death Do Us Part"

Michael helps a pair of bickering society ghosts (Joyce, Everett) find their murderer; Annie announces her engagement.

Roland Barker......................................................Chad Everett
Stephanie Barker..................................................Elaine Joyce
Hobson.............................................................Richard Narita
Sutton Reigert.....................................................Michael Cole
Walker Evers......................................................Daniel Greene
Stacy.................................................................Devon Ericson
Dr. Ted Kolfax, Annie's fiance..............................Dean Butler
        Also orig. announced:
        Miss Christopher West (Treadway)

Director: Chris Pechin      Writers: Brenda Lilly & Renee Palyo

SLA 0617. "Ten Little Thespians"

At a house party/murder-mystery weekend, Michael encounters the shade of a novelist (Rescher) really killed at the house.

Albert................................................................Clive Revill
Anna Kaplan.................................................Dee Dee Rescher
Heather.............................................................Crystal Carson
Raymond.........................................................Henry Woronicz
Gary...............................................................Kenny Johnson
Katherine.........................................................Fern Fitzgerald
        Also orig. announced: Miss Christopher West (Treadway)

Director: Chuck Bowman              Writer: William Bleich

SLA 0618. "The Really Big Sleep"

A tough, old-time private eye (Stroud), killed 50 years ago,
wants Michael's help in nailing the louse that bumped him off.
Ware reprises her role from ep. 0611.

Sam Doyle..........................................................Don Stroud
Veronica Brandis..................................................Mary Fanaro
James Browning..................................................Stephen Elliott
Thomas Browning........................................Michael Anderson, Jr.
Paula Browning......................................................Joan Leslie
Candy Carson........................................................Susan Ware
Attorney............................................................Robert Broyles
Intruders...........................................Ted Mehous, Wiley Pickett

Director: Richard L. O'Connor              Writer: Bruce Rush

SLA 0619. "Line of Fire" Part 1

A TV evangelist (Parks), seeking an incriminating videotape of
his murder of a call girl, stalks the TV-news-producer widow
(Kitaen) of Michael's former partner (Jones).

Announced cast includes:
Detective Robert "B.J." Makowski.........................Sam Jones
Linda Makowski..................................................Tawny Kitaen
Andrew Makowski, her and B.J.'s son.................Brian Bonsall
Jimmy Scarborough.............................................Michael Parks
Tucker..............................................................James Nixon
George..............................................................Duke Moosekian
Josef.............................................................Vahan Moosekian
Dr. Robbins.....................................................Michael Boatman
And: Ava Dupree (Receptionist), Kathleen Bonsall (Call girl)

Director: NA   Writer: NA

SLA 0620. "Line of Fire" Part 2

B.J.'s ghost, jealous over Linda and Michael's fledgling romance, nonetheless helps Michael save her from Scarborough.

Announced cast includes:
Detective Robert "B.J." Makowski.........................Sam Jones
Linda Makowski..................................................Tawny Kitaen
George..............................................................Duke Moosekian
Josef.............................................................Vahan Moosekian
Dr. Robbins.....................................................Michael Boatman
And: Ava Dupree (Receptionist), Kathleen Bonsall (Call girl)

Director: NA   Writer: NA

## Shannon's Deal

NBC          Tuesdays, 10-11 p.m.

Premiere (as a TV-movie): June 4, 1989
Series premiere: April 16, 1990
Final telecast: May 21, 1991

Law drama of a divorced, disillusioned Philadelphia attorney with a gambling addiction, who has abandoned his partnership in a corporate law firm for what he considers a more ethical, if far less lucrative, solo practice.

Jack Shannon..................................................Jamey Sheridan
Secretary Lucy Acosta.........................................Elizabeth Pena
Neala Shannon, Jack's daughter..........................Jenny Lewis
Wilmer Slade..................................................Richard Edson

*Recurring:*
Lt. Menke (ep. 2-3,6)........Ronald G. Joseph a.k.a. Ron Joseph

Stan Rogow Productions in assoc. with NBC Productions
Executive producer: Stan Rogow
Co-executive producer: Marvin Kupfer
Supervising producer: Jerry Patrick Brown, Allan Arkush
Producer: Gareth Davies
Associate producer: Peter Chomsky
Director of photography: Michael Gershman
Creative consultant: David Greenwalt
Legal consultant: Alan Dershowitz
Music: Tom Scott (ep. 1,5,6); Wynton Marsalis (ep. 3); David
    Benoit (ep. 7); Lee Ritenour (ep. 4); composed by Russell
    Ferrante, performed by the Yellowjackets (ep. 2)
Theme: "Shannon's Theme" (instrumental, with voiceover by
    star Sheridridan): Wynton Marsalis
End-theme: "Live and Learn" by Alan and Marilyn Bergman
    (words) and David Benoit (music); performed by Diane
    Schuur
Creator [and] executive script consultant: John Sayles

––––––––––––––

1. "Bad Beat"  Saturday, March 23, 1991   10-11 p.m.

Shannon is tempted by his old gambling demons when he volunteers to investigate a girlfriend's gambling ex-husband.

Peter J. Reilly................................................Darrell Larson
Bara Reilly.................................................Mary Jo Keenen
Sean Gardner...............................................Spencer Garrett
Howie..........................................................Milton Murrill
Eddie Wong..................................................Bill Cho Lee
Madame Dloran...........................................Rosalie Claudio
Process server.................................................Richard Assad
Dealer...........................................................Milan Nicksic
Card player.....................................................Farrell Mayer
Benny.....................................................Captain Mike Gordon
Panhandler.....................................................Jack Denbo
Young man....................................................James Bershad
Mack Reilly (child)..........................................(uncredited)
    Also orig. announced: Jack Orend (Testa)

Director: Eugene Corr    Writers: Eugene Corr & Ruth Shapiro

2. "Greed"  April 9, 1991

Cash-poor Jack joins a corporate law firm, neglecting two old men (Mayo, Lane) being evicted from his building.

Kennedy.....................................................Whitman Mayo
With: Charles Lane
Baker......................................................Stephen Tobolowsky
With: Juanin Clay, Tom Towles, Kurt Fuller
Bill Miller..................................................Charles Bateman
Vivian.....................................................Caroline Williams
Ingrid...........................................................Anna Bjorn
Mrs. Rigatti....................................................Mary Portser
And: Burton Collins (Postal worker), Harry Cohn (Bum)

Director: Allan Arkush        Writer: David Greenwalt

3. "Strangers in the Night: A 'Shannon's Deal' Mystery Movie"
    April 16, 1991  9-11 p.m.

Shannon files a wrongful-death suit after a shootout in which two cops kill a store-owner and nearly Lucy as well. Orig. scheduled for March 17. Working title: "Wrongful Death."

Mr. Kee.........................................................B.D. Wong
Griggs.........................................................Victor Love
Mercer.........................................................Clark Gregg
Tomko......................................................Steve Vinovich
With: Randle Mell
Madame Cure.............................................Dee Dee Rescher
Mirovich.......................................................Barry Kivel
Mrs. Oh....................................................June Kyoko Lu
Green hightops.......................................Charles Bailey-Gates
And: Sally Prager (Joyce), Wendy Bowers (Normal lady),  Ralph
    Ahn (Mr. Oh), Chi-Muoi Lo (Red bandana), Anthony
    Johnson (Officer), Macka Foley (Cop), Elly Enriquez (Korean man), Desi Reilly (Billings' daughter)

Writer-director: Tom Rickman

4. "First Amendment"  April 23, 1991

A loud, Arab-baiting TV personality (Kapelos) is charged with inciting a young man (Hinkley) to kill a Syrian store-owner.

Turner Bryce...................................................John Kapelos
Vince Mooney..................................................Brent Hinkley
Ted McCarthy..................................................Stuart Pankin
Julia............................................................Kimberly Scott
Daoud Hasan.....................................................Avner Garri
Laila Hasan...................................................Janet Graham
Wayne Wilson.................................................Richard Grove
And:  James Staskel (Joe), Eric Kohner (Don), Sonny Carl Davis (Larry), Dirk Tanner (Dean), Don Neason (Eddie),
    John Brian Flanagan (Roger), Sean Whalen (Sam), Sarah
    Lilly (Demonstrator), Zephra Dunn (Woman in minimart), Lisa Kaminir, Marabina Jaimes, Nancy Meyer
    (Reporters), Gary Bryson, Carl Gilliard (Officers)

Director: Allan Arkush        Writer: Barry Pullman

5. "The Inside Man"  April 30, 1991

Representing a farm worker burned by illegal chemicals, Shannon discovers his corporate-law past is partly a root cause of the accident.  Scott reprises her role from last episode.

Luther Yates..................................................Paul Whitthorne
Bruce......................................................Michael McManus
Nina...........................................................Julie Garfield
With: Michelle Forbes, James Lashly, Richard Roat, David
    Spielberg
Julia............................................................Kimberly Scott
Attersly..........................................................Paul Kent
And: Vincent Lucchesi (Di Falci), Colette Kilroy (Hunter), Paul
    Collins (Aston), Angela Paton (Oriana), Lea Floden (Sue
    McPherson), Frank Smith (Freddy), Carl Prickett (Little
    Freddy), Bee-Be Smith (Iris)

Writer-director: Corey Blechman

**preempted May 7**

6. "Matrimony"  May 14, 1991

Shannon dates a prosecutor (Callan), and helps a pal's cheating wife (Pawk), who had a hit-and-run accident after a tryst. Director Thomas is a former cast-member of *Hill Street Blues*.

Jodie............................................................Cecile Callan
Tyler Scott..................................................Barry Cullison
Andrea Scott, his wife................................Michele Pawk
Lamont.....................................................Cleto Augusto
Linette....................................................Kathleen Garrett
And: Eric Lawson (Thad), Gene Wolande (Grover), Doug Frank-
    lin (Eugene), Camila Griggs (Margie), Leon Simmons, Jr.
    (Cop), Arland Russell (Waiter)

Director: Betty Thomas          Writer: Kathy McCormick

7. "Trouble" May 21, 1991

Neala's rich, troubled pal (Warren) is unwillingly commited to
a mental hospital by her dad (Jackson), Shannon's old enemy.

Eva Melville.................................................Meg Foster
With: Kiersten Warren, John M. Jackson, Dietrich Bader
Judge.........................................................Ray Reinhardt
Dr. Kennedy.............................................Kandis Chappell
Dr. Tyrell..................................................Jeames Higgins
Freddy.....................................................Gerald Hopkins
And: Rocco Spinelli (Mark), Blanche Rubin (Mrs. Appratto),
    Janette Caldwell (Gwen), G. Malcolm Houston (Bailiff)

Writer-director: Joan Tewkesbury

## She-Wolf of London

Quasi-syndicated*   One-hour

* Initially, only on the MCA-owned stations KCOP/Los Angeles and WWOR/New York City. In New York, primetime
  airings were Tuesdays, 9-10 p.m. from Oct. 9-23, Nov. 6-
  Dec. 11, and Dec. 25, 1990; and Fridays, 8-9 p.m. from
  Jan. 4-March 1, 1991, after which title and format changed
  to *Love & Curses* (see that entry). Airdate order different in
  New York than Los Angeles. Episodes listed in order of production number.

New York City premiere: Oct. 9, 1990
Final telecast in this format (NYC): March 1, 1991

Lighthearted fantasy-drama of an American student in London
who teams with a young parapsychologist in an occult-investi-
gation firm, while seeking to cure her periodic transformations
into a supernatural wolf-being. "Freely adapted from" the
movie *She-Wolf of London* (1946). Filmed in England.

Randi Wallace..............................................Kate Hodge
Prof. Ian Matheson......................................Neil Dickson
*Cast-members listed in end-credits:*
Julian Matheson, Ian's teenaged nephew................Scott Fults
Mum Matheson.........................................Jean Challis
Dad Matheson.............................................Arthur Cox
Aunt Elsa..............................................Dorothea Phillips
Randi as she-wolf........................................Diane Youdale

Finnegan • Pinchuk, MTE, and Hollywood Premiere Network in
  assoc. with HTV International
Executive producers: Sheldon Pinchuk, Pat Finnegan, Bill
  Finnegan, Patrick Dromgoole, Paul Sarony (latter early in
  season)
Producer: David Roessell
Supervising producers: Tom McLoughlin, Lee Goldberg,
  William Rabkin
Associate producer (early in season): Keith Webber
Executive consultant: Mick Garris
Prosthetics and special-effects makeup: Christopher Tucker
  (early in season)

Special make-up effects: Bryan Moore (later in season)
Director of photography (variously): Mike Thomson (ep. 1);
    Brian Morgan; Howard Block
Music [and] Theme (instrumental): Steve Levine
Creators: Mick Garris & Tom McLoughlin

––––––––––––

SW 0701. "She-Wolf of London"

After acquiring the lycanthropic curse, Randi meets a fortune-
teller remarkably familiar with a supernatural ring Randi has.

Pitak.........................................................Pete Lee Wilson
Madame Elena.........................................Annabelle Lee
Dr. Stevens...............................................Pavel Douglas
Inspector Majid......................................Phillip Manikum
And: Jane Cunliffe (Stewardess), David Plummer (Custodian),
    Alexander Forte (Boris), Neil Betts, Julian Howarth (Boys)

Director: Dennis Abey
Writers: Mick Garris & Tom McLoughlin

SW 0702. "The Bogman of Letchmoor Heath"

The reanimated corpse of a long-dead hanged man found in a
peat bog begins murdering denizens of an English village.
Manikum reprises his role from last episode.

Announced cast includes:
P.C. Leary................................................Richard Coleman
Rev. Goodbody.........................................Adrian Cairns
Gertie.......................................................Pamela Duncan
Inspector Majid......................................Phillip Manikum
And: Roger Winslett (Oates), Charles Lewson (Angus), John
    Hallam (Fergus), Eve Ferret (Abigail)

Director: Roger Cheveley          Writer: Anthony Adams

SW 0703. "The Juggler"

A satanic priest (Knight) steers the daughter (Bryan) of a minister (Carlin) to a murderous "devil clown" apparition (Parker).

The Juggler..............................................Gary Parker
Rev. Palfrey..............................................John Carlin
Liza Palfrey.............................................Claudia Bryan
Peter Griscombe....................................Anderson Knight
Baker/Charles.......................................Jonathan Rickard
Miss Rigby................................................Carol Kirkland
Teacher.................................................Christine Pollon
And: Daniel Pope (Rod), Steve Edwards (Mick), Tina Pyne (Sac-
    rificed woman), Blaise Doran (Ghost priest), Anna Carras
    Wilson (Mother), Jared Morgan (Mourner ghost)

Director: Gerry Mill          Writer: Jim Henshaw

SW 0704. "Moonlight Becomes You"

Randi and Ian help the twin sister (Tracey) of a werewolf (Sharrock) held by a scientist (Guard) as an experimental subject.

Announced cast includes:
Diane Westbury.........................................Ingrid Tracey
Derek Westbury as werewolf...................Mark West
Dr. Nigel Hatchard..................................Chris Guard
Derek Westbury........................................Ian Sharrock
And: Daphne (Mary), Tim Kirby (Burt), Peter Greeves (Otto),
    Susie Anne Watkins (Miss Stone)

Director: Brian Grant          Writer: Valerie West

**SW 0705. "Nice Girls Don't"**

A succubus -- female sexual demon -- (Robertson) is turning young men into withered old shells. Cast-member Youdale, normally in special makeup, plays an additional role sans.

Announced cast includes:
Ernest.................................................Stuart Linden
Nurse Robin.......................................Rachel Robertson
And: Diane Youdale (Morgana), April Olrich (Isadora)

Director: Roger Cheveley
Writer: Lee Goldberg, William Rabkin, Abbie Bernstein

**SW 0706. "Little Bookshop of Horrors"**

An antiquarian book-shop owner (Brierly) uses demonic tomes to create murderous versions of famous literary characters.

Announced cast includes:
Hope...................................Serena Scott Thomas
Mel Berger.......................................Ron Berclass
Michael Westfield................................Pavel Douglas
Gordon Ganza....................................Roger Brierly
Dave McConnell..............................Patrick O'Connell

Director: Gerry Mill
Writers: Lee Goldberg & William Rabkin

**SW 0707. "The Wild Hunt"**

The murderous ghost of a huntsman wreaks vengeance on the descendants of the townspeople who killed him.

Announced cast includes:
Dave...................................................Mark Drewry
Mary.................................................Cathy Murphy
Waitress Betty...............................Philippa Haywood
Mechanic...............................................Al Ashton

Director: Brian Grant   Writers: Diana Ayers, Susan Sebastian

**SW 0708. "Can't Keep a Dead Man Down" Part 1**

Randi's ex-fiance movie producer (Saxon) falsely promises to option Ian's book; Ian's department head (Faulkner) apparently kills him, adding him to her horde of cannabalistic zombies.

Charlie Beaudine......................................Rolf Saxon
Dr. Samantha Stevens.........................Sally Faulkner
John Decarlo...........................................Gary Olsen
Lily Decarlo.............................................Jenny Jay
Marilyn Decarlo..........................Bernadette Milnes
Andre.............................................Jon Cartwright
And: Terence Bayler (Sir Robert), Richenda Carey (Zelda), Gary Rice (Waiter), Matthew Sharp (Caretaker)

Director: Roger Cheveley
Writers: Lee Goldberg & William Rabkin

**SW 0709. "Can't Keep a Dead Man Down" Part 2**

Ian returns as an apparent zombie, and thwarts Dr. Stevens' plan to use Randi as a human sacrifice to her zombie horde.

Announced cast includes:
Charlie Beaudine......................................Rolf Saxon
Dr. Samantha Stevens.........................Sally Faulkner

Director: Roger Cheveley
Writers: Lee Goldberg & William Rabkin

**SW 0710. "What Got Into Them?"**

The spirits of a Russian noble, her husband, and Ian's murdered colleague possess members of the Matheson household.

Guest cast NA.

Director: Dennis Abby
Writers: Lee Goldberg & William Rabkin

**SW 0711. "Big Top She-Wolf"**

A demonic, seductive circus ringmaster (Carter), who has stolen the souls of his performers, attempts to steals Randi's.

Caleb Wakefield....................................Jason Carter
Danny..............................................Mark Dawson
Selena................................................Chloe Treeno
And: the performers of the Jay Miller Circus

Director: Brian Grant            Writer: Kate Boutilier

**SW 0712. "She-Devil"**

An experimental synthetic aphrodisiac turns a former classmate of Ian's (Forbes) into a deadly, savage beast.

Kristen McCord....................................Natlie Forbes
Ed Decker........................................Kevin Drinkwater
And: Tony Hughes (Tom Nile), Sion Tudor Owen (Peter), Don Gallagher (Dave), Martin Dee (Repairperson)

Director: Dennis Abey
Writers: William Rabkin & Lee Goldberg

**SW 0713. "Voodoo Child"**

One of Ian's new students (Edwards), an arrogant expert in Guarani Indian ways, uses voodoo to torment Randi and Ian.

Greg.................................................Keith Edwards
Phil.................................................Stephen Tredre
Laura.............................................Debra Beaumont
And: Kim Fenton (Page), Simon Jessop (Tim), Amber Beezer (Maggie), Christopher Benjamin (Dr. Morris)

Director: Roger Cheveley               Writer: Terry Erwin

**SW 0714. "Beyond the Beyond"**

The creator (McBain) of the cult-favorite science-fiction series *Beyond the Beyond* is apparently killed at a fan convention.

Guy Goddard........................................Edward DE SOUSZA
Conrad Stipe.......................................Robert McBain
And: Gordon Milne (Jim), Graham Seed (Derby Winthrop), Kate Harper (Nicole), Hugh Walters (Snork)

Director: Brian Grant
Writers: Lee Goldberg, Bill Rabkin, Arthur Sellers

**Changed format and title; see *Love & Curses***

## The Simpsons

Fox  Thursdays, 8-8:30 p.m.

Series premiere: Jan. 14, 1990

Animated comedy of a blue-collar family in Springfield, U.S.A.:

Nuclear-plant worker Homer, housewife Marge, school-age siblings Bart and Lisa, and baby Maggie (silent except for pacifier sucking noises by cartoonist/executive producer Matt Groening). Series began as segments (starting April 19, 1987) on *The Tracey Ullman Show* (Fox, 1987-1990), followed by a December 17, 1989 half-hour special. Note: Director Wes Archer uses several variations of his name; only the specific one for each episode is listed.

Voice of Homer Simpson...........................Dan Castellaneta (1)
Voice of Marge Simpson..................................Julie Kavner (2)
Voice of Bart Simpson............................Nancy Cartwright (3)
Voice of Lisa Simpson......................................Yeardley Smith
Assorted voices.............................................Harry Shearer (4)

(1)  Also Abraham J. (Grandpa) Simpson (Homer's dad), Krusty the Klown, Homer's drinking companion Barney Gumble, Diamond Joe Quimby, Scott Christian, school groundskeeper Willy

(2)  Also Patty Bouvier and Selma Bouvier, Marge's sisters

(3)  Also Bart's friends: Todd Flanders, Nelson, Kearney

(4)  Including recurring characters Montgomery Burns (Homer's boss), Smithers (Burns' lackey), Kent Brockman, Dr. Marvin Monroe, Jasper, Herman, Otto the bus driver, Dr. Julius Hibert, Principal Skinner, neighbor Ned Flanders, Rev. Lovejoy, Dr. Pryor, Marty

*Recurring vocal performers,*
*all or virtually all episodes:*
Assorted voices.................................................Hank Azaria (1)
*Other recurring vocal performers:*
Assorted voices
    (ep. 4,6-9,12,15,17-20,22)....................Maggie Roswell (2)
Assorted voices
    (ep. 1-2,5,8-9,13-15,19-21).................Pamela Hayden (3)
Assorted voices
    (ep. 1,14,19)........................................Marcia Wallace (4)

(1)  Including Apu the convenience store clerk, Moe the bartender, Prof. John Frink, Police Chief Wiggum, Dr. Nick Riviera, Smitty, Cabbie, Lenny

(2)  Including Helen Lovejoy

(3)  Including Bart's friend Milhouse

(4)  Including teachers Elizabeth Hoover, Mrs. Krabapple

Gracie Films in assoc. with 20th Century Fox Television
Executive producers: Matt Groening, James L. Brooks, Sam Simon (latter two early in season)
Supervising producers: Al Jean, Mike Reiss
Producers: Richard Sakai, Larina Jean Adamson, Jay Kogen, Wallace Wolodarsky
Co-producer: George Meyer
Associate producer: J. Michael Mendel
Executive story editor: Jon Vitti
Story editors: John Swartzwelder, Jeff Martin
Executive creative consultant (later in season): James L. Brooks
Creative supervisor (later in season): Sam Simon
Executive consultant: Brad Bird
Creative consultant (later in season): David Stern
Visual consultant: Stephen Lineweaver
Animation company: Klasky-Csupo; Gabor Csupo, executive animation producer; Sherry Gunther, animation producer
Overseas animation directors: Mike Girard, S.J. Kim
Korean production company: Akom Production Co.

Music (variously): Arthur B. Rubinstein; Patrick Williams; Alf Clausen
Theme (instrumental): Danny Elfman
Creator: Matt Groening
Developed by: James L. Brooks, Matt Groening, Sam Simon

---

1. "Bart Gets an F" Oct. 11, 1990

On the verge of flunking fourth grade, Bart recruits brainy Martin to prep him for an exam.

Voices of Martin; Twins; Grandmother.................Russi Taylor
And: Jo Ann Harris

Director: David Silverman
Writers: David M. Stern (Matt Groening and Sam Simon orig. announced)

2. "Simpson and Delilah" Oct. 18, 1990

When Homer scams his company insurance to buy a miracle hair-growth product, he gains confidence and climbs up the corporate ladder -- for as long as his hair holds out.

Karl, Homer's secretary....................................Harvey Fierstein

Director: Rich Moore                          Writer: Jon Vitti

3. "Tree House of Horrors" Oct. 25, 1990

In their tree house, Bart and Lisa try to top each other with three scary Halloween stories: "Bad Dream House" (director: Wes Archer; writer: John Swartzwelder), "Hungry are the Damned" (director: Rich Moore; writers: Jay Kogen & Wallace Wolodarsky) and "The Raven" (director: David Silverman; writer: Sam Simon, adapting the Edgar Allan Poe poem).

Mover........................................................James Earl Jones

4. "Two Cars in Every Garage and Three Eyes on Every Fish" Nov. 1, 1990

Homer's nuclear-plant boss Mr. Burns runs for governor. Orig. scheduled for Oct. 25.

Director: Wes Archer
Writers: Sam Simon, John Swartzwelder

5. "Dancin' Homer" Nov. 8, 1990

Homer's popularity as the mascot for the Springfield Isotopes baseball team sends him to the big leagues in Capital City.

Himself...............................................................Tony Bennett
And: Tom Poston, Daryl L. Coley, Ken Levine

Song: "Capital City" by Jeff Martin

Director: Mark Kirkland
Writers: Ken Levine & David Isaacs

6. "Dead Putting Society" Nov. 15, 1990

Homer and next-door neighbor Flanders bet on their sons' performance against each other in a miniature-golf tournament.

Director: Rich Moore                          Writer: Jeff Martin

7. "Bart vs. Thanksgiving" Nov. 22, 1990

Bart leaves home after his family and relatives get upset at him for spitefully destroying Lisa's elaborate centerpiece.

With recurring vocal performers and: Greg Berg

Director: David Silverman                  Writer: George Meyer

8. "Bart the Daredevil" Dec. 6, 1990  8-8:33 p.m.

Homer steps in when Bart plans to duplicate the stunts of a professional daredevil. Episode ran overtime due to the inclusion of a video-clip for the pop single "Do the Bartman" (director: Brad Bird; song written by Bryan Loran).

With recurring vocal performers, and, in "Do the Bartman," Pamela Hayden, Marcia Wallace

Director: Wesley Meyer Archer
Writers: Jay Kogen & Wallace Wolodarsky

9. "Itchy & Scratchy & Marge" Dec. 20, 1990

Marge crusades against producers of violent TV cartoons.

With recurring vocal performers and: Alex Rocco

Director: Jim Reardon                  Writer: John Swartzwelder

10. "Bart Gets Hit by a Car" Jan. 10, 1991

When Homer's boss accidentally runs over Bart, slightly injuring him, Homer envisions big money in a lawsuit.

With recurring vocal performers and: Phil Hartman, Doris Grau

Director: Mark Kirkland                  Writer: John Swartzwelder

11. "One Fish, Two Fish, Blowfish, Blue Fish" Jan. 24, 1991

Homer thinks he's fatally poisoned, and reassesses his life. Guest King is the radio and CNN television personality.

Voice of Bible narrator............................................Larry King
And: Sab Shimono, George Takei, Joey Miyashima, Diana Tanaka

Director: Wesley M. Archer                  Writer: Nell Scovell

12. "The Way We Was" Jan. 31, 1991

Homer and Marge reflect on their 1974 high-school courtship.

With recurring vocal performers and: Jon Lovitz, Tress MacNeille

Director: David Silverman
Writers: Al Jean & Mike Reiss and Sam Simon

13. "Homer vs. Lisa and the Eighth Commandment" Feb. 7, 1991

Lisa is disheartened when her dad breaks the Commandment "Thou shalt not steal" by pirating cable TV.

Cable installer......................................................Phil Hartman
And: Tress MacNeille

Director: Rich Moore                  Writer: Steve Pepoon

14. "Principal Charming" Feb. 14, 1991

Principal Skinner falls for Marge's sister Patty.

Director: Mark Kirkland                  Writer: David Stern

15. "Oh, Brother, Where Art Thou" Feb. 21, 1991

After the family discovers Homer's illegitimate half-brother, an auto tycoon in Detroit, Homer's car design bankrupts him.

Herb Powell................................................Danny DeVito

Director: W.M. "Bud" Archer                  Writer: Jeff Martin

16. "Bart's Dog Gets an F" March 7, 1991  8-8:33 p.m.

Homer threatens to get rid of the family dog, Santa's Little Helper, unless he shapes up at obedience school. Episode ran overtime due to the inclusion of a video-clip for the pop single "Deep, Deep Trouble" (director: Gregg Vanzo; song written by Matt Groening and D.J. Jazzy Jeff; animation producer: K.S. Park; animation associate producer: Ken Tsumura).

Dog trainer Emily Winthrop................................Tracey Ullman
And: Frank Welker

Director: Jim Reardon                  Writer: Jon Vitti

17. "Old Money" March 28, 1991

Grandpa Simpson falls in love with a woman (Meadows) at his rest home, who dies and leaves him $106,000.

Bea Simmons................................................Audrey Meadows
And: Phil Hartman

Director: David Silverman
Writers: Jay Kogen & Wallace Wolodarsky

18. "Brush with Greatness" April 11, 1991

While Homer tries to lose weight, Marge rekindles an art talent inspired by her admiration for Ringo Starr, the rock musician and former Beatle, and is assigned to paint Mr. Burns' portrait.

Himself................................................Ringo Starr
Art teacher................................................Jon Lovitz

Director: Jim Reardon                  Writer: Brian K. Roberts

19. "Lisa's Substitute" April 25, 1991

Bart runs for class president; Lisa falls for her subsitute teacher (Hoffman), making Homer feel neglected. Voice guest Hoffman used the pseudonymous credit "Sam Etic."

Mr. Bergstrom..........................Dustin Hoffman (uncredited) •
And: Jo Anne Harris, Russi Taylor

• Harry Shearer erroneously credited in Fox press materials for April 22 rerun.

Director: Rich Moore                  Writer: Jon Vitti

20. "The War of the Simpsons" May 2, 1991

Leaving the kids with Grandpa, a fed-up Marge takes Homer to a mountaintop marriage-retreat, where he'd rather fish.

     Also orig. announced: Marcia Wallace (Mrs. Krabapple)

NOTE: Fox announced Azaria as Rev. Lovejoy (normally done

by Shearer); unconfirmed.

Director: NA                           Writer: John Swartzwelder

21. "Three Men and a Comic Book"  May 9, 1991

Bart does odd jobs to raise money to buy the scarce *Radiation Man #1*. Stern is the adult narrator of *The Wonder Years*.

Mrs. Glick.................................................Cloris Leachman
Adult narrator.........................................Daniel Stern
And: Russi Taylor

Director: Wes M. Archer                 Writer: Jeff Martin

22. "Blood Feud"  July 11, 1991

Bart is the only matching blood donor for Homer's mortally ill boss, Mr. Burns.

Director: David Silverman               Writer: George Meyer

**renewed for 1991-92; new episodes begin Sept. 19, 1991**

## Sisters

NBC       May 11-June 20, Aug. 3-on      Saturdays, 10-11 p.m.

Series premiere: May 11, 1991

Drama of four sisters in Winnetka, Ill.: a wealthy plastic-surgeon's wife (Kurtz); a single-mother artist and recovering alcoholic (Ward); a wealthy marketing analyst (Phillips); and the even-keeled mother/part-time real-estate agent and family mediator (Kalember).

Alex Reed Halsey...........................................Swoosie Kurtz
Georgie Reed Whitsig.................................Patricia Kalember
Francesca "Frankie" Reed............................Julianne Phillips
Theodora "Teddy" Reed...................................Sela Ward
Beatrice Reed, their mother........................Elizabeth Hoffman
Mitch Margolis, Teddy's ex-husband...................Ed Marinaro
John Whitsig, Georgie's husband................Garrett M. Brown

*Recurring:*
Dr. Wade Halsey (ep. 2-3,5-7)..............................David Dukes
Cat Margolis (15), Tracy and Mitch's
    daughter (ep. 1-3,5-7)...........................Heather McAdam
Trevor Whitsig, Georgie and John's son............Ryan Francis •
Evan Whitsig, Georgie and John's son..........Dustin Berkovitz •
Reed Halsey, Alex and Wade's daughter
    (ep. 1-2,5-7)...........................................Kathy Wagner
Teenage Alex (flashback)
    (ep. 1)..................................................Alexandra Lee
    (ep. 2-4,7)..............................................Sharon Martin
Teenage Teddy (flashback)
    (ep. 1)..................................................Devon Pierce
    (ep. 2-4,7)...............................................Jill Novick
Young Georgie (flashback; ep. 1-5,7)........................Riff Regan
Young Frankie (flashback)
    (ep. 1)................................................Rhianna Janette
    (ep. 2-4,7)..............................................Tasia Schutt
Judge Truman Ventner (ep. 3-4,6).....................Philip Sterling

• In every episode, but contractually and per screen credit not a cast-member.

Lorimar Television
Executive producers: Ron Cowen, Daniel Lipman, Robert Butler, Anita Addison

Producer: David Latt (ep. 1); Kevin Inch (ep. 2-on)
Co-producer: Randall Zisk
Supervising producer (ep. 2-on): Eric Overmyer
Associate producer (ep. 2-on): Jessie Ward
Director of photography: Neil Roach (ep. 1); Brian Reynolds (ep 2-on)
Music [and] End-theme (instrumental): Jay Gruska
Creators: Ron Cowen & Daniel Lipman

————————————

1. "Moving In, Moving Out, Moving On"  May 11, 1991

As the sisters help their recently widowed mom, Teddy returns from living in California, hoping to win back her ex-husband but discovering his romance with little sis Frankie.

Dr. Thomas Alton Reed, their late father............John McCann
Mrs. Winfield...............................................Peggy Pope
Irv.......................................................Charles Walker
D.C.....................................................Philip Brown
Mrs. Emerson........................................Donna Lowre
Prostitute.............................................Susie Singer
Moving persons.........................George C. Simms, John Lyons
Bargain hunter...........................Patrick Waddell, Delia Salvi
Women.............Pamela Brown, Tamar Cooper, Jody Price
And: Lyndsey Fields (Waitress), Sheridan Gayr (Young Alex)

Director: Robert Butler   Writers: Ron Cowen & Daniel Lipman

2. "80%"  May 18, 1991

While throwing a 15th-anniversary party for herself and Wade (Dukes), Alex finds evidence her husband is cheating on her.

Robert Costanzo.........................................Sidney Getz
Bellperson.............................................Charles Hutchins
Woman in sauna...........................................Jody Price
Young Wade....................................Mark Patrick Gleason
Mrs. Christian............................................Myrna Niles

Director: Robert Butler   Writers: Ron Cowen & Daniel Lipman

3. "A Thousand Sprinkles"  May 25, 1991

Frankie hires Teddy as her secretary, exacerbating the tension between them; the Halseys join a support group for cross-dressing husbands.

Dr. Faith Newton........................................Lois de Banzie
Rita......................................................Deborah Strang
Salesperson.............................................Kathryn White
Harvey Sanderson......................................Robert Neches
Waitress.................................................Jan Gan Boyd
Brad, Frankie's secretary..................................Tuc Watkins

Director: Steven Robman
Writers: Eric Overmyer and Ron Cowan & Daniel Lipman

4. "Devoted Husband, Loving Father"  June 1, 1991

Georgie's tempted by her old college flame (Converse-Roberts); Frankie encounters a woman (Van Patten) in dad's past; Teddy loses her job; John wants to record a homemade album. A different actor than in ep. 1 portrays the sisters' late father.

Alan "Bingo" Bing............................William Converse-Roberts
Belle Adderly................................................Joyce Van Patten
Dr. Thomas Alton Reed....................................Stanley Grover
Collegiate Bingo.........................................Jonathan Emerson
Joy Simmer...................................................Nancy Lenehan

Stu Zimmer.....................................................Lorry Goldman
Franco Gelati......................................................Eddie Fontaine
And: Tamar Cooper (Sauna lady), Hugh Holub (He)

Director: Jan Eliasberg   Writers: Ron Cowen & Daniel Lipman

5. "Of Mice and Women" June 8, 1991

After arguing with Frankie, Mitch unwittingly tells all to a psuedononymous Teddy on a 900 line; Wade reveals he's broke, and vanishes; Georgie invites her boss home for dinner.

Fred Tuttwyler........................................................Cliff Bemis
Didi Poncell...........................................................Hildy Brooks
Wesley Picard..........................................................Bruce Gray
Salesperson........................................................Sarah Simmons
And: Nina Mann (Lila Tuttwyler), Doug Franklin (Ralph), Will Kepper (Car reposessor), Lisa Williams (Sexy woman)

Director: James Contner          Writer: Diana Gould

6. "Deja Vu All Over Again" June 15, 1991

As Frankie's wedding nears, Teddy shoots up Alex's house; Frankie calls off her nuptials; Wade returns from Honduras. Watkins reprises his role from ep. 3.

Tony Jennings...........................................................Roy Fegan
Dr. Larwin, Wade's partner..............................Raymond Singer
Dr. Simmons, Wade's partner...........................Stephen Mendel
Mrs. Margolis, Mitch's mother.................................Erica Yohn
Jeweler................................................................Robert Nadder
And: Annie Barker (Flower girl Frankie), Tuc Watkins (Brad), Cristian Letelier (Cop), William B. Jackson (Minister)

Director: Arlene Sanford         Writer: Eric Overmyer

7. "Some Tuesday in July"
    Thursday, June 20, 1991 10-11 p.m.; June 22, 1991

Teddy announces she's moving on, and that she's leaving Cat with the more stable Mitch; Georgie tries to remain stoic over Evan's hospitalization for leukemia.

Dr. Eisenberg.........................................................Mark Hutter
Dr. Reinholdt.........................................................Lenny Wolpe
Pilsner....................................................................I.M. Hobson
D.C.......................................................................Philip Browne
First person........................................................Lewis Dauber
Ronald Rasmussen..........................................J.G. Buzanowski

Director: Anita Addison
Writers: Ron Cowen & Daniel Lipman

**on hiatus until reruns begin Aug. 3; renewed for 1991-92; new episodes begin Sept. 21, 1991**

## Sons and Daughters

CBS         Fridays, 10-11 p.m.

Series premiere: Jan. 4, 1991
Final telecast: March 1, 1991

Ensemble drama of a three-generation family in Portland, Ore., centering on three grown siblings: single mother Tess; Gary; and Patty. Spud's high school: La Porte High. Cast-member Wallace listed as a guest performer in ep. 1. Orig. scheduled to premiere Oct. 25, 1990, and air Thursdays, 9-10 p.m. Working title: *The Hammersmiths*.

Interior designer Tess Hammersmith......................Lucie Arnaz
Coach Spud Lincoln.............................................Rick Rossovich
Patty Hammersmith Lincoln, his wife.............Peggy Smithhart
Rocky Lincoln.........................................................Paul Scherrer
Paulette Lincoln.................................................Kamaron Harper
Ike Lincoln.........................................................Billy O'Sullivan
Gary Hammersmith.................................................Scott Plank
Lindy Mercer Hammersmith, his wife..............Stacy Edwards
Astrid, Tess' adopted daughter............................Michele Wong
Bing Hammersmith, Sr............................................Don Murray
Mary Ruth Hammersmith, his new wife.................Lisa Blount
Bing Hammersmith, Jr., their son................Aaron Brownsten
Grandpa Hank Hammersmith (ep. 2-on).......George D. Wallace

*Recurring, all or virtually all episodes:*
Dakota Hammersmith, Gary and Lindy's
     baby.........................................the Bull Twins (uncredited)

B&E Enterprises in assoc. with Paramount Pictures
Executive producers: Brad Buckner, Eugenie Ross-Leming
Supervising producer: Ronald Rubin
Coordinating producer (ep. 2-on): Roger Bondelli
Producers: Frederic W. Brost (ep. 1); Peter Levin, Robert Cochran
Associate producers: Bernie Laramie (ep. 1); Randy S. Nelson (ep. 2-on)
Creative consultant (ep. 2-on): E. Jack Kaplan
Director of photography (variously): John McPherson, A.S.C. (ep. 1); King Baggot, A.S.C.; Stanley Lazan
Music: Steve Dorff
Theme (instrumental): Steve Dorff
Creators: Eugenie Ross-Leming & Brad Buckner

---

1. "Sons and Daughters" Jan. 4, 1990

Reaction is mixed to the prodigal return of Bing Sr. with his new family.

Grandpa Hank Hammersmith......................George D. Wallace
Daisy Mercer, Lindy's mother................................Marj Dusay
Scout leader..........................................................Brook Bundy
Man with bullhorn..................................................Joe Farago
Girls.........................................Sabrina Harper, Kristen Corbett
Minister......................................................................Jack Loo

Director: David Carson
Writers: Eugenie Ross-Leming & Brad Buckner

2. "Crime and Punishment" Jan. 11, 1991

A woman (Yasutake) shows up claiming to be Astrid's biological mother; Rocky wants to move in with Gary and Lindy.

Lillian Park..........................................................Patti Yasutake
Muriel Kroft..........................................................Olivia Negron
Security guard...................................................Garret Pearson
Sean....................................................................Derek Stewart
Georgia...........................................................Michelle Bronson
Young woman........................................................Laura Austin
Jailer....................................................................Blumen Young
Huge men..............................Brogan Young, Rocky Giordani

Director: Bill Bixby         Teleplay: Ronald Rubin
Story: Ronald Rubin and Ken Carlton

3. "The Dating Game" Jan. 18, 1991

Tess agrees to a date with a teacher (Kilner) from Spud's school; Gary and Lindy try to take a romantic weekend away.

Michael Morgan................................................Kevin Kilner
Roger................................................................Todd Susman
Waiter...........................................................Peter Elbling
And: Megan Ward (Dee Dee), Shawn Phelan, Annemarie Mc-
    Evoy (Students), Michael Lee Owens (Cody Morgan)

Director: Betty Thomas          Story: Deborah Starr Seibel
Teleplay: Eugenie Ross-Leming & Brad Buckner and Deborah
    Starr Seibel

4. "Throw Mama from the Terrain" Jan. 25, 1991

Bing's first wife (Garland), who'd abandoned the family 23
years ago, shows up unexpectedly; Lindy takes her breast-
feeding fight public.

Marcy Hammersmith........................................Beverly Garland
Sheila Albright...............................................Dori Brenner
Michael Valdez...............................................Richard Chaves
Maitre d'.........................................................Brian George
Bill Sanders....................................................Les Lannom
And: Julie Inouye (Anchorperson), Marianne Muellerleile
    (Makeup person), Justin Shenkarow (Roy Sanders)

Director: King Baggot              Writer: E. Jack Kaplan

**preempted Feb. 1**

5. "Melanie" Feb. 8, 1991

Rocky and his twentysomething supervisor at his part-time
job (Pelikan) fall for each other; a stray dog Astrid's adopted
wreaks household havoc; Grandpa babysits.

Melanie............................................................Lisa Pelikan
Burt.................................................................David Dunard
And: Stephen Root (Stevey), Ed Crick (Yard person), Mik
    Scriba (Cop), Patrick LaBrecque (Boy)

Director: Bill Bixby               Writer: Kathryn Baker

6. "The Thing" Feb. 15, 1991

Bing takes a camping trip with his sons, leaving Tess and
Mary Ruth to face a contractor building a Jacuzzi. Susman reprises his role from ep. 3, Lannom and Shenkarow from ep. 4

Roger................................................................Todd Susman
Slasher Martin...................................................Don Gibb
Bill Sanders.......................................................Les Lannom
And: Justin Shenkarow (Roy Sanders), Eli Rich (Parent)

Director: Paul Lynch              Teleplay: Robert Cochran
Story: Jeff Stepakoff

**preempted Feb. 22**

7. "Deep Throat" March 1, 1991

Mary Ruth and Bing visit a fertility clinic; Ike and Spud both
go to get tonsils removed; Lindy's neurotic mother (Dusay,
reprising her role from ep. 1) wants to move in.

Daisy Mercer.....................................................Marj Dusay
Dr. Baumgarten..................................................Scott Bryce
Debbie.............................................................Kathleen Freeman
And: Stephen Prutting (Raoul Cleese), Norma Maldonado (Ms.
    Martinez), Susan Mackin (Judy Jolly)

Director: Peter Levin
Writers: Eugenie Ross-Leming & Brad Buckner

Unaired

Title NA

Mary Ruth asks Tess to help her cook a fancy dinner; Ike in-
vents an imaginary pal (Gorman); Gary puts Dakota's college
fund in a get-rich-quick scheme. Orig. scheduled for March 8.

Announced personnel includes:
Harold..............................................................Robert Hy Gorman
Dr. Barnett.......................................................Lane Davies
Jim Brookhurst..................................................Woody Eney
Paul Chapman....................................................Stanley Grover
Elaine Chapman..................................................Susan Brown
And: Cameron Thor (Greg), Daniel Bardol (Todd), Patricia Bar-
    ry, (Grace Brookhurst), David Belafonte (Terry)

Director: Nick Havinga            Writer: Jim Wells

## Star Trek: The Next Generation

Syndicated                     One-hour

Series premiere: Sept. 1987

The voyages of the starship *Enterprise*, approximately 85 years
after those of its namesake in the original series, *Star Trek*
(NBC, 1966-69), the source also of six feature films from 1979-
91. Season began syndication week of Sept. 24, 1990. Episode
production number and week of release given in parentheses
following title. Frakes is married to actress Genie Francis.

Capt. Jean-Luc Picard........................................Patrick Stewart
Commander William Riker..............................Jonathan Frakes
Lt. Commander Geordi La Forge.......................LeVar Burton
Lt. Worf (Klingon)............................................Michael Dorn
Chief Medical Officer Dr. Beverly Crusher.......Gates McFadden
Ensign Wesley Crusher, her son (ep. 1-9)..............Wil Wheaton
Counselor Deanna Troi (Betazoid).......................Marina Sirtis
Lt. Commander Data (android).............................Brent Spiner

*Recurring:*
Guinan (ep. 1,4,10,14,16-17,25-26)...............Whoopi Goldberg
Transporter Chief O'Brien
    (ep. 1,3-6,11-12,14,17,22,24-25).................Colm Meaney
Keiko (ep. 11-12,17,25)....................................Rosalind Chao
Nurse Ogawa (ep. 8,14,18,23)..........................Patti Yasutake
* Transporter technician (ep. 7-8,11,16).................April Grace

* Identified as Transporter Chief Hubbell, ep. 11 only.

Paramount Television
Executive producers: Gene Roddenberry, Rick Berman,
    Michael Piller
Supervising producer (later in season): Jeri Taylor
Producers: Lee Sheldon, David Livingston
Co-producer: Peter Lauritson
Line producer (later in season): Merri Howard
Associate producer: Wendy Neuss
Executive story editor: Ronald D. Moore, Joe Menosky
Story editors (later in season): David Bennett Carren, J. Larry
    Carroll
Director of photography (variously): Marvin Rush; Thomas F.
    DENOVE; Joe Chess
Technical consultants: Rick Sternbach, Michael Okuda
Make-up designer-supervisor: Michael Westmore
Music (variously): Ron Jones; Dennis McCarthy; Jay
    Chattaway
Theme: Jerry Goldsmith, Alexander Courage
Creator: Gene Roddenberry

1. "The Best of Both Worlds, Part 2" (Sept. 24, 1990) (175)

Continued from last season. The malevolent Borgs, having turned Picard into an evil Borg-human hybrid called Locutus, utilize him in their plot to conquer Earth; in his absence, Riker is promoted to Captain and names Shelby his First Officer.

Lt. Commander Shelby...............................Elizabeth Dennehy
Admiral Hanson...........................................George Murdock
Gleason.................................................................Todd Merrill

Director: Cliff Bole                    Writer: Michael Piller

2. "Suddenly Human" (Oct. 15, 1990) (176)

Picard risks war when he refuses to return a human boy (Allen) to the Talarian foster-father (Howard) who raised him, and possibly abused him.

Endar.............................................................Sherman Howard
Jono/Jeremiah Rossa.........................................Chad Allen
Connaught..................................................Barbara Townsend

Director: Gabrielle Beaumont        Story: Ralph Phillips
Teleplay: John Whelpley & Jeri Taylor

3. "Brothers" (Oct. 8, 1990) (177)

After being summoned home by his elderly creator, Data clashes with his evil "brother," Lore. Co-star Spiner, playing three roles, reprises the part of Lore from two seasons previous.

Lore [and] Dr. Noonian Soong...............................Brent Spiner
Jake Potts.........................................................Cory Danziger
And: Adam Ryen (Willie Potts), James Lashly (Ensign Kopf)

Director: Rob Bowman                    Writer: Rick Berman

4. "Family" (Oct. 1, 1990) (178)

While the *Enterprise* undergoes repairs on Earth, crew members reunite with their families: A bitter reunion with Picard's older brother in their hometown French village; an uncomfortable meeting with Worf's adoptive human parents (Brown, Bikel); a holographic-disc message for Wesley from his late dad.

Robert Picard......................................................Jeremy Kemp
Marie Picard...................................................Samantha Eggar
Sergey Rozhenko.............................................Theodore Bikel
Helena Rozhenko.............................................Georgia Brown
And: Dennis Creaghan (Louis), David Tristan Birkin (Rene Picard), Doug Wert (Jack Crusher, Wesley's late father)

Director: Les Landau                    Writer: Ronald D. Moore
Based in part on a premise by Susanne Lamboin & Bryan Stewart

5. "Remember Me" (Oct. 22, 1990) (179)

When Wesley's warp-field experiment goes awry, Dr. Crusher unknowingly is catapuled into a universe created by her own mind.

Dr. Dalen Quaice....................................................Bill Erwin
The Traveller.......................................................Eric Menyuk

Director: Cliff Bole                    Writer: Lee Sheldon

6. "Legacy" (Oct. 29, 1990) (180)

On a mission to Turkana Four, home planet of their late comrade Tasha Yar, the crew finds Tasha's sister, a guerilla in the clash between her own Coalition and the opposing Alliance.

Ishara Yar........................................................Beth Toussaint
Hayne.................................................................Don Mirault
And: Vladimir Velasco (Tan Tsu), Christopher Michael (Man)

Director: Robert Scheerer          Writer: Joe Menosky

7. "Reunion" (Nov. 5, 1990) (181)

When Picard must mediate a power struggle between potential successors to the Klingon Empire, Worf is reunited with his half-human former mate (Plakson) and their son (Steuer).

Ambassador K'Ehleyr...........................................Suzie Plakson
Gowron...............................................................Robert O'Reilly
Duras................................................................Patrick Massett
Klington leader K'Mpec....................................Charles Cooper
Alexander.............................................................Jon Steuer
Security guard...................................................Michael Rider
Klingon guards............Basil Wallace, Mirron E. [Edward] Willis

Director: Jonathan Frakes
Story: Drew Deighan and Thomas Perry & Jo Perry
Teleplay: Thomas Perry & Jo Perry and Ronald D. Moore & Brannon Braga

8. "Future Imperfect" (Nov. 12, 1990) (182)

After a mission he leads goes awry, Riker awakens in Sickbay to find 16 years have apparently passed, and that he now commands the Enterprise, has a son (Dementral) by a woman now dead, and is negotiating a treaty with the Romulans. Merrill reprises his role from ep. 1.

Romulan Commander Tomalak....................Andreas Katsulas
Jean-Luc/Ethan/Barash...............................Chris Dementral
And: Carolyn McCormick (Mutant), Todd Merrill (Gleason), George O'Hanlon, Jr. (Transporter Chief)

Director: Les Landau
Writers: J. Larry Carroll & David Bennett Carren

9. "Final Mission" (Nov. 19, 1990) (183)

Wesley, now accepted to Starfleet Academy, accompanies Picard to mediate a dispute on Pentarus Five, and the two get stranded on a desert moon with a planet representative (Tate).

Dirgo..................................................................Nick Tate
Songi..............................................................Kim Hamilton
Ensign Tess Allenby.........................................Mary Kohnert

Director: Corey Allen                    Story: Kacey Arnold-Ince
Teleplay: Kacey Arnold-Ince and Jeri Taylor

10. "The Loss" (184; Dec. 31, 1990)

With the ship on a collision course with a black hole-like "cosmic string," Deanna loses her empathic ability and wants to resign as counselor. Kohnert reprises her role from ep. 9.

Janet Brooks......................................................Kim Braden
Ensign Tess Allenby.........................................Mary Kohnert

Director: Chip Chalmers                    Story: Hilary J. Bader
Teleplay: Hilary J. Bader and Alan J. Adler & Vanessa Greene

11. "Data's Day" (185; Jan. 7, 1991)

O'Brien's last-minute cold feet regarding his wedding to Data's friend Keiko confuses the android; the crew believes they've accidentally killed a Vulcan ambassador (Pecheur).

T 'Pei..............................................Sierra Pecheur
Romulan Commander Mendak..............................Alan Scarfe
V'Sal..............................................Shelly Desai

Director: Robert Wiemer          Story: Harold Apter
Teleplay: Harold Apter and Ronald D. Moore

12. "The Wounded" (186; Jan. 28, 1991)

A renegade Federation ship, the *Phoenix*, led by a former captain of O'Brien's, is making unprovoked attacks on vessels of former Federation enemies the Cardassians.

*Phoenix* Capt. Maxwell.............................Bob Gunton
Cardassian Capt. Gul Macet..............................Marc Alaimo
Telle..............................................Marco Rodriguez
And: Time Winters (Daro), John Hancock (Adm. Haden)

Director: Chip Chalmers          Teleplay: Jeri Taylor
Story: Stuart Charno & Sara Charno and Cy Chermak

13. "Devil's Due" (187; Feb. 4, 1991)

A shape-changing woman (Dubois) claiming to be the Devil informs the panicked planet Ventax that she has arrived to fulfill the enslaving terms of a thousand-year-old contract.

Ardra............Marta DuBois (misspelled "Du Bois" in *TV Guide*)
Dr. Clarke......................................Paul Lambert
Jared..............................................Marcelo Tubert
Devil monster......................................Thad Lamey
Klingon monster......................................Tom Magee
     Also orig. announced: William Glover (Marley)

Director: Tom Benko          Teleplay: Philip LaZebnik
Story: Philip LaZebnick and William Douglas Lansford

14. "Clues" (188; Feb. 11, 1991)

After the *Enterprise* passes through a "worm hole" that knocks everyone save Data unconscious, the crew awakens to find evidence Data is lying to them about how long they were out.

Ensign..............................................Pamela Winslow
Trixie..............................................Rhonda Aldrich
Gunperson..........................................Thomas Knickerbocker

Director: Les Landau          Story: Bruce D. Arthurs
Teleplay: Bruce D. Arthurs and Joe Menosky

15. "First Contact" (189; Feb. 18, 1991)

On the planet Malcoria, Riker, undercover, is critically injured, stranded, and hospitalized during a first-contact mission. Neuwirth is a recurring guest on *Cheers*.

Chancelor Durken..............................George Coe
Science Minister Mirasta Yale......................Carolyn Seymour
Berel..............................................George Hearn
Internal Security Minister Krola......................Michael Ensign
Nilrem..............................................Steven Anderson
And: Sachi Parker (Tava), Bebe Neuwirth (Lanel)

Director: Cliff Bole
Teleplay: Dennis Russell Bailey & David Bischoff and Joe
     Menosky & Ronald D. Moore and Michael Piller
Story: Marc Scott Zicree

(Orig. announced: Story: Marc Zicree and David Bischoff & Dennis Russell Bailey; teleplay: Joe Menosky & Ronald D. Moore and Michael Piller)

16. "Galaxy's Child" (190; March 11, 1991)

While Geordi finds that his brilliant dream woman (Gibney) can't stand him, the crew becomes surrogate mother to an energy-lifeform baby whose mother they had to destroy.

Senior Design Engineer, Theoretical
     Propulsion Group, Dr. Leah Brahms...........Susan Gibney
Ensign Estevez.................................Lanei Chapman
Ensign Pavlik..................................Jana Marie Hupp

Director: Winrich Kolbe          Teleplay: Maurice Hurley
Story: Thomas Kartozian

17. "Night Terrors" (191; March 18, 1991)

After locating the marooned science vessel *Brattain*, the crew finds itself in a "Tyken's Rift," an energy-draining space rupture where dream deprivation threatens to drive them insane.

Hagan..............................................John Vickery
Gillespie..........................................Duke Moosekian
Peeples..............................................Craig Hurley
Kenny Lin..........................................Brian Tochi
And: Lanei Chapman (Ensign Rager), Deborah Taylor (Zaheva)

Director: Les Landau          Story: Shari Goodhartz
Teleplay: Pamela Douglas and Jeri Taylor

18. "Identity Crisis" (192; March 25, 1991)

A parasite Geordi and an old Starfleet friend (Plunkett) absorbed on the planet Tarchannen may turn them into aliens.

Susanna Leijten.................................Maryann Plunkett
Hickman..............................................Amick Byram
Transporter technician (orig.
     Transporter Chief Hedwek)...................Dennis Madalone
Ensign Graham......................................Mona Grudt
     Also orig. announced:
     Whoopi Goldberg (Guinan), Paul Tompkins (Ensign Breville)

Director: Winrich Kolbe          Teleplay: Brannon Braga
Story: Timothy DeHaas

19. "The Nth Degree" (193; April 1, 1991)

While trying to repair the Argus Array telescope, a shy, unassuming crew-member (Schultz) is transformed by an alien probe into a dangerous, overconfident, super-intelligent being.

Barclay..............................................Dwight Schultz
Holodeck Albert Einstein..........................Jim Norton
Alien..............................................Kay E. Kuter
Lt. Linda Larson..................................Saxon Trainor
Ensign April Anaya................................Page Leong
Ensign Brower......................................David Coburn

Director: Rogert Legato          Writer: Joe Menosky

20. "Qpid" (194; April 22, 1991)

The near-omnipotent prankster Q (de Lancie, reprising his role from past seasons) transforms Picard into Robin Hood, his crew into Merry Men, and Picard's adventuress old-fling (Hetrick, reprising her role from last season) into Maid Marian.

Vash............................................................Jennifer Hetrick
Sir Guy............................................................Clive Revill
Q/Sheriff of Nottingham.................................John de Lancie
Servant................................................................Joi Staton

Director: Cliff Bole                              Teleplay: Ira Steven Behr
Story: Randee Russell and Ira Steven Behr

21. "The Drumhead" (195; April 29, 1991)

A retired Starfleet Admiral stages a witch hunt against a suspected traitor (Garrett) aboard the *Enterprise* after an explosion occurs and a visitng Klingon officer admits to spying.

Admiral Norah Satie..........................................Jean Simmons
Sabin Genestra, her Betazoid aide.......................Bruce French
Simon Tarses......................................................Spencer Garrett
Klingon officer J'Ddan....................................Henry Woronicz
And: Earl Billings (Starfleet Admiral), Ann Shea (Nellen Tore)

Director: Jonathan Frakes                          Writer: Jeri Taylor

22. "Half a Life" (196; May 6, 1991)

Deanna's visiting mother (Barrett, a cast-member of the original *Star Trek* and wife of series creator Roddenberry) tries to
keep her new lover (Stiers) from returning to his planet, Kae-
lon Two, and committing the ritual suicide, "The Resolution."
Barrett reprises her guest role from 1988.

Lwaxana Troi.....................................................Majel Barrett
Dr. Timicin..............................................David Ogden Stiers
Dara Timicin, his daughter.............................Michelle Forbes
B'Tardat.....................................................Terence E. McNally
Mr. Homm......................................................Caryl Struycken

Director: Les Landau                          Teleplay: Peter Allan Fields
Story: Ted Roberts and Peter Allan Fields

23. "The Host" (197; May 13, 1991)

Dr. Crusher falls in love with a Trillian ambassador (Luz) medi-
ating a dispute between the moons of the planet Peliar, but
discovers his exterior is simply the mannequin-like host body
of a small, gelatinous lifeform she must transplant into Riker.
Director Rush is one of the series' regular cinematographers.

Ambassador Odan....................................................Franc Luz
Leka..............................................................Barbara Tarbuck
Kareel.......Nicole Orth-Pallavicini a.k.a. Nicole Orth Pallavicini
Kalin Trose...................................................William Newman
Lathal.............................................Robert Harper (uncredited)

Director: Marvin V. Rush                       Writer: Michel Horvat

24. "The Minds Eye" (198; May 27, 1991)

Geordi, kidnapped and brainwashed by a Romulan (Fleck) stir-
ring anti-Federation sentiment on the rebelling Klingon colony
Krios, unwittingly allies with a Klingon traitor (Dobkin).
Voiceover-guest Barrett played a different role in ep. 22

Ambassador Kell.................................................Larry Dobkin
Taibak..................................................................John Fleck
Krios Governor Vagh..........................................Edward Wiley
Computer voice.................................................Majel Barrett

Director: David Livingston                     Teleplay: Rene Echevarria
Story: Ken Schafer and Rene Echevarria

25. "In Theory" (199; June 3, 1991)

While the ship encounters a nebula that creates gaps in the
fabric of space, Data experimentally programs himself to pursue a romance with a fellow crew-member (Scarabelli). Barrett
reprises her voiceover role from last episode.

Ensign Jenna Anaya....................................Michele Scarabelli
Ensign...........................................................Pamela Winslow
Computer voice................................................Majel Barrett

Director: Patrick Stewart
Writers: Joe Menosky & Ronald D. Moore

26. "Redemption" (200; June 17, 1991)

Civil war erupts as the Klingon Empire installs a new Leader
of the High Council (O'Reilly); Worf confronts the son (Cullum)
of the rebel, Duras, responsible for his discommendation.

Gowron..........................................................Robert O'Reilly
Kurn, Worf's brother...............................................Tony Todd
Lursa............................................................Barbara March
B'Etor........................................................Gwynyth Walsh
K'Tal.................................................................Ben Slack
And: Nicholas Kepros (Movar), J.D. Cullum (Toral), Tom Or-
meny (Klingon First Officer), Clifton Jones (Helmsperson)

Director: Cliff Bole                          Writer: Ronald D. Moore

**renewed for 1991-92; new episodes begin week of Sept.
23, 1991**

## Stat

ABC                              Tuesdays, 9:30-10 p.m.

Series premiere: April 16, 1991
Final telecast: May 21, 1991

Ensemble comedy of the skilled, dedicated and borderline
neurotic doctors and nurses of the trauma center at New York
City's fictional Hudson Memorial Hospital. The title is medical
code for "immediately." Actor Dannel Arnold and co-creator
Danny Arnold are not the same person.

Dr. Tony Menzies.......................................Dennis Boutsikaris
Dr. Elizabeth Newberry.....................................Alison La Placa

*Recurring:*
Dr. Lewis "Cowboy" Doniger (ep. 1,3-4).................Casey Biggs
Jeanette Lemp (ep 1-3,6)........................................Alix Elias
Desk nurse Anderson "Mary" Roche
     (ep. 2-3,5-6)................................................Ron Canada
Dr. Werner (ep. 1,4-6).......................................Dannel Arnold
Dr. Ron Murphy (ep. 1,3-4)..............................Wren T. Brown
Orderly Julio Oscar (ep. 2-5)....................Julio Oscar Mechoso

Tetragram, Ltd., in assoc. with Touchstone Television
Executive producer: Danny Arnold
Producers: Chris Hayward, John Bunzel
Executive story consultant: John Bunzel
Director of photography: Vincent E. Contarino
Technical advisors: Gary Sugarman, M.D., Lance Gentile, M.D.
Music [and] Theme (instrumental): Jack Elliott
Creators: Tony Sheehan, Danny Arnold, Chris Hayward

---

1. "Psychosomatic" April 16, 1991

A man (Koss) has all the same symptoms as his wife (Ponterotto), who's about to give birth; a lawyer (Willrich), needing an emergency operation, won't sign the consent papers.

Mickey Weller..................................................Kurt Fuller
Dougherty........................................................Alan Koss
Mrs. Dougherty..........................................Donna Ponterotto
Felicia Brown..............................................Jenifer Lewis
Rita Falco.......................................................Talia Balsam
Leland Fisk................................................Rudolph Willrich
Paramedics............................Wayne Duvall, Duke Moosekian
Nurses.......Arva Holt, Yuri Ogawa, Cynthia Lea Clark, Carol A.
    Payton

Director: Danny Arnold
Writers: Samuel Shem, M.D. and Chris Hayward & John Bun-
    zel & Danny Arnold

2. "Fantasy"  April 23, 1991

Newberry's date (McGillin) finds her upset after she inadvertently nearly kills a patient; Menzies treats a fellow doctor
(Graham); a mental case (Opatoshu) thinks he's a psychiatrist.

Dr. Gus Rivers..........................................Gerrit Graham
Sidney Wolff...........................................David Opatoshu
Chief of Psychiatry Dr. Herschel "Hesh" Cooper.....Allan Arbus
Randall Forbes..........................................Howard McGillin
Distrubed woman..........................................Anne Haney
Woman on gurney.........................................Lucille Bliss
Drunk man..................................................Jack Kutcher
And: Eric Kohner (Paramedic), Arva Holt (Nurse)

Director: Alan Bergmann          Story: Samuel Shem, M.D.
Teleplay: Samuel Shem, M.D. and Chris Hayward & John
    Bunzel & Danny Arnold

3. "Ladyfinger"  April 30, 1991

An accident victim's missing finger is lost; a doctor hits the
hospital administrator; a patient attacks Newberry.  Graham
reprises his role from last episode.

Dr. Gus Rivers..........................................Gerrit Graham
Eddie Diaz.....................................................Jose Perez
Hospital administrator Leonard Sorkin............David Margulies
Cassidy......................................................Robert Symonds
Dr. Willie Burns.........................................Angela Bassett
Stan Malkowski...........................................Larry Hankin
Jorge Rosario...........................................Maurice Benard
Police officer...............................................George Wallace
Orderlies................Carlos Lacamara, Tony Rolon, Rita Gomez
Paramedic......................................................Bill Miller
Alzheimer's patient........................................Vance Colvig
And: Robina Suwol (Upstairs nurse), Marabina Jaimes (Nurse)

Director: Danny Arnold
Writers: John Bunzel, Chris Hayward, Danny Arnold

4. "The Wilding"  May 7, 1991

Patients keep dying on a surgeon (Garfield) now operating on a
brutally assaulted jogger; Doniger tries to keep a man (Rich)
from arguing himself to death.  Bassett and Lacamara reprise
their roles from last episode.  Orig. scheduled for April 30.

Charles Bauer................................................Allan Rich
Dr. Harold Frohman......................................Allen Garfield
Tilda Barclay............................................Loretta Divine
Dr. Willie Burns.........................................Angela Bassett
Warren Neff..................................................David Bowe
And: Carlos Lacamara (Orderly), Marabina Jaimes (Nurse)

Director: Danny Arnold
Teleplay: Chris Hayward, John Bunzel, Danny Arnold and
    Barry Sandler and Samuel Shem, M.D.
Story:  Chris Hayward, John Bunzel, Danny Arnold and  Barry
    Sandler

5. "High Society"  May 14, 1991

Menzies may be leaving for a better job, after he performs surgery on a wealthy woman (Thayer).  Arndt is a recurring guest
on *L.A. Law*; Margulies reprises his role from ep. 3; director
Glass was a cast-member of co-creator Arnold's *Barney Miller*.

Leonard Sorkin...........................................David Margulies
Dr. Stanley Deardorf.......................................Denis Arndt
Katherine Faraday........................................Brynn Thayer
Frank Resnick...............................................Brian Smiar
Sherry Fazio.........................................Jana Marie Hupp
Nurse Winona Booth.......................................Ann Weldon

Director: Ron Glass
Writers: Chris Hayward & John Bunzel & Danny  Arnold  and
    Andrew Smith

6. "Safe Smuggling"  May 21, 1991

Menzies wants to have Newberry removed to another unit; a
smuggler (Bara) is carrying swallowed drugs in his stomach.
Arbus reprises his role from ep. 2, Perez from ep. 3.

Ira Newmark............................................Peter Michael Goetz
Eddie Diaz.....................................................Jose Perez
Jose Ramos...................................................Fausto Bara
Chief of Psychiatry Dr. Herschel "Hesh" Cooper.....Allan Arbus
Dimitri Ivanovich.....................................Savely Kramarov
And: Adilah Barnes (Nurse Barnes), Michael Lewis (Paramedic)

Director: Danny Arnold
Writers:  Chris Hayward & John Bunzel & Danny  Arnold  and
    Andrew Smith

## Stephen King's Golden Years

CBS              Thursdays, 10-11 p.m.

Series premiere: July 16, 1991
Last scheduled telecast: Aug. 22, 1991

Serialized fantasy-drama of a 70-year-old custodian at the
government's secret Falco Plains "Agricultural Testing Facility"
experimental lab in upstate New York, who begins growing
younger after a lab explosion exposes him to an unknown
combination of chemicals.  Series creator King is a horror-fan-
tasy novelist. Episodes are untitled. Filmed in Wilmington, N.C.

Harlan Williams.........................................Keith Szarabajka
Gina Williams, his wife............................Frances Sternhagen
Security Chief Terrilynn (Terry) Spann............Felicity Huffman
Gen. Louis Crewes............................................Ed Lauter
Government investigator Jude Andrews.....................R.D. Call
Dr. Richard Todhunter.....................................Bill Raymond

*Recurring:*
Maj. Moreland (ep. 1-2,5-7)............................Stephen Root
Dr. Ackerman (ep. 1-2,4)...............................John Rothman
Fredericks (ep. 2-5)..........................................Tim Guinee
Billy DeLois (ep. 1-2,4,6-7)............................Phil Lenkowsky
Rick Haverford (ep. 1-2,4-5)............................Graham Paul
Burton (ep. 5-7)..................................................Erik King
Hawkins (ep. 4,6-7).....................................Randell Haynes

Laurel Productions, a unit of Spelling Entertainment / Laurel-
    King
Executive producers: Richard P. Rubenstein, Stephen King
Producers: Mitchell Galin, Peter R. McIntosh
Supervising producer: Josef Anderson
Director of photography: Alex Nepomniaschy
Special make-up effects consultant: Dick Smith
Harlan's make-up designed by: Carl Fullerton, Neal Martz
Music: Joe Taylor
Theme: "Golden Years," performed by Davie Bowie (the 1976
    recording, a #10 hit on the *Billboard* pop chart)
Creator: Stephen King

––––––––––––––

1. Tuesday, July 16, 1991   9-11 p.m.

After accidental exposure to youth-giving exerpimental chemicals in Dr. Todhunter's lab, Harlan finds himself pursued.

Redding......................................................Matt Molloy
Jackson.....................................................Adam Redfield
Lt. Vester....................................................Jeff Williams
Lt. McGiver.............................................Peter McRobbie
Mrs. Rogers................................................Sarah Melici
And: Lili Bernard (Harlan's nurse), J.R. Horne (Dr. Eakins),
    Rick Warner, Mark Miller, Graham Smith (Shop persons),
    Howard Kingkade (Redding's nurse), Michael Burgess
    (Soldier), Cress Horne (Pilot)

Director: Kenneth Fink          Writer: Stephen King

2. July 18, 1991

Andrews works to keep Harlan's condition under wraps, while
Harlan discloses to Gina their lives may be in danger.

With  recurring guests and: J.R. Horne (Dr. Eakins), Cathleen
    Cohen (Receptionist), Susan King (Ackerman's nurse),
    Richard K. Olsen (Watchperson), Kathleen Piche (Rita)

Director: Allen Coulter          Writer: Stephen King

3. July 25, 1991

Terry, suspecting her ex-partner Andrews as the person killing
those who know the truth about Harlan, urges Harlan and
Gina to skip town with her, putting Andrews on their trail.

Sheriff Mayo.........................................Mert Hatfield
Steven Dent..........................................Brad Greenquist
And: Michael P. Moran (Trucker), Alberto Vazquez (Janitor),
    Stephen Ayers (Cop), Pat Brady (Security guard), Steve
    Coley (Boy), Bob Pentz (State trooper)

Director: Michael Gornick          Writer: Stephen King

4. Aug. 1, 1991

Harlan's change accelerates; another witness is killed; the
murderous Andrews takes over the investigation.

Sheriff Mayo.........................................Mert Hatfield
With: Steve Ryan
And: Susan King (Ackerman's nurse), Don Bland (Technician),
    Todd Brenner (Man), Tim Parati (Attendant), David Dwyer
    (Father), Rick Zieff (Paramedic)

Director: Allen Coulter          Writer: Stephen King

5. Aug. 8, 1991

Harlan and Gina go their separate ways, planning to reunite
at their daughter Francie's home, while Andrews closes in.
Series creator King and producer Anderson have bit parts.

Capt. Marsh............................................Paul Butler
And: Dylan Haggery (Trooper Lyon), Josh Liveright (Trooper
    Arnie), Matthew Ryan (Trooper Jack), Josh Fardon
    (Trooper Shawn), D. Garen Tolkin (Technician), Stephen
    King (Bus driver), Josef Anderson (Janitor), Caroline Dol-
    lar (Little girl), Sarah Melici (Mrs. Rogers), Troy Winbush
    (Tanker driver), Keith Diamond (Security guard), Lucile
    McIntyre (Sunrise reactor), Doug Richards (Lab tech)
    Also orig. announced:
    Harriet Sansom Harris (Francie Williams)

Director: Stephen Tolkin
Writer: Stephen King   (orig. announced: teleplay: Josef Ander-
    son; story: Stephen King)

6. Aug. 15, 1991

In Chicago, Andrews and Crewes separately close in, as Gina
arrives with Terry to hide with Gina's blind daughter (Harris).

Announced cast includes:
Francie Williams....................................Harriet Sansom Harris
And: Anne Pitoniak (Flo), Richard Whiting (Ernie), Margo Ma-
    rindale (Waitress)

Director: Allen Coulter          Teleplay: Josef Anderson
Story: Stephen King

7. Aug. 22, 1991

Francie tries to hide Harlan, Gina, Terry and new ally Crewes
with her '60s radical friends, as Andrews stages a showdown.

Francie Williams....................................Harriet Sansom Harris
Cybil......................................................Kaiulani Lee
And: Jonathan Teague Cook (Cap'n Trips), Peter McIntosh
    (Shop commander), Judson Camp (Tom Hayman), G.W.
    Rooney, Stephanie Rogers, Jason Robards III (Hippies)

Director: Michael Gornick          Teleplay: Josef Anderson
Story: Stephen King

## Sunday Best

NBC          Sundays, 7-8 p.m.

Series premiere: Feb. 3, 1991
Final telecast: Feb. 17, 1991

Lighthearted magazine about television programming, focusing nonexclusively on NBC shows, and including themed clips
from current and historic series. Host: Carl Reiner. Performers (variously, each edition): Jeff Cesario, Harry Shearer, Merrill Markoe, Linda Ellerbee. Announcer: Andre Baruch. Orig.
schduled to premiere Jan. 13. Production company name is
as onscreen.

The (TBA) Co. in assoc. with NBC Productions
Executive producer: Garth Ancier
Supervising producers: Cissy Baker, Bruce Handy
Producers: Joe Stillman, Eddie October
Coordinating producer: Sue Silkiss
Segment producers: Andy Aaron, Noah Edelson, Neil
    Krupnick, Lisa Tauger
*Ellerbee segment:* Supervising producer: Rolfe Tessem;
    producers: Carolyn Everett, John Fuller; associate

producers: Debbie Diclementi, Lucy Lehrer; for Lucky Duck Productions

*Markoe segment:* Producers: Markoe, Chuck Stepner

*Shearer segment:* Director: Rick Locke; cast: Dan Castellenetta, Kurtwood Smith, Orlando Bonner; producers: Kevin Bright, Michael Stokes

*Cesario segment:* Director: Stephen Kessler; additional cast (ep. 1): Rick Dempsey, Whitby Hertford

Associate producers: Al Kennedy, Gregney Gordon

Music: Front Page

Director: Paul Miller

Writers: Joseph E. Toplyn, Bill Oakley, Joshua M. Weinstein, Bruce Handy, Joe Stillman, Eddie October

------------

1. Feb. 3, 1991

Cameos: George Wendt, Park Overall

"Jane Pauley Spectacular": lyrics by Bill Oakley and Joshua M. Weinstein; choreographer: Diane Arnold

2. Feb. 10, 1991

Guest: Anne-Marie Johnson

3. Feb. 17, 1991

## The Sunday Comics

Fox                Sundays, 10-11 p.m.

Series premiere: April 28, 1991 *

* retitled, reformatted version of *Comic Strip Live: Primetime*

Stand-up comedians, taped before audiences at the Palace theater, Hollywood, Calif. and occasionally at other locations, plus short film pieces featuring a loose recurring pool of comics. Hosts: Jeff Altman (April 28-June 16); Lenny Clarke (June 30-on). Announcer: John Cramer.

Film-segment comics include (variously, generally two to four per edition): Bruce Baum, Brian Haley, Gilbert Gottfried, Dana Gould, Rich Hall, Dom Irrera, Carol Leifer, Mike MacDonald, Bill Maher, John Mariano, Andrew Hill Newman, Rick Overton, Paul Provenza, Jeff Schimmel, Robert Schimmel, Ritch Shydner, Carol Siskind, Fred Wolf

The Sunday Comics Band: Eric Daniels, Mitch Reilly, Bob Wackerman, Denny Fongheiser (initially); Nathan East, Michael Thompson, Danny Pelfrey, Kevin Cloud, Randy Waldman (later)

Fox Television Stations / FA Productions

Film segments produced (some editions) in assoc. with Dakota North Entertainment

Executive producers: Ken Ceizler, Joe Revello

Producer: Troy Miller

Coordinating segment producer: Eric Zappia

Segment producers (variously, several each edition): Craig Armstrong, Bruce Baum, Roger Eschbacher, Kevin Goodman, Barry Marder, T.P. Mulrooney, Ken Rogerson, Marty Rudoy, Mark Steen, Brian Stoller, Joanne Toll, Adam Tyler

Line producer (some editions): Oak O'Connor

Floor producer (some editions): Linda Zwick

Field producers (variously, two or three each on some editions): Craig K. Armstrong, Tom Sherren, Jagene Simmons, Joanne Toll, Patrick Dempsey

Associate producer: John Saade

Location associate producer (early editions): Craig Armstrong

Creative consultant: Jim Sharp

Director of photography: Clyde Smith

Segment directors of photography (variously, one or both per edition): Clyde Smith, Bill Dill

Theme (instrumental): Nathan East, Randy Waldman

Music: Dick Bright

Special material (ep. 1-8): Jeff Altman

Segment directors (variously, one or more each edition): Bruce Baum, Michael Davis, John Lawton, Rick Overton, Stacy Peralta, Clyde Smith

Director (variously): Ken Ceizler, Michael Tobin

------------

1. April 28, 1991

Franklyn Ajaye, Dom Irrera, Monica Piper, and Mark Schiff.

2. May 5, 1991

Gilbert Gottfried, Dennis Wolfberg, Pam Stone, and The Amazing Jonathan.

3. May 12, 1991

Lenny Clarke, Carol Leifer, George Lopez, and Rondell Sheridan at the Marine Corps Air Ground Combat Center, Twentynine Palms, Calif.

4. May 19, 1991

Jeff Dunham and Peanut (puppet), Jeff Foxworthy, John Mendoza, Rosie O'Donnell, and Steve White.

**preempted May 26**

5. June 2, 1991

Max Alexander, Bruce Baum, Brian Haley, Jeff Joseph, and Bobby Slayton.

6. June 9, 1991

A. Whitney Brown, Paul Provenza, Carol Siskind, and George Wallace.

7. June 16, 1991

Ritch Shydner, David Strassman and Chuck Wood (puppet), and Judy Tenuta.

8. June 30, 1991

Michael Finney, Rich Hall, Pam Matteson, and Tommy Sledge.

9. July 7, 1991

The Flaming Idiots, Diane Ford, Jack Gallagher, and Mike MacDonald. (Also orig. announced: Bobby Slayton).

10. July 14, 1991

Ellen DeGeneres, The Higgins Boys and Gruber, A.J. Jamal, and Bill Maher.

11. July 21, 1991

Wayne Cotter, Brad Garret, Dan Horn, and Cathy Ladman.

12. July 28, 1991

Jimmy Aleck, Steve Odekerk, Jeff Stilson, Michael Winslow.

**preempted Aug. 4**

13. Aug. 11, 1991

Bob Dubac, Bill Engvall, Jedda Jones, and the Raspyni Brothers.

**preempted Aug. 25**

**renewed for 1991-92; new episodes begin Sept. 8, 1991**

## Sunday Dinner

| | | |
|---|---|---|
| CBS | June 2-June 23 | Sundays, 8-8:30 p.m. |
| | June 30-July 7 | Sundays, 8:30-9 p.m. |

Series premiere: June 2, 1991
Final telecast: July 7, 1991

Comedy of the Benedict family, whose widowed, 56-year-old, printing-business patriarch (Loggia) returns from a six-month vacation engaged to a beautiful, 30-year-old environmental attorney (Hatcher) with a highly spiritual bent, causing distress and consternation among his three grown children. Locale: Great Neck, L.I.

Ben Benedict.........................................Robert Loggia
Thelma Todd ("T.T.") Fagori...................Teri Hatcher
Diana Benedict.......................................Kari Lizer
Vicky...................................................Martha Gehman
Kenneth Benedict................................Patrick Breen
Rachel, Vicky's daughter.....................Shiri Appleby
Martha, Ben's sister.........................Marian Mercer

Act III Television Venture and Columbia Pictures Television
Executive producers: Norman Lear, James Andrew Miller (also
      orig. announced: Jack Elinson)
Supervising producer: George Burditt
Producers: Stuart Silverman, Patricia Fass Palmer
Creative consultant: Charles Hauck
Executive story consultant: Marie Therese Squerciati
Executive story editor: Wayne Lemon
Story editor: Fred Graver, Vincent Ventola, Rosanne
      Allessandro-Ventola
Director of photography: Mikel Neiers
Music: uncredited/inapplicable
Theme: "Love Begins at Home" by John Davis and Ellen
      Shipley (words and music); performed by Kim Carnes
T.T.'s art by: Jane Gottlieb
Director unless otherwise noted: Jack Shea
Creator: Norman Lear

———————————————

1. "Welcome, T.T."  June 2, 1991

Ben, returning from a six-week vacation, gathers the family for Sunday dinner to break the news of his engagement to T.T.

Killer Karuso...................................Calvin Remsberg

Director: Peter Baldwin          Writer: Norman Lear

2. "Guess Who's Coming to Sunday Dinner"  June 9, 1991

Ben's daughters align with T.T. when Ben wants to print a billionaire publisher's (Lee) environmentally odious magazines.

Donald Bascomb.....................................Stephen Lee

Director: Peter Baldwin          Writer: Howard Gould

3. "In Sickness and in Health"  June 16, 1991

After having hernia surgery, Ben vents his pain and frustration on his family during his convalescence.

Writers: Marta Kauffman & David Crane

4. "My Dinner with Jack and Delores"  June 23, 1991

Vicky tries to sabotage Ben and T.T.'s relationship by inviting her deceased mother's best friend (Roberts) to dinner.

Dolores...............................................Doris Roberts
Jack, her husband...............................Paul Dooley

Writer: Fred Graver

5. "The Write Stuff"  June 30, 1991

When Rachel encounters writer's block over a school essay, working mother Vicky gets angry when T.T. gives Rachel help.

Writer: Wayne Lemon

6. "Whose House Is It Anyway?"  July 7, 1991

A famous fashion designer (Leachman) hires Kenneth as an executive, but she's interested in other than his professional talents; Diana and T.T. set a wedding date.

Georgianna Romani.......................Cloris Leachman

Writer: Marie Therese Squerciati

## Swamp Thing

| | | |
|---|---|---|
| USA | July 27, 1990-June 28, 1991 | Fridays, 10:30-11 p.m. |
| | July 5-on | Fridays, 10-10:30 p.m. |
| | (in both cases, rerun Sunday afternoons) | |

Series premiere: July 27, 1990

Science-fiction drama of a scientist accidentally changed by his bio-restorative formula from Dr. Alec Holland to an intelligent, articulate, mobile plant-creature living in a swamp near the small town of Houma, Fla., where he befriends an 11-year-old boy (Zeigler) and is challenged by would-be world dominator Arcane. Based on the DC Comics character, the basis also of the theatrical movies *Swamp Thing* (1982) and *The Return of Swamp Thing* (1989). Utility player Duhame, in several episodes, is also the series' stunt coordinator. Series went on hiatus immediately after the premiere ("The Emerald Heart"), returning Sept. 7 with ep. 2. Beginning ep. 14, the storyline was modified and the cast partly changed. New cast-member Garrison was a guest in ep. 13. Filmed in Orlando, Fla.

Swamp Thing.........................................Dick Durock
Dr. Anton Arcane..............................Mark Lindsay Chapman
Jimmy Kipp (ep. 1-13)...........................Jesse Zeigler
Tressa Kipp, his mother.....................Carrell Myers
Oboe Hardison (ep. 1-13)..................Anthony Galde
Will (ep. 14-22)..................................Scott Garrison
Abigail (ep. 14-22)..............................Kari Wuhrer

*Recurring:*

Dr. Hollister (ep. 14-22)...............................William Whitehead
Graham (ep. 14-15,17-22)...........................Kevin Quigley •
Sheriff Andrews (ep. 3,9-11)........................Marc Macaulay

• Also appeared in a different role ("Thug") in ep. 3.

Batfilm Productions & DIC Enterprises and Villa di Stefano
    Productions, BBK Productions and MTE (ep. 13-on, all
    same minus Villa di Stefano)
Executive producers: Benjamin Melniker, Michael Uslan, Andy
    Heyward, Tom Greene (latter ep. 13-on)
Supervising producer: Joseph Stefano (early in season)
Producer: Boris Malden
Executive story editors (later in season): Sandra Berg, Judith
    Berg
Story editors (early in season): Sandra Berg, Judith Berg
Director of photography: Geoff Schaaf
Music: Christopher L. Stone
Swamp Thing created by: Len Wein and Berni Wrightson
Swamp Thing bodysuit designed by: Carl Fullerton and Neal
    Martz
Developed for television by: Joseph Stefano

---

2. "The Living Image" Sept. 7, 1990

Arcane lures the bio-restorative formula from Swamp Thing
through the wiles of a lookalike of Dr. Holland's late wife
(Smith, the July 1973 *Playboy* Playmate).

"Linda Mason Holland"......................................Martha Smith
Dr. Alec Holland.................................................Lonnie Smith
Minister..............................................................Rex Benson
Real estate salesperson......................................Robert Small
Buyer.................................................................Billy Gillespie
Intruders.............................................Doc Duhame, John Hoye

Director: John McPherson
Teleplay: David Braff and Judith Berg & Sandra Berg
Story: Joseph Stefano & Judith Berg & Sandra Berg

3. "The Death of Dr. Arcane" Sept. 14, 1990

Swamp Thing must revive Arcane, killed by his latest mutant,
in order to learn from the doctor wherhere he's hidden Jim.

Coroner.............................................................Pat Cherry
Coroner's assistant........................................George Colangelo
And: Darren Dollar (Deputy), Andrew Clark (Thug)

Director: John McPherson          Story: Joseph Stefano
Teleplay: Judith Berg & Sandra Berg

4. "Legend of the Swamp Maiden" Sept. 21, 1990

Jim and Oboe witness the arrival of the mythical Swamp
Maiden, whose seduction turns Oboe into a monster.

Greg...................................................................Tom Nowicki
Swamp Maiden.....................................................Heide Paine

Director: Yuri Sivo          Writer: Lorenzo Domenico

5. "Spirit of the Swamp" Sept. 28, 1990

Arcane enlists a voodoo expert (Browne) against Swamp Thing.

Duchamp................................................Roscoe Lee Browne
Mutants.........................................Sandy Beach, Tony Marini

Director: Yuri Sivo
Teleplay: Judith Berg & Sandra Berg
Story: Michael Reaves and Judith Berg & Sandra Berg

6. "Blood Wind" Oct. 5, 1990

Tressa accidentally sniffs a potion created by Arcane, that
makes everyone she comes in contact with lust for her.

Crown Prince................................................Michael Champlin
Mrs. Spritzler....................................................Lori Logan
And: Jay Glick (Minister), Bill Orsini (Gardener)

Director: Walter Von Huene          Writer: Marc Scott Zicree

7. "Grotesquery" Oct. 12, 1990

Jim's grandmother (Helwick) lobbies city officials to clean the
polluted swamp; Jim becomes an aide at a "freak show."

Savanna Langford..........................................Patricia Helwick
Simon.............................................................Jacob Witkin
Amos.............................................................Joshua Sussman
Clair.....................................................Kathy Gustafson-Hilton
And: Christopher Alan (Kid brother), Brad Abrel, Dennis Neal
    (Workers), Judy Clayton (Gardenia)

Director: David Jackson          Writer: Michele Barinholtz

8. "Natural Enemy" Oct. 19, 1990

Jim falls gravely ill when bitten by a mutant fly.

Dr. Cass Muir...................................................Chase Randolph
Dr. Bloom...........................................................Bill Cordell
Nurse.................................................................Carolyn Jett

Director: Tony Dow          Writer: Robert Goethals

9. "Treasure" Oct. 26, 1990

Jim takes in an ailing man claiming to be Tressa's brother,
who says he's stashed stolen money in the swamp.

Eleanor...........................................................Cynthia Garris
Buckholt..........................................................Kevin Corrigan

Director: Tony Dow          Writer: Jon Ezrine

10. "New Acquaintance" Nov. 2, 1990

Jim befriends a strange and troubled little girl (Phoenix, the
sister of performers River Phoenix and Rainbow Phoenix).

Lily.................................................................Summer Phoenix
Boys.....................Chris Lobban, Danny Gura, Jordan Kessler

Director: David Jackson
Writer: Lawrence G. DiTillio and Wade Johnson & Daniel Ken-
    nedy

11. "Falco" Nov. 9, 1990

Swamp Thing encounters an assassin out to kill Arcane, who
he claims transformed him from a bird into a human. Glick
reprises his role from ep. 6.

Falco.......................................................Peter Mark Richman
And: Jay Glick (Minister), Doc Duhame (Mutant)

Director: Fritz Kiersch          Writer: Joseph Stefano

**12. "From Beyond the Grave"  Nov. 16, 1990**

At the same time Jim and Tressa share dreams about the recently deceased Mrs. Langford, they learn they're being evicted. Helwick reprises her role from ep. 7.

Savanna Langford...........................................Patricia Helwick
Everett Baxter.......................................................Brett Price
Young Tressa.......................................................Jamie Cuffe
Young Savanna.....................................................Lisa Miller

Director: Tony Dow
Writers: Wade Johnson & Daniel Kennedy

**13. "The Shipment"  Nov. 23, 1990**

When Jim is abducted while spying on Arcane's lab, his stepbrother (Garrison) bands with Swamp Thing to find him.

Announced cast includes:
Will...................................................................Scott Garrison

Director: Walter Von Huene
Teleplay: Judith Berg & Sandra Berg
Story: Joseph Stefano and Judith Berg & Sandra Berg

**14. "Birth Marks"  Feb. 1, 1991**

Tressa takes in an enigmatic young woman (new cast-member Wuhrer) who, along with an infant, are the sole survivors of a ship Arcane destroyed.

Kiefer.................................................................Doc Duhame

Director: Walter Von Huene          Writer: Tom Greene

**15. "Dark Side of the Mirror"  Feb. 8, 1991**

Arcane creates a second Swamp Thing, which murders the town's district attorney. Writer Whitehead is a recurring guest.

Eric Matthews.................................................Jordan Williams
Hammett.......................................................Danny Hanemann
Kiefer.................................................................Doc Duhame
Deputy Javert.....................................................Steve Zurk
And: John Hoye (New Swamp Thing), Bob Sokoler (Reporter)

Director: Bruce Seth Green          Writer: W.M. Whitehead

**16. "Silent Screams"  Feb. 15, 1991**

Arcane creates an invisible "stealth shield," trapping two of Tressa's friends. Champlin played a different role, ep. 6.

Melissa........................................................Catherine Haderder
Ilene..........................................................Elizabeth Fendrick
Commander Hammer...........................................Roger Pretto
Alexander.....................................................Michael Champlin

Director: Walter Von Huene
Writer: Judith Berg & Sandra Berg

**17. "Walk a Mile in My Shoots"  Feb. 22, 1991**

Arcane swaps bodies with Swamp Thing, in the hope of finding the secret of Holland's bio-restorative formula.

Gorley.............................................................Robert Reynolds
Wilkes..............................................................Doc Duhame

Director: Bruce Seth Green          Writer: Jonathan Torp

**18. "The Watchers"  March 1, 1991**

Arcane sends cyborgs (Higgs, Palmer) after Tressa and then Abigail. Co-scripter Whitehead is a recurring guest.

Lamar..............................................................Scott Higgs
And: Peter Palmer (Orvin), Steve DuMoucher (Officer Donnelly)

Director: Lyndon Chubbuck
Writers: Tom Greene & W.M. Whitehead

**19. "The Hunt"  March 8, 1991**

Will's long-lost father (Coufos) steals a rare swamp flower, a component in Arcane's plot to decimate the world food supply.

Brydon Kipp........................................................Paul Coufos

Director: Bruce Seth Green
Writers: Wade Hohnson & Daniel Kennedy

**20. "Touch of Death"  March 15, 1991**

Arcane injects a dead man (McCracken) with a serum that restores his life, and gives him the power to accelerate a victim's aging. Co-scripter Whitehead is a recurring guest.

Abraham MacCyrus.........................................Mark McCracken
Sentry hunter.....................................................Ralph Wilcox

Director: Walter Von Huene
Writers: Tom Greene & W.M. Whitehead

**21. "Tremors of the Heart"  March 22, 1991**

A treacherous employee (Bergman) uses Arcane's earthquake device to set off a tremor, trapping Tressa and Swamp Thing. DuMoucher had appeared in a different role, ep. 18.

Sienna............................................................Sandahl Bergman
Guard.............................................................Steve DuMoucher

Director: Mitchell Bock
Writers: Wade Johnson & Daniel Kennedy

**preempted March 29**

**22. "The Prometheus Parabola"  April 5, 1991**

Arcane's old adversary (Funk) arrives to try to liquidate him. Co-scripter Whitehead is a recurring guest.

J.J. Dax...............................................................Terry Funk

Director: Walter Von Huene
Writers: Tom Greene & W.M. Whitehead

**preempted April 12 and April 19**

**reruns continue through at least Sept. 6; new episodes scheduled to begin January, 1992**

# Tales from the Crypt

HBO          Wednesdays, 10-10:30 p.m.

Series premiere: June 1989

Horror anthology, inspired by the 1950s EC Comics comic book of the same name, and featuring adaptations of stories from various EC Comics. Host the Crypt-Keeper is an animatronic puppet created by Kevin Yagher. Information (incomplete) primarily from HBO.

Tales from the Crypt Productions
Executive producers: Richard Donner, David Giler, Walter Hill, Joel Silver, Robert Zemeckis
Producer: Gil Adler
Co-producers: Jennie Lew Tugend, Barry Josephson
Story editor: Alan Katz
Directors of photography include: Don Burgess
Theme: Danny Elfman
Music: Peter Allen, Gary Scott (ep. 1); Jimmy Webb (ep. 2); Jay Ferguson (ep. 5); David Mansfield (ep. 6); Cliff Eidelman (ep. 7); J. Peter Robinson (ep. 8); Nicholas Pike (ep. 9); Craig Safan (ep. 13); Alan Silvestri (ep. 14)
Crypt-Keeper sequences directed by: Kevin Yagher

---

1. "The Trap" Saturday, June 15, 1991 10-10:30 p.m.

A debt-ridden loser (McGill) involves his wife (Garr) and brother (Kirby) in an insurance scam. The half-hour directorial debut for actor Fox, following a short for a David Letterman special. Adapted from a story in *Shock SuspenStories*.

Announced cast includes: Teri Garr, Bruno Kirby, Bruce McGill, Carroll Baker, Michael J. Fox

Director: Michael J. Fox          Teleplay: Scott Alexander

2. "Loved to Death" Saturday, June 15, 1991, 10:30-11 p.m.

A fledgling screenwriter (McCarthy) uses a love potion on the girl of his dreams (Hemingway), with too-perfect results. Adapted from a story in *Tales from the Crypt*.

Announced cast includes: Mariel Hemingway, Andrew McCarthy, David Hemmings

Director: Tom Mankeiwicz
Teleplay: Joe Minion, John Mankeiwicz

3. "Carrion Death" Saturday, June 15, 1991 11-11:30 p.m.

An escaped convict (MacLachlan) heads for the Mexican border, handcuffed to a dead police officer (Deloy) and eyed by a hungry vulture. Adapted from a story in *Shock SuspenStories*.

Announced cast includes: Kyle MacLachlan, George Deloy

Director: Stephen E. de Souza    Teleplay: Stephen E. de Souza

4. "Abra Cadaver" June 19, 1991

A doctor (Bridges) takes revenge for a horrifying practical joke by conducting a life-after-death experiment on his brother. Adapted from a story in *Tales from the Crypt*.

Announced cast includes: Beau Bridges, Tony Goldwyn

Director: Steven Hopkins          Teleplay: Jim Birge

5. "Top Billing" June 26, 1991

An actor (Lovitz) plans to murder a rival (Boxleitner) for the role of Hamlet. Adapted from a story in *The Vault of Horror*.

Announced cast includes: Jon Lovitz, Bruce Boxleitner, John

Astin, Sandra Bernhard, Louise Fletcher, Paul Benedict, Kimmy Robertson

Director: Todd Holland          Teleplay: Myles Berkowitz

6. "Dead Wait" July 3, 1991

A doublecrossed con-artist (Remar) who's stolen a priceless black pearl turns to an island "medicine woman" (Goldberg) for help. Adapted from a story in *The Vault of Horror*.

Announced cast includes: James Remar, Whoopi Goldberg, Vanity a.k.a. D.D. Winters, John Rhys-Davies

Director: Tobe Hooper          Teleplay: A.L. Katz, Gilbert Adler

7. "The Reluctant Vampire" July 10, 1991

A mild-mannered vampire (McDowell) takes a job in a blood bank. Adapted from a story in *The Vault of Horror*.

Announced cast includes:
Longtooth....................................................Malcolm McDowell
And: George Wendt

Director: Elliot Silverstein          Teleplay: Terry Black

8. "Easel Kill Ya" July 17, 1991

An eccentric art dealer pays a starving artist (Roth) to paint twisted portraits of the dead. Adapted from a story in *The Vault of Horror*.

Announced cast includes: Tim Roth, William Atherton

Director: John Harrison          Teleplay: Larry Wilson

9. "Undertaking Palor" July 24, 1991

A pharmacist (Jarvis) and an undertaker (Glover) team up in a murder-for-profit scheme involving lethal prescriptions. Adapted from a story in *Tales from the Crypt*.

Announced cast includes: John Glover, Graham Jarvis

Director: Michael Thau          Teleplay: Ron Finley

10. "Mournin' Mess" July 31, 1991

An alcoholic, down-on-his-luck reporter (Weber) stumbles onto the mystery of a serial killer at a cemetery for the homeless. Adapted from a story in *Tales from the Crypt*.

Announced cast includes: Steve Weber

Director: Manny Coto          Teleplay: Manny Coto

11. "Split Second" Aug. 7, 1991

A lumberjack (Wirth) has a liaison with his boss' (James) new wife (Johnson). Adapted from a story in *Shock SuspenStories*.

Announced cast includes: Billy Wirth, Michelle Johnson, Brion James

Director: Russell Mulcahy
Teleplay: Richard Christian Matheson

12. "Deadline" Aug. 14, 1991

An alcoholic crime reporter (Jordan) gets an ultimatum to find and report a juicy homicide. Adapted from a story in *Shock SuspenStories*.

Announced cast includes:
Charlie.............................................Richard Jordan
And: Marg Helgenberger, John Capodice

Director: Walter Hill
Writers: Mae Woods, Walter Hill

13. "Spoiled" Aug. 21, 1991

A workaholic surgeon (Rachins) gets revenge on his cheating wife (Grant) and her cable-TV-installer lover (LaPaglia). Adapted from a story in *The Haunt of Fear*.

Announced cast includes: Faye Grant, Alan Rachins, Anthony LaPaglia, Anita Morris, Annabelle Gurwitch

Director: Any Wolk     Writers: Connie Johnson, Doug Ronning

14. "Yellow" Aug. 28, 1991

A WWI general and his unit corporal discipline the general's son for panicking during battle. The Douglases are real-life father and son. Adapted from a story in *Shock SuspenStories*.

Announced cast includes:
Gen. Calthrob.......................................Kirk Douglas
Lt. Calthrob..........................................Eric Douglas
And: Dan Aykroyd (Unit Corporal), Lance Henriksen (Corporal), Dominick Morra, Steve Boyum, Charles Picerni Jr., Anthony Gall, R. David Smith, John Kassir

Director: Robert Zemeckis
Teleplay: Jim Thomas & John Thomas and A.L. Katz & Gilbert Adler

**renewed for 1991-92**

## They Came from Outer Space

Quasi-syndicated*          One hour

New York City premiere: Oct. 9, 1990

* Premiered on the MCA-owned stations KCOP/Los Angeles and WWOR/New York City. In New York, primetime airings were Tuesdays, 8-9 p.m, Oct. 9, 1990-March 26, 1991; continued afterward on Saturday afternoons. Airdate order different in New York than in Los Angeles. Episodes listed below in order of production number.

Adventure-comedy of two radical-dude brothers from the planet Crouton, who, en route to attend Cambridge, decide to skip college and tool around California in a 1957 Corvette (license plate: RWE 2KL), pursued by two Air Force UFO-chasers.

Bo................................................Dean Cameron
Abe...............................................Stuart Fratkin
Col. Tom Barker...............................Allan Royal
Lt. Pat Wilson..............................Christopher Carroll
Dad................................................Victor Brandt
Mom.............................................Rosalee Mayeux

Finnegan ● Pinchuk, MTE, Hollywood Premiere Network
Executive producers: Sheldon Pinchuk, Pat Finnegan, Bill Finnegan
Supervising producers: Tom McLoughlin, Peter Baloff
Coordinating producer: Gary M. Lapoten (ep. 1); Chuck Murray

Producer: Lori-Etta Taub
Associate producer: Ellen Pinchuck
Creative consultant: Dave Wollert
Director of photography (variously): Michael Hofstein, Clinton Doughterty
Music: Gary Stockdale
Theme: "They Came from Outer Space" by Gary Stockdale & Marie Cain (words and music); performers uncredited
Creator: Tom McLoughlin

———————————————

TC 0501. "They Came from Outer Space"

The guys flee gangsters and the military when they arrive on earth and hook up with a blonde (Knight) on the run.

Karin..............................................Tuesday Knight
Jordan.............................................Harris Laskawy
Sheriff............................................Beau Billingslea
Quincy..............................................Paul Short
And: Delia Salvi (Waitress), Catherine Dao (Tech)

Director: Sidney Hayers          Story: Tom McLoughlin
Teleplay: Tom McLoughlin and Peter Baloff & Dave Wollert

TC 0502. "The Beauty Contest"

In the small town of Miranda, the guys judge a beauty contest.

Polly Peckham........................................Leah Lail
Mayor Duffy.....................................William Lanteau
Charlie Hawkins..................................Johnny Dark
Sheriff Meecham..................................Jeff Doucette
George Lockhart...................................Stuart Nisbet
John Peckham.......................................Paul Brinegar
Red Baxter..........................................Robert Keith
And: Jocelyn Seagrave (Molly Meecham), Patty Burtt (Dolly Duffy), Geri Betzler (Holly Hawkins)

Director: Bruce Bilson     Writers: Peter Baloff & Dave Wollert

TC 0503. "Undressed for Success"

While working backstage at a male strip club, the guys help a law student/stripper (Johansson) decide between two women.

Doug/"Legal Eagle".............................Paul Johansson
Toni.................................................Starr Andreeff
Kimberly........................................Julie Ann Lowery
Ramona............................................Fern Fitzgerald
And: Mary-Ellen Dunbar (Melissa), Sky Anderson (Bouncer), LaRue Stanley, Rosalie Claudio (Ladies)

Director: Chuck Bowman          Writer: Tony Reitano

TC 0504. "Rodeo Romeos"

Bo dreams he and Abe have a New Mexico rodeo adventure.

Willie Tyrell..............................George "Buck" Flower
Julia Clearwater.................................Elaine Bilstad
Ellen Clearwater...................................Bettina Bush
George Clearwater..................................Ivan Naranjo
J.M. Berkhardt......................................Steve Welles
And: Jon Sharp (Roy), Chip Campbell (Rodeo hand)

Director: Sidney Hayers
Writer: Paul Chitlik & Jeremy Bertrand Finch

TC 0505. "The Legend"

In Las Vegas, Abe thinks he's a famous Elvis-type singer (Hochberg). Dunbar played a different role in ep. 0503.

| | |
|---|---|
| Cassandra | Debi A. Monahan |
| Tony Maroni | Peter Iacangelo |
| Billy Bob | Kent Perkins |
| Telly Martin | Jack Carter |
| Psychiatrist Dr. Kendall | Marvin Kaplan |
| Clerk | Thomas C. Garner |
| Carney | Daily Pike |
| Ginger | Lori A. Fox |

And: Steve DeVorkin (Photographer), Richard Hochberg (Arlen Frazier #1), Robert Kim (Arlen Frazier #2), Robert Gentili (Casino manager), Mary-Ellen Dunbar (Woman), Stephen Burrell (Roulette player)

Director: Jefferson Kibbee
Writers: Peter Baloff & Dave Wollert

TC 0506. "Something Personal"

Through the personals, Bo and Abe are captivated and captured by a busty dominatrix (Burch).

| | |
|---|---|
| Melvin | Doug Dale |
| Patty | Llyn Llewelyn |
| "Sarge" Butkus | Tracey Burch |
| Jessica | Caroline Williams |

And: Ron Pearson (Waiter), Jennifer Van Buskirk (Surfer girl)

Director: Dennis Donnelly
Writers: Peter Baloff & Dave Wollert

TC 0507. "School Fools"

The guys enroll at the newly co-ed Cambridge School for Girls (in California) and join the basketball team.

| | |
|---|---|
| Miss Baron | Jo Ann Dearing |
| Wendy | Brooke Theiss |
| Norma | Debbie Barker |

Director: Sidney Hayers    Writers: Peter Baloff & Dave Wollert

TC 0508. "Tennessee Lacey"

On the boys' mutual birthday, they find themselves up against a biker chick (Whitman) and a UFO-tabloid publisher (Kaiser). No teleplay credit given.

Announced cast includes:

| | |
|---|---|
| Quincy Sullivan | Brian Kaiser |
| Tennessee Lacey | Kari Whitman |
| Tracey | Terri Hendrickson |

Director: Chuck Bowman    Story: Dan Levine & Peter Baloff

TC 0509. "Trading Faces"

In Beverly Hills, a crooked, soon-to-be-sentenced millionaire who looks exactly like Bo tries to trick his double into prison.

| | |
|---|---|
| Max Travis | Dean Cameron |
| Julie Carter | Andrea Elson |
| Laura Travis, Max's wife | Teresa Ganzel |
| Gerta | Christina Whitaker |
| Conky Young | Sara Ballantine |

And: Robert Casper (Maitre d'), Kim Maxwell (Nirvana), Julian Stone (Jeweler), Mitch Hara (Salesperson), Frank Simmons (Waiter), Rick Garia, Michael Halberg (Cops), David Benbow (Security guard)

Director: Sidney Hayers
Writers: Tracy Newman & Jonathan Stark

TC 0510. "Mr. Geek"

In a plot to help a polite, unimposing wrestler (Gibb) get his girl, the guys go into the ring against "The Executioner."

Announced cast includes:

| | |
|---|---|
| Mr. Geek | Don Gibb |
| The Executioner/Wreck Riley | Tony Longo |
| Athena | Rose Nevin |
| George | Pepper Martin |

Director: NA    Writer: NA

TC 0511. "Ads 'R Us"

The guys become consultants to a toy company.

| | |
|---|---|
| Rod Smeckles | Ron Masak |
| Hodge Blakely | Jonathan Schmock |
| Doreen | Cathy McAuley |
| Melody | Stacey Cortez |
| Wanda | Jodi Russell |
| Tammy-Lynne | Kathy Hartsell |

Claire Berger (Waitress), Charles C. Meshack (Cashier)

Director: Chuck Bowman
Writers: Peter Baloff & Dave Wollert

TC 0512. "Animal Magnetism"

After feigning insanity to try to avoid jail, the arrested brothers wind up in a mental hospital, injected with truth serum.

| | |
|---|---|
| Art Decko | Charlie Brill |
| Nurse Crockett | Pamela Brull |
| Carol | Ruth Buzzi |
| Peterson | John Fiedler |

And: Mark Holton (Frank), Elizabeth Keifer (Paula), Eva LaRue (Juanita Gillespie), Adriane Rogers (Becky)

Director: Dennis Donnelly
Writers: Antoinette Stella & Thomas Sheeter

TC 0513. "High Five"

The guys take over a small, failing, independent TV station and make it successful. The character name "Bill Rabkin" is an in-joke reference to the supervising producer of *She-Wolf of London*, from the same production company.

| | |
|---|---|
| Kate McCord | Barbara Brighton |
| Mimi | Catherine Carlen |
| Westbrook Kensington | I.M. Hobson |
| Dino Manze | Joe Marinelli |
| Bill Rabkin | Barry Pearl |

And: Susie Singer (Tina), Debbie Naughton (Tanya), Eric Poppick (Squeezemier), Eugene Williams (Store manager)

Director: Gary Walkow
Teleplay: Jeffrey Peter Bates and Peter Baloff & Dave Wollert
Story: Jonathon Torp & Tom Chapman and Peter Baloff & Dave Wollert

TC 0514. "Cozy Cove"

An old map, indicating a buried treasure where a yacht club now stands, prompts the guys to work there while searching. Naughton played a different role last episode.

Announced cast includes:
Jeffrey....................................................Jordan Brady
Elizabeth Baldwin........................................Karen Person
And: Ron Ulstad (Smythe), Jim Whittle (Man), Franklin Cover (Renick), Debbie Naughton (Mrs. Smythe)

Director: Dennis Donnelly
Teleplay: Peter Baloff & Dave Wollert
Story: Peg Mohone & Jack Shapiro and Peter Baloff & Dave Wollert

TC 0515. "Look Who's Barking"

Via telepathic communication, the guys "talk with" and help save a famous movie dog, Oscar, from his owner (Wayne, the son of late actor John Wayne).

Harry Miller..............................................Tom Henschel
Detective Martin.......................................Darrow Igus
Voice of Oscar............................................Bob Ridgely
Voice of Bushman the gorilla................Edgar Small
Lester Kerwick..........................................Patrick Wayne
Cindy...................................................Pamela Winslow
And: Cindy Brooks (Marianne), Howard French (Sheriff), Anthony Russell (Cassidy), John Lykes (Ace)

Director: Jefferson Kibbee
Teleplay: Peter Baloff & Dave Wollert
Story: Howard Friedlander & Ken Peragine and Peter Baloff & Dave Wollert

TC 0516. "Hair Today, Gone Tomorrow"

Bo and Abe become hair-styling stars, to the consternation of the embezzling salon owners (Polic, Currie).

Val Vincent..............................................Henry Polic II
Sylvia Vincent........................................Sondra Currie
Rene..........................................................Halle Berry
And: Rick Lieberman (Tab), Robin Greer (Fana Forrest), Penelope Crabtree (Mrs. Weston), Bobbi Phillips (Mrs. Morley), Judi Lynne Alley (Mrs. Stein)

Director: Chuck Bowman
Teleplay: Peter Baloff & Dave Wollert
Story: Frank Dandridge and Peter Baloff & Dave Wollert

TC 0517. "Play Doctor"

The guys help a pretty diet doctor expose plagiarists who appropriated her research.

Dr. Traif..................................................Barry Dennen
Desk clerk...................................................Jim Jansen
Dr. Felicia Ramsey.............................Karen Lynn Scott
Janine Gregor.........................................Brenda Thomson
Dr. Milshick.............................................Dick Yarmy
Dr. B.L. Hinten (misspelled "Hinton" in end-credits)...........................Louan Gideon
Dr. H.J. Pretzel......................................Jenilee Harrison
Cop...........................................................Bo Sabato
And: Kathy Hartsell (Call girl), Carl Ciarfalio (Bruno)

Director: Dennis Donnelly
Teleplay: Peter Baloff & Dave Wollert
Story: Stephen Lord and Peter Baloff & Dave Wollert

TC 0518. "Double Jeopardy"

As detectives (company name: Snoop Brothers), the guys investigate the theft of a rich couple's (Faison, Cattell) jewelry.

Connie Watkins........................................Nadia Capone
Doreen Dorrick....................Christine Cattell (Cathy McAuley orig. announced)
Donald Dorrick.........................................Matthew Faison
Mrs. Rutherford............................Kim Morgan Greene
And: Ace Mask (Jarvis), Dina Sherman (Daphne), George Woods (Capt. Potter), David Shelton (Bishop Harvey)

Director: Gary Walkow
Teleplay: Peter Baloff & Dave Wollert
Story: George Gilbert & Gregg Sherman and Peter Baloff & Dave Wollert

TC 0519. "Sex, Lies and UFOs, Part 1"

On a woodsy getaway, the guys encounter breathtaking female aliens who must mate-and-kill to repopulate their planet.

Shtarka..................................................Debrae Barensfeld
Kitten......................................................Kendra Booth
Ranger Binkley...........................................Tim Dunigan
Betty.........................................................Terry Ivens
And: Sharon Lee Jones (Shpilka), Lisa Melilli (Shneka), Natalie Lennox (Roger), Preston Scott Lee (Robber)

Director: Dennis Donnelly
Writers: Peter Baloff & Dave Wollert

TC 0520. "Sex, Lies and UFOs, Part 2"

Bo must keep Abe from marrying an alien (Melilli), after his lovemaking of which Abe will turn green and die. Guest Smith is the July 1973 *Playboy* Playmate.

Neville Nessen...........................................John Astin
Shtarka..................................................Debrae Barensfeld
Shpilka................................................Sharon Lee Jones
Monica Bates...........................................Tawny Kitaen
And: Lisa Melilli (Shneka), Martha Smith (Vicki McVicker), Milton Demel (Henry), Jerry Tullos (Willoughby)

Director: Dennis Donnelly
Writers: Peter Baloff & Dave Wollert

# thirtysomething

ABC                    Tuesdays, 10-11 p.m.

Series premiere: Sept. 29, 1987
Final telecast: Sept. 3, 1991

Ensemble drama of young urban professional friends and families, in a Philadelphia suburb. The ad agency for which Michael works: DAA (Drentell, Ashley & Arthur). Co-stars Olin and Wettig are husband and wife, as are co-creator Zwick and co-story editor Godshall; Harris is married to *Equal Justice* cast-member Cotter Smith. Title is as onscreen.

Advertising executive Michael Steadman....................Ken Olin
Hope Murdoch Steadman, his wife...........................Mel Harris
Photographer Melissa Steadman, his cousin....Melanie Mayron
Advertising executive Elliot Weston...............Timothy Busfield
Nancy Krieger Weston, his wife.........................Patricia Wettig
City Hall administrator Ellyn Warren...................Polly Draper
English professor Gary Shepherd.........................Peter Horton

*Recurring:*
DAA head Miles Drentell
   (ep. 3,5-6,9,16,18-19,21,23)....................David Clennon
Susannah Hart, Gary's wife (ep. 4,15,18)......Patricia Kalember

Billy Sidel, Ellyn's fiance/husband
   (ep. 8,10-16-17,20)....................................Erich Anderson
Janey Steadman, Hope and Michael's
   daughter (ep. 1,4-6,10-11,14,
   16-17,19-22)................................Brittany/Lacey Craven
Ethan Weston, Nancy and Elliot's son
   (ep. 1,4,5,7,9-10,13-14,16-17,19,23)..............Luke Rossi
Brittany Weston, their daughter
   (ep. 4-5,7)..........................Jordana "Bink" Shapiro
   (ep. 9-10,13-14,16-17,19))........................Lindsay Riddell
Angel (ep. 2,5,9-10,18-19,21)............................Andra Millian
Peter Montefiore (ep. 5,10,18)..........................Peter Frechette
Mark Harriton (ep. 5,10,21)..................Richard Cummings, Jr.

The Bedford Falls Co. in assoc. with MGM/UA Television
Executive producers: Marshall Herskovitz, Edward Zwick
Supervising producer: Scott Winant
Producers: Ellen S. Pressman, Richard Kramer, Ann Lewis
   Hamilton, Joseph Dougherty
Coordinating producer: Lindsley Parsons III
Associate producer: Jeanne Byrd Hall
Story editors: Liberty Godshall, Winnie Holzman
Executive story consultant: Susan Shilliday (early in season)
Director of photography: Kenneth Zunder
Melissa's photo art by: Deborah Roundtree
Music: Stewart Levin
Theme (instrumental): W.G. Snuffy Walden & Stewart Levin
Creators: Marshall Herskovitz & Edward Zwick

---

1. "Prelude to a Bris"  Sept. 25, 1990

Hope gives birth to a son, Leo, and Michael confronts his Jewish faith when the issue of a bris (ritual circumcision) arises.

Barbara Steadman, Michael's mother...............Barbara Barrie
Dr. Ben Teitleman..................................................Alan King
Catherine................................................................Robin Morse
Dr. Silverman.................................................Patricia Heaton
Rabbi Frankel..................................................Philip Sterling
And: Joshua Smith (Young Leo), Janet Borrus (Pregnant lady)

Writer-director: Richard S. Kramer

2. "Life Class"  Oct. 2, 1990  10:16-11:14 p.m.

Nancy lacks sexual desire for Elliot, but is drawn to a fellow art student; Hope, with two children now, feels overwhelmed. Late start due to a Presidential address.

Art.........................................................................Eric Rosse
Hollis.................................................................Holly Fulger
Dr. Silverman.................................................Patricia Heaton
Model............................................................Deborah D'Allessio
DAA drones.............................Malcolm Groome, Una Kim
   Also orig. announced: Christopher Curry (Dr. Eilertson)

Director: Scott Winant          Writer: Winnie Holzman

3. "Control"  Oct. 9, 1990

When Melissa photographs Miles for a magazine article, the two begin to date; Ellyn and her old boyfriend Jeffrey decide to move in together. Gilliland, reprising his role from past seasons, is the husband of Designing Women co-star Jean Smart.

Jeffrey Milgrom...........................................Richard Gilliland
Jerry..........................................................Christopher Duncan

Director: Ellen S. Pressman          Writer: Ann Lewis Hamilton

4. "The Distance"  Oct. 16, 1990

Gary's wife (Kalember, reprising her role from last season) is offered a job in New York; Ellyn has doubts about her relationship with Jeffrey. Gilliland reprises his role from ep. 3.

Jeffrey Milgrom...........................................Richard Gilliland
Kate.............................................................Elizabeth Kemp
Judge Allen....................................Beverly Hope Atkinson
Gail...................................................................Lauren Tom
   Also orig. announced:
   Anthony Thomas Mitchell (Security guard)

Director: Melanie Mayron          Writer: Joseph Dougherty

5. "The Haunting of DAA"  Oct. 30, 1990

As Michael struggles to comply with Miles' directive to trim the DAA staff, he's visited by the ghost of an agency founder. Fulger reprises her role from ep. 2.

Hollis.................................................................Holly Fulger
Janitor.................................................................John Ingle
Kevin.................................................................Neal Lerner
Hairless party-goer....................................David Snizek
And: Sean Morgan (Frog), Patty Toy ("I'm Madonna!")

Director: Joseph Dougherty          Writer: Ann Lewis Hamilton

**preempted Nov. 6**

6. "The Guilty Party"  Nov. 13, 1990

A flustered Hope plans a surprise birthday party for Michael.

Electra.................................................................Renee Taylor
Ernest.................................................................Andrew Lauer
Janusz..............................................Vladimir Skomarovsky
Preceptor.....................................................Deborah Mooney
Miss Jackie....................................................Heidi Swedberg
Wattanabe...................................................Rodney Kageyama
Students................................Leila Kenzl, Amy Moore Davi
Grendel (dog)........................................................Maxx

Director: Norman Seef          Writer: Winnie Holzman

**preempted Nov. 20**

7. "Photo Opportunity"  Nov. 27, 1990

Melissa is torn between family and job when her mom (Newman) is badly hurt just as Melissa's offered her biggest gig. Guest Holzman is one of the series' story editors.

Elaine, Melissa's mom......................................Phyllis Newman
Jill, Melissa's sister................Gail Mayron a.k.a. Gale Mayron
Brendan Norris.................................................Joseph Maher
Assistant.........................................................Nicholas Miscuso
Expectant grandma.................................Dianne Turley Travis
Ms. Alexander...............................................Roberta Wallach
And: Cynthia Frost (Aunt Muriel), Anna Berger (Lotte Strauss),
   Douglas Dirkson (Irvin Nessel), Tom Klunis (Sheldon Tei-
   tler), Winnie Holzman (Sherry Eisen)

Director: Ellen S. Pressman          Writer: Racelle Rosett Schaefer

8. "Never Better"  Dec. 4, 1990

Gary and Ellyn begin an unlikely friendship, and Ellyn is drawn to a man (new recurring guest Anderson) she'd dated just once, years before.

Claire.................................................................Jill Novick
Therapist.......................................................Frank DiElsi

Director: Ann Lewis Hamilton          Writer: Joseph Dougherty

9. "Guns & Roses"  Dec. 11, 1990

Nancy's problems with her therapy take a toll on her kids; Elliot becomes envious when Michael gets an award nomination.

Group leader.......................................................Laura Owens
Ted Brunel.....................................................Joseph Brutsman
And: Carey Eidel (Man), Sally Prager (Young woman)

Director: Ken Olin                     Writer: Liberty Godshall

10. "Happy New Year"  Dec. 18, 1990

At Michael and Hope's New Year's Eve party, the guests reflect and ruminate, and Ellen receives a mysterious phone call.

Patsy Klein....................................................Mary Kay Place
Russell.....................................................David Marshall Grant
Melody Klein....................................................Heather McComb
Kate Harriton........................................................Cynthia Bond

Director: Victor Du Bois              Writer: Richard Kramer

**preempted Jan. 1**

11. "Melissa and Men"  Jan. 8, 1991

Melissa's joy over a gallery show of her photographs is short-lived when she discovers it chronicles her failed relationships.

Cindy...............................................................Noelle Parker
Leonard..............................................................Mark Nelson
Lee Owens, Melissa's estranged boyfriend.............Corey Parker
Young Melissa....................................................Alexandra Lee
And: David Glasser (Young Leonard), Kristen Trucksess (DAA person), Siobhan McCafferty (Debbie), Valerie Long (Fan)

Director: Randall Miller               Writer: Winnie Holzman

12. "Advanced Beginners"  Jan. 22, 1991

After Ellyn and Billy decide to live together for a week, Billy's old flame (Godshall, a series story editor) suddenly arrives.

Madison Arnold...............................................Liberty Godshall
Dr. Rawlings.......................................................Bruce Winant
Mr. Gomez..........................................................Adrian Sparks
Person in elevator.........................................Norma MacMillan
And: April Ortiz (Lina), Josh Richman (City clerk), Maureen Kelly (City official), William Vincent Kulak (Administrator)

Director: Deborah Reinisch
Writers: Liberty Godshall and Winnie Holzman

13. "Sifting the Ashes"  Feb. 5, 1991

Nancy prepares for a final round of chemotheraphy; Elliot, in his hometown, stirs up old conflicts with his mother (Brennan).

Margaret Weston...............................................Eileen Brennan
Tommy........................................................................Jeff Perry
Father Tearney..............................................Richard Brestoff
Sally.........................................................................Cecile Callan
Susie...............................................................Alexandra Johnson
And: Kathleen McMartin (Anna), Colin Drake (Wohlman), Mari (Receptionist), King Moody (TV evangelist)

Director: Martin Nicholson
Writers: W.H. Macy & Steven Schachter and Joseph Dougherty

14. "Second Look"  Feb. 12, 1991

Nancy's second-look surgery shows her cancer is in remission; Gary, on the way to the hospital visit her, is killed in a car accident on the Schuylkill Expressway when a tractor-trailer's wheels lock up. Heaton reprises her role from ep. 2.

Eleanor Krieger, Nancy's mother..................Elizabeth Hoffman
Dr. Silverman........................................................Patricia Heaton
Nurses..................Cheryl Carter (Kathleen McMartin also orig. announced)

Director: Ken Olin                    Writer: Ann Lewis Hamilton

15. "Fighting the Cold"  Feb. 19, 1991

On the evening after Gary's funeral, the group tries to comfort a hostile Susannah.

Writer-director: Joseph Dougherty

16. "The Difference Between Men and Women"  Feb. 26, 1991

The guys throw a bachelor party for Billy, and the gals try to come up with an alternative to a bachelorette party for Ellyn.

George......................................................................Chris Mulkey
Hostess........................................................................Laura Tate
Dancer....................................................................Roxanne Bell
And: Ron Kologie (Sofabed salesperson), Michael A. Nickles (Italian waiter), Cameron (Stripper)

Director: Timothy Busfield            Writer: Winnie Holzman

**on hiatus after a rerun March 5**

17. "A Wedding"  April 9, 1991

Ellyn has cold feet on her wedding day, and Billy's family harbors skepticism about her. Parker reprises his role from ep. 11.

Lee Owens.............................................................Corey Parker
Mrs. Warren, Ellyn's mother....................................Lois Smith
Mr. Sidel, Billy's father...............................................Len Lesser
Mrs. Sidel, Billy's mother...........................................Rita Zohar
Rev. Taylor.......................................................John Resenhouse
Uncle Sy................................................................Maury Cooper
And: Harriet Medin (Grandma), Lynne Charnay (Aunt Sarah), Michael Siegel (Stan), Cayce Callaway (Agnes)
Also orig. announced: Jack Bruskoff (Uncle Erwin)

Director: Scott Winant                  Writer: Jill Gordon

18. "Closing the Circle"  April 16, 1991

Gary's ghost helps Michael deal with his estate, and with a friend (recurring guest Frechette) getting AIDS-tested. The character name Larry Tate is an homage to the advertising-agency boss of Bewitched (ABC, 1964-72)

Catherine.............................................................Deborah Offner
Insurance person......................................................Phil Leeds
Claire...................................................................Madelyn Cates
Larry Tate..........................................................John C. Moskoff
Jessica...............................................Catherine Chacon Sjolund
Young man............................................................Chris Hardwick
Ad people.........Stanley De Santis, Maureen Kelly, Dave Edison

Director: Richard Kramer
Writers: Paul Monette and Richard Kramer

19. "Out the Door" April 30, 1991

Mike sides with Miles in rejecting his Elliot's ad proposal, straining their friendship and leading to Elliot's resignation.

Ernst Verdoring...............................................Reiner Schone
Jerry...................................................................Michael Ayr
Mary...............................................................Stephanie Segal
And: Warren Harris (Mark), Nick Brooks (Prop person)

Director: Mel Harris          Writer: Ann Lewis Hamilton

20. "Hopeless" May 7, 1991

Hope volunteers at a homeless shelter, and tries befriending a woman (Coy) and her daughter (Fontaine) living there.

Mary.................................................................Suzanne Coy
Alice...........................................................L. Scott Caldwell
Jenna.........................................................Brooke Fontaine
Homeless Hispanic man..............................Darryl Henriques
Doctor..........................................................Lawrence Cook
And: Wendy Rhodes (Wendy), Oscar Jordan (Clinic worker), David Correia (Guard), Paul Desmond (Homeless man)

Director: Mark Harris          Writer: Liberty Godshall

21. "A Stop at Willoughby" May 14, 1991

In a partial homage to the same-titled episode of the original *The Twilight Zone* (CBS, 1959-65), Michael's job stress, and a moral choice regarding a blacklisted actor, brings him to re-sign DAA. Film excerpt seen in episode: *Jail Bait* (1954).

Lars Durstin.......................................................Ken Jenkins
Rita..............................................................Shawn Weatherly
Randy Towers..............................................Richard Comeau
And: Dierk Torsek (Doctor), Raeann Emery (Miles' assistant), Dave Edison (DAA employee)

Director: Timothy Busfield          Writer: Joseph Dougherty

22. "Melissa in Wonderland" May 21, 1991

Melissa encounters Hollywood weirdness when she's sent there to photograph the star (Adams) of a hit TV sitcom. Guest Hamilton is the daughter of actress Carol Burnett.

Bree Ann Pratt.................................................Brooke Adams
Warren......................................................Matthew Laurance
Callie Huff.........................................................Carrie Hamilton
Daniels Diggs......................................................David Brisbin
Friendly.........................................................Mark Lowenthal
Boss...................................................................Jordan Myers
And: Nealla Gordon (Co-worker), Colleen Camp (Debrah Diggs), Harry Woolf (Guard), Casey Sander (Jack)

Director: Ellen S. Pressman          Writer: Winnie Holzman

23. "California" May 28, 1991

As their marriage narrowly avoids dissolving, Michael is interviewed by the Chiat/Day agency's Los Angeles office (where he and Elliot make up), and Hope is wooed by a Washington, D.C., group for the homeless. In-joke references are made to an agency named "Scott Winant" (the name of this episode's director), and to a "Kenny Zunder" (the series' director of photography). Guest Parsons is the series' coordinating producer.

Robert Gould Shaw.................................................David Bowe
Willa..................................................................Rosalind Chao
Fiona Simms Porter...........................................Dana Stevens
Laurence.................................Peter Henry Schroeder
Secretary (listed as "Miles' assistant," ep. 14)....Raeann Emery
Bruno................................................................Steve Broussard
"Not Nancy"..........................................................Taylor Leigh
"Not Elliot"...........................................................Michael Mitz
"Not Ethan".............................................................Trek Potter
"Not Brittany"..................................................Rhianna Janette
Wendy...............................................................Wendy Rhodes
Taxi driver................................................Lindsley Parsons III
        Also orig. announced:
        Gregory Cooke (TV commercial assistant director)

Director: Scott Winant
Writers: Marshall Herskovitz & Edward Zwick & Liberty Godshall & Susan Shilliday & Joseph Dougherty & Winnie Holzman & Richard Kramer & Ann Lewis Hamilton

**cancelled; reruns begin July 23**

# Toon Nite

CBS          April 17-24, June 5          Wednesdays, 8-8:30 p.m.
                 May 1-May 29                  Wednesdays, 8-9 p.m.

Series premiere: April 17, 1991
Final telecast: July 3, 1991

Umbrella title for a series of half-hour cartoon specials, both original and rerun. After two weeks, the series expanded to two successive half-hour specials.

**Bugs Bunny's "Overtures to Disaster"**
CBS          Wednesday, April 17, 1991  8-8:30 p.m.

Compilation: new sequence featuring Bugs Bunny as an orchestra conductor framing the theatrical cartoon shorts "Rabbit of Seville" (1950) and "What's Opera, Doc?" (1957), plus two other segments, "Sylvester's Hungarian Rhapsody" and "Baton Bunny."

Theatrical shorts voice characterizations: Mel Blanc
Voice recreations: Jeff Bergman
Other voices: June Foray, Stan Freberg

New animation story and direction: Greg Ford, Terry Lennon
"William Tell Overture" sequence director: Daniel Haskett
"Baton Bunny" directors: Chuck Jones, Abe Levitow
"Sylvester's Hungarian Rhapsody" director: Friz Freleng
Theatrical shorts director: Chuck Jones
Additional dialog: Ronnie Scheib

Warner Bros. Animation
Executive producer: Kathleen Helppie-Shipley
Producer: Greg Ford
Associate producers: Veronica Chiarito, Christopher Walsh
Music: Carl Stalling, Milt Franklyn

**Snoopy's Reunion**
CBS          Wednesday, May 1, 1991  8-8:30 p.m.

Seriocomedy of a reunion party thrown by Charlie Brown for his beagle Snoopy and siblings Spike, Olaf, Belle, Molly, Rover, Andy and Marbles. Latest of many specials based on the comic strip "Peanuts" by Charles M. Schulz. Working titles: *Your Dog is Born, Charlie Brown*; *Snoopy is Born, Charlie Brown*.

Voice of Charlie Brown.......................................Philip Shafran

Voice of Sally Brown, his younger sister.............Kaitlyn Walker
Voice of Farmer [and] Bus driver..........................Steve Stoliar
Voice of Linus................................................Josh Weiner
Voice of Lila's mother..........................................Laurel Page
Voice of Lila.................................................Megan Parlen
Voice of Snoopy [and] Woodstock......................Bill Melendez

Director: Sam Jaimes                 Writer: Charles M. Schulz

Lee Mendelson-Bill Melendez Productions in assoc. with
    Charles M. Schulz Creative Associates and United Media
    Productions/United Feature Syndicate
Executive producer: Lee Mendelson
Producer: Bill Melendez
Music: Judy Munsen

## Garfield Gets a Life
CBS          Wednesday, May 8, 1991  8:30-9 p.m.

Comedy of the lazy, manipulative, corpulent cat, as his owner,
Jon, enrolls in a self-improvement course and hits the singles
scene. Latest of many specials based on the comic strip "Garfield" by Jim Davis. Orig. scheduled for May 15.

Voice of Garfield..............................................Lorenzo Music
Jon.............................................................Thom Huge
Odie [and] Stinky [and] Announcer......................Gregg Berger
Girl in library [and] Receptionist...........................Julie Payne
Lorenzo [and] Gunner........................................Frank Welker
Mona [and] Librarian........................................June Foray
And: Kim Campbell, Kevin Campbell

Director: John Sparey                  Writer: Jim Davis

Film Roman Productions in assoc. with United Media/
    Mendelson, and Paws, Inc. / United Features [sic]
    Syndicate
Executive producer: Jim Davis
Producer: Phil Roman
Animation: Wang Film Productions, Cuckoo's Nest Studio
Music: David Benoit, Desiree Goyette
Songs: "Monday Morning Blues," by Patrick Devuona, Darlene
    Koldenhoven (words and music); performed by B.B. King;
    "Shake Your Paw" by Tim Camp (words and music),
    performed by The Temptations; "Get a Life" (writers
    uncredited), performed by Lou Rawls
Creator: Jim Davis

## preempted May 15 and May 22

## Will Vinton's Claymation Comedy of Horrors
CBS          Wednesday, May 29, 1991  8:30-9 p.m.

Clay-animated comedy of blustery schemer Wilshire Pig and
timid Sheldon Snail, as they brave a convention of the undead
at the castle of mad Dr. Frankenswine, in search of Frankenswine's Monster. Orig. scheduled for October. Working title:
Will Vinton's Claymation Halloween.

Principal voices: Tim Conner, Brian Cummings, Krisha Fair-
    child, Michele Mariana, Todd Tolces

Director: Barry Bruce
Writers: Barry Bruce, Mark Gustafson, Ryan Holznagel

Will Vinton Productions/Claymation
Executive producer: Will Vinton
Producer: Paul Diener
Director of photography: Bruce McKean
Lead animators: John Ashlee Prat, Teresa Drilling, Chuck
    Duke, Jeff Mulcaster

Reruns:

April 24: Teenage Mutant Ninja Turtle cartoons from Sept. 8,
    1990
May 1, 8:30-9 p.m.: Daffy Duck Goes Hollywood from Nov. 20,
    1980 (as Daffy Duck's Thanks-for-Giving)
May 8, 8-8:30 p.m.: The Bugs Bunny Mother's Day Special
May 29, 8-8:30 p.m.: Compilation from The Bullwinkle Show
June 5: Compilation from The Bullwinkle Show

**unscheduled preemption June 12; preempted June 17 and
June 26**

July 3: Compilation from The Bullwinkle Show

# Top of the Heap

Fox          Sundays, 9:30-10 p.m.

Series premiere: April 14, 1991
Final telecast: July 21, 1991

Comedy of an urban Chicago tenement superintendent (Bologna) trying to better his station in life by getting his dense but
good-hearted son (LeBlanc) married into money. The characters were introduced in the March 17 and April 7 episodes of
Married With Children. Orig. scheduled to premiere March 31.

Charlie Verducci..............................................Joseph Bologna
Vinnie Verducci....................................................Matt LeBlanc
Mona Mullins.........................................................Joey Adams
Rolling Hills Country Club
    Manager Alixandra Stone............................Rita Moreno
Mr. Fluffy (cat)............................................S.H. III (uncredited)

Recurring:
Security guard Emmet Lefebvre (ep. 1-3,5,6)........Leslie Jordan

Columbia Pictures Television / ELP Communications
Executive producers: Arthur Silver, Ron Leavitt
Co-executive producer: Lenny Ripps
Co-producer: Harriette Ames-Regan
Executive script consultant: Mike Scully
Executive story editor: Wayne Kline
Story editors: Johnathan Collier, Kimberly Young
Director of photography: Thomas W. Markle
Animal trainer: Scott Hart
Theme: Pop standard "Puttin' on the Ritz" by Irving Berlin
    (words and music); performed by Kenny Yarbrough
Creators: Arthur Silver & Ron Leavitt

---

1. "The Agony and the Agony" April 14, 1991 (102)

Vinnie gets a country-club job as gofer/assistant to the manager (cast-member Moreno). Faustino's character crosses over
from Married With Children.

Bud Bundy.......................................................David Faustino
Frank (orig. Hal) Clayton......................................Rod Arrants
Mrs. Epstein.................................................Mary Pat Gleason
Fred Epstein...................................................Richard Fancy
Lupe Hernandez...........................................Irene Olga Lopez
And: Greg Lewis (Gil Gilbert), Alisha Fontaine (Mrs. Gilbert),
    Anita Mann (Bee Bee), Jeff Reilly (Carlo Dupree.)

Choreographer: Diane Arnold

Director: Linda Day          Writers: Lenny Ripps & Mike Scully

2. "Behind the Eight Ball" April 21, 1991 (103)

The sucker (Jaffe) Charlie hustles at pool might be a Mafiaso. Applegate's character crosses over from *Married With Children*.

Kelly Bundy.................................................Christina Applegate
Warren Pardo..................................................Seth Jaffee
Romona, his niece........................................Pamela Anderson
Sherry, his niece.........................Heather Elizabeth Parkhurst
Arnie...............................................................Gabriel Bologna

Director: Linda Day                    Writer: Kimberly Young

3. "Stocks and Bondage" April 28, 1991 (TH-104)

Charlie borrows $10,000 from a loan shark when Vinnie overhears a "sure thing" stock tip at the club. Carlton is the July 1985 *Playboy* Playmate.

• Hal Clayton...................................................Rod Arrants
Ray...............................................................Chuck Bergansky
And: Hope Marie Carlton (Terry Lynn), Robin Angers (Gina),
    Therese Kablan (Lotus), John Hostetter (Newscaster)

• Character listed as Frank Clayton, ep. 1.

Director: Linda Day                    Writer: Jonathan Collier

4. "The Last Temptation of Charlie" May 5, 1991 (TH-101)

Believing bad guys get rich quicker than good, Charlie tries to shed his good image by selling Mr. Fluffy. Applegate reprises her role from ep. 2. Onscreen disclaimer: "The American Humane Association warns pet owners to check washers and dryers before turning them on. These appliances can be fatal to your pet."

Kelly Bundy.................................................Christina Applegate
Mrs. O'Miley.........................................Marianne Muellerleile
Deliverperson.............................................Martin Kachuck
And: Thelma Lee (Nun), K.C. Calloway (Housewife)
    Also orig. announced: Tony Steedman (Atwell)

Director: Gerry Cohen      Writers: Arthur Silver & Lenny Ripps

5. "The Marrying Guy" May 12, 1991 (TH-105)

Before a wedding at the club, Vinnie finds the bride-to-be (Ryan) was his long-ago first love, and rekindles the romance.

Tyler................................................................Jeri-Lynn Ryan
Minister.......................................................Warren Munson
Stuie......................................................................Phil Diskin
Brian....................................................................Adam Mills
Amber Spagler...................Starr Young a.k.a. Rori Starr Young
Frank..................................................................Frank Lloyd

Director: Tony Singletary
Writers: Jonathan Collier & Wayne Kline & Mike Scully &
    Kimberly Young

6. "Mona by Moonlight" May 19, 1991 (TH-106)

Vinnie has to break a prom date with the lascivious, underage Mona to escort his boss' stepdaughter (Udenio) to it instead.

Mrs. Fairchild.................................................Joan Leizman
Claudia......................................................Fabiana Udenio
Bobby Grazzo.................................................Robert Torti
Candi............................................................Christina Nigra
And: Eric Harrison (Chester), Josh Goddard (Cute guy)

Dance music: "Prom Dilly Dally" by Cooley Jackson
Choreographer: Cooley Jackson

Director: Tony Singletary
Writers: Kimberly Young & Mike Scully & Wayne Kline & Jon
    athan Collier

**on hiatus after June 9 rerun; reruns begin again July 14 for two weeks; orig. scheduled to run through Aug. 18.**

## The Trials of Rosie O'Neill

CBS         Sept. 17-Jan. 28; March 25 Mondays, 10-11 p.m.
            June 9-July 7                Sundays, 10-11 p.m.
            July 11-on                   Thursdays, 9-10 p.m.

Series premiere: Sept. 17, 1990

Drama of a former Los Angeles corporate lawyer, a blue-blood who becomes a public defender after a tough divorce from her husband and law partner, who left her for a younger woman. Recurring guest Bridget Gless is a niece of star Sharon Gless; producer Rosenzweig occasionally cameos as the mostly silent, unseen psychiatrist to whom Gless speaks in the openings; the two were married after this season's production ended.

Rosie O'Neill.................................................Sharon Gless
Hank Mitchell..............................................Dorian Harewood
Ben Meyer......................................................Ron Rifkin
Charlotte O'Neill, Rosie's mother................Georgann Johnson
Doreen Morrison, Rosie's sister.......................Lisa Banes
Kim Ginty, her ex-husband's daughter..................Lisa Rieffel

*Recurring:*
Carole Kravitz (ep. 1-15,17-18)...........................Elaine Kagan
Udell Corey, III (ep. 4,6-8,10-14,16-18)..............Geoffrey Lower
Barbara Navis (ep. 1-8,11,13-15,17-18)...............Bridget Gless
Investigator George Shaugnessy (ep. 3,5,7-15,17)....Al Pugliese
Dr. Jim Wyman (ep. 13-14,17)...................Arthur Rosenberg
Pedro "Pete" Ramos (ep. 1-2,4-6)...........................Tony Perez
JoJo "Gags" Gagliardi (ep. 1,10-11)...................Louis Mustillo
Jeff Kemper (ep. 1-4)..............................................Tim Choate
Judith Yamamoto (ep. 1-2,4)...................................Josie Kim
D.A. Linda Vargas (ep. 3,9,13-15)...................Marisa Redanty
D.A. Duncan Watts (ep. 5-6,8,18)......................Jim Knobeloch
D.A. Deb Grant (ep. 10,12,17).............................Meg Foster
Judge Spencer Martin (ep. 3,6,8,17).....................John Carter
Judge Binghampton (ep. 7,9,11)........................George Furth
Judge Cervantes (ep. 12,15-16)........................Carmen Zapata
Court clerk (ep. 1,7-8)................................Charles Champion
Bailiff (ep. 1,4,8,11)..........................................Skip O'Brien

MTM Enterprises and The Rosenzweig Co.
Producer: Barry Rosenzweig
Associate producer: Paula Marcus
Executive story supervisor: Beth Sullivan
Director of photography: Jack Priestly, A.S.C.
Artwork provided by: Tobey C. Moss Gallery; Feingarten
    Galleries (paintings by Ron Blumberg)
Consultant to the producer (later in season): Ron Danton
Music: Ron Ramin
Theme: "I Wish I Knew" by Carole King; performed by Melissa
    Manchester
Creators: Beth Sullivan & Joe Cacaci
Developed by: Barney Rosenzweig

---

1. "Starting Over" Sept. 17, 1990; Wednesday, Sept. 26, 1990
    11:30 p.m.-12:30 a.m.

To her distaste, Rosie, on one of her first cases, must defend a young unmarried mother accused of killing her newborn child and tossing the body into a dumpster.

Louise Walker...............................................Heather Fairfield
Steve Cunningham...........................................Doug Wert
Women.....................Shelley Taylor Morgan, Barbara Lusch
Judge Haggerty...............................................Anne Gee Byrd

Director: Ron Lagomarsino
Writers: Beth Sullivan & Joe Cacaci

2. "The Rapist" Sept. 24, 1990

Rosie's defense of a rapist may yield an acquittal when she uncovers fraudulent prosecution evidence; Doreen has a girl.

Gilbert Lonner.................................................Gary Swanson
Dr. Blanchette...............................................Carolyn Seymour
Todd Morrison................................................Bruce Fairbairn
And: Ron Leath (William), Claudia Wick (Nurse)

Director: Sharron Miller
Writers: Beth Sullivan & Joe Cacaci & Dawn Prestwich & Nicole Yorkin

3. "So Long Patrick" Oct. 1, 1990

Though skeptical, Rosie finds herself the victim of a voodoo curse that seems to be working.

Johann..........................................................John Calvin
Bill Abbott.......................................Gregory "Mars" Martin
Amos...........................................Abdul Salaam El Razzac
Salazar...........................................................Gregory Millar
D.A. Nordwind...................................................Martin Grey
Maria Salazar.................................................Montrose Hagins
Judge Cooper....................................................Lori Caldwell
And: Richard Grove (Officer Baxter), Reginald Ballard (Bailiff), Michael Halpin (Messenger), Dino Andrade (Paramedic)

Director: David Carson                    Writer: Josef Anderson

4. "Late Night Callers" Oct. 15, 1990

While Rosie's boyfriend (Wert) chafes at her lack of commitment, her defense of a young man accused of assault erroneously persuades the lad her interest isn't just professional. Byrd and Wert reprise their roles from ep. 1.

Julio..............................................................Tony Acierto
Steve Cunningham.............................................Doug Wert
Judge Haggerty...............................................Anne Gee Byrd
Officer Shaheun..............................................John Hostetter
Dr. Atkinson.....................................................Joe Faust
And: James R. Sweeney (Jury foreperson), Rana Ford (Salesperson), Lucy Vargas (Waitperson)

Director: Reza Badiyi
Writers: Dawn Prestwich & Nicole Yorkin

5. "Shalom" Oct. 22, 1990

Rosie defends an all-American boy accused of desecrating a Jewish cemetary, while Ben faces cutbacks and a confrontation with Hank, and Doreen has postpartum depression.

Loni Sanders..................................................Tyra Ferrell
Judge Beller.....................................................James Avery
Evan Andrews..............................................Michael Sharrett
Harriet Meyer...................................................Susan Merson

Lisa Dodd.........................................................Lara Lyon
Judge Brenda Pomaroy.....................................Selma Archerd
Ilana Meyer.....................................................Jamee Natella
Mark Meyer................................................Michael Kopelow
     Also orig. announced: Doug Wert (Steve Cunningham)

Director: Reza Badiyi
Teleplay: Nicole Yorkin & Dawn Prestwich & Joe Cacaci
Story: Kip Orgullo and Beth Sullivan & Joe Cacaci & Nicole Yorkin & Dawn Prestwich

6. "An Act of Love" Oct. 29, 1990

Rosie meets the woman (Hunt) for whom her ex-husband deserted her, and defends a man accused of killing his AIDS-ravaged companion. Ferrell reprises her role from last episode.

Bridget Kane.....................................................Helen Hunt
With: Andrew Parks
AIDS counselor...............................................Christine Healy
Loni Sanders..................................................Tyra Ferrell
Woman with AIDS..........................Gordana Rashovich
Helen.............................................................Pamela Kosh

Director: Joel Rosenzweig
Writers: Judy Merl & Paul Eric Myers

7. "When I'm 44" Nov. 5, 1990

Her 44th birthday near, Rosie defends a man (Covarrubias) accused of child rape.

Diane Phelps...................................................Lynne Moody
Craig Weisberg..............................................Richard Gates
Frank Delgado..........................................Robert Covarrubias
Ann Martinez..................................................Maria Strova
Melvin..............................................................John T. Olson
Records clerk...............................................Michael Heimos
Winkler...........................................................Steven Hack
Marshall............................................................John King
     Also originally announced: Tim Choate (Jeff Kemper)

Director: Sharron Miller
Writers: Beth Sullivan & Josef Anderson & Joe Cacaci & Dawn Prestwich & Nicole Yorkin

**preempted Nov. 12**

8. "Rosie Gets the Blues" Nov. 19, 1990

Rosie faces her first Thanksgiving alone, and defends a blues singer (Cobbs) charged with extorting money from a heavy-metal performer (Sanville) he alleges stole his song.

"Fish Fry Baby"/Luther Little.................................Bill Cobbs
Mongoose.......................................................Rick Zumwalt
King Death................................................Michael Sanville
Receptionist..................................................Malissa Novak

Songs: "The Worm and the Apple" by Terry Abrahamson; "A Million Miles from Nowhere" and "Things May Go Your Way" by Barry Goldberg and Ron Ramin, performed by Merry Clayton

Director: James Frawley                    Writer: Terry Abrahamson
(Orig. announced: "Teleplay and story by Terry Abrahamson and revised by Nicole Yorkin & Dawn Prestwich")

9. "The Gang's All Here" Nov. 26, 1990

Rosie defends a former gang-member (Slaughter) accused of

assault, and tries placating her mom by joining her social club.  Furth reprises his role from ep. 7.

| | |
|---|---|
| Sam Marshall | Sam Scarber |
| Reggie Brown | Lance Slaughter |
| Detective Yaniger | Gary Wood |
| Roscoe Williams | Derek Mitchell |
| Buffy | Sue Casey |
| Frank Fryler | Ed Evanko |
| Delivery person | Paul Roache |
| Desk clerk | Gyl Roland |
| Airline agent | Nancy Black |
| Caroline | Barbara Lusch |
| Gang-members | Kimble Jemison, Mark Adair |
| Prisoner | Lee Dupree |
| Jurors | Ron Chovance, Lisa Dinkins (Angel Harper orig. announced), Dorothy Blass |

Director: Nancy Malone          Writer: Josef Anderson

10. "Mr. Right"  Dec. 3, 1990

As she tries hard to quit smoking, Rosie defends an underage prostitute accused of killing her pimp in self-defense.  Mustillo reprises his role from ep. 1.

| | |
|---|---|
| Detective John Santos | Richard Chaves |
| Roland Cooper | Rick Lenz |
| Leah Davis | Alix Koromzay |
| Maxine Clark | Kim Braden |
| Velma Warfield | Jada Pinkett |
| And: Keenan B. Thomas (Boxer), Armand Asselin (Desk clerk), Esther Scott (Nurse), Lindsey Lombardi (Patient) | |

Director: Reza Badiyi          Writer: Joe Cacaci

11. "The Man from E.L.F."  Dec. 17, 1990

On Christmas Eve, as she's in court defending a member of the Exceptional Life Foundation (E.L.F.), Rosie considers skipping midnight Mass to avoid seeing her ex-husband, Patrick, and his new love.  Grey reprises his role from ep. 3.

| | |
|---|---|
| Sven Ingerson, E.L.F. | Paul Williams |
| Elvira Nivens | Zelda Rubinstein |
| Gabriel | William Lanteau |
| D.A. Nordwind | Martin Grey |
| Gas station attendent | John Fahey |

Director: Reza Badiyi          Writer: Josef Anderson

12. "Mother Love"  Dec. 31, 1990

The impending marriage of Rosie's ex-husband helps Rosie and Kim bond; Rosie defends a woman (Johns) who murdered her child.  Braden reprises her role from ep. 10.  Orig. scheduled for Jan. 7.

| | |
|---|---|
| Rene Bridges | Sheila Johns |
| Maxine Clark | Kim Braden |
| Tristan | Wayne Pere |
| Movers | Dale Swann, Bobby Kosser |

Director: Victoria Hochberg
Writers: Nicole Yorkin & Dawn Prestwich

13. "State of Mind"  Jan. 7, 1991

Rosie becomes romantically attracted to a psychiatrist (recurring guest Rosenberg) who might be able to help a psychotic client (McCay).

| | |
|---|---|
| Irene Hayes | Peggy McCay |
| Emily Warner | L. Scott Caldwell |
| Todd Morrison | Bruce Fairbairn |
| Dr. Eric Phillips | Marcus Smythe |
| Guard | Cheryl Waters |
| And: Naomi Caryl (Receptionist), Lacey Bevarly (Nurse) | |

Director: Sharron Miller          Teleplay: Beth Sullivan
Story: Beth Sullivan & Barbara Schiffman

14. "Time Will Tell"  Jan. 14, 1991

A shocked Rosie discovers her father has had an affair; Kim tags along with Rosie for a school project on the legal system.

| | |
|---|---|
| Thompkins | Philip Abbott |
| Barrett | Grant Cramer |
| Judge Grant Watson | Henry G. Sanders |
| Sal | Joseph Reale |
| Emilio Sanchez | Jason Miranda |
| And: Ken Del Conte (Bailiff), Judy Jean Berns (Court clerk) | |

Director: Gwen Arner
Writers: Debbie Smith & Danna Doyle

**preempted Jan. 21**

15. "Reunion"  Jan. 28, 1991

Rosie defends a man charged with torching a crack house, and at her 25th high school reunion encounters a Broadway-star old friend (Daly, Gless' former *Cagney & Lacey* co-star).  Fahey, Daly's real-life personal assistant, played a different bit part, ep. 11.  Guest King sings the theme within the episode.

| | |
|---|---|
| Vicky Lindman | Tyne Daly |
| Tobey Kalow | Carole King |
| Judith Ann Bacon | Marianne Muellerleile |
| Madeline McDaniel | Gretchen Corbett |
| Jesse Abadia | Miguel Sandoval |
| Adam Lippman | Byrne Piven |
| Bobby Reeves | Michael Anthony Rawlins |
| Kent Baker | James Bartz |
| Nancy Butler | Annie O'Donnell |
| Lynn Lombardi | Elizabeth Hansen |
| Joanie Stuart | Teri Ralston |
| Simon Christian | Dusty Rhoads |
| And: Dom Magwill, Darwyn Carson (Neighbors), Sam Goldstein (Pianist), John V. Fahey, Marina Palmiter (Fans) | |

Directory: Nancy Malone          Story: Michael Corey
Teleplay: Dawn Prestwich & Nicole Yorkin & Josef Anderson

**on hiatus until June 9, except for a rerun on March 25**

16. "Conflict of Interest"  June 9, 1991

When Hank's younger brother (Davis) is arrested, Hank is compelled to turn his defense over to a reluctant Rosie.

| | |
|---|---|
| Paul Kelly | Yaphet Kotto |
| Willie Mitchell | Kevin N. Davis |
| Malcolm | Charlie Messenger |

Director: Joel Rosenzweig          Writer: Joe Cacaci

17. "Environmental Robin Hood"  June 16, 1991

An environmental activist (Foxworth) admits to sabotaging a dangerous toxin-incinerator plant.  Guests Walker and Machado are real-life newscasters.  Orig. scheduled for Jan. 21.

Mark Roxman...............................................Robert Foxworth
John Devey.......................................................Erik Holland
D.A. John Robinson..........................................Jesse Doran
Stan Roberts.................................................George Ceres
Reporters...........................Bree Walker, Mario Machado, Terry
   Kingsley-Smith, Kriss Turner
Tommy Smith..................................................Greg Natale
D.A. Bureau Chief Morton Henderson...................(uncredited)

Director: Reza Badiyi            Writer: Barry Schkolnick
(Orig. announced writers: Barry Schkolnick with revisions by
   Beth Sullivan)

18. "Special Circumstances" June 23, 1991

When Hank is hospitalized, Rosie, solo, must handle a death-
penalty case against an abused and neglected teen.

Jamal Bell....................................................K. Todd Freeman
Judge............................................................Liam Sullivan
Dana Hayden..............................................Gammy L. Singer
Conrad........................................................Jahary Bennett
Police officers......................Dino J. D'Annibale, Terry Jackson,
   David Anthony Smith

Director: Sharron Miller
Writers: Nicole Yorkin & Dawn Prestwich

**renewed for 1991-92; new episodes begin Sept. 12, 1991**

## True Colors

Fox        Sept. 2-June 16    Sundays, 7-7:30 p.m.
           June 20-on         Thursdays 8:30-9 p.m.

Series premiere: Sept. 2, 1990

Comedy of a newlyed interracial couple in Baltimore, Md.,
their three teenage children, and the wife's live-in mother.

Dentist Ron Freeman.....................................Frankie R. Faison
Kindergarten teacher Ellen Bower Davis Freeman.....Stephanie
   Faracy
Sara Bower.....................................................Nancy Walker
Terry Freeman...............................................Claude Brooks
Katie Davis...............................................Brigid Conley Walsh
Lester Freeman..................................................Adam Jeffries

*Recurring:*
Junior Taylor (ep. 2-3,7,17)....................................Vonte Sweet

Hanley Productions in assoc. with 20th Century Fox Television
Executive producer: Michael J. Weithorn
Co-executive producer: Lloyd GarverAlan Uger
Producers: Faye Oshima Belyeu
Co-producer: Anne Convy
Associate producer: Cathy Rosenstein
Story editor: Peter Freedman
Story consultant: Regina Y. Hicks
Script consultant: Stan Seidel
Director of photography: Bryan Hays
Music (variously): Gordon Lustig, Lennie Niehaus
Theme: Lennie Niehaus
Creator: Michael J. Weithorn

———————————

1. "True Colors -- Pilot"  Sept. 2, 1990  8:30-9 p.m.

Ron's and Ellen's families try to adjust to the marriage, while

Lester befriends a turkey scheduled to become dinner.

Turkey farmer Mr. Lukins......................................Parley Baer
Delivery person................................................Joey Miyashima
Cop...............................................................Jack Lindine
Turkey from Critters of Cinema

Director: Stan Lathan            Writer: Michael J. Weithorn

2. "A Pair of Cranks" Sept. 9, 1990

Sara comes to Lester's defense when he is mistakenly accused
of stealing a pair of expensive basketball shoes.

Salesperson..........................................................J.J.

Director: Stan Lathan            Writer: Michael J. Weithorn

3. "One of the Girls" Sept. 16, 1990

Lester starts seeing things like his step-grandmother when he
starts joining Sara and her friends for mah-jongg.

Rita..................................................................Connie Sawyer

Director: John Sgueglia          Writer: Lloyd Garver

4. "A Dog's Life" Sept. 23, 1990

Katie inadvertently jeopardizes Terry's chance for a student
athletic scholarship. Originally scheduled for Sept. 16.

Penelope Atwater...........................................Ernestine Mercer

Director: John Sgueglia          Writer: Michael J. Weithorn

5. "Step Lightly"  Sept. 30, 1990

When Ron and Sara both are out of town, Terry is forced to
turn to Ellen for motherly help.

Director: John Sgueglia          Writer: Michael J. Weithorn

6. "Life with Fathers" Oct. 7, 1990

Ron befriends Ellen's ex-husband.

Leonard Davis...........................................................Paul Sand
Beverly...............................................................Jada Pinkett
And: Rose McGowan (Suzanne), Jennifer Milmore (Marcy)

Director: John Sgueglia          Writer: Anne Convy

7. "What's Wrong With That Boy?" Oct. 21, 1990

Lester is daydreaming and cartooning in history class.

Mr. Dinski.............................................................George Wyner

Director: John Sgueglia          Writer: Michael J. Weithorn

8. "Tooth or Consequences" Oct. 28, 1990

Sara converts to Ron as her new dentist, and sits in for his
vacationing receptionist.

Guest cast NA

Director: Rob Schiller           Writer: Gregory Allen Howard

9. "Soft Shell" Nov. 4, 1990

Katie falls for the much older leader (Lucas) of an environmental group.

Jonathan........................................................Joshua Lucas
And: Carol Arthur

Director: Arlene Sanford          Writer: Stan Seidel

10. "Young at Heart" Nov. 11, 1990

When a tongue-tied Lukins takes Sara to a wedding, Lester plays Cyrano for him. Baer reprises his role from ep. 1.

Lukins..........................................................Parley Baer
And: Bunny Summers, Rhonda Aldrich, Doug Cox, Monty Ash, Ed Cambridge, Troy Fromin, Alan Shearman

Director: Peter Bonerz          Writer: Peter Freedman

11. "Occasional Wife" Nov. 18, 1990

Ellen's ex (Sand, reprising his role from ep. 6) never told his aged aunt about the divorce, and begs Ellen to keep it secret.

Leonard Davis....................................................Paul Sand
Aunt Sylvia......................................................Frances Bay

Director: Peter Bonerz          Writer: Anne Convy

12. "High Anxiety" Nov. 25, 1990

Terry's invitation to interview at a West Coast college is jeopardized by his fear of flying; Ron and Ellen attend a funeral.

With: Troy Curvey Jr., Don "Bubba" Bexley, Lillian Hightower Domio, Minnie Summers Lindsey, Gail Neely, Eric Drachman

Director: Carol Scott
Writers: Peter Freedman and Regina Y. Hicks

13. "Puppet Regime" Dec. 16, 1990

The family helps Ron's cousin (Mitchell) join a puppet troupe.

Toby..........................................................Kathleen Mitchell
With: Louis Guss, Carl J. Johnson

Director: Rob Schiller          Writer: Peter Freedman

14. "Christmas Show '90" Dec. 23, 1990

A flashback to the first meeting of the Bowers and Freemans.

"Silent Night" performed by Darryl Phinnessee

Director: Rob Schiller          Writer: Michael J. Weithorn

15. "Moment of Ruth" Jan. 13, 1991

A black awards committee-member (Lifford) asks white Ellen not to appear during Ron's interviews and the awards function.

Ruth Dixon......................................................Tina Lifford
Leon............................................................Mark Nordike
    Also orig. announced:
    Thomas Webb (Father Hoskins)

Director: Ron Schiller          Writer: Regina Y. Hicks

16. "A Real Pain" Feb. 3, 1991

An hysterical Sara is hospitalized for a gallbladder operation.

Nurse Radcliffe................................................Diana Bellamy
Nurse Tanya......................................................Kavi Raz
Donald Jenkins............................................Tom Roberts Byrd
Dr. Patel.......................................................Patricia Clipper
Sonia Jenkins................................................Victoria Hoffman
Dr. Smith........................................................David Crisler

Director: Rob Schiller (Michael J. Weithorn orig. announced)
Writers: Lloyd Garver & Regina Y. Hicks

17. "The Tender Trap" Feb. 10, 1991

Dating novice Lester is torn between a plain girl (McClelland) and trying for a date with the school's most popular (Shawel).

A.J............................................................Tamika McClelland
Keisha..........................................................Saba Shawel
And: John Petlock (Pilot), Richard Penn (Co-pilot)

Director: Carol Scott
Writers: Peter Freedman & Anne Convy

18. "Opposites Attract" Feb. 17, 1991

While he's on a date, Terry's car breaks down on a back road where he had to give Katie and her friend (Pancake) a ride.

Shep............................................................John Fleck
Cletis..........................................................Pete Schrum
Howard..........................................................Sam Pancake
Chardonnay....................................................Jeanine Michelle
Cop............................................................Marvin J. McIntyre
Dog from Critters of the Cinema

Director: Rob Schiller          Writer: Stan Seidel

19. "Homies Alone" March 3, 1991

With Ron, Ellen and Terry at an awards banquet, Lester and Katie stay home alone, and get scared by a horror movie.

Officer Bolton..............................................Wesley Thompson
Officer Dehling..............................................Jim Doughan
Bellperson....................................................James MacNerland
    Also orig. announced: Patrick Gorman (Repairperson)

Director: Arlene Sanford          Story: Peter Freedman
Teleplay: Regina Y. Hicks & Stan Seidel

20. "Daughter Dearest" March 24, 1991

Katie and Ellen go on a skiing trip together, leaving Sara at home on her birthday with all the guys.

Maury..........................................................Murray Rubin
Lou............................................................Michael Fox
And: Kevin Wixted (Brett), Vanessa Brown (Waitress)

Director: Peter Bonerz          Writer: Regina Y. Hicks

21. "Matter of Principal" April 14, 1991

Ellen's suggestion of Ron as a "Career Day" role-model hits a roadblock when a parent (Brull) objects to his being black.

Mr. Warner......................................................Raye Birk
Mrs. Fairchild (orig. Daniels)...............................Pamela Brull
And: Clara Bryant (Jessica), Jared Segawa (Kevin)
    Also orig. announced: Tara Thomas (Lauren)

Director: Peter Bonerz                    Writer: William Schifrin

22. "Superman, Superego" April 21, 1991

Terry turns in an old school paper written by Katie, but his conscience bothers him after a dream sequence with God.

Roxanne...............................................Gretchen Palmer
        Also orig. announced: Greg Allen Johnson (Nixon)

Writer-director: Michael J. Weithorn

23. "Prisoners of Love" April 28, 1991

Terry and Lester are arrested after sneaking into an apartment to retrieve a precious keepsake Sara mistakenly gave as a gift.

Sadie.................................................Ellen Albertini Dow
Officer Potchski (orig. Coley).....................Vito D'Ambrosio
Bertram.................................................Rick Zumwalt

Director: Rob Schiller              Story: Regina Y. Hicks
Teleplay: Peter Freedman & Stan Seidel

24. "Favorite Son" May 12, 1991

On Ron's birthday, Ellen thinks his visiting parents (Cobbs, Dubois) dislike her because she's white.

Bernard Freeman.....................................Bill Cobbs
May Freeman...........................................Ja'net Dubois
Wayne Covington/"Butterman".....................Charles Brown
Renee (orig. Veneta) Freeman..................Cyndi James Gosset
Young Terry..........................................Jason Bose Smith
Young Lester........................................Joseph J. Bryant

Director: Rob Schiller              Writer: Kermit Frazier

**renewed; begins its 1991-92 season Aug. 22.**

## Twin Peaks

ABC           Sept. 30-Feb. 16   Saturdays, 10-11 p.m.
              March 28-April 18  Thursdays, 9-10 p.m.
              June 10            Monday, 9-11 p.m.

Series premiere: April 8, 1990
Final telecast: June 10, 1991

Absurdist, serialized drama/primetime-soap parody of FBI agent Dale Cooper's investigation of strange goings-on in a Northwest logging town, following the murder of homecoming queen Laura Palmer. Twin Peaks High School team: Scalphunters. Warren Frost is the father of series co-creater Mark Frost and of actress Lindsay Frost; Da Re is the son of actor Aldo Ray; cast-member Laurie returned as a guest in ep. 7, and to the regular cast in ep. 8; Wise left the cast after ep. 9, returning for the final episode. Exteriors filmed in Washington state.

Dale Cooper............................................Kyle MacLachlan
Sheriff Harry S. Truman............................Michael Ontkean
Shelly Johnson.........Madchen (pronounced may-chen) Amick
Bobby Briggs.............................................Dana Ashbrook
Benjamin Horne......................................Richard Beymer
Donna Marie Hayward..............................Lara Flynn Boyle
Audrey Horne, Benjamin's daughter.................Sherilyn Fenn
Dr. William Hayward, Donna's father.................Warren Frost
Diner owner Norma Jennings............................Peggy Lipton
James Hurley...........................................James Marshall
"Big Ed" Hurley, his uncle..................................Everett McGill

Pete Martell.............................................Jack Nance
Sheriff's Dept. secretary Lucy Moran...........Kimmy Robertson
Leland Palmer (ep. 1-9,21)...............................Ray Wise
Jocelyn (Josie) Packard...................................Joan Chen
Catherine Packard Martell (ep. 8-on)..............Piper Laurie *

*Recurring, all or virtually all episodes:*
Leo Johnson, Shelly's husband..............................Eric Da Re
Deputy Andy Brennan.....................................Harry Goaz
Deputy Tommy "Hawk" Hill.........................Michael Horse
Nadine Hurley, Ed's wife....................................Wendy Robie

*Other prominent recurring guests:*
Annie Blackburne (ep. 17-21).........................Heather Graham
Maj. Garland Briggs, Bobby's father
    (ep. 1-2,9-10,12-14,17,19,21)....Don (a.k.a. Don S.) Davis
DEA Agent Dennis/Denise Bryson
    (ep. 11-13)....................................David Duchovny
Windom Earle (ep. 14-15,17-21)..............Kenneth Welsh
Thomas Eckhardt (ep. 14-16)......................David Warner
Madeleine Ferguson (ep. 1-9)......................Sheryl Lee **
Phillip Michael Gerard (ep. 1,3,6-9)......................Al Strobel
Eileen Hayward, Donna's mother
    (ep. 1,10,17-21)..............................Mary Jo Deschanel
Jerry Horne, Ben's brother
    (ep. 1-2,8,14-16)..........................David Patrick Kelly
Dr. Lawrence Jacoby (ep. 1,3,10,14-15,17,21)....Russ Tamblyn
Hank Jennings, Norma's ex-convict husband
    (ep. 1,2,4-5,8,10-11,13,16)........................Chris Mulkey
The Log Lady/Margaret
    (ep. 1-2,7,11,17-18,21)...............Catherine E. Coulson
Evelyn Marsh (ep. 11-15).......................Annette McCarthy
Ernie Niles (ep. 8,10-13).................................James Booth
One-Eyed Jacks manager Blackie O'Reilly
    (ep. 1-3,5)....................................Victoria Catlin
Andrew Packard (ep. 11-12,14,19-21).................Dan O'Herlihy
Sarah Palmer, Laura's mother
    (ep. 1,2,5,7-8,10,21).............................Grace Zabriskie
Jean Renault (ep. 3-5,10,13)............................Michael Parks
Agent Albert Rosenfield
    (ep. 1-3,9,15-16)..............................Miguel Ferrer
Harold Smith (ep. 3-6)................................Lenny Von Dohlen
Vivian Smythe (ep. 8-10)....................................Jane Greer
Richard Tremayne (ep. 3-4,9-14,17,19,21)..........Ian Buchanan
John (Jack) Justice Wheeler (ep. 16-20)....................Billy Zane

*Other recurring guests:*
Asian man ("Jonathan"/"Mr. Lee")
    (ep. 1-4,6)....................................Mak Takano
Emory Battis (ep. 2-4)............................Don Amendolia
Bob (ep. 1,7-8 [all uncredited], 9,16,20-21)............Frank Silva
Betty Briggs, Bobby's mother (ep. 11-12,21)..Charlotte Stewart
Lana Budding (ep. 11-12,14,19,20)......................Robyn Lively
FBI agent Gordon Cole (ep. 6-7,18-
    19 [plus uncredited voiceover, ep. 11]).........David Lynch
The Giant (ep. 1,7,9,20-21).......................Carel Struycken
Jones (ep. 14,15,17,18)......................................Brenda Strong
Malcolm (ep. 12-13,15)...................................Nicholas Love
Man from Another Place ("The Dwarf")
    (ep. 9,16,21).............................Michael J. Anderson
Dougie Milford (ep. 10-12)...................................Tony Jay
Mayor Dwayne Milford (ep. 10-11,14,19-21).........John Boylan
Mike Nelson (ep. 7,11-13,17-19,21)...............Gary Hershberger
Nancy O'Reilly, Blackie's sister (ep. 1,3,5)...............Galyn Gorg
Ronette Pulaski (ep. 1-3,21).......................Phoebe Augustine
Randy St. Croix (ep. 14,16-17,20).........................Ron Blair
Tojamura (ep. 4-7).................................Fumio Yamaguchi
The Waiter (ep. 1,7,11,21)..............................Hank Worden

* Also as one of two performers playing Tojamura, ep. 8-9.
** Also as Laura Palmer in photos and dream sequences.

Lynch/Frost Productions in assoc. with Propaganda Films and Spelling Entertainment / Twin Peaks Productions
Executive producers: Mark Frost, David Lynch
Supervising producer: Gregg Fienberg
Producer: Harley Peyton
Co-producers: Robert D. Simon, Robert Engels, Philip Neel (latter two later in season)
Associate producer: Philip Neel (early in season), John Wentworth (later in season)
Coordinating producer: Tim Harbert
Executive story editor: Robert Engels (early in season)
Director of photography: Frank Byers
Theme (instrumental) and music: Angelo Badalamenti
Creators: Mark Frost, David Lynch

---

1. Sunday, Sept. 30, 1990   9-11 p.m.

Continued from last summer: A shot and bleeding Agent Cooper has visions of a giant; Audrey is imprisoned at the casino/bordello One-Eyed Jacks; Donna receives a strange message; Josie and Catherine are missing; a stirring Ronette sees "Bob," who apparently killed Laura.  Dedication: "To the memory of Kevin Young Jr."

Pie eater..............................................Stephen C. MacLaughlin
Doctor..............................................................Charles Miller
Harriet Hayward..........................................Jessica Wallenfels
Nurse..................................................Sandra Kaye Wetzel
Gersten Hayward....................................................Alicia Witt

Director: David Lynch                    Teleplay: Mark Frost
Story: Mark Frost & David Lynch

2. Oct. 6, 1990

Cooper learns his ex-partner, Windom Earle, has escaped from a mental asylum;  Maj. Briggs gives Cooper a message from outer space ("The owls are not what they seem"); Donna meets an eerie old woman (Bay) and her grandson (Austin Jack Lynch, son of co-creator David Lynch); Ben orders Leland killed; Deputy Andy thinks he's sterile; Audrey learns more about Laura, but is uncovered by a vengeful Blackie.

Mrs. Tremond........................................................Frances Bay
Little boy....................................................Austin Jack Lynch
Ice-bucket girl............................................................Jill Pierce

Director: David Lynch                    Writer: Harley Peyton

3. Oct. 13, 1990

Donna finds a diary of Laura's at the agoraphobic Harold Smith's house; Blackie holds Audrey hostage, and wants Renault to murder Cooper; James and Madeleine become close, to Donna's dismay; Lucy lunches with Tremayne, the apparent father of her unborn child; Dr. Jacoby undergoes hypnosis, leading to Leland's arrest.

Director: Lesli Linka Glatter                    Writer: Robert Engels

4. Oct. 20, 1990

Cooper is stymied by an unsual request from Ben Horne to save Audrey's life; Josie introduces her "cousin" Jonathan from Hong Kong; Renault kills Battis.

Clinton Sternwood.................................................Royal Dano
Daryl Lodwick.....................................................Ritch Brinkley
And: Belina Logan (Desk clerk), Claire Stansfield (Sid)

Director: Todd Holland
Writers: Jerry Stahl and Mark Frost & Harley Peyton &  Robert Engels

5. Oct. 27, 1990

Cooper and Truman stage a raid on One-Eyed Jacks, resulting in Renault killing Blackie; Leland attends his court hearing; Donna and Madeleine plot to steal Laura's secret diary from Harold Smith; Ben gets a business proposition.

Clinton Sternwood...................................................Royal Dano
Tim Pinkle.......................................................David L. Lander
Jack Racine....................................................Van Dyke Parks
Daryl Lodwick....................................................Ritch Brinkley
Sid...............................................................Claire Stansfield
Outside bodyguard..............................................Mike Vendrell
Bodyguard on stairs.....................................................Bob Apisa

Director: Graeme Clifford                    Writer: Barry Pullman

6. Nov. 3, 1990

Donna and Madeleine fear an enraged Harold Smith; Shelly and Bobby, planning on government caretaker money, hold a "welcome home" party for the comatose Leo; Cooper's hard-of-hearing boss (played by co-creator Lynch) visits to warn Cooper of threats;  Josie gets $5 million from Ben for helping to burn the mill, and leaves with Jonathan; Gerard's split-personality surfaces, with news of the supernatural killer "Bob," and a cryptic poem: "Through the darkness/of future past/The magician longs to see/One chance out between two worlds/Fire, walk with me."

Trudy...................................................................Jill Engels
Cappy.....................................................................Ron Kirk
Lounge local......................................................Leonard Ray
Brett Vadset....................................................Joey Paulsen
And: Ian Abercrombie

Director: Lesli Linka Glatter
Writers: Harley Peyton & Robert Engels

7. Nov. 10, 1990

Ben is brought in for questioning after Audrey confronts him about One-Eyed Jacks and passes the information to Cooper; Harold Smith is found hanged; having misjudged the money due them, Shelly and Bobby are cash-strapped; Bobby finds a microcassette of Leo's; Laura's killer is revealed as Bob inhabiting the body of Leland, who then kills Madeleine (who continues to appear as a corpse or in flashback, ep. 8-9); Tojamura reveals "himself " to Pete as his wife Catherine in disguise.

Tojamura/Catherine Martell...................................Piper Laurie
Singer....................................................................Julee Cruise
White horse by: Steve Martin's Working Wildlife

Songs: "The World Spins" and "Rockin' Back Inside My  Heart" by David Lynch (lyrics) and Angelo Badalamenti (music); performed by Julee Cruise

Director: David Lynch                    Writer: Mark Frost

8. Nov. 17, 1990

Norma's visiting mother (Greer) introduces her new husband (Booth), unaware he knew Hank in prison; Lucy returns, with her sister (Wilhoite); Bobby decides to blackmail the jailbound Ben, charged with Laura's murder, who also gets a tape-recorded ultimatum from Catherine; Madeleine is found dead.

Gwen................................................Kathleen Wilhoite
Louise Dombrowski................................Emily Fincher

Director: Caleb Deschanel          Writer: Scott Frost

**preempted Nov. 24**

9. Dec. 1, 1990

From a piece of Laura's secret diary, Cooper discovers he and she shared the dwarf dream (from last season), with her message in it leading to Leland/Bob's arrest and Leland's death; Catherine tricks a freed Ben into signing away the mill; Lucy, Andy and Tremayne confront each other over her pregnancy.

Mr. Zipper.......................................Clive Rosengren
Mrs. Tremond....................................Mae Williams

Director: Tim Hunter
Writers: Mark Frost & Harley Peyton & Robert Engels

10. Dec. 8, 1990

As Cooper says his goodbyes, an FBI agent arrives to suspend him and investigate the unauthorized One-Eyed Jacks affair; at the wake for Leland, the publisher (Jay) of the *Twin Peaks Gazette* argues with his brother, the Mayor; Reanult recruits Hank and Ernie to frame Cooper; Nadine, deluded that she's a teenager, enrolls in high school; Maj. Briggs, fishing with Cooper, vanishes amid light and an owl, recalling "Bob."

FBI Agent Roger Hardy.....................Clarence Williams III
Mountie........................................Gavan O'Herlihy
Vice Principal Greege............................Don Calfa
Physical Education teacher....................Lisa Cloud
Cheerleader....................................Tiffany Muxlow
Samantha.......................................Susan Sundholm

Director: Tina Rathborne          Writer: Tricia Brock

11. Dec. 15, 1990

Cooper is investigated by the FBI and the DEA; Nadine falls for teen Mike Nelson; James gets room and board for helping a beautiful blond (McCarthy); Hank confronts Ben; Tremayne becomes Big Brother to a terror (Harris); Catherine forces Josie to become her maid; Andrew Packard turns up alive.

FBI Agent Roger Hardy.....................Clarence Williams III
Reverend.....................................Royce D. Applegate
Coach Wingate..................................Ron Taylor
And: Jill Engels (Trudy), Joshua Harris (Nicky)
    Also orig. announced:
    Lisa Cloud (Phys. Ed. teacher), Nicholas Love (Malcolm)

Director: DUWAYNE Dunham          Writer: Barry Pullman

**preempted Dec. 29 and Jan. 5**

12. Jan. 12, 1991

Cooper finds cocaine at a deserted house Renault uses; Andy and Tremayne confront concerns over Nicky's past; a mentally decaying Ben has Bobby tail Hank; Dougie Milford dies of a wedding-night heart attack; supernaturally superstrong Nadine joins the wrestling team; Maj. Briggs returns.

Announced cast includes several recurring guests and:
Coach Wingate..................................Ron Taylor
Nicky..........................................Joshua Harris
And: Tony Burton

Director: Caleb Deschanel
Writers: Harley Peyton & Robert Engels

13. Jan. 19, 1991

Cooper is held hostage by Renault, but kills him with Bryson's help; Andy and Tremayne pry into Nicky's past; Catherine professes her love for Ben; James succumbs to a treacherous Evelyn; Ed and Norma succumb to each other; Nadine rescues Ed from Hank; Cooper's ex-partner Windom Earle makes a move.

Mountie........................................Gavan O'Herlihy
M.P............................................J. Marvin Campbell
Brunston......................................Will Seltzer
Dead man......................................Craig MacLachlan

Director: Todd Holland          Writer: Harley Peyton

**preempted Jan. 26**

14. Feb. 2, 1991

Cooper confides to Truman how he'd fallen in love with the wife of his then-partner, Windom Earle, who he believes killed the woman and who now takes in a revived and vicious Leo; Audrey strikes a business deal with Bobby; James realizes Evelyn set him up for her husband's murder; Josie's dangerous old lover, Thomas Eckhardt, appears.

Jeffrey Marsh, Evelyn's husband.........................John Apicella
Dead man........................................Craig MacLachlan
    Also orig. announced: Nicholas Love (Malcolm)

Director: Uli Edel          Writer: Scott Frost

15. Feb. 9, 1991

Cooper finds evidence that Josie shot him, and gets help from Pete in matching wits with Earle in a deadly chess game; Donna makes a desperate plea to save James' life; Nadine walks in on Ed and Norma; Catherine uses a helpless Josie as booty before Eckhardt. Director Keaton is better known as an actress; see also *China Beach*, Nov. 3, 1990.

Johnny.........................................Robert Bauer
Cop............................................Matt Battaglia
Bartender......................................Gerald L'ECUYER

Director: Diane Keaton
Writers: Harley Peyton & Robert Engels

16. Feb. 16, 1991

Ed proposes to Norma; James and Donna break up; Audrey meets a handsome, wealthy admirer (Zane) from her past; Earle mails a puzzle to Audrey, Shelly and Donna; after killing Eckhardt, Josie confesses to shooting Cooper and to killing Jonathan, then apparently dies in Truman's arms, momentarily disappearing with him then reappearing surreally within a dresser knob, as "Bob" and the dwarf reappear.

With recurring guests; also orig. announced: Brenda Strong (Jones)

Director: Lesli Linka Glatter          Writer: Tricia Block

**on hiatus**

17. March 28, 1991

Cooper is attracted to Norma's sister (Graham), returning to the world from a convent; Truman grieves for Josie; Donna receives a macabre family visitor; Audrey falls for Wheeler; Nadine and her teenage beau Mike Nelson check into the Great Northern Hotel; Ben hosts an environmental benefit.

Tim Pinkle.................................................David L. Lander
Model.....................................................Julie Hayek
Teen model..........................................Betsy Lynn George

Director: James Foley            Writer: Barry Pullman

18. April 4, 1991

Cooper and the Sheriff's Dept. go spelunking in Owl Cave; Truman awakens in the murderous embrace of a naked woman; Windom Earle insinuates himself into the lives of potential victims; Audrey and Donna see Mrs. Hayward meet with Ben.

Director: DUWAYNE Dunham
Writers: Harley Peton & Robert Engels

19. April 11, 1991

Cooper and Truman try to decipher the hieroglyph from Owl Cave; the Miss Twin Peaks contest gets underway; Tremayne holds a wine-tasting at the Great Northern Hotel; Cooper falls for Annie, and Gordon for Shelley; Windom Earle gruesomely leaves a victim in a giant pawn piece.

Heavy metal youth/Rusty.............................Ted Raimi
Bellhop.................................................John Charles Sheehan

Director: Jonathan Sanger
Writers: Mark Frost & Harley Peyton

20. April 18, 1991

Cooper and Truman continue to investigate the mystery of Owl Cave; Windom Earle snares Maj. Briggs; Cooper romances Annie; Donna finds no father listed on her birth certificate; Wheeler leaves, saying his partner's been murdered.

Heavy metal roadie.................................Willie Garson
Cappy...................................................Ron Kirk
Heavy metal youth/Rusty.............................Ted Raimi
Pilot.....................................................Layne Robert Rico
    Also orig. announced:
    Wendy Robie (Nadine Hurley), Gary Hershberger (Mike Nelson), David L. Lander (Tim Pinkle)

Director: Stephen Gyllenhaal
Writers: Harley Peyton & Robert Engels

**on hiatus**

21. Monday, June 10, 1991  9-11 p.m.

Cooper and Truman decipher part of the secret of the Black Lodge, and rush to save Miss Twin Peaks there; Dr. Jacoby holds a therapy session; Catherine continues her battle with the black box; Donna discovers she's Ben Horne's daughter; Audrey stages an act of civil disobedience, at a bank blown up by Eckhardt; Lucy chooses Deputy Andy; Nadine regains her senses; Cooper is taken over by Bob. Orig. scheduled as two episodes, for April 25 and May 2.

Tim Pinkle.................................................David L. Lander
Black Lodge performer..............................James V. Scott
Dell Mibbler...........................................Ed Wright
Sylvia Horne.........................................Jan D'Arcy
Trudy....................................................Jill Engels

Heidi.....................................................Andrea Hays
Security guard........................................Arvo O. Katajisto
Caroline................................................Brenda E. Mathers

Songs: "Sycamore Trees" by David Lynch (words) & Angelo Badalamenti (music); performed by The Legendary Jimmy Scott

Directors: Tim Hunter (first hour); David Lynch (second hour)
Writers: Barry Pullman (first hour); Mark Frost & Harley Peyton & Robert Engles (second hour)

## Uncle Buck

| CBS | Sept. 10-Nov. 12 | Mondays, 8-8:30 p.m. |
| | Nov. 16- Nov. 23 | Fridays, 8-8:30 p.m. |
| | Jan. 26-March 9, April 6 | Saturdays, 8-8:30 p.m. |

Series premiere: Sept. 10, 1990
Final telecast: April 6, 1991

Comedy of an ill-mannered, irreverent uncle heading his late brother's household. Based on the 1989 movie. Recurring guest Meadows appears in the opening credits as a cast-member on her episodes only. For unspecified reasons, the production company would not supply titles, except for one.

Uncle Buck...........................................Kevin Meaney
Tia (16).................................................Dah-ve Chodan *
Miles (9)................................................Jacob Gelman
Maizy (6)..............................................Sarah Martineck

*Recurring:*
Mrs. Hogoboom (ep. 1,3,8,11-12,15)..............Audrey Meadows
Skank (ep. 1,4-6,10,12,14,16).......................Dennis Cockrum
Rafer Freeman
    (ep. 4,6,10-11)......Thomas Mikal Ford a.k.a. Tommy Ford
Lucy (ep. 2,7,12,14,17)......................................Rachel Jacobs
Darlene (ep. 3,11,16)...........................................Laurel Diskin

* Spelling as confirmed by production company; CBS press materials and *TV Guide* spell her first name Dah-Ve.

Verbatim Productions in assoc. with Universal Television, an MCA Co.
Executive producers: Tim O'Donnell, Richard Gurman
Producers: Rick Newberger (ep. 2-on), Jack Seifert
Associate producer: Lori Motyer
Executive script consultant: Kevin Abbott
Director of photography: George LaFountaine (ep. 1); Wayne Kennan
Theme: "Uncle Buck" by Steve Dorff (music), John Bettis (lyrics); performed by Ronnie Milsap
Music: Steve Dorff
Director unless otherwise noted: James Widdoes
Developed by: Tim O'Donnell

---

1. Sept. 10, 1990

Buck confronts the kids' no-nonsense grandmother (Meadows), who reluctantly agrees to let him live with and care for them, though she vows to pop in with a watchful eye.

Ms. Crappier.........................................Lu Leonard
Doreen Douche.......................................Jill Jacobson
David....................................................David Coburn

Director: John Tracy            Writer: Tim O'Donnell

2. Sept. 17, 1990

When scantily dressed Tia gets promoted on her first day of work at a boutique, Buck gets suspicious.

Julius...................................................................Carmen Filpi
Jack......................................................................Lou Richards
Laura..................................................................Brooke Theiss
And: Ryan Todd (Boy), Raffaella Commitante (Mother)

Writer: Caryn Lucas

3. "The Grey Fox" Sept. 24, 1990

Buck's old flim-flam pal (Carney) comes to visit, and romances Mrs. Hogoboom. A rare series appearance together for Carney and Meadows, of *The Honeymooners*.

Pete..........................................................................Art Carney
Mechanic..................................................Michael Gilbert Lewis

Writers: Tim O'Donnell & Richard Gurman

4. Oct. 1, 1990

Contest-winner Buck co-announces a Chicago Cubs baseball game, and turns the city against him with a caustic comment. Caray is the real-life announcer; Jacobson, a WBBM anchor.

Himself...................................................................Harry Caray
Himself.............................................................Walter Jacobson
Jason.......................................................................Scott Duffy

Writer: Rick Newberger

5. Oct. 8, 1990

In a deal to prevent Tia from dropping out, Buck must earn the high-school diploma he never received. Leonard reprises her role from ep. 1.

Ms. Crappier..........................................................Lu Leonard

Director: Art Dielhenn          Writer: Kevin Abbott

6. Oct. 15, 1990

Buck's old girlfriend, a flight attendant, visits and rekindles the old flame.

Stacy.............................................................Deborah Harmon

Writer: Rick Newberger

7. Oct. 22, 1990

Tia tries to play matchmaker between Buck and her English teacher (Bergan).

Ms. Gail Wilcox.......................................Judith-Marie Bergan
Louis.........................................................................Eric Taslitz

Director: Art Dielhenn          Writer: Warren Bell

*unscheduled preemption Oct. 29*

8. Nov. 5, 1990

Mrs. Hogoboom is oddly ecstatic after her house burns down.

Bernie...............................................................Robert Costanzo

Director: Art Dielhenn          Writer: Kevin Abbott

9. Nov. 12, 1990

Tia makes friends with her bookish algebra tutor (Ponce), and gets arrested with her shoplifting at the mall. Dedication: "In Loving Memory of Dr. Ben Gurman, 1910-1990."

Julie.....................................................................LuAnne Ponce
Desk Sgt. Levine........................................F. William Parker
Mrs. Hollander.......................................................Ann Gillespie
Mr. Hollander.........................................................Murphy Dunne

Writer: Caryn Lucas

10. Nov. 16, 1990

Buck and his buddies combine their race-track winnings to buy a racehorse. Orig. scheduled for Nov. 19.

Kroger.................................................................Sam Anderson
Wanda.................................................................Colleen O'Hara

Writer: Rick Newberger

11. Nov. 23, 1990

Buck becomes Maizy's "Bluebell Mom" so she can join the neighborhood troop of Girl Scouts-like "Bluebells."

"The Doc"/Bernard..........................................Beans Morocco
Kimberly....................................................................Taylor Fry

Director: John Tracy          Writer: Warren Bell

*on hiatus*

12. Jan. 26, 1991

So he can go fishing, Buck reluctantly leaves Tia in charge of the household for one night. Orig. scheduled for Dec. 7.

Detective Chapman...............................Jeffrey Allan Chandler
Ed Hartley..................................................................Bill Erwin
Tommy...................................................................Nicholas Katt

Writer: Warren Bell

13. Feb. 2, 1991

Buck, playing matchmaker, finds a clean-cut guy (Scherrer) for Tia, whose preferences run to guys in leather and chains.

Paul....................................................................Paul Scherrer
Serena........................................................................Lela Ivey
And: Bill Stevenson (Crash), Bruce Baum (Bouncer)

Writer: Kevin Abbott

14. Feb. 9, 1991

Tia, who to Buck's dismay plans on skipping college to become a model, falls and gets a vision of herself 50 years hence.

Writers: Tim O'Donnell & Richard Gurman

**preempted Feb. 16; unscheduled preemption Feb. 23**

15. March 2, 1991

Furious that Buck won't let her go on an overnight ski trip

with her friends, Tia moves in with her grandmother.

Writer: Caryn Lucas

16. March 9, 1991

Buck, the coach of Maizy's basketball team, goes to court over a property dispute regarding her practice backboard. Abdul-Jabbar is a former pro basketball player; Anderson reprises his role from ep. 10. Orig. scheduled for Feb. 9 and Feb. 23.

Judge Nathan Wells.................................Kareem Abdul-Jabbar
Kroger.................................................................Sam Anderson

Director: John Tracy                    Writer: Warren Bell

**off the schedule**

17. April 6, 1991

Tia pays a modeling agency for a photo session, with Buck tagging along to make sure the pictures aren't "over-exposed." Orig. scheduled for March 9.

Gwen....................................................................Cristine Rose

Writer: Warren Bell

Unaired

While tending bar for Skank, Buck foils an attempted holdup. Orig. scheduled for Nov. 30.

Rafer Freeman..............Thomas Mikal Ford a.k.a. Tommy Ford
Skank.......................................................Dennis Cockrum
Keating.......................................................Jonathan Coogan
Michelle Patterson.................................................Toni De Rose

Writer: Kevin Abbott

Also: CBS announced a planned episode teaming Audrey Meadows and her actress sister Jayne Meadows in a rare TV appearance together.

## Under Cover

ABC          Jan. 7-Feb. 16      Saturdays, 9-10 p.m.
             July 6, July 20     Various

Series premiere: Jan. 7, 1991
Final telecast: July 3, 1991

Drama of covert operatives in the C.I.A.-like National Intelligence Agency, trying to balance their family lives with the dangers and rigors of the spy profession. Cast-member Lemmons was listed a guest star ep. 7; consultant Snepp is a former C.I.A. agent. Creator Broyles is former editor-in-chief of *Newsweek*. Working title: *The Company*.

Agent Dylan Del'Amico.........................Anthony John Denison
Agent Kate Del'Amico, his wife..............................Linda Purl
Agent Flynn..........................................John Rhys-Davies
Graham Parker.......................................John Slattery
Alex Robbins (ep. 2-6).....................................Kasi Lemmons
Stewart Merrimen.................................................Josef Sommer
Lisa Koufax (ep. 1)...............................................Colleen Flynn
Fyodor (ep. 1)................................................Bozidar Smiljanic

*Recurring:*
Director Waugh (ep. 2-4,7-8)................................G.W. Bailey

Tim Grimbach (ep. 1,4,8)...............................................Raye Birk
Marlon Del'Amico, Kate and Dylan's son
     (ep. 1)..............................................................Joshua South
     (ep. 2-3,5-8)..............................................Adam Ryen
Emily Del'Amico, Kate and Dylan's daughter
     (ep. 1).............................................................Sumer Stamper
     (ep. 3-6,8)................................................Marne Patterson
Gen. Hausman (ep. 2,4,7)....................................Salome Jens
Megan (ep. 1,3,5,8)................................................Arlene Taylor

Paint Rock Productions and Sacret, Inc. in assoc. with Warner Bros. Television
Executive producers: John Sacret Young, William Broyles, Jr.
Supervising producers: Stuart Cohen, Terry Curtis Fox, Don Carlos Dunaway (latter two, not all episodes)
Producers: Terry Morse (ep. 1); Kevin Droney, Michael Fresco, Thania St. John (latter two, not all episodes)
Co-producer: David Simmons (ep. 2-on), Terry McDonnell, Thania St. John (latter two, ep. 8 only)
Executive story editor (some episodes): Thania St. John
Creative consultant (some episodes): Don Carlos Dunaway
Director of photography (variously): Thomas Olgeirson (ep. 1); Geoffrey Erb; Roy H. Wagner, A.S.C.
Technical advisor: Frank Snepp
Music: Bill Conti (ep. 1); Cameron Allan
Creator: William Broyles, Jr.

1. "Under Cover"  Monday, Jan. 7, 1991  9-11 p.m.

Ten years after being caught by the KGB in Iran and being returned to America, Del'Amico tries to prevent the assassination of a high-ranking Soviet reformer, while Flynn, believing best friend Del'Amico is a double agent, has been assigned by the agency to kill him. Filmed in Yugoslavia.

Announced cast includes:
Dakin Matthews
Boris...............................................................Milos Kirek
Caddie Varner.....................................................Dawn Comer
FBI agent.........................................................Michael Whaley

Director: Harry Winer              Writer: William Broyles, Jr.

2. "Sacrifices" Part 1   Jan. 12, 1990

Dylan is stuck in Iraq after the invasion of Kuwait, where Kate and new N.I.A. recruit Alex are taken hostage. Part 2, scheduled for the following week, was preempted with this onscreen notice: "Due to the similarities between real events in the Middle East and the fictional story in tonight's part II episode of *Under Cover*, it will be rescheduled at a later date. Now stay tuned for a special [rerun] episode of *MacGyver*." Part 2 telecast July 13, when it and Part 1 were combined into a two-hour episode, "Before the Storm."

Sam Hamadi.......................................................Jesse Borrego
Col. Sabri................................................................Nick Faltas
Omar......................................................Jorian J. Husayn
Abdul.....................................................Duke Moosekian
Bing Tupper................................................Randolph Mantooth
Fasir..................................................................Shelly Desai
And: Mary Ellen (Flight attendant), Vida Ghahremani (Arab woman), Ray Nazzari (Customs), Faras Rabadi (Solider)

Director: Michael Fresco              Writer: Thania St. John

**preempted Jan. 19**

3. "Truth and Consequences"

A former agent's suicide prompts psychological reevaluations of the task-force team; Dylan considers telling Emily his real profession. Orig. scheduled for Feb. 2.

Dr. Hernandez..........................................Ivonne Coll
Dr. Sullivan..........................................Matthew Fasion
Molly..........................................Mariangela Pino
Dr. Filbert..........................................Steve Franken
Mail clerk..........................................Shannon Day
Uncle Howard..........................................Kedric Robin Wolfe
Dr. Sommers..........................................Saxon Trainor

Director: NA    Writer: NA

4. "War Game"  Feb. 2, 1991

Dylan and a KGB colonel (Freeman) search for a terrorist who has kidnapped Waugh and tortured him into making video-taped statements. Orig. scheduled for Jan. 26.

Col. Ilysevich Kalganin...................Paul Freeman (uncredited)
Dr. Jurgens..........................................Norbert Weisser
Patricia..........................................Teresa Gilmore
Security persons...................James Oden Hatch, Peter Lewis
Old woman..........................................Elizabeth Talbot-Martin
      Also orig. announced:
      Adam Ryen (Marlon Del'Amico)

Director: Jonathan Sanger        Writer: Frank Snepp

5. "Family Album"  Feb. 9, 1991

The agency recruits Kate's old flame (Hove), a Russian scientist, by making him believe an unmarried Kate has been raising their child in America.

Andrei Andreivich..........................................Anders Hove
Miss Gresham..........................................Fran Ryan
Andy..........................................Tim Eyster
John Neuman..........................................Bernard Kates

Director: Vern Gillum        Writer: Kevin Droney

6. "Mr. Butterfly"  Feb. 16, 1991

In Shanghai, Dylan and Kate try to smuggle out a dissident by disguising the person as a member of the opposite sex.

Walter Austin..........................................John Calvin
Wills..........................................Alan Haufrect
Chen Ling..........................................Nonie
Chen Lee..........................................Ping Wu
Claudette..........................................Brandis Kemp
Tiny..........................................F. William Parker
Marine..........................................Ed Beechner
U.S. translator..........................................George Kee Cheung
Security person..........................................Brian Fong
And: Nancy Chen (Old woman), Lang Yun (Translator)

Director: Jonathan Sanger        Writer: Scott Kaufer

**off the schedule, then cancelled**

7. "Before the Storm"  Saturday, July 6, 1991  9-11 p.m.

Dylan escapes Iraq and meets Flynn in Kuwait to rescue the hostaged Kate and new recruit Alex, leaving a second inexperienced agent (Borrego) behind to try to pinpoint an Iraqi launch site for chemical missiles. Comprised of the two-part episode orig. titled "Sacrifices," part 1 of which ran Jan. 12. Orig. scheduled for this date, rescheduled to July 6, then returned to July 13.

Sam Hamadi..........................................Jesse Borrego
Col. Sabri..........................................Nick Faltas
Dr. Gutman..........................................Dana Gladstone
Omar..........................................Jorian J. Husayn
Abdul..........................................Duke Moosekian
Bing Tupper..........................................Randolph Mantooth
And: Shelly Desai (Fasir), Said Naber (Sabri's soldier), Faras Rabadi, Bruce Jalili (Soldiers), Shaun Toub (Jeep soldier), Adam Angeli (Officer), Mary Ellen (Flight attendant), Vida Ghahremani (Arab woman), Larry Marks (Mr. Suit), Ray Nazzari (Customs), Elyse Nicole Sherman (Jenny)

Director: Michael Fresco        Writer: Thania St. John

8. "Spy Games"  Sunday, July 20, 1991  9-11 p.m.

An elite group of operatives once led by Kate's late father are on the hit list of a murderous rogue agent. Orig. designed as two one-hour episodes. Stamper, who plays 8-year-old Kate, had played Kate and Dylan's daughter, ep. 1; Kathryn Kimler-Monks is the series' stunt coordinator, as Kathryn Kimler.

Randall Cobb..........................................Kevin Tighe
Dieter..........................................Walter Addison
Rockwell..........................................Michael Cavanaugh
Juro..........................................John Apicella
Singleton..........................................William Cain
Caretaker..........................................Lilyan Chauvin
Kurt..........................................Alan Goetschkes
Leisel..........................................Kathryn Kimler-Monks
Agent Frank Graham..........................................(unidentified)
And: Orlando Bonner (Police officer), Patricia Conklin (Cobb's wife), Jenny Marie DuBasso (German woman), Nancy Grevich (Kate's mom, home movie), Charles Holman (Clerk), C. Darnell Rose (Pizza deliverer), Sumer Stamper (8-year-old Kate, home movie)
      Also orig. announced:
      Bonnie Bartlett (Margaret Singleton)

Directors: Christopher Leitch (first hour); Michael Fresco (second hour)
Writers: William Broyles, Jr. (first hour); Thania St. John (second hour)

## Who's the Boss?

ABC        Sept. 18-Aug. 6        Tuesdays, 8-8:30 p.m.
           Aug. 13-on             Tuesdays, 8:30-9 p.m.

Series premiere: Sept. 20, 1984

Comedy of a live-in male domestic (Danza) and his quasi-romantic relationship with his ad-executive employer (Light).

Tony Micelli..........................................Tony Danza
Angela Bower..........................................Judith Light
Samantha Micelli, Tony's daughter...................Alyssa Milano
Jonathan Bower, Angela's son..........................Danny Pintauro
Mona Robinson, Angela's mother...............Katherine Helmond

*Recurring:*
Billy (ep. 4,6-25)..........................................Jonathan Halyalkar
Kathleen Sawyer, Tony's girlfriend (ep. 1-2,4)........Kate Vernon
Andy, Angela's boyfriend (ep. 4-7)..........................Doug Ballard
Mrs. Rossini (ep. 4,6,21)..........................................Rhoda Gemignani
Ernie (ep. 1,6,10)..........................................Ralph P. Martin
Joey (ep. 7,9,20)..........................................Josh Byrne

Hunter/Cohan Productions in assoc. with Columbia Pictures Television / ELP Communications

Executive producers: Martin Cohan, Blake Hunter, Danny
    Kallis, Phil Doran
Producers: Bob Rosenfarb, Clay Graham, John Maxwell
    Anderson
Associate producer: Michael Greenspon
Executive script consultants: Gene Braunstein, Daniel
    Palladino
Story editors: David Lesser, Matthew Swerdlick, Linda Va
    Salle, Mike Teverbaugh, Michele J. Wolff (latter three
    later in season)
Director of photography: Mark Levin
Music: Jonathan Wolff
Theme: "Brand New Life" by Larry Carlton and Robert Kraft
    (music), Martin Cohan and Blake Hunter (lyrics); per-
    former uncredited
Director: Tony Singletary
Creators: Blake Hunter and Martin Cohan

---

1. "Ridiculous Liaisons"  Sept. 18, 1990

Tony comes unglued when it appears Angela has found the
perfect mate.

Peter Gerber.............................................Stan Ivar
Maitre d'.........................................Oliver Muirhead
Attendant........................................Alfred Dennis
And: Chris Paul Davis (Christopher), Bill Stevenson (Young
    man), Michael Gilbert Lewis (Busboy), Sierra Samuel
    (Girl)

Writer: Daniel Palladino

2. "Hey Dude"  Sept. 25, 1990

Samantha plans to marry a dude-ranch cowboy (Muldoon).

Matt...............................................Pat Muldoon
Guest...........................................Patrick Waddell
Mrs. Albrecht.....................................Jean Sincere

Writers: Richard Albrecht & Casey Keller

3. "The Fabulous Robinson Sisters"  Oct. 2, 1990

Tony persuades Mona to include Angela on Mona's wild nights
out.  Guest Vale is a singer.

Himself...............................................Jerry Vale
Waitress..........................................Mindy Seeger
Suit...............................................Daniel Moriary
Leonard Tibbs......................................Dean Hill
Gorgeous girl.....................................Krista Tesreau
And: Geno Michellini (Guy), Colette Duvall (Cello teacher), Eric
    Kohner (Fedora), Mick E. Jones (Sunglassed musician),
    Fred Asparagus (Del Moore), Mark Sivertsen (Damien),
    Michael Meyer (Man at bar)

Writer: Michael Swerdlick

4. "Did You Ever Have to Make Up Your Mind?"  Oct. 9, 1990

Tony's nervous about meeting Kathleen's dad; Tony and Angela
meet the 5-year-old grandson (new recurring guest Halyalkar)
of Mrs. Rossini's (recurring guest Gemignani) very sick neighbor.  Orig. scheduled for Sept. 18.  Story continues in ep. 6.

Jack Sawyer.....................................Mitchell Ryan
Nurse.............................................Brenda Ballard
Minister.........................................Wilfred La Voie

Writer: Clay Graham

5. "One Flew Over the Empty Nest"  Oct. 16, 1990

When Samantha leaves for college, Tony's loneliness makes
him hang out with her, and butt-in between Angela and Andy.

Melinda...........................................Andrea Elson
Laurie..............................................Ria Pavia
Jennifer........................................Jennifer McComb
Janie and Jeanie.....................Samantha and Jackie Forrest
Girl (listed as Abby in press materials)............Abigail Franken

"The Brady Bunch Theme" performed by: Emily Forman, Ni-
    cole Haggard, Symphony Smart

Writers: Mike Teverbaugh & Linda Va Salle

6. "The Kid"  Oct. 23, 1990

Continuing the story from ep. 4: A now-elderly and incapaci-
tated boyhood neighbor (Lockwood) of Tony's wants him to
raise her 5-year-old grandson, Billy.

Mrs. Napoli ("Grandma Napoli").....................Vera Lockwood
Nurse Heather...................................Denise Gentile
And: Carlease Burke (Nurse), Jean Adams (Nun)

Writer: Bob Rosenfarb

7. "Parental Guidance Suggested"  Oct. 30, 1990

Trying to help Billy adjust to his new home and preschool,
Tony and Angela overzealously pile on activities.

Ms. Adams..........................................Jane Leeves
Herb.............................................Ray Reinhardt
Willa...........................................DeVera Marcus
Chris.............................................Dave Florek
Diane.........................................Mary Pat Gleason
Greg..........................................Robert Clotworthy
Laurie (orig. Linda)..............................Janice Kent

Writer: Gene Braunstein

8. "Roomies"  Nov. 6, 1990

Sam's boyfriend (Muldoon, reprising his role from ep. 2) is out-
raged that her new college roommate (Perry) is male.

Benjamin..Matthew Perry (Christopher Collet orig. announced)
Beth.............................................Mary Tanner
Matt...............................................Pat Muldoon

Writer: David Lesser

9. "Four Alarm Tony"  Nov. 13, 1990

Tony becomes an overly competitive volunteer firefighter.

Chief Baxter.......................................Bryan Clark
Sid..............................................Harris Laskawy
Jake................................................Barry Kivel
Arthur...........................................Kyle Heffner
Clarence.......................................Michael Goldfinger
And: Ross Malinger (Rory), Craig Stepp (Johnson), Dale Hari-
    moto (Laurie Lee), Billye Ree Wallace (Woman)

Song: "The Fireman," performed by Michael Stanton

Writer: Neil Lebowitz

10. "Starlight Memories" Nov. 20, 1990

Tony and Angela fantasize about what their love life might have been like if played out in a 1940s Hollywood movie.

Nick......................................................Jerry Orbach
Jenny..................................................Gretchen Wyler
Tom......................................................Michael Cutt
And: Brenda Varda (Lizzie), Cherie Franklin (WAC)

Writer: Clay Graham

11. "Inherit the Wine" Nov. 27, 1990

To claim an inheritance from his Uncle Aldo, Tony takes Samantha and Billy to Italy, where he finds the family name besmirched. Orig. scheduled for Nov. 20.

Dominic.................................................Louis Guss
Aunt Rosa..............................................Antonia Rey
Lido................................................John La Motta
Lawyer.......................................................Joe Lala
And: Anthony Ponzini (Dante), Ivan Kane (Deliveryperson), Al Sapienza (Tomato person), Valerie Fedi (Lucia), Benito Prezia (Vineyard worker), Harriet Medin (Older woman)

Writer: Daniel Palladino

12. "Who's Minding the Kid" Dec. 4, 1990

When a social worker (Lerner) appears unexpectedly, Tony and Angela fear they'll be judged too incompetent to keep Billy.

Charlie................Ed Winter (George Lazenby orig. announced)
Leonard Marshall.....................................Ken Lerner
Prof. Wallace.....................................Ellen Crawford
Jack Dodds.............................................Cliff Emmich
Abbie......................................................Ria Giuliani
Ben.................................................David Michael Mullins
Greg....................................................Tahj D. Mowry

Writers: Barry Vigon & Deborah Leschin

13. "Broadcast Blues" Dec. 18, 1990

Tony wants to bow out when he discovers he and Samantha are both vying for a college broadcaster position.

Chappy..................................................Pat Buttram
Steve Barton............................................Scott Bryce
And: Ted Davis (Rashid), Rob Grader (Student)

Writers: Linda Va Salle & Mike Teverbaugh

**preempted Jan. 1**

14. "Days of Blunder" Jan. 8, 1991

While passing off Tony's prize jeep as his own to impress a girl, Jonathan badly scratches it. Orig. scheduled for Dec. 18.

Patricia...............................................Heather McComb
Officer Norton..........................................Justin Lord

Writers: Deborah Leschin & Barry Vigon

15. "You Can Go Home Again" Jan. 22, 1991

Overjoyed that pressured college student Samantha has agreed to live at home again, Tony and Angela overindulge her. Orig. scheduled for Jan. 15.

Bonnie..............................................Shana Lane-Block
Michael Haynes.........................................Paul Walker
And: Shonda Whipple (Gina), Mary Valena Broussard (J.J.)

Writer: Carol Starr Schneider

16. "Ms. Mom" Jan. 29, 1991

When Tony begins a two-week teaching internship, he and Angela temporarily exchange roles around the house.

Mr. Kimball.........................................Franklin Cover
Ms. Clover...............................................Eve Brent
Kyle.................................................Chris Paul Davis
Wild kids.........................................Ross Malinger, Jesse Stock

Writers: Richard Albrecht & Casey Keller

17. "The Unsinkable Tony Micelli" Feb. 5, 1991

Billy wants to go swimming with Tony, who doesn't know how.

Pam...................................................Jeri Lynn Ryan
Boys......................................Zachary La Voy, Andrew Van Wey
Fathers...........................................David Morin, Frank Kopyc
Woman at pool.......................................Christy Barrett

Writer: Gene Braunstein

18. "Tony and Angela Get Divorced" Feb. 12, 1991

When Tony and Angela find that for tax purposes the IRS considers them a married couple, they start acting like one. Garlington is a cast-member of *Lenny*.

Judge................................................Dakin Matthews
Mrs. Foster.........................................Lee Garlington
Peterson...............................................John Mansfield
Ben......................................................Dick Christie
And: Charles Champion (Parker), Thomas Babson (O'Malley), Kenneth Zane (Groom), Sondra Baker (Bride)

Writer: Michele J. Wolff

19. "Let Her Tell You 'Bout the Birds and Bees" Feb. 19, 1991

Tony teaches a seventh-grade sex education class, with help from worldly Mona. Cover played a different role, ep. 16.

Campbell...........................................Franklin Cover
Plumber............................................Clive Rosengren
Mrs. Barker........................................Andrea Walters
Mrs. Gallagher.........................................Jessie Jones
Todd...................................................Cory Danziger
Mickey...............................................Silvio Luciano
And: Yunoka Doyle (Linda), Cynthia Marie King (Carrie), Lewis Dauber (Rev. Markham), Hal Rayle (Narrator)

Writers: Linda Va Salle & Mike Teverbaugh

20. "Party Politics" Feb. 26, 1991

When Tony and Angela attempt to make Billy's sixth-birthday party special, they begin a "can-you-top-this?" competition. The characters of guests Clark and Fetrick cross over from the syndicated *American Gladiators* stunt/competition series.

Mark Harper..........................................Sam McMurray
Pam Harper..............................................Leah Ayres
Bobo the Clown.........................................Ryan Stiles
The Amazing Dave......................................Jim Doughan

Travis..............................................................Ross Malinger
And: Shannon Farrara (Audrey), Nathan Lorch (Adam), Dan Clark (Nitro), Lori Fetrick (Ice)

Writers: Phil Doran and Bob Rosenfarb and Gene Braunstein

21. "Choose Me" March 12, 1991

When Mona and Mrs. Rossini fall for the same guy (Frank), Angela and Tony choose sides and compete to help.

Clifford..............Charles R. Frank (Ian Ogilvy orig. announced)

Writers: Dawn Aldredge & Mona Marshall

22. "Tony and the Princess" March 26, 1991

Tony teaches domestic responsibility to a mobster's gorgeous 20-year-old daughter (Mitchell), who falls for him. Matty Danza is Tony Danza's brother. Orig. scheduled for March 12.

Gus Stone (orig. Grant)....................................Raymond Serra
Claudia Stone (orig. Grant)...........................Shareen Mitchell
Father Marconi....................................................Tom Troupe
Bartender Marty.......................................Matt (Matty) Danza
Chauffeur...........................................................Mik Scriba
And: Michael Andrew Kelly (Carl), Adam Wylie (Child)

Writers: Danny Kallis & Clay Graham & Daniel Palladino

**preempted April 2**

23. "Between Rock and a Hard Place" April 16, 1991

When promoter Samantha needs a headline act for a college concert, Tony gets a cheesy doo-wop group. Orig. scheduled for April 9.

Al.................................................................William Gallo
Steve Mueller.....................................................Chris Barnes
M.C. Too Big................................................Lamont Johnson
Screaming girl.........................................Charmaine Charles
"The Mighty Echoes":
    John Hostetter (Satch), Jonathan Rubin (Benny), Charles G. Davis (Jimbo), Harvey Sheild (D.J.)

Writers: Linda Va Salle & Mike Teverbaught and Michele J. Wolff

24. "The Road to Washington" Part 1  April 30, 1991

Tony's desire to protect an elderly friend (Buttram, reprising his role from ep. 13) facing Medicare cutbacks winds up putting the whole household on a train ride to a Senate hearing.

Chappy...............................................................Pat Buttram
Conductor...............................................John Cothran, Jr.
Senator Stewart..................................................Ken Smolka
Senator Mars..................................................Mimi Cozzens
And: Dona Hardy (Lena), Ralph Manza (Francis)

Writer: Daniel Palladino

25. "The Road to Washington" Part 2  May 7, 1991

Angela gets jealous when Tony falls for the gorgeous chief of staff (Ulrich) of the senator he's lobbying.

Christine Morris......................Kim Johnston Ulrich a.k.a. Kim Johnston-Ulrich a.k.a. Kim Ulrich
Chappy...............................................................Pat Buttram

Liz.....................................................................Pat Sturges
White House tour guide....................................Kimberly Chase
Women................................................Hope Garber, Gerry Lock

Writer: Gene Braunstein

**renewed for 1991-92; new episodes begin Sept. 28, 1991**

# Wings

NBC          Sept. 28-Dec. 21    Fridays, 9:30-10 p.m.
             Jan. 3-March 28     Thursdays, 9:30-10 p.m.

Series premiere: April 19, 1990

Comedy of two contrasting brothers who run the one-plane Sandpiper Air commuter airline out of Tim Nevers Field in Nantucket, Mass. Lowell's unseen wife: Bunny.

Joe Hackett...........................................................Timothy Daly
Brian Michael Hackett...........................................Steven Weber
Lunch-counter owner Helen Chappel..............Crystal Bernard
Aeromass owner Roy Biggins..........................David Schramm
Reservationist Faye Evelyn Cochran................Rebecca Schull
Mechanic Lowell Mather.....................Thomas Haden Church

*Recurring:*
Kenny Margaret McElvey
    (ep. 9, 14, 17-18)...............................Michael Manasseri

Grub Street Productions in assoc. with Paramount Television
Executive producers: David Angell, Peter Casey, David Lee
Supervising producer: Dave Hackel
Producer: Roz Doyle, Philip LaZebnick, Bruce Rasmussen
Associate producer: Maggie Randell
Executive story consultants: Bill Diamond, Michael Saltzman
Director of photography: Ken Lamkin, A.S.C.
Air technical assistance: Air L.A.
Music: Bruce Miller
Theme (instrumental): "Piano Sonata in A Major" D959 by Franz Schubert; adapted by Antony Cooke
Director: Noam Pitlik
Creators: David Angell & Peter Casey & David Lee

---

1. "The Puppetmaster" Sept. 28, 1990

Frustrated by Helen's not dating pilots, Brian hires an actor (Bierko) to romance her and then "reveal" he's a pilot.

Matt Sargent......................................................Craig Bierko

Writer: Philip LaZebnik

2. "The Story of Joe"  Oct. 5, 1990

Brian dazzles a reporter from *American Flyer* with tales of aeronautic adventures; barflies Norm and Cliff (in a crossover from *Cheers*) make the rounds.

Norm Peterson....................................................George Wendt
Cliff Clavin..................................................John Ratzenberger
Ted Cobb......................................................Charles Hallahan

Writer: Bruce Rasmussen

3. "A Little Nightmare Music" Oct. 12, 1990

The guys urge aspiring cellist Helen to deliver a symphony

conductor's "lost" luggage to his honeymoon suite, in hopes of being granted an audition.

Edward Tinsdale..........................................David Ogden Stiers
Mrs. Tinsdale.....................................................Kelly Miller
Passenger..............................................William B. Jackson

Writer: Bryan Winter

4. "Sports and Leisure"  Oct. 19, 1990

Roy tries to be more likable.

Writer: David Angell

5. "A Stand Up Kind of Guy"  Oct. 26, 1990

Joe, Brian and Helen can't recall the high school classmate who arrives asking Joe to be best man at his wedding.

Jerry Stark...........................................................Kelly Connell
Marilyn................................................................Amanda Carlin
Monsieur Busard...................................................Roger Til
And: Leslie Cook (Roberta), Walter Wiliford (Larry)

Writer: Dave Hackel

**preempted Nov. 2**

6. "It's Not the Thought, It's the Gift"  Nov. 9, 1990

Brian and Joe try to outdo each other in getting a sensational birthday gift for Helen.

Young Joe in home movie (no lines)...................Adrian Arnold
Young Brian in home movie (no lines)...........Spencer Vrooman
Young Helen in home movie (no lines).......................Valentino
Mrs. Hackett in home movie (no lines)................Valri Jackson

Writers: Peter Casey & David Lee

7. "Hell Hath No Fury..."  Nov. 16, 1990

When Brian charms his way out of a parking ticket, the infatuated and obsessive female cop begins harassing him.

Off. Coleen Thomas...............................................Sharon Barr
Fisherman...............................................................Dave Florek

Writers: Bill Diamond & Michael Saltzman

8. "High Anxiety"  Nov. 23, 1990

Joe, grounded by high-blood pressure, splits with Brian, whom he deems too irresponsible to run the airline.

Deke Braverman..................................................Robert Colbert
Dr. Bennett............................................................Harris Shore
Nurse Carrie................................................................Jo Brewer
Young Joe (no lines)..........................................Spencer Smith
Young Brian (no lines)...............................................Ryan Bish

Writer: Bruce Rasmussen

**preempted Nov. 30**

9. "Friends or Lovers"  Dec. 7, 1990

Childhood pals Joe and Helen try succumbing to their 15-year romantic attraction; Joe hires a young backup pilot (new recurring guest Manasseri).

Mr. Stubbs.........................................................Charles Dugan
Doug...................................................................Jeremy Roberts

Writer: David Lloyd

10. "There's Always Room for Cello"  Dec. 14, 1991

Roy won't allow his strapping teenage son (Benrubi, a cast-member of *Parker Lewis Can't Lose*) to take "sissy" cello lessons. Preempted in New York City by a local holiday special.

R.J. Biggins.....................................................Abraham Benrubi
Rudy..........................................................Ferdinand Carangelo

Writers: Peter Casey & David Lee

11. "A Terminal Christmas"  Dec. 21, 1990

Joe, Brian and Helen crash Faye's supposed Christmas party, only to find her alone and mourning her late husband, George, on her first holiday without him. Orig. scheduled for Dec. 14.

Frank....................................................................George Furth
Passenger...............................................................Chuck Sloan

Writers: Bill Diamond & Michael Saltzman

12. "Airport '90"  Jan. 3, 1991

Helen wants to learn flying, and has to land the plane when Brian gets knocked unconscious during a lesson.

Walter................................................................Ralph Bruneau
Cathy Windsor..................................................Elizabeth Ince
Brutus, Roy's dog..........................................................Rascal

Writer: Bruce Rasmussen

13. "Love Is Like Pulling Teeth"  Jan. 10, 1991

Joe, now dating Helen, risks missing a night with all the gang from out of town when she needs him following dental surgery.

Mr. Tupperman.........................................................Ace Mask
Art.....................................................................Patrick Massett

Writer: Dave Hackel

**unscheduled preemption Jan. 17**

14. "The Tennis Bum"  Jan. 24, 1991

After her defeat in the Nantucket Women's Tennis Championships, Faye trounces Brian; Joe wrecks Lowell's model blimp.

"Audrey".........................................................Christopher Best
Passenger..............................................................Craig Benton

Writer: Peter S. Mehlman

15. "My Brother's Back, and There's Gonna Be Trouble"
     Jan. 31, 1991

Joe, in traction with an injured back, trusts the airline to Brian, who loses the plane.

FAA inspector Hanson.............................Jonathan McMurtry
Candy striper....................................................Dana Andersen
Mrs. McCloskey..................................................Karen Hensel
And: Dai Kornberg (Greely), Michael Rogen, Marilyn Child (Travel agents), Peggy Mannix (Woman)

Writers: Bill Diamond & Michael Saltzman

16. "Plan Nine from Nantucket"  Feb. 7, 1991

After Brian tells the FAA about his and Joe's possible UFO sightings, UFO fanatics converge on Sandpiper Air. Orig. scheduled for Jan. 17. McMurtry reprises his role from ep. 15.

Al..........................................................................John Vickery
John........................................................................Teddy Wilson
FAA inspector Hanson..............................Jonathan McMurtry
Tom........................................................................James Whitson
Mary......................................................................Roberta Farkas
Reporter.................................................Michael Eugene Fairman

Writer: Philip LaZebnik

17. "Looking for Love in All the Wrong Places"  Feb. 14, 1991

On Valentine's Day, Helen and Joe agree to meet at their "special place" -- each inadvertently going to a different one.

Karen.....................................................................Deborah May
Antonio..................................................................Tony Shalhoub
Stephanie...............................................................Claire Yarlett
Giacomo.................................................................Perry Anzilotti
High school football player................................Ed Beechner
Deliveryperson......................................................David Fullmer

Writers: Bill Diamond & Michael Saltzman

18. "Love Means Never Having to Say Geronimo"  Feb. 21, 1991

Brian impetuously decides to marry an adventurer (Darr) who goads Joe and Helen into nearly doing likewise.

Gwendolyn Susanne Holmes.................................Lisa Darr
Mr. Beekman..............................................Robert Alan Browne
Mrs. Beekman................................................Laurel Lockhart

Writer: Bruce Rasmussen

**preempted Feb. 28**

19. "All in the Family"  March 7, 1991

Brian goes on a date with a woman (Marshall) who turns out to be the mother of a highly concerned Kenny.

Melinda McElvey.................................................Marie Marshall
Customer..............................................................Gordon McManus
Woman....................................................................Donna Fuller
Blonde woman................................................Sharon Lee Jones
Passenger......................................................Christopher Darga

Writer: Bryan Winter

20. "Mother Wore Stripes"  March 14, 1991

The brothers' mom visits, currently out of prison for embezzlement after shucking them and domestic life 18 years before.

Mae Hackett................................................Barbara Babcock

Writer: David Lloyd

21. "Murder, She Roast"  March 21, 1991

Brian, forced by fumigation to room with Faye, gets scared when he sees her dead ringer on TV's (fictional) *Fugitives from Justice.* Guest Povich is a real-life tabloid-TV anchor.

Himself/host of *Fugitives from Justice*................Maury Povich
Customer......................................Christopher Michael Moore
Carl Torley.........................................................Andrew Bilgore

Writer: Dave Hackel

22. "Duet for Cello and Plane"  March 28, 1991

When an ecstatic Helen lands a spot in an out-of-state symphony, she must choose between the cello and Joe.

Becky.....................................................................Olivia Burnette
Mooshta...................................................................Ivonne Coll
And: Adam Gregor (Yonni), Roger Keller (Man)

Writer: Philip LaZebnick

**on hiatus, then reruns begin June 20**

**preempted Sept. 12**

**renewed for 1991-92; new episodes begin Sept. 19, 1991**

## WIOU

CBS                 Wednesdays, 10-11 p.m.

Series premiere: Oct. 24, 1990
Final telecast: March 20, 1991

Serialized ensemble drama of a news director and news staff of a large Midwestern city's struggling TV station, WNDY/Channel 12.  Co-star Phil Morris is the son of actor Greg Morris.

News director Hank Zaret.........................................John Shea
Co-anchor Kelby Robinson...................................Helen Shaver
Co-anchor Neal Frazier.............................................Harris Yulin
Executive producer Liz McVay........................Mariette Hartley
Weatherperson Floyd Graham..........................Dick Van Patten
Field producer Ann Hudson..................................Jayne Brook
Intern Willis Teitlebaum..................................Wallace Langham
Reporter Eddie Bock...................................................Phil Morris
Reporter Taylor Young..............................................Kate McNeil
Public relations person Tony Pro (Provenza)............Joe Grifasi
Station manager Kevin Dougherty..................Robin Grammell

*Recurring:*
Sportscaster Lucy Hernandez (ep. 6,8,10-11)..........Rosie Perez
Field cameraperson Marc Adamson (ep. 9-13).....Eric Pierpoint
Frances Frazier, Neal's wife (ep. 5-6,12)................Anita Morris
Michael McVay, Liz's husband (ep. 3,10-12).....Stephen Kahan
Rick Singer, Ann's fiance (ep. 4,10,12-13).......Steven Eckholdt
Trudy Blades (ep. 1-3,5,9-10)...............................Liane Curtis
Tom Gerson (ep. 1,4,12).......................................John Hammil
Ernie Valens (ep. 6-8).......................................Visili Bogazianos
Floor director Ralph (ep. 1-12)............................Scott Harlan
* Director (ep. 1,2,4-7,9,13)..............................Robert Crow
Security guard Mel Guthrie (ep. 1,3,5,7-8)....................Al Fann
Cameraperson (ep. 1-2,12)..................................Richie Allan

* Given onscreen as "Floor director," ep. 5,7,9,13.

GTG Entertainment a.k.a. The Grant Tinker Group in assoc. with Orion Television
Executive producers: Kathryn Pratt, John Eisendrath, Scott Brazil
Supervising producer: Joe Viola
Producers: John Heath, Michelle Ashford, Michael Cassutt
Line producer: Tony Brown
Associate producers: Scott Citron, Augie Hess

Executive story consultant: Tammy Adler
Director of photography: William Wages (ep. 1); Jonathan West
   (ep. 2-on)
Music: Gary Chang (ep. 1); (variously) Gary Chang, Laura
   Karpman, Jay Ferguson
Theme (instrumental): Gary Chang
Creators: Kathryn Pratt, John Eisendrath

---

1. "Pilot"  Oct. 24, 1990  (0100)

Newcomer Zaret faces in-fighting to fill the seat of a news anchor who died on-screen, plus new sparks from an old love affair with Kelby, plus his dotty father, plus an executive producer who wanted his job; Kelby must report a shady, long-ago incident by a friend (Eckhouse, a cast-member of *Beverly Hills, 90210*) about to become school-board president.

| | |
|---|---|
| Bob Lorwin | James Eckhouse |
| Alice Lorwin, his wife | Margaret Gibson |
| Jo Finc | Fran Drescher |
| Gus Zaret, Hank's father | Eddie Jones |
| Bear | Wayne Federman |
| Marla | Francis Fisher |
| Herb | David Wohl |
| Curtis Warden | Peter D. MacLean |
| Ben Jones | Earl Billings |
| Stan | Joe A. Dorsey |
| Firefighter | Rick Goldman |
| Cameraperson | Ronald William Lawrence |
| Paul Szymanski | Mik Scriba |
| Chris Lorwin (child) | Tiffany/Krystle Mataras |

And: Lee Arenberg (Tech director), Pierre Gonneau (Fire Chief), Ken Butler (School person), Jerome Guardino (Engineer), Alan Charof (Rabbi), Chris Bensinger (Associate producer), William Cort (Reporter), Marvyn Byrkett (Worker), Deborah Greene (Hooker), Ric Sarabia (Gang member)

Director: Claudia Weill
Writers: John Eisendrath & Kathryn Pratt

2. "Appearances"  Oct. 31, 1990  (0101)

Taylor discovers Eddie's story about a local hero is inaccurate; Kevin hires an image consultant; Floyd hosts a behind-the-scenes report on the news staff; lovelorn Willis takes in a financially strapped Ann as a temporary roommate. Director Mark Tinker is the son of production-company head Grant Tinker.

| | |
|---|---|
| Denise Meyers | Katy Boyer |
| Frank | Gregg Henry |
| Bud Hoover | Andrew White |
| Motel clerk | Owen Bush |
| Maureen Scott | Gloria Cromwell |
| Drunk driver/Jerry Craft | Dan Desmond |

And: Ellen Albertini Dow (Tour woman), Louisa Abernathy (Nurse/Joyce Newman), Orlando Bonner (Cop), Chauncey Leopardi (Tour member), Marty Madler (Landlord), Moria Turner (Telethon worker), Blumen Young (Sheriff)
Also orig. announced:
Lee Arenberg (Tech director), Al Fann (Mel Guthrie)

Director: Mark Tinker                     Writer: John Eisendrath

3. "The Inqusition"  Nov. 7, 1990  (0102)

Hank and Kevin try to appease a group protesting a lack of minorities at WNDY; Liz too soon assigns a story on a priest accused of child molestation; Taylor seduces Neal; a circus elephant dies at the station. Jones reprises his role from ep. 1.

| | |
|---|---|
| Leonora Gates | Fran Bennett |
| Daniel McVay | Grant Gelt |
| Stuart McVay | Bobby Jacoby |
| Janet Harper | Randee Heller |
| Gus Zaret | Eddie Jones |
| Father Brian Flyte | Paul Joynt |
| Pete Welsh | Ron Karabatsos |
| PRISM members | Irene Olga Lopez, Monica H. Hsu |

And: Jamie McEnnan (Jeffrey Harper), Annie O'Donnell (Sister Sue), John Del Regno (Ringmaster/Elmer), Wayne Pere (Dispatcher), Louis A. Rivera (Paramedic)

Director: Arthur Seidelman              Writer: Michael Cassutt

4. "Do the Wrong Thing"  Nov. 14, 1990  (0103)

Kelby's story on a jailhouse confession attained via beating could set free an alleged rapist-murderer (Gordon); Kevin discovers his favorite candidate (Carrington) for sports anchor is three feet tall; Taylor, to Neal's chagrin, reports on impotence; a man (Adams) holds Floyd at gunpoint for bad forecasting.

| | |
|---|---|
| Hal Krasner | Mason Adams |
| Andrea Morgan | Cynthia Bain |
| Carla | Debbie Lee Carrington |
| Mrs. Deerfield | Dorothy Fielding |
| Howard | Ken Foree |
| George Lewis | Keith Gordon |
| Det. Bleekler | Alyson Reed |
| Greg Hemmerkin | Pete Koch |

And: Michael Francis Clarke (Reporter), Mary Pat Gleason (Millie), Jordan Myers (Desk Sergeant), Dan Peters (Officer)
Also orig. announced: Anne Curry (Buffy)

Director: Mark Tinker                     Writer: Tammy Ader

**preempted Nov. 21 and Nov. 28**

5. "One Point No Light"  Dec. 5, 1990  (0104)

Hank and Kelby are rattled by Hank's ex-wife (Wilson, the wife of actor Tom Hanks), who's writing a magazine story about him; a mental patient (Polis) commits suicide; Neal takes desperate measures to try to satisfy the sexually ravenous Taylor; Willis unknowingly beds Neal's wife. Arenberg reprises his role from ep. 1. Orig. scheduled for Nov. 28.

| | |
|---|---|
| Stanley Corman | Joel Polis |
| Ellen Zaret | Rita Wilson |
| Tech director | Lee Arenberg |
| Dr. Ortland | Mark Arnott |
| Dr. Pierce | Earl Boen |
| Maxie | John Fleck |
| Channel 9 reporter Laurel Cassidy | Dale Weston |

And: Debbie Gregory (Melanie), Taylor Leigh (Nurse)
Also orig. announced: Steven Eckholdt (Rick Singer)

Director: Scott Brazil                    Writer: Michelle Ashford

6. "They Shoot Sources, Don't They"  Dec. 12, 1990  (0105)

A savings-and-loan scandal suspect (Allport) is murdered while dining with Taylor; the station holds auditions for sports anchor; Hank is pressured to reveal Kelby as the source of the police-brutality allegation; Floyd sees an eye doctor.

Announced cast includes:
| | |
|---|---|
| Frank Kozyck | Daniel Ziskie |
| David Natelson | Christopher Allport |
| Arnold Elkins | Earl Theroux |
| Old guy | Herb Smith |

Jesus Hernandez....Jimmy Medina a.k.a. James Medina a.k.a. Jimmy Medina Taggert
Quentin Mandel...................................................Richard Fancy
Dr. Kajita...........................................................Steve Park
And: Gabe Cohen (Demure guy), Dale Swann (Byron), James Mathers (Detective Biaggi), Edgar Small (Judge Searcy), Julie Hayek (Kimberly Deville), Vinnie Curto (Guido), Anthony Mangano (Mike), Don Craig (Reporter), Gene Freedman (Biff Randall), Raoul Rizik (Organ grinder), Manny Kleinmuntz (Shlomo), Faizon Love (Rapper)

Director: Ben Bolt                    Writer: Gardner Stern

7. "Diamond Dogs" Dec. 19, 1990 (0106)

Willis has a menorah placed in a park where Tony puts a nativity scene each year; Hank is pressured for not revealing the source of Kelby's story; Kelby must choose between Hank or her rock-star beau; Floyd quits over his growing blindness.

Announced cast includes:
Jimi Slavin.........................................................Richard Cox
Buffy..............................................................Anne Curry
Monica Shriver.....................................................Jane Daly
Lew Gold...........................................................Mark Lonow
Skinhead...........................................................Mark Pellegrino
Sheriff............................................................Reid Cruickshanks
Kleigmore/Santa....................................................Frederick Long
Cops....................................Christopher Darga, Lou Palumbo
Detective..........................................................Jason Edwards
Luigi Provenza, Tony's cousin........................Anthony Mangano

Director: Jan Eliasberg              Writer: Matt Dearborn

8. "Mother Nature's Son" Dec. 26, 1990 (0107)

Hank risks a jail sentence for contempt, as Kelby weighs whether to reveal a source; Liz and Neal battle for newsroom control; a boy, adopted after a series on children needing homes, shows up looking for a new family; Taylor asks for Floyd's help when she becomes the "weather bunny." Reed and Gordon reprise their roles from ep. 4, Fancy and Small from ep. 6.

With: Julie Ariola, Gabriel Damon
George Lewis......................................................Keith Gordon
With: Terri Hanauer
Det. Bleekler.....................................................Alyson Reed
Billy Randfield.......................................Dick Anthony Williams
District Attorney.................................................Nick Eldredge
Quentin Mandel....................................................Richard Fancy
And: Carlos Lacamara (Dale Martinez), Edgar Small (Judge Searcy), Jarrett Lennon (Zachary Newman), Frank Smith (Fred Jones), Danny Trejo (Jail inmate)

Director: Donna Deitch          Teleplay: Michael Cassutt
Story: Katie Crusoe (Kathryn Ford orig. announced) and Michael Cassutt

9. "Ode to Sizzling Sal" Jan. 2, 1991

A murderer (Williams, reprising his role from last episode) wants Kelby to witness his execution; Tony's publicity stunt sours Taylor on weather-bunnydom; Taylor meets a highly ambitious cameraperson (new recurring guest Pierpoint). Guest Crosby is a granddaughter of singer-actor Bing Crosby.

With: Denise Crosby, Kenneth Tigar
Janine Stabler....................................................Millie Slavin
Billy Randfield.......................................Dick Anthony Williams
Pulkie............................................................Christine Jansen
Tech director.....................................................Vince Melocchi

And: John Towey (Warden), Anita Bascelli (Margena), Charles Bouvier (Merle), Skip Strellrecht (Young man)

Director: David Carson               Writer: Kathryn Ford

10. "Labored Relations" Jan. 9, 1991 (0109)

The staff goes on strike, with Liz and her union-rep husband on opposite sides; Lucy and Trudy are attacked by a gang during a live shoot; Willis is moved to propose when Ann and Rick talk engagement. Bennett reprises her role from ep. 3.

Leonora Gates.....................................................Fran Bennett
Teresa.............................................................Patty Neumeyer
Zee-bo.............................................................Phillip LaMarr
Kyle Mellis........................................................Arthur Eckdahl
Fred Barrett...........................................Michael Hungerford
Emil Castillo......................................................Shawn Munoz

Director: Bethany Rooney Hillshafer a.k.a. Bethany Rooney
Writer: Joe Viola

**unscheduled preemption Jan. 16**

**on hiatus**

11. "Bleeds, It Leads" Monday, March 4, 1991 (0110)

Marc and Taylor's works leads to a coveted "Crime Watch" segment; Lucy's attacked on the street; an estranged wife (Peterson) threatens to microwave her fertilized eggs to keep them from her husband (Ward). Medina reprises his role from ep. 6, Neumeyer from ep. 10. Orig. scheduled for Jan. 16 and 30.

Jesus Hernandez....James Medina a.k.a. Jimmy Medina a.k.a. Jimmy Medina Taggert
Teresa.............................................................Patty Neumeyer
Cindy..............................................................Robin Peterson
Sgt. Bellows.......................................................Vic Polizos
Ricardo............................................................Marco Rodriguez
Wes................................................................Lyman Ward
Kate McVay, Liz and Michael's daughter..........Michelle Collins
Carmen.............................................................Stephanie Eustace
And: Terry Jackson (Cop), Michaelangelo Kowalski (Harold White), Tino Michaels (Tito), Laura P. Vega (Marta)

Director: Ben Bolt                    Writer: Michelle Ashford

12. "Pair O' Guys Lost" March 13, 1991 (0111)

Neal concedes to demands for sensationalism, but finds a real story; a bachelorette party is thrown for Ann, who asks Willis to be her Man of Honor; Liz suspects she's pregnant; a woman (Stansfield) claims to be an alien. Orig. scheduled for Feb. 6 and March 6, the latter an unscheduled preemption.

With: Matthew Faison, Mike Genovese, Theodocia Goodrich, Rick Lieberman, Armin Shimerman, Lynne Marie Stewart
Councilperson Gehrity.................................Charles McDaniel
Landor.............................................................Claire Stansfield
Charles Hamlin....................................................Thomas Wagner
Monique............................................................Elizabeth Whitcraft

Director: Ed Sherin                   Writer: Gardner Stern

13. "Three Women and a Baby" March 20, 1991 (0112)

Kelby's report on an illegal adoption may jeopardize a crack baby's new home; Hank suspects Taylor and Marc are supplying information to a rival station; Ann calls off the marriage at the last minute. Orig. scheduled for Feb. 13 and March 13.

With: Rae Allen, Francis X. McCarthy, Daniel O'Shea
Jasmine, Kendra's mother.................................Kelly Jo Minter
Mr. Hudson, Ann's father.................................Greg Mullavey
Susan Green...........................................Cristina Raines-Crowe
Beatrice Hudson, Ann's mother.......................Gail Strickland
Rabbi Greenblatt.............................................Nat Bernstein
Photographer....................................................Gary Dubin
Clark.............................................................Phillip Simon
Kendra/Sarah Green (infant)...............................(uncredited)

Director: Bethany Rooney a.k.a. Bethany Rooney Hillshafer
Writer: Kathryn Pratt

Unaired

Ann's human-interest story about a local Arab community
stirs up violent prejudice; Liz discovers she's menopausal, and
entertains notions about an affair with a young producer (Ruginis); Hank helps secure a child's foster placement with Kelby. Orig. scheduled for March 20 and March 27, the latter a
last-minute preemption by a two-hour Jake and the Fatman.

Announced cast includes:
Beatrice Hudson...............................................Gail Strickland
Dana Burton.......................................................Vyto Ruginis
Omar (Mark) Hussein..........................................Josh Lozoff
Ahmad Hussein...................................................Aharon Ipale
Adele Kenny......................................................Lorinne Vozoff
Jolleen.................................................................April Grace
Derelict.............................................................Harvey Vernon

Director: Fred Gerber    Writers: Tammy Ader, Gary Goldstein

## Wiseguy

CBS                    Saturdays, 10-11 p.m.

Series premiere: Sept. 16, 1987
Final telecast: Dec. 8, 1990

Serialized drama of a disbarred federal prosecutor who joins
the government's Organized Crime Bureau (OCB) as an undercover operative. Presented in miniseries-like "arcs" of varying
lengths (though only one aired this season before the series
was cancelled). Series previously starred Ken Wahl (1987-90)
as operative Vinnie Terranova. Banks and Byrnes were cast-
members since the series' inception.

Michael Santana...............................................Steven Bauer
Frank McPike...................................................Jonathan Banks
Attorney Hillary Stein.........................................Cecil Hoffman
"Lifeguard"/Daniel Benjamin Burroughs...............Jim Byrnes

Stephen J. Cannell Productions
Executive producers: Stephen J. Cannell, Peter Lance
Supervising producers: James Wong, Glen Morgan, Jo
    Swerling, Jr.
Producers: Alex Beaton, Ted Mann
Associate producer: Alan Cassidy
Story editor: James Kearns
Technical consultant: Rafael Lima
Music: Ray Velton Bunch
Theme (instrumental): Mike Post
Director of photography (variously): Tom Priestley, Jr.; John
    Elton
Creators: Stephen J. Cannell & Frank Lupo

First arc: Investigating Terranova's apparent murder by a Sal-

vadoran death squad, McPike uneasily allies with Santana,
who infiltrates the operation of a Cuban-American kingpin
(Schell) for whom Santana's father (Villaverde) works. Arc co-
star Martika is a singer-songwriter. Filmed in Miami, Fla.

First-arc supporting cast:
Dahlia Mendez....................................................Martika
Rafael Santana............................................Manolo Villaverde
Amado Guzman............................................Maximilian Schell

1. "Fruit of the Poisonous Tree"  Nov. 10, 1990  9-11 p.m.

McPike, recently out of the hospital, begins an unauthorized
investigation into Terranova's disappearance, leading him to
disbarred federal prosecutor whom Terranova contacted shortly before vanishing. Jenkins, Raven and Petrie reprise their
roles from last season. Orig. scheduled for Nov. 17.

Announced cast includes:
Mark, McPike's boss...........................................Ken Jenkins
Wyler White....................................................James Rebhorn
Carlotta Terranova Aiuppo, Vinnie's mother............Elsa Raven
Don Aiuppo, Vinnie's stepfather.....................George O. Petrie
Ted Brownell...................................................Stephen Markle
Father Tom Gallagher.......................................James Baldwin
Mrs. Gallagher....................................................Jody Wilson
And: Mario Ernesto Sanchez (Col. Guerrera), John Archie
    (Digger), Alex Panas (Martinez-Gacha), Chaz Mena (Pilot),
    Iris Acker (Judge Laverty), Ellen Beck (Astrid)

Director: Jan Eliasberg              Teleplay: Peter Lance
Story: Stephen J. Cannell & Peter Lance & Rafael Lima

2. "Black Gold"  Nov. 17, 1990

Haitian boat people arrive at a warehouse staked out by Santana and McPike, interfering with their plan to sting Guzman.

Etoile De Joi.......................................................Badja Djola
Dag Machado...................................................Carlos Gomez
Chaput..........................................................Colson F. Gilkes
Digger..................................................................John Archie
Carmine.........................................................Joshua Sussman
And: Fabienne Rousseau (Haitian girl), Dana Mosher (Wait-
    ress), Julian Byrd (Farmer), Felecia Rafield (Julie), Reggie
    Pierre (Assailant), Glenn Witcher (Haitian man), Sara
    Rogers (Bikini-clad woman), Charles Matheny (Agent
    McSorley), Gail Allen (Haitian woman)

Director: Jorge Montesi
Teleplay: Bill Bludworth (Peter Lance also orig. announced)
Story: Stephen J. Cannell & Peter Lance & Rafael Lima

3. "The Gift"  Nov. 24, 1990

Santana commits to working with McPike, and is introduced
to Lifeguard; Machado, seeking revenge for being replaced in
Guzman's organization, discovers Santana's fed connections.

Dag Machado...................................................Carlos Gomez
Cruz Machado, his brother...................................Tony Bolano
Blair Biggs.......................................................Kevin Quigley
And: Lynn Ladner (Fed), Nelson Oramos (Captain)

Director: Jorge Montesi
Writer: Stephen J. Cannell (Orig. announced: Story by Ste-
    phen J. Cannell & Peter Lance)

4. "La Mina"  Dec. 1, 1990

After Guzman reveals to Santana he's laundering money for a

mysterious client, Santana and McPike have Stein start invest-
ing the money badly in order to draw the client out.

Wyler White.................................................James Rebhorn
Jack Schine.................................................Marc Macaulay
Andrew Mendoza...........................................Rene Rokk
Martinez-Gacha.............................................Alex Panas
And: Raul Santidrian (Albino), Jeff Breslauer, Robert Escobar
    (DEA Agents), Christopher Grant (Judge), Felecia Rafield
    (Julie), Raphael Rey Gomez, Omar Cabral (Pistolocos),
    Tim Powell (Chief), Chaz Mena (Paco), Stephen Neal (FBI
    agent), Becca Allen (Screaming woman), Donatella Dillon
    (Barber), Mark Blanchard (Bartender)


Director: Colin Bucksey
Writer: Peter Lance (Orig. announced: Story by Stephen J.
    Cannell & Peter Lance

5. "Witness Protection for the Archangel Lucifer"  Dec. 8, 1990

Santana returns Guzman from El Salvador for trial, but a
powerful attorney (Lehne) arranges a deal for his immunity,
and McPike learns Guzman may know who killed Terranova.

Winston Chambers III.....................................Fredric Lehne
Jack Schine.................................................Marc Macaulay
Andrew Mendoza...........................................Rene Rokk
Martinez-Gacha.............................................Alex Panas
Killebrew....................................................Shawn McAllister
And: Michael Champlin (Prior), Bobby Rodriguez (Raul), Luis
    Valderrama (Guard), Guillermo Gentile (Servant), Mal
    Jones (Judge), Arnie Cox (Bailiff), Avery Sommers (Fore-
    person), Crystina Wyler (TV reporter)


Director: Jorge Montesi
Teleplay: Peter Lance and Rafael Lima
Story: Stephen J. Cannell & Peter Lance

## The Wonder Years

ABC          Sept. 19-Aug. 14   Wednesdays, 8-8:30 p.m.
             Aug. 21-on         Wednesdays, 8:30-9 p.m.

Series premiere: Jan. 31, 1988

Seriocomedy of a suburban boy in the 1960s, as reminisced
by his adult self in voiceover narration. His school: Robert F.
Kennedy Junior High. Team: Wildcats. Cast-member d'Abo is
the cousin of actress Maryam d'Abo. Recurring guest Crystal
McKellar is the sister of cast-member Danica McKellar; Picardo is a cast-member of China Beach; Stein is primarily known
as a writer-attorney. The title and spelling of character Asst.
Principal Diperna is taken from onscreen artifacts (office door);
misspelled "DiPerna" in ABC press material.

Kevin Arnold...............................................Fred Savage
Jack Arnold, his father...................................Dan Lauria
Norma Arnold, his mother................................Alley Mills
Wayne Arnold, his older brother.........................Jason Hervey
Karen Arnold, his older sister............................Olivia d'Abo
Winnie Cooper..............................................Danica McKellar
Paul Pfeiffer.................................................Josh Saviano
Voice of adult Kevin.......................................Daniel Stern (uncredited)

*Recurring:*
Coach Ed Cutlip (ep. 2-3,8-9,22).......................Robert Picardo
Science teacher Mr. Cantwell (ep. 5,11,22)............Ben Stein
Asst. Principal Diperna (ep. 17,19,22)..................Raye Birk
Doug Porter (ep. 1,3-4,6,9-11,14,18,22)...............Brandon Crane
Randy Mitchell (ep. 3,5-6,9,10-11,22)..................Michael Tricario

Tommy Kisling (ep. 8-10,14)............................Jay Lambert
Madeline Adams (ep. 2,5,11-12).........................Julie Condra
Becky Slater (ep. 2,10,22)...............................Crystal McKellar
Tony Barbella (ep. 2,17,22).............................Tony Nittoli

The Black/Marlens Co. in assoc. with New World Television
Executive producer: Bob Brush
Co-executive producer: Jill Gordon
Producers: David Chambers, Michael Dinner
Supervising producer: Ken Topolsky
Associate producers: Bruce J. Nachbar, Sue Bea Belknap
    a.k.a. Sue Bea Montgomery
Executive story editor: Mark B. Perry
Story editors: Eric Gilliland (early in season), Jeffrey Stepakoff
    (most of season), Mark Levin
Directors of photography (variously): Rene Ohashi; Russell
    Carpenter; Tim Suhrstedt
Music (variously): J. Peter Robinson; W.G. Snuffy Walden
Theme: "With a Little Help from My Friends" by John Lennon
    & Paul McCartney, a 1967 composition for the Sgt. Pep-
    per's Lonely Hearts Club Band album; performed by Joe
    Cocker (the 1969 recording, a #1 British hit, and #68 on
    the Billboard U.S. pop chart)
Creators: Neal Marlens and Carol Black
    Also orig. announced:
    Creative consultant: Bob Bendetson

---------------

1. "Growing Up"  Sept. 19, 1990

The Arnolds attend Jack's office picnic.

Walter McCafferty.........................................John Anthony
Mimi Detweiler.............................................Soleil Moon Frye
Angela.......................................................Meredith Scott Lynn
And: Jay Byron (Umpire), Mark Drexler (Big guy), John T. Ol-
    son (Man), Rick Hurst (Harry Detweiler)

Director: Michael Dinner              Writer: Bob Brush

2. "Ninth Grade Man"  Sept. 26, 1990

Kevin has a rough first day of ninth grade.

Shop teacher Mr. Nestor..................................Charles Tyner
Mrs. Falcinella.............................................Julie Payne
Shop kid.....................................................Blake Soper
And: Josh Berman (Guillaume), Greta Brown (Nurse)

Director: Daniel Stern                 Writer: Jill Gordon

3. "The Journey"  Oct. 3, 1990

Kevin and his friends try to crash a girls' slumber party. Anthony reprises his role from ep. 1.

Walter McCafferty.........................................John Anthony
Girls.........................................................Sarah Lundy, Stacey Young

Director: Peter Werner                 Writer: Jeffrey Stepakoff

4. "The Cost of Living"  Oct. 10, 1991

Kevin gets a golf caddying job, and finds himself toting clubs
for his dad's work rival (Fudge), who's playing against his dad.
Orig. scheduled for Oct. 3.

Ken Stein...................................................Alan Fudge
Mark Kovinski..............................................Justin Whalin
And: Cal Gibson (Caddy master), Eric Foster (Kid)

Director: Nick Marck                      Writer: Mark Levin

5. "It's a Mad, Mad, Madeline World" Oct. 24, 1990

Kevin inadvertently leaves an ID bracelet, a grift from Winnie, in the home of a pretty new girl from school. Berman played a different character, ep. 2; Payne reprises her role from ep. 2.

Mrs. Falcinella.....................................................Julie Payne
Jeweler..............................................................John O'Leary
Harold Gurtner...................................................Josh Berman

Director: Rob Thompson
Writers: Eric Gilliland & Jeffrey Stepakoff

**preempted Oct. 31**

6. "Little Debbie" Nov. 7, 1990

A humiliated and embarrassed Kevin escorts Paul's little sister to a seventh-grade cotillion. Orig. scheduled for Oct. 17.

Debbie Pfeiffer, Paul's sister.........................Torrey Anne Cook
Alvin Pfeiffer, their father..............................John C. Moskoff
Ida Pfeiffer, their mother................................Stephanie Satie
Teacher............................................................Annie Waterman
Punch lady.......................................................Vanessa Brown
Girls.................................Stephanie Scott, Alexandra Kurhan
        Also orig. announced:
        Jennifer Banks, Jessica Puscas, Kellie Parker (Little girls)

Director: Michael Dinner                  Writer: Mark B. Perry

7. "The Ties That Bind" Nov. 14, 1990

Though his dad is away on a crucial business trip, Kevin's dejected mom still cooks an elaborate Thanksgiving dinner.

Ned........................................................................Biff Yeager

Director: Peter Baldwin                    Writer: Mark B. Perry

**preempted Nov. 21**

8. "The Sixth Man" Nov. 28, 1990

Kevin, not accepting that Paul has grown up considerably, tries to prove Paul isn't good enough for the basketball team.

With some recurring guests (see list).
        Also orig. announced:
        Richard J. Baker (Referee)

Director: Nick Marck                       Writer: David Chambers

9. "A Very Cutlip Christmas" Dec. 12, 1990

Kevin spots Coach Cutlip working as a shopping-mall Santa.

Elf...................................................................Aron Eisenberg
Hall monitor...........................................................April Dawn
Little boy................................................................Sean Ryan

Director: Michael Dinner                   Writer: Mark Levin
Suggested by material by: Gene Wolande

10. "The Candidate" Jan. 9, 1991

Paul tricks Kevin into running for Student Council President against arch-rival Becky (McKellar, reprising her role from previous seasons). Orig. scheduled for Dec. 26.

Shop kid.................................................................Blake Soper
Mr. Altman....................................................Willie C. Carpenter
Mrs. Ritvo..................................................................Linda Hoy
And: Marguerite Moreau (Julie), Josh Peden (Student)

Director: Neal Israel                      Teleplay: Eric Gilliland
Story: David Chambers & Eric Gilliland

**preempted Jan. 16**

11. "Heart Break" Jan. 23, 1991

On a class museum trip, Kevin realizes he and Winnie have grown apart since she began attending a crosstown school, Lincoln. Orig. scheduled for Jan. 9 and Jan. 16.

Roger.....................................................................Art Hoffman
Sean.......................................................................Aaron Lohr
And: Robin Lynn Heath (Tina), Keira Montell (Marsha)

Director: Andy Tennant                     Writer: David Chambers

12. "Denial" Jan. 30, 1991

Kevin is distraught when Winnie brings her new boyfriend (Hoffman, reprising his role from last episode) to a party. Director Masur is primarily known as an actor.

Roger.....................................................................Art Hoffman
Kids.................................................Josh Peden, Michael Bower

Director: Richard Masur                    Teleplay: Mark Levin
Story: Mark Levin & David Chambers

13. "Who's Aunt Rose?" Feb. 6, 1991

At a funeral for a relative his family never knew, Kevin comes face-to-face with the thought of mortality. Huddleston reprises his previous-season role as Jack's father.

Grandpa Albert Arnold................................David Huddleston
Lloyd Arnold.................................................Arlen Dean Snyder
Mr. Lively.............................................................Wesley Mann
Opal Arnold..................................................Helen Page Camp
Phillip Arnold....................................................John Brandon
And: Earl Boen (Pastor), Danny Breen (Ray McKinsey), Ben Kronen (Gentleman), Eda Reiss Merin (Woman)

Director: Rob Thompson                     Teleplay: Mark B. Perry
Story: Jill Gordon

14. "Courage" Feb. 13, 1991

Kevin goes to the dentist.

Dental hygienist Janet Hasenfuss.................Whitney Kershaw
Dr. Tucker..........................................................Gerrit Graham
Mrs. Craw..................................................................Mary Gillis

Director: Daniel Stern                     Writer: Mark B. Perry

**preempted Feb. 20**

15. "Buster" Feb. 27, 1991

Kevin agonizes over whether to have the family dog fixed to try to remedy its chronic misbehavior. Tyner reprises his role from ep. 2. Orig. scheduled for Feb. 13.

Dr. Ferleger.........................................................Cristine Rose
Shop teacher Mr. Nestor....................................Charles Tyner

Director: Nick Marck              Story: Jeffrey Stepakoff
Teleplay: Jill Gordon & Mark B. Perry

16. "Road Trip" March 6, 1991

When Kevin and his father get lost while driving to a store, they realize they don't know how to talk with each other.

Waitress...................................................Melora Walters
Attendant................................................J. Andrew Bilgore

Director: Ken Topolsky            Writer: David Chambers

17. "When Worlds Collide" March 20, 1991

Kevin is highly embarrassed when his mom takes a temporary job at his school. Orig. scheduled for March 13.

Director: Lyndall Hobbs           Writer: Eric Gilliland

18. "Separate Rooms" April 3, 1991

With Karen at college, Kevin and Wayne can't agree on who's going to get her old room.

Director: Michael Dinner          Teleplay: Bob Brush
Story: Jill Gordon & Bob Brush

19. "The Yearbook" April 10, 1991

Kevin gets used by "the popular kids" on the elite Yearbook Committee to take the blame for insulting captions. Carpenter reprises his role from ep. 10; recurring guest Raye Birk's first name is misspelled "Ray" in the end-credits.

Peter Armbruster...............................................Michael Bower
Brad Patterson.......................................................Chad Allen
Marci Doran (last name erroneously given
    as Donovan onscreen)............................Sandy Alexander
Steve.................................................................Jonathan Brandis
Susan...................................................................Ami Foster
Julius......................................................................Sonny Kelly
Mr. Altman.................................................Willie C. Carpenter
Mr. Armbruster.............................................James O'Connell
Mrs. Armbruster.................................................Gerry Lock

Director: Neal Israel             Writer: David Chambers

20. "The Accident" April 24, 1991

Kevin senses Winnie is going through an upheaval in her life, but she rejects his attempts to help her.

Mrs. Cooper, Winnie's mother.............................Lynn Milgrim
Mr. Cooper, Winnie's father........................H. Richard Greene
Rex.......................................................................Nicolas Read
William................................................................Shawn Phelan

Director: Richard Masur          Teleplay: Jill Gordon
Story: Jill Gordon & Bob Brush

21. "The House That Jack Built" May 1, 1991

Jack clashes with Karen over her decision to share a rundown house with a male roommate (Schwimmer).

Michael Keillor..............................................David Schwimmer

Director: Ken Topolsky   Writers: Mark B. Perry & Mark Levin

22. "Graduation" May 8, 1991

As they graduate, Kevin is distressed when Paul says he's going to a local prep school; Kevin helps his pregnant former English teacher (Meldrum, reprising her role from last season) reach a hospital. Satie and Cook reprise their roles from ep. 6.

Mrs. Heimer ("Miss White").............................Wendel Meldrum
Ida Pfeiffer [no lines].........................................Stephanie Satie
Debbie Pfeiffer [no lines]................................Torrey Anne Cook

Director: Michael Dinner          Writer: Bob Brush

23. "Looking Back" May 15, 1991

Kevin looks back on his three years in junior high, via clips of past episodes and new narration.

*From past-episode clips, various seasons:*
    Dante Basco, Maia Brewton, Torrey Anne Cook, Brandon Crane, Lindsay Fisher, Steven Gilborn, Linda Hoy, David Huddleston, Donnie Jeffcoat, Michael Landis, Crystal McKellar (misspelled "Crystall" onscreen), Wendel Meldrum, Krista Murphy, Tony Nittoli, Robert Picardo, Holly Sampson, Ben Stein, Michael Tricario, Andrea Walters

Director: Nick Marck      Writers: Mark B. Perry & Mark Levin

**renewed for 1991-92; new episodes begin Oct. 2, 1991**

## Working It Out

NBC       Aug. 22-Nov. 10      Saturdays, 8:30-9 p.m.
          Nov. 28-Dec. 12      Wednesdays, 9:30-10 p.m.

Series premiere: Aug. 22, 1990
Final telecast: Dec. 12, 1990

Romantic comedy of the relationship between a divorced mother with a nine-year-old child, and a divorced father of two grown daughters. Sarah's apartment: 9G. Cast-member Colton was a guest performer ep. 1. Set and shot in New York City. Working title: *The Jane Curtin Show*.

Sarah Marshall........................................................Jane Curtin
David Stuart.....................................................Stephen Collins
Molly Marshall (9).......................................Kyndra Joy Casper
Stan......................................................................David Garrison
Andy (orig. Gail)..............................................Mary Beth Hurt
Gail (ep. 1)..............................................................Randy Graff
Sophie (ep. 2-on)..................................................Chevi Colton

*Recurring, virtually all episodes:*
Lynda..........................................................Jane Summerhays
Cooking teacher Mr. Giamelli ("Mr. G")...............Dick Latessa

*Other recurring guests:*
Chuckie (ep. 3,6,9,11)............................................David Klein
Bob (ep. 3,6,8,10)............................................Charles Gemmill

A Dan Jali Production in assoc. with Twentieth Century Fox
Executive producers (ep. 2-on): Bill Persky, Marshall Karp
Producers (ep. 1): Bill Persky, Steven Haft
Executive story consultants: Adriana Trigiani, David Handler, Peter Gethers (latter two early episodes), Marie Squerciati (later episodes)
Creative consultants: Chuck Ranberg, Anne Flett
Supervising producer: George Barimo
Coordinating producer: Gabe Kennedy Abel
Music: uncredited/inapplicable
Theme: John Leffler & Ralph Shuckett; performed by John Leffler

Director: Bill Persky
Creator: Bill Persky

--------------------

1. Wednesday, Aug. 22, 1990, 9-9:30; Sept. 8, 1990

Sarah meets David at an Italian cooking class.

Sophie.................................................................Chevi Colton
Amy.....................................................................Christina Ricci

Writer: Bill Persky

2. "And Now, My Non-Love"  Sept. 22, 1990

Friends convince Sarah and David to avoid getting entangled
in a romance, and to be friends with each other instead.

Lesley................................................................Christina Haag
Judd........................................................................Jim Gillis
Nurse..................................................................Frances Foster
And: David Gautreaux (Phillipe), Joseph Palmas (Clerk)

Writers: Peter Gethers & David Handler

3. "Who Asks First"  Sept. 29, 1990

Sarah and David face the embarrassing dilemma of who to
bring to their cooking-class dinner party.

Phillip.................................................................David Bailey
Susan................................................Kathleen Bridget Kelly
And: Ed Fry (Reed), Michael Miceli (Alex)

Writer: Lee Kalecheim

4. "First Date from Hell"  Oct. 6, 1990

Sarah and David finally synchronize their schedules for a dinner date.

Jean Paul.........................................................Edmond Genest
Nurse...............................................................Saundra McClain
Sheila...............................................................Catherine Perry
Love Child (rock group)............Tony Andresakis, Joel Chaiken,
     Bryan Larkin
Repairperson.............................................................Bob Ari
Restaurant captain...........................................Richard Ferrone
Guests...................................Marlon Hoffman, Roswell Smith
And:  Mike Hodge (Haggerty), Nicholas Levitin (Elliot), Marcell
     Rosenblatt (Gladys), Phil Stein (Hospital worker)

Writer: Marshall Karp

5. "What Next, My Love"  Oct. 13, 1990

Sarah and David enjoy their second date, then both become
anxious about the dreaded "third date syndrome."

Announced cast includes some recurring guests and: Alan
     Dysert (Emcee/stage performer)

Writers: Peter Gethers & David Handler

6. "Old Boyfriends"  Oct. 20, 1990

An old boyfriend (Muenz) invites Sarah to spend the weekend
with him in Los Angeles.

Brian Burnell...................................................Richard Muenz

Teleplay: Nina Shengold & Jeffrey Sweet and Chuck Ranberg
     & Anne Flett

Story: Nina Shengold & Jeffrey Sweet

7. "Ageless Love"  Oct. 27, 1990

Sarah feels as smothered by David as David's daughter
(Lange) feels by her college beau.

Jody Stuart...........................................................Robin Lange

Writer: Adriana Trigiani

8. "It Almost Happened One Night"  Nov. 3, 1990

Sarah and David attempt to spend the night together.

With some recurring guests and: Marjorie Lovett, Danielle
     Marcot

Writers: Peter Gethers & David Handler

9. "Instructions"  Nov. 10, 1990

In their attempts to assemble a cider mill, Sarah and David
discover troubling differences in their approaches to tasks.

Announced cast includes some recurring guests and:  Michael
     Higgins, Dan Lounsbery

Director: NA    Writer: NA

10. "Take My Girlfriend..."  Nov. 28, 1990

Sarah doesn't think David's favorite comic is funny.

Announced cast includes some recurring guests and:  Henny
     Youngman (Himself)

Writers: Peter Gethers & David Handler

**unscheduled preemption, Dec. 1, 8:30-9 p.m.**

11. "Molly and David"  Dec. 12, 1990

When Molly starts calling David "Pop" after a photo shoot,
Sarah worries that Molly likes modeling.

With some recurring guests and: Catherine Hyland, Linda
     Kerns, Heather Zolvick, Arline Miyazaki, Robert Hogan.
     Gwendolyn Coleman, Cynthia Darlow

Writer: Adriana Trigiani

**preempted Dec. 19; unscheduled preemption Dec. 26,
then cancelled**

Unaired

"Surprise! I Hate Your Friend"

At their first meeting, making preparations for David's surprise birthday party, Sarah and Stan are cat and dog.  Orig.
scheduled for Nov. 17.

Lynda.........................................................Jane Summerhays
Cooking teacher Mr.  Giamelli ("Mr. G")...............Dick Latessa
Bob..................................................................Charles Gemmill

Director: NA    Writer: NA

"Foxhole"

Sarah and David have their first big argument. Orig. scheduled for Dec. 26, 1990; preempted by the last half of an unscheduled one-hour *Dear John...* rerun.

Director: NA   Writer: NA

## You Take the Kids

CBS          Saturdays, 8-8:30 p.m.

Series premiere: Dec. 15, 1990
Final telecast: Jan. 12, 1991

Comedy of the blue-collar Kirkland (orig. Metcalf) family in Pittsburgh, with a school-bus driver dad and a piano-teacher mom married 17 years.

Nell Kirkland......................................................Nell Carter
Michael Kirkland..............................................Roger E. Mosley
Raymond Kirkland (16)...........................................Dante Beze
Lorette Kirkland (14)..............................................Caryn Ward
Peter Kirkland (12)..............................................Marlon Taylor
Nate Kirkland (10)..............................................Trent Cameron
Helen, Nell's mother............................................Leila Danette

CBS Entertainment Productions in assoc. with Paul Haggis
    Productions and MTM Enterprises
Executive producer: Paul Haggis
Supervising producer: Stephen Nathan
Producers: Stephen C. Grossman (and Bill Levinson, ep. 1)
Coordinating producer: Matt Dinsmore (ep. 2-on)
Executive story editor: Kathy Slevin
Story editor: John DeBellis
Executive consultant: Joel Thurm
Director of photography: Bill Williams, S.O.C.
Music: Jeff Jones and Bob Mithoff
Theme: Jeff Moss (words and music); performed by Nell Carter
Creators: Paul Haggis & Stephen Nathan

--------

1. "You Take the Kids"  Dec. 15, 1990

Nell and Michael's plans for a romantic getaway are complicated by Nate's new job delivering stolen audio equipment.

Director: Paul Haggis   Writers: Paul Haggis & Stephen Nathan

2. "Merry Christmas to All and a Pointy Hat to You"
   Dec. 22, 1990

The Christmas tree and gifts are stolen by a homeless family.

Officer Ernst..........................................................James Lorinz
Mother............................................................MaryLou Saltonstall
Father..............................................................Dennis O'Sullivan
Children....Cheney Shapiro, Samantha Jordan, Ryan Sheridan

Director: Frank Bonner
Writers: Paul Haggis & Stephen Nathan

3. "The Eggs and I"  Dec. 29, 1990

When Lorette teams with a cute boy (Tate) in a school parenting project involving the care of eggs, her folks misunderstand.

Terry.......................................................................Larenz Tate
Carol......................................................................Sunny Gorg

Director: J.D. Lobue                          Writer: Kathy Slevin

4. "Fishes Are Like Sisters...You Can't Flush Them Without
   Feeling Guilty"  Jan. 5, 1991

Lorette asks out Raymond's cool but sexually active friend (Payne); Nate has plans to assassinate an unwanted goldfish. Orig. scheduled for Dec. 22.

Spunk...................................................................Carl Payne II

Director: Peter Baldwin
Writers: Paul Haggis & Stephen Nathan

5. "Bad Boy"  Jan. 12, 1991

Peter steals the family car to get his parents' attention. Orig. scheduled for Jan. 19.

Director: J.D. Lobue                          Writer: Marcia L. Leslie

Unaired

"What I Did for Love"

Raymond borrows from a high school loan shark (Baker) to take out the most materialistic girl in school (Campbell), then steals to try to repay. Orig. scheduled for Jan. 19.

Loraleen.............................................................Tisha Campbell
Dewayne...................................................................Shaun Baker

Director: J.D. Lobue                          Writer: Bill Levinson

## The Young Riders

ABC          Saturdays, 8-9 p.m.

Series premiere: Sept. 20, 1989

Western drama of a group of young men -- and a young woman (Suhor) masquerading as one -- in the Pony Express of the 1860s. New cast-members Wren and Franklin were guests ep. 1-2. Occasional director James Keach is the brother of actor Stacy Keach and the son of actor Stacy Keach, Sr. Filmed near Tucson, Ariz.

William Cody....................................................Stephen Baldwin
Jimmy Hickok..........................................................Josh Brolin
Ike McSwain.............................................................Travis Fine
Noah Dixon (ep. 3-on)..........................................Don Franklin
The Kid......................................................................Ty Miller
Buck Cross...........................................................Gregg Rainwater
Lou McCloud.........................................................Yvonne Suhor
Rachel Dunne (ep. 3-on)...........................................Clare Wren
Teaspoon Hunter......................................................Anthony Zerbe

*Recurring:*
Tompkins (ep. 4-5,9-10, 15-17,19).........................Don Collier

Pendragon and the Ogiens/Kane Co. and MGM/UA Television
Executive producer: Jonas McCord
Producer: Christopher Seitz
Co-producers: Raymond Hartung, Steven Baum
Coordinating producer: Larry Rapaport
Associate producer: Tony Palermo
Executive story editor: Charles Grant Craig
Director of photography: Earl L. Clark
Theme (instrumental) and music: John Debney
Creator: Ed Spielman

1. "Born to Hang"  Sept. 22, 1990

The riders try to recapture gold stolen from a woman (Reese) spearheading a venture to send escaped slaves to Africa.

Noah Dixon.....................................................Don Franklin
Rachel Dunne...................................................Clare Wren
Stagecoach Sally...............................................Della Reese
Barnes...........................................................Barry Cullison
McKenna........................................................Ron Phillips
Helga............................................................Francesca Jarvis
And:  Mildred J. Brion (Idabel), Elijah N. Crane (Young Noah), Lillie Richardson (Mother), Adam Frank (Undertaker)

Director: George Mendeluk          Writer: Delle Chatman

2. "Ghosts"  Sept. 28, 1990

The "ghost" of one of Teaspoon's victims returns for revenge.

Noah Dixon.....................................................Don Franklin
Rachel Dunne...................................................Clare Wren
"The Buzzard Eater".........................................David Carradine
Thad Browing...................................................James Healy
Henry.............................................................James Lancaster
Dennis Browning..............................................Jeff Bennett
Ethan Browning...............................................Mark Jeffreys
Angus Browning...............................................Jay Bernard
And:  Brad Jarrell (Deputy), Jake Walker (Blue Creek Sheriff), Billy Joe Patton (Replacement)

Director: James Keach          Writer: Steven Baum

3. "Dead Ringer"  Oct. 6, 1990

Hickok sets out to catch a vicious gunman impersonating him.

Henry Muncie...................................................John Slattery
Jake Colter......................................................William Shockley
Fuller............................................................Ken Bridges
Ranch hands...................................Wally Welch, Robin Wayne
Wrangler........................................................Ed Adams
And: David Richards (Bank manager), Paul Threlkeld (Clerk)

Director: Virgil W. Vogel          Teleplay: Raymond Hartung
Story: Elaine Newman & Ed Burnham

4. "Blood Moon"  Oct. 13, 1990

Fear of a cholera outbreak turns the citizens of Sweetwater into a mob intent on lynching a deaf-mute boy (Hutchison) suspected of being the carrier. Orig. scheduled for Oct. 6.

Elijah Quinn....................................................George Hearn
Danny............................................................Doug Hutchison
Flynn.............................................................Seth Foster
Doc Barnes.............................Bill T. (a.k.a. Travis) Middleton
Blacksmith......................................................Tommy Townsend
And: Erol Landis (Brody), Casey Van Patten (Clint)

Director: Virgil W. Vogel
Writers: Christopher Thinnes & Deirdre Le Blanc

**preempted Oct. 20**

5. "Pride and Prejudice"  Oct. 27, 1990

Buck finds Tompkins' long-missing wife (O'Hara) and child (O'Neill) assimilated with the Sioux tribe that had taken them.

Sally Tompkins.................................................Jenny O'Hara
Jennifer Tompkins.............................................Amy O'Neill
Running Bear...................................................Joaquin Martinez
Black Wolf......................................................Joseph Runningfox
Peter.............................................................Richard Comeau
April.............................................................Charmaine Blakely
2nd Lieutenant.................................................Craig Reay
Citizens.............................Warner McKay, Owen O'Farrell

Director: Joseph L. Scanlan          Teleplay: Christopher Thinnes
Story: Randy Holland

6. "The Littlest Cowboy"  Nov. 3, 1990

Ike, bitter after being beaten by men who take advantage of his handicap, befriends a terminally ill boy (Graas).

Helen............................................................Judith Hoag
Arthur...........................................................John Christian Graas
Sims.............................................................George O. Petrie
Mary Jane.......................................................Kathy Fitzgerald
Sheriff...........................................................Tom Noga
And: Marian Gibson (Elderly woman), David Bukunus (Flunky), Jay Bernard (Biggers), Dick Bellarue (Deputy)

Director: Virgil W. Vogel          Writer: Steven Baum

7. "Blood Money"  Nov. 10, 1990  (3314)

The Kid catches a would-be horse thief (Patton), who apparently hangs himself while in the custody of a corrupt marshal.

Marshal Cole Lambert.........................................Sherman Howard
Sutter............................................................John Nesci
Emily.............................................................Pierrette Grace
Foster............................................................George Dobbs
Dyson............................................................Billy Joe Patton
And: Nick Nichols (McBride), Jarrod Wilson (Matthew), William Spies (Mayor), Ken Kolb (Kane)
Also orig. announced: Leon Palles (Perkins)

Director: Joseph L. Scanlan          Writer: Raymond Hartung

8. "Requiem for a Hero"  Nov. 17, 1990

Cody meets and learns from his doomed Old West hero (Roberts). Threlkeld played a different role in ep. 3.

Hezekiah Horn..................................................Pernell Roberts
Webster..........................................................Norm Skaggs
Doc Barnes.............................Travis (a.k.a. Bill T.) Middleton
Barker...........................................................Don Pendergrass
And: George Salazar (Indian Police), Paul Threlkeld (Manager), Betsabe Moore (Squaw), Jonathan Gill (Brave)

Director: Virgil W. Vogel          Writer: Bruce Reisman

9. "Bad Company"  Dec. 1, 1990  (3309)

Hickok leaves to become sheriff of the lawless town of Regrets, hoping to meet death quickly as retribution for accidentally killing a young woman (Risley) during a gunfight.

Jennifer.........................................................Michelle Joyner
Luke Rinehart..................................................Stephen Root
Angel............................................................Karen Person
Sheriff of Benton...............................................Hank Fletcher
Preacher.........................................................William J. Fisher
Thatcher.........................................................Charles Gunning
Cora Rinehart..................................................Anna Risley
Sheriff of Regrets..............................................Mike Shanks

Director: Stephen L. Borey          Writer: James L. Novack

10. "Star Light, Star Bright"  Dec. 15, 1990

At Christmastime, the riders believe they own half a gold mine, a repayment for Hickok's kindness to a prospector (Keith).

Cyrus............................................................Brian Keith
McPhalen......................................................Richard Zobel
Sarah........................................................Jaime Lyn Bauer
And:  Craig Reay (Jorgenson), Ed Adams (Perkins), Grant Wheeler (Dodd), Mike Casper (Blacksmith/Otis)

Director: Joseph L. Scanlan          Writer: Raymond Hartung

11. "The Play's the Thing"  Dec. 29, 1990

Cody considers joining a theater troupe, and unknowingly enters a plot to assassinate a U.S. General. Co-writer Graham is known primarily as an actor. Orig. scheduled for Oct. 13.

Margaret......................................................Tammy Grimes
Jenny St. Clair............................................Rebecca Staab
Edmund.........................................................Grant James
Jonathan..................................................Dane Christopher
Eastman.....................................................Richard Glover
General Fremont..........................................Jim Newcomer
Walker.........................................................William Lang
        Also orig. announced:
        Ric San Nicholas (Guard), Jimmy Cox (Drunk)

Director: George Mendeluk          Teleplay: Charles Grant Craig
Story: Gerrit Graham & Chris Hubbel

12. "Judgment Day"  Jan. 5, 1991

Cody, still affected by Hezekiah Horn's death, seeks guidance from a preacher-vigilante (Massett). Working title: "The Regulators." Guest Overall is a cast-member of Empty Nest.

Gideon Poole.............................................Patrick Massett
Lucius............................................................James Lashly
Millie Owens..................................................Park Overall
Horace Pullman..........................................David Richards
Deputy Barnett..............................................Monty Stuart
Oscar Flagler.............................................Gerald Burgess
Caleb..........................................................Andy Sherman
Simon Poole.....................................................Jim Cody
William Matthew.......................................Nick Sean Gomez

Director: Corey Blechman          Writer: Donald Marcus

13. "Kansas"  Jan. 12, 1991

Noah is taken into slavery when he tries to free his former teacher (Roundtree). Cullison reprises his role from ep. 1.

Calvin.....................................................Richard Roundtree
Barnes.........................................................Barry Cullison
Andrew.....................................................Andre Marcellous
Nathan Smith.............................................Ric San Nicholas
And:  Jason Kenny (J.B. Higgins), Lee E. Wells Jr. (Robert), Burney Starks (Thomas), Roger Carter (Preacher)

Director: Virgil W. Vogel          Teleplay: Steven Baum
Story: James L. Crite

14. "The Peacemakers"  Jan. 19, 1991

Hickok falls for a woman (Bakke) from an ostracized religious group, and settles an old score with a gunfighter (Railsback).

Tyler...........................................................Steve Railsback
Jacob......................................................James Cromwell
Alice............................................................Brenda Bakke
Marcus............................................................Joe Sikorra
Estes.............................................................Alan McRae
Marshall Scruggs.........................................Blake Conway
Carter......................................................Kenneth Bridges
And: Gregg Brazzel (Redneck), George K. Sullivan (Rancher)
        Also orig. announced:
        Tiffany Westlie (Girl), John Hajck-Doggett (Boy)

Director: James Keach          Writer: Charles Grant Craig

15. "Daisy"  Feb. 2, 1991

Tracked by a riverboat gunslinger (Hoy), Rachel's former lover (Russ) leaves his nine-year-old daughter in Rachel's care.

Roger..........................................................William Russ
Daisy, his daughter........Lexi Randall a.k.a. Lexi Faith Randall
Mingus......................................................Robert F. Hoy
Livery man................................................Sydney Warner
Waiter.....................................................Gerry Glombecki
Clerk...................................................Michael F. Woodson
Faith..................................................Kellye Chapman Bell

Director: Michael Preece          Writer: Steven Baum

16. "Color Blind"  Feb. 9, 1991

After Lou and the Kid break up, she gets close to Hickok, and the Kid falls for the town's troubled new schoolteacher (Valen).

Samantha Edgars............................................Nancy Valen
Martha.................................................Olivia Virgil Harper
Robert Andrew.......................................David Patrick Wilson
Neville Hopkins................................................Seth Foster
Mrs. Evans...................................................Linda Jurgens
William...........................................................Sid Dawson
And: Wolfe Bowart (Juggler), Gene Collins (Top Hat)

Director: Virgil W. Vogel          Writer: Delle Chatman

17. "Old Scores"  Feb. 16, 1991

Ike hunts the man (Deloy) involved in the gang-style murder of his family, while the other riders track a strange beast.

Rawlings.....................................................George Deloy
Jeremy.......................................................Brian Bonsall
Nicholson..................................................Daniel Martine
Molly..........................................................Peppi Sanders
P.J. Curtis......................................................Gary Clarke
And: Bob Holland (Mr. Mike), James Tarwater (Henchperson)

Director: Guy Magar          Writer: Linda J. Cowgill

18. "The Talisman"  Feb. 23, 1991

Outlaws attack a minister's (Haynie) mission; a woman (Mahaffey) is haunted by visits from a mountain hermit (Crawley). Stuart reprises his role from ep. 12. On initial airing, episode cut short by a news report.

Father Peter Reilly..............................................Jim Haynie
Lottie......................................................Valerie Mahaffey
Miguel...........................................................Julian Reyes
Stoltz..................................................Robert Sonne Browne
Pedro...........................................................Fredrick Lopez
Maria.............................................................Ana Arthur
Nils Petersen..............................Michael Benjamin Crawley

And: Monty Stuart (Deputy Barnett), Wanda Dittman (Elena)
    Also orig. announced:
    George W. Pompa (Santo), Alejandra Garcia-Lohr (Pregnant woman)

Director: Virgil W. Vogel          Writer: Donald Marcus

19. "The Noble Chase" March 9, 1991

Hickok and his bounty-hunter nemesis (Shockley, reprising his role from ep. 3) compete to bring in an alleged bank robber (Maggio). Orig. scheduled for Feb. 23.

Jake Colter.....................................................William Shockley
Lon Chase.....................................................Tony Maggio
Gov. Phelan...................................................Dave Adams
Marshal Steiger.............................................Ed Beimfohr
Secretary Davis.............................................Mark Lang
Investor.........................................................Ronald L. Colby
Marshal Hurston...........................................Jake Walker

Director: Michael Preece          Writer: Christopher Thinnes

**preempted March 16**

20. "Face of the Enemy" April 6, 1991

When Teaspoon's war-hero friend (Carhart) orders an attack upon a Sioux delegation, Indians threaten to retaliate. Comeau played a different role, ep. 5.

Army Col. Matthew Curtis..............................Timothy Carhart
Nigel Bunthorn.............................................Steeve Arlen
Ben Cleveland...............................................Richard Comeau
Spotted Horse...............................................Bob Cota
Doc................................................................David Carey Foster
Runs Like Deer.............................................Jonathan Gill
And: Paul Klein (Haliwell), George Salazar (Dancing Hawk)

Director: James Keach          Writer: Raymond Hartung

21. "The Exchange" May 4, 1991 8:01-10:12 p.m.

When Teaspoon arranges for a bank robber (Knott) to be hanged, the man's brother (Nordling) kidnaps Teaspoon's would-be daughter (Leeds), precipitating a massive showdown. Late start and end due to a news bulletin and a live telecast of a White House press conference.

Frank Pike....................................................Jeffrey Nordling
Ramirez.........................................................Tony Acierto
Hack..............................................................Peter Phelps
Amanda O'Connel..........................................Sue-Ann Leeds
Emory Pike, Frank's brother..........................Robert Knott
Jane...............................................................Lisa Rubin
Redfern..........................................................Pat McCord
Sheriff Dooley................................................Tommy Townsend
Grave digger..................................................George Dobbs
Hangman........................................................Michael B. Crawley
Mayor of Benton.............................................David Richards
Desk clerk......................................................Sonya Austin

Director: Virgil W. Vogel          Writer: Charles Grant Craig

**preempted May 18**
**preempted July 13**
**preempted Aug. 3**
**preempted Aug. 17**
**preempted Aug. 31**

**renewed for 1991-92; new episodes begin Sept. 28, 1991**

# UNSOLD COMEDY AND DRAMA PILOTS

## Hammer, Slammer & Slade

ABC          Saturday, Dec. 15, 1990 9-10 p.m.

Seriocomic adventure featuring characters and some performers from executive producer Wayans' film parody, *I'm Gonna Git You Sucka* (1988): Three black crimefighters come out of retirement to vindicate a retiring cop (O'Neal) accused of robbery. Dedication: "To the memory of Tony Bishop, 1943-1990."

"Hammer" Wilson..............................................Isaac Hayes *
"Slammer" Jenkins.............................................Jim Brown *
John Slade........................................................Bernie Casey *
Ray Samuels......................................................Ron O'Neal
Joanne.......................Ja'net DuBois (played Ma Bell in film) *
Leonard............................................................Bentley Evans **
Jack Spade........................................................Eriq LaSalle #
Willie...............................................................Martin Lawrence ##
Sgt. Hill...........................................................Ron Dean
With: Steve James* (played Kung Fu Joe in film), Ron Karabatsos, Mark Palston, Sandy Simpson
And: Alma Yvonne (Coretha Jones), Sam Menning (Homeless man), Margaret Wheeler (Mary), Carlos Cervantes (Man), Blackie Dammett (Weasel), Jack Axelrod (Valend)

\*      appeared in film.
\*\*    played by Dy Damon Wayans in film.
\#     played by Keenen Ivory Wayans in film.
\#\#   played by Kadeem Hardison in film.

Director: Michael Schultz          Writer: Keenen Ivory Wayans

Ivory Way Productions in assoc. with Robert Greenwald and MGM/UA Television
Executive producer: Keenen Ivory Wayans
Producer: Tony Bishop
Associate producer: Carl Craig
Director of photography: Charles Mills
Music: Stanley Clarke

## The Brotherhood

ABC          Tuesday, Jan. 2, 1991 10-11 p.m.

Drama of two Italian brothers in the New York City borough of Queens, who grow up on opposite sides of the law -- one (La Paglia) as a crime boss, the other (Meek) as a police officer.

Nicholas Gennaro.............................................Anthony La Paglia
Salvatore Gennaro.............................................Jeffrey Meek
Teresa Gennaro.................................................Teri Hatcher
Ian Geller.........................................................Patrick Massett
Irene Gennaro...................................................Pamela Dillman
Maria Gennaro...................................................Rose Gregorio
Antonio Santangeletta.........................................Richard Sarafian
Police lieutenant................................................Richard Marcus
Carrie Embers...................................................Kimberly Foster
Joey Piselli...........James Medina a.k.a. Jimmy Medina Taggert
And: Rene Assa (Jilly), Peter Onorati (Priest), Jack Ong (Paul Chen), Maria Cavaiani (Ariana Gennaro), Christina Cocek (Anchorperson), Paolo Piazzardi (Frank Gennaro)

Director: Robert Butler          Writer: Richard DiLello

Gangbuster Films and Dark Ink in assoc. with Citadel Entertainment and Lorimar Television

Executive producers: Robert Butler, Richard DiLello
Producer: Ronald L. Schwary
Supervising producer: Anita Addison
Coordinating producer: Jessie Ward
Executive consultants: Lawrence Gordon, Charles Gordon
Director of photography: Paul Onorato, A.C.S.
Music: Lee Holdridge

## The Steven Banks Show

Showtime    Saturday, Jan. 12, 1991    10-10:30 p.m.

Comedy of a Walter Mitty-like copywriter for the Cutting Edge Catalogue Company: Steven prepares for a date while on deadline with an emergency work project. Based on Banks' stage production and later Showtime special *Home Entertainment Center* (1989).

Steven Brooks.................................................Steven Banks
Landlord Victor Ullman................................David Byrd
Wendy Ullman, his daughter............................Signy Coleman
Dennis..........................................................Alex Nevil

*Guest cast:*
Martha..........................................................Dana Andersen
Froller..........................................................Christopher Collins
Cop..............................................................Michael Rider
With: Christiane Carman, Catherine Dent, Nancy Rubin

Director: Tom McLoughlin
Writer: Steven Banks & Douglas McGrath

Touchstone Television
Executive producer: Bob Young
Supervising producer: Mark Brull
Producers: Douglas McGrath, Susan Dietz
Associate producer: David Z. Sacks
Director of photography: Vance Conterino
Music: Gary Stockdale
Song: Steven Banks

## Tag Team

ABC            Saturday, Jan. 26, 1991    10-11 p.m.

Action-adventure of two pro wrestlers, unjustly drummed out of the profession, who become undercover police officers. Co-stars Piper and Ventura are professional wrestler-actors; guest Tweed is the November 1981 *Playboy* Playmate and 1982 Playmate of the Year. Information (incomplete) primarily from ABC.

"Tricky" Rick MacDonald......................."Rowdy" Roddy Piper
Billy "The Body" Youngblood............Jesse "The Body" Ventura
Lt. Steckler...................................................Robin Curtis
Sgt. Harrigan................................................Michael Genovese
Hatch..........................................................Raymond O'Connor

*Guest cast:*
Officer Ray Tyler.............................................Phill Lewis
Rita Valentine.................................................Jennifer Runyon
Leona..........................................................Shannon Tweed
Barney..........................................................Michael M. Vendrell
Riker............................................................Robert Hanley
Instructor......................................................Kathy Kinney
Patrol officer..................................................Randy Olea
"The Orient Express" wrestling team......Pat Tanaka, Akio Sato
And: Tawny G. Little (Newscaster), Bill Anderson (Announcer), Joey Marella (Referee), Mr. Fuji (Manager), Sean Baca, Mark Gintner, Mark Lenow

Director: Paul Krasny            Writer: Robert L. McCullough

The IndieProd Co. in assoc. with Touchstone Television
Executive producers: Reuben Leder, Bruce Sallan
Producer: Ric Rondell
Music: Jay Ferguson
Creator: Robert L. McCullough

## Clippers

CBS            Monday, June 3, 1991    10:30-11 p.m.

Comedy of the proprietor, employees and customers of a once-elegant hotel's barbershop in St. Louis, Missouri: Mel tries to avoid his visiting ex-wife, who'd walked out on him years before, until he discovers she is stricken with cancer.

Barber-proprietor Mel Haig.......................................John Amos
Barber Teddy Jackson................................................Shabaka
Barber Charles Robinson...........................................Phill Lewis
Hotel night clerk Leonard Sarkin.........................Arnold Stang
T.J., Mel's nephew....................................................Larenz Tate
Renee Haig, Mel's attorney daughter...................A.J. Johnson
Manicurist Esther................................Phyllis Yvonne Stickney

*Guest cast:*
Mel's ex-wife........................................................Cicely Tyson
Bubba..........................................................Sy Richardson
Franklin....................................Don "Bubba" Bexley
And: Jon Clair (Marcus), K.C. Amos (Hector)

Director: Matthew Diamond            Writer: Robert Moloney

Moloney Limited (but not very) in assoc. with Eddie Murphy Television and Paramount Television.
Executive producers: Robert Moloney, Eddie Murphy
Supervising producer: Mark McClafferty
Producer: Henry Lange Jr.
Coordinating producers: Mark E. Corry, Clint Smith
Co-producer: Jason Shubb
Director of photography: Donald A. Morgan
Theme (words and music) and music: Paul Pilger, Dennis Pollen, William Moloney; theme performed by Joe Williams

## Our Shining Moment

NBC            Sunday, June 2, 1991    7-8 p.m.

Seriocomic drama of a middle-class Midwestern family in the early 1960s, centered on the Catholic schoolboy son (Brandis): Scooter, temporarily and unjustly expelled from school, runs into his secretly out-of-work dad in the park. Director Tinker is the son of producer Grant Tinker. Filmed in Vancouver.

Betty McGuire....................................................Cindy Pickett
John McGuire......................................................Max Gail
Scooter McGuire (13)....................................Jonathan Brandis
Wheels, his friend................................................Seth Green
Maureen McGuire.................................................Luanne Ponce
Papa McGuire, John's father................................Don Ameche
And: Shawn Levy

*Guest cast:*
Father Hogan....................................................Alec Burden
Lois Jessel..........................................................Sonia Banman
Officer Hamsen....................................................George Catalano
Teenager..........................................................Mike Iacobucci
And: Bill Dow (Barney), Alvin Lee Sanders (Rahill)

Director: Mark Tinker                Writer: Patrick Hasburgh

Patrick Hasburgh Productions in assoc. with Walt Disney
    Television
Executive producer: Patrick Hasburgh
Producer: Mark H. Ovitz
Co-producer: Justin Greene
Director of photography: Laszlo George, C.S.C.
Music: Peter Bernstein

## 5 Up, 2 Down

CBS          Wednesday, June 5, 1991  8:30-9 p.m.

Comedy of a young, married Los Angeles couple (Sams, Roberts) faced with the birth of triplets and the sudden presence
of their own feuding parents (Little, Yancy), who announce
they intend to settle in to help bring up the babies.

Sam Tyler, Nick's blue-collar father.....................Cleavon Little
Daphne Fitzgerald, Angie's upscale mother...........Emily Yancy
Angie Tyler.................................................Jackie Mari Roberts
Nick Tyler...............................................Jeffrey D. Sams
Infants Sophie, Lisa and George...........................(uncredited)

Director: Linda Day
Writers: Richard Ommanney and Winifred Hervey-Stallworth

Winifred Hervey-Stallworth Productions in assoc. with D.L.
    Taffner Productions and Orion Television Entertain-
    ment / Up and Down Productions
Executive producer: Winifred Hervey-Stallworth
Co-executive producer: Richard Ommanney
Producer: Shelley Jensen
Associate producer: Annette Sahakian
Music: Steve Tyrell
Theme (instrumental): Barry Coffing, Michael Lent, Steve
    Tyrell
Based upon characters from the BBC television series *Three
Up, Two Down*, created by Richard Ommanney

## The Hit Man

ABC          Saturday, June 29, 1991  9-10:30 p.m.

Action-adventure drama of a Steven Spielberg-like Hollywood
filmmaker (Boutsikaris) who enlists his special effects team in
an elaborate scheme to outfox a vicious loan shark (Pryor) out
to foreclose on a widowed mother (Gago).  Guest Leach is the
host of syndicated celebrity-lifestyles shows.

Roger Woods..............................................Dennis Boutsikaris
Spider......................................................Daryl Anderson
Billy.......................................................Eagle Eye Cherry
Jerry Wilson...................................................Tim Dunigan
Vigo.......................................................Ferdinand Mayne
Sara..........................................................Gail O'Grady
Gordon Padway...................................................Nick Pryor
Otto.........................................................Robert Donner
Pauly Arando (14)..............................................Dante Basco
Rita Arando, his mother........................................Jenny Gago
Judge.........................................................Charles Lane
Josh..........................................................Josh Richman
Himself.......................................................Robin Leach
Annie........................................................Deena Freeman
Kentucky.................................................Branscombe Richmond
Connie......Nicole Orth Pallavicini a.k.a. Nicole Orth-Pallavicini
And:  Gregg Berger (Neal), Elyse Donalson (Mrs. Stoner), Doug
    MacHugh (Harry), Jake Jacobs (Alien), Bernie Pock (Tour

guide/driver), David Spade (Usher), Robert Hanley (Cop),
Dean Wein (Highway patrol officer), Michael J. London
(Deputy), Jenny Nauman (Penelope)

Director: Gary Nelson
Writers: George Schenck & Frank Cardea

Schenck/Cardea Productions in assoc. with the Christopher
    Morgan Co. and ABC Circle Films and MGM/UA / ABC
    Productions
Executive producers: Frank Cardea, George Schenck
Producer: Gary Nelson
Co-producer: Steve Barnett
Associate producer: Murray Miller
Director of photography: Jack Priestley, A.S.C.
Music: Arthur Kempel

## Maverick Square

ABC          Saturday, June 29, 1991  10:30-11 p.m.

Comedy of two Italian, inner-city pals in the East Boston
neighborhood of Maverick Square: Fat Nicky and Sal believe a
recently deceased friend may have purchased a winning lot-
tery ticket.  Guest LeNoire is a cast-member of *Family Matters*;
Casella, of *Doogie Howser, M.D.*.

Fat Nicky.................................................Michael Chiklis
Sal.......................................................David Marciano
Rochelle...................................................Sharon Cornell
Althea....................................................Karla Tamburrelli

*Guest cast:*
Mrs. Lewis..............................................Rosetta LeNoire
And: Will Le Bow, Max Casella, Kay Janes, Richard Pitts-
    Wiley, Barry Rossen, Tina Bruno, Jack Lucero, Cheryl
    McMahon, Ingrid Sonnichsen, Ed Mason, Anthony Mi-
    chael Ruivivar

Director: Steve Miner              Teleplay: Frank Renzulli
Story: Frank Renzulli & Steve Miner

Stephen C. Miner Films in assoc. with Lorimar Television
Executive producer: Steve Miner
Producer: Peter Schindler
Director of photography: Nick McLean
Music: Tom Scott
Theme (lyrics but mostly instrumental, plus voiceover by
    co-star Chiklis): "Welcome to My World" by Ray Winkler
    and John Hathcock (words and music); performer un-
    credited

## K9000

Fox          Monday, July 1, 1991  8-10 p.m.

Science-fiction adventure of a maverick cop (Mulkey) teamed
with a beautiful research scientist (Oxenberg) to rescue her
prize creation: a German shepherd with a computer-enhanced
brain.  Filmed in 1989 as a series pilot, unaired until now.

Eddie Monroe...................................................Chris Mulkey
Dr. Aja Turner...........................................Catherine Oxenberg
Nick Sanrio.................................................Dennis Haysbert
Police Capt. DeLillo.........................................Dana Gladstone
Voice of Niner (dog).............................................Jerry Houser
Anton Zeiss.....................................................Judson Scott
With: Anne Haney, Thom McFadden, David Renan, Ivan E.
    Roth, Danny Weselis

And: Rick Aiello (Waller), Ted Barba (Factor), Ed Evanko (Butler), Mitch Hara (Dijon), Jim Ishida (Rocky Aroki), Waldemar Kalinowsky (Zeiss doctor), Henri King (Zeiss enforcer), Fred Ottaviano (Dock worker), Patricia Raymond (Charity person), Nicholas Shaffer (Zeiss tech), Sammy Thurman (Store owner), Charles Walker (Johnson), Steve Whiteford (Waiter), Deborah Wilkes (Nurse), Jim Burk, Jason Corbett, Kenny Endoso, Jeff Imada, Dave Perna, Danil Torppe (Zeiss personnel).

Note: The dog who played the character Niner was uncredited; per Fox press materials, it was played by two German shepherds from the Family Channel series *Rin Tin Tin K-9 Cop.*

Director: Kim Manners
Writers: Steven E. de Souza & Michael Part

de Souza Productions and Fries Entertainment
Executive producer: Steven E. de Souza
Producer: J. Rickley Dumm
Co-producer: Michael Part
Director of photography: Frank Raymond, A.S.C.
Music: Jan Hammer
Niner furnished by: Birds & Animals Unlimited/Gary Gero
Animal trainers: Roger Schumacher, Bryan Renfro

## In the House

NBC          Monday, July 1, 1991 8:30-9 p.m.

Comedy of a recent college graduate (Cheadle) who returns to live with his father and try make an entrepreneurial go of it in his old Detroit neighborhood, though his conservative, working-class dad wants him to enter the corporate world.

Derrick Brantley.................................Don Cheadle
Ike Brantley, his father......................Bruce A. Young
Charlotte, Ike's sister.........................Loretta Devine
Ike's friends.....................Gilbert Lewis, Hugh Dane
Daphne.............................................Leilani Fields
Dave Collins, Derrick's partner.........Troy Allan Burgess
Roxie, Daphne's older sister...............Viveca A. Fox

*Guest cast:*
Shep.................................................Dietrich Bader
And: Sean Gavigan (Mitch), Michael Carrington (Kenny)

Director: Matthew Diamond
Writer: Susan Borowitz & Andy Borowitz

The Stuffed Dog Company in assoc. with NBC Productions
Executive producer: Andy Borowitz, Susan Borowitz
Producer: Werner Walian
Coordinating producer: Pamela Oas Williams
Associate producer: Mara Lopez
Music: Kenny Finch
Theme: "My Way/Business as Usual" by Don Cheadle and Kenny Finch (words and music); performed by Don Cheadle and Kenny Finch

## The Danger Team

ABC          Wednesday, July 3, 1991 8:30-9 p.m.

Light fantasy-drama, blending clay animation and live action, of a pragmatic bookkeeper (Beller) at the Carl Stalling Detective Agency, who with the help of three tiny, clay-figure-like aliens -- brainy Spex, brawny Truk and playful Nit -- overcomes her boss' resistance to become a "junior detective."

Cheryl Singer.....................................Kathleen Beller
Animator Chris Norman.........................Steve Levitt
Mr. Weidner, Cheryl's boss...............Steven Gilborn
Voice of Spex.............................John Wesley Shipp
Voice of Truk............................Christopher Collins
Voice of Nit...........................................June Foray

*Guest cast:*
Peterson...................................Christopher Neame
Wayne....................................................Lee Ryan
Alan.....................................................Robert Mangiardi
Leonard Rossiter.................................Mark Lonow
Bar patron.......................................Patrick Culliton
Receptionist.........................................Cheryl King
Agency worker..................................Richard Kuller

Director: Helaine Head
Teleplay: Michael Wagner and Harley Peyton
Story: Tom Greene and Michael Wagner

Tom Greene Productions in assoc. with Lorimar Productions
Executive producer: Tom Greene
Producers: David Bleiman, Ken Pontac, Bob Bain
Director of photography: Brian Reynolds
Special effects: Ken Speed
Music: Brian Banks, Anthony Marinelli
Clay characters created by: David Bleiman, Ken Pontac

## Belles of Bleecker St.

ABC Friday, July 5, 1991 9-9:30 p.m.

Comedy of two 13-year-old friends in New York City's Greenwich Village, a Spanish girl (Gonzales) and a WASP (Clayton): Against parents' wishes, Lindsey and JoJo sneak off to a celebrity party to glimpse Miller and Baldwin of *The Young Riders.*

Lindsey...........................................Melissa Clayton
JoJo..............................................Barbara Gonzales
Chris, Lindsey's photographer father.............David Naughton
Holly, Lindsey's mother.........................Breon Gorman
Carmen, JoJo's mother.............................Ivonne Coll
Serena, JoJo's older sister....................Tasia Valenza
Porter..................................................Shawn Phelan
Austin, JoJo's little brother.....................Max Supera
Jerry, JoJo's cab-driver father.................Luis Avalos

*Guest cast:*
Themselves.....................Ty Miller, Stephen Baldwin
Society matron.........................................Anna Lisi

Director: Matthew Diamond
Writers: Anne Beatts and Eve Brandstein

B-Girls Productions in assoc. with Steven J. Cannell Productions
Executive producers: Eve Brandstein, Anne Beatts
Producer: Henry Lange Jr.
Associate producer: Suzy Friendly
Director of photography: Andy Kassan
Theme: Deborah Holland (music), Anne Beatts, Eve Brandstein (words)

## K-9

ABC          Saturday, July 6, 1991 9-10 p.m.

Lighthearted drama of an erratic police officer and an equally erratic German shepherd police dog: Jack and Jerry Lee arrest a car thief, and stumble onto a carnival-based drug operation. Based on the 1989 action-comedy movie.

| | |
|---|---|
| Officer Jack Bergin | Robert Carradine |
| Jerry Lee (dog) | Rondo (erroneously credited as "Jerry Lee" onscreen) |
| Margaret Slater | Lisa Darr |
| Lt. Emmett Broussard | Jason Bernard |

*Guest cast:*

| | |
|---|---|
| Larry Overby | Ken Foree |
| Bernardo | Larry Hankin |
| Ray | Scot Casey |
| Simon | Gregory Wagrowski |
| Monice Du Tour | Gigi Rice |
| Mrs. Pitman | Ellen Albertini Dow |

With: Scott Jaeck, Pierrino Mascarino
And: Stewart J. Zully (Sgt. Sonny Pualtz), Patricia Conklin (Lila Grissum), Jimmie F. Skaggs (Bones), Dallas Cole (Barmaid), Ron Howard George (Lea), Bill Moser (Bart), Nicholas Shaffer (Clerk), Lisa Melilli, Kelly Jerles (Students), Cody Glenn (CHP officer), Julio Ochoa (Danny), Louis Elias (Security guard), Mark Mooring (DEA agent)

Directors: Vincent McEveety and Beth Hillshafer a.k.a. Bethany Rooney Hillshafer a.k.a. Bethany Rooney (orig. announced: Vincent McEveety)
Writers: Maurice Hurley & Wilton Crawley (orig. announced: Maurice Hurley & John Mankiewicz)

Universal Television, an MCA Co.
Executive producers: Maurice Hurley (also orig. announced: Chuck Gordon, Larry Gordon)
Co-executive producers: John Mankiewicz
Supervising producer: John G. Stephens (orig. announced as Co-executive producer)
Coordinating producer: Paul Cajero
Director of photography: Lloyd Ahern II
Technical advisor: Mark Mooring
Jerry Lee [sic] furnished by: Canine Paws, Inc.
Music: Kenny Edwards
Theme (instrumental) written and performed by: Taj Mahal
Based on characters created by: Steven Siegel & Scott Myers

## Silverfox

ABC          Saturday, July 6, 1991  10-11 p.m.

Action-adventure of a veteran U.S. intelligence agent: Fox must untangle a web of murder, romance and international crime, while an assassin dogs his trail. Mack is the wife of actor and series co-creator Tom Selleck; guest Nickson-Soul is the wife of actor David Soul. Orig. scheduled for 9-10 p.m.

| | |
|---|---|
| Robert Fox | James Coburn |
| Charles Blankenship | M. Emmett Walsh |
| Joanie | Jillie Mack |

*Guest cast:*

| | |
|---|---|
| Shimoi Chen | Julia Nickson-Soul |
| Tom | Christopher Allport |
| Klaus Gerhardt | Gianni Russo |
| Jeffrey Campbell | Geoffrey Lower |
| Nita Davenport | Leigh Taylor-Young |

And: Stephen Poletti (Sonny Meyerson), Bruce Reed (Rake), Tricia Long (Caterer), Mary Watson (Newscaster), William Piletic (Bishop), Paula Murad (Bride)

Director: Rod Holcomb          Teleplay: Chris Abbott
Story: Tom Selleck & Chas. Floyd Johnson & Chris Abbott

Banana Road Productions and BBK Productions in assoc. with Universal Televison, an MCA Co.
Executive producers: Tom Selleck, Chas. Floyd Johnson, Chris Abbott
Supervising producer: Rod Holcomb
Producer: Rick Weaver
Associate producer: Scott Ejercito
Director of photography: Robert Steadman
Music: Jay Gruska

## Sunday in Paris

NBC          Monday, July 8, 1991  8:30-9 p.m.

Comedy of a New York City soap-opera actress (Allen), the single mother of daughters Alison and Taylor and son Brandon, who gives up her career to try to regain sight of her familial values by moving back with her extended family on the farm in Paris, Texas. Working title: *Fresher Pastures*.

| | |
|---|---|
| Sunday Chase | Debbie Allen |
| Momma | Diahann Carroll |

With: Jenifer Lewis

| | |
|---|---|
| O.S. Dixon, Sunday's grandfather | Oscar Brown, Jr. |

With: John Witherspoon, Essence Atkins, Brandon Adams, Jurnee Smollett

Guest cast: NA

Director: Hugh Wilson (Debbie Allen orig. announced)
Story: Jeff Stetson          Teleplay: Jeff Stetson and Susan Fales

Production data (incomplete) per ABC:
Columbia Pictures Television
Executive producer: Hugh Wilson
Producer: Debbie Allen
Creators: Hugh Wilson, Jeff Stetson

## Miss Jones

ABC          Friday, July 12, 1991  9:30-10 p.m.

Comedy of an attorney trying to juggle her life as a single parent and as a lawyer for a firm representing pampered professional athletes: Thea joins the firm, and is assigned to rehabilitate a troubled star baseball pitcher (O'Leary). Orig. scheduled for July 5, 9:30-10 p.m.

| | |
|---|---|
| Thea Jones | Christine Ebersole |
| Buddy Ryan, her boss | Ken Welsh |
| Larry Shapiro | Larry Haines |
| Mrs. Mayo | Lynn Milgrim |
| Rob Nettles | Robert Prescott |
| Spencer Jones, Thea's son | Charlie Newmark |
| Evinrude Johnson | Ernie Hudson |

*Guest cast:*

| | |
|---|---|
| Doggie Dolan | William O'Leary |
| Attorneys | John Cowans, Allan Hunt |
| Boys | Christian Hunt, Adam Jeffries |

Director: Will Mackenzie          Writer: Robert Moloney

Moloney Limited (but not very) in assoc. with Paramount
Executive producer: Robert Moloney
Line producer: Jason Shubb
Director of photography: Gary Scott
Music [and] Theme: Paul Pilger, Dennis Polen, William Moloney (words and music); performed by Christine Ebersole

## The Julie Show

NBC        Sunday, July 28, 1991  7-7:30 p.m.

Comedy of a vivacious actress who goes to extreme lengths to interview a teen singer (Walker), in hopes of landing a job as a celebrity reporter on the tabloid TV show *Inside Scoop*. Star Brown is the singer-actress, not the MTV veejay. Working title: *The Julie Brown Show*.

Julie Robbins...................................................Julie Brown
June (orig. Janet), her mother...........................Marian Mercer
*Inside Scoop* reporter Debra Deacon..............DeLane Matthews
Cheryl, Julie's roommate..................................Susan Messing
*Inside Scoop* producer Tony Barnow.................Kevin O'Rourke

*Guest cast:*
Kiki..................................................................Kim Walker
Hotel desk clerk...............................................Don Sparks
Kimba.............................................................Robin Angers
Tawny Tuttle..................................................Deborah Driggs

Director: David Mirkin
Writers: Charlie Coffey & Julie Brown and David Mirkin

MIrkinvision and New World Television
Executive producer: David Mirkin
Producers: John Ziffren, Julie Brown
Co-producer: Charlie Coffey
Associate producer: Hudson Hickman
Director of photography: Wayne Kennan
Music: Stewart Levin
Theme (words and music): Ray Colcord, Julie Brown, Charlie Coffey, David Mirkin; performed by Julie Brown

## Lookwell

NBC        Sunday, July 28, 1991  7:30-8 p.m.

Comedy of an acting teacher and former star of a TV crime drama (*Bannigan*) who has trouble letting go of his fictional past and gets involved in real-life police work. Co-star Frazier is the series supervising producer.

Ty Lookwell....................................................Adam West
Detective Kennery............................................Ron Frazier
Hyacinth, Ty's housekeeper................................Ann Weldon

*Guest cast:*
Jason..............................................................Todd Field
Albert..........................................................Bart Braverman
Miss Royster.................................................Deborah Richter
Alex..............................................................Brian Bradley
And: Jeff Austin, Chris Barnes, John Capodice, Molly Cleator, Brick Karnes, Sal Lopez, John Riggi, Steve Schubert, Terry Beaver, Audree Chapman, Sip Culler, Tom Dahlgren, Rif Hutton, Michael Milhoan, Steve Prutting, Ami Rothschild, Jack Yates
   Also orig. announced:
   Robert Wagner, Donna Rice

Director: E.W. Swackhamer
Writers: Robert Smigel, Conan O'Brien

Brillstein • Grey Productions and Broadway Video
Executive producer: Lorne Michaels
Producers: Robert Smigel, Conan O'Brien
Supervising producer: Ron Frazier
Executive consultant: Sandy Wernick
Director of photography: Ken Peach, Jr.

## Deadline

ABC        Wednesday, July 31, 1991  10-11 p.m.

Drama of a San Francisco TV reporter (Russ) and his romantically involved researcher (Pollak): Malone and Parker pursue the links between the murders of a fellow crime reporter (Martinet) and a call girl (York). Orig. scheduled for Saturday, July 6, 10-11 p.m. Working title: *Bay City Story*.

Jim Malone....................................................William Russ
Sarah Parker..................................................Cheryl Pollak

*Guest cast:*
Tony Cefalu.....................................................Paul Regina
Douglas Turner..............................................Squire Fridell
Marci Fenner...................................................Rachel York
Sally Turner......................................................Liza Hella
Fowler..........................................................Nathan Roberts
Muffy Giardino...............................................Jean Montanti
Bob Crisman.......................................................Don West
Allison Conry......................................................Ann Block
Art Ronstadt...............................................Charles Martinet
Vito Rovenaazno..................................................David Piel
Sepolcro.......................................................Howard Stephens
And: Ed Holmes (Nimmo McCracken), Mark Leigh Stevens (H.T. Harlow), Miguel Najera (Opingdon), Mollie Stickney (Flower girl), Tracy Heffernan (Uniformed officer), Joe Cole (Cab driver), Paul Ghiringhelli (Dennis Snow)

Director: Robert Butler        Writer: Stephen Zito

Lorimar Television in assoc. with Gangbuster Films, Green River Productions and Cosgrove-Meurer Productions
Executive producer: Robert Butler
Co-executive producers: Stephen Zito, John Cosgrove, Terry Meurer
Producer: Kevin Inch
Associate producer: Jessie Ward
Director of photography: Geoffrey Erb
Music: Jay Gruska

## Howie and Rose

ABC        Friday, Aug. 2, 1991  8:30-9 p.m.

Comedy of a New York City radio talk-show host (Mandel) whose life abruptly changes when his streetwise 11-year-old niece comes to live with him after her bookie parents are sent to prison. Station: WCRY. Episode title: "The Music Box."

Howie Newman..................................................Howie Mandel
Rose Haber..................................................Shanelle Workman
Co-host Lawrence Fine.......................................Stephen Furst

*Guest cast:*
Lisa Hubbard.....................................................Margot Rose
Rita Haber, Rose's mother..............................Dee Dee Rescher
Receptionist.........................................................Judy Toll
Morris Haber, Rose's father.............................Randy Oglesby
And: John C. Moskoff, Lou Bonacki, Jan Rabson, Benji Schulman

Director: Noam Pitlik        Writer: Nat Mauldin

Sandollar and Pronoun Trouble, Inc. in assoc. with 20th Century Fox Television
Executive producer: Nat Mauldin
Producers: Sandy Gallin, Candace Farrell, Faye Oshima-Belyeu

Associate producer: Cathy Rosenstein
Executive consultant: Marc Flanagan
Director of photography: Richard Brown
Music [and] Theme (instrumental): Gordon Lustig

## New York Mounted

CBS          Saturday, Aug. 3, 1991  8-10 p.m.

Lighthearted adventure-drama of a former Montana cop (Gauthier) who with his prized rodeo horse, Blaze, joins the New York Police Dept. Mounted Police, and is paired with a Brooklyn-born officer (Franz).  Title is as onscreen; widely reported, erroneously, under its working title, *N.Y.P.D. Mounted.*

Anthony (Tony) Spampatta...................................Dennis Franz
Lonnie "Lucky" Wellington.................................Dan Gauthier
NYPD Lieutenant................................................Roxann Biggs
Capt. Smithers.................................................Cliff De Young

*Guest cast:* Mariangela Pino (Madeline Spampatta), Karla Montana, Dana Wheeler-Nicholson, Evan Mirano, Spike Alexander, Johnny Pinto, James MacDonald, John Leguizamo, Joseph R. Sicari, Arnie Mazer, Adrian Bailey (Impersonator), George Bamford (Dave Baker), Anna Berger (Woman), Kristin Davis (Young lady), Gary Eimiller (Cop), Martin Garner (Man), Jack Haley, Verna Hampton, Evan O'Meara (New Yorkers), Sal Jenco (Doorperson), Frank Licato (Bullhorn cop), Kathleen McNeeny (Holly Hartley), Nick Muglia (Burns), Patricia O'Connell (Mom), Joe Pentangelo (Henderson), James Pritchet (Judge), Michael Santoro (Cameraperson), Peter Schuck (Store manager), Joseph Siravo (Mugger), Sean Whitesell, Scott Sowers (Joggers), Jason Stuart (Vincent), Christopher Wynkoop (Vendor)

Director: Mark Tinker (Sam Weisman orig. announced)
Teleplay: Patrick Hasburgh
Story: Patrick Hasburgh & Alfonse Ruggiero, Jr.

Patrick Hasburgh Productions and Orion Television
Executive producers: Patrick Hasburgh (Alfonse Ruggiero, Jr. also orig. announced)
Producer: Mark H. Ovitz
Co-producer: Jodi Rothe
Director of photography: Constantine Makris
Music [and] Theme (instrumental): Peter Bernstein

## The Owl

CBS Saturday, Aug. 3, 1991  10-11 p.m.

Fantasy-drama of a former investigative reporter who becomes a vigilante-for-hire when, after his wife and daughter are murdered, he develops a rare disease, "insomnolence," preventing him from sleeping: The Owl tries to find a young girl's (Flores) father, the victim of a kidnapping related to a new street drug. Based on characters from the book by Robert Forward.

The Owl.........................................................Adrian Paul
Danny Santerre, his police contact.........Patricia Charbonneau
Bartender Norbert.........................................Brian Thompson

*Guest cast:*
Lisa...............................................................Erika Flores
Cool Ice.................................................Jacques Apollo Bolton
Bobby B..........................................David Anthony Marshall
Gullett...........................................................Billy "Sly" Williams
Dr. Clements...................................................David Selburg

Dr. Miller..........................................................Mark Lowenthal
Hutchins..............................................................Alan Scarfe
Morito.......................................................Thomas Rosales, Jr.
Gosset...........................................................Alejandro Quezada
And:  Gregory Scott Cummins (Trash) Rick Zumwalt (Packer), Bridget Klappert (6-year-old), Jill Pierce (Dark-haired woman), Sandra Spriggs (Black woman)

Writer-director: Tom Holland

LeMasters Productions in assoc. with Todman-Simon Productions and Lorimar Television
Executive producers: Kim LeMasters, Tom Holland
Producers: Bill Todman Jr., Joel Simon, Michael Green
Co-producer: Robert Forward
Associate producer: John Anthony LeMasters
Director of photography: Steve Yaconelli
Music [and] Theme (instrumental): Sylvester Levay

## Big Deals

ABC          Saturday, Aug. 3, 1991  10:30-11 p.m.

Comedy of two eternally broke scam artists in Hollywood, one Brit, one American, forever concocting get-rich-quick schemes: Chris, needing money to buy his son a birthday gift, teams with Dash to try to return a runaway dog for the reward.

Christopher Nizzle..............................................Tim Curry
Dashiel "Dash" Ryan...........................................Corey Parker
Diner-owner Earl Radulavitch...............................Troy Evans
Topaz Radulavitch, his daughter...........................Amy Sedaris

*Guest cast:*
Ernst.............................................................Jonathan Schmock
Brian Nizzle, Christopher's son.........................Aaron Metchik
Pepper.........................................................Robin Lynn Heath
Announcer.....................................................Dennis Seiwell
Mrs. Bluett.....................................................Holland Taylor
        Also orig. announced: Britt Leach (Mr. Bluett)

Director: Robert Berlinger          Writer: Chris Thompson

Christopher Thompson Productions in assoc. with Viacom
Executive producer: Chris Thompson
Producer: Marie Connolly
Director of photography: Mikel Neiers
Music: uncredited/inapplicable
Theme: classical music

## Coconut Downs

ABC          Tuesday, Aug. 6, 1991  8:30-9 p.m.

Comedy of the small Van Buren Hotel, the clientele for which has turned colorful with the opening of a racetrack across the street.  Orig. scheduled for Wednesday, July 24, 8:30-9 p.m.

Julie Van Buren..................................................Robin Bartlett
Gambler Tony Formica.....................................David Gianopoulos
Track announcer Jimmy Dugan..................David Huddleston
Eric Van Buren (16), Julie's son......................Jayce Bartok
Sara Van Buren (10), her daughter................Jaclyn Bernstein
Sally Van Buren, Julie's mother.....................Carole Shelley

*Guest cast:*
Nicky Fish...................................................Dominic Chianese
Gamblers...............Marty Davis, Bill Saluga, Vincent Lucchesi
Porterhouse...................................................Mitchell Edmonds

And: J.C. Brandy (Jockey/Cindy), Shanelle Workman (Jane)

Director: David Steinberg          Writer: Elliot Shoenman

ABC Productions / a.k.a. Productions, Inc.
Executive producer: Elliot Shoenman
Producer: Stephen C. Grossman
Coordinating producer: Matt Dinsmore
Director of photography: Wayne Kennan
Music [and] Theme (instrumental): J.A.C. Redford
Creator: uncredited onscreen

## Claws

CBS          Saturday, Aug. 10, 1991  8-8:30 p.m.

Comedy of three Mesa, Ariz. cats, whose thoughts we hear in voiceover: jaded wiseguy Merv, imperious Petey (who prefers the name Harrison) and naive Crystal: Amzie's daughter and family, including a slob husband allergic to cats, move in.

Amzie..................................................Barbara Barrie
Phil, her son-in-law................................Stephen Lee
Patti, her daughter..................................Nana Visitor
Ashley (15)..........................................Melissa Clayton
Mitch (13)..............................................Sean Baca
"Themselves"......Merv, Crystal, Petey (vocal artists uncredited)

*Guest cast:*
Burly torso..............................................Joe Costanzo

Director: Pat Patchett
Writers: Vicki S. Horwits and Rebecca Parr

Patchett Kaufman Entertainment
Executive producers: Tom Patchett, Kenneth Kaufman
Producers: Rebecca Parr, Vicki S. Horwits
Coordinating producer: Steve Lamar
Associate producer: Susan Polmanski
Director: Ted C. Polmanski
Music [and] Theme (instrumental): Mark Mothersbaugh

## The Vidiots

CBS          Saturday, Aug. 10, 1991  8:30-9 p.m.

Three Stooges-like farcical comedy of three down-on-their-luck siblings who unexpectedly inherit their late long-lost brother's employment agency, and his eight-year-old son (Zuckerman).

Lenny Plotz..............................................Roger Kabler
Lester Plotz..............................................John Kassir
Louie Plotz............................................Peter Pitofsky
Lazlo Plotz...........................................Alex Zuckerman
*Cast-member listed in end-credits:*
Mutt (dog)....................................................Chopper

*Guest cast:*
Zwertlow Cruntagg.................................Roy Brocksmith
Bertha....................................................Ellen Gerstein
Judge Thelma Canago........................Dorian LOPINTO
And: Beans Morocco (Mail deliverer), Lou Wills (Sam)

Director: Howard Storm          Writer: Peter Tilden

CBS Entertainment Productions in assoc. with the Steve Tisch
     Co. and MGM/UA
Executive producer: Steve Tisch
Producers: Mireille Soria, Peter Tilden

Line producer: Ronald B. Colby
Director of photography: Robert Elswit
Music [and] Theme (instrumental): John Debney
Dog trainer: Kim Lindemoen

## Passion

CBS          Saturday, Aug. 17, 1991  10-10:30 p.m.

Romantic comedy of the feisty new editor (Seymour) of *Lady's Day* magazine, who reconfigures it under the title *Passion* to the consternation of the playful, nonconformist publisher (Terry).  Set in New York City.  Orig. scheduled for July 27.

Amanda Brooks.................................................Jane Seymour
Jack Keenan.......................................................John Terry
Veronica Andrews.................................................Cristine Rose
Former editor Maryedith Sweetzer....................Nancy Lenehan
Jenny Colomby..................................................Janeane Garofalo
Kirby Taylor, Jack's partner..................................Josh Mostel

Director: Will Mackenzie          Writer: Pamela Pettler

Quirky Productions in assoc. with Columbia Pictures
     Television / ELP Communications
Executive producer: Pamela Pettler
Co-producer: Craig Knizek
Director of photography: George LAFOUNTAINE
Music: David Kitay
Cat photographs featuring: Buster Pettler, Leo Mackenzie
Creator: Pamela Pettler

## Acting Sheriff

CBS          Saturday, Aug. 17, 1991  10:30-11 p.m.

Comedy of a B-movie Western star turned real-life sheriff in rural Lomacita County.  Some (fictional) McCord movies: *Guadalcanal Picnic* (Warner Bros., 1964); *Get Al Capone!*; *The Long So Long* (MGM); *A Fistful of Courage*.  Working title: *Make My Day*.  Unannounced preemption of pilot *Word of Mouth*.

Sheriff Brent McCord...........................................Robert Goulet
Deputy Mike Swanson...........................................John Putch
Asst. D.A. Donna.......................................Hillary Bailey Smith
Receptionist-dispatcher Helen Munson.................Ruth Kobart
Deputy Judith Mahoney.......................................Diane Delano

*Guest cast:*
Capt. Van Patten...............................................Art La Fleur
Fred.......................................................Michael McManus
Harper......................................................Daniel O'Shea
And: Page Leong (Anne Wong-Fowler), Barney Burman (Doug),
     Buck Herron (Burns), Lee Tergesen (Robbie)

Director: Michael Lembeck
Writers: Gary Murphy & Larry Strawther

Gary Murphy Larry Strawther Productions in assoc. with
     Touchstone Television
Executive producers: Larry Strawther, Gary Murphy
Producer: Tim Steele
Director of photography: Mike Berlin
Music [and] Theme (instrumental): Ed Alton

## Mimi & Me

CBS          Saturday, Sept. 7, 1991  10-11 p.m.

A free-spirited woman and a stiff orthodontic student (on probation from dental school) take over his late uncle's detective agency after the uncle's killed helping them solve a murder involving Germanic killers and an ancient piece of jewelry. Guest Yarbrough is a folk-rock singer.

Mimi............................................................Terry Farrell
Howard..................................................Howard McGillin
Rula, Mimi's friend............................................Belina Logan

*Guest cast:*
Prof. Sauer..........................................Basil Hoffman
Amy, Howard's fiancee....................................Kari Lizer
Al Marr, Howard's uncle...................................Kenneth Mars
With: Jack McGee, Alan Scarfe, Patricia Smith, Jimmie F. Skaggs, Jonathan Coogan, Wilson Raiser, Sonny Craver, Glenn Yarbrough

Director: Sam Weisman                    Writer: Roger Director

Cherub Productions in assoc. with Warner Bros. Televison
Executive producer: Roger Director
Producer: Artie Mandelberg
Director of photography: Laszlo George
Music: David McHugh

UNAIRED

### News at Twelve

NBC

Comedy of a 12-year-old (Gerard) delivering the highlights of his life via newscasts from a makeshift studio in his bedroom. Orig. scheduled for Aug. 4, 1991, 7:30-8 p.m; unscheduled preemption by a rerun of the July 7, 1990 unsold pilot *Turner & Hooch.*

Announced cast includes:
Danny Peterson.................................................Danny Gerard
And: Christine Sutherland, Gary Basarabe, Sam Gray

Creator-executive producer: Bill Persky

### Love & Money

NBC

Comedy of a once-respected author trying to maintain his rich Manhattan lifestyle by grinding out romance novels. Working title: *Paperback Writer.* Orig. scheduled for Aug. 19, 1991, 10:30-11 p.m.; unscheduled preemption by a news report.

Announced cast includes:
Michael Wyatt....................................................Robert Wagner
Sam Wyatt, his opinionated father.................Barnard Hughes
Audrey Bishop, his aggressive assistant........Marietta DePrima
Veronica Chapman, his patronizing agent.........Robin Strasser

### Word of Mouth

CBS

Comedy of a young, enthusiastic White House speechwriter (Newbern) and his more jaded colleagues. Orig. scheduled for Aug. 17, 10:30-11 p.m.

Jim Smith.......................................................George Newbern
Executive Office Building head B. Laurence Taylor.......William Daniels
Hammond Egley................................................Lewis Black
Office manager Bonnie Cole.................................Gladys Knight
Alyson McCleod.............................................Haviland Morris
Roxanne Robinson..................Michele Lamar Richards
Steve Nadelman.............................................Joshua Rifkind

Director: Terry Hughes
Writers: John Tinker, Tom Fontana, Bruce Paltrow

The Paltrow Group in assoc. with Columbia Pictures Television
Executive producers: Bruce Paltrow, Tom Fontana, John Tinker

# UNSOLD COMEDY AND DRAMA PILOTS WITH NO SCHEDULED TELECASTS

### Against the Odds

NBC

"Reality-based" program featuring the exploits of people who have attempted to overcome amazing odds both for socially responsible and irresponsible ends. Executive producers: John Cosgrove, Terry Meurer. Cosgrove/Meurer Productions.

### Ball$

CBS

Restoration comedy, set in the 1890s, about a wealthy, eccentric family running a factory that produces sports equipment and tennis balls. Starring Raquel Welch, Robert Klein. Executive producer: Norman Lear. ACT III Communications.

### Baltimore

NBC

Comedy with music about two sisters -- a singer (Megan Gallagher) with a struggling jazz group called Baltimore, and her prodigal, free-spirited younger sibling -- with little in common except for their love of music and a penchant for falling in love with the same men. Characters also include their musician brother, a hypochondriac with stage fright. Creator-producer: Jay Tarses; executive producers: Bernie Brillstein, Brad Grey, Sandy Wernick. You and Me Kid Productions.

### Esme's Little Nap

CBS

Comedy of a woman (Debbie Reynolds) who must take care of her grandchildren when her daughter goes into a catatonic shock after a freak accident. Writers-executive producers: Carrie Fisher, Janis Hirsch. 20th Century Fox Television.

### Empire City

CBS

Crime drama of a pair of emotionally involved homicide detectives (Michael Pare, Mary Mara) who work on sensational murder cases involving New York City's rich and famous. Executive producer: Mark Rosner. Warner Bros. Television.

## The Fifth Corner

NBC

Drama of amnesiac Richard Baum (Alex McArthur), who struggles to recall his true identity while serving as an identity-changing operative in a sinister espionage web manipulated by a reclusive billionaire (E.G. Marshall). Also starring Kim Delaney as his former partner and lover, and J.E. Freeman as his rumpled chauffeur. Executive producers: Gary Adelson, Craig Baumgarten, John Herzfeld (latter also pilot writer-director). Adelson-Baumgarten Productions and New World Television.

## Grey Guns

CBS

Drama of two old friends and veteran cops (Wilford Brimley, Richard Farnsworth) who are the law in a small Rocky Mountain town.

## The Human Touch

CBS

Drama of a a dedicated physician and teacher (John Mahoney) who leaves a lucrative practice to join an inner-city teaching hospital. Executive producer: Dick Wolf. Universal Television, an MCA Co.

## I-Witness

NBC

"Interactive" half-hour mystery that follows investigative reporter Jack Barnett (Robert Firth) as he covers a weekly crime story, with all the action seen through the lens of video cameraperson Mike (Larry Hankin), whose face is never revealed. Designed to end each week with the solution unrevealed, and a 900 number supplied to allow viewers to attempt answering "whodunit" for a prize. Executive producers: John Cosgrove, Terry Meurer; co-executive producer and pilot writer: Jeff Melvoin. Cosgrove/Meurer Productions.

## Jack of Hearts

CBS

Drama of a charismatic and mysterious owner (David Beecroft) of a major Las Vegas casino-hotel. Executive producer: Aaron Spelling. Aaron Spelling Productions in assoc. with Orion Pictures Television.

## Love Child

NBC

Comedy of a U.S. Senator (John Forsythe) whose career and family life are turned upside town when his illegitimate adult daughter meets him for the first time. Executive producer: Norman Lear. Producers: Marta Kauffman, David Crane. Columbia Television.

## Mr. Lyle

NBC

Drama of a dapper master of the supernatural, who, upon instruction from his mysterious leader, Dr. George, does battle against the omnipresent Dr. Coma, a demonic force who materializes on TV screens to instruct and dispatch his violent "sleeper" agents and his personal assassins, the Men in Black. Writer-executive producer: Robert Crais; supervising producer: Stuart Cohen. 20th Century Fox Television.

## Ruth Harper

CBS

Comedy of a widow (Susan Sullivan) who takes over her husband's business. Writers-executive producers: Mark Egan, Mark Solomon. MTM Productions in assoc. with CBS Entertainment Productions.

## Stand By Your Man

CBS

Comedy of two sisters whose husbands are in jail for bank robbery; adapted from the British series Birds of a Feather. Starring Rosie O'Donnell. Executive producers: Nancy Steen, Neil Thompson. Witzend Productions in assoc. with 20th Century Fox Television.

## Tequila and Boner

CBS

Drama of hip, irreverent cop T.T. Boner (Rick Rossovich) and his canine partner, Tequila. Executive producer: Don Bellisario; co-executive producer: Michael Zinberg. Belisarius Productions in assoc. with Universal Television, an MCA Co.

## Three Blind Mice

CBS

TV-movie drama of a lawyer who turns detective to free a client accused of murdering three Vietnamese men he believed raped his wife. Based on the book by Ed McBain a.k.a. Evan Hunter. Executive producer: Philip D'Antoni. D'Antoni Production Group in assoc. with Viacom Productions

## Toonces and Friends

NBC

Surreal comedy of Toonces the driving cat, from the puppet and live-action recurring sketch on the latenight series Saturday Night Live. Executive producer: Lorne Michaels; pilot writer: Jack Handy. Broadway Video Productions in assoc. with NBC Productions.

## Untitled Leavitt and Moye Project

NBC

Sketch comedy/variety show featuring four farcical, irreverent running skits including "Cro-Magnon Man at Oxford," "Married Man" and "Teen Witch." Executive producers: Ron Leavitt, Michael Moye. Columbia Pictures Television.

## Untitled Tom Clancy Project

ABC

TV-movie thriller of a high-tech military command force, based on an original story by novelist Tom Clancy. Executive producer: Philip D'Antoni; pilot writer-producer: Derek Marlowe. D'Antoni Production Group in assoc. with Viacom Productions.